The Economic Way of Thinking

The Economic Way of Thinking

PAUL HEYNE
University of Washington

PETER J. BOETTKE
George Mason University

DAVID L. PRYCHITKO
Northern Michigan University

Eleventh Edition

Prentice Hall
Upper Saddle River, NJ 07458

Library of Congress Cataloging-in-Publication Data

Heyne, Paul T.
The economic way of thinking / Paul Heyne, Peter J. Boettke, David L. Prychitko.—11th ed.
p. cm.
Includes index.
ISBN 0-13-154369-5 (alk. paper)
1. Economics. I. Boettke, Peter J. II. Prychitko, David L. III. Title.

HB171.5.H46 2005
330—dc22 2004057294

Executive Editor: David Alexander
Editorial Director: Jeff Shelstad
Editor: Jon Axelrod
Project Manager: Marie Mchale
Editorial Assistant: Katy Rank
Media Project Manager: Peter Snell
Executive Marketing Manager: Sharon M. Koch
Marketing Assistant: Tina Panagiotou
Managing Editor (Production): Cynthia Regan
Production Editor: Melissa Owens
Permissions Supervisor: Charles Morris
Manufacturing Buyer: Arnold Vila
Design Director: Maria Lange
Interior and Cover Design: Pat Smythe
Cover Illustration/Photo: Juliana Heyne "Sol" oil on paper; © 2004
Courtesy Francine Seders Gallery
Photo: Spike Mafford
Director, Image Resource Center: Melinda Reo
Manager, Rights and Permissions: Zina Arabia
Manager: Visual Research: Beth Brenzel
Manager, Cover Visual Research & Permissions: Karen Sanatar
Image Permission Coordinator: Frances Toepfer
Manager, Print Production: Christy Mahon
Composition: GGS Book Services, Atlantic Highlands
Printer/Binder: R.R. Donnelley
Typeface: 10/12 New Aster

Credits and acknowledgments borrowed from other sources and reproduced, with permission, in this textbook appear on page 558.

Pearson Education LTD.
Pearson Education Singapore, Pte. Ltd
Pearson Education, Canada, Ltd
Pearson Education–Japan
Pearson Education Australia PTY, Limited
Pearson Education North Asia Ltd
Pearson Educación de Mexico, S.A. de C.V.
Pearson Education Malaysia, Pte. Ltd

10 9 8 7 6 5 4 3

ISBN 0-13-154369-5

In memory of Paul Heyne

Paul Heyne

1931–2000

a tribute

On a rare occasion, if you are fortunate, you will run across an individual who lives and acts upon the ideals that we profess. I was fortunate. Paul Heyne came into my life in 1975. Out of the blue, he sent me a letter that began as follows:

I'm going to be moving to Seattle at the end of the current academic year and I'd like to find a college or university in the city at which I could be an economics teacher. Those are two separate decisions. I'll be moving to Seattle whether or not I find a position in an economics department there. But teaching and especially the teaching of introductory economics is one of the things I think I do well and something I would continue doing.

I had assumed the chairmanship of the department of economics at the University of Washington in 1967 and set out to make it one of the best in the country. My definition of best included not only scholarly eminence, which we were in the process of achieving, but the effective, caring teaching of the multitude of undergraduates that populated a large state university. The University played lip service to good teaching but the reward system was geared to publication and most, but not all, of my colleagues acted accordingly. Shortly after assuming the chairmanship, I decided I should go back to teaching the introductory course to see just what we did. I was dismayed to find that it had not changed an iota from my undergraduate days. The textbooks were full of the formal jargon of economic theory elucidating the perfectly competitive model, imperfect competition a la Chamberlin and Joan Robinson, and monopoly replete with all the marginal analysis and appropriate graphs. Following the tradition, I was in the midst of my fourth lecture on perfect competition illustrating it with the case of American agriculture when a student in the back of the auditorium noisily took exception to what I was saying. I thought I would teach him a lesson and invited him to address the class, explaining himself. He did, describing effectively the myriad of price supports, milk marketing acts, sugar production subsidies, etc. that pervaded agriculture and made it far from the competitive model. I slunk back to my office and began a search for a more effective teaching program. I was some years into an attempt when Paul's letter arrived. I wrote back asking what he would like to do as a teacher. His reply, in part:

I would like to teach at a college whose faculty was enthusiastically committed to providing a liberal education for undergraduates. I would like to be a member of a faculty that was continuously asking about the nature and significance of liberal education and looking critically at its own efforts to provide one. The members of such a faculty would use their own disciplines as bases for venturing into other disciplines and not as castles within which to enjoy untroubled lives. In the college of my fantasies, there would be some core requirements for all to satisfy; not so much because anyone can specify particular knowledge that a liberally educated person must have as because a liberal arts college requires some common core if it wants to be a lively intellectual community, Mastery of the core would be expected first of all of faculty members. (I've often thought how much more profitable faculty curriculum discussions would be if every faculty member knew that he would be taking all courses imposed on undergraduates and that his colleagues would be evaluating any course he himself wanted to offer in the common core.)

Paul left a tenured professorship at Southern Methodist University to come to Washington as a non-tenured lecturer and he retained that untenured rank until he died in March 2000. I am not sure we lived up to Paul's fantasies of the ideal faculty; I know we didn't but he did change the way economics was taught at the University; revamping the undergraduate program, overhauling the introductory course, and meeting regularly with the graduate teaching assistant to improve the quality of their teaching. But much more than that, Paul was a continuing inspiration for those of us who took seriously a quality liberal education for undergraduates.

The Economic Way of Thinking embodies Paul's approach to economics and to a liberal education. It was a radical change from the textbooks of the time. Its focus on the problems of a society and the way in which economic reasoning could shed light on those problems made economics interesting to the students. More than that, the book recognized that the strength of economics was precisely described in the title of the book—as a way of thinking. Comprehending that way of thinking was, and continues to be, the revolutionary contribution of economics to the social sciences and to a better understanding of the world around us.

I open the seminar for freshmen that I teach every fall with a lecture on Paul, the human being—his Seminary education, ordination, the way he got drawn into economics, and the way he combined a rigorous economics (and make no mistake about it, Paul's economics is rigorous) with a broad and active concern for community and social welfare. He believed in individual freedom and the demands that that freedom imposed on responsible human beings. And he and his wife, Julie, lived their lives accordingly.

Douglass C. North
Washington University, St. Louis
Nobel Prize in Economic Sciences, 1993

Contents

Preface

The Economic Way of Thinking continues to enjoy a steady and dedicated following, one that has lasted for more than three decades. It looks different, feels different, and reads different compared to the mainstream fare.

Indeed, this book *is* different.

This text introduces students to the skills of the economist. It teaches students through example and application. It even teaches by showing students how *not* to think, by exposing them to the errors implicit in much popular reasoning about economic events. The text is designed primarily for a one-semester survey course in general economics although it can also be used as a micro principles text. *The Economic Way of Thinking* develops the basic principles of micro- and macroeconomic analysis and rigorously employs them as *tools* rather than ends unto themselves.

Authors of other introductory texts, understandably eager to display the formal beauty of economic analysis, unwittingly tend to overload students with abstract technical details. One principles text, written by an eminent economist, emphasizes in the first chapter that "economists build models." And, in fact, we all *do* build models. But the uninitiated college freshman probably won't share our excitement over the models. Most, in fact, sit through our courses merely hoping to get a prerequisite out of the way. Let's show them *why* they're in the seats and we're at the podium. Let's show them why others who designed the curriculum believe economics is an important area of study. In the end, economics is not about production functions, perfectly competitive equilibria, or Phillips curves. Economics explains the logic of both the economizing process and the exchange process—it is about the everyday world around us. Students using this book will get that message not only at the end of their studies. They'll get it at the very beginning, too.

Paul Heyne never shied away from making his strategy explicit. In previous editions he insisted that "we must show them from the first day how the principles of economics make sense out of buzzing confusion, how they clarify, systematize, and correct the daily assertions of newspapers, political figures, ax grinders, and coffee shop pontificators." For more than 30 years *The Economic Way of Thinking* has taught students how to see through the nonsense, and begin to understand the complex world around them. The eleventh edition continues that tradition.

Accomplishing More with Less

This text accomplishes more—more thinking, more application, more insight—with less emphasis on formal modeling. But don't get us wrong. This is not an easy and watered-down exploration of economics. The eleventh edition offers a solid discussion and development of economic principles and a wealth of probing, illuminating applications to the everyday world around us. Even professional economists have informed the coauthors that *they* have learned more about economics by reading this book. And that's *after* they've acquired their Ph.D.s.

This book is designed to develop our students' skills in *thinking* like an economist. If they become hooked, they will have ample opportunity to hone their modeling skills as they advance to other economics course offerings. May we hope that the students continue their pursuit of this wonderful discipline—or at least retain its basic lessons.

Changes to the Eleventh Edition

The Economic Way of Thinking is Paul Heyne's baby, his pedagogical legacy. It is richly steeped in the property rights and coordinationist tradition of Alchian and Allen's *University Economics*, which is long out of print. It also has an Austrian School flair, emphasizing the dynamic, entrepreneurial nature of the market process, themes developed by Ludwig von Mises, F. A. Hayek, Israel Kirzner, and Murray Rothbard. These and other insights, such as the Public Choice approach of James Buchanan and the Monetary Disequilibrium theory of Gunnar Myrdal, are further developed in this new edition.

Specific changes to the eleventh edition:

- The concept and role of property rights is now introduced up front, in Chapter 1.
- A clearer discussion of economic goods and bads, and the concept of economic efficiency, in Chapter 2 on "Efficiency,

Exchange, and Comparative Advantage." We've added a new appendix introducing students to the issue of economic growth.

- Also a focus on transaction costs and the role of middlemen has been moved into Chapter 2 and further applied in following chapters. (The discussion of middlemen and speculation was originally introduced in Chapter 7 in the previous edition. Those topics have now been developed and integrated among the first seven chapters, rather than receiving a chapter of their own.)
- A much more detailed discussion of the factors that shift the demand curve is developed in Chapter 3, and the factors that shift the supply curve in Chapter 4. The importance of monetary calculation is also first introduced in these chapters and further developed in later chapters.
- The market for credit is introduced as an example of supply and demand at work, in Chapter 5, along with an appendix on time preference and interest rates.
- Minimum wage and agricultural price supports have been added to Chapter 6.
- Chapter 7 on "Profit and Loss" has been reorganized. The discussion of professional speculators and futures markets are merged into this chapter, along with an appendix on discounting.
- The macro material, beginning with Chapter 14 on GDP accounting (which was one of the weakest chapters in previous editions), has been substantially reorganized and rewritten. Chapter 14 now contains new, detailed discussions of the GDP concept, in its expenditures, income, and value-added measurements. The limitations of national income accounting, and aggregate analysis in general, is discussed in much greater detail as part of a new appendix to Chapter 14. Previous discussions of intercountry GDP comparisons have been moved into the appendix of a later chapter on economic growth. We feel this chapter is more accessible now for the introductory student, while at the same time it provides a more rigorous discussion of the GDP concept.
- Several of our users cover the chapter on unemployment immediately after completing the GDP chapter, which in previous editions meant skipping over several chapters. (In fact, one of the coauthors has done this himself for many years.) That inconvenience has been corrected. The material on employment and unemployment, originally Chapter 19 in the previous edition, is now Chapter 15.
- Chapter 16 on the Federal Reserve and the supply of money has been substantially reorganized. We believe it reads better and is more user-friendly for the student. We've added a much more detailed discussion of reserve

requirements, the discount rate, and open market operations. The discussion of the gold standard has been reorganized into an appendix.

- Chapter 17 on monetary and fiscal polices has a new discussion using a monetary disequilibrium approach, and a criticism of functional finance.
- We've done some further rearranging of the macro chapters by making "Economic Performance and Political Economy" follow as Chapter 18.
- Chapter 19 on "National Policies and International Exchange" comes next, with a new discussion of the globalization and outsourcing debates.
- Chapter 20 follows, on "Promoting Economic Growth." We've added an appendix on the difficulties of international comparisons.
- Data in the macro and international chapters have been updated through 2003.
- Finally, we've heard from several students who requested a real glossary be added to the book. We are happy to oblige. This edition has a glossary with definitions of more than 100 terms used in the book.

Acknowledgments

We shall always be indebted to the late Paul Heyne. We are thankful that new generations of students *continue* to have the opportunity to learn from Paul's text. We thank Juliana Heyne for her cover art and assistance with the chapter photos.

We wish to acknowledge those who have reviewed or commented on earlier editions. They are: Terry Anderson, Yoram Barzel, Roger Beck, Robert Bish, Walter Block, Samuel Bostaph, Barry Boyer, Ronald Brandolini, Henry Bruton, Judith B. Cox, Arthur DiQuattro, John B. Egger, Theo Eicher, Mary Eysenbach, Horst Feldmann, Joe Furhig, Andrew Hanssen, Robert Higgs, P. J. Hill, Laurie Johnson, Thomas Johnson, Edward A. Kaschins, Ronald Krieger, Charles Lave, Ian Laxer, Frank Machovec, Howard Miller, Glenn Moots, Charles Nelson, Marilyn Orozco, E. C. (Zeke) Pasour, Potluri Rao, Andrew Rutten, Haideh Salehi-Esfahani, Howard Swaine, Peter Toumanoff, Stephen J. Turnovsky, T. Norman Van Cott, Donald Wells, Sidney Wilson, Michelle Wyrick, Harvey Zabinsky, and M. Y. (Zak) Zaki.

We thank Paul Briggs, Windward Community College, Shawn Carter, Jacksonville State University, John McArthur, Wofford College, Tom Means, San Jose State University, and Reed Reynolds, University of Toledo, who provided us clear, detailed comments and reviews for this new edition. Sam Bostaph, Art Carden, P. J. Hill (again), Ted Holmstrom, and Mark Skousen provided helpful unsolicited comments on the text and its supplements. We probably couldn't please everybody, but we seriously considered all their comments, criticisms, and suggestions. Any remaining errors are the coauthors' responsibility. In a *market* economy, mismanaged property rights tend to move into more effective hands, and so we have every incentive to minimize errors and add value to the project. Information, nevertheless, remains a scarce good. We welcome your comments, criticisms, and suggestions. Feel free to email Boettke (pboettke@gmu.edu) or Prychitko (dprychit@nmu.edu).

We thank David Alexander, our editor at Prentice Hall, for the continued opportunity, and Katy Rank, Prentice Hall's editorial assistant in economics, for cheering us on and keeping us up to schedule at a time when other professional commitments and warm sunny weather competed for our attention. We thank Melissa Owens, our pleasant production editor, Marie McHale for coordinating the supplements, and Elena Picinic for coordinating the marketing of the book. (We should also take this opportunity to thank all those who have translated the tenth edition into Hungarian. A Russian translation is in the works, and a Japanese translation appeared for the ninth edition. Translating *The Economic Way of Thinking* must be a rather difficult task, given the idiomatic language used throughout the text and the rather esoteric references to American pop culture.)

We thank Isaac Dilanni, Nick Schandler, Chris Coyne, and Peter Leeson for tracking down and updating the data used in the text.

We are grateful to the J. M. Kaplan Fund, the Atlas Foundation, and the Earhart Foundation. Over the years they have provided financial support for our research and teaching activities, activities which continue to shape this project as well.

Pete thanks his wife, Rosemary, and sons, Matthew and Stephen. Dave thanks his wife, Julie, and kids, Sonja, Emily, Anthony, and Anna. This project would not have been possible if it weren't for their love, support, and understanding. We like economics, but we *love* our families, although it might not always appear that way at the margin.

Pete Boettke and Dave Prychitko

1 The Economic Way of Thinking

Good mechanics can locate the problem in your car because they know how your car functions when it *isn't having any problems*. A lot of people find economic problems baffling because they do not have a clear notion of how an economic system works when it's working well. They are like mechanics whose training has been limited entirely to the studying of malfunctioning engines.

When we have long taken something for granted, it's hard even to see what it is that we've grown accustomed to. That's why we rarely notice the existence of order in society and cannot recognize the processes of social coordination upon which we depend every day. A good way to begin the study of economics, therefore, might be with astonishment at the feats of social cooperation in which we daily engage. Rush-hour traffic is an excellent example.

Recognizing Order

You are supposed to gasp at that suggestion. "Rush-hour traffic as an example of social *cooperation*? Shouldn't that be used to illustrate the law of the jungle or the *breakdown* of social cooperation?" Not at all. If the association that pops into your mind when someone says "rush-hour traffic" is "traffic jam," you are neatly supporting the thesis that we notice only failures and take success so much for granted we aren't even aware of it. The dominant characteristic of rush-hour traffic is not jam but movement, which is why people venture into it day after day and almost always reach their destinations. It doesn't work perfectly, of course. (Name one thing that does.) But the remarkable fact at which we should learn to marvel is that it works at all.

Thousands of people leave their homes at about eight in the morning, slide into their automobiles, and head for work. They all choose their own routes without any consultation. They have

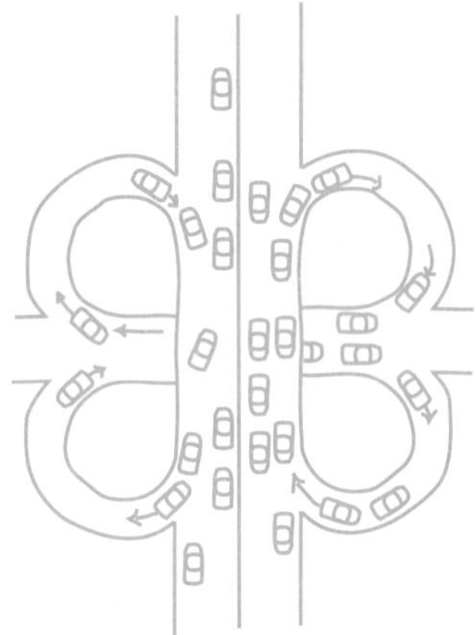

diverse skills, differing attitudes toward risk, and varying degrees of courtesy. As these passenger automobiles in their wide assortment of sizes and shapes enter, move along, and exit from the intersecting corridors that make up the city's traffic veins and arteries, they are joined by an even more heterogeneous mixture of trucks, buses, motorcycles, and taxicabs. The drivers all pursue their separate objectives, with an almost single-minded devotion to their own interests, not necessarily because they are selfish but simply because none of them knows anything about the objectives of the others. What each one does know about the others is confined to a few observations on the position, direction, and velocity of a changing handful of vehicles in the immediate environment. To this they add the important assumption that other drivers are about as eager to avoid an accident as they themselves are. There are general rules, of course, that everyone is expected to obey, such as stopping for red lights and staying close to the speed limit. That's about it, however. The entire arrangement as just described could be a prescription for chaos. It ought to end in heaps of mangled steel.

Instead we witness a smoothly coordinated flow, a flow so smooth, in fact, that an aerial view from a distance can almost be a source of aesthetic pleasure. There they are—all those independently operated vehicles down below, inserting themselves into the momentary spaces between other vehicles, staying so close and yet rarely touching, cutting across one another's paths with only a second or two separating a safe passage from a jarring collision, accelerating when space opens before them and slowing down when it contracts. Rather than anarchy and chaos, the movement of rush-hour traffic, or indeed of urban traffic at any time of day, really is an astounding feat of social cooperation.

The Importance of Social Cooperation

Everyone is familiar with traffic but almost no one thinks of it as a cooperative endeavor. We depend on processes of coordination for far more than what we usually think of as "economic" goods. Without institutions that encourage cooperation, we couldn't enjoy the benefits of civilization. "In such a condition," as Thomas Hobbes observed in an often-quoted passage of his book, *Leviathan* (1651), there is no place for industry, because the fruit thereof is uncertain; and consequently no culture of the earth; no navigation, nor use of the commodities that may be imported by sea; no commodious building; no instruments of moving and removing such things as require much force; no knowledge of the face of the earth; no account of time; no arts; no letters; no society; and, which is worst of all, continual fear and danger of violent death; and the life of man—solitary, poor, nasty, brutish, and short.

Because Hobbes believed that people were so committed to self-preservation and personal satisfaction that only force (or the threat of it) could keep them from constantly assaulting one another, his writings emphasize only the most basic form of social cooperation: abstention from violence and robbery. He seems to have supposed that if people could merely be induced not to attack one another's persons or property, then positive cooperation—the kind that actually produces industry, agriculture, knowledge, and art—would develop of its own accord. But will it? Why should it?

How Does It Happen?

How do people encourage one another to take precisely those complexly interconnected actions that will eventually produce the multitude of goods and services that we all enjoy? Even a society of saints must use some procedures for inducing positive cooperation *of the right kind* if the life of each saint is to be more than "solitary, poor, nasty, brutish, and short." Saints must, after all, somehow find out exactly what ought to be done and when and where it ought to be done before they can play an effective part in helping others.

Three hundred and fifty years have passed since Hobbes examined society. Hobbes probably failed to see the importance of this question for understanding life in the "commonwealth" because the society he knew was far simpler, more bound by custom and tradition, and less subject to rapid and disruptive change than the societies in which we have grown up. Not until well into the eighteenth century, as a matter of fact, did any significant number of thinkers begin to wonder why it was that society "worked"—that individuals pursuing their own interests, with extremely limited information, nonetheless managed to produce not chaos but a remarkably ordered, productive society.

One of the most perceptive and surely the most influential of these eighteenth-century thinkers was Adam Smith. Smith lived in an age when most educated people believed that only the careful planning of political rulers could prevent a society from degenerating into disorder and poverty. Smith did not agree. But in order to refute the accepted opinion of his day, he had to describe the process of social coordination that he saw operating in society—a process that not only functioned, in his judgment, without the constant attention of government but also worked so powerfully that it often canceled the effects of contrary governmental policies. Adam Smith published his analysis in 1776 as *An Inquiry into the Nature and Causes of the Wealth of Nations* and thereby established his claim to the title Founder of Economics. He did not *invent* "the economic way of thinking" but he developed it more extensively than any of his predecessors had done, and he was the first writer to use it in a comprehensive analysis of social change and social cooperation.

An Apparatus of the Mind—The Skill of the Economist

What exactly do we mean by *the economic way of thinking*? To begin with, it is exactly what the term suggests: an approach, rather than a set of conclusions. John Maynard Keynes phrased it aptly in the statement quoted in the front of this book:

> The Theory of Economics does not furnish a body of settled conclusions immediately applicable to policy. It is a method rather than a doctrine, an apparatus of mind, a technique of thinking which helps its possessor to draw correct conclusions.

But what is this "technique of thinking"? It's a little hard to describe in any way that is both brief and clear. You will come to see what it is by practicing it yourself. Perhaps it can best be summarized as a set of concepts derived from one fundamental presupposition: *All social phenomena emerge from the actions and interactions of individuals who are choosing in response to expected additional benefits and costs to themselves.*

That's a rather sweeping assertion. *All* social phenomena? You bet. The fact is, and it might as well be admitted at the outset, that economists believe that their theory explains a lot more than what people usually have in mind when talking about "the economic sector" of society. Economics is not only about money and profit, business and finance. Nor is it only a study of people's competitive behaviors. In fact, economics studies people's choices and the unintended consequences—the unanticipated side effects—of their choices. Rush-hour traffic and international trade can both be studied using the economic way of thinking; so, too, can nonprofit businesses and socially concerned charities and government bureaus. If we have found a way to explain the behavior of International Business Machines and the American Farm Bureau Federation, why shouldn't it also explain the behavior of the Internal Revenue Service and the Department of Agriculture in the United States government? Isn't every branch and agency of government made up, just like any other social group, of individuals who choose on the basis of expected benefits and costs to themselves?

Don't misunderstand. Economic theory does not assume that people are selfish or materialistic or shortsighted or irresponsible or interested exclusively in money. None of these is implied by the assumption that individuals choose on the basis of expected benefits and costs to themselves. Everything depends on what people take to be benefits and costs and the relative values they place upon these benefits and costs. Economic theory does not deny the reality or importance of generosity, public spirit, or any other virtue. Economists would be foolish if they denied the facts.

The economic way of thinking, when put to work, displays three aspects, one focusing on *actions*, the second on *interactions*, and the third on *consequences*, whether those consequences are intended or unintended. The focus on actions emphasizes *economizing* and *trade-offs*, or sacrifices. To economize means to use resources in a way that extracts from them the most of whatever the economizer wants. Scarcity makes economizing necessary. Although someone with access to unlimited resources would not have to economize, keep in mind that time is a scarce resource, at least for mortals, so that even people with more money than they know how to spend must economize. Because a week on the ski slopes in Utah is a week that cannot be spent on the beaches of Acapulco, you must choose, no matter how large your money income. Even Bill Gates must choose how to best use his time and wealth—shall he search next month for more investment opportunities or take a hard-earned vacation on a remote island? Even he can't have everything all at once. Even he faces trade-offs. In fact, he even faces trade-offs—choices—when deciding what to do with the next billion dollars he earns. Shall he stuff it in his mattress, invest it in another Microsoft venture, or place it in his charitable foundation? His options may be very different from yours, but like you, Bill Gates still faces scarcity. As we shall see in the chapters ahead, the economic way of thinking clarifies the economizing process, the actions of choosing under the constraints that scarcity imposes.

Economizing actions

It also clarifies a lot of puzzling but important *inter*actions. If the core problem for economic actions is scarcity, the core problem for economic *inter*actions is a *multiplicity of diverse and even incompatible individual projects*. We deal with scarcity by economizing. We deal with the fact that we require the cooperation of millions of other people whom we don't even know by participating in a coordinating process. The urban traffic example illustrates both aspects. When they are planning their route, thinking about a lane change, or deciding whether to speed up or slow down as the traffic light turns orange, commuters are engaged in economizing actions. They are making choices—doing what each thinks is best under the circumstances. But their actions get coordinated through a process that is much more than the simple sum of each driver's behavior. No driver (and no central traffic planner!) controls this process with all its interactions, and yet the process manages to coordinate all those individual decisions. Although the process is never perfect, most people successfully reach their destinations.

And this leads us to consider the idea of *unintended consequences*. Each and every driver intends to reach his or her destination, each makes decisions along the way, and each interacts with others on the road. The *overall flow of traffic*, however, is not intended by anyone. It is not in any single driver's control. Nor does some fictional central traffic planner tell everybody exactly what to do to ensure an orderly flow. The complex pattern of traffic emerges spontaneously, as an unintended consequence of people "merely driving." Much of what motivates the economic way of thinking is in asking the question "How can such an orderly pattern of events emerge, not on purpose, but as a by-product of people pursuing their own separate interests?"

In modern industrial societies, people's economizing actions occur in the context of extreme specialization. Specialization, or what Adam Smith called the division of labor, is a necessary condition for the increases in production that have so expanded "the wealth of nations" in recent centuries. But specialization in the absence of coordination is the road to chaos, not wealth. How is it possible for millions of people to pursue the particular projects in which each of them is interested, on the basis of their own unique resources and capabilities, in almost total ignorance of the interests, resources, and capabilities of almost everyone else upon whose cooperation their own projects depend for success?

commerical society as defined by Adam Smith

Economic theory will turn out to be most illuminating when used to answer this question, to explain the often mysterious working of what Adam Smith called *commercial society*. "When the division of labour has been once thoroughly established," Smith observed early in *The Wealth of Nations*,

> it is but a very small part of a man's wants which the produce of his own labour can supply. He supplies the far greater part of them by exchanging that surplus part of the produce of his own labour, which is over and above his own consumption, for such parts of the produce of other men's labour as he has occasion for. Every man thus lives by exchanging, or becomes in some measure a merchant, and the society itself grows to be what is properly a commercial society.

Interactions: exchange

The successful coordination of activity in such a society, where everyone lives by specializing and exchanging, is a task of extraordinary complexity. Think for a moment about the activities that had to be precisely coordinated in order for you to enjoy this morning's breakfast. Farmers, truck drivers, construction workers, bankers, and supermarket checkers are just a few of the multitude of people whose efforts contributed to the production, processing, transportation, and distribution of your breakfast cereal or toast. (It gets even more fantastic: Think of all the miners who unearthed the iron ore that made the steel that made the trucks that drove the bricks that built the factory that made the tractor that the farmer used to harvest his wheat. We can write an entire book on the countless individuals and organizations that made the farmer's tractor itself, and we still wouldn't have accounted for them all.) How were all these people induced to do exactly the right thing at precisely the right time and place? Economic theory originated and developed largely out of efforts to answer that question. And despite all its imperialistic adventures in recent years, economics still does most of its useful work in explaining the functioning of commercial society, which is what most people probably have in mind when they talk about "the economy."

Cooperation Through Mutual Adjustment

Economic theory asserts that the economizing actions people take in the pursuit of their own interests create the alternatives available to others and that social coordination is a process of continuing mutual adjustment to the changing net advantages that their interactions generate. That is a very abstract argument. We can make it more concrete by referring once more to traffic flow.

Picture a freeway with four lanes in each direction and with all the entrances and exits on the right. Why don't all the drivers stay in the far-right lane? Why do some of them go to the trouble of driving all the way over to the far left when they know they'll have to come back to the right lane to exit? Anyone who has driven on a freeway knows the answer: The traffic flow is impeded in the far-right lane by slow-moving vehicles entering and exiting, so people in a hurry get out of the right lane as quickly as possible.

Which of the other lanes will they choose? Although we can't predict the action of any single driver—we are instead trying to understand the overall patterns that might arise—we know that the drivers will disperse themselves quite evenly among the three other lanes. But why does this happen? How does it happen? The answer is also the explanation of what we meant just now by *a process of continuing mutual adjustment to the changing net advantages that their actions generate*. Drivers are alert to the net advantages of each lane and therefore try to move out of any lanes that are moving slowly and into those that are moving faster. This speeds up the slow lanes and slows down the fast lanes until all lanes are moving at the same rate or, more accurately, until no driver perceives any net advantage to be gained by changing lanes. It all happens quickly, continuously, and far more effectively than if someone at the entrances passed out tickets *assigning* each vehicle to a particular lane.

The same basic principles are at work in the rest of society. Individuals choose their actions on the basis of the net advantages they expect. Their actions alter, however minutely, the relative benefits and costs of the options that others perceive. When the ratio of expected benefit to expected cost for any action increases, people do more of it. When the ratio falls, they do less. The fact that almost everyone prefers more money to less is an enormous aid in the process, an extremely important lubricant, if you will, in the mechanism of social coordination. Modest changes in the monetary cost and monetary benefit of particular options can induce large numbers of people to alter their behavior in directions more consistent with what other people are concurrently doing. And this is the primary system by which we obtain cooperation among the members of society in using what is available to provide what people want. This is what the market economy is all about.

Rules of the Game

Economic systems—the ways and means through which citizens pursue and coordinate their projects and plans—are shaped by the "rules of the game," a phrase you're going to meet repeatedly in this book. The rules of the economic game go a long way in explaining whether people will use scarce resources effectively or wastefully.

Rules affect incentives. Take Major League Baseball, for example. Why do National League pitchers practice bunting while American League pitchers don't engage in batting practice at all? Because the rules of the game are different with respect to pitchers: National League pitchers step up to the plate during the game; the American League substitutes designated hitters for its pitchers. The designated hitter rule provides no incentive for an American League pitcher to become a better batter.

All interactions presuppose some "rules of the game."

Whether the "game" is business, government, science, family, school, traffic, baseball, or chess, it can't be played satisfactorily unless the players know at least roughly what the rules are and generally agree to follow them. The rules must be reasonably stable. Although rules can and will change over time, they must have a fair degree of stability so that they can be known and relied upon (imagine the problems that would emerge were the designated hitter rule to be dropped during the middle of an American League ball game or even during midseason). Often it takes time for participants to understand and adjust appropriately to new rules of the game. Consider, for example, the recent expansion of the strike zone by umpires in Major League Baseball. Players are beginning to adjust their expectations of what counts as a ball and a strike and will adjust their batting strategies in light of the evolution of the rule. Pitchers and catchers are adjusting their strategies as well.

Most social interaction is directed and coordinated by the rules that participants know and follow. When the rules are in dispute or inconsistent or simply not clear, the game tends to break down. This is true not only of a child's game of Go Fish or a professional ball game but for production and trade as well. In the 1990s, the countries of central and eastern Europe that were trying to move from centrally planned and bureaucratically controlled systems of production to decentralized, market-coordinated systems faced no greater obstacle than the absence of clear and accepted rules for the new game they were attempting to play. If you have ever traveled in a foreign country with a culture radically different from your own and a language that you didn't understand, you have some sense of what happens when the rules of the game in a society are suddenly and dramatically upset. People don't know exactly what is expected of them or what they can expect from others. Social cooperation declines quickly in such a setting, as mutually beneficial exchanges under the rules give way to hesitant attempts to find out what the rules are and, in the worst cases, destructive struggles to establish rules that will work in one's own favor.

Property Rights as Rules of the Game

Property rights form a large and important part of the rules governing most of the social interactions in which people regularly engage. A market exchange economy is based upon *private property rights*—rights assigned to specific individuals in the form of legal ownership. They clearly specify who legally owns what. As a private property right owner, no other person may use or alter the physical characteristics of your property without your permission. The neighbor down the street is not allowed to drive your car without your permission, nor is he allowed to jump on the car, repaint it, flatten the tires, or even put in a better stereo system without your approval. (Nor, of course, are you allowed to drive all over his beautiful front yard without his permission.) Moreover, private property rights can be voluntarily *traded or exchanged* for similar rights to other goods and services. The purchase of your car, or a bag of groceries for that matter, is, in the economic way of thinking, an exchange of property rights. You are now assigned ownership of the car, groceries, and so on, and the seller is now assigned ownership of the cash payment.

Property rights are rules of the game.

In former socialist economies, citizens often enjoyed private property rights to consumer goods (clothing, food, radios, etc.), but the means of production—natural resources, land, factories, machinery and other material inputs in the production process—were typically designated as *social property rights*. Here, *ownership is legally assigned to "society" as a whole, and therefore to nobody in particular.* Social property rights are not freely exchangeable. With these rules, it is unclear who is legally allowed to do what with the goods owned by society. Who decides (and through which process of agreement) that a socially owned factory should produce cars or trucks or ships or bombs, or that the factory should be doubled in size, reduced in size, or even continue to operate at all? Can "society as a whole" *really* be expected to make these decisions—not only for a single factory but for *all* of the socially owned means of production—in ways that would tend to encourage economic growth and prosperity?

By deciding exactly what belongs to whom under which circumstances, private property rights provide the members of a society with dependable information and incentives. But a system of satisfactorily clear property rights cannot be created overnight; it will almost inevitably be the product of an evolution over time, in which law, custom, morality, technology, and daily practice interact to establish reliable patterns. A movement away from socialism entails the abolition of old property rights but not necessarily the creation of new ones. The consequence may be chaos rather than market coordination. The road from bureaucratic control of the economy to market control has been a treacherous one for the nations of the former Soviet bloc, with many potholes, washouts, earth slides, and unmapped sections.

In the economic way of thinking, the emergence of clearly defined and enforced property rights does encourage the effective use of already existing scarce resources. Clear property rights also spark efforts to discover *new* resources, to innovate by introducing new cost-cutting technologies, to develop new talents and skills. We shall also demonstrate in the next chapter that the voluntary exchange of property rights can also expand the opportunities and wealth of the trading parties. Of course, economic decay is possible. An outright reduction in resources can reduce a country's production possibilities (consider, for example, the civil wars in Bosnia and Kosovo in the 1990s, and the physical and human destruction that followed, or the massive destruction of lives and property from the earthquake in Iran in 2003, or the bombing of Baghdad that same year, or even the temporary breakdown of the U.S. electrical grid that same year).

The Biases of Economic Theory: A Weakness or A Strength?

Okay, so you're on your way to thinking like an economist. One caveat: Our theory about society is not perfect nor unbiased. (Are you aware of one that is?). It does not offer an unprejudiced view, in which *all* the facts are presented and *all* values are given the same weight. Think again about what we suggested was the fundamental presupposition of economic theory, that all social phenomena emerge from the actions and interactions of individuals who are choosing in response to expected benefits and costs to themselves.

Isn't that a biased perspective? Consider the emphasis on *choice*. Economic theory is so preoccupied with choice that some critics have accused it of assuming people choose to be poor or choose to be unemployed. When we come to the issues of poverty and unemployment, you can decide for yourself whether this is a fair criticism or a misunderstanding. But there can be no doubt that economic theory attempts to explain the social world by assuming that events are the product, and typically the unintended product, of people's choices.

People choose.

Closely related to this focus on choice is the emphasis economic theory gives to the *individual*. Our everyday language sometimes muddies this up. Because only individuals actually choose, economists try to dissect the decisions of such collectives as businesses, governments, or nations until they locate the choices of individual persons within them. For example, you chose to attend your present college, but surely the college itself didn't "choose" to admit you as a student. The college itself is composed of a number of individuals with diverse roles and responsibilities. Some individuals within the college, acting in the *name of the college*, made that choice. The groundskeepers, the secretaries, and most if not all of the faculty and other students probably played no part in the choice of admitting you as a new student. Similarly, neither Microsoft, the Red Cross, New York City, nor the Al Qaeda terrorist organization makes choices. Individuals within those collectives make choices. (Could you imagine any of those organizations making decisions if they weren't composed of individual people? And even if you could, do you think that would lead to an insightful way of explaining how they operate?) Just as any good physics student learns to see through our everyday language about the sun "rising" and "setting" (she instead knows that the earth rotates around the sun and that makes it appear that the sun goes up and down), so, too, a good economics student ought to quickly learn that individuals make choices and decisions, rather than organizations themselves.

Only individuals choose.

Economic thinking is also criticized by some as false or misleading because of its emphasis on the economizing process, on calculation and consistency of ends and means. Economists assume that people act with a purpose in mind, that they compare the expected costs and benefits of available opportunities before they act, and that they learn from and therefore do not repeat their mistakes. But are people really that calculating? Aren't our actions guided more by unconscious urges and unexamined impulses than all this would admit? And is every action really a means to some end, a pursuit of some clearly given goal? Although economists do not claim that people know everything or never make mistakes, the economic way of thinking does indeed assume that people's actions follow from comparisons of benefits and costs. And it does emphasize the instrumental character of human action while neglecting the fact that many important

Individuals choose after weighing benefits and costs.

activities—a spirited conversation, perhaps, or a friendly game of tennis—are not engaged in as a means to some other end.

Another charge often leveled against the economic way of thinking is that it harbors a *pro-market* bias. This criticism, too, calls attention to a genuine and significant characteristic of economic theory, although this characteristic may not be altogether what it seems to be. Economic theory originated as a study of markets, of complex exchange processes, and economists have learned a great deal over the years about the conditions under which exchange works poorly or well. The economist's alleged pro-market bias is probably better seen as a preference for those social institutions and rules of the game that make exchange mutually beneficial and production more efficient—a process from which all participants derive benefit.

Biases or Conclusions?

Are they really biases or prejudices? Why couldn't we call them convictions (or even conclusions) and simply say that economists explain social phenomena by observing scarcity, choice, trade-offs, and consequences, because this enables us to understand those phenomena? Do we say that physicists are biased when they argue that energy cannot be created nor destroyed, or that biologists are biased because they assume that DNA molecules control the development of organisms?

The questions we're raising now are important and interesting.[1] But we cannot follow them further without pushing this introductory chapter to an intolerable length. It has long seemed obvious to the authors that the search for knowledge of any kind necessarily begins with some *commitments* on the part of the inquirer. We cannot approach the world with a completely open mind, because we weren't born yesterday. And completely open minds would in any event be completely empty minds, which can learn nothing at all. All discussion, every inquiry, and even each act of observation are rooted in and grow out of convictions. We must begin somewhere with something. Even economists face limited resources and therefore make choices and trade-offs. We proceed from where we find ourselves and on the basis of what we believe to be true, important, useful, or enlightening. We may, of course, be wrong in any of these judgments. Indeed, we are always wrong to some extent, since every "true"

[1]The thoughtful student who would like to pursue these issues further might wish to consider reading *The Structure of Scientific Revolutions* by Thomas S. Kuhn (Chicago: University of Chicago Press, 1970). This highly readable essay on the history and philosophy of science has had an enormous influence on the thinking of social scientists, include these three authors, about the respective roles of assumption and evidence in their investigations.

statement necessarily leaves out a great deal that is also true and thus errs by omission. The most detailed road map is a simplification of reality.

We cannot avoid this risk, as some people suppose, by steering clear of theory. *Economics is a theory of choice and its unintended consequences*. People who sneer at "fancy theories" and prefer to rely on common sense and everyday experience are often in fact the victims of extremely vague and sweeping hypotheses. Common sense might lead someone to believe that pot smoking *leads to* more powerful drugs, because most hard drug users started on pot. Yet, most pot users had previously been milk drinkers—does milk drinking therefore *lead to* pot smoking? Even though milk has heavy amounts of L-tryptophane—the same amino acid in turkey that leads to drowsiness—surely these "facts," by themselves, cannot prove that one fact caused the other. Or, consider the so-called "Superbowl Effect." Financial journalists often report, during Superbowl week, an interesting set of facts. When an NFC team wins the Superbowl, the Dow Jones Industrial Average does well over the course of the year; when an AFC team wins, the Dow does poorly that year. This held about 100 percent of the time until the Green Bay Packers (an NFC team) messed it up in 1998. Today, it is said to hold about 80 percent of the time. *Hold what?* The *fact* that the Dow had often done well after an NFC victory and poorly after an NFC loss provides little insight about financial markets and the Dow. It doesn't necessarily follow that the Superbowl outcome *causes* (or "leads to") the value of Dow stocks to rise or fall. To conclude otherwise is to fall victim to the all-too-common but profoundly mistaken reasoning that the association or statistical correlation among groups of facts establishes some kind of causation among those facts. It may, in fact, be a mere coincidence.

Economics defined.

No Theory Means Poor Theory

The point is a simple but important one. We can observe facts, but it takes a theory to explain the causes. It takes a theory about cause and effect to weed out the irrelevant facts from the relevant ones (and so, although the facts clearly show that most pot smokers were former milk drinkers, milk drinking is probably not a relevant fact in explaining pot smoking; similarly, the Superbowl is likely irrelevant when explaining Wall Street interactions). Our observations of the world are in fact drenched with theory, which is why we can usually make sense out of the buzzing confusion that assaults our eyes and ears. Actually, we observe only a small fraction of what we "know," a hint here and a suggestion there. The rest we fill in from the theories we hold: small and broad, vague and precise, well tested and poorly tested, widely held and sometimes peculiar, carefully reasoned and dimly recognized.

This textbook developed out of a growing suspicion that when students found economic theory mystifying and tedious, it was largely because we economists were trying to teach them too much. This book very consciously sets out, therefore, to achieve more by attempting less. It is organized around a set of concepts that collectively make up the economist's basic kit of intellectual tools. The tools—actually, the skills—are all related to the fundamental assumption we have discussed and are surprisingly few in number. But they are extraordinarily versatile. They unlock such mysteries as foreign exchange rates, business firms that make profits by accepting losses, the nature of money, and different prices charged for "identical" goods—mysteries that are generally conceded to be in the economist's province. But they also shed light on a wide range of issues that are not ordinarily thought of as economic at all—traffic congestion, environmental pollution, the workings of government, and the behavior of college administrators—to mention just a few that you will encounter in the chapters ahead.

It's important to realize, however, that economic theory *by itself* cannot answer any interesting or important social questions. The economic way of thinking has to be supplemented with knowledge drawn from other sources: knowledge about history, culture, politics, psychology, and the social institutions that shape people's values and behavior. Learning the mere techniques of economic analysis is far easier than mastering the art of applying them sensibly and persuasively to actual social problems in their infinite complexity. The best economists and students of economics aren't mere technicians. They are skilled users of the economic way of thinking.

But this is not the time to worry about the fact that intelligent applications of economic theory will always be difficult and uncertain. The primary goal of this book is to get you started in the practice of thinking the way economists think, in the belief that once you start you will never stop. Economic thinking is addictive. Once you get inside some principle of economic reasoning and make it your own, opportunities to use it pop up everywhere. You begin to notice that much of what is said or written about economic and social issues is a mixture of sense and nonsense. You begin to think "outside the box," which tends to be a scarce, powerful, and rewarding intellectual skill.

Can you connect all points together with straight lines without retracing or taking your pen off the paper? (Hint: Think outside the box.)

Once Over Lightly

The economic way of thinking was developed by social theorists largely to explain how order and cooperation emerge from the apparently uncoordinated interactions of individuals pursuing their own interests in substantial ignorance of the interests of those with whom they are cooperating. Economics is a theory of choice and its unintended consequences.

The fundamental assumption of the economic way of thinking is that all social phenomena emerge from the actions and interactions of individuals who are choosing in response to expected benefits and costs to themselves. Only individuals make choices. They may make those choices on their own or by collaborating in groups (households, business firms, government bureaus, and so on). But that should not lead us to lose sight of the fact that the choices in the name of a group were really made by individuals who evaluate trade-offs and economize in the pursuit of their plans and projects. Individuals economizing in the face of scarcity create the alternatives available to others, and their interactions are coordinated by a process of continuing mutual adjustment to the changing net advantages that their actions generate.

The perspective of economic theory on human actions and interactions places a strong emphasis on choices by individuals who continually compare expected additional benefits and costs. We often call this economizing behavior. While this is a biased or limited perspective, theory of some kind is indispensable for anyone who wants to understand the complex phenomena of social life.

The economic way of thinking also emphasizes the importance of the rules of the game, and the way those rules tend to influence our choices. By legally assigning ownership of scarce goods, property rights are a key element of the rules of the game. Social property rights assign ownership to society in general, and therefore nobody in particular. But the problem is, society by itself never makes choices and decisions. Only individuals can do that. A system of private property rights assigns rights to specific individuals, rights that can be voluntary traded. Being freely exchangeable, private property rights help clarify our options and opportunities and form the foundation of the market-exchange economy.

QUESTIONS FOR DISCUSSION

1. How much do people have to know about one another in order to cooperate effectively? Contrast the situation of two family members who are planning to take a vacation together with the situation of motorists who are simultaneously using intersecting streets. How are "collisions" avoided in each case? What do you know about the interests, the personality, or the character of the people whose cooperation supplied your breakfast this morning?
2. What do you predict would happen if planners in Dallas decided to reserve one lane on each of its freeways for "urgent vehicles," with an urgent vehicle defined as any vehicle whose driver might be late for an important event if the vehicle were to be delayed by congestion in the

regular lanes? Do you think drivers would stay out of the urgent vehicle lane? Or would it become just as congested as all the other lanes? Would such an idea be more likely to succeed in practice if drivers were generally less selfish and more considerate?

3. When Mother Teresa accepted the Nobel Prize for Peace in October 1979 and decided to use the $190,000 award to construct a leprosarium, was she acting in her own interest? Was she behaving selfishly? Was she economizing?
4. A newspaper item reported that two-thirds of all mothers who work outside the home "do it for the money, not by choice." Are those really alternatives? Either for the money or by choice?
5. How important are monetary motives? A story in the *Wall Street Journal* of May 1, 1995 reported the results of a survey conducted by Kaplan Educational Centers of its students preparing to take the Law School Aptitude Exam. They were asked what attracted them to a career in law. Only 8 percent said they were attracted by the financial rewards. But 62 percent thought that *others* were attracted by the financial rewards. How would you interpret this disparity?
6. Why do most people want larger money incomes? Former British Prime Minister Margaret Thatcher once suggested that people are motivated by money not because they are greedy, but because money gives them more control over their lives. What do *you* think most people are ultimately after when they make sacrifices in order to increase their money incomes?
7. What happens when the rules of the game (written or unwritten) decree that important student government meetings won't start until everyone is present and that late arrivals will incur no penalty? Is it in anyone's interest to be punctual? Are these rules of the game likely to prove satisfactory over time?
8. What are some of the more important rules that coordinate the actions of all those playing the "game" of this economics course? Who decided where and when the class would meet, who would teach it, who would enroll as students, what the textbook would be, when the exams would be given, and so on? Who decides where each student will sit? Do you find it odd that two students rarely try to occupy the same seat?
9. Have you ever noticed that the grounds of city-owned parks are often more polluted than those of country clubs?
   (a) Is it simply because people who use parks are less concerned with pollution compared to those who golf? Is that even true?
   (b) Might the property-rights assignments have something to do with it? Who owns the city park? Who owns the country club?
   (c) Though their grounds are often impeccably clean, country clubs tend to use powerful fertilizers that eventually seep into and pollute the water table below, causing problems for others in the surrounding community. Who owns the water table?
10. What do we mean when we say, "That's just a coincidence; it doesn't prove anything"? How does theory enable us to distinguish relevant evidence from mere coincidence?

11. Would you say that physicians who don't believe acupuncture works are biased if they reject it without trying it? If someone told you that you can get a perfect grade in this course, without studying, just by regularly chanting the mantra "invisible hand," would you believe it? Would it be a sign of bias or prejudice on your part if you totally ignored this advice even though you are extremely eager for a high grade in the course?
12. Someone has calculated that American women with four years of college have twice as many babies on average as women with five years of college. Assume the data are correct. What conclusions would you draw? Would you infer that going to college for a fifth year reduces female fertility? Would you caution a woman who has just completed four years of college not to take a fifth year if she is determined to have children? What theories are you using?

2

Efficiency, Exchange, and Comparative Advantage

Economists generally favor free trade, but trading has long had an unsavory reputation in the Western world. This is probably the result of a deep-seated human conviction that nothing can *really* be gained through mere exchange. Agriculture and manufacturing are believed to be genuinely productive: They seem to create something new, something additional. But trade only exchanges one thing for another. It seems to follow that the merchant, who profits from trading, must be imposing some kind of tax on the community. The wages or other profit of the farmer and artisan can be obtained from the alleged real product of their efforts, so that they are entitled in some sense to their income; they reap what they have sown. But merchants seem to reap without sowing; their activity does not appear to create anything and yet they are rewarded for their efforts. Trading, some have thought, is therefore social waste, the epitome of inefficiency.

This line of argument strikes a deeply responsive chord in many people who still retain the old hostility toward the merchant in the form of a distrust of the "middleman." People often want to bypass the middleman, who is pictured as a kind of legal bandit on the highways of trade, authorized to exact a percentage from everyone foolish or unlucky enough to come his way. (And in a market system they often are free to avoid the middleman; yet, more often than not, people choose to use the middlemen's services.)

However ancient or deep-seated this conviction of the unproductiveness of trade, however, it is completely mistaken. There is no defensible sense of the word *productive* that can be applied to agriculture or manufacturing but not to trading. Exchange is productive! It is productive because it makes available more of what people want.

The exchange of private property rights is fundamental to market processes. This chapter explores the central reason why people voluntarily trade goods and services. We shall show that trade increases the wealth of the trading parties, that trade generates efficiency. We shall also introduce you to your first graphs—the production possibilities frontiers. Graphs are a useful tool to recognize trade-offs and to clarify the growth in wealth that occurs through specialization and exchange.

Goods and Bads

The act of cooperative exchange is fundamentally an agreement to swap property rights—ownership—of goods and services. Your purchase of oranges at the local grocery provides you the opportunity to consume the oranges as you now wish and provides the grocer the opportunity to use the cash payment as best he sees fit. What were his (the oranges) are now yours; what was yours (the 3 dollars) are now the grocer's. In many of our everyday exchanges there is no explicitly written contract. (It is simply understood that you now own the oranges.) In other exchanges, such as the purchase of a car or a home, or the rental of an apartment unit, contracts and agreements will be drafted giving clear account of who owns what and how the property can be used.

Economists are fascinated with the everyday exchange of goods, and, thankfully, we have a very clear meaning of the word *good*. In the economic way of thinking, something is a *good* if, in the eyes of the chooser, *more of it is preferred to less*. It's that simple. We can analyze the concept of a good a little further by distinguishing between a "free good" and a "scarce good." *A free good is a good that can be acquired without sacrifice; a scarce good can only be acquired by sacrificing some other good.*

A good is anything whereby more of it is preferred to less.

Your voluntary purchase of oranges, for example, suggests that oranges are a good to you, and, moreover, they're a scarce good because you sacrificed something else you value (the 3 dollars) to gain ownership of the oranges. Your roommate's willingness to stand in line for "free" concert tickets suggests that those tickets are a scarce good for her. She'd prefer to have them, and she sacrifices her time that could have been devoted to some other activity that she values. Think of it this way. A good is *scarce* if one must incur a *sacrifice* to obtain it.

A scarce good can be obtained only through sacrifice.

Something represents a free good only if it is acquired without any sacrifice whatsoever. Free goods are harder to imagine, but they do exist. It's all a matter of context. Air is a scarce good to a scuba diver, but air is typically a free good to students in the college classroom. Lovely tropical sunshine is a free good to the child born and raised in the Bahamas, but it's a scarce good for the family that travels from Milwaukee to enjoy a few hot days during the winter holidays.

If only all goods were free goods! Then none of us would face scarcity, none of us would have to make sacrifices, trade-offs, or choices. We would have everything that we could possibly desire, automatically. Heaven is often depicted that way. The problem is, here on earth, we face scarcity. We can't have everything we desire all at once. We must choose.

The economic problem: scarcity.

And not only that, economic "bads" also exist. If a good is something in which more is preferred to less, then, you've guessed it, *a bad is something in which less is preferred to more*. Summertime mosquito bites, Los Angeles smog, and the terror of 9/11 are just a few examples of bads. In all of this, don't forget that the notion of an economic good—or bad—is subjective. Consider your authors here. Boettke detests bluegrass music. Prychitko loves it. We're not sure if Paul Heyne had any strong opinion of it either way. What's considered a bad to one person might very well be a good to somebody else, and neither a good *nor* a bad to yet another person.

The Myth of Material Wealth

If we are going to demonstrate that trade, and therefore market exchanges of scarce goods in general, creates "wealth," it is also best to clarify what we mean by that word, too.

Of what does wealth consist? What constitutes your own wealth? Many people have drifted into the habit of supposing that an economic system produces "material wealth," *things* such as Palm Pilots, Sun workstations, John Deere tractors, Ford minivans, Martin guitars, Sunbeam toasters, Jim Beam whiskey, Game Boys, and Harry Potter novels. But none of these is wealth unless it is available to someone who values it. *Wealth, in the economic way of thinking, is whatever people value.*

Wealth is whatever people value.

And value is in the eyes of the chooser. Buddha, we are reminded, wanted nothing—and that's pretty much what he got. Since he had found what he wanted, he had greatly increased his wealth. He had found nirvana. But different people can, and do, have quite different values. Additional water is additional wealth to a farmer who wants to irrigate; it is not wealth to a farmer caught in a Mississippi River flood. Two feet of fresh snow is additional wealth to the owner of a ski resort, but perhaps only a backbreaking burden to the driveway shoveler. An accordion is wealth to a front man in a polka band, but not to the boys in Metallica.

Economic growth consists not in increasing the production of *things*, but in increasing the production of *wealth*. Material things can contribute to wealth, obviously, and are in some sense essential to the production of wealth (accordions are made of material things; snow can be made by snowmaking machines). Even such "nonmaterial" goods as health, love, and peace of mind do, after all, have some material embodiment. But there is no necessary relation between the growth of wealth and an increase in the volume or weight or quantity of material objects. The claim that "wealth = material things" must be rejected at root. It makes no sense. And it blocks understanding of many aspects of economic life, such as specialization and exchange—the heart of what Adam Smith called the commercial society.

Trade Creates Wealth

Those suspicious of trade, going at least as far back as Aristotle, tended to believe that voluntary exchange is always (or *should* be) the exchange of equal values. The exact reverse is true: Voluntary exchange is never an exchange of equal values. *If it were, it would not occur.* Traders cooperate with one another to enjoy the opportunity to gain *more* of what each values. The opportunity for each to gain provides the incentive. In an informed and uncoerced exchange, both parties expect to gain by giving up something of lesser value for something of greater value. If Jack swaps his basketball for Jim's baseball glove, Jack values the glove more than the ball, and Jim values the ball more than the glove. We observe each person freely sacrifice one good he values for some other good he values more. Viewed from either side, the exchange was unequal, for the traders have differing values; otherwise, they wouldn't have rearranged their property rights of the ball and glove ("the glove is now *yours*"). And that is precisely the source of its productivity. Jack now has greater wealth than he had before, and so does Jim. The exchange was productive because it increased the wealth of both parties.

"Not really," says a contentious voice from the rear of the classroom. "There was no real increase in wealth. Jack and Jim feel better off, it's true; they may be happier and all that. But the exchange didn't really produce anything. There is still just one baseball glove and one basketball, regardless of who the new owner is."

True, nothing physically new has been manufactured by the swap. But what is manufacturing, anyway? Factories, raw material inputs, workers' sweat and toil, and the packaging of final products immediately leap to mind. We tend to picture the technical element of production—looking only "inside the box," as it were. We are inclined to ignore that manufacturers of the baseball glove and the basketball technically try to rearrange those materials into *more valuable combinations*. That's the economic element—they are trying to *add* value—that's why they're manufacturing in the first place. All it takes is a little thought outside the box.

The swapping of the ball for the glove didn't produce a new material thing—it didn't require an additional technical feat—but it did produce a rearranged pattern valued more highly by both Jack and Jim, and that's why they traded. It added value, wealth, for Jack and for Jim. Think of exchange as being an alternative way of producing something. Jack used the basketball as an "input" to obtain the "output" of a baseball glove. For Jim the glove was the input and the ball the output.

Each traded a scarce and valuable good for a more valuable good. Each incurred a cost. In fact, any choice or action entails a trade-off, a forsaken opportunity. In the economic way of thinking, *the cost of obtaining anything is the value placed on whatever must be sacrificed in order to obtain it*. We call that, for emphasis, an *opportunity cost*. Jack valued the basketball, but he freely sacrificed that for something he valued even more, the glove. Jim valued the glove, but sacrificed that for something he valued more, the ball. Each found that the benefit outweighed the cost. They each enjoyed a net benefit—an increase in their wealth.

Any choice implies a sacrifice, an opportunity cost.

Where did the additional wealth come from? If Jack enjoys more wealth after the trade, it might seem that it must have come from Jim. But notice that Jim also enjoys more wealth. It could not have been taken away from Jack. Instead, the voluntary trade was an opportunity that created more wealth for both traders. Each found a way to increase his own wealth by cooperating in an exchange.

The result of the productive process (the exchange) was an output value greater than input value for both parties. Nothing further is required to make an activity productive. The exchange expanded real wealth. It was an efficient way for the two parties to get more of what they wanted.

Is It Worth It? Efficiency and Values

Economists speak a lot about efficiency. So let's try to answer this question: Which is more efficient, a car that gets 25 miles per gallon or a car that gets 75 miles per gallon? At first blush it seems that higher miles per gallon necessarily means higher efficiency. And, in some technical sense, that's true. A gallon of fuel "input" goes further, provides greater "output," with the more "fuel-efficient" car. And those figures, the "objective data," as it were, are an important piece of information for the prospective car buyer. But the decision maker will surely ask another question: "Is it worth it?" After all, the greater fuel efficiency often comes at a greater cost. When making a decision, an individual tends to weigh all the expected additional benefits against all the expected additional costs.

The additional *cost* of acquiring the car with the higher miles per gallon is an important piece of information for the chooser. Suppose the auto that gets 75 miles per gallon is priced at $80,000, while the auto that gets only 25 miles per gallon is priced at $20,000. Most prospective buyers might feel that the higher mileage is simply not worth the higher price. For them, the additional costs of acquiring such a vehicle outweigh the additional benefits provided by the greater fuel savings. The concept of technical efficiency, which only focuses on the objective data (such as miles per gallon), does not account for the *values* that the chooser places on the inputs and the outputs. The economist's notion of efficiency—call it *economic efficiency*, for emphasis—compares, from the chooser's own perspective, the additional benefits against the additional costs. A decision or plan of action is said to be economically efficient if the chooser judges that the expected additional benefits will exceed the expected additional costs.

Something is economically efficient if the additional benefits outweigh the additional costs.

Simply put, a question that asks "Is it worth it?" is a question about economic efficiency. And each of us might answer that question very differently. One office worker drives a Hummer to work, another takes the bus, and a third rides a bicycle. Each worker compared the additional costs and benefits and selected the form of travel that they thought was best. Each is pursuing an "economically efficient" way to get to work. Their disagreements at the office about the best way to get to work are ultimately disagreements over values.

That's right. An economist cannot definitively answer questions such as "Which is more efficient, a nursing degree or a philosophy degree? A cell phone or a pay phone? Clear-cutting forests or selective thinning?" In fact, stated this way, these questions are *meaningless*. It all depends on the situation at hand.

What we value determines what we will consider efficient or inefficient. Disagreements in society about the relative efficiency of particular projects will usually be disagreements about the relative value to be assigned to particular goods—or the relative disvalue of particular nongoods. Knowing this won't settle any controversial issue. But failing even to recognize what we're arguing about surely makes the resolution of controversy more difficult.

The question is not "What is *really* more efficient?" but rather "Who has the *right* to make particular decisions?" Crawling out of a sleeping bag to climb a mountain is atrociously inefficient to someone who plans to crawl back into that sleeping bag in the evening and is merely looking for the shortest distance between those two points. Fans of mountain climbing strenuously disagree, of course. But that creates no social conflict, because we all agree that individuals should have the right to decide for themselves whether it's more valuable to put their bodies on mountain peaks or to keep them in bed during vacations. It is when we do not agree on who has which rights that we get into vehement arguments about whether it is "really" efficient, for example, to clear-cut forests or to strip-mine coal. Or whether extensive use of the single-occupant vehicle is "incredibly inefficient in a world of rapidly depleting natural resources."

When the rules of the game establish clear and secure property rights, they implicitly decide by what process prospective benefits and costs are to be evaluated for decision-making purposes. If Mom decides to open her windows and turn up the thermostat on a cold winter day, she is using resources efficiently as long as she has an uncontested right to allocate all the resources she's using. If, on the other hand, she is cooling off someone else's living space, or if someone else is paying her heating bills, her property rights are likely to be challenged. Then the issue becomes not the efficiency of her preferred arrangements but rather her exclusive right to value the inputs and the outputs in what she does.

When property rights are clear, stable, and exchangeable, scarce resources tend to acquire money prices that reflect their relative scarcity. Decision makers then pursue efficiency by using these prices as information, the subject of the next few chapters. To say that the prices are "wrong" because they don't reflect the real value of certain costs or benefits amounts to rejecting the entire market process by which those prices were determined. It is a critique not of efficiency, but of the existing system of property rights and of the rules of the game of which they form a part.

Recognizing Trade-Offs: Comparing Opportunity Costs of Production

Economists can safely argue that individuals who engage in voluntary exchange do so because *they* think it's worth it. They find exchange to be an efficient way of enjoying greater wealth. Let's consider this a bit further using the following example.

In a house on Elm Street, Jones makes two kinds of beer, a lager and a stout. (A lager is a rather light beer; a stout is dark and heavy.) Every three months he can make *either* 10 gallons of quality lager *or* 5 gallons of quality stout, or any linear combination in between. This is illustrated by Jones's production possibilities frontier in Figure 2–1. *The production possibilities frontier illustrates the maximum combination of stout and lager that Jones can produce using a given set of resources and talent.*

The production possibilities frontier.

Meanwhile Brown, who lives on Oak Street, also makes lager and stout. Given her skills and resources, every three months she can make either 3 gallons of quality lager or 4 gallons of quality stout, or any linear combination in between. We illustrate Brown's production possibilities frontier in a separate graph in Figure 2–1, given her resources and talent. When all is said and done, Jones's stout tastes just as good as Brown's, and the same for their lagers.

At first glance it appears that Jones is more efficient at brewing both lager and stout. After all, he can make more of either one than Brown. *But the ability to make more, in itself, is not a measure of efficiency*. We must compare what is *sacrificed* against what is *gained,* for neither beer is a free good. We must, in other words, look at the *opportunity costs* of producing lager and stout, and compare those costs between Jones and Brown.

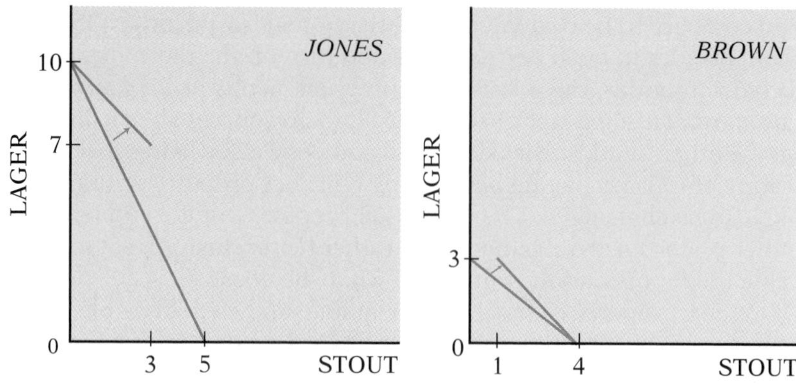

Figure 2–1 **Simple production possibilities frontiers**

These graphs illustrate the production possibilities frontiers of Jones and Brown. If Jones specializes in producing lager (10 gallons) and Brown specializes in producing stout (4 gallons), and they trade 3 lagers for 3 stouts, each enjoys a combination of lager and stout that lies beyond his or her own frontier.

Okay, then, just what are Jones's costs of production? Suppose Jones decides to produce only lager. He can make 10 gallons. *But he sacrifices the opportunity to make 5 gallons of stout.* That's his *cost* of brewing 10 gallons of lager. For each gallon of lager, he sacrifices the opportunity to make 1/2 gallon of stout. (Suppose, instead, that he brews only stout. He can make 5 gallons, but he would *sacrifice the opportunity to make 10 gallons of lager*. For each gallon of stout, he gives up the chance to make 2 gallons of lager.) If Brown makes only stout, she can make 4 gallons, but she sacrifices the opportunity to make 3 gallons of lager. For every gallon of stout, Brown sacrifices 3/4 of a gallon of lager. (Likewise, 1 gallon of lager costs Brown one and 1/3 gallons of stout.)

Let's put this information in Table 2–1:

Table 2–1

Brewer	Gallons of Stout	Gallons of Lager	Opportunity Cost of Stout	Opportunity Cost of Lager
Jones	5	10	2 gallons of lager	1/2 gallon of stout
Brown	4	3	3/4 gallon of lager	4/3 gallon of stout

comparative advantage: the ability to produce something at a lower cost, compared to somebody else.

Now we are prepared to ask the critical question: *Who produces lager at a relatively lower opportunity cost?* It's there in the table—Jones does. He sacrifices only 1/2 gallon of stout, while Brown gives up 1 1/3 gallons of stout, to brew a gallon of lager. *Jones is the lowest opportunity cost producer of lager, compared to Brown*. In the economic way of thinking, Jones has a "comparative advantage" in lager production. He is relatively more efficient at producing lager, *compared to* Brown.

Our conclusion that Jones is more efficient at brewing lager probably doesn't come as a surprise to you. But get this. Brown is more efficient at producing stout, compared to Jones! Notice Brown produces a gallon of stout at a cost of 3/4 of a gallon of lager; it costs Jones a whole 2 gallons of lager to make a gallon of stout. *Brown is the lowest opportunity cost producer of stout, compared to Jones*. Stout brewing is *Brown's* comparative advantage.

We can imagine their own choices as if they each face a fork in the road. Choosing one path means sacrificing the other. Jones has a choice—brew stout or lager. Brewing a gallon of stout (pursuing *that* path) means sacrificing the next-best opportunity—brewing 2 gallons of lager (the *forsaken* path). Brown also faces a similar choice, but her costs are different. Brewing a gallon of stout costs her only 3/4 of a gallon of lager. That's what we mean by opportunity cost.

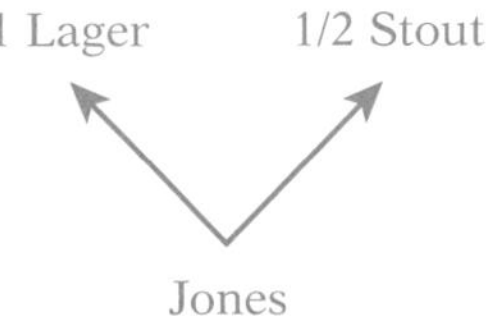

1 Lager 4/3 Stout

Brown

Think of choice as standing at a fork in the road.

The Gains from Specialization and Exchange

With a little analysis, we've found that Jones is clearly the least-cost producer of lager, Brown of stout. What would happen if each were to *specialize* in the activity each is relatively more efficient at doing and trade between each other? Suppose, for example, that Jones and Brown run into each other at the home brewery supply store in town and discuss their brewing experiences. After some negotiation, they agree to try the following arrangement: Jones will produce only lager, Brown only stout, and they'll trade on a one-for-one basis. Jones will trade 3 gallons of his lager for 3 gallons of Brown's stout.

Three months pass and Jones bottles 10 gallons of lager; Brown bottles 4 gallons of stout. Each specialized completely in the product of his or her comparative advantage. Notice, in Figure 2–1, that they are originally constrained by their own production possibilities frontiers. But, when they trade 3 lagers for 3 stouts, *each enjoys a combination of beers that lies beyond his or her own original frontier*. Jones has more of what he wants—his wealth has increased—as he now enjoys 7 gallons of lager and 3 gallons of stout. *He could not have done that on his own.* Brown's wealth increased too, as she now enjoys 3 gallons of lager and 1 gallon of stout, *which she could not have accomplished on her own.*

Specialization and exchange expand people's production possibilities.

Why Specialize?

Specialization is another word for "following one's comparative advantage." We now understand the incentive. People specialize

Specialization: the pursuit of one's comparative advantage.

because they can increase their wealth by doing so. Specialization allows producers to expand their possibilities by trading for something that is more costly for them to produce on their own—the rules of the market economy allow people to trade their private property rights in this manner. This is so fundamental to the economic way of thinking that economists have called this insight the "law of comparative advantage." Comparative advantage explains the incentive to specialize and the economic growth that results. It explains why people forsake being "a jack of all trades" for highly specialized activities such as those undertaken by accountants, nurses, entertainers, pilots, carpenters, dental assistants, longshoremen, teachers, plumbers, and even designated hitters. People expect to enjoy greater wealth (more of what *they* value) by specializing in activities in which they believe themselves to have a comparative advantage. If you have ever asked yourself, "What major is best for me, and what opportunities will I enjoy after I graduate?," you've asked a question about your own comparative advantage.

From Individual Trade to International Trade, and Back Again

In our story it is clear that both Jones and Brown gain by specialization and exchange. Although neither of them has heard of the "law of comparative advantage," they are nevertheless eager to follow its principle. David Ricardo, the British economist and a successor to Adam Smith, was among the first to articulate the law of comparative advantage in his 1817 book *Principles of Political Economy and Taxation*, where he applied it chiefly to the issue of international trade. We see, however, that it actually applies to specialization and exchange in general. If we wish, for example, we could say that the Jones household "exported" lager and "imported" stout, paying an "exchange rate" of one lager for one stout. Similarly, the Brown household exported stout and imported lager at the same exchange rate. We could go a step further than that. We immediately notice that *each party ultimately pays for its imports with its exports*.

But even arguments are subject to diminishing returns, and we might push our luck if we pursue this line of thought much further. We said earlier that Jones lives on Elm Street, Brown on Oak. One wonders if we would gain any additional insight, or just add confusion, were we also to say, "Elm Street imported stout from Oak Street, and Oak Street imported lager from Elm Street." What does it even mean to say, "Elm Street traded with Oak Street"? *It means nothing more than Jones traded with Brown*. Strictly speaking, streets don't trade, nor do neighborhoods. Individuals trade and benefit, not the streets.

What if Jones lived in Kansas and Brown in Pennsylvania, and Jones and Brown met virtually on an Internet home-brewing discussion list and made the same deal? Perhaps we could say that "Kansas imported stout from Pennsylvania" and the like, but does that provide more insight or confusion? It still means nothing more than Jones traded with Brown. Like streets or neighborhoods, states don't trade and benefit. People trade, typically across city, county, and state borders.

only individuals choose!

What, then, does it mean when we say that the United States trades with Finland, Germany, Canada, or Asia? It means U.S. citizens trade with citizens of another country. Finland doesn't produce and export Nokia cell phones. People do. There's nothing necessarily wrong with the terms *interstreet trade, intercity trade, intercounty trade, interstate trade, international trade* (or, perhaps someday, even *intergalactic trade*, though the authors have their doubts about that possibility). Economists are often called upon to discuss complex international trade issues and do so with various degrees of sophistication. It is *convenient* to say that the United States trades with Finland, for example. It would be prudent to keep in mind, however, that this is a shorthanded expression for a fantastic number of exchanges among a huge number of people, many acting in the name of larger organizations, across different regions and political borders.

Transaction costs

Certainly it gets quite complicated, and we'll have ample opportunity to discuss international exchange policies in a later chapter. But our insights remain unshaken. Voluntary trade is mutually beneficial; otherwise, it wouldn't be undertaken. In a private property system, people have strong incentives to specialize because comparative advantage generates personal wealth. The rules of the game encourage those activities.

Our story discussed and compared opportunity costs of production. But aren't there also costs of *finding* that other trader? We intentionally assumed those costs were low. Jones and Brown lived in the same community. Were Jones and Brown to live in different parts of the country, the discovery of an exchange opportunity is not so apparent. Physical distance might add a hurdle to trade; so, too, does *ignorance* of existing trading opportunities. We call these transaction costs. *Transaction costs are the costs of arranging contracts and agreements—trades in general—among interested parties.*

Transaction costs are just as real, just as important impediments to the production of additional wealth, as any other kind of cost. The Internet discussion list effectively lowered the transaction cost when we considered the example of Jones and Brown living in Kansas and Pennsylvania. Without it they might not discover their potential opportunities for trade.

Incentives to Reduce Transaction Costs: Middlemen

Suppose you own 10 shares of Yahoo! stock and want to sell. You could go around to your friends and try to peddle it, or you could put an ad in the newspaper. But it is very likely that you would obtain a higher price—even after paying the commission—by using the services of a middleman, in this case a stockbroker. No doubt if you advertised long enough and wide enough you could find a buyer willing to pay the price the stockbroker obtained for you. But it is most improbable that the cost of your search would be less than the broker's fee. Moreover, new technology has allowed Internet brokers to emerge and compete against traditional brokers by substantially lowering their fees and commissions.

"Getting it wholesale" is a popular pastime for many people who think that they're economizing. Perhaps they are. If they enjoy searching for bargains (and many people do), then they may well gain from their activities. That's their choice. Free markets allow for those buying strategies. But for most people, retailers are an important low-cost source of valuable information. Market competition among suppliers and middlemen encourages them to find ways of informing potential customers and reducing their transaction costs. The retailer's inventory reveals something of the range of opportunities available, information that is often difficult to obtain in any other fashion.

Middlemen expand the range of opportunities available to us.

Much the same is true of job-placement agencies. People frequently resent the fee charged by private agencies for finding them a job. Unless they had expected the information obtained through the agency to be worth more than the fee, they presumably would not have used the agency's services. But they choose to use it. However, as soon as they have established contact with a suitable employer, the agency seems useless—as it now is, of course—and its fee begins to look like an unwarranted imposition.

A large part of the middleman's bad press stems from our habit of comparing actual situations with nonexistent better ones. The exchanges we make are rarely as advantageous as the exchanges we could make if we knew everything. So we conclude that the middleman takes advantage of our ignorance. But why look at it that way? Using the same argument, you could say that doctors take advantage of your illnesses and that they should receive no return for their services because they would be unable to obtain a return if you were always healthy. That is both true and irrelevant. We are neither always healthy nor all-knowing. Physicians and middlemen are consequently both producers of real wealth, for they create more desirable options for us.

Middlemen Create Information

One of the continuing themes of this book will be that supply and demand, or the market process of competing bids and offers, unintentionally creates indexes of value for decision makers by placing price tags on available resources. The capacity of participants in the market to generate high-quality information at low cost is one of its most important but least appreciated virtues. Middlemen are important agents in this process. The process reveals their comparative advantage.

Some markets, like stock markets and commodity markets, are "well organized," which means that the bids and offers of many prospective buyers and sellers have been brought together to create a single price for a fairly uniform good over a wide geographic area. Other markets, like the market that even the least practiced eye can see operating in a singles bar, are much less well organized: The precise good to be exchanged and the terms of the exchange have to be negotiated for each separate transaction, and transaction costs are consequently very high. The market for used furniture is relatively unorganized: Transactions take place at prices that vary greatly, because buyers and sellers are not in extensive contact. The market for retail groceries, on the other hand, is far along toward the well-organized end of the spectrum, so that prices for ground beef will vary much less over a given area than will used-furniture prices.

It is sometimes said that stock markets and commodity markets are more nearly "perfect" than retail grocery markets and used-furniture markets. This is a misleading way to describe the difference, because it implies that the latter markets ought to be changed (perfection is better than imperfection). Such a recommendation only makes sense, however, if the costs of improving the markets are less than the gains from less costly exchanges made possible by the improvement. It is often the case, however, that we simply don't know of any way to improve a particular market except at transaction costs too high to make it worthwhile. Moreover, some efforts to "improve" markets through government action look suspiciously like efforts to promote special interests. We'll encounter some examples in Chapter 10.

Every price is a piece of potentially valuable information to other people about available opportunities. The more such prices there are, the more clearly and precisely they are stated, and the more widely they are known, the greater will be the range of opportunities available to people in the society. The greater will be their wealth, in short. Is that not what we finally mean by an increase in wealth? It is a wider range of available opportunities, the ability to do more of whatever it is we want to do.

Middlemen have the kind of comparative advantage that lowers our transaction costs.

Middlemen are specialists in the organization of markets and hence in the creation of valuable information. They presumably specialize in this way because they think they have a comparative advantage in information production. Just consider eBay, the

Internet auction site. Its developers have discovered a way of lowering transaction costs and producing valuable information for those people who choose to use its services. In short, middlemen—whether they fully realize it or not—tend to lower the hurdles that get in the way of exchange, which in itself provides further opportunities for *others* to specialize and exchange. Thanks to the grocer-middleman, the accountant finds an alternative way of obtaining milk for the family. After all, she *is* free to raise and milk her own dairy cattle. But she chooses not to. She'd rather pursue her own comparative advantage and trade a small portion of her income for the services of the local grocer. She doesn't have to learn how to raise her own dairy cattle. Nor does she have to drive to Wisconsin to purchase milk directly from the source. The local grocer arranges all those deals and thereby relieves the accountant of such burdens, not to mention the burden of the dairy farmer cooperative trying to find buyers for thousands of gallons of milk.

Buying milk from a grocer is an alternative way of producing milk for yourself.

Markets as Discovery Processes

Such are the incentives of the market system. Economists rarely, if ever, know what someone else's comparative advantage is outside of the market-exchange process. In fact, economists aren't necessary for markets to work well! Individuals in markets pursue what they think is their comparative advantage. Individuals assess their own costs and benefits and act accordingly. Economists try to explain the principles and logic that guide people's choices. Our graphs help shed some light on the logic that others use out there in the real world. In nonmarket systems, where property rights are not held and traded by individuals, but instead are owned by "society as a whole," a central economic planner—attempting to produce and deliver goods and services for the betterment of society as a whole—would have to draw up graphs and do all these mind-numbing calculations for millions of individuals and plans and projects—and where would he obtain all the necessary information to do it rapidly and productively?

In the real world, people pursue their comparative advantages simply by choosing the option that they find most attractive, all things considered. Sammy Sosa plays baseball rather than football; R. L. Stine writes children's horror stories rather than American history textbooks; Jay Leno hosts *The Tonight Show* rather than manage a Harley-Davidson plant. Americans buy shirts made in Asia, and Asians purchase grain from the United States because, in each case, they believe that is the best way to obtain what they want. Comparative advantages, and the efficiencies that they engender, are *discovered* not on the chalkboard but through real market exchanges of property rights.

Comparative advantage is discovered in markets.

In most of these decisions, relative prices provide fundamental information. We consider our various abilities and the wages we can command at the different tasks we are capable of performing and choose the job that we think will best further the projects in which we are interested. Students want to know, for example, the kinds of careers and opportunities available to them, as well as the constraints, with their political science degree, nursing degree, or philosophy degree. None of this implies that people pay attention *exclusively* to prices, or that they are in it "only for the money," which would be an absurd and impossible way to behave. It means rather that relative prices guide people's decisions when other things are equal. American clothing stores find Asian products less expensive than domestically produced shirts of similar quality. Asian farmers choose not to raise wheat because they know that they could not raise enough to earn a satisfactory living, given the fact that they could not sell it above the price at which U.S.-grown wheat is available. In short, they behave as if the least costly way to achieve a given goal is the most efficient way. And in doing so they continuously coordinate these processes of cooperative interaction and mutual accommodation that comprise the economy.

An Appendix: *ECONOMIC GROWTH: SPECIALIZATION, EXCHANGE, AND THE RULE OF LAW*

Believe it or not, except for a tiny handful of privileged people, poverty has been the rule rather than the exception throughout almost all of human history. One of the big questions in economics, therefore, is not what keeps people poor, so much as what has enabled some to become rich. Why was it that a few nations situated on the protruding northwest corner of the great Asian landmass suddenly, about 300 years ago, embarked upon the process that we now call economic growth? Why did it happen? Why did it happen first in Europe and for a long time afterward outside of Europe only in nations founded on a European heritage?

Searching for an Explanation of Economic Growth

What exactly happened? Adam Smith, surveying the situation toward the end of the eighteenth century, summed up the matter in the first chapter of *The Wealth of Nations*:

> It is the great multiplication of the productions of all the different arts, in consequence of the division of labour, which occasions, in a well-governed society, that universal opulence which extends itself to the lowest ranks of the people.

In other words, wealth came from the huge increases in production caused by the division of labor. Economic growth was a consequence of the evolution of commercial society, a society in which everyone specializes and then lives by exchanging.

The most distinguished nineteenth-century student of economic growth employed a different terminology but delivered a similar verdict. Karl Marx attributed the enormous increases in production that had occurred in some countries in the eighteenth and nineteenth centuries to development of the system of commodity production. By commodities Marx meant goods produced for profit by private owners of capital rather than for use, which is what occurs, of course, when the division of labor has thoroughly extended itself through society. What Smith called commercial society Marx referred to as bourgeois society. In case you thought that Marx had nothing good to say about such a society, here is what he and Friedrich Engels wrote in *The Communist Manifesto*:

> The bourgeoisie, during its rule of scarce one hundred years, has created more massive and more colossal productive forces than have all preceding generations together. Subjection of Nature's forces to man, machinery, application of chemistry to industry and agriculture, steam-navigation, railways, electric telegraphs, clearing of whole continents for cultivation, canalisation of rivers, whole populations conjured out of the ground—what earlier century had even a presentiment that such productive forces slumbered in the lap of social labor?

Marx thought he saw deep flaws in a society characterized by the private ownership of capital and production for profit, flaws that would ultimately destroy the system. But he had no doubts about its ability to produce wealth. And in the century and a half since publication of *The Communist Manifesto*, the productive achievements of bourgeois or commercial society have dwarfed the achievements that Marx and Engels observed in 1848.

The Evolution of Rules That Encourage Specialization and Exchange

But to say that nations grew wealthy by practicing specialization makes the issue seem much more simple than it is. If specialization is the solution to the problem of poverty, one might well ask why every nation doesn't adopt the division of labor and thereby become wealthy. The answer is that "nations" don't actually "adopt" systems as complex as a commercial society. And neither do individuals. Adam Smith once again put the matter succinctly, this time in the second chapter of *The Wealth of Nations*:

> The division of labour, from which so many advantages are derived, is not originally the effect of any human wisdom, which foresees and intends that general opulence to which it gives occasion.

The division of labor evolves over time, slowly and gradually, by an evolutionary process that no one designed or even intended.

Particular individuals expect to obtain advantages from specializing, so they specialize in specific ways. Their decisions facilitate the decisions of others. Meanwhile, still other individuals are advancing their interests by contributing to the development of social institutions that make exchange easier by lowering transaction costs.

Complex social institutions evolve—without a blueprint in advance.

Money is one such institution, and an especially crucial one, as we shall discuss later in the book. But crucial though it is, no one in fact invented the institution of money. It evolved in the same way that the division of labor evolved, through individuals acting to further the projects in which they happened to be interested and encountering others whose interactions generated a monetary system. One of Adam Smith's teachers, Adam Ferguson, correctly observed in his work *An Essay on the History of Civil Society*, published in 1767, that "nations stumble upon establishments, which are indeed the result of human action, but not the execution of any human design"; that communities often experience "the greatest revolutions where no change is intended"; and that even government officials "do not always know whither they are leading the state by their projects."

This is not to say that foresight is unimportant, much less that government has nothing to contribute toward the development of a successful economic system. Adam Smith certainly did not believe that. It is only "in a well-governed society," he maintained, that we see the evolution of extensive specialization, increases in production, and "universal opulence." Government must maintain conditions that allow the evolution of a commercial society. As Smith stated in the 1755 manuscript that served as the basis of *The Wealth of Nations*: "Little else is requisite to carry a state to the highest degree of opulence from the lowest barbarism, but peace, easy taxes, and a tolerable administration of justice; all the rest being brought about by the natural course of things."

Private property rights and the rule of law.

Thus we return once more to the important concept introduced in Chapter 1, the *rules of the game* and their economically most important feature, clearly defined and adequately defended property rights. People will not invest for the future, organize useful projects, or initiate any other costly undertakings in the absence of reasonably secure property rights. In practice this means at a minimum that governments must protect the members of a society against theft and robbery by other individuals, maintain a reasonably fair and predictable judicial system to settle disputes among individuals, and somehow assure citizens that government will not itself engage in arbitrary acts of plunder. Those of us who have lived all our lives in societies characterized by "the rule of law" usually don't realize how rarely governments have lived up to these standards.

Reasonably secure property rights and their important corollary, freedom to exchange those rights, are necessary conditions for the evolution of a successful commercial society, in which people cooperate effectively in creating and using resources to serve one another's wants, so that economic growth occurs. In the absence of these conditions, poverty is assured, except, perhaps, for a tiny minority that is able to enjoy affluence by wringing it from the labors of the vast majority.

Other factors matter, too. Climate can be a major aid or impediment to a people's endeavors to better their condition. Natural resources make a difference, even if not as large a difference as many have supposed. And war has made a huge difference, largely by destroying the wealth of the warring nations, but also by subjecting some people to the tyranny and exploitation of others. But if we choose to look backward in order to ask what ought to be done now, one large part of the answer seems clear. Governments must establish the rule of law, so that individuals within the boundaries of their control can expect to enjoy the benefits (and pay the costs!) of their own efforts and investments. A commercial society cannot develop successfully in the absence of the rule of law.

Once Over Lightly

The exchange of a good is fundamentally an exchange of ownership, an exchange of property rights. Property rights are an important part of the "rules of the game," in this case rules that clarify who owns what and how the property can be used. A social system with clear property rights and few restrictions on exchange generates money prices that help people who are pursuing their comparative advantage to discover in exactly which direction their advantage lies. Market processes inform people of their opportunities and thereby lead to discoveries of efficient ways of creating net benefits for their participants.

A good is anything whereby more of it is preferred to less, and a bad is just the opposite: anything whereby less of it is preferred to more. A scarce good is a good that can be obtained only by sacrificing some other good, something else that a chooser values. We contrast that with a free good, which is a good that can be obtained without any sacrifice. A scarce good, then, is acquired through an act of choosing, selecting, incurring some kind of trade-off; a free good is not an object of choice. Economics, being a theory of choice, focuses on the production and exchange of scarce goods. There would be no economic problem were we to live in a world without scarcity.

The term *opportunity cost* is often used in the economic way of thinking to emphasize that the cost of an action is the value one places on the next-best opportunity that one sacrifices when making a choice.

Wealth, in its broadest sense, is whatever people value. People voluntarily exchange property rights because they feel it is an efficient way to create personal wealth. Voluntary exchange always involves the sacrifice of what is less valued (input) for what is more valued (output). It is never an exchange of equal values. Exchange is as much a wealth-creating transformation as is manufacturing or agriculture. In fact, exchange is an alternative way of producing something.

Economic efficiency depends on valuations. Although physical or technological facts are certainly relevant to the determination of efficiency, they can never by themselves determine the relative efficiency of alternative processes. When considering a project or activity, decision makers tend to ask themselves whether or not the project or activity is worth the cost. This is another way of asking whether they feel the activity is economically efficient, for the concept of economic efficiency weighs the expected additional benefits against the expected additional costs.

Disagreements about whether some process or arrangement is efficient are at root disagreements about the relative weights that should be given to different people's evaluations. They are therefore often disagreements about the rules of the game or about who should have what rights over which resources.

Comparative advantage is determined by opportunity costs. People specialize in order to exchange and thereby further increase their wealth. They specialize in activities in which they believe themselves to have a comparative advantage. They exchange for goods and services that they believe are too costly to produce themselves. The increase in wealth can be illustrated with the help of the production possibilities frontier. The "law of comparative advantage" holds whether individuals are engaged in local trade or international trade.

A great deal of economic activity is best understood as a response to the fact that information itself is a scarce good, which adds to transaction costs—the costs of arranging contracts, agreements, and trades. The cost of producing information is not the same for everyone. If a system of appropriate incentives is allowed to evolve—particularly the market process—people will specialize in the production of those kinds of information in which they have a comparative advantage.

The much-abused "middleman" is in large part a specialist in information production and thereby the lowering of transaction costs. That's the middleman's comparative advantage. Just as the stockbroker enables prospective buyers and sellers to locate one another, so the typical retailer provides customers with knowledge of the goods sellers are offering and brings sellers into contact with those who want the sellers' offerings. Middlemen—those who feel they have a comparative advantage in providing the kinds of information that reduce transaction costs—coordinate market exchanges across regions, integrating local markets into the larger economic system.

The rules of the game help determine the ways we can cooperate (and compete) with one another. A rule of law that recognizes private property rights allows the freedom to exchange and provides incentives for individuals to specialize in the activities of their comparative advantage. Market specialization, and the rise of the division of labor, creates the conditions for economic growth and helps explain why wealth is greater in some nations as opposed to others.

QUESTIONS FOR DISCUSSION

1. Serena Dippity has all the luck. She woke up this morning to find an ounce of gold under her pillow, which greatly pleased her. Because she didn't incur any sacrifice, the gold is a free good for Serena. Later that day she learns that the gold is worth $400, which she can sell if she wishes. If she chooses to continue to own the gold, rather than sell it, does the gold remain a free good for Serena?
2. Suppose a gasoline station offers the following promotion on the 4th of July: "TODAY ONLY: FREE GASOLINE FROM NOON UNTIL 3:00 P.M.! HAPPY BIRTHDAY, AMERICA!" Is that gasoline a free good to the owner of the station? Is it a free good for all the drivers who wait in long lines to fill up? Countless others might decide to avoid the "free" gas and fill up at other stations that charge $1.85 per gallon. In your opinion, are they foolish to pass up the opportunity? In the economic way of thinking, would they be failing to economize?
3. A bully clobbers Jack over the head and steals his new baseball glove. Who gains? Who loses?
4. In the economic way of thinking, which is more efficient?
   (a) A remarkably clean and beautiful-sounding 1956 Fender Stratocaster guitar or a brand new but tinny-sounding 2005 El Cheapo electric guitar? (Would it make any difference if the Fender sells for $12,000 and the El Cheapo sells for $175?)
   (b) Booking a concert at Madison Square Garden or booking a gig at the local bar? (Would it make any difference if the entertainer were Eric Clapton or your own garage band?)
   (c) Purchasing bananas from the local grocer or purchasing bananas directly from the growers themselves?
   (d) An eight-cylinder SUV or a solar-battery-powered car?
5. Is it efficient to feed a family using large quantities of frozen "convenience" foods? Under what circumstances could these expensive grocery items provide the least-cost inputs for producing the output of a family dinner? What questionable premise is being used by someone who says that shoppers are wasting money by paying twice as much for convenience foods as they would have to pay for dinner items they prepare themselves?
6. Many Americans regularly drive their own cars to work rather than use public transportation or form a car pool.
   (a) How do you know that each person in a single-passenger vehicle during the rush hour is behaving efficiently?
   (b) The people riding the bus are also behaving efficiently. How can (a) and (b) both be true simultaneously?
   (c) What is actually being asserted by someone who says that it's inefficient for so many commuters to take their own cars to work?
7. In seeking to show that population growth threatens to exhaust the world's agricultural resources, the Worldwatch Institute has pointed out that in 1988, for the first time in its history, the United States ate more food than it grew.

(a) By what measure do you suppose the United States ate more food than it grew in 1988? Volume? Weight? Calories? Or monetary value?
(b) If official trade accounts show that U.S. food imports exceeded food exports in any given year, this will mean that the dollar value of the imports was greater than the dollar value of the exports. Why would such figures not be persuasive evidence that the United States had lost the ability to feed itself?

8. During the gasoline "crises" of the 1970s and early 1980s, many people asked why, in view of the gasoline shortage, such "utterly wasteful uses of gasoline" as auto racing were still permitted. Many urged that such "obvious waste" be curtailed in the public interest. Is auto racing an utter and obvious waste of gasoline? Try to construct a clear and defensible definition of waste that would indict auto racing but exonerate other uses of automotive gasoline at a time when there might be a gasoline shortage.
9. Grain farmers have many options when it comes to preparing the soil. They can plow and then thoroughly harrow a field before planting, they can practice minimum tillage, or they can go so far as to plant without preparing the ground at all. Heavy tilling buries and thus kills weeds and insects. No-till farming requires careful and extensive use of herbicides and pesticides and also produces slightly lower yields. Explain how each of the following will affect the relative efficiency of maximum tillage and no-till farming:
   (a) Higher prices for diesel fuel.
   (b) Improved herbicides and pesticides.
   (c) Tougher government controls on stream and lake pollution caused by chemicals used in agriculture. (*Note*: Untilled ground is more likely to retain the chemicals put into it.)
   (d) Farmers adopt the same attitude toward their fields that some suburban homeowners have toward their lawns: They find satisfaction in looking at a broad, well-tended expanse of land.
   (e) Higher prices for land.
10. The Sevier River in Utah has been used for about a century to irrigate farmland in central Utah. A 3,000-megawatt, coal-fired electrical generating plant, which would require about 40,000 acre-feet of water per year from the Sevier River, was proposed for this area. Operation of the generating plant would mean less water for agriculture.
   (a) Is the water of the Sevier River used more efficiently when it grows food or when it generates electricity?
   (b) Can you answer this question by comparing the value of food with the value of electricity? (*Hint*: Value is determined at the margin.)
   (c) If farmers who own rights to Sevier River water sell their rights to the power company, is the water allocated to its most valuable use?
   (d) Who are some of the parties who might be adversely affected by the farmers' decisions to sell their water rights?
11. Have you ever noticed how few gasoline stations are to be found in the center of large cities? With such heavy traffic one ought to be able to do an excellent business.

(a) Why are there so few gasoline stations in the center of large cities?
(b) Would it be efficient for city governments, which have the right of eminent domain, to take over a small amount of downtown land in order to provide gasoline stations in areas where the demand is obviously great?

12. Airlines are willing to overbook flights because they know that people who make reservations do not always show up. Sometimes, however, this results in more people holding reservations at the gate than there are seats on the flight.

(a) Is overbooking efficient from the airlines' standpoint?
(b) Is overbooking efficient from the standpoint of passengers?
(c) As a consequence of a 1976 court case that Ralph Nader won against an airline that had "bumped" him, the federal government adopted a rule requiring airlines to compensate people who were denied boarding despite holding a confirmed reservation. As a result, the airlines started to ask for volunteers who were willing to take a later flight whenever a flight turned out to be overbooked. Who benefited from this new regulation?
(d) If passengers can in effect sell their confirmed reservations when a seat shortage arises, why can't passengers sell their right to land at a crowded airport when a shortage of landing slots arises?
(e) Before 1976, the airlines often denied boarding to passengers who were flying on urgent business in favor of passengers who were not in any particular hurry to reach their destinations. This would seem to be a cooperative failure. What was the crucial step that lowered transaction costs sufficiently to transform the frustrating situation before 1976, when the last persons to show up at the gate were denied boarding, into the current system, where only volunteers are denied boarding?

13. Attorney Fudd is the most highly sought after lawyer in the state. He is also a phenomenal typist who can do 120 words per minute. Should Fudd do his own typing if the fastest secretary he can hire does only 60 words per minute? Can you provide an argument (no graphs are necessary) that Fudd is not twice as efficient as his secretary at typing, that he is, in fact, less efficient at typing and that he should therefore retain a secretary?

14. Gomer can make either 200 bushels of corn (C) or 200 bushels of strawberries (S) every six months. Goober can make only 100 bushels of corn (C) or 50 bushels of strawberries (S) every six months.

(a) Draw their corresponding production possibilities curves.
(b) What is Gomer's opportunity cost of making one bushel of corn?
(c) What is Gomer's opportunity cost of making one bushel of strawberries?
(d) What is Goober's opportunity cost of making one bushel of corn?
(e) What is Goober's opportunity cost of making one bushel of strawberries?
(f) Who has a comparative advantage in making corn?
(g) Who has a comparative advantage in making strawberries?
(h) Provide terms of trade between corn and strawberries that would be mutually beneficial to both Gomer and Goober if each specialized and exchanged the product of his comparative advantage.

15. "Specialization and free trade within our country is fine. But free international trade is another beast altogether. Cheap foreign imports do not increase our own nation's production possibilities frontier and create economic growth. Instead, cheap imports create a loss of jobs in our country." Carefully evaluate this statement
16. Students frequently complain about the low prices the campus bookstore pays for used texts.
    (a) Why then do they sell their used textbooks to the bookstore?
    (b) How can we decide whether the bookstore is providing a useful service with its used-book operation or merely ripping off students?
    (c) Why do campus bookstores commonly sell all used copies of a particular textbook at an identical price, regardless of condition? Sellers of used cars don't do that. How would you explain the difference between the policies of campus bookstores and car dealers?
17. If you found that you could reduce your bills for groceries 10 percent by buying exclusively from the Internet, would you do it? Why would some people be unwilling to take advantage of this "savings"? What do people do when they go "shopping"? How often have you discovered what you were looking for by seeing what sellers were offering?
18. Would you expect prices for goods of similar quality offered in garage sales to vary more than prices for goods offered in regular retail outlets? Why? Do the differences in prices mean that someone is being cheated or that someone is taking unfair advantage of someone else?
19. A man approaches you in a busy airport terminal, shows you a handsome wristwatch, which he says is worth $135, and offers to let you have it for $25. Would you buy it? Would you be more willing to buy it if you had better information? What do you "know" when you buy a watch from an established local jeweler that you do not know in this situation?
20. Why does a new car lose so much of its value in the first year? Is it because Americans have an irrational attachment to cars that are new rather than used?
    (a) Which year-old car is more likely to be on the used-car market: one that performed handsomely for its owner or one that had to be taken in regularly for repairs during its first year?
    (b) Which set of vehicles being offered for sale will contain a larger percentage of vehicles with defects known to the seller but unknown to the buyer: new cars or year-old cars?
    (c) What does all this imply about the prices sellers are willing to accept and that buyers are willing to offer for year-old cars, relative to what they would be if all buyers and sellers had complete information?
    (d) Why do used-car dealers sometimes provide warranties with the cars they sell and at other times advertise "As Is—No Warranties, All Sales Final"?

Бранденбург
Кюстрим
Потсдам
Центр
Унтер ден Линден
Рейхстаг

Substitutes Everywhere: The Concept of Demand

3

So far we've discussed trade-offs quite a bit. We've learned that *most goods are scarce,* which means that they can be obtained only by sacrificing some other good, something else of value. In this chapter, we will consider a further implication of scarcity—*there are substitutes for anything*. Yes, anything. It follows that intelligent choice—choice that obtains the most of what is wanted from what is available, economizing choice—requires comparing the expected additional costs of using alternative means against the expected additional benefits of doing so. *Everyday choice entails trade-offs*. We shall develop the notion of consumer demand to explain how buyers face trade-offs and how market price signals encourage buyers to economize.

On the Notion of "Needs"

What is the relationship between our claim that people face "trade-offs" versus the claim that people have genuine "needs"? Consider, for example, these four statements:

- The average person needs eight glasses of water per day in order to maintain optimal health.
- All citizens should be able to obtain the medical care they need regardless of their ability to pay.
- A diabetic needs insulin.
- You need to read your economics textbook.

These statements all have the notion of *necessity* in common. Although the economic way of thinking doesn't deny that real people have real needs, it does suggest that these statements can be seriously misleading. We could use a little thinking "outside the box."

Consider the last statement first. *You need to read your economics textbook*. Your professor who put this on her syllabus surely believes it's true. Indeed, failure to keep up with the reading often does explain poor grades. And, after all, if your professor holds a Ph.D., then you the student received your doctor's orders—something like a prescription. But the issue isn't merely what your professor believes you need to do in order to pass the class; the issue is what will students actually do? Students face scarcity and therefore an array of trade-offs. Are you aware of any students who chose *not* to even purchase a textbook because its price was too high? Or what about any students who paid full price for the text but never bothered to open it up during the semester? (They must have considered their expenditure a "sunk cost"—something we'll discuss in a later chapter.) What of the students who valiantly attempt to read their econ book but also "need" to read their calculus, philosophy, and physics textbooks as well, and therefore merely skim rather than carefully read each assigned chapter? An upcoming physics midterm raises the cost of reading the assigned chapter in economics.

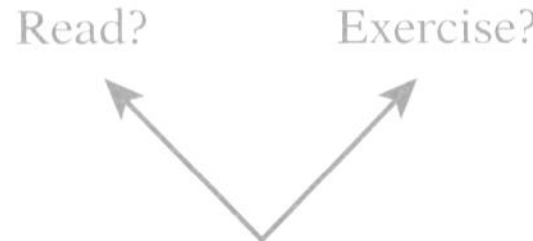

All students face this kind of problem. *Reading the economics textbook entails sacrifices*. As the sacrifice or cost increases, students tend to do less. They search, instead, for *substitutes*. For example, you might ask a classmate (who read the chapter) about the textbook's main points; you might sleep with it under your pillow and hope you absorb its contents; you might wish for pure luck when you take your exams; or, if you're really brave, you might go to your professor's office hours and ask her to clarify the issues in the chapter, insinuating that you've read the material but still don't completely understand it (we know all of the tricks). These are all substitutes for reading the book.

While that might resonate with your own experience, what about the first statement? *The average person needs eight glasses of water per day in order to maintain optimal health*. Surely the medical authorities have demonstrated this as true. And now we're talking about a person's *health*, rather than mere grades in a college class. Still, another fact remains. Even the "average person" might be willing to drink less water in favor of more coffee, beer, or soda. Or someone might eat a tangerine instead. None of these are water; they are *substitutes* for water. (By the way, have you also managed to eat your required daily servings of fruit and vegetables lately? If not, why not?) And what of the person who currently does drink eight glasses of water per day? Is this person likely to continue to do so if the price of water jumps to, say, 2 dollars a glass? 5? 50?

Okay, now on to the apparently tougher statements. *All citizens should be able to obtain the medical care they need regardless of their ability to pay*. But how much medical care does any person need? We might all agree that a woman with a terribly inflamed appendix and no money should have an appendectomy completely at the taxpayers' expense if she is unable to meet any of the costs herself. But what of the teenager with a mild case of acne? The services of physicians and others in the medical community are scarce goods, and they would not cease being scarce even if every physician were required to treat patients without charging them. There just would not be enough physicians to go around if everyone consulted a doctor for every minor ailment. Indeed, the lower the price of visiting a doctor, the more frequently people substitute a trip to the doctor for such other remedies as going to bed, eating enough fruits and vegetables, taking it easy, or waiting and hoping. One could confidently predict that lower monetary fees would result in higher costs of *other* sorts—such as waiting in line for many hours, being whisked through the office exam, and so on, because the services of physicians are scarce goods.

A diabetic needs insulin. True. Without it the diabetic would be terribly uncomfortable at the least and most likely face death. So surely a diabetic, although he might substitute other goods for eight glasses of water a day, or sacrifice reading his textbook for discussions with classmates, surely *he* faces no substitutes for insulin, right? Not so fast. Common substitutes include a better diet and appropriate exercise. Holistic care and organic medicines are also increasing in popularity (even if they are not as effective as insulin, the fact remains that people do use these in place of insulin, not unlike the student who might wish for luck rather than read the textbook). Because even insulin is a scarce good for most diabetics, its use entails *trade-offs*, or the sacrifice of *other goods* they value.

Scarce goods can be obtained only by sacrificng other goods.

Marginal values

Which is more valuable, water or diamonds? Most people who are asked that question answer without hesitation: "water." But follow up with a slightly altered question and they waver: Which is more valuable, a glass of water or a glass of diamonds? If they again answer "water," we can ask which they would take if offered the choice between a glass of water and a glass of diamonds. Diamonds win every time.

How can people say that water is more valuable than diamonds when they would, without a moment's hesitation, take diamonds rather than water if offered the choice? Because, they say, water is a necessity for life; diamonds aren't. True, the water would be more valuable than another diamond if they were in the middle of a desert dying of thirst. But that response confuses the different contexts, and trade-offs, within which our choices are conducted. *Our choices depend upon the situations we face.*

An old newspaper is more valuable than the collected works of Shakespeare if you are trying to swat a mosquito intent on giving you a case of yellow fever. A toothpick is more valuable than a computer if the piece of corn stuck between your teeth is driving you insane. Just about anything could be more valuable than anything else *under appropriate circumstances*, because, like our choices, *values depend upon the situation, too*.

Economists have their own way of saying the same thing. *The values that matter are marginal values*. Economic analysis is basically marginal analysis. Many economists even use the word *marginalism* to refer to what we have called "the economic way of thinking." *Marginal* means "on or at the edge" (the margin on this page is the edge of the page). A marginal benefit or a marginal cost is an *additional* benefit or cost. Economic theory is marginal analysis because it assumes that people make decisions by weighing expected additional benefits against expected additional costs, all measured from the frontier on which the decision maker currently stands. Nothing matters in economic decision-making except marginal benefits and marginal costs.

What do I expect to gain? What do I expect to sacrifice?

Everyday Choices Are Marginal Choices

A bit too abstract? Okay, then, suppose that a good friend phones you at 9:00 in the evening while you're studying desperately for tomorrow's physics exam. (You've already given up your assigned, required reading for your economics class.) Your friend wants to come over for a couple of hours. You say you have to study. Your friend pleads. You say no. Your friend asks plaintively, "Is physics more important than I am?" And if you've grasped the economic way of thinking, you respond without hesitation: "Only at the margin."

If that doesn't stop the whining, tell your friend to enroll next term in an economics class and go back to your studies. The issue of your friend's value versus the value of physics just doesn't arise in this situation. The question, rather, is whether an additional two hours with your friend on this margin—on this particular evening—is worth more than an additional two hours with your physics text.

Study — Visit friend

How should I spend the next two hours?

Your friend is making a common mistake: thinking in terms of "all or nothing." "Me" versus "physics." But that just isn't the choice when your friend phones on the evening before your exam. In fact, that is rarely the choice we face when we're called upon to make decisions. It's usually more of this and less of that versus more of that and less of this, measured from the position in which we find ourselves when called upon to decide. The economic way of thinking rejects the all-or-nothing approach in favor of attention to marginal benefits and marginal costs. This is true for people who economize on *any* scarce good, including a basic "necessity" such as water.

The Demand Curve

The concept of "needs" encourages all-or-nothing thinking and fails to appreciate the idea of marginal thinking. People *do* have needs. But, in a world of scarcity individuals incur trade-offs—choosing less of one good for more of another. That's why economists have developed the idea of "demand." Demand is a concept that relates amounts people want to obtain to the sacrifices they must make to obtain these amounts. It is a further, and very important, application of marginal analysis.

Consider, for example, Table 3–1, which depicts the amount of water people plan to use, at various prices, in a "typical" American town:

Table 3–1

Price per Gallon	Gallons per Day (millions)
$0.07	23
0.04	40
0.02	80
0.01	160
0.005	320

We can all agree that people do need water. But take a good look at the table. The table illustrates an interesting relationship, a relationship that has to do with the way those townspeople alter their planned water use when the price of water changes. If water is priced at 7 cents per gallon, a total of 23 million gallons would be used per day. Should the price of water fall—for whatever reason—people would plan to use more water. At 2 cents per gallon, people would plan to consume 80 million gallons per day; at a half a cent per gallon, they'd consume 320 million gallons per day. (The word *consume* doesn't necessarily mean they are all trying to drink that much water per day! It simply means they are trying to *acquire and use* that much water for *a variety of different purposes*.)

Things become more interesting when we illustrate the information in our table with the aid of the graph in Figure 3–1. The vertical axis shows those possible prices that might be charged for water, in cents per gallon. The horizontal axis shows the quantity of water that people in the community would plan to purchase at those prices. By plotting those points from the table, and connecting them together, we get a downward-sloping curve.

Economists call that a *demand curve*. A demand curve *illustrates the amount of a good that consumers plan to purchase at any given price*. We "read" a demand curve by taking some specific price and finding the corresponding point on the horizontal axis. That quantity represents the amount that people would plan to purchase. We call that the *quantity demanded*. The demand curve in our graph shows, for example, that if the price of water is $0.005 per gallon, people will want to use about 320 gallons each day. That's their quantity demanded. They will use water as if it had no value at all, or, more accurately, as if its value was about one-half cent per gallon, because that is in fact what they must pay to obtain water. When it's relatively cheap, people will of course use water for drinking, bathing, cooking, and washing clothes, but also for countless *other purposes*, such as filling

Quantity demanded: the amount that consumers plan to purchase at a given price.

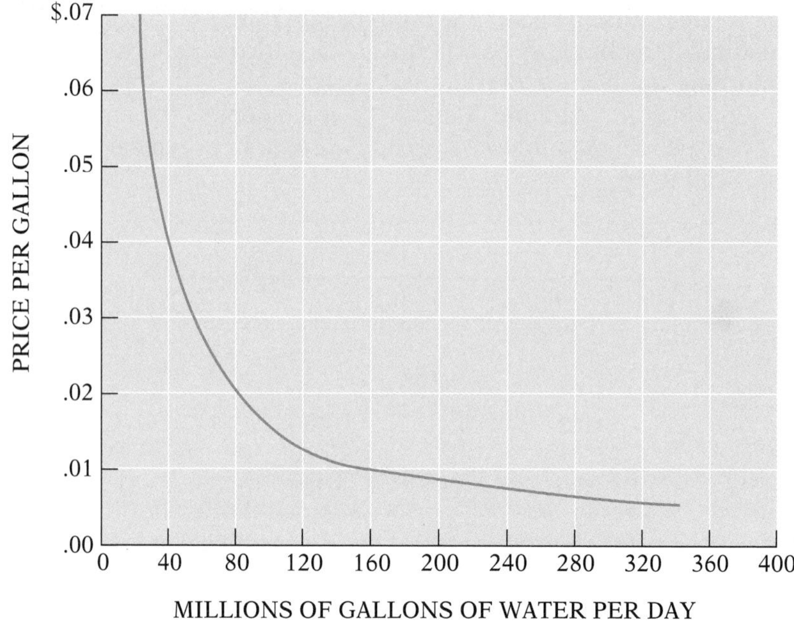

Figure 3–1 **Demand for water for a "typical" American town**

swimming pools, watering lawns, washing cars, and so on. (These, too, are all acts of *consumption*.) Many homeowners will hose off rather than sweep the driveway and sidewalks after mowing the lawn; they will flush their toilets after each use; they will take long showers; and they will let the washing machine fill with water to do just a quarter load of laundry.

Double the price of water to $0.01 per gallon, however, and households will begin to behave quite differently. People will tend to *alter their plans*. The quantity demanded will change. They will give up their least valuable uses for water and, according to the graph, cut their daily water consumption in half. Double the price again to $0.02 and they will economize further. The same pattern unfolds at $0.04 per gallon. Now the quantity demanded is only 40 million gallons per day. Many might water their lawns or wash their cars less frequently. Washing machines might be run only with full loads of dirty laundry. Others might decide not to fill their swimming pools at such high prices. Notice, even if the price were to reach $0.07 per gallon, people do not go *completely* without water. Some 23 million gallons will still be consumed per day, most likely being devoted to the "most important" or most highly valued purposes in the eyes of the individual choosers.

Looking at the graph, can you determine how much water this community *needs*? The economic way of thinking provides no special insights into how much water people need. We'll leave that up to physiologists. That's a part of *their* comparative advantage, not ours. But, the concept of demand, and the illustration of the demand curve for water, does offer a rather underappreciated insight: the economist's emphasis on *marginal analysis*. We find in this example that *consumers make marginal adjustments to changes in the price of water. They don't normally engage in all-or-nothing trade-offs.*

Instead, as *economizers*, people tend to *conserve* water when they face higher prices. *They seek out substitutes for water.* As water becomes more costly to acquire, they'll strive to "waste less water." *They'll decide that some of their uses are no longer worth it.* They'll seek out *more economically efficient* ways of accomplishing their goals. (Don't forget the ideas you learned in Chapter 2!) Those who washed off the grass clippings on the driveway may now be inclined to use a broom. They'll be more likely to install high-pressure shower heads. Rather than frequently water their lawns, some might decide for the longer run to plant more shade trees. A swimming pool might be replaced by a backyard trampoline. In these cases, we can say that brooms, shower heads, shade trees (and, with a bit of a stretch, even trampolines) are used as substitutes for water.

A broom can be a substitute for water!

The Law of Demand

The pattern of which we're speaking is so fundamental that some economists have been willing to assign it the status of a law: *the law of demand*. We call it a "law" because it applies not only to water but to *all* scarce goods. It states: *If the price of a good increases, holding other things constant, the quantity demanded will decrease. Likewise, if the price of a good decreases, other things constant, the quantity demanded will increase.*

Law of demand: Negative relationship between price and quantity demanded, other things being constant.

This law asserts that there is a negative or inverse relationship between the amount of anything that people will want to purchase and the price (sacrifice) they must pay to obtain it. *Price and the amount demanded move in opposite directions.* At higher prices, consumers will plan to purchase less; at lower prices they will strive to purchase more. Would you agree that this generalization can be called a law? Or can you think of exceptions? (What about insulin? Not yet—we want to tantalize you a bit longer!) Why would people be indifferent to the sacrifices they must make? Or prefer more sacrifice to less? That is what a person would be doing who bought more of something when the cost of obtaining it increased. Other things being constant, fewer CDs will be purchased at $14.99 compared to $10.99 each; more people will subscribe to Internet access providers when the rates come down; Old Navy is more likely to be crowded with eager buyers during a storewide sale.

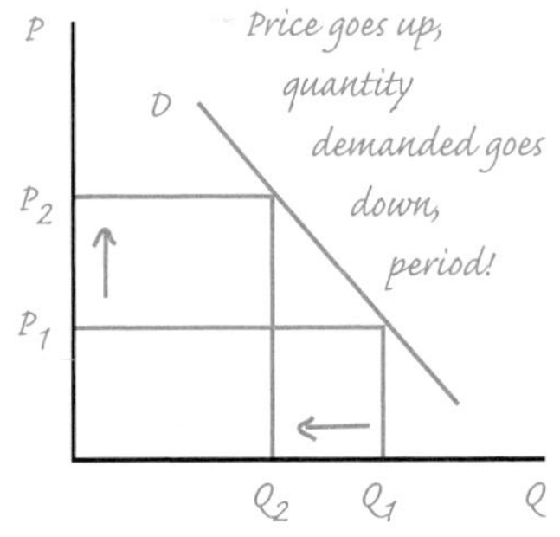

Demand and Quantity Demanded

In using the concept of demand, you must remain alert for the possibility that something else has changed in addition to the price. Your best protection is a clear grasp of the distinction between *demand* and *quantity demanded*. Commentators on economic events often use the word *demand* as a shorthand term for *quantity demanded*. That can and often does lead to error, as we shall see later.

Demand in economic theory is a relationship between two specific variables: price and the amount people want to purchase. You can't state the demand for any good simply as an amount. Demand is always a *relationship* that connects different prices with the quantities (or amounts) that people would want to purchase at each of those prices. We express that fact by saying that demand is a schedule or a curve. A movement from one row of the schedule to another, or from one point on the curve to another point on the curve, should always be called a change in the quantity demanded, not a change in the demand. *Pay close attention to how we state the law of demand*. We don't say that *demand* increases when the price decreases, for example. Instead, we say that the *quantity demanded* increases.

Demand is a schedule or curve. Quantity demanded is a specific amount at a specific price.

We see this all at work in Figure 3–1. If the price had been set at $0.01 per gallon and was then lowered to $0.005 per gallon, the *quantity demanded* would increase from 160 to 320 gallons per day. At a price of $0.04, the *quantity demanded* would be only 40 gallons per day. That's what the households strive to purchase at the 4-cent price. But the *demand* would be unchanged through all this, because *the demand is the whole curve or schedule*. Notice in our graph that the demand curve didn't move or shift or change. *We moved along the given demand curve.* The demand curve itself illustrates the different quantities the consumers plan to purchase at various prices. Perhaps the best way to keep this distinction straight is to remember that the word *curve* or the word *schedule* should always be able to follow the word demand. If you say "demand" but cannot, in the context, say "demand curve," you have made a common mistake. You probably mean not *demand*, but *quantity demanded*.

Demand Itself Can Change

"Are you telling us that demand itself *never* changes?," asks the skeptic from the back of the classroom. "Didn't you say that people will probably buy more high-pressure showerheads or whatever when water itself becomes expensive? They are buying those things because *water* is more expensive, *not* because showerheads are cheaper, right? So then your 'law of demand' doesn't apply to showerheads—because people are buying more of those even though their price hasn't changed!"

This student raises a good question. And, although his conclusion is in error, we respect the fact that he's paying close attention to everything we've said so far. So let's continue to pay attention as we try to further develop the demand concept.

The law of demand does hold true, across the board. It says that if the price of a good changes, *holding other things constant,* the quantity demanded for that good will also change. The key here is the phrase *other things constant*. Price is an important influence on our choices, but we also recognize that there are *other influences, besides the price itself*, that might encourage people to increase or decrease their consumption of goods and services. *If people's willingness to buy changes even though the price of the good in question remains constant, then overall demand for that good must have changed.* The demand curve itself *can* shift. Demand for any particular good *can* increase or decrease.

Let's return to our original example regarding the townspeople's demand for water itself. All along we were assuming that the only important source of change is the change in the price of water. We held constant all other influences on the townspeople's willingness to purchase water. Quantity demanded changed *only* because the price of water changed. For the overall *demand* to increase, something would have to occur that made the households want to purchase more water than before at each price. At a price of $0.005 per gallon, people might choose to consume *more than* the original 320 million gallons per day, if, for example, they strive to water their lawns more often due to a drought in the region. *The demand (curve) would shift* upward and to the right. Or suppose, instead, that the community discovers some trace contaminants in the water supply. Households might reduce their uses of water. (Drinking? No. Showering? Only briefly. Maintaining the swimming pool? No. Watering lawns, why not?) Were this to occur, people would tend to consume less water than before, at any given price. Their overall demand would decrease. The *curve itself* would shift downward and to the left.

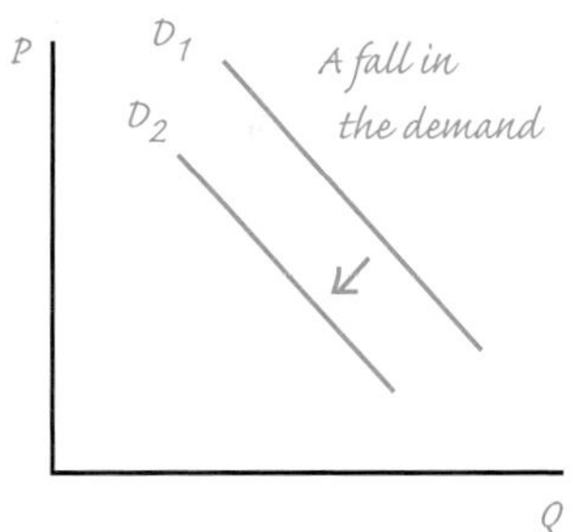

If you would like to graph an increase in the demand for water, plot the quantities in the second column shown in Table 3–2. (Feel free to mark up the book. It's yours, not ours.) If you prefer to graph a decrease in demand, practice with the third column. You shall see, in either case, that for any given price per gallon, the quantity demanded would be higher or lower than before. *The law of demand still holds*. We still depict a *downward-sloping demand curve*. In each case there's an inverse relationship between price and quantity demanded. But the curve itself shifts to a new position.

Table 3–2

Price per Gallon	Gallons per Day	Gallons per Day
$0.07	40	15
0.04	60	25
0.02	140	55
0.01	240	100
0.005	400	200

Everything Depends upon Everything Else

We can clearly isolate several influences that can cause a change in the demand for a good, influences that can "shift the demand curve," as it were. Any good student of economics ought to be aware of these. Let's start with the most obvious.

A change in the number of consumers (demanders). A growing population among our townspeople would tend to increase the demand for water within the township; a shrinking population would tend to reduce it. As more teens receive their driver's licenses, and beg for the old man's car, that adds to the overall population of drivers, and the demand for gasoline would tend to rise. A growing elderly population, on the other hand, would tend to put some downward pressure on the demand for gasoline. It would also likely lead to an increase in the demand for nursing-home care services.

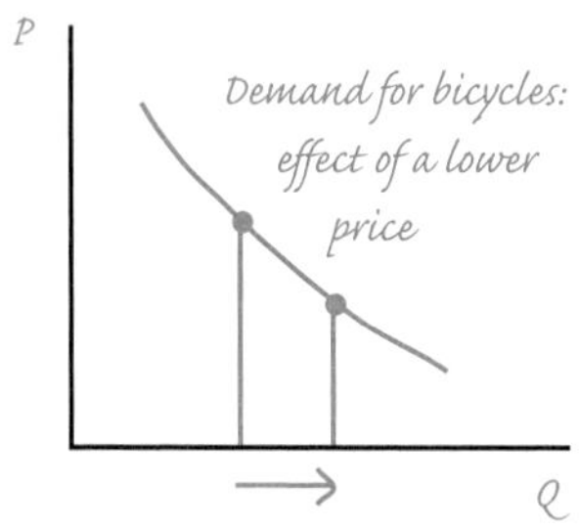

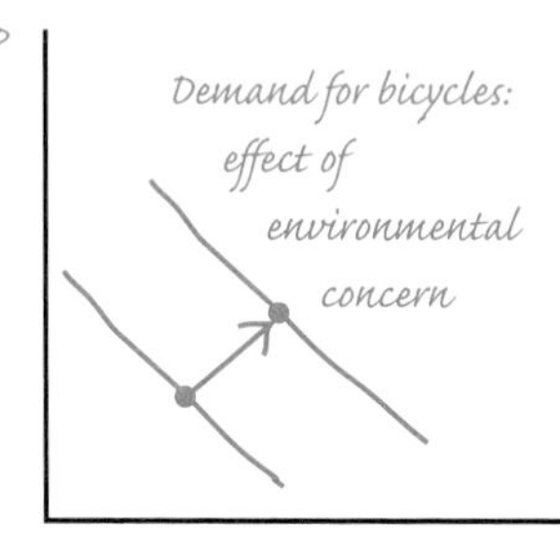

A change in consumer tastes and preferences. As your authors revise this chapter, we see that the current Atkins Diet craze is killing Krispe Kreme donut sales. Demand has fallen as health-conscious consumers have begun to shy away from such foods. They aren't buying fewer donuts because donut *prices* have increased. They're buying less because their *tastes* have changed. They now prefer to eat foods with fewer carbohydrates. (Also, the overall demand for low-carb beer has increased for much the same reason.) There are probably a few students in your class who were once big fans of Britney Spears but now wouldn't even consider obtaining her new CDs, even if those were being given away. People's tastes can and do change over time, and that can cause shifts in demand.

A change in income. Of course our demand is driven not only by our tastes but also by our incomes. And, normally, we might expect that an increase in income would lead to an increase in the demand for a particular good or service, while a decrease in income would lead to a decrease in demand. You might tend to buy more fine clothing while working your summer job but reduce your purchases when you're back in school full-time and your income is low. More people are likely to travel to Disney World when the economy is doing well and their incomes are up. In a sluggish economy, with more people out of work, the demand would likely fall. But be careful here. *Changes in income are positively related to changes in demand for a "normal" good.* But not all goods are "normal" goods. There are also a whole array of goods in which the opposite pattern occurs. Economists call those *inferior goods*. A good is an inferior good if consumers demand *less* when their income rises. Likewise, they demand *more* when their income falls. For example, college students on low budgets often eat macaroni and cheese or ramen noodles. After graduation, and landing that first great job, they might choose to spend their income differently, buying much less macaroni and cheese and more restaurant meals that they can now afford. For *those* students, macaroni and cheese would be an inferior good: As their income rises, their demand for that good falls.

Let's not forget, however, that value is in the eyes of the chooser. What is an inferior good for one consumer might in fact be a normal good for another. The term *inferior* is an unfortunate one, because it seems to imply that the good must be of poor or inferior quality. But the "inferior" label is *not* necessarily tied to quality at all. For better or worse, we're stuck using that label. *Economists distinguish normal from inferior goods exclusively by the way consumers respond to changes in income*. Consider the case of Jones and Brown, our home-brewing neighbors from Chapter 2. Suppose they both received substantial pay raises. Jones can now afford to send his kids to the local community college. His household demand for that good has increased. Brown, on the other hand, now encourages her child to leave the community college and apply to Ivy College. Her household demand for community college has now decreased. Community college is, therefore, a normal good for the Jones household, and an inferior good for Brown's.

The economic way of thinking appreciates the fact that everything is interconnected. Economists like to say that *everything depends upon everything else*. And they mean it. We've seen so far that consumers' willingness to purchase a good is connected to the price of the good in question, as well as their tastes and preferences and their income. But there's more. While selecting among different options, consumers will also *compare* the prices of *other* goods. Changes in the prices of other goods can very well generate a change in the demand for a given good under consideration. After all, *the price of any single good has meaning only when considered against the prices of the vast array of other goods and services that a chooser considers*.

"That has become too expensive!"

This leads us to a fourth factor that changes demand: *A change in the price of a substitute good.* Look what happened when the price of water increased in our township: The demand for water-saving, high-pressure showerheads increased. People bought more of those not because their price decreased, but instead because the price of *water* increased. Or consider hamburger and steak. Suppose hamburger were originally priced at 2 dollars per pound while steak is priced at 4 dollars per pound. What would tend to happen if, for whatever reason, hamburger alone became more expensive? Suppose its price rises to 3 dollars per pound. The law of demand suggests people will buy less hamburger. The quantity demanded would fall. At the same time, many may be more inclined to purchase steak, a substitute for hamburger. The *demand for steak* would tend to increase. Or take a very different example. Cheaper foreign cars imported into the United States tend to *reduce the demand* for American-made vehicles. No wonder U.S. automobile producers insist upon a series of quotas or taxes to raise the prices of their foreign competitors. *All else being constant, a rise (or fall) in the price of a given good will tend to increase (or decrease) the demand for the substitute good*.

A change in the price of a complementary good can also generate a demand shift. Complementary goods are goods that "go together," like hot dogs and hot dog buns, water and swimming pools, or gasoline and eight-cylinder SUVs. The grocer who puts hot dogs on sale will likely sell more hot dogs. That's the law of demand at work: The quantity demanded of hot dogs will tend to rise. He is also more likely to sell more hot dog buns (the complement) even if he doesn't put those on sale. More hot dog purchases will lead to more bun purchases. Since bun prices are constant, the overall demand for buns will increase. Higher water prices would likely *reduce the demand* for swimming pools. Higher gasoline prices would tend to reduce the demand for gas-guzzling vehicles. *Everything else being constant, a rise (or fall) in the price of a given good will tend to decrease (or increase) the demand for the complementary good.*

"Let's buy more now before the price goes even higher."

And, finally, *a change in the expected price of a good* can cause a change in the overall demand for that good. The demand for gasoline surged on the day of the terrorist attack on New York City and Washington, D.C. People's *expectations* regarding the *future price* of gasoline changed suddenly and dramatically. They now expected the price to jump. They acted upon their new expectation by rushing off to buy more gasoline, attempting to fill up now before the price rises. In other words, their *demand for gasoline increased on 9/11*. This occurred throughout the United States. (And, in fact, that surge in gasoline demand brought about a surge in gasoline prices!) Or consider a different situation. Suppose you're considering buying an LCD television. As you're shopping, and prepared to purchase one today, you come across a classmate who works at the store. She quietly tells you that those TVs will be put on sale next week, at 20 percent off the current price. How would you respond? If you decide to *wait until the price falls*—acting upon your *new expectation of next week's lower price*—then your *current demand* for the LCD television *decreases* in light of that new expectation.

Misperceptions Caused by Inflation

One major reason why many people think that the law of demand doesn't operate is that they have forgotten to take the effects of inflation into account. In a period of rapid inflation, most apparent price increases are not real price increases at all. The nature, causes, and consequences of inflation will be examined in detail later in this book (beginning with Chapter 14), but inflation so distorts our perceptions of relative price and cost changes that we'd better think about it before going any further. An ounce of anticipation may prevent a pound of confusion.

Inflation means *an increase in the average money price of goods*. But because we're accustomed to think of the price of anything as the quantity of money we have to sacrifice to get it, we easily conclude that twice as much money means twice as large a cost or sacrifice. That isn't the case, however, if twice as many dollars have only half as much purchasing power. If the money price of each and every good, including human labor and whatever else people sell or rent to obtain money, were to double, then no good would have changed in real price—except money, of course, which would have fallen by one-half. And so a doubling of the price of gasoline won't necessarily induce people to use any less gasoline—*if at the same time their incomes and the prices of all the other goods they use have also doubled*.

Consider this very simple situation. Suppose you make $5 per hour (after tax) working at the college library. Also suppose you can purchase ramen noodles at five packs for $1.00 and hamburger at $2.50 per pound. Your hour's worth of work, and particularly the income it generates, provides you the power to purchase up to 25 packs of ramen noodles *or* at most 2 pounds of hamburger. Suppose instead that *all prices*, including your own hourly wage, were to double. Now you earn $10 per hour. Anybody would rather earn $10 as opposed to $5 per hour, *other things being constant*. But if the prices of the goods that others provide *also* double, then, in fact, you are no richer than before. You can still purchase, at most, up to 25 packs of noodles or 2 pounds of hamburger with your new $10 hourly money income. In this overly simple example, we clearly see that the *relative price* of your labor, ramen noodles, and hamburger has not changed.

"In the good old days, a movie cost only 50 cents." (But grandpa, didn't you earn only 50 cents an hour back then?)

All money prices do not, in fact, change in equal proportion as a result of inflation—which is one of the reasons inflation creates problems. But they do tend to move together. Consequently, if we want to examine the effect of a particular price increase, we must first abstract from the effects of a general increase in prices. Suppose, for example, that a college that had been charging its students $5,000 per year tuition in 1975 was charging $15,000 in the year 2005. By how much did the college raise tuition over this period? The answer is that it did not raise its tuition at all. If its tuition charges had just kept pace with the rate of inflation, they would have increased from $5,000 to more than $15,000 per year.

Time Is on Our Side

If you are at all a suspicious sort of person, you might be wondering whether people really are as flexible and ready to adjust as all these examples suggest. That is a healthy suspicion. Changes in the quantity demanded will be greater for any given price change the longer the time period allowed for adjustment.

Consider the price of gasoline. How high did the price of gasoline have to go before Americans reduced their consumption during the OPEC crisis of the 1970s? Don't answer without first noting that the price did not go up by nearly as much as the numbers suggest. Once again, *it's the relative price that matters,*

Carpooling was unheard of before the jump in oil prices in the 1970s.

and much of the increase in the price of gasoline was merely an inflation-induced rise in its money price. The 1972 price of 38 cents per gallon for regular would be about $1.35 currently *if gasoline prices had merely gone up at the rate of inflation*. The question is nonetheless a good one: How large a relative price increase will it take to cut gasoline consumption by 10 percent or 25 percent or even 50 percent? The answer clearly depends on the time allowed for adjustments. People will buy cars that use less fuel, will move closer to work, and will arrange car pools if the price of gasoline rises far enough; but they won't do so at once. It will also take time for automotive engineers to increase the fuel efficiency of cars and for buses and airlines to expand their schedules, thereby providing automobile users with more and better substitutes for gasoline. In the short run, we're in trouble. But over time (in the longer run), we learn to seek out substitutes for gasoline (car pools, six- and four-cylinder engines, shorter pleasure drives through the country, and so on). We find new ways to economize.

By taking our examples almost entirely from the area of household decisions, we may have obscured the important fact that customers include producers as well as households. Business firms use water and gasoline, too, and they sometimes use so much that they are exceptionally sensitive to price changes. You'll be neglecting some of the major factors that cause demand curves to slope downward if you overlook the contribution producers make to the demand for many goods. In the case of water, location decisions are often made on the basis of the expected price of water, and those decisions then affect the quantities demanded in different geographic areas.

It takes time to discover substitutes.

But it takes time for customers to find and begin to use substitutes. It also takes time for producers to devise, produce, and publicize substitutes. As a result, the amount by which people increase or decrease their purchases when prices change depends very much on the time period over which we are observing the adjustment. Occasionally, even a rather large price increase (or decrease) will lead to no significant decrease (or increase) in consumption—*at first*. And this sometimes causes people to conclude that price has no effect on consumption. A very mistaken conclusion! Nothing in this world happens instantly. People, creatures of habit that they are, must be allowed time to discover for themselves that there are substitutes for anything.

Price Elasticity of Demand

It is quite cumbersome to talk about "the amount by which people increase or decrease their purchases when the price changes." But this is an important relationship with many useful applications. So economists have invented a special concept that summarizes the relationship. The formal title of the concept is *price elasticity of demand*. That's an appropriate name. Elasticity means responsiveness. (A golf ball is more elastic than a marble when hit by a three iron.) If the amount of any good that people want to purchase changes substantially in response to a small change in price, demand is said to be elastic. If even a very large price change results in little change in the amount demanded, demand is said to be inelastic.

Price elasticity of demand is defined precisely as *the percentage change in quantity demanded divided by the percentage change in price*. Thus, if a 10 percent increase in the price of eggs leads to a 5 percent reduction in the number of eggs people want to buy, the elasticity of demand is 5 percent divided by 10 percent, or 0.5. (To be completely accurate, it is *negative* 0.5, since price and amount purchased vary inversely. But for simplicity we shall ignore the minus sign and treat all coefficients of elasticity as if they were positive.)

$$\text{Price elasticity of demand} = \frac{\%\text{ change in } Q}{\%\text{ change in } P}$$

Whenever the coefficient of elasticity is greater than 1.0 (ignoring the sign)—that is, whenever the percentage change in quantity demanded is *greater* than the percentage change in price—demand is said to be elastic. Whenever the coefficient of elasticity is less than 1.0, which means whenever the percentage change in quantity demanded is *less* than the percentage change in price, demand is said to be inelastic. Compulsive learners will want to know what is said when the percentage change in quantity demanded is exactly equal to the percentage change in price, so that the coefficient of demand elasticity is exactly 1.0. You may file away the information that demand is then *unit elastic*.

Elasticity is influenced by three factors:

Time (as already discussed). The longer the period people have to adjust to price changes, the more elastic demand will become.

The availability and closeness of known substitutes. Consumers economize in face of a higher price by seeking substitutes. There are, indeed, substitutes for everything, but some things have more known substitutes than others. The more the substitutes, the greater the elasticity of demand. Fewer substitutes lead to lower elasticity of demand. (Can you see how time and the availability of known substitutes are related to each other? It often takes time for us to consider and discover appropriate substitutes.)

The proportion of one's budget spent on a good. The smaller the proportion of one's budget spent on a good, the less sensitive consumers will be to price changes. Demand will be less elastic. If a larger proportion of one's budget is spent on a good, buyers will likely be more careful and discerning shoppers—more sensitive to changes in price—and therefore the demand will tend to be more elastic.

You can begin to familiarize yourself with the uses of this concept by asking whether demand is elastic or inelastic in the circumstances described next. Each case is discussed in the subsequent paragraphs.

- "The price of salt could double, and I'd still buy the same amount—so much for the alleged law of demand."
- The demand for minivans.
- The demand for Ford minivans.
- The demand for red Ford minivans.
- "The university's total receipts from tuition would actually increase if tuition rates were cut by 20 percent."
- The demand for insulin.

Thinking About Elasticity

"The price of salt could double and I'd still buy the same amount—so much for the alleged law of demand." Sure, for many consumers hooked on salt, in their view there are very few good substitutes for salt. Moreover, consumers of many cheap things, such as salt, toothpicks, ramen noodles, perhaps even pencils, aren't very sensitive to changes in price. It's not so much the "cheapness" itself that creates a highly inelastic demand, however, as it is the proportion of one's budget spent on an item. Chances are your yearly purchases of table salt make up a miniscule portion of your yearly grocery purchases, let alone your total purchases. You might not even know offhand how much you spend on salt each year. You have little incentive to be a careful, "picky" shopper of salt. But we bet you have a pretty good idea how much you spend on tuition or rent each year, because they're likely to be a much more significant percentage of your budget. (Of course, you might not know if your parents are footing your bills, but surely they do!)

If salt increases from 50 cents to a dollar per pound, many people will continue to purchase as usual; they won't respond dramatically, if at all. But pay attention to two things: (1) This does not violate the law of demand, for it is a relationship that unfolds over the entire range of possible prices. Would households continue to buy as usual if the relative price of salt continued its ascent, to, say, 5 dollars? 10? (2) Other users of salt—consider some restaurants or prepared-food establishments—who use a larger portion of their budget to purchase salt would be much more likely to economize on salt as its price rises. Surely the "salt potato" industry in parts of the Northeast would attempt to economize more carefully.

The demand for minivans. Let's consider this example, and the next two, in the context of availability of known substitutes. Can you list some substitutes for minivans? A short list might include delivery vans, conversion vans, sport utility vehicles, cars, public transportation, even motorcycles and bikes. If the price of minivans *in general* were to increase, people would seek out substitutes such as these.

Now consider the *demand for Ford minivans*. Notice that we've narrowed the product class from minivans in general to only Fords in particular. What would happen if the price of Ford minivans *alone* were to increase? People could switch to substitutes, such as those in our list. But now there are actually *more* substitutes than those. We can now add Chrysler, Dodge, Chevy, Toyota, and a host of other non-Ford minivans to the list. Clearly, these are not substitutes for "minivans" as a product class, but they *are* substitutes for Ford minivans. Because consumers have a wider range of good substitutes to consider, the demand for Ford minivans would be more elastic than the demand for minivans as a whole.

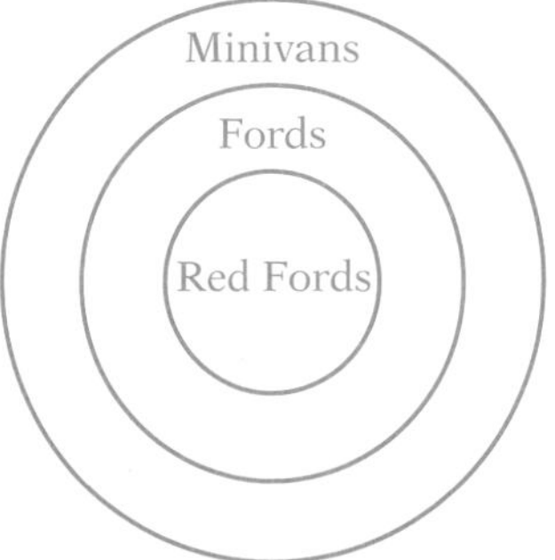

Finally, *the demand for red Ford minivans*. The product class is even narrower. But that means the number of substitutes is necessarily larger—now we can add green, blue, purple, black, and all other nonred Ford minivans to our list. The demand curve for red Ford minivans would be even more elastic than the demand for Ford minivans, which means consumers would be even more price sensitive to increases in the price of red Ford minivans alone.

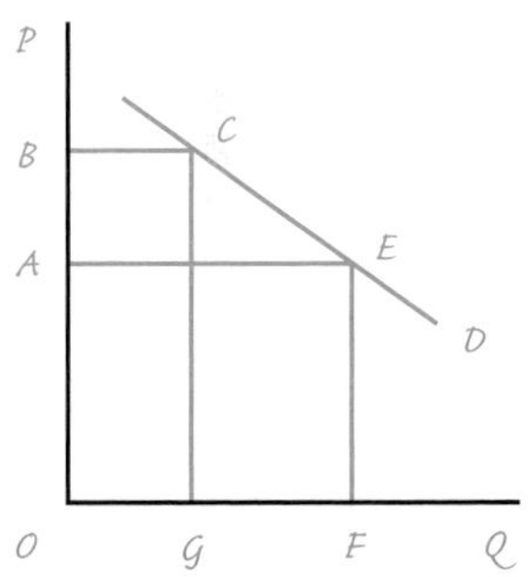

Demand is elastic between C and E, because OBCG < OAEF.

Elasticity and Total Receipts

"The university's total receipts from tuition would actually increase if tuition rates were cut by 20 percent." The university's total receipts from tuition are the product of the tuition rate and the number of students who enroll. If a 20 percent decrease in the tuition rate results in an increase in tuition receipts, then there must have been a more than 20 percent increase in enrollment. The percentage change in quantity demanded is greater than the percentage change in price, so demand is elastic.

This suggests a simple way of thinking about elasticity. Keep in mind that the quantity demanded will always move in the opposite direction from the price. *If the price change causes total receipts to move in the opposite direction from the price change, demand must be elastic.* The change in the quantity demanded has to be larger in percentage terms than the price change because total receipts are nothing but the product of price and quantity. And that is the definition of an elastic demand. *If a price change causes total receipts to move in the same direction as the price change, demand must be inelastic*. The change in the amount demanded was not large enough to outweigh the change in price. And that is the meaning of an inelastic demand.

Don't jump to the conclusion that the university will always be in a better financial position, given an elastic demand, if it lowers its tuition. It is true that lower tuition charges will mean larger receipts whenever demand is elastic, but a larger enrollment probably also means higher total costs. The university must decide in such a case whether the addition to total receipts will be larger than the addition to total costs. (But problems of pricing strategy must be deferred until we reach Chapter 9.)

On the other hand, the relationship between elasticity and total receipts does lead us to question a common mistake: Many people believe that all that a firm needs to do to "make more money" is raise its price. But if a firm raises price by, say, 20 percent, and quantity demanded falls (the law of demand!) by more than 20 percent, total receipts will fall.

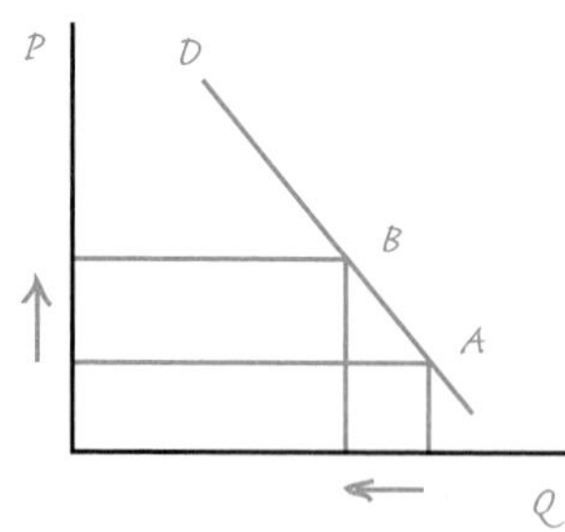

Demand is inelastic between points A and B.

The Myth of Vertical Demand

Demand curves are not *completely inelastic* over the *entire* price range. No exceptions. A completely inelastic demand curve would graph as a vertical line, suggesting there are *no* substitutes for the good in question. You would be wise not to look for such demand curves in the real world. It would be like looking for a unicorn in a world of horses.

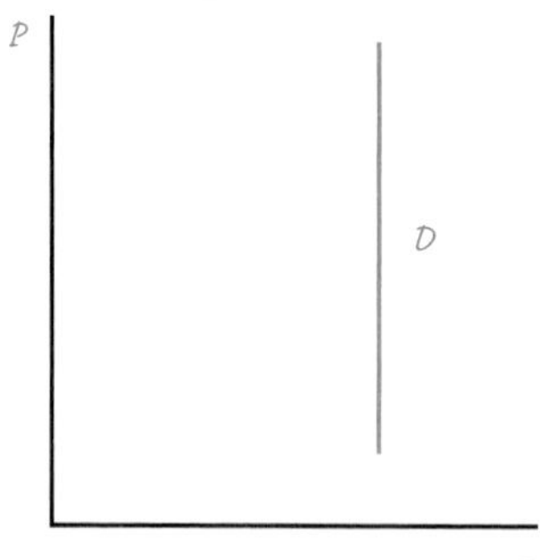

Which finally leads us, as promised, to *the demand for insulin*. Is it a vertical line? Well, we already recognized that a better diet and holistic health care are considered substitutes, and we could, if we like, perhaps add prayer, the power of positive thinking, and a slew of others to the list. But suppose you're still skeptical. Let's assume—temporarily—that diabetics do not consider any of these as potential substitutes. If we *assume* the demand for insulin is completely vertical, what are the implications? Diabetics would fill their prescriptions (again, on doctor's orders) *regardless of the price they themselves have to pay for insulin*. If their prescription costs 3 dollars a week, they'll do it. If the same prescription costs 30 dollars a week, they'll do it. If it costs 300 dollars a week, they'll do it. *Or will they?* Is it safe to assume people really behave this way? The economic way of thinking suggests, instead, that prayer would look like an increasingly attractive alternative as the price of insulin rose.

Look at it from another way. Suppose, instead, that the price of insulin is 30 dollars a week and then drops substantially to only a dollar a week. Would more diabetics use insulin *now*? Yes. But what does *that* imply? Diabetics are more likely to fill their prescriptions when their out-of-pocket cost is lower. The quantity demanded increases as the price they pay decreases. Of course, that means the demand for insulin is *downward-sloping*, rather than a vertical line. And, in fact, it is.

The law of demand can now be expressed in the language of elasticity: *There is no such thing as a completely inelastic demand over the entire range of possible prices*. Most purchasers will respond at least a little to changes in the cost to them, and all purchasers will respond to a sufficiently large change. If this seems too obvious to bother mentioning, consult your daily newspaper for evidence that it is by no means obvious to everyone. Well-intentioned people and some not so well intentioned talk constantly of basic needs, minimum requirements, and absolute necessities. But demand curves are rarely as inelastic as they suppose. This does not imply, of course, that demands are always elastic. That is a more difficult question, to be answered by looking at each case. But as we shall subsequently discover, it is a very important question for anyone who wants to decide how well our economic system functions.

All Scarce Goods Must Be Rationed Somehow

We have so far been using market prices, and willingness to pay them, as our primary criteria for rationing scarce goods and services, from water to minivans to insulin.

If a good is scarce—if people cannot obtain as much of it as they would like to have without sacrificing something else that they also value—that good has to be rationed. In other words, a criterion or rule of some kind must be established for discriminating among claimants to determine who will get how much. Willingness to pay money for the good is one such criterion, but there are many other systems that we actually use. It's a *property rights* issue.

Many ways to ration scarce goods.

The idea of "rationing according to need" appeals instinctively to many people but will appeal less to anyone who has read the first part of this chapter or who has simply thought about how vague, subjective, arbitrary, relative, uncertain, and subject to abuse this criterion would become in any society that tried to employ it on a large scale. Another system is "first come, first served." Whenever you see people standing in line to purchase something, you're observing the operation of a rationing system that employs this criterion, usually as a supplement to willingness to pay money. Another system for rationing scarce goods is a lottery. That strikes many of us as a fair way to ration a scarce good when none of those who want it seem to have better claims than anyone else. Sometimes we ration using the criterion of equal shares for all. We cut the cake or the pizza into slices of equal size and let everybody have just one. Animals interested in feeding on a carcass regularly employ the criterion "might makes right" as their way of rationing a scarce good, as do human beings on some occasions. Humans also employ the criterion of merit in some contexts: Scarce goods go to those who deserve them, for whatever reason. Can you think of examples where goods and services are rationed according to political power?

Each of these rationing systems has advantages. But each also has some serious disadvantages when considered as a *general system* for allocating scarce goods, especially among the members of what Adam Smith called "a commercial society." People would spend an awful lot of time standing in line if most goods were rationed by the criterion of "first come, first served." Although a lottery commends itself to us on fairness grounds when no one has any special claim to the scarce goods, allocating by chance pays no attention to diversity of desire and condition. Equal shares for all makes little sense when goods cannot easily be divided into equal shares, or when shares cut up into equal parts would be too small to be of much value to any user. The principle that might makes right has obvious drawbacks, not only for the weak but also for the strong, who are compelled to expend valuable resources to seize and defend their portion. Rationing according to merit is a sensible system for people who agree both on what constitutes merit and on a procedure for deciding exactly how much merit each person possesses; but those conditions are rarely satisfied outside of very small social circles, such as a closely knit family.

Most important, rationing by any of the criteria just mentioned ignores the problem of *supply*. Because very few goods fall from heaven like manna, how much will be available is rarely independent of the system used to ration. Most goods are produced by people who want to be rewarded for their efforts. A system for rationing scarce goods that does not produce appropriate rewards for those whose decisions create the goods will eventually collapse. But we're postponing consideration of supply in order to focus in this chapter on the concept of demand. Even when viewed exclusively from the demand side, a system that rations scarce goods to those who are willing to pay the most money has important advantages that are too often overlooked. Most basically, it tends to expand people's freedom and power by enabling individuals to economize as their own particular circumstances suggest. Consider the case of gasoline.

There are many ways to economize on gasoline: walk more, take the bus, ride a bicycle, form a car pool, move closer to work, reduce highway speed, tune the engine, eliminate certain activities (like waterskiing and joyriding), plan more carefully, consolidate trips, take vacations closer to home, or purchase a smaller or more fuel-efficient car. The cost or sacrifice that each of these economizing steps will entail is going to vary, sometimes enormously, among individuals. Those with access to good bus service may sacrifice little by taking the bus—unless riding a bus induces nausea. Those who have work colleagues in their neighborhood may be able to form a car pool at low cost—unless they do some of their best thinking all alone on the daily commute while listening to loud music. Those who were already planning to buy a new car may find little inconvenience in replacing a large car with a small car—unless they have a huge family or regularly use their car to transport large paintings. There is no formula that will fit everyone and no one best way to economize. Europeans have long tolerated more mixing of residential housing with business in the same or adjacent buildings and walking or taking the elevator to work. If we think it's important that people economize on gasoline and that they economize in ways that are not enormously costly, we ought to look favorably on an increase in the relative money price for gasoline.

When the price of a good rises, users of the good don't have to be *told* to economize—*they don't need economists to tell them what to do*. Instead, they find it in their *own* best interest to economize, even if they have never heard that word before. They also don't have to be told to cut back first on the most wasteful uses of the good; that's *exactly* what they will want to do, though they might differ extensively on what constitutes a wasteful use. They won't have to be watched to make certain that they really do economize; those who "cheat" will be cheating themselves. Raise the price of water and they will have the incentive to find and fix the leak. They won't, for the most part, have to suffer greatly in order to "do their part," because they will naturally choose those ways to economize that entail the smallest sacrifice; and since they know their own circumstances far better than anyone else does, they will be in the best position to pick and choose among all the alternative ways of economizing.

Incentives

Is Money All That Matters? Money Costs, Other Costs, and Economic Calculation

None of our discussion in this chapter implies, however, that the price in money that must be paid for something is a complete measure of its cost to the purchaser. Indeed, sometimes it is a very inadequate measure. Economists know this at least as well as anyone else. The concept of demand definitely does not suggest that money is the only thing that matters to people. Confusion about this point has done so much to create misunderstanding that we might profitably take a moment to clarify the matter.

To assert that people purchase less of anything as the cost to them increases does not imply that people pay attention *only* to money, or that people are selfish, or that concern for social welfare does not influence behavior. The economic way of thinking suggests instead that *as the opportunity cost of an action increases, the chooser will tend to undertake less of that action; as the opportunity cost of an action decreases, the chooser will tend to undertake more of that action*. People respond not merely to changes in expected *benefit*; they compare the expected additional benefit against the expected additional cost, *in whatever way that cost is conceived*. In a commercial market economy, money is a common denominator. It is a "yardstick" that is fairly easy to understand. More specifically, it allows individuals to *calculate* relative costs and benefits. It is something to which everyone pays attention because all can use it to further whatever projects they happen to be interested in.

Prices measured in money allow for economic calculation.

If man can't live on bread alone, then he certainly can't live on money alone, either. But that doesn't imply that bread or money fails to provide important advantages and uses. Changes in money prices are useful signals that coordinate people's consumption and production plans. That's why economists give such changes so much of their attention.

Once Over Lightly

Trade-offs, trade-offs, trade-offs—most goods are scarce, which means that they can be obtained only by sacrificing other goods.

There are substitutes for any good. Economizing is the process of making trade-offs among scarce goods by comparing the expected additional benefits and the expected additional costs from alternative ways of pursuing one's objectives. Marginal benefits and costs are the additional benefits and costs expected in the existing situation.

The concept of "needs" overlooks what the concept of demand emphasizes: the great variety of means for achieving ends and the consequent importance of considering trade-offs.

The "law of demand" asserts that people economize: They will want to purchase more of any good at lower prices and less at higher prices.

The demand for a good expresses the relationship between the price that must be paid to obtain the good and the quantity of the good people will plan to purchase. Demand is a schedule or curve and should not be confused with the specific quantity that will be demanded at any particular price.

Don't confuse a change in quantity demanded with a change in overall demand! If the price of a specific good changes, holding everything else constant, only the quantity demanded for that good is subject to change. Overall demand itself can change, however, when something other than the price of the good in question changes. Those other influences on overall demand—influences that the law of demand holds constant—include a change in the number of consumers, a change in tastes and preferences, a change in income, a change in the prices of substitutes and complements, and, finally, a change in expected prices.

The extent to which people will want to increase or decrease their purchases of a good in response to a change in its price is expressed by the concept of price elasticity of demand, which is the percentage change in the quantity demanded divided by the percentage change in the price.

When the percentage change in quantity demanded is greater than the percentage change in price, demand is said to be elastic, and price changes will lead to changes in dollar expenditures on the good that move in the opposite direction from the price change. When the percentage change in the quantity demanded is less than the percentage change in the price, demand is said to be inelastic, and price changes will lead to changes in dollar expenditures on the good that move in the same direction as the price change.

The price elasticity of demand for a good depends primarily on the availability of substitutes. The better the substitutes for a good, the greater will be the elasticity of the demand for it. Often it takes time to seek out and discover such substitutes, so time, too, plays a role in determining the price elasticity of demand. Also, the proportion or percentage of one's budget devoted to a good has an effect on elasticity.

Scarce goods must be rationed since, by definition, everyone cannot have as much as he or she would like. Although many criteria can be used to ration scarce goods—to determine who gets what—rationing through the voluntary exchange of private property rights and by the criterion of money price tends to enhance the economic freedom and power of individuals. Such rules, and the information signals they generate, allow people to calculate and therefore better economize on the basis of the particular facts of their unique situation.

QUESTIONS FOR DISCUSSION

1. What do people have in mind when they talk about "needs"?
   (a) According to a Gallup survey, the average U.S. family says it needs at least $387 per week after taxes "to get by." College graduates reportedly need $462 a week on average, but high school graduates need only $384 a week. While Democrats say they could get by on $386 a week, Republicans claim to need $458. Do you think college graduates and Republicans really have more needs, or more expensive needs, than high school graduates and Democrats? What explains these differences?
   (b) According to a National Automobile Safety Study conducted some years ago by Northeastern University, 16 percent of all surveyed consumers said they would "definitely buy" an air-bag safety system for their automobiles if one were available for $500. Only 5 percent of them would "definitely buy," however, at a price of $1,000. What does this imply about the "need" for air bags on the part of those people who are convinced that air bags will work? What does the study suggest in general about the "need" for lifesaving goods?
   (c) Would you agree with the results of a survey showing that about 60 percent of all middle-income Americans have "unmet legal needs"? What are some "legal needs" that many people will have only if they can hire a lawyer cheaply?
   (d) Here is a paragraph from a front-page story that was published in *Workers World* during a record-breaking heat wave in the midwestern United States:

   > Shouldn't air-conditioning be a right? Why should it only be accessible to those who can afford it? Only a system which defines human

worth based on how much money you have would reject the simple solution that in these crisis weeks everyone who needs air-conditioning must have it.

Who "needs" air-conditioning? Do people in wealthy nations such as the United States "need" air-conditioning more than people in much hotter but also much poorer nations, such as Bangladesh or Niger? Did anyone "need" air-conditioning before it had been invented?

2. The contention that certain goods are "basic human needs" carries a strong suggestion that access to those goods should be a matter of right, not of privilege. But the assertion of rights logically entails the assertion of obligations. Your right to vote, for example, entails the obligation of election officials to accept and count your ballot; your right to use your own umbrella implies an obligation on the part of others not to borrow it without your permission.
   (a) The American Medical Association officially proclaims that "health care is the right of everyone." What quantity and quality of health care do you suppose the AMA is talking about? Is a liver transplant, for example, the right of everyone with a diseased liver?
   (b) If "health care is the right of everyone," who has the obligation to provide health care to everyone? Who currently accepts the obligation to provide people with health care? How are they persuaded to accept these obligations?
   (c) Here are three news items relating to the cost of medical care: (i) Use of primary care services at a leading health maintenance organization fell 11 percent when the HMO imposed a $5 charge per office visit. (ii) University researchers found that disability claims for lower-back pain rose or fell with the local jobless rate. (iii) When Sweden's welfare system reduced sick-leave insurance benefits from 100 percent of pay to 75 percent for the first three sick days and 90 percent for each day thereafter, the number of sick-leave days fell nearly 20 percent. What does all this suggest about the "need" for health care?
3. When asked if there are any substitutes for water, students often respond with "Yeah—death!" Explain why that answer misunderstands what economists mean by "substitutes."
4. Someone says: "It's not true that there are substitutes for anything. If you want omelets, you need eggs. There are no substitutes for eggs in an omelet." How would you respond?
5. "The *Mona Lisa* is a priceless painting." Evaluate.
6. Do you think more cancer patients would elect chemotherapy treatment if the price they pay for chemotherapy falls? Do you think fewer would elect the treatment if the price they pay triples? What does this say about the demand curve for chemotherapy? Is it vertical?
7. "According to the law of demand, the lower the price of meals, the more meals I'll eat. But I always eat three meals a day. Obviously the law of demand doesn't apply to me." Has this person found an exception to the law of demand?
8. Would you embark on a 2,000-mile journey through the mountain states without a spare tire? To answer this question, wouldn't it be nice to know if the spare tire costs 50 dollars, 500 dollars, or 1,000 dollars?

9. A letter to the editor of a newspaper from a citizen interested in curbing Americans' consumption of gasoline recommends the elimination by law of nonessential uses and mentions as an example rural mail deliveries six days a week. Would we be eliminating a nonessential use of gasoline if all rural carriers took Saturdays off? Why don't we eliminate Tuesday and Thursday deliveries as well and save even more gasoline?
10. According to a report by the American Planning Association, the average four-member household uses about 345 gallons of water daily. The report broke that down into 235 gallons for inside use and 110 for outside use. Of the "inside" water, about 95 gallons per day went to flush toilets. Drinking and cooking used 9 to 10 gallons per day. Water rates vary, but they are rarely higher than 0.1 cent (that's $0.001) per gallon (which is a *much lower* price than we used in our hypothetical township example!). Would a doubling or even a quadrupling of water rates from the $0.001 level work a serious hardship on poor people?
11. "Landlords have been known to place a couple of bricks in the water tanks of toilets to economize on water when its price rises. Therefore, bricks are substitutes for water in this context." True or false?
12. Evaluate the following argument against a call for Congress to repeal the 1993 increase in the national gasoline tax:

    Repealing the 4.3-cents-per-gallon tax will give oil companies an additional incentive to raise prices. If skyrocketing gas prices are due to supply and demand factors, as oil companies argue, a reduction of 4.3 cents will increase demand on a product already in short supply. The increased demand will contribute to increased pump prices.

    What mistake has the author of that argument made?
13. Is it strictly true that a change in the price of a good causes a change in the quantity of that good demanded but *not* a shift in the demand curve for the good?
    (a) What effect do you suppose the large increases in the price of gasoline in the 1970s had on the demand (curve) for fuel-efficient cars?
    (b) What effect did this have after several years on the original demand (curve) for gasoline?
    (c) How did the huge increase in the price of home heating oil during 2003 affect the demand for housing insulation? How did this eventually shift the demand for heating oil?
    (d) Can you think of similar processes through which changes in the price of a good would lead, over time, to shifts in the demand for the good?
    (e) If the price of a good returned to its previous level after a time but the quantity demanded did not, would this be evidence that the demand had changed in the interim?
14. The graphs in Figure 3–2 show the demand for bus services (left) and the demand for downtown parking space (right) in an imaginary city. If the city raises bus fares from P_1 to P_2, the demand curve will not change, but the quantity demanded will fall. With fewer people riding the bus, what will happen to the demand for downtown parking? What effect will this have on downtown parking rates? With higher parking rates, more people

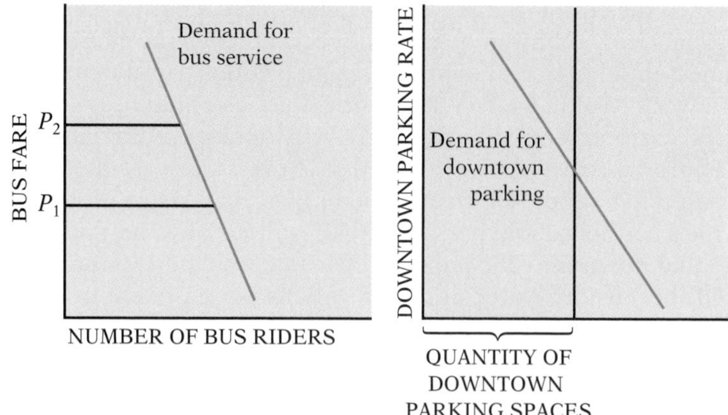

Figure 3–2 **Demand curves for bus service and downtown parking**

will want to ride the bus. So what effect will the higher bus fares have after all on the demand for bus service?

15. If customers always want to purchase less at higher prices, why would any seller publicize the fact that its prices are high?
    (a) The advertising slogan of Maker's Mark Whiskey is: "It tastes expensive. . . and it is." Isn't the firm foolish to advertise its high price? Or will people buy more if they think Maker's Mark is more expensive than other whiskeys? If so, does this contradict the law of demand?
    (b) A waiter at Jean-Louis, a restaurant in Washington, D.C. often patronized by eminent politicians, says: "It is good to be known as expensive. People know they can impress their guests here." What does he think people are purchasing when they go to Jean-Louis for dinner?
    (c) Robert Cialdini reports the following event in his book *Influence: The Psychology of Persuasion*. The owner of an Arizona jewelry store was unable to move some fine-quality turquoise jewelry that was selling at low prices in the height of the tourist season. So she instructed her assistant to cut the prices in half just before leaving on a business trip. But the assistant misunderstood and doubled the prices. When the owner returned a few days later, every piece had been sold. Can you explain this in a way that does not contradict the law of demand?
16. A change in expectations can cause a change in demand. Explain how this could lead to a situation in which a price increase was followed by an increase in the amount people want to purchase.
17. What makes demand curves elastic or inelastic?
    (a) How do you think e-mail has affected the elasticity of demand for snail mail provided by the U.S. Postal Service? Do you think the Postal Service is pleased by the results?
    (b) The demand for aspirin at currently prevailing prices seems to be highly inelastic. What do you think would happen to the elasticity of

demand if the price of aspirin relative to everything else were five times as high? Fifty times as high? Why?

(c) Is the demand for prescription drugs elastic or inelastic? Why? Do you agree with the statement sometimes made that the prices charged for prescription drugs can be freely set by the manufacturers, since people must buy whatever the doctor prescribes?

(d) CD NOW, the Internet music retailer, can be accessed all across the country. What effect does that have on the elasticity of demand for music retailers in local shopping malls?

(e) In the 1980s, a number of IBM clones appeared in the PC industry. What effect would that have had on the elasticity of demand for IBM personal computers?

18. One estimate of the price elasticity of demand for cigarettes puts it at 0.4: A 10 percent increase in the price of cigarettes will lead to a 4 percent decline in the quantity demanded.

(a) Does this imply that an increase in the tax on cigarettes is an effective way to reduce smoking?

(b) Does it imply that an increase in the cigarette tax is an effective way for the government to increase its revenue?

(c) If government officials would like both to reduce smoking and to increase government revenue from the tax on cigarettes, how elastic or inelastic do they want the demand for cigarettes to be?

19. Studies have shown that states with higher cigarette taxes have lower rates of teenage smoking. But subsequent studies that excluded the states of North Carolina, Kentucky, and Virginia found no significant relationship between the tax on cigarettes and the incidence of teenage smoking. Can you think of a plausible explanation? Why is there no significant difference in the incidence of teenage smoking between high-tax and low-tax states when North Carolina, Kentucky, and Virginia are excluded from the study?

20. Some people have suggested that we can distinguish between luxuries and necessities in the following way: Luxuries are goods for which the demand is very elastic, and necessities are goods for which the demand is very inelastic. Do you agree that relative elasticity of demand provides an effective criterion for distinguishing luxuries from necessities? Think of some specific items that most people would classify as luxuries and some that most people would classify as necessities and then ask yourself whether the demand curves would generally be elastic or inelastic in each case.

21. According to an article on the abuse of statistics that appeared in *The Economist* (April 18, 1998), the government of Mexico City in the late 1970s increased the capacity of the *Viaducto*, a four-lane expressway, by repainting the lines to make it six lanes wide: a 50 percent increase in capacity. But after this resulted in more fatal accidents, the government switched back to four lanes: a reduction in capacity of one-third, or 33 percent. Did the successive changes produce a net 17 percent increase in capacity, as the government allegedly claimed in a report on social progress? (If you're wondering what this has to do with economics, go on to question 22.)

22. Price elasticity of demand can be calculated by dividing the percentage change in the quantity demanded by the percentage change in the price.
    (a) What is the coefficient of elasticity between the two points of the demand schedule in each of the cases shown in Table 3–3?

Table 3–3

Price per Ticket	Tickets Demanded	Price per Cup of Coffee	Cups of Coffee Demanded
$2	200	35¢	600
$1	400	70¢	300

    (b) If you divided 100 percent by 50 percent in the ticket case, and 50 percent by 100 percent in the coffee case, you got very different coefficients (2 and 0.5, respectively) for what are actually identical relative changes. The different results come from using the larger price and the smaller quantity as the base from which to calculate the percentage change in the ticket case, and using the smaller price and the larger quantity as the base in the coffee case. But the coefficient of elasticity should be the same between two points regardless of the direction in which the change is measured. How can this problem be handled?
    (c) What is the coefficient of elasticity in each of these cases if you use the *average* of the prices and quantities between which the change is occurring as the base for calculating the percentage changes?

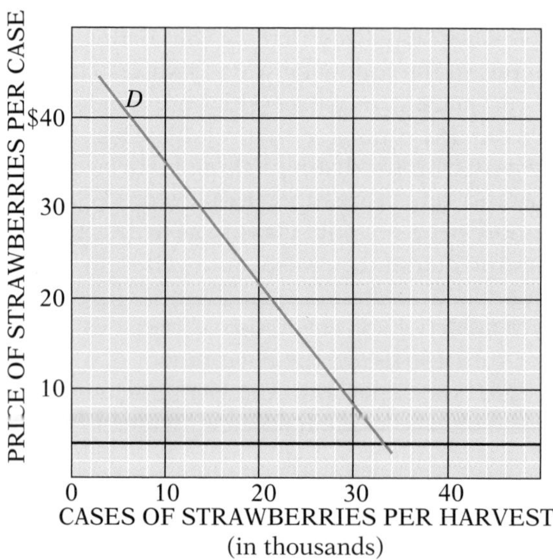

Figure 3–3 **Demand curve for strawberries**

(d) In both cases, total expenditure (price times quantity) does not change when the price changes. What does this imply about the elasticity of demand between the prices given? Does this implication agree with your answer in (c)? (It should.)

23. Figure 3–3 shows a hypothetical demand curve for strawberries.

(a) What price per case would maximize the gross receipts of strawberry growers? [Peek at part (d) of this question rather than waste too much time trying all sorts of different prices. The price that maximizes gross receipts will be found at the midpoint of a straight-line demand curve when the curve is extended to the axes. If you see why, good. If not, it's a bit of knowledge with only academic usefulness anyway.]

(b) If the price of strawberries is determined by the total quantity harvested in conjunction with the demand, what size crop will result in the price quoted in part (d)?

(c) What would the gross receipts of strawberry growers be if the crop turned out to be 30,000 cases?

(d) Can you prove that the demand for strawberries is elastic above a price of $24 per case and inelastic below that price?

(e) If strawberry growers can make more money by selling fewer than 30,000 cases, why would they ever market that much? Why wouldn't they destroy some of the crop rather than "spoil the market"?

24. See if you can clarify this analysis: "If half of our forests were destroyed in a fire, the value of the remaining lumber would be greater than the value of all the lumber in the country before the fire. This absurdity—that the whole is worth less than a half—shows that values are distorted in a market economy."

Opportunity Cost and the Supply of Goods

4

The theory of supply in economics is not essentially different from the theory of demand. Both assume that decision makers face alternatives and choose among them and that their choices reflect a comparison of expected benefits and costs. The logic of the economizing process is the same for producers as it is for consumers. We shall discuss how the incentive to produce and supply scarce goods is shaped by opportunity costs and the market prices that reflect and inform us of those costs.

Refresher on Opportunity Costs

First, let's see if you can further apply the notion of opportunity cost developed in the previous chapters to explain typically puzzling events.

Why are poor people more likely to travel between cities by bus and wealthy people more likely to travel by air? A simple answer would be that taking the bus is cheaper. But it isn't. It's a very costly mode of transportation for people for whom the opportunity cost of time is high (think of a lawyer who values her time at $100 an hour); and the opportunity cost of time is typically much lower for poor people than for those with a high income from working.

Why is it often so much harder to find a teenage baby-sitter in a wealthy residential area than in a low-income area? The frustrated couple unable to find a baby-sitter may complain that all the kids in the neighborhood are lazy. But that is a needlessly harsh explanation. Teenage baby-sitters can be found by any couple willing to pay the opportunity cost. That means bidding the baby-sitters away from their most valued alternative opportunity. If the demand for baby-sitters in the area is large because wealthy people go out more often, and if the local teenagers receive such generous allowances that they value a date or leisure more than the ordinary income from baby-sitting, why be surprised to find that the opportunity cost of hiring a baby-sitter is high?

Why do more college students continue on to graduate school during a recession? Poor job prospects reduce the opportunity cost of staying in college; therefore, more students are inclined to consider spending another year or two to obtain an M.A. or M.B.A. rather than accept a job offer as overnight manager of a twenty-four-hour gas station.

Why are more young people from low-income regions more likely to join the military? Do you have the idea?

Costs Are Tied to Actions, Not Things

It is clear from these examples that costs are not tied to *things*. Costs are always tied to actions, decisions, choices. It is for this reason that the economic way of thinking recognizes no objective costs. That offends common sense, which teaches that things do have "real" costs, costs that depend on the laws of physics rather than the vagaries of the human psyche. It's hard to win a battle against common sense, but we must try. Again, we could profit by thinking outside the box of common sense.

A "thing" cannot have a cost. Only actions (or decisions) have costs.

Perhaps we can disarm common sense most quickly by pointing out that "things" have no costs at all. Only actions do. If you think that things do indeed have costs and are ready with an example to prove it, you are almost certainly smuggling in an unnoticed action to give your item a cost.

For example: What is the cost of a baseball? "Ten dollars," you say. But you mean that the cost of *purchasing* an official major league baseball at the local sporting goods store is 10 dollars. Since purchasing is an action, it can entail sacrificed opportunities and thereby have a cost. But note the smuggled-in action. With other actions, the cost of a baseball changes. The cost of *manufacturing* a baseball is quite different. *Selling* one has yet another cost. And what about the cost of *catching* one at the ballpark? Just consider what the fan unintentionally did to himself, and the Chicago Cubs, during the 2003 playoffs!

Consider college education. What does it cost? The answer is that "it" cannot have a cost. We must first distinguish the cost of *obtaining* a college education from the cost of *providing* one. As soon as we make that distinction, we should also notice something that has been implicit in everything we've said so far about costs, either in this or the preceding chapters: Costs are always costs to *someone*. The cost of obtaining an education usually means the cost to the student. But it could mean the cost to the student's parents, which is not the same. Or, if that student's admission entailed the rejection of some other applicant, it could even mean the cost to John (who was refused admission) of

There are no "objective" costs. All costs are costs to someone who places value on forgone opportunities.

Marsha's obtaining entrance to the first-year class. Those will all be different.

A great deal of fruitless argument about the "true cost" of things stems from a failure to recognize that only actions have costs and that actions can entail different costs for different people.

What Do I Do Now? The Irrelevance of "Sunk Costs"

You learned in Chapter 3 that the value of goods is always determined *at the margin*. The value of water, for example, is not what people would sacrifice to obtain it if their only alternative was to do without water altogether. The value of water to people is what they would be willing to pay for an additional amount in the actual situation in which they find themselves. The same marginal principles apply to costs. In the case of goods or benefits, most people who go astray do so by confusing the total value of a good or benefit with its marginal value. In the case of costs, the most common error is confusing costs *previously* incurred with additional or marginal costs. The proper stance for making cost calculations is not looking back to the past, for the past is filled with sunk costs, irretrievable costs. The proper stance is looking forward to current opportunities.

Mary's parents put up a $5,000 nonrefundable deposit for her wedding reception. Two weeks later, Mary and her parents discover that her fiancé is a cheater and a louse. They cancel the wedding and the reception. Did the family therefore *lose* $5,000 by canceling the reception? Common sense leads us to say yes. But would they have gotten that deposit *back* if they had decided to have the reception without the wedding? No. That deposit represented an exchange of property rights. It was no longer the parents' from the moment it was paid.

Suppose you pass through the cafeteria line, pick up the tuna lasagna, and pay the cashier $1.90. You are willing to pay that cost because you expect the satisfaction obtained to be greater than the satisfaction from spending the $1.90 on anything else. Then you take your first bite and realize you have made a serious mistake. The tuna lasagna is *awful*. What will it cost you to leave the lasagna on your plate?

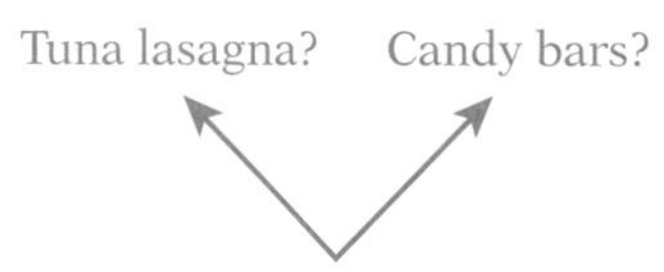

It will not be $1.90. The cash you gave to the cashier is no longer yours; it's the cafeteria's. It's gone, and it won't come back if you continue to eat all your lasagna and claim to "get your money's worth." Instead, once the cash is the cafeteria's and the lasagna is yours, *you confront a new set of choices*. Do you now wish to dispense with your next class (should eating this meal make you sick)? Do you wish to dispense with your life (should you fear getting struck by a lightning bolt if you don't finish your meal)? Or do you wish to dispense with the lasagna, feel somewhat guilty for not

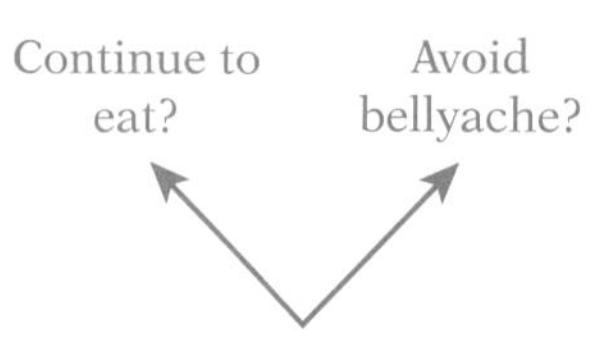

cleaning your plate, but at least reduce your chance of getting ill? The choice is all yours. But that's the point—you now face new choices, and no matter what you do, your $1.90 is gone for good.

The price you paid is what economists dismiss as a *sunk cost*. Sunk costs are irrelevant to economic decisions. Bygones are bygones. The only costs that matter in decision making are marginal costs—additional costs—and *marginal costs always lie in the future*. Like your $1.90, the $5,000 nonrefundable deposit for Mary's wedding reception is also a sunk cost *after it has been paid*. Chalk that up as one of life's important lessons. You now stand at a new fork in the road.

Of course, we must be certain that a cost is really sunk, or fully sunk, before we decide to regard it as irrelevant to decision making. The student who paid $100 for the calculus textbook and drops the course after the midterm cannot get his "money's worth" by trying to *read* the entire book. He might, however, be able to sell it back to the campus bookstore for $20. *That's the choice he now faces*—continue to own the book versus transferring ownership back to the bookstore. The student hasn't sunk $100; $20 is recoverable. His sunk cost is $80.

In the economist's way of thinking, sunk cost is a piece of history, for it represents no opportunity for future choice. It may be cause for bitter regret (at the calculus professor, the bookstore, college life), but it is no longer a cost in any sense relevant to the economics of present decisions. It is a piece of information, a lesson in life. Don't get us wrong—the lesson is certainly not irrelevant, only the cost is. *The question is what do you do now?*

Producers' Costs as Opportunity Costs

When we think about producers' costs—asking ourselves, for example, why it costs more to manufacture a mountain bike than a redwood picnic table—we tend to think first of what goes into the production of each. We think of the raw materials, of the labor time required, perhaps also of the machinery or tools that must be used. We express the value of the inputs in monetary terms and assume that the cost of the bike or the table is the sum of these values. That isn't wrong, but it leaves two questions unanswered. Why did the producers of the bike or the table choose to use precisely these inputs in just this combination? And why did it cost the producers whatever it did cost, in monetary terms, to use these inputs?

There are substitutes for everything in production as well as in consumption. Technology creates possibilities and sets limits to what we can do; but it does not decree a single, uniquely correct process for producing anything. In New Delhi, men using short-handled hoes dig the foundations for highway overpasses and women haul the dirt away in baskets on their heads. Imagine that. *Why do they do it in that way?* Contractors choose this technology because they believe it's the least costly way to dig and haul the dirt they want to remove. Human labor moves dirt in India at a lower cost than heavy machinery can do the job because human labor can be hired in India at a very low wage. It is too costly to devote heavy machinery to that particular activity.

Why is the wage rate for unskilled labor in India so low? It's low because so many potential workers in that country have no opportunity to employ their labor in any manner that would produce something of substantial value to others. The concept of opportunity cost asserts that the amount of money a producer must pay for any resource, human or physical, will depend upon what the owner of that resource can obtain from *someone else* and that this will depend upon the value of what that resource can create for someone else.

So manufacturers' costs of producing a bike will be determined by what they must pay to obtain the appropriate resources. And, because these resources have other opportunities for employment, the manufacturers must pay a price that matches the "best opportunity" value. The value of forgone opportunities thus becomes the opportunity cost of manufacturing a mountain bike.

All costs relevant to decisions to supply lie in the future.

Consider the example of the picnic table. Part of its cost of production is the price of redwood. Assume that the demand for new housing has increased recently and that building contractors have consequently been purchasing a lot more redwood lumber. If this causes the price of lumber to rise, the cost of manufacturing a picnic table will go up. Nothing has happened to affect the physical inputs that go into the table, but its cost of production has risen. Because houses containing redwood lumber are now more valuable than formerly, table manufacturers must pay a higher opportunity cost for the lumber they want to put into their picnic tables. When Hurricane Andrew devastated southern Florida in 1992, the price of plywood quickly rose across the entire United States. Plywood took on a greatly increased value for people whom Andrew had made homeless, and everyone who wanted to use plywood for other purposes now had to pay this new and higher opportunity cost. Of course, this also gave everyone an incentive to economize on the use of plywood.

A skilled worker will be paid more than an unskilled worker because and only insofar as those skills make the skilled worker more valuable somewhere else. Workers who can install wheel spokes while standing on their heads and whistling "Dixie" are marvelously skilled. But our mountain bike manufacturer will not have to pay them additional compensation for that skill unless their unusual talent makes them more valuable somewhere else. That could happen. A circus might bid for their talents. If the circus offers them more than they can obtain as bike producers, their opportunity cost to the manufacturer rises. In that case, the manufacturer will probably wish them good-bye and good luck and replace them with other workers whose opportunity cost is lower.

When the National Basketball Association and the American Basketball Association merged into one league, what happened to the opportunity cost of hiring physically coordinated seven-footers? With two leagues, each player had two teams bidding for his services. What either team was compelled to pay to get him was determined by what the other team was willing to pay, and both were willing to pay a lot if they thought he would make a big difference in ticket sales. When the leagues merged, however, the right to hire a particular player was assigned to a single team, and the opportunity cost of hiring a well-coordinated seven-footer fell. When the players' union subsequently secured the right of players (under certain circumstances) to switch to another team if they chose, the opportunity cost of hiring basketball stars rose again. It's not surprising that owners of professional athletic teams prefer one league to two and vehemently argue that giving players the right to switch teams will destroy balance and hence the quality of the game.

Let's take a more ordinary case. If a large firm employing many people (such as a Wal-Mart or Target) moves into a small town, the cost of hiring grocery clerks, bank tellers, secretaries, and gasoline station attendants in the town will tend to go up. Why? Because grocery stores, banks, offices, and gasoline stations must all pay the opportunity cost of the people they employ, and these people might find better opportunities for employment in the new firm. It might be better wages, better conditions, better health care plans. The new firm might attract potential employees in this manner. Owners of gasoline stations, for example, will tend to find it more difficult to retain their workers, or attract new replacements at the same old wage, as workers find more valuable opportunities elsewhere. If a military recruitment office moves into town and cannot attract people away from their current employers, it might indeed face very real recruitment challenges.

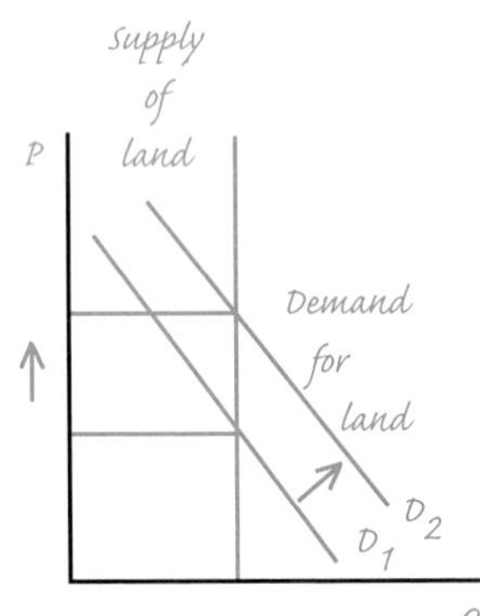

How demand affects the cost of buying land

The resource that most clearly illustrates the opportunity-cost concept is probably land. Suppose you want to purchase an acre of land to build a house. What will you have to pay for the land? It will depend on the value of that land in alternative uses. Do other people view the acre as a choice residential site? Does it have commercial or industrial potentialities? Would it be used for pasture if you did not purchase it? The cost you pay for the land will be determined by the *alternative opportunities* that people perceive for its use.

Marginal opportunity costs

Mantra on costs: Only actions have costs; all costs are costs to someone; all costs lie in the future.

If you are wondering at this point about the relationship between opportunity cost and marginal cost, you are wondering about the appropriate question. *All opportunity costs are marginal costs and all marginal costs are opportunity costs*. Opportunity cost and marginal cost are the same thing, viewed from different angles.

Opportunity cost calls attention to the value of the opportunity forgone by an action; marginal cost calls attention to the change in the existing situation that the action entails. The full name for any cost that is relevant to decision making is *marginal opportunity cost*.

All such costs are costs of actions or decisions, all are attached to particular persons, and all lie in the future.

Costs and Supply

And now we get to the heart of the chapter—using our notion of marginal opportunity cost to explain the decisions to supply goods and services on the market. Just as demand curves indicate the marginal costs or sacrifices that people are willing to incur in order to obtain particular goods, so supply curves show the marginal costs that must be covered to induce potential suppliers to make particular goods available. We can use our familiar production possibilities frontier in Figure 4–1 to illustrate our logic.

A small Iowa farmer, let's call him Smith, considers producing soybeans and corn this season. If he devotes all his acreage to soybean production, he can produce 14.5 units. If he produces only corn instead, he can produce 10 units. His production possibilities

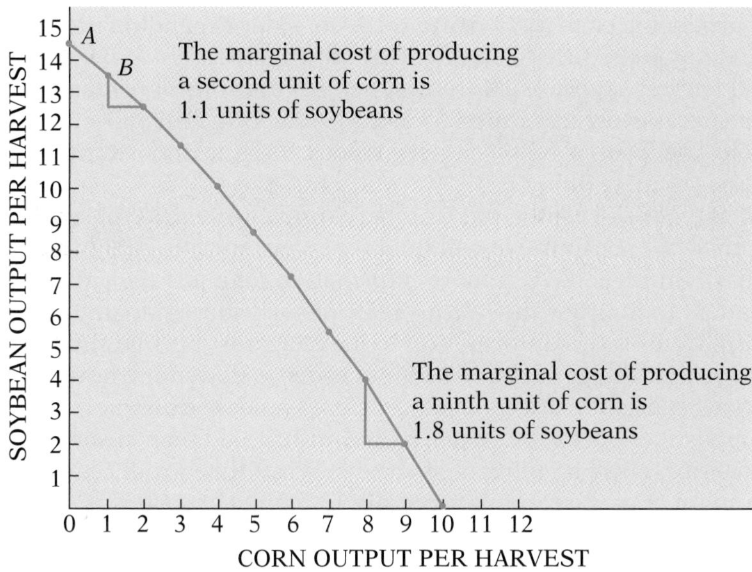

Figure 4–1 **The production possibilities frontier with rising marginal cost**

Smith's production possibilities frontier for corn and soybeans. He can produce at most 14.5 units of soybeans (and 0 units of corn) or 10 units of corn (and 0 units of soybeans), or any combination of the two on the frontier. Notice the bend to this particular frontier. It illustrates that corn can be produced only at higher and higher marginal cost.

frontier represents those two combinations, as well as all other possible combinations, given his acreage, the suitability of the soil for either crop, farm machinery, talents, and so on. Table 4–1 shows the actual combinations on Smith's frontier:

Table 4–1

Soybean Output per Harvest	Corn Output per Harvest
14.5	0
13.5	1
12.4	2
11.2	3
9.9	4
8.5	5
7.0	6
5.4	7
3.7	8
1.9	9
0	10

(You might notice that the frontier in Figure 4–1 is a curve, not a line. This illustrates that Smith faces increasing opportunity costs of producing each good. Were he to consider expanding his corn production, he sacrifices, of course, the opportunity to produce and harvest soybeans. Moreover, he uses portions of his farm that are successively less suited for corn production. The movement along the frontier represents the trade-offs—the opportunity costs—that Smith faces.)

Suppose—keeping our numbers simple—the price of soybeans is $1 per unit (we will hold that constant throughout our story). Smith could use more information than just that. What matters to Smith is the *relative price* of soybeans compared to corn. He uses that information to judge against his marginal opportunity costs of production, in order to determine how much of soybeans and corn to produce. Here's an easy example. Suppose corn sells for $0 per unit. Smith would then clearly produce say, only 14.5 units of soybeans. Why? If he produces 1 unit of corn, he can produce only 13.5 units of soybeans (we move downward along the frontier). His marginal cost would be $1 (the sacrificed market value of 1 unit of soybeans). *What would he gain?* A unit of corn, with a *zero* market value. What's important is that the *marginal cost* of producing the first unit of corn is $1. What if, instead, corn were priced at 90 cents per unit? If Smith willingly produced 1 unit of corn, he would gain an additional 90 cents, but at an additional cost of $1—the value of his sacrificed unit of soybeans. Smith wouldn't be enticed to produce corn at *that* relative price.

Market prices help us economize more effectively.

Suppose, instead, that the price of corn were also $1 per unit. Then Smith would be inclined to produce *up to but no more than* 1 unit of corn. At most, he would plan to harvest 13.5 units of soybeans and 1 unit of corn. He would move downward along the frontier, from point *A* to *B*. He would sacrifice $1 worth of soybeans and gain $1 worth of corn.

What is Smith's marginal cost of producing a second unit of corn? He'd have to reduce soybean output from 13.5 to 12.4 units. That's a difference of 1.1 units, with a market value of $1.10 (again, holding the price of soybeans constant at $1.00 per unit). *Smith would consider producing a second unit of corn only if the market price of corn were to compensate for his marginal opportunity cost of producing corn—in this case if the price of corn were $1.10 per unit.* What is Smith's marginal cost of producing a third unit of corn? He'd sacrifice 1.2 units of soybeans, with a market value of $1.20. Smith would be willing to increase corn output to 3 units only if he were compensated for *that* additional cost. *Smith would consider producing a third unit of corn only if the market price of corn were $1.20 per unit.*

We can summarize all of this in Table 4–2 below:

Table 4–2

Corn Output (units)	Marginal Opportunity Cost (holding price of soybeans = $1.00)
1	$1.00
2	$1.10
3	$1.20
4	$1.30
5	$1.40
6	$1.50
7	$1.60
8	$1.70
9	$1.80
10	$1.90

We're now ready to draw three important conclusions. First, *producers consider marginal costs of production when deciding upon which outputs, and which levels of output, to produce.* Second, *relative prices further inform producers of the marginal costs, and marginal benefits, of their alternative production plans.*

The Supply Curve

Our third conclusion is best represented by the information in Figure 4–2, which simply plots the information from our Table 4–2. The bars in the graph show Smith's marginal opportunity costs of

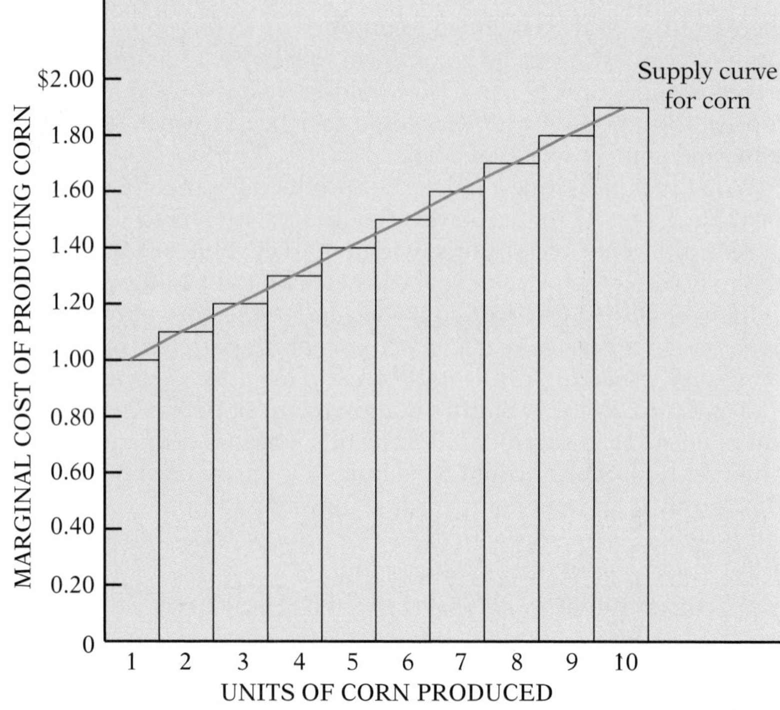

Figure 4–2 **The supply curve is the marginal opportunity cost curve of making various quantities of a good available**

The bars in the graph depict the marginal cost (measured in dollars) of producing each unit of corn. Smith will want to ensure that the price he can receive compensates him for his last unit produced. Therefore, if the price is $1.10, he'll produce 2 units. A price of $1.80 will encourage him to produce 9 units. In this way we derive an upward-sloping supply curve for corn. The higher prices increase his quantity supplied, reflecting the law of supply.

producing corn, measured in market values when the price of soybeans is given at $1.00 per unit. (The height of the first bar is $1.00, the second is $1.10, the third is $1.20, and this continues to the tenth, which has a height of $1.90.) We've seen how Smith would supply 0 units of corn if the relative price of corn were under $1.00 per unit; he'd supply 1 unit only if the price rose to $1.00 per unit; he'd supply 2 units if the price were $1.20. The upward-sloping line illustrates Smith's *supply curve for corn*. Each bar represents the marginal cost of producing corn. The total area underneath the supply curve represents Smith's *total costs of production* (the adding up of all the marginal costs of production).

The supply curve illustrates the alternative amounts of a good supplied at alternative prices. In our story, they represent Smith's planned outputs at different corn prices. Because he faces higher marginal opportunity costs of production, Smith would plan to increase corn production only if he expected to be compensated by higher corn prices. Smith would produce up to 10 units of corn if he expected to receive $1.90 per unit.

This story about farming tells in a simplified way what underlies all supply curves. Supply curves are the marginal opportunity cost curves of making various quantities of a good available. As the price people are willing to pay for a good rises, that price persuades people with a marginal opportunity cost of supplying the good that is less than the price to shift the resources they own or control into supplying the good in question. *Other things being constant, a change in price of the output increases quantity supplied, not the overall supply curve.*

Supply Itself Can Change

But the supply curve itself can change. *Anything that changes the marginal cost of production will tend to change (or shift) the overall supply curve, too.* A rise (or fall) in the *price of a factor of production* would raise (or lower) marginal costs, and thereby lead to a shift of the overall supply curve. Higher marginal costs would shift the supply curve upward and to the right; lower marginal costs would shift it downward and to the left. *Technological changes*, such as new innovations that reduce marginal costs, would tend to *increase* overall supply. Technological deterioration, on the other hand, would likely *decrease* overall supply.

Notice from our tables and graphs that *a change in the relative price of an alternative product will tend to generate a change in the supply curve*. It will provide the producer an incentive to reconsider his options. Suppose, for example, that the price of soybeans alone falls from $1.00 (as in our original example) to $0.50 per unit. *The lower market value of soybeans reduces the farmer's marginal opportunity cost of growing corn*, as shown in Table 4–3. It will be cut in half for each unit of corn output. That would shift the supply curve for corn downward and to the right. That's an *increase in overall supply.* The corn farmer will now be willing to deliver any given unit of corn at a *lower price* than before. We can view it in another way as well: The farmer will be willing to *supply a larger quantity of corn at any given price.* If you would like to practice graphing this increase in the supply of corn, plot the quantities shown onto Figure 4–2.

Do you recall from the previous chapter how consumer demand may change if consumers expect higher or lower prices in the future? The same holds true for producers. We all act upon our expectations. *A change in the expected price of the producer's output will tend to change the overall supply of that output.* If producers expect lower prices for their outputs six months from now, they may strive to *increase* deliveries of their present output to the market, attempting to "supply more while the price is still high." Likewise, if they expect more favorable prices six months from

Table 4–3

Corn Output (units)	Marginal Opportunity Cost (holding price of soybeans = $0.50)
1	$0.50
2	$0.55
3	$0.60
4	$0.65
5	$0.70
6	$0.75
7	$0.80
8	$0.85
9	$0.90
10	$0.95

now, they may choose to supply *less today*, which would shift the supply curve upward and to the left. By postponing their present supply, they are not necessarily reducing their *current production*. In anticipation of the higher future price, they are reducing the *current quantities that they plan to deliver to today's market*.

And finally, *a change in the overall number of suppliers tends to shift the market supply curve*. The entry of more competitors would tend to increase overall supply, whereas exit would tend to decrease overall supply. Typically, expected profits will encourage entry and thereby increase market supply. Expected losses will encourage exit and reduce market supply, as producers search for more profitable uses of their resources. We shall discuss the role of profit and loss quite extensively in Chapter 7.

Marginal and Average Costs

It's important not to get the marginal concept mixed up with the notion of *average*. If you have no intention of doing that, what follows may only plant in your head the seeds of a bad idea. Let's hope it doesn't. Consider Farmer Smith one more time. Table 4–4 illustrates Smith's total cost of producing corn (which is merely the sum of his marginal costs), his marginal cost, and his average cost (which is merely the total cost divided by the level of output) for up to 3 units of output.

It is clear that marginal cost can differ substantially from average cost. But average cost didn't guide Smith's choice to produce more corn; marginal costs did. Shall he produce more? Or less? Marginal cost is the consequence of action; it should therefore be the guide to action.

Are businesspeople then not interested in average costs? Unless they receive sufficient revenue to cover all their costs, they

Table 4–4

Units of Corn Produced	Total Cost of Producing Corn	Marginal Cost	Average Cost
0	$0	$0	$0
1	1.00	1.00	1.00
2	2.10	1.10	1.05
3	3.30	1.20	1.10

will sustain a loss. They won't willingly commit themselves to any course of action unless they anticipate being able to cover their total costs. They might therefore set up the problem in terms of anticipated production cost per unit against anticipated selling price per unit. But notice that the *anticipated* costs of any decision are really *marginal* costs. Marginal cost need not refer to the additional cost of a single unit of output. It could also refer to the additional cost of a batch of output, or the addition to cost expected from a decision regarding an entire process. Decisions are often made in this "lumpy" way.

For example, no one plans to build a soda-bottling factory expecting to bottle only one case of soda. There are important economies of size in most business operations, so that unless businesspeople see their way clear to producing a large number of units, they won't produce any. They won't enter the business. They won't build the bottling factory at all. The entire decision—build or don't build, build this size plant or that, build in this way or some other way—is a marginal decision at the time it is made. Remember that additions can be very large as well as very small. The lump of output could even be the sales your favorite hangout would enjoy if it stayed open until 2:00 A.M. instead of closing an hour earlier.

Whether or not businesspeople cast their thinking in terms of averages, it is expected marginal costs that guide their decisions. Averages can be looked at after the fact to see how well or poorly things went, and maybe even to learn something about the future if the future can be expected to resemble the past. But this is history—admittedly an instructive study—whereas economic decisions are always made in the present with an eye to the future.

The Cost of a Volunteer Military Force

Let's consider the supply of something very different from corn. Here's a timely example. The U.S. military faced recruitment and reenlistment difficulties and shortages in the late 1990s (the 1990s were economically prosperous times!). In 1999, Floyd Spence, the House Armed Services Committee chairman, argued

You may be called to serve!

that the military confronted "a desperate situation that keeps getting worse." He favored the possible abandoning of the all-volunteer forces for some form of military draft—compulsion. That's something the people of the United States hadn't practiced since the early 1970s. After the attack on the World Trade Center and the Pentagon in 2001, the call for a renewal of the military draft gained momentum. With the current U.S. military deployments in both Afghanistan and Iraq, and an improving economy once again at home (as we revise this chapter in the summer of 2004), the call to reinstate the military draft of young men and women is greater now than it has been in decades.

Perhaps a draft—simply forcing able-bodied young men and women to serve in the military—is a "cheaper" way to get the number of personnel that we need. (*Need?*) Of course, outright compulsion often works, but is it necessarily a less costly way to organize a military force?

There may be good arguments for the draft, but the familiar argument that an adequate volunteer army[1] costs too much is not one of them. The Department of Defense and others who worry about the relative costs of a conscripted and a volunteer military are conveniently bypassing the question of *cost to whom*. Are we talking about the cost to taxpayers, enlisted personnel, Congress, or the Pentagon? They are very different.

What is the cost to a young person of becoming a soldier? The best way to find out would be to offer a bribe and to keep raising it until it was accepted. If Marshall would enlist for $5,000 per year, Carol for $8,000, and Philip for no less than $60,000, these represent the opportunity costs of Marshall, Carol, and Philip. The cost of drafting all three, *to them*, would then be $73,000, even though the government can conceal this fact by offering far less in wages and then compelling each to serve.

The opportunity cost is a function of forgone alternative employment opportunities and all sorts of other values: preferences with respect to lifestyle, attitude toward war, degrees of cowardice or bravery, and so on. When the government bids for military personnel, raising its offer until it can attract exactly the desired number of enlistments, the government in an important sense actually minimizes the cost of its program. For it pulls in those with the lowest opportunity costs of service—everyone like Marshall but no one like Philip. Under a draft, this could occur only through the most unlikely of coincidences. Figure 4–3 provides a simple way to grasp the argument.

The graph depicts a supply curve of military volunteers. It summarizes the number or quantity that would be supplied at various prices. The argument that people won't voluntarily risk their lives is refuted by the fact that people do—not only military

[1]In some contexts, a volunteer means a person who works without pay (volunteer firefighters, hospital volunteers). That is *not* the case with the volunteer military force, where payment of an attractive wage is the key to its success.

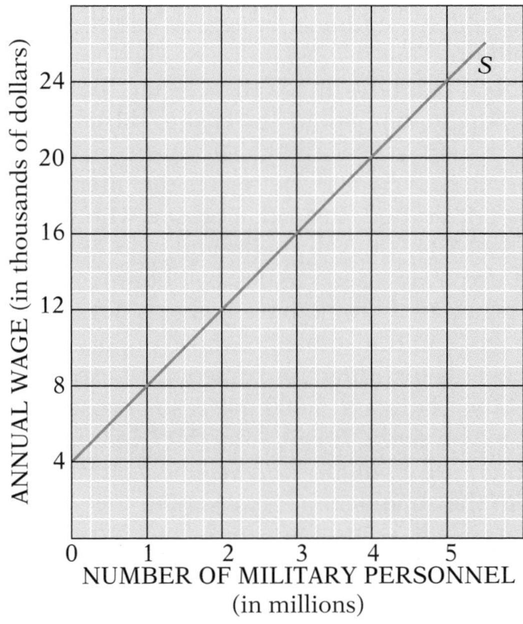

Figure 4–3 **Supply curve of military volunteers**

volunteers but also police, steeplejacks, and even skiers. Whatever its precise position and slope, the supply curve will certainly incline upward to the right. Some people (those who assign low value to their available alternatives) will volunteer at a very low wage. But 3 million volunteers can be secured, on our assumptions, only if the wage offer is at least $16,000 per year. That would mean a wage bill of $48 billion annually. But because taxpayers don't like to have their taxes raised, Congress is reluctant to approve such a huge appropriation. And the people in the Department of Defense care very much about the likes and dislikes of the people in Congress. They can cut that upsetting bill in half by offering only $8,000 and *compelling* enlistments. The published cost will now be only $24 billion. Hurrah for cost savings!

But what about the costs to those who make up the armed forces? The cost of the volunteer army *to the volunteers* under our assumptions would be $30 billion. That is the value of the area under the supply curve up to 3 million men and women, or the sum of the values of the opportunities forgone by those who enlisted. The other $18 billion paid out by the government is a transfer of wealth from taxpayers to members of the military who would have enlisted at a lower wage but who nonetheless receive the higher wage that is required to induce the enlistment of the 3-millionth volunteer.

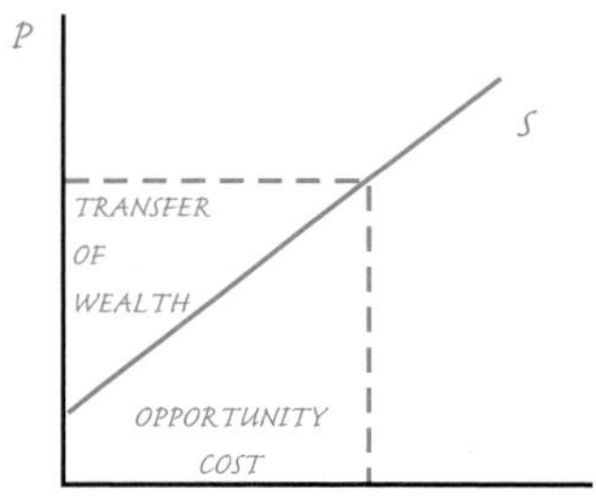

What will be the cost of a *conscripted* army to those who are drafted? We can't say, except that it will certainly be larger. Only if the draft happened to hit exactly those and only those who would have enlisted under a volunteer system would the cost be as low as $30 billion. That is most unlikely. The more draftees who are grabbed from the upper, rather than the lower, end of the supply curve, the higher will be the cost to the conscripts. For example, a man who would have volunteered at a wage of $9,000 is offered only $8,000. He rejects the offer, and he is subsequently not drafted. Instead, a person who would have volunteered only at $24,000 is drafted—and paid $8,000. The net result is that taxpayers save $16,000 by obtaining for only $8,000 services for which they would have had to pay $24,000 under an all-volunteer system. But someone whose opportunity cost is $24,000 has been substituted for someone whose opportunity cost was only $9,000. That's a $15,000 increase in cost from the standpoint of those who serve. *The military draft does not reduce "the cost" of maintaining a military establishment*. It rather transfers that cost from the shoulders of taxpayers to the shoulders of the draftees. That may in your judgment be one of the least of its faults, or it may be outweighed in your mind by presumed advantages. But at least it's a consequence that economists can point out.

Again, that bothersome voice from the back of the room asks, "But what about patriotism? Shouldn't we all do our part?"

Perhaps we all *should* do our part. But in fact we don't. Even in wartime more than half of the age-eligible group never serves in the military due to physical characteristics, occupational exemptions, and various deferments. We could better "all do our part" if we would pay the military personnel their opportunity costs, just as industry does. And the fact is most of us *do* have feelings of patriotism. If there were enough patriotism, we could attract volunteers who would see service as a patriotic duty and serve at zero or nominal cost. There undoubtedly are many such persons but far fewer than "needed" to staff our military. But all is not lost in this respect. Recall that a few paragraphs back we said that opportunity cost is a function of alternatives "and all sorts of other values," one of which is patriotism. The greater the degree of patriotic feeling, the lesser the monetary wage it would take to induce voluntary enlistments.

Price Elasticity of Supply

Price elasticity of supply = $\frac{\text{\% change in quantity}}{\text{\% change in price}}$

The concept of elasticity is every bit as important in the case of supply as it is in the case of demand. The formal definitions are the same. *Price elasticity of supply is the percentage change in the quantity supplied divided by the percentage change in the price*. In the case of supply, price and quantity will vary in the same direction, reflecting the fact that it takes a higher price to induce suppliers to offer for sale a larger quantity. The supply is relatively elastic if the percentage change in the quantity supplied is greater than the percentage change in the price, and it is relatively inelastic if the percentage change in the quantity supplied is less than the percentage change in the price.

This book puts completely inelastic *demand* curves in the same family as unicorns: the family of nonexistent phenomena. Completely inelastic *supply* curves are another matter. Although it takes no time to start demanding less when the price of a good rises, it does take time and often quite a bit of time to start *supplying* more when the price of a good rises. Even a significant increase in the price of a good may consequently produce no increase at first in the quantity of the good supplied. With time, however, potential suppliers will reorganize the resources available to them and will eventually be able to supply a larger quantity in response to a higher price.

If additional quantities of the resources required to produce a particular good can be readily obtained at no higher cost, the supply curve for the good will be close to completely elastic. In such a case a very modest rise in the price will induce suppliers to increase by a very large amount the quantity offered for sale.

The supply curve of military volunteers portrayed in Figure 4–3 is an in-between case. The price elasticity varies along the curve, decreasing steadily from 2.0 between $7 and $9 to 1.2 between $23 and $25. (If you want to check these numbers for yourself, use as the base in calculating percentage changes the average of the two prices and quantities between which the change is occurring.)

Pause for a moment to be sure you have understood the concept of price elasticity of supply. As we shall see in the next chapter, it is the relative elasticities of supply curves and demand curves that determine what effects changing circumstances will have on the quantities of goods exchanged and the prices at which they exchange.

Cost as Justification

The economic analysis of costs is an especially treacherous enterprise for the unwary, because costs often have an ethical and political as well as an economic dimension. Many people seem to believe that sellers have a right to cover their costs, have no right to any price that is significantly above their costs, and are almost surely pursuing some unfair advantage if they price above or below cost. This way of thinking, in which cost functions as *justification*, has even infiltrated our laws. Legislated price controls, for example, usually allow for price increases when costs go up but refuse to permit any price hikes that are not justified by higher costs. And foreign firms selling in the United States can be penalized for "dumping" if a government agency determines that they sold in this country at prices "below cost." In circumstances such as these, when costs become a rationalization rather than a genuine reason for decisions, all statements about costs must be inspected for evidence of special pleading.

Prices *ought* to be closely related to costs, in popular thought, because costs supposedly represent something real and unavoidable. The most enthusiastic advocates of rent control will agree, at least in principle, that landlords should be allowed to increase their rents when the cost of heating fuel goes up. They will never agree—if they did, they wouldn't advocate rent controls—that landlords should be allowed to raise rents merely because the demand for apartments has increased faster than the supply. That would be "gouging," "profiteering," or "a rip-off," because it is unrelated to cost. But such a rental increase is just as surely related to cost as is an increase in response to higher heating bills. When the demand for rental apartments increases, tenants bid against one another for available space, thereby raising the cost to the landlord of renting to any particular tenant. What another tenant would be willing to pay for the third-floor apartment in the Hillcrest Arms is the landlord's marginal opportunity cost of continuing to rent to the present occupant. The case seems to be different with higher heating-fuel prices but really is not. The cost of fuel oil is also determined ultimately by the bids of competing users in relationship to the offers of suppliers. Cost is always the product of demand and supply. That will be the continuing theme of the next two chapters.

Costs are never independent of demand.

Once Over Lightly

Supply curves as well as demand curves reflect people's estimates of the value of alternative opportunities. Both the quantities of any good that are supplied and the quantities that are demanded depend on the economizing choices people make after assessing the opportunities available to them.

Costs are always the value of the opportunities that particular people sacrifice. Conflicting assertions about the costs of alternative decisions can often be reconciled by agreement on whose costs are under consideration.

Past expenditures cannot be affected by present decisions: They are sunk costs and hence irrelevant to decision making. All costs relevant to decision making therefore lie in the future.

Opportunity costs are necessarily marginal costs: They are the additional costs that an action or a decision entails.

Supply depends on cost. (What doesn't?) But the cost of supplying is the value of the opportunities forgone by the act of supplying. This concept of cost is expressed in economic theory by the assertion that all costs relevant to decisions are opportunity costs—the value of the opportunities forsaken in choosing one course of action rather than another.

Supply curves slope upward to the right because higher prices must be offered to resource owners to persuade them to transform a current activity into an opportunity they are willing to sacrifice.

Anything that alters the marginal cost of production would tend to shift the supply curve. The market supply curve is also subject to shift if the producers' price expectations change, or if the overall number of producers within an industry changes.

Price elasticity of supply is the percentage change in the quantity supplied divided by the percentage change in the price.

Many disagreements about what something "really" costs could be resolved by the recognition that "things" cannot have costs. Only actions entail sacrificed opportunities, and therefore only actions can have costs.

Never forget to ask yourself "cost to whom?" "cost of doing what?" By so doing, you'll be well on your way to thinking like an economist.

QUESTIONS FOR DISCUSSION

1. What is the true cost of an Old Navy T-shirt, a Linkin Park concert ticket, or your *Economic Way of Thinking* textbook?
2. While fishing your favorite stream, you find an 8-ounce nugget of gold. What price would you ask for it? Why? What did it *cost* you?
3. The acres of grass surrounding the Taj Mahal in Agra, India, are often cut by young women who slice off handfuls with short kitchen blades. Is this a low- or high-cost way to keep a lawn mowed?
4. By taking an airplane one can go from D to H in one hour. The same trip takes five hours by bus. If the airfare is $120 and the bus fare is $30, which would be the cheaper mode of transportation for someone who could earn $6 an hour during this time? For someone who could earn $30 an hour?
5. The photocopy machine in the library costs $295 per month to rent. The rental fee covers repair service, toner, developer, and 20,000 copies per month. The library also pays 1 cent for every copy beyond 20,000, plus 1/2 cent for every sheet of paper used.

   Harriet Martineau has to read a 20-page journal article for tomorrow's class. She is willing to pay 50 cents for a photocopy of the article, but she will read it in the library if she has to pay more than that.

   (a) What is the highest price per page Harriet will be willing to pay to use the copier?
   (b) What is the lowest price per page the library should be willing to accept? What additional information must you have in order to answer?
   (c) Harriet just found out she is supposed to read a second article for tomorrow's class, an article full of complex graphs. Harriet badly wants her own copy of this article and will pay whatever she has to pay to get one. What is now the highest price Harriet will be willing to pay to use the library copier? (You must supply some information from your own experience to answer.)
   (d) How does the $295 monthly rental fee affect the price the library will want to charge users of its copier?

6. If the firm for which you work pays you 20 cents for every mile you drive your own car on company business, should you use your own car or a company car? Which of the following costs are relevant to your decision?
   (a) Purchase price of your car
   (b) Vehicle license fee
   (c) Insurance premiums
   (d) Depreciation
   (e) Gasoline
7. Should the casualties already incurred in a war be taken into account by a government in deciding whether it is in the national interest to continue the war? This is obviously not a trivial question. And it is a much more difficult question than you might at first suppose, especially for a government depending on popular support.
8. The economist's rule, "sunk costs are irrelevant," is like a string around your finger. It reminds you to consider only marginal costs, but it cannot identify the marginal costs. That requires informed judgment. You could sharpen your judgment by trying to enumerate and assess the marginal costs of retaining or not retaining your college apartment over the summer vacation. Try to calculate the minimum rental from subleasing that would persuade you to retain it for fall reoccupancy.
9. Here is a statement from the textbook by Francis Wayland that was the most widely used economics text in American colleges before 1860:

   > The qualities and relations of natural agents are the gift of God, and, being His gift, they cost us nothing. Thus, in order to avail ourselves of the momentum produced by a waterfall, we have only to construct the water-wheel and its necessary appendages, and place them in a proper position. We then have the use of the falling water, without further expense. As, therefore, our only outlay is the cost of the instrument by which the natural agent is rendered available, this is the only expenditure which demands the attention of the political economist.

   (a) What was the cost to a nineteenth-century mill owner of using a waterfall to power his mill if he owned the site of the waterfall?
   (b) What was the cost to the mill owner if someone else owned the site?
   (c) Under what circumstances would use of a waterfall to power a mill actually have cost nothing?
   (d) Why do modern "political economists" disagree with Francis Wayland and pay attention to the cost of using "natural agents"?
10. Explain the following statement by a military recruiter: "There's nothing like a good recession to cure our recruiting problems."
11. It has been argued that a volunteer army would discriminate against poor people, because they tend to have the lowest-value alternatives to military service and hence would dominate the ranks of volunteers.
    (a) Do you agree with the analysis and the objection?
    (b) Some critics have argued that if the military relied exclusively on volunteers, the armed forces would be filled with people of such low intelligence and skills that they could not operate sophisticated weapons. International Business Machines relies exclusively on

"volunteers," and *its* employees are not predominantly people of low intelligence and skills. What's the difference between the armed forces and IBM? How would you reply to the argument of these critics?

(c) Another frequent criticism of a volunteer military is that we don't want "an army of mercenaries." How high does the military wage have to be before the recipient becomes a mercenary? Are officers compelled to remain in the armed services? Why do they stay in? Are they mercenaries? Is your teacher a mercenary? Your physician? Your minister?

12. In recent years more and more Americans have begun to evade jury duty, creating a serious problem in some courts, which have been forced to postpone trials because an adequate number of jurors was not available.
   (a) What is the cost to a citizen of serving as a juror?
   (b) For whom will the net cost be very low or even negative? For whom will the net cost be very high, perhaps even prohibitively high?
   (c) Can you think of any simple system for reducing the average cost to citizens of jury service?
   (d) What consequences would you predict if we moved to a completely volunteer jury system, under which the courts paid jurors a daily wage sufficient to obtain the services of as many qualified jurors as the court required?
   (e) Many citizens who faithfully answer every summons to jury duty have complained of their treatment at the hands of court officials who behave as if the time of jurors had no value whatsoever. For example, prospective jurors may be required to sit for days in a waiting room without ever seeing the inside of a courtroom. What is the cost to court officials of behaving inconsiderately toward jury candidates?
13. Why might a multinational corporation with identical plants in different countries pay different wage rates to workers in the two countries even though their skill levels are the same? Does this strike you as unjust? Why might the *higher-paid workers* object?
14. Rising commercial rents in San Francisco in recent years have induced many corporations to move their offices out of the city. Can a San Francisco firm that owns its own office building simply ignore rising rents?
15. Why do parking lot fees vary so widely from city to city in the United States? The all-day rate in Manhattan, for example, is often $20. In Atlanta, it is likely to be less than $5. Does this difference reflect the greater greed of New York City parking-garage owners?
16. If people are offering to pay $100 for $10 (face-value) tickets to the Big Game and someone gives you a ticket, what does it cost you to attend the game? Would you be more likely to attend if someone gave you a ticket than if you had to purchase one for $100? Would you be more likely to attend if someone gave you a ticket than if you had to purchase one that you could buy (through an inside source) for $10?
17. From the opportunity-cost perspective, there is no difference between paying money and forgoing an opportunity to receive money. That does not fully accord, however, with a lot of our intuitions. Consider the following cases:

(a) Dave and Pete are friends. Dave asks Pete to lend him $1,000 for a year and Pete does so. Would it be proper for Pete to charge Dave interest on the loan if Pete himself had to borrow the money and pay interest? Would it be any less proper for Pete to charge Dave interest if he obtained the funds by cashing a certificate of deposit on which he had been earning interest?

(b) Friedrich bought a large painting by Turner that was on display at a major exhibition, but he had to agree not to take possession until the show ended six months later. When the show finally ended and Friedrich brought the painting home, he made two discoveries: The show had so increased Turner's prestige that the painting was now worth twice what he had paid for it, and the painting was too large to fit on any of his walls. Karl has larger walls in his home and would like to purchase the painting from his friend Friedrich. What is the proper price for Friedrich to charge Karl? What he himself paid for the painting or what he could now get for it if he put it on the market?

18. What does it cost you to sleep through one of 30 lectures in a course for which you paid $300 in tuition? What does it cost you to attend?

19. Do students put more effort into courses when they have to pay higher tuition to take the courses?

20. In order to decide whether or not to drop intercollegiate football, your school undertakes a study of the program's cost. To what extent do you think the following budget items represent genuine costs?

(a) Tuition scholarships to players
(b) Payments on the stadium mortgage
(c) Free tickets to all full-time students
(d) Salaries of the athletic director, ticket manager, and trainer

21. The supply curve on the graph in Figure 4–4 shows the wage rates that would have to be offered by business firms to obtain various quantities of hours of envelope stuffing on any given day.

(a) What wage rate will firms have to offer if they want to hire 400 hours of envelope stuffing?
(b) What will be the firms' total expenditure on the wages of envelope stuffers?

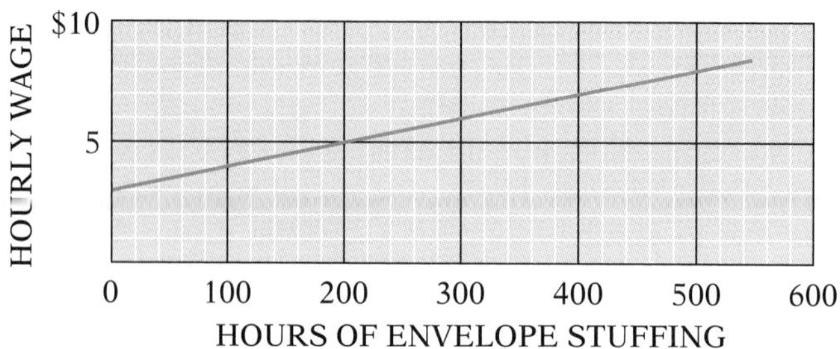

Figure 4–4 **Supply curve for envelope stuffing**

(c) What will be the total opportunity cost to the envelope stuffers of stuffing envelopes? (*Hint*: Each square represents $20: 20 hours times $1.)

(d) What is the price elasticity of supply between $4 and $6? Between $6 and $8?

22. When does it make sense to give up?

(a) How long will you search for a $20 bill that you lost if you value your time at $5 an hour? Suppose you know that you lost it somewhere in your bedroom. Would it ever be rational for you to search more than four hours? Use the concepts of expected marginal benefit and expected marginal cost to explain how a rational person who values time at $5 an hour could *search indefinitely* for a lost $20 bill.

(b) A dispute between a tenant in a Manhattan apartment cooperative and the cooperative's board over who should pay the $909 cost of installing childproof window guards was taken to court in 1987. Seven years later, the dispute had not yet been resolved but the lawyers' fees exceeded $100,000. Do you think this reflects stubborn stupidity? Under what circumstances could people rationally run up legal fees of more than $100,000 in trying to settle a $909 dispute?

5

Supply and Demand: A Process of Cooperation

Specialization is what distinguishes every wealthy society the world has ever known. As Adam Smith observed when reflecting on the economic growth that had occurred in Britain during the eighteenth century:

> It is the great multiplication of the productions of all the different arts, *in consequence of the division of labour* [emphasis added], which occasions, in a well-governed society, that universal opulence which extends itself to the lowest ranks of the people.

A society becomes wealthy when its members acquire the ability to specialize effectively, to "divide" their labor, as Smith put it.

How does the division of labor—specialization—arise? Chapter 1 posed that as a central question of economics. In Chapter 2 we began answering that question when we explored the incentives to specialize and exchange and the increase in opportunities or wealth that specialization generates. We called that the "law of comparative advantage." But how exactly do the people in a wealthy, highly specialized commercial society encourage one another to take those interconnected actions that wind up producing the incredible array of goods and services that they enjoy?

Knowledge and information is a scarce good—for everybody.

The basic problem is massive ignorance. Specialists, by their very nature, don't know how to do everything. (Can you name one person, specialist or otherwise, who *does* know how to do everything, or at least can productively *order* everybody to produce goods and services efficiently?) The fact is, people *do* have some skills and abilities *and* they remain genuinely ignorant of countless other skills and abilities. Consider this incredible example, one thoroughly rooted in the real world: Probably no single person anywhere in the world knows how to produce something as simple as an ordinary no. 2 pencil.

That sounds crazy at first, but go outside the box and think about it. Lots of specialists know how to assemble a pencil *once* the wood, graphite, rubber, paint, glue, tin ferrule, appropriate tools, and machinery are all in the pencil factory. But specialists in pencil assembly don't know how to produce *those* essential inputs. Consider the wood itself. It took loggers to fell the trees. And the loggers depend upon specialized, high-tech equipment, as well as coffee, meals, clothing, health care, and countless other goods and services to do their job adequately. The logging equipment is made, in part, from steel. So steelworkers had a hand in the making of pencils, too, whether they know it or not. The steel is made from iron ore—which was probably mined in Michigan's Upper Peninsula (if not imported by other specialists abroad) and sent first by rail on the Lake Superior & Ishpeming Railroad and then by hundreds of ships down Lakes Superior and Michigan to ports in Gary, Indiana, and elsewhere. Who made the trains, the tracks, the ships, the varieties of food that fed the crews (let alone the soap, toilet paper, and so on)? Who contributed to producing the fuel, the ports, or the sophisticated communications systems that guided the ships? The answer is countless *other* specialists, individuals pursuing their comparative advantage, acting on *their* limited knowledge and skills, and cooperating with still other specialized input providers.

Imagine the number of different people, from different races, colors, and creeds, with different opinions, skills, and goals, within the country and abroad, whose goods and services contributed to the production of a simple no. 2 pencil. All those people cannot possibly know one another, they may not even speak the same language, yet no. 2 pencils get produced. And we consumers generally know where to find them, cheap.

The miracle of the market, as some have quite properly described it, is that millions of people who don't even know of one another's existence manage to cooperate and produce not only no. 2 pencils but also innumerable other goods of *much* greater complexity, and to do so in ways that make them readily and abundantly available. And people are encouraged to cooperate not by obeying the orders of some comprehensive, national economic plan issued in part, say, from a government Writing Implement Bureau. The government's role is much more limited. Recall that Adam Smith said, "in a well-governed society." The government plays an important role in all of this, especially in monitoring and enforcing private property rights and contracts—the overall rules of the game—that allow for these countless exchanges to take place.

People often tend to take this orderly, nonchaotic network of exchanges for granted ("What do you mean you're *out* of pencils?"). Surely a market system is much more complex than the smooth flow of traffic (also taken for granted) that we discussed in Chapter 1. While the orderly nature of markets might appear miraculous, it is not, however, mysterious. What are the key signals, the traffic lights, if you will, that help people in a commercial society coordinate their varied production and consumption plans? The answer is prices. Millions of people receive important information and signals, as well as incentives to act on those signals, from prices formed in the market. Market prices emerge through the interplay of supply and demand, which we introduced separately in Chapters 3 and 4. In this chapter we put supply and demand together and describe the principles of the market process itself.

Market prices convey useful information.

The Market Is a Process of Competing Bids and Offers

Many people often think of "the market" as a *place* or forum, such as a baseball card and collectible show at Gateway Center in St. Louis or a cattle auction at the fairgrounds in Kansas City or the New York Stock Exchange in the Wall Street district. But all of these are really elements of markets that stretch across regions, around the globe, and even into cyberspace. Formal markets might have emerged with town fairs during the Middle Ages, but it makes little economic sense to view markets as mere places or forums today.

Journalists and those in the financial community use many mixed metaphors to describe markets, often making it sound as if a market is a *person*. How many times have we heard some expert on the evening news or the financial channels say that Wall Street was "excited" or "nervous" about the latest economic data, or that the stock market "hopes" or "expects" that Alan Greenspan at the Federal Reserve will cut interest rates? Perhaps someday when the conditions are right, one of those experts will report that "the stock market has awakened bloated, with terrible cramps and a bad headache, and has called in sick today." Although that kind of statement might make the news more interesting, the economic way of thinking recognizes that *individuals* have hopes, expectations, cramps, and headaches; *markets* don't.

"Wall Street woke up with a hangover today."

Even economists themselves use misleading metaphors. They often refer to market systems as "automatic" or "self-adjusting," giving the impression that markets function without the intervention of human beings! Many economists make it sound as if the market is some kind of mechanical *thing*, like a thermostat. That's wrong. Market systems are *entirely composed* of demanders and suppliers, who are real human beings pursuing the projects that interest them, economizing on the basis of the relative scarcities that they confront, and negotiating arrangements to secure what they want from others by offering others what they in turn want to obtain.

It is best to avoid these common but misleading interpretations of markets. The market is not a person, place, or thing. *The market is a process of competing bids and offers*. When economists use the terms *supply* and *demand*, they are really talking about these kinds of continual, ongoing negotiations among individuals. Think of the various exchanges on the Web.

• Bids and offers

The negotiations rarely take place in committee meetings. They are rather the daily bids and offers that we extend in the many societies in which we participate. These bids and offers usually presuppose well-defined rules of the game, including well-defined property rights. We take for granted most of the relevant rights and obligations when we enter into a negotiation. "Will you do this for me if I do that for you?" Usually we don't even have to ask. We just walk uninvited into the pizzeria, seat ourselves at an unoccupied table, and instruct an attendant to prepare a medium pizza with green peppers, black olives, and extra cheese. The attendant doesn't ask what we're willing to do in return, but simply assumes we will pay the posted money price.

Transaction Costs, Again

Let's remind ourselves of Chapter 2's notion of *transaction costs*. The fact that people want something done and are more than willing to pay what others want for doing it does not necessarily mean that it will get done. Nothing may occur despite the fact that the value to the demanders is great enough to cover the opportunity costs of the suppliers. Here is a simple example of a type that all of us have probably encountered. Each day several hundred cyclists use the bicycle lane to cross the bridge. Every now and then an accident will scatter broken glass all over the bicycle lane. Each one of those several hundred cyclists, encountering the broken glass for the first time, would willingly pay 1 dollar to have it swept up. That means the cyclists would be collectively willing to pay several hundred dollars to obtain an action that any number of people would be happy to perform for less than $10. Nonetheless, hundreds of bicycles will probably ride through that broken glass day after day until weather and traffic finally disperse it. This is obviously a failure of cooperation. Why does it occur?

It occurs because *the costs of arranging the transaction are too high*. It isn't enough that demanders are *willing* to pay what suppliers would require. Someone must arrange the actual transaction: collect money from the cyclists and see to it that the glass gets swept up. And that's not easy to do, as it turns out. If it were easy, we wouldn't see so much glass in bicycle lanes. An enterprising person who resolved to profit from repairing this failure of cooperation would have to flag down cyclists, explain the situation, persuade them of his own honesty, induce them to admit how much they want to see the glass removed, and finally talk them into handing over a sum of money that reflects the strength of their desire, while all the time most of the cyclists are wondering to themselves why *they* should pay when the benefits are going to go to so many others.

Failures of this sort are the consequences of *transaction costs: the costs of arranging contracts or transaction agreements between demanders and suppliers.*

Transaction costs cause failures of cooperation.

Transaction costs explain why commuters with comfortable, air-conditioned cars that sport superb stereo systems and who don't mind at all sitting in traffic jams on the way home in the evening do not get off the road and clear the way for those in a much bigger hurry. They explain why people who care sincerely and deeply about the environment nonetheless contribute to its degradation. The concept of transaction costs enables us to explain why the majority of the voters in a democracy often fail to get their way. The concept is especially important for those societies that are now attempting to make a transition from central economic planning and bureaucratic control of economic decisions to market-coordinated systems.

In the early 1990s, as the system of central economic planning in the USSR disintegrated, news reports regularly told about unharvested food rotting in rural areas while grocery store shelves stood empty in the cities. How could a thing like this occur? Why didn't someone transport that food to the cities where it was so much in demand? Collapse of the system of bureaucratic control does not provide an adequate explanation. People should be able to move food out of the fields and into the hands of hungry people without explicit orders from above.

Or so one would suppose. But think more carefully and concretely. Who owned the food that was going to waste? Who had authority to harvest it? Who owned harvesting equipment? Who could authorize the use of the equipment? Who owned trucks to transport the food to the cities? Who had fuel for the trucks? How was the food to be distributed once it arrived in the cities? The mere fact that food is going to waste in the fields while people are hungry in the cities is not enough to get food actually moving from farms to urban pantries. The right people must first acquire the appropriate information and incentives.

Transaction costs explain that "wasteful" situation. The word *wasteful* is set within quotation marks because it's not at all clear that what happened really was wasteful. It's not wasteful to let food rot rather than consume it if the costs of getting the food to consumers exceed the value of the food. And that was apparently the case. Transaction costs are just as real and no less important than the costs of harvesting and transporting.

Property Rights and Institutions

Such a situation would be much less likely to develop in the United States, where fields, food, farm machinery, trucks, warehouses, and retail stores are privately owned. The rules of the game are different. Under a system of clearly defined property rights, people with information about the situation would have strong incentives to acquire control of whatever resources were needed to move the food from where it had no use to where it did. And within a system that allows for free exchange among property owners, the necessary resources will quickly and at low cost come together under the control of those who can put them to valuable uses.

- Clearly defined property rights
- The ability to exchange rights

Contrast the frustrating situation in the former USSR with the way that people, tractors, construction equipment, and everything else needed for emergency relief and reconstruction moved into Miami when Hurricane Andrew struck in 1992; into Fargo, North Dakota, and Davenport, Iowa, when the Mississippi River flooded in 1998 and 2001; or into lower Manhattan after the attack on the World Trade Center in 2001. The crucial difference is the well-established system of clearly defined property rights in the United States along with the extensive freedom that people have to trade those rights as they choose. This has produced over the years a vast network of institutions—profit and not-for-profit—in the United States that keeps transaction costs low for almost all the exchanges in which people engage with any frequency or regularity. (The thoughtful reader will shrewdly note that people frequently and regularly engage in particular transactions only *because* the transaction costs are low.)

Think again about how easy it usually is to obtain the precise pizza on which your hungry heart is set. The many transactions that make your pizza possible—that constructed the pizzeria, grew the peppers, shipped the olives, milked the cows, and arranged the requisite lines of credit for all these activities—all had to be negotiated. These negotiations succeeded because the transaction costs were sufficiently low. And the transaction costs were low because the transactions occurred within an extensive set of institutions that evolved over time as market participants worked to lower the costs of the transactions in which they wanted to engage. Think of specialized manufacturers, specialized Internet retailers, specialized providers of every kind of service; the principles of financial accounting, the rules of the road, the customs of the trade in varied lines of business; banks, credit reporting agencies, highly organized stock exchanges; the classified sections of daily newspapers, the telephone companies' Yellow Pages, lists of brokers and suppliers that can be obtained on a moment's notice; the rules of the common law, police to enforce these rules and courts to resolve disputed issues, plus private systems of arbitration to supplement the system of public law.

In those nations where central planning has failed, market systems seem to be evolving. Achievement of those market systems faces the enormous obstacle of high transaction costs at almost every turn precisely because many of the institutions that are crucial are still lacking. Can individual transactors (ordinary people) in these nations now create by design what evolved without design in long-established market economies? Can they create quickly the complex institutions that have elsewhere come into existence through a slow, evolutionary process? Can they overcome the problem of high transaction costs rapidly enough to satisfy the aspirations of their citizens, who are impatient to enjoy the promised rewards of a market system? The success of the reform programs in many of the nations of the former Soviet bloc depends largely on the answers to these questions.

The Coordinating Role of Money Prices

Why do almost all the exchanges in a market system take place for money? Why don't more people engage in barter, trading what they produce directly for what they want? Why do business owners sell goods and services for money, and workers accept payment in money, even though money is of little use *in itself*. (As recent protesters of the World Trade Organization put it, "You can't eat money." Perhaps, but where it's legal, you *can* foolishly roll it up and smoke it.)

The answer is that money lowers transaction costs. *Money is a general medium of exchange*. It pervades all markets, licit and illicit. The advantages of using money rather than relying solely on a barter system are enormous. The cost of arranging exchanges would be far greater, and our wealth as a consequence far less, if there were no money in our society to facilitate the process. (Don't forget, wealth is not defined as money or material things; wealth is *whatever* people value.) In an economic system limited to barter, people would have to spend a tremendous amount of time searching for others with whom they could make a trade. A guitar maker would have to find a farmer, toilet paper manufacturer, logging mill owner, toolmaker, glue supplier, building contractor, among many others, each willing to accept guitars in return for the goods that he or she produces. All that time spent on searching would be time not available for guitar making, and the production of guitars would decline steeply. So, too, would the production of all those *other* goods whose owners must also search for the right people to barter with.

Aware of the high transaction costs attached to almost every exchange, people would increasingly try to produce for themselves most of whatever they wanted. Specialization would decline dramatically in a society confined to barter, an exchange system without the facility of money, and everyone would be much poorer. The evolution of some kind of money system in almost every known society, even when conditions were extremely unfavorable to it, is eloquent testimony to the advantages of using money.

Money has another important advantage. The amount of money offered in exchange can be adjusted up or down by very small or very large amounts. Imagine the guitar maker wanting one concert ticket in a pure barter economy. Can he offer only 1/10 of a guitar for the ticket and trade the remaining portions of his guitar for a six-pack, Big Mac and fries, gasoline, and the many other things he values? Or must he trade a whole guitar for, say, 10 concert tickets, and *then* find ways to exchange the extra tickets for the six-pack, burger, and so on? Think of the ridiculously large transaction costs! No wonder Buddha gave it all up. But if the guitar maker sells guitars for money, he can buy a little bit more or a little bit less of what he wants with no trouble at all. And he can raise the exchange value—the money price—of his guitars by a small amount if he senses that his customers are willing to pay more for them than before, or lower their exchange value by just a little if he thinks this would secure some sales that he wouldn't otherwise get.

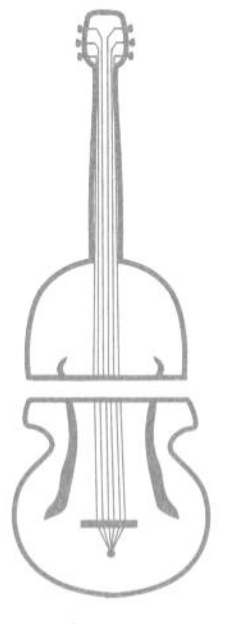

Two halves do not equal a whole.

The ability to make small adjustments is essential to the coordination of a commercial society. Consider a gallon of gasoline. If we are to be able to fill our tanks at the self-service island on Tuesday evening at 5:30, just the right number of people with just the right abilities and command over just the right physical resources must cooperate at just the right times and in just the right ways to explore, drill, pump, pipe, refine, truck, and store. That intricate system is coordinated basically by means of the responses people make to adjustments in money prices. The people who regularly accomplish this spectacular feat of coordination don't do it because they love us and know how much we want gasoline, but to further the innumerable and diverse projects in which they themselves happen to be interested. Their efforts mesh because those efforts are coordinated by the continually changing signals that money prices emit.

The role of monetary calculation.

We must insist once again that the crucial importance of money prices to the working of our society implies *nothing* about the character or morality of our citizens. People pay attention to money prices insofar as they want to economize, that is, to get as much as possible of what they value from the resources they command. Money prices help consumers establish budgets and clarify their options. Money prices help producers calculate expected costs and expected revenues. People don't pay attention *exclusively* to money prices, of course; that wouldn't make sense. They do, however, change their behavior when prices change in order to "take advantage" of the new situation signaled by the new prices. This is what causes coordination to occur and self-interested (again, not necessarily selfish) behavior to become cooperative action.

The Basic Process

We're now ready to consider, with the help of a graph, the supply and demand process. Let's consider the market for relatively inexpensive acoustic guitars, the kinds bought by beginning and

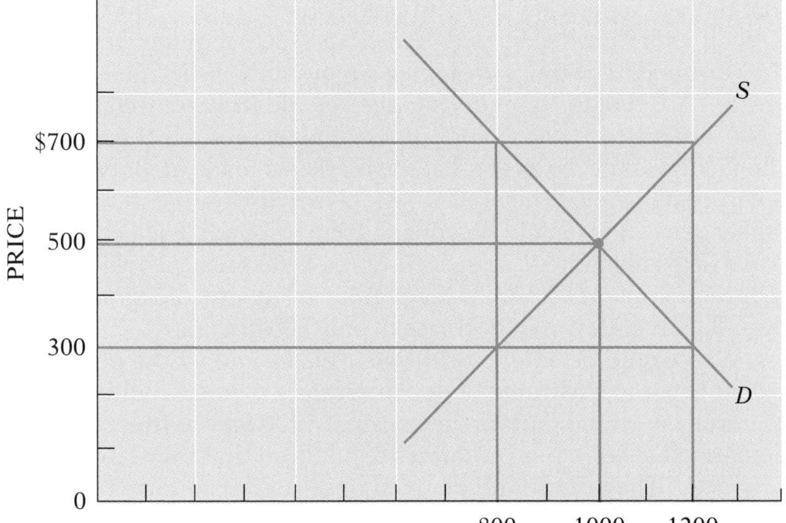

Figure 5–1 **Supply and demand in the acoustic guitar market**

The market clears at $500. A surplus of 400 guitars exists at the $700 price, and a shortage of 400 guitars occurs at the $300 price.

intermediate pickers throughout the country. Figure 5–1 depicts the market. Notice the downward-sloping market demand curve. That reflects an essential point from Chapter 3—the law of demand. People would plan to purchase more guitars as the relative price falls and plan to purchase fewer guitars as the relative price increases. The *quantity demanded* increases or decreases, not the overall demand curve, when only the price of guitars changes. Next, notice the upward-sloping supply curve. Recall from Chapter 4 that supply curves generally slope upward, which reflects the increasing marginal opportunity costs of producing more guitars. Making more acoustic guitars requires many specialized resources, from specific grades of spruce and mahogany to the highly skilled labor of the workers. For guitar producers to obtain spruce and mahogany, they must *bid* those resources away from *other* productive uses, such as Christmas trees, fine cabinets, incense holders, and the many other goods that people desire that can also be made from those materials. Higher prices for the guitars will induce producers to make more guitars.

Notice where the supply and demand curves intersect. There, the market price is $500 per guitar and the market output is 1,000 guitars. At the $500 price, note that the quantity demanded is 1,000 guitars, which is exactly equal to the quantity supplied. In this event, the plans of guitar buyers are *fully coordinated* with the plans of guitar producers.

Full market coordination: X marks the spot.

In a free market, of course, producers can charge any price they wish, and consumers can offer any price they wish. So let's suppose that the market price were substantially higher than $500. Say it's $700. If guitar producers plan to receive $700 per guitar, how would they respond? The upward-sloping supply curve helps illustrate the answer. At $700, the quantity supplied would increase well beyond 1,000 guitars, to 1,200. (Supply doesn't increase—only the quantity supplied!) But never forget that the market is made up of two sides, sellers and buyers. While sellers would increase output at the higher price, how would potential buyers respond? The demand curve helps illustrate *that* answer: At the $700 price, people would reduce their planned purchases of guitars. Quantity demanded (not overall demand!) would decrease to only 800 guitars.

Who would be able to fulfill their plans, and whose plans would become frustrated? Consumers, as a whole, would be able to purchase all the guitars they wish at $700 apiece (the quantity demanded is 800), but producers would find that they have overproduced. They made and planned to sell 1,200 guitars (the quantity supplied). That's a difference of 400 guitars, guitars that are undesirably piling up in the manufacturers' inventories. Here, the market is not fully coordinated. A *surplus* of guitars has emerged. *A surplus occurs when the quantity supplied is greater than the quantity demanded*. In our example, there is a surplus of 400 guitars. Sellers often become aware of a surplus by the unplanned piling up of their inventories. They simply aren't selling as much as they had counted on.

Surplus: $Q_d < Q_s$ (frustrated sellers).

How can producers unload their unplanned inventories of guitars? Perhaps they can point guns to the heads of terrified people and force them to purchase the remaining guitars for $700 apiece. But that goes against the *rules* of the free market. Perhaps one manufacturer can sell more guitars by burning down another competitor's guitar-making facilities. But that, too, breaks the rules of the game. Perhaps they can seek legislation requiring children to learn how to play guitars, which might improve demand and sales. That is an effort of manipulating and changing the rules of the game in their favor, but that takes quite a lot of time and political maneuvering and is a costly activity. What they can do, and what generally happens in free markets, is that producers will *cut their own prices*.

Sellers compete with sellers.

Indeed, we would predict that the market price of guitars would fall from $700 to $500. As the price falls, potential buyers would be more receptive: The quantity demanded (not the overall demand!) would increase from 800 to 1,000 guitars. At the same time, quantity supplied (not the overall supply!) would decrease from 1,200 to 1,000. Then the surplus would disappear: The plans of both buyers and sellers would fully mesh; the market would become fully coordinated at the $500 price. Sellers would have no further incentive to compete against other sellers by lowering their prices.

Finally, consider the opposite case. Suppose the current market price were well *below* $500. At a price of $300 per guitar, people would eagerly plan to purchase a total of 1,200 guitars (the quantity demanded), but producers would produce and plan to sell only 800 guitars (the quantity supplied). While the plans of the producers would be achieved, many customers would be frustrated as they try to purchase a guitar but find them sold out. Here we have a *shortage*, which is the opposite of a surplus. *A shortage occurs when the quantity demanded is greater than the quantity supplied*. Customers might sense a shortage by facing unusually long lines or finding items out of stock. Sellers might have to unexpectedly dip into their planned inventories, discovering that they are selling more than they originally expected.

Shortage: $Q_d > Q_s$ (frustrated buyers).

What can a frustrated buyer do? Breaking into the shop and stealing is a violation of the law. So is putting sand in the gas tank of another customer who might race out before you to purchase the last remaining guitar in stock. People are, however, free to offer a higher price for a guitar. If consumers begin bidding up the price of guitars, how will sellers respond? By producing more guitars. As the market price rises from $300 to $500, notice that the quantity supplied will increase, from 800 to 1,000 guitars. At the same time, the increased price will reduce quantity demanded from 1,200 to 1,000 guitars. Whether people actually begin to bid the price up, or sellers find that they can substitute for the consumer bidding process by raising their own prices *and* selling more guitars, there are tendencies for the market price to rise and the overall shortage to disappear.

Buyers compete with buyers.

Competition, Cooperation, and Market Clearing

People often argue that buyers compete with sellers in the market economy. Is this true? Back in Chapter 2 Brown and Jones *cooperated* with each other by exchanging stouts and lagers. Does the exchange for *money* alter that cooperative relationship between two trading parties? No. If you voluntarily purchase a guitar for $20, $200, $500, or whatever, you and the seller have found a way to cooperate with each other—that's the essence of mutually beneficial exchange, whether the exchange takes place through money or barter. Money facilitates the *ability* to induce these acts of cooperation.

Competition does, of course, occur, and like cooperation, competition is rampant throughout the market process. Rather than competition between buyer and seller, however, buyers tend to compete with other buyers, and sellers tend to compete with other sellers.

Consider the case of a shortage. Frustrated guitar shoppers compete with one another by offering higher money prices or by demonstrating their own willingness to pay the higher posted price. The bidding process eliminates the shortage. The sellers of guitars would like, of course, the highest prices they can receive and will eagerly try to accommodate buyers who are offering more money. In the opposite case of a surplus, sellers compete among themselves by trying to attract customers and move excess inventories. It is not a rivalry between buyer and seller; it's a rivalry between guitar sellers. The rivalry works itself out not through violence and mayhem—as long as the rules of the game are respected and enforced!—but by price reductions. "Every other shop is charging $700 for this guitar. Because I see you love this guitar, I'll give you a break. $595. And I'll even throw in a free pick." Even though you know the extra pick is b.s., the seller is finding a way to compete against other sellers *and* cooperate with you. The competitor who was only offering free picks with its $700 guitar will soon find that's not enough. She will soon lower her price as well. (When you shop for a car, is the seller intent on competing with you or the dealer down the street? You want a low price but do you fear the seller, or do you fear that your offer may be too low and the car may be sold to a buyer who offered $100 more than you did?)

Therefore, the price tends to rise during times of shortages and fall during times of surpluses. The competitive bidding process runs its course once the shortage or surplus is alleviated. In our example, that ends at the $500 price. Individual buyers will have no incentive to increase their bids without the shortage. Individual sellers will have no incentive to lower their price without the surplus. Economists typically refer to that price as an *equilibrium price*, as the "forces" of supply and demand have worked themselves out and there is no further tendency for the price to change. But again, that sounds a bit too mechanical, as if the market were a thing. The authors instead prefer the term *market clearing price*. To say that the market is clear is to say there is neither a shortage nor a surplus. The plans of buyers have become fully coordinated with the plans of sellers.

Market clearing: $Q_d = Q_s$ (plans of buyers and sellers are fully coordinated).

The economic way of thinking emerged in part to explain the phenomenon of market clearing. It's not only the market for guitars that tends to clear. *Free markets for any good or service show a tendency to clear.* The "laws" or principles of supply and demand help us explain *why* and *how* markets generally tend to clear, how people with limited information nevertheless find ways to accomplish many of their plans.

One final but crucial point. *A commercial society doesn't require expert economists to clear markets. It instead requires that there are effective rules of the game that allow people to buy, sell, and trade their property—to coordinate their own plans—as they best see fit*. Economists are useful in explaining how market processes coordinate peoples' plans and generate wealth and economic growth, something that a lot of people still don't understand. People often fail to see that *market clearing is an unintended consequence* of the specific choices that individuals make. Guitar buyers couldn't care less about the overall state of the market. They want guitars at an acceptable price. They can't possibly know everything there is to know about the state of the guitar industry. Same for guitar sellers. They pursue their own goals, too, geared toward making a living and a profit. *The tendency for market clearing is not planned and engineered by economists, government agencies, nor even producers or consumers. Markets tend to clear as an unintended consequence of people competitively bidding and cooperatively exchanging, following their own projects, plans, and goals, with inescapably limited information and knowledge.*

No need for experts!

Changing Market Conditions

And now for a little further practice. Our discussion centered around the tendency for the market to clear with *given* supply and demand curves. But, as you learned in Chapters 3 and 4, supply and demand curves themselves can shift. Let's practice a couple of those shifts.

Suppose, for example, the price of spruce fell, with other prices (for skilled labor, mahogany, and other materials) unchanged. Your first challenge is to decide whether this would affect the supply or the demand curve. Lower spruce prices would tend to reduce the marginal opportunity costs of making guitars. More guitars would be produced as a result. And, recall that the supply curve is derived from the "height" of those marginal costs. Lower marginal costs mean a rightward shift of the supply curve. As more guitars come on the market, and the *overall supply* increases, the price would fall from \$500 to \$400. (What would happen if supply increased but the price stayed at \$500? A surplus would emerge. Sellers would compete by lowering their prices until the surplus is eliminated.) A *new* market clearing price would emerge, at \$400 per guitar. (Notice that the demand curve for guitars has not changed. The *quantity demanded* increased as the price fell from \$500 to \$400.)

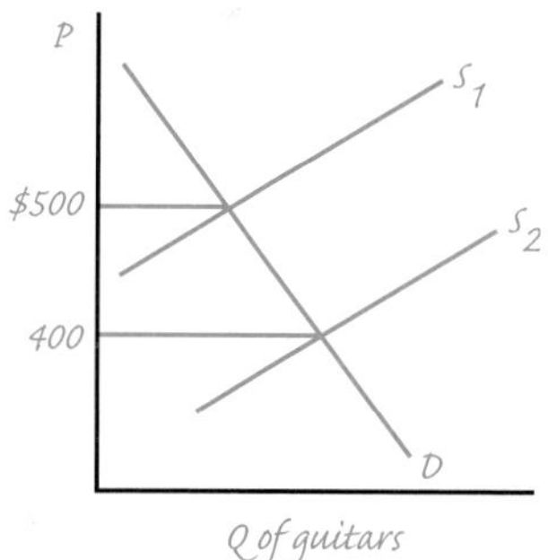

Consider a different example. What if the price of *electric* guitars were to increase? How would this initially affect the market for acoustics? Electric and acoustic guitars are generally considered good substitutes. People who planned to buy electric guitars would revise their plans in light of the higher price. Some would switch to acoustic guitars instead, while a couple of others would consider trombones, accordions, or other things to purchase with their money. Nevertheless, this raises the *overall demand for acoustic guitars*. We could depict that with a rightward shift of the demand curve in the market for acoustic guitars. A new market clearing price would emerge, at \$600 per acoustic guitar.

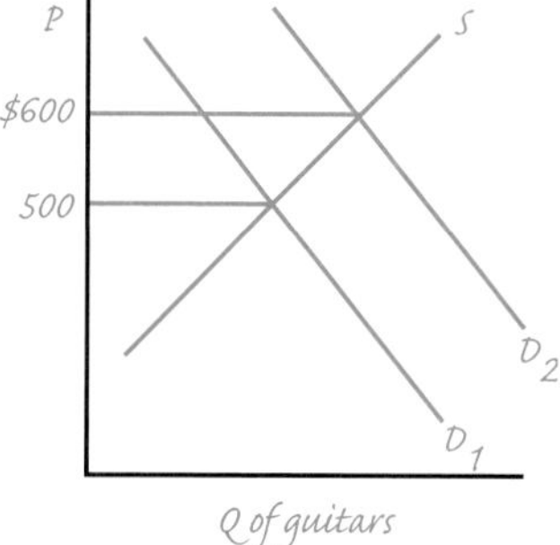

The Market for Credit

Market processes coordinate not only our planned production and consumption of guitars, of course. The same basic process is at work for a countless variety of scarce goods and services.

Consider, for example, the market for credit. We depict this in Figure 5–2. As for any scarce good, the demand curve for credit is

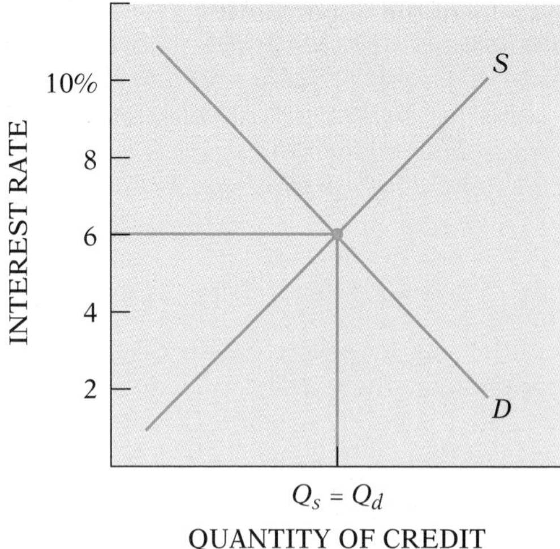

Figure 5–2 **Supply and demand in the market for credit**

downward-sloping. A lower interest rate (the price of credit) will tend to increase the quantity of credit demanded; a higher interest rate will reduce the quantity demanded. The supply of credit tends to be an upward-sloping curve. A higher interest rate will tend to increase the quantity supplied; a lower interest rate will reduce the quantity supplied. The market for credit clears when the plans of the lenders are coordinated with the plans of borrowers (the quantity supplied would equal the quantity demanded). In our graph, that's at the 6 percent interest rate. Other things being constant, were the rate to be *below* 6 percent, a shortage of credit would emerge. Borrowers would tend to compete with other borrowers for loans in short supply. The interest rate would therefore tend to be bid up to the market-clearing level. Were the rate instead to be above the market-clearing rate, say at 8 percent, a surplus of credit would emerge. Bankers would be planning to offer more loans than households and others are willing to take on at the 8 percent rate. Competition among banks would tend to reduce the interest rate until it reaches the 6 percent market-clearing level.

Suppose we continue by practicing a shift in demand. For example, let's assume that the interest rate is currently at the 6 percent level, which clears the market, but people begin to expect that interest rates will rise within the next several months. *If people expect higher interest rates in the future, what may likely happen to their demand for loans in the present?* Well, it's similar to the "buy now before prices rise" example from Chapter 3. Those borrowing money for cars, homes, vacation property, business investment projects, and so on may wish to jump in and commit themselves to today's relatively lower interest rates. This change in *price expectations* would tend to *increase the demand for credit*.

The demand curve would therefore shift upwards and to the right. (Feel free to draw the new demand curve in Figure 5–2.) This leads to the rather interesting result that *a change in expectations about tomorrow's price* (in this case, tomorrow's interest rate) *can actually alter today's price*. The rise in today's demand itself will lead to a higher market-clearing interest rate.

Of course, if demanders expect higher interest rates within the next several months, it's likely that the *suppliers* also have similar expectations. Recall from Chapter 4 that suppliers also act on price expectations. In the case of the credit market, they would tend to *supply fewer loans today* in anticipation of the higher interest rates in the coming months. Here, *the overall supply curve of credit would shift upward and to the left.* The decrease in the supply of credit would put further upward pressure on the current interest rate.

(In all of this you might be asking yourself, *why do people pay—and charge—interest on a loan?* It might make sense why a person would pay a price for something like a guitar, or a gallon of gasoline, or even for somebody else's labor service or rental property. But why pay a price, with the rather unusual name of *interest,* for a loan? What did the lender do, for example, to *deserve* the interest return? After all, the craftsman spent hours making the guitar. The shop owner incurred the transaction costs to make guitar shopping more convenient for you. If you borrowed the \$500 to purchase a guitar, you would now owe \$500 *plus interest*. What did the lender do to justify the additional interest return? We address these and other questions surrounding the phenomenon of interest in the appendix.)

Competition Results from Scarcity

No one blames the thermometer for low temperatures or seriously proposes to warm up the house on a cold day by holding a candle under the furnace thermostat. That's because they have a more-or-less correct understanding of how those things work. People do, however, often blame high prices for the scarcity of certain goods and act as if scarcity could be eliminated by enforcing price controls. We will discuss price controls in the next chapter.

For now, let it be understood that *scarcity is a relationship between desirability and availability, or between demand and supply*. A good is scarce whenever people cannot obtain as much of it as they would like without being required to sacrifice something else of value. Market prices inform us of relative scarcities. *But don't confuse scarcity with rarity*. Something is *rare* if it is available in a relatively small quantity. Eight-track cassette tapes, therefore, are rarer than compact discs. *Desirability is not a component of rarity*. Who really wants eight tracks any more? The demand just isn't there. Old eight tracks sell for a buck or two at urban flea markets.

For Sale: Barry Bonds autographed baseball, $150
For Sale: Dave Prychitko autographed baseball, 50 cents

The same music on compact discs fetches much higher prices. People are willing to sacrifice more cash for the disc. It is therefore more scarce than an eight track. (If you still can't see it, consider this. Suppose one of the authors—Prychitko—autographs a baseball. It will be much rarer than a Barry Bonds ball, because there would be only one in existence, whereas Bonds has signed hundreds, if not more. But nobody wants to pay as much for a Prychitko as for a Bonds. In fact, Prychitko's signature probably reduces the value of the ball close to zero. It is therefore nowhere near as scarce as a Bonds.)

Now it follows immediately, as Chapter 3 insisted, that if a good is scarce, it must be rationed. In other words, a criterion of some kind must be established for discriminating among claimants to determine who will get how much. The criterion could be age, eloquence, swiftness, public esteem, willingness to pay money, or almost anything else. We most commonly ration scarce goods in our society on the basis of willingness to pay money. But sometimes we use other criteria in order to ration.

For example, Harvard University each year has many more applicants than it can place in the freshman class, so Harvard must ration the scarce places. It discriminates on the basis of high school grades, test scores, recommendations, relationship to important alumni, and other criteria. Joe College is the most popular man on campus and has young women clamoring for his favor. He must therefore ration his attentions. Whether he employs the criterion of beauty, intelligence, geniality, or something else, he must and will discriminate in some fashion.

Scarcity makes rationing necessary.

The other side of rationing is competition. Once Harvard announces its criteria for discrimination, freshman applicants will compete to meet them. If the women eager to date Joe College believe that beauty is his main criterion, they will compete with one another to seem more beautiful.

Rationing (by means of discriminatory criteria) makes competition inevitable.

Competition is obviously not confined to capitalist societies or to societies that use money. *Competition results from scarcity and can be eliminated only with the elimination of scarcity.* Whenever there is scarcity, there must be rationing. Rationing is allocation in accordance with some criteria for discrimination. *Competition is what occurs when people strive to meet the criteria that are being used to ration scarce goods.*

The criteria that are used make a difference, sometimes a huge and important difference. If a society rations on the basis of willingness to pay money, members of that society will strive to make money. If it uses physical strength as a primary criterion, members of the society will do bodybuilding exercises. If it rations on the basis of people's ability to play brass instruments, members will try to learn how to play bugles. If the better colleges and universities use high school grades as an important criterion for selection, high school students will compete for grades. They might be competing for grades to acquire other goods as well (status among classmates, compliments from teachers, use of the family car or the old man's credit card), but the rationing criteria used by these schools will certainly encourage students to compete for higher grades.

Surpluses and Scarcity

We've spoken a lot about shortages. What about surpluses? Many people use the word *surplus* to suggest that a particular good is not scarce. But this doesn't make a lot of sense. The only sensible definition of a surplus is a quantity supplied that exceeds the quantity demanded, which always implies *at some price*. In our original acoustic guitar example, guitars were still scarce even at the $700 price—people were willing to make a sacrifice to obtain one—even though the overall market experienced a surplus.

A surplus is a sign of discoordination, not an elimination of scarcity!

The American Medical Association has long been warning about an imminent surplus of physicians. If we don't stop training so many physicians, says the AMA, we will soon be burdened with more than we need. But there is no precise number of physicians "needed" by any population. When members of a profession talk about the number "needed," they almost always mean the quantity demanded at the current price. Of course, a lower price for their services is precisely what they don't want to see. And that makes them reluctant to admit that lower prices would also produce lower incomes for physicians and an eventual reduction in the number of physicians practicing.

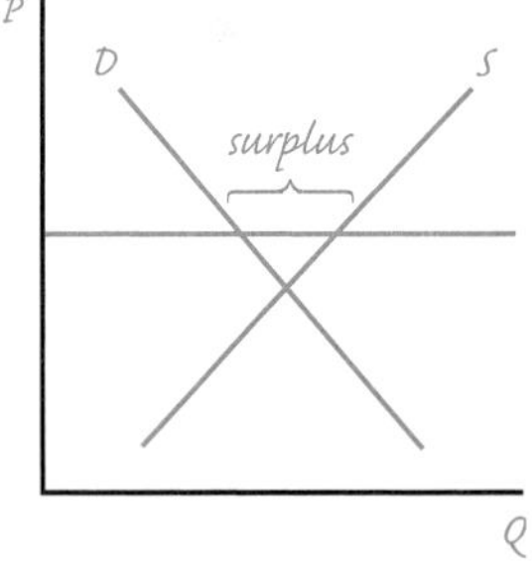

Market Processes Versus Central Planning

The central economic task for a society is to secure cooperation among people in using what is available to obtain what is wanted. Effective cooperation among large numbers of people who barely know each other requires that the terms of exchange be clear, simple, and standardized so that transaction costs can be kept down.

We live in a world of people with highly diverse skills, interests, values, and preferences; where resources have many different potential uses and opportunity costs vary infinitely; where continual change and constant discovery are the features of everyday life. Imagine an alternative economic system of socialist central planning, in which all the means of production—resources, machinery, factories, and so on—are not owned privately but by society as a whole, with decisions about the best uses of these scarce goods deposited in the hands of a group of expert economists, sociologists, chemists, and so on who would form a central planning board and decide what to produce, how to produce, and for whom to produce. The entire socialist economy would be run like one huge nonprofit organization. Markets would be abolished. So, too, would the use of money. *What information and signals would central planners use to effectively and efficiently produce and distribute the massive array of goods and services desired by millions of citizens?*

After all, the engineers on the planning committee could announce that it is physically possible to make buses out of gold, to make train tracks out of platinum, and to make wedding rings out of tin. In a free market system, bus producers, railroad builders, and jewelers are both politically and economically free to make these goods in this way.

Economic calculation informs people of the relative scarcity of goods and services.

A socialist economy abolishes economic calculation and the information that it provides.

So why don't they commonly do that in a market economy? *Because it would be ridiculously unprofitable to do so*. The market prices of those resources, compared to the prices people are willing to pay for the final goods, help *inform* producers that these will likely generate losses in *advance* of actually undertaking the activity. That's what monetary calculation is all about. Those same prices emerge by millions of people's daily acts of voluntary exchange and negotiation in the market process. But socialist central planning abolishes that process. What signals and information will be readily available to the planners? They might enjoy reams of engineering principles and equations, huge warehouses stockpiled with material resources, an eager and fit-for-work population, and sophisticated computer systems tracking all the data, but will the data be economically useful? The data show that tin wedding rings are remarkably rare. Should more be produced? Or less? At what cost? *Just how scarce are tin wedding rings?* Platinum provides less friction than steel, but does that inform planners that platinum is best used to make railroad tracks? What are all the *alternative uses of platinum and the associated costs of using platinum for medical equipment, railroad tracks, or whatever?* Indeed, what are the associated costs of producing a railroad track when those materials and workers could be devoted to producing hospitals, toasters, pencils, and countless other scarce goods and services? Without money and market pricing, planners cannot effectively engage in economic calculation.

The collapse of central planning in the former USSR and its client states illustrated what economic theory has long suggested: Central economic planners, even if they are brilliant and loving people, don't even begin to know enough to manage effectively the day-to-day business of a commercial society. The issue is not getting better people to plan our way to economic growth; it's getting more effective institutions and rules of the game that encourage people to discover their own comparative advantage and make the most effective use of their limited knowledge, information, and resources.

Why is Interest Paid?

It is fairly obvious that both wages and rents represent payments for a specific service or good. We generally understand why a worker's services, and a renter's property, might be valued in the marketplace, but why is *interest* paid? Just what is interest?

Recently, a financial journalist declared on television: "If Alan Greenspan at the Federal Reserve lowers interest rates, the price of money will go down." We hear these kinds of stunning statements all the time. This might catch the attention of some channel surfers, but the statement is entirely wrong from the perspective of the economic way of thinking.

The notion that interest is a payment for the use of money, the way that a Hertz or Avis fee is a payment (a rent!) for the use of a car, is quite mistaken. Your employer offers you money in return for your services. You hand that money over to grocers, utility companies, and others to secure goods that they supply and you want; they in turn use the money you provide them to pay their employees, and so on. None of us pays any interest for the use of the money that changes hands in this way. Moreover, if you choose to put a pair of $20 bills into your sugar bowl for a rainy day and it doesn't rain for several years, the Federal Reserve Bank that had those bills printed up and then put them into circulation doesn't charge you for their use during this period. Contrast that with the probable reaction of Hertz or Avis if you stored one of its cars in your garage for a rainy day.

Interest is not "the price of money" or a payment made for the use of money.

We pay interest only when we *borrow* money. *Borrowing is a matter of obtaining purchasing power that we have not yet earned. Borrowers want money now though they currently have no valuable service to offer in exchange for it.* They persuade lenders to provide them with money *now* by promising to pay later. They enter a mutually agreed-upon contract. The ratio between what is given back later and what is obtained now determines the interest rate.

Interest is thus the price that people pay to obtain resources now rather than wait until they have earned the purchasing power with which to buy the resources. The best way to think about interest is to view it as *the premium paid to obtain current command of resources.* It surely is not "the price of money."

Current resources are generally more valuable than future resources because having resources now usually expands one's opportunities. Present command of resources will often enable us to do things that cause our earning capacity to increase over time, so that we will have more resources at some future date than we would otherwise have had. When we see such a prospect, we want to borrow. And we are willing to pay, if we have to, a premium—interest—as long as the interest is less than what we expect to gain as a result of borrowing.

People pay interest in order to obtain current command over resources. Present command of resources is generally worth more than future command of the same resources.

Interest is consequently not something unique to capitalist economies, much less a result of the greed and power of bankers and other moneylenders. Above all, it is not something that could be eliminated merely by making more money available. Making more money available to everyone would just reduce the purchasing power of money, which is why we have kept stressing the fact that borrowers want purchasing power, not mere money. Interest rates are generally talked about as if they were the cost of borrowing money simply because money is the usual means by which people acquire possession of present goods. But interest would exist in an economy that functioned without money, because it's fundamentally the difference in value between present and future goods.

Time Preference

We don't want to leave the impression that it's only the productivity of capital that makes resources now generally more valuable than the same resources at some future date. People also seem to display what the economist calls a *positive rate of time preference*; that is, they place a higher value on present enjoyment than on enjoyment in the distant future.

Here are two little tests you might use to find out whether you are among that overwhelming majority with a positive rate of time preference. Imagine your boyfriend gives you a simple kiss on Valentine's Day and says the dozen roses will arrive next week. A dozen roses might be a dozen roses, but if you feel that a dozen roses arriving a week late is *not the same* as a dozen roses arriving on Valentine's Day, chances are you have a positive rate of time preference. Or imagine that you have responded to one of those innumerable promotions that come in the mail with large and gaudy announcements on the envelope stating that YOU MAY ALREADY HAVE WON A BRAND-NEW $45,000 SPORTS CAR. And to your own utter astonishment, you find out that you have actually won the grand prize! You are very happy, of course. Then you learn that the car won't be delivered to you until about one year from now. You are still happy, but you are probably a lot less happy than you were when you imagined yourself driving that sports car next week. In fact, you would most likely be willing to pay a substantial sum of money to get the car now rather than having to wait a year. If all this describes you, then you have a positive rate of time preference.

Some critics have interpreted positive time preference as evidence of shortsightedness, or of inability to imagine the distant future with as much vividness and force as one contemplates the immediate future, or of an innate human tendency to view the future through rose-tinted glasses. Each of these interpretations casts suspicion on the ultimate "rationality" of time preference. Given the facts of human mortality, however, and all the contingencies of life, it isn't necessarily irrational or shortsighted to prefer a bird in the hand to two in the bush. Moreover, if people have reason to believe that their income will increase over time, they could very logically conclude that giving up something now entails a larger subjective sacrifice than giving up quite a bit more of the same thing at a future date when they expect their income to be larger. Economists do not say that people *should* have a positive rate of time preference. They instead observe that people *do* place greater value on a good today compared to the "same" good in the future. We generally are not indifferent between eating now (when we are hungry) or going to sleep now (when we are tired) as opposed to eating later or sleeping later, all else being constant.

If you place the same value on $1,000 now as on $1,250 one year from now, you have a 25% rate of time preference.

Interest is paid, then—to answer the question with which we began this section—to induce people to give up present command of resources. It is a payment for the value of the opportunity that lenders forgo, a payment that borrowers are willing to make because of the opportunities that borrowing opens up for them.

The Risk Factor in Interest Rates

The rates charged by banks to corporate borrowers, by department stores to customers with revolving charge accounts, or on credit cards all reflect the net rate of time preference in a particular society. But they also include risk premiums of various sizes plus differences in the cost of negotiating loans. It will ordinarily cost you more per dollar to borrow from a commercial bank than it will cost a large and successful corporation. This doesn't really mean that you're paying a higher rate of interest, however. You are paying for the costs incurred by the bank in investigating your credit standing and doing the bookkeeping entailed by your loan, as well as a kind of insurance premium that the bank collects from the borrower in anticipation of losses through costs of collection and defaults. If the bank could not charge this premium, it would refuse to make loans to customers in higher-risk categories. So when legislators impose ceilings on the "annual interest" that lenders may legally charge, they don't reduce interest rates so much as they exclude certain categories of borrowers from contracting for loans. Because the borrowers wouldn't contract for the loans unless they deemed them advantageous, it's difficult to discover in what way maximum-interest-rate laws benefit low-income borrowers.

Interest rate ceilings reduce opportunities for high-risk borrowers.

Real and Nominal Interest Rates

The quoted interest rates that you see in market contracts also include one other component that is not really interest but is, nevertheless, very important. They incorporate an additional amount to compensate the lender for any expected decrease in the purchasing power of money ("inflation" is another word for the decrease in the purchasing power of money; how and why it occurs will be discussed carefully in a later chapter). If a lender wishes to earn 3 percent annually, and expects zero inflation (and thus a constant purchasing power of money), he will charge borrowers a 3 percent nominal interest rate. And he will "really" earn 3 percent on the loan. Again, the nominal rate is the quoted rate—the rate on the lending contract, the rate that you see posted on the walls behind the tellers in your own bank. If the lender expects a 2 percent rate of inflation—meaning the purchasing power of the dollar would fall by 2 cents over the course of the year—he would charge a nominal interest rate of 5 percent. The lender isn't "really" earning 5 percent—remember, each dollar that he collects for principal and interest will be worth 2 cents less. So his "real" interest rate—his real rate of return—is 3 percent.

The formula for calculating the real interest rate is straightforward:

The real rate of interest is the market rate (the nominal rate) minus the rate of inflation.

The real interest rate = the nominal interest rate minus the rate of inflation

(In our preceding example, we determined the real interest rate by subtracting the expected rate of inflation, 2 percent, from the nominal rate of interest, 5 percent, leaving us with a real rate of 3 percent.)

Once Over Lightly

The coordination of decisions in a society characterized by extensive division of labor is a task of enormous complexity, requiring the continuous daily negotiation, renegotiation, and monitoring of millions of agreements to exchange.

The market is best thought of as a process of competing bids and offers, rather than being depicted as a person, place, or thing. Supply and demand is the process of interaction through which relative prices are determined. It is a process of mutual adjustment and accommodation.

An effective market economy features numerous institutions that have evolved to reduce transaction costs and thus facilitate voluntary exchange. Transaction costs are the costs of arranging contracts or transaction agreements between suppliers and demanders. Money is a general medium of exchange that reduces transaction costs. A corresponding system of money prices that change readily in response to changing conditions of supply and demand transmits the kind of information that allows for people to coordinate their plans efficiently in highly specialized economic systems.

Markets clear when the plans of buyers are coordinated with the plans of sellers, in other words, when quantity demanded equals quantity supplied. When a price is below its market-clearing level, a shortage occurs, defined as quantity demanded exceeding quantity supplied. The market price will tend to increase, thereby reducing the shortage. When a price is above its market-clearing level, a surplus occurs, defined as quantity supplied exceeding quantity demanded. The market price will tend to decrease, thereby reducing the surplus. Market clearing is an unintended outcome of buyers and sellers pursuing their own objectives. Economists are helpful in explaining how this process works; economists aren't necessary, however, for free markets to work effectively.

Interest represents the cost of obtaining present command of resources, or the difference in value between present and future goods. It is usually attached to money loans simply because money represents general command over present or future goods.

Quoted interest rates also incorporate the costs of arranging and insuring the loan plus the expected rate of inflation. The real interest rate is the nominal rate minus the expected rate of inflation.

The rate of interest in a society is typically positive because people generally find present goods more valuable than future goods.

Exchange is a cooperative activity. Buyers and sellers cooperate with one another by agreeing to the terms of trade. Buyers compete with buyers by bidding up prices or finding other non-monetary ways to gain access to scarce goods, which is evident during a shortage. Sellers compete with sellers in their search for profit. During shortages they typically compete by reducing their prices.

Rarity shouldn't be confused with scarcity. Something is rare if it exists in relatively small quantities, such as a Prychitko autographed baseball or a Boettke autographed tennis racket.

Scarcity is a relationship between availability and desirability, or between supply and demand. A good ceases to be scarce only when people can obtain all they want at a zero opportunity cost to themselves.

Scarce goods must be rationed in some fashion. Rationing entails the use of discriminatory criteria to determine who gets how much. Competition is the attempt to satisfy whatever discriminatory criteria are being used to ration scarce goods. Surpluses don't imply an end of scarcity. Surpluses, like shortages, imply a lack of coordination of plans among buyers and sellers.

Prices established in an open market process transmit important information regarding the relative scarcities of goods and services. By attempting officially to abolish private ownership, money, and markets, centrally planned economies also destroyed precisely those market signals that allow people to discover their comparative advantage and effectively coordinate their production and consumption plans.

QUESTIONS FOR DISCUSSION

1. Here is a good question to get you thinking about supply and demand as a process of coordination. Millions of Americans change their residences each year, many moving long distances to new and strange areas. How do they all find places to live?
   (a) Who sees to it that every individual or family moving to a new state finds someone in that state willing to sell or rent them a house or apartment that suits their tastes and circumstances?
   (b) Who oversees construction planning so that those states that are growing most rapidly manage to expand their stock of housing at a rate that matches their population growth?
   (c) List some of the institutions that lower transaction costs for Americans who must sell a house and buy another house in order to move from one city to another.
   (d) During the years when the communist government of China claimed ownership of all housing in the nation, it also maintained housing-exchange stations in all the major cities. Why would transaction costs be much higher with a housing exchange than with a system of private ownership and changing prices when it comes to facilitating trades among millions of people who want to move?
2. The deputy chairman of the Russian Red Cross complained in the 1990s that food aid sent to the country by Western nations was being stolen. "Russian swindlers are the most experienced in the world," he said. The deputy director of the Russian aid commission expressed the need for a centralized system to ensure proper distribution. Which do you think is likely to get into the mouths of hungry people faster and with less loss through spoilage: food that is distributed through government agencies and charity organizations or food that has been stolen? Why?
3. If the desire for more money is an indication of a selfish and materialistic attitude, as many people seem to think, why do churches and charitable organizations work so hard to acquire more of it? (If your first response is "they're just as greedy as anyone else," you might want to think again.)
4. Explain how, in a barter economy, a toilet paper manufacturer would have a little easier time bartering compared to a guitar maker.
5. It might take only one person to screw in a lightbulb, but how many people does it take to eventually produce lightbulbs?
6. You know it took ink, paper, computers, and money to write this edition of *The Economic Way of Thinking*. But *Andy Griffith Show* reruns, a Merle Haggard concert, coffee beans, and several hours in the sauna among *countless* other goods and services were also used to eventually produce this edition of the book. Could you offer a plausible economic explanation?
7. Here's further practice in shifting supply and demand curves. What would happen to the market-clearing price of acoustic guitars in Figure 5–1 if
   (a) People turned on to some accordion craze and started losing interest in learning to play the guitar?
   (b) The price of electric guitars were to fall substantially?

(c) A number of acoustic guitar makers decide to exit the market and make violins instead?

8. Suppose the short-term supply of lakefront cottages is fixed, depicted by a vertical supply curve (those aren't mythical beasts—only vertical demand curves are). What would happen to the market-clearing price if rising incomes induce many additional families to look to buy vacation cottages?
9. More and more colleges are converting to WebCT and other online testing programs. What effect would this have on the price of old-fashioned no. 2 pencils? Would you expect the price change to be small or quite large? What does that say about the price elasticity of supply of no. 2 pencils?
10. "When the price of apples falls, the supply falls and the demand increases." Evaluate this statement.
11. "If there is a shortage of platinum, its price will rise. The shortage will eventually disappear because the higher price will reduce demand and increase supply." Evaluate this statement.
12. If gasoline prices continue above $2.00 a gallon, what would tend to happen to the demand for eight-cylinder SUVs? What would that tend to do to the market price of those SUVs?
13. Many people believe that in the event of another oil crisis brought on by war in the Middle East or elsewhere, gasoline should be rationed by the government by the criterion of *need*. How would you propose that the rationing authorities determine need?
14. There are no toll charges for driving on many urban expressways during the rush hour. How is the scarce space rationed?
15. Parking space is sometimes made available on college campuses at a zero price even when parking space is quite scarce.
    (a) What exactly does it mean that parking space is scarce? Does it mean that parking spaces are not available?
    (b) How is scarce parking space rationed in the absence of parking fees?
    (c) If a college charged all students who wanted to park on campus $200 for a yearly parking permit, would that fee effectively ration scarce parking space?
    (d) Suppose the college placed parking meters along all the campus streets. How could these be used to ration scarce parking space effectively? Keep in mind that some parking spaces will be in much greater demand than others.
16. Ricky Martin concerts were selling out all over the country a few years ago. Believe it or not, young kids skipped school, camped out in overnight lines, and did who knows what else to try to obtain tickets before they sold out. Were they competing against Ricky Martin? His managers and promoters? His sponsors? The ticket agency? The concert hall? Were they competing at all?
17. Here are the first three sentences from a booklet titled "The Arithmetic of Interest Rates," published by the Federal Reserve Bank of New York: "Everything has a price. And money is no exception. Its price—the interest rate—is determined in the marketplace where money is borrowed and lent." Is it correct to speak of interest as the price of money?

(a) If interest is the price of money in the same way in which 35 cents is the price of an orange, then we should expect an increase in the quantity of money to lead to lower interest rates just as an increase in the quantity of oranges leads to a reduced price for oranges. Why then are interest rates very high in nations that allow the quantity of money in circulation to increase very rapidly?

(b) A large increase in the quantity of money available will indeed have an effect on "the price of money" similar to the effect that a large increase in the quantity of oranges supplied will have on the price of oranges—if by "price" we mean value relative to other goods. The term we use to describe a fall in the value of money relative to other goods is *inflation*. If an increase in the amount of money in circulation creates expectations of inflation, what will happen to interest rates?

(c) Interest is the price of something, but not of money. What is the good whose price has gone up when the interest rate rises?

(d) The law of demand says that a higher price for a good causes less of that good to be demanded. What is the good for which the quantity demanded decreases when the interest rate increases?

18. "When lenders extend credit to high-risk borrowers, they must raise the interest rates they charge low-risk borrowers in order to cover their losses from defaults." Does this claim make sense?
19. Far fewer babies are currently offered for adoption in the United States than couples want to adopt. Would you be willing to let the available children go to the highest bidder? What consequences would you predict from such a system? By what criteria are scarce babies currently assigned to prospective adopters?
20. Federal law currently prohibits the sale of human organs for transplant purposes. At the present time, people are dying while waiting for suitable organs to become available. It seems almost certain that more organs would become available if financial incentives were offered to prospective donors. Would you be in favor of allowing this? What consequences would you predict?
21. Utah annually sells 27 licenses to hunt buffalo in a 1,500-square-mile area of the state. The fee is $200 for residents and $1,000 for nonresidents. Because the state receives more than a thousand applications each year, it holds a drawing to decide who will get the 27 licenses.

    (a) Why do you suppose Utah doesn't sell the licenses to the highest bidder?

    (b) Do you think people who receive a license should be allowed to sell it to someone else?

    (c) What effects do you think a lottery system with *freely transferable licenses* would have?
22. If the supply of turkeys in a particular November turned out to be unusually small, do you think a turkey shortage would result? Why or why not?
23. If you travel through the western United States in the summer, you are much more likely to encounter a shortage of camping spaces than of motel rooms. Why?

24. Which is more scarce, an ounce of gold or an ounce of plastic? What information did you use to reach your conclusion?
25. "Central planners were more effective than your free-market-loving textbook authors let on. Planners in the former Soviet Union never even considered making railroad tracks out of platinum or ships out of gold. They already knew that would be a waste of those scarce resources. They were informed by the world market prices for platinum and gold." We never said ships. We said buses. But anyway, how would you respond to that statement? What does it actually say about the importance of market processes and market prices?

Supply and Demand: Issues and Applications

6

Physicists don't have to encourage apples to fall to the ground. Apples seem to do it all by themselves, for a process is at work whether physicists exist or not. Physicists discovered the principle behind that process and named it the law of gravity. The economic way of thinking is somewhat similar in that it uncovers the principles at work with regard to people's choices and the consequences of their choices. Economics helps us understand how individuals, in their economizing pursuit of plans and projects, are able to coordinate their plans through cooperative and competitive activities in the market process. As we emphasized in the last chapter, economists aren't necessary to make markets clear. This is accomplished instead through the principles of supply and demand.

Economists play another important role by debunking some common misperceptions about market processes. Economists tend to think outside the box. We've been doing that since Chapter 1. But hopefully it will become especially clear to you as we continue that activity in this chapter and explore new themes such as price controls, prohibition on booze and drugs, taxation, and the all-too-common claim that costs determine prices.

The Urge to Fix Prices

Let's consider something that a lot of people depend upon: gasoline. As we revise this chapter, the average price for a gallon of regular gasoline in the United States is over $2.00. (In many parts of the country prices are well above $2.80.) Let's stick with that average as the market-clearing price of gasoline in the overall U.S. market.

Like you, the authors grumble about paying such high prices. (Funny we don't grumble about paying a lot more for a gallon's worth of beer, but that's another story.) Maybe it's time we all do something about it. Forget "market forces" and "market processes." How about if we *legislate* a price control? We could change the rules of the game—intervene in free markets and make it *illegal* for people to charge, or offer, a price above the federally mandated maximum price!

What's a fair price for a gallon of gasoline? $1.50? $1.25? 99 cents? Fair *to whom?* Forget about the suppliers. We outvote them. What is fair to us consumers? Suppose we all finally agree (*How? Using what arguments?*) that $1.00 a gallon is a "fair and reasonable price" for a gallon of gasoline, and, after a lengthy and debated political process, it becomes a new rule: Sellers can charge no more than $1.00 a gallon. Economists call a legally maximum price a *price ceiling*—the price is not allowed to rise *above* a certain level. Let's first get that enacted, and maybe later we can call for price ceilings for beer, food, clothing, medicine, guitars, and trombones.

But let's not get too excited. It's a joy to *imagine* being able to pay only $1.00 for a gallon of gasoline, but imagination and reality aren't always perfect complements. Often they're not even close substitutes. We would be wise to employ our economic way of thinking about market processes and unintended consequences. Figure 6–1 gives us a good start.

The market-clearing price is $2.00 per gallon. Using small numbers for simplicity, suppose the quantities supplied and demanded were equal at 1 million gallons per day. But sellers can only charge, and customers only offer, $1.00 a gallon with the price ceiling. The new rules are being enforced. Any higher and they're breaking the new law. What's the result? People will plan to buy more gas, envisioning longer pleasure rides through the country, an end to having to car pool to work or take the bus to college, perhaps purchasing a new gas-sucking eight-cylinder SUV, and so on. People's plans to purchase more gas at the lower $1.00 price are reflected by the movement down and along the demand curve. Quantity demanded (not demand!) increases to 1.5 million gallons per day. *But will all or even most of them be able to accomplish those plans?* Will the market remain coordinated? Quantity supplied rises when the price increases and falls when the price decreases, whether *that price is established on the free market or directly by law*. Sellers' inventories would be depleted with the new surge in buying, and daily output would drop from 1 million gallons to 500,000 per day. Sellers would be frustrated by their fall in sales, revenues, and profits as a result of the new price control (but recall, we assumed we didn't care about *them*). They respond by economizing, by cutting back output—if they don't, most would go out of business. We can make suppliers lose money—temporarily—but we can't make them stay in a money-losing enterprise. The consumers, the ones we *did* care about in this story, however, would find that they can't satisfy their planned purchases as a whole. Instead, a

Plans change when price changes.

Unintended consequence: shortage of gasoline.

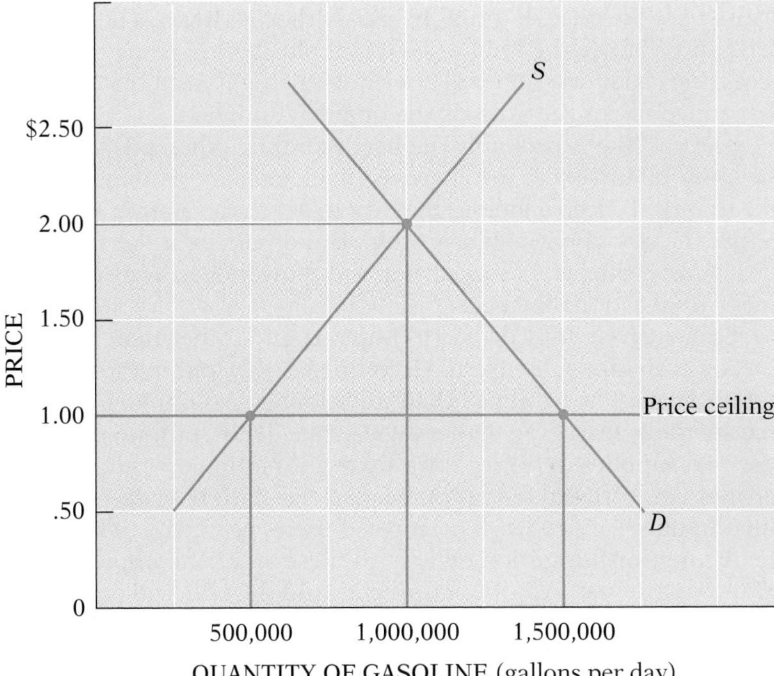

Figure 6–1 **Price control on gasoline**

The market clears at $2.00 per gallon. A price ceiling is set at $1.00 per gallon. Quantity demanded rises to 1.5 million gallons per day, while quantity supplied falls to 500,000 gallons per day. A shortage of 1 million gallons emerges as an unintended consequence of the price control.

shortage would occur, of about 1 million gallons per day (the difference between quantity demanded and quantity supplied).

Competition When Prices Are Fixed

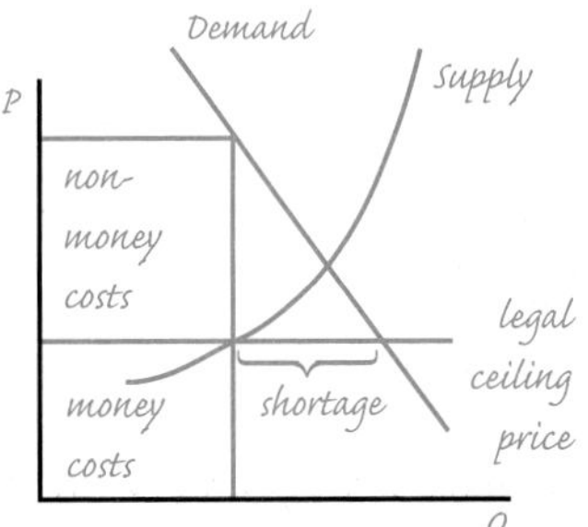

In a free market, the price would tend to rise during the shortage, and as an unintended consequence the market would tend to clear. The price ceiling, however, generates a different unintended consequence: a persistent shortage of gasoline. Relative market prices send important information about a good's relative scarcity. The mandated $1.00 maximum price makes it *appear* that gasoline is less scarce than it was at $2.00 per gallon, but it just isn't so. How will people deal with the shortage when they are not allowed to charge or bid higher prices? We will certainly see increases in the *nonmonetary costs* of purchasing it, for gasoline is scarce and therefore *must* be rationed. If by law we suppress the rationing device of monetary price, other rationing criteria will have to be used, whether by drift or by design. Potential purchasers of gasoline will attempt to discover the new criteria being used to discriminate among buyers, and they will compete against one another in trying to satisfy those criteria. Their competition will raise the total cost—price plus nonmonetary costs of acquiring gasoline—and will continue raising it until the quantity demanded no longer exceeds the quantity supplied.

The gas line is probably the best example. When people think they may be unable to purchase as much gasoline as they would like to buy at $1.00 a gallon, they try to get to the station early before the stocks have all been sold. But others have the same idea, so that the lines form earlier and grow longer. Waiting in line is unquestionably a cost.

Some drivers may decide to hunt around rather than wait in line, or even hire someone to sit in line, as they did in the 1970s in California. They will pay their additional cost in time and gasoline spent on searching. Others will strike deals: a fill-up out of reserved supplies in return for a tip to the station operator, or the payment of a special fee for parking at the station, or an agreement to have service work performed there, or maybe tickets to the theater for the station owner. All these ways of competing for gasoline raise the cost of obtaining it. And the cost will continue rising until it finally reduces the quantity demanded to match the quantity supplied.

Competition among people—whose combined desires to purchase a good cannot all be fully satisfied at the prevailing money price—will bid up the cost of purchasing it. Usually it is the money price that rises in such a situation. Whenever other components of the cost of purchasing a good start to climb, we can be fairly certain that some kind of social pressure (such as legislated price controls) is holding down the money price. And when that occurs—that is, when lengthening lines, longer searching, or special arrangements come into play to ration a good because the quantity demanded is greater than the quantity supplied *at the prevailing money price*—we have a *shortage* of that good.

Scarcity is unavoidable; shortages can be prevented by letting prices rise.

The economist's concept of shortage zeros in on the money price. Shortages exist only when money prices are not able to perform the function of rationing scarce goods to competing demanders. *We spot a shortage in real life whenever we find the nonmoney costs of acquisition rising to ration scarce goods.*

Appropriate and Inappropriate Signals

FRED'S FRIENDLY SERVICE

Open for ~~your~~ my convenience

~~24~~ 3 hours daily

What will suppliers do if the law prevents them from raising their prices in a situation of obvious shortage? They will probably look for alternative ways to turn the situation to their advantage. Gasoline retailers may decide to lower the cost *to themselves* of selling by reducing their daily hours of operation and closing altogether on weekends. If they can sell their entire weekly allocations in 20 hours, why should they bother to stay open for 120 hours a week? This response to the shortage will tend further to increase the cost *to buyers* of purchasing gasoline: They will face even longer lines, will be forced to cancel or curtail weekend traveling, will more frequently find themselves stranded because of the inability to obtain fuel, and will pay additional costs through searching, worrying, and even endangering their lives by improperly siphoning and storing gasoline.

We are extremely dependent on changing money prices to secure effective cooperation in our complex, interdependent society and economy. When prices are not permitted to signal a change in relative scarcities, suppliers and demanders receive inappropriate signals. They do not find, because they have no incentive to look for, ways to make accommodations to one another more effectively. It is important that people receive some such incentive, because there are so many little ways and big ways in which people *can* accommodate—ways that no central planner can possibly anticipate, but which in their combined effect make the difference between chaos and coordination. Changing money prices, continuously responding to changing conditions of demand or supply, provides just such an incentive.

Looking for an Apartment in the City? Read the Obituary!

Let's now turn to a rather bizarre fact. People struggle to find apartments in New York City. The struggle itself isn't bizarre. It's the rather creative ways that the struggle unfolds. For example, people often turn to the daily *obituaries* listed in the *New York Times* and *New York Post* to track down a potentially vacant apartment for rent. No, they're not trying to channel some dead spirit for clues in their search. They're trying to beat the competition to a lease on a newly vacated apartment. There's been a persistent shortage of apartments in New York City for decades, not because the free market process hasn't worked. It's because city commissioners imposed rent controls decades ago and continue their public-spirited crusade to maintain apparently low-cost housing for the middle class. Reading obituaries is part of the high nonmonetary costs of finding a rent-controlled apartment.

Suppose you live in a community where rents were $380 per month, but a growing population over the past year or two has increased demand and has driven rents up to $500 per month for the same units. People begin to ask, "What have the landlords done to deserve the higher rent?" and grow indignant about the price increase.

Figure 6–2 depicts the current situation. The market-clearing price, or rent in this case, is $500 per month. Notice the vertical supply curve. That represents a fixed stock of 750 apartment units. Whether the rent is $400, $500, or $800 per month, the quantity supplied remains 750 units in the short run. Over time,

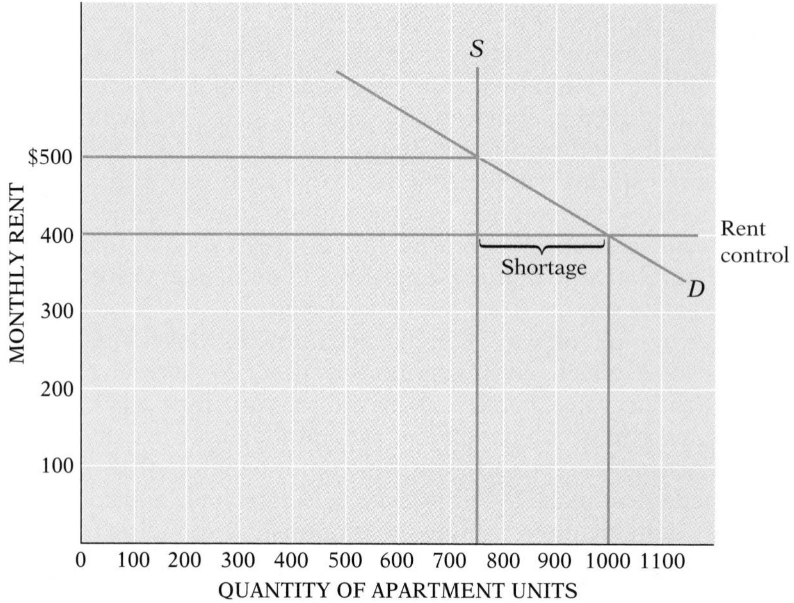

Figure 6–2 **Unintended consequence of rent control**

of course, the quantity supplied could decrease or increase, but, like a snapshot in time, the current market supply is relatively fixed. It is inelastic in the short run.

Suppose enough influential people in the community decide to do more than just complain about the higher rents they or others pay. Their protests to the landlords fell upon deaf ears. Now they seek the city commissioners. After all, they insist, people need a place to live, and the city commissioners begin to agree, dismissing all the counterarguments of the existing landlords (after all, the number of tenants well outweighs the number of landlords). If the landlords were happy two years ago with $380 a month, they should be quite happy with $400 a month today (they've even allowed for the landlords to keep up with the rate of inflation and higher taxes).

Now the landlords' protests fall on deaf ears. ("What did you do to deserve rents higher than $400 a month anyway?") A rent control of $400 a month is imposed by city law. Landlords and tenants are free to negotiate leases at or below that level, but not above.

All demand curves slope downward!

What's the intention or goal of the rent control? To make housing more affordable to tenants. But look at what unfolds. The quantity supplied remains 750 units, as before, but the quantity demanded grows to 1,000 units. What explains the increase in quantity demanded? Why, the lower price, of course! A shortage of 250 units emerges (can you see how we arrived at that number?). This is an *unintended consequence* of the rent control. Landlords will now be flooded with applicants, all competing among themselves to obtain what they want—an apartment

Rent controls unintentionally create shortages.

rental contract. Without the rent control, applicants would compete on the basis of price, and rents would be bid up to the $500 market-clearing level. But now that's illegal.

Apartments are no less scarce than they were before. When law or custom keeps money rents below the level at which the quantity demanded equals the quantity supplied, other ways of rationing must evolve. Landlords might discriminate on the basis of age, sexual preference, racial preference, personal habits, family size, letters of reference, pet ownership, length of residence in the community, or willingness to abide by petty regulations.

Consider a racist landlord. Without the rent control, and the shortage that emerged, were he to turn down a Muslim, a Ukrainian, or an Asian applicant, the landlord would be turning down $500 a month. The apartment would go vacant. But at the imposed $400 rent control, and the corresponding long list of eager applicants, a racist landlord can turn down any applicant and still find someone else eager to pay the full $400 rent. *The costs of discriminating according to the landlord's personal preferences are greatly reduced*. We predict, and indeed we observe, that prejudiced landlords will therefore engage in more of that activity.

Landlords will discriminate using nonprice criteria.

Tenants who were lucky enough to be in a rent-controlled apartment when the controls were imposed will hoard as much space as possible for as long as they can and will try to pass the unit on to a friend or to sublease when they do vacate. Meanwhile, landlords have little incentive to maintain quality or replace leaky pipes, drafty windows, or malfunctioning thermostats, for those activities come at an additional cost to the landlord. What's the additional benefit? Landlords would have an incentive to bear the costs of upkeep if, without the rent control, the tenants threatened to leave (for then a landlord would have to bear the forgone monthly rent on the vacated apartment). With the rent control the landlord can confidently say, "You don't like? Leave. There are many others banging down my door for this apartment!"

Unintended consequences!

All these responses will lead to demands for costly administrative review boards and for additional legislation prohibiting particular landlord responses. The long-term result may be the eventual disappearance of landlords, as existing buildings are allowed to deteriorate or are torn down for parking lots or are turned into condominiums or office buildings, and new rental units are not constructed. If that were to happen, the overall supply would be reduced. What would *that* do to the shortage? (Draw a new vertical supply curve in Figure 6–2 at, say, 500 units, to help you make the prediction.)

Strong Booze, Stronger Drugs: Criminal Incentives

Incentives clearly change when the rules of the game change. In completely "dry" counties, it's illegal for adults to produce, sell, and perhaps even consume alcohol. Did you ever wonder why individuals in dry counties tend to make moonshine and white lightning for distribution and sale, rather than beer or wine? Is it because the typical drinker *likes* moonshine more than a six-pack? Did you ever wonder why the production of beer and wine fell precipitously during the "Roaring Twenties" of the last century while, at the same time, gin and whiskey were readily available? Or why the death rate from alcohol poisoning was much higher then compared to now, or why liquor producers and distributors engaged in brutal violence all across the streets of Chicago back then, but not today?

Answers to these questions aren't reserved exclusively for sociologists, social psychologists, historians, or scholars of criminal justice. Economists can learn something from them. But the economic way of thinking contributes its own perspective as well. We've already let the cat out of the bag by mentioning incentives and rules of the game. Keeping that idea in mind, and our notions of supply and demand, let's get to work.

Fact: The prohibition of alcohol in the 1920s didn't abolish the supply and demand process; it made it illegal. People coordinated their activities through *underground* market processes. Production fell into the hands of very powerful criminals, as opposed to many independent, legitimate distillers, criminals who also controlled the distribution and sale of their products. Thinking in terms of our supply and demand concepts, Prohibition primarily affected the elasticity of supply of alcoholic drinks, as output or quantity supplied was not as responsive to small changes in price as it had been with flourishing and open markets for liquor. Supply became much more inelastic. The demand curve for alcohol, however, remained relatively stable during Prohibition; people were willing to sneak off to a "speakeasy" or other outlets for a drink and entertainment. The result was a surge in price and considerable profit opportunities for those willing to take the huge risks and break the law.

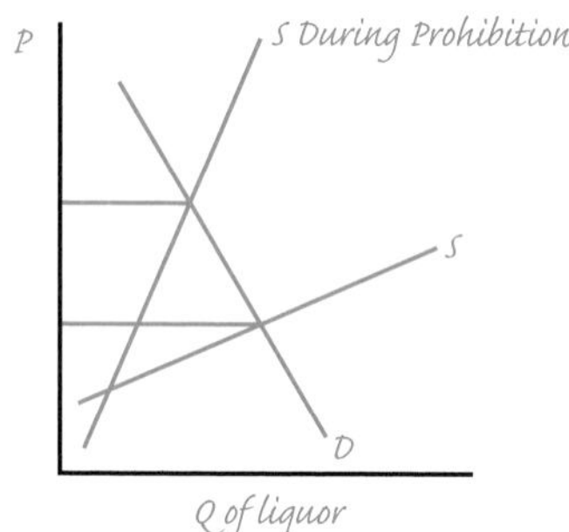

People pursue their comparative advantage. This is not meant to be an evaluative term, but an analytical term that appropriately accounts for the facts. *When production and distribution go underground, those with a comparative advantage in crime rise to the top of the heap.* Nice guys get weeded out of this competitive process. A successful bootlegger must know *how* to break the law, how to keep his friends close and his enemies closer, *whom* to threaten with violence or buy off with payola, whom to trust and distrust. He must not only determine who's to do the bookkeeping, marketing, and dealing, but who's to do the threatening, beating, and killing. He'll select comrades on the basis of their own comparative advantage.

And not only that. He of course must know just what to produce. Beer or whisky? Wine or gin? Production will be geared toward the stronger drinks. If one is equally likely to get caught hauling a truckload of beer or a truckload of whisky, better, from the point of view of the economizing criminal, to produce and transport whisky, because whisky fetches a *much higher* black market price. Is it any wonder, from the economic way of thinking, that the more powerful and dangerous liquor was widely available during Prohibition while weak drinks were much more rare, and therefore why the rate of alcohol poisoning was terrifyingly high?

Compare the prohibition of alcohol to the current war on drugs. *Nobody* tries to illegally sneak truckloads of coca leaves into our country. Powdered cocaine is more efficient. With the current war on drugs (fought with $20 billion annually), an even more highly refined and dangerous form—crack—has emerged in response. We can only imagine what's around the corner. The current drug laws do not demolish the supply of drugs, nor the demand. Like other forms of prohibition of truly dangerous substances, they have the unintended consequence of unleashing more powerful and more profitable substances to replace less powerful and less profitable ones. While the alcohol wars ended many, many decades ago, the drug wars continue to escalate.

Skim Milk, Whole Milk, and Gangster Milkmen

Perish the thought, but what if the production, distribution, and consumption of milk were prohibited? We predict these activities would be driven underground, too. The demand for milk wouldn't change substantially, but the supply would become quite inelastic and prices would increase considerably. Skim milk and 2 percent milk would fall out of production in favor of whole milk and cheese, as criminal risk takers would find it more profitable to ship trucks and planes loaded with the purer and therefore pricier stuff. Although stronger milk will still lead to strong bones and teeth, one might wonder about the quality. And certainly those with a comparative advantage in crime would weed out, either through intimidation or bloody violence, any remaining friendly milkmen who had worked hard all those years before the prohibition.

Supports and Surpluses

Our earlier examples of price controls on gasoline and rents looked at price ceilings, or legislated *maximum* prices set on a particular good or service. We've found that an *effective* price ceiling—one that actually makes a difference by being set *below* the market-clearing price—tends to generate an unintended shortage. We're now ready to consider an example or two of a *price floor*. A price floor is a *legally mandated minimum price* set on a particular good or service. In principle, nobody is allowed to bid or offer a price *below* the established floor. Whereas price *ceilings* are often established with the goal of improving prospects for consumers, price *floors* are established to improve prospects for suppliers. *Both floors and ceilings represent an attempt to transfer wealth from one group in the market to the other.*

Consider, for example, the wheat industry. Suppose the market-clearing price is $1.50 per bushel and that yields a cacophony of complaints from the farming community. Wheat farmers would much rather enjoy a $2.00 price per bushel, but they stand at the mercy of the forces of the marketplace. If these complaints are felt to be legitimate, the Department of Agriculture might decide to establish a $2.00 price floor as a way to support not only the price that farmers receive but the incomes and wealth that they enjoy.

How would consumers respond to the higher price of wheat? They would plan to purchase *less*, as the higher price sets off a decrease in quantity demanded. That's simply the law of demand at work once again, whether or not the higher price is established by free market negotiation or by federal farm policy. At the same time, how would *wheat farmers* respond to the more favorable price? If you understand the concept of the supply curve by now, you would be correct in predicting that the quantity of wheat produced would increase. The problem is, in this case *planned consumption decreases while planned output increases*. In other words, the market becomes *discoordinated* through the production of a *surplus* of wheat.

Again, plans change when price changes!

Wheat farmers get $2.00 per bushel that they sell to consumers, but what happens to their unsold (surplus) wheat? Because consumers have bought all that they planned to buy at the current price, the government must step in and purchase the surplus output—at $2.00 per bushel. (What the government officials decide to do with the wheat that they purchase is largely irrelevant for the effectiveness of the price support program. They can send it off to other nations or they can dump it in the ocean, just as long as they don't try to sell it to domestic consumers at a price below the support price.)

Agricultural price supports unintentionally create surpluses.

Price supports on agricultural goods *do* benefit producers, but that benefit comes from a corresponding *loss* to others. Consumers will now be paying higher prices. Taxpayers will also have to "tighten their belts" in light of the higher tax burden imposed upon them to finance the government purchases of surplus output. An effective agricultural price support transfers wealth from consumers and taxpayers to producers.

Supply, Demand, and the Minimum Wage

The demand for the services of productive resources is like any other demand curve: It slopes downward to the right. Other things remaining equal, a larger quantity will be demanded at lower prices and a smaller quantity at higher prices. The demand for unskilled labor, for example, is a downward-sloping curve. Firms, whether they are for-profit or not-for-profit, will be more inclined to hire more unskilled workers at a lower hourly wage rate, other things being constant.

The supply of unskilled labor is upward-sloping. A higher hourly wage tends, other things being constant, to increase the quantity of labor supplied. A market-clearing wage for unskilled labor is established where supply meets demand. *X marks the spot*, as it were. Here, the quantity of labor supplied equals the quantity demanded, which is a shorthand way of saying that those searching for work at the market-clearing wage are able to find work and those seeking to hire are able to find employees.

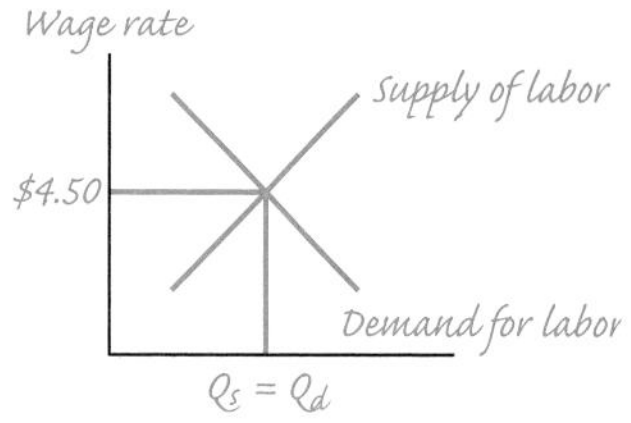

But suppose the market clears at a $4.50 hourly wage rate. Wouldn't workers be better off if, instead, a *minimum wage*, of say $5.35 per hour, were established by federal law? A minimum wage is another example of a *price floor*. It is illegal for somebody to offer, or accept, a wage rate below the established minimum. For the minimum wage to work, it must be set *above* the market-clearing wage rate. But if it's effective, it does generate unintended consequences. A *surplus of labor* will result, from two directions. First, the quantity demanded will fall in response to the higher wage rate. That's another way of saying that some workers will be fired. Second, the quantity supplied will increase, as more people seek employment at the more attractive wage rate. Notice we said they *seek* employment. Their prospects of actually *finding* employment will fall as the surplus of labor emerges. This unintentionally generates *unemployment* in the unskilled labor market. (We have ample opportunity to discuss other causes of unemployment in Chapter 15.)

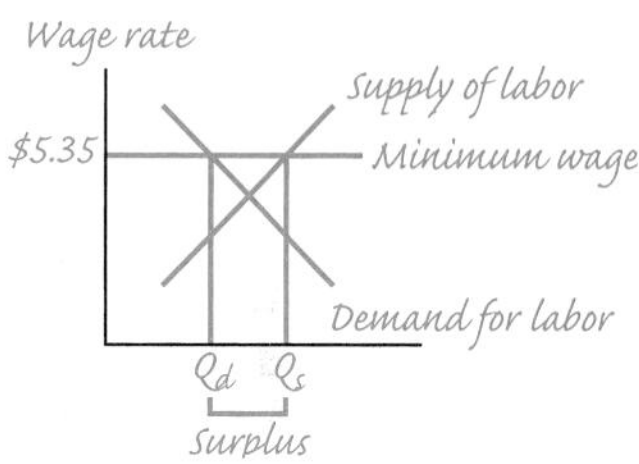

The minimum wage has been around for decades. Do poor people really benefit from legislated increases in the minimum wage? If the legal minimum is no higher than what employers are already paying, it has no effect. It will have an impact only if some covered employers are paying less than the legal minimum. But won't these employers lay some workers off if they're compelled to pay a higher wage, or at least not replace workers who quit?

"They wouldn't have to" isn't a good answer. It's a common answer, because so many people believe that employers pay wages "out of profits" and can therefore refrain from laying workers off when wage rates rise, as long as profits are adequate to cover the increased wages. This seems to imply that the quantity of labor services demanded is a constant, dictated perhaps by technology, so that the only options before employers are either to pay the higher wage rates or to close down the operation. But the demand for labor services is not perfectly inelastic and will at times be highly elastic, because employers can almost always find substitutes, within some range, for labor services of any particular type.

Most voters seem to reason about the minimum wage as if both the number of unskilled persons willing to work and the number of unskilled workers that employers want to hire are constants. Below some low minimum wage ($4 an hour?), no one will be willing to work. Above some maximum ($8 or $9 an hour?), employers who rely on unskilled labor will have to close their doors. Between these limits, the demand curve for unskilled labor is completely inelastic. If all this were true, whoever had the most bargaining power would determine the wage for unskilled labor, and one might reasonably ask why that power should be left in the hands of employers. Why not let the law step in and decree a minimum so that employers are compelled to pay at least a living wage?

Supply and demand!

The traditional (some would say notorious) hostility of most economists to a high legal minimum wage is rooted in their conviction that supply curves slope upward to the right and demand curves slope downward. The number of unskilled persons willing to supply their labor services is not a constant but *increases* when the wage rate rises, so more people will be competing for the available jobs when the prevailing wage is higher. And at higher wages, employers of unskilled workers will find all sorts of ways to economize on the help they "need."

Consider what the owners of a fast-food franchise might do if an increase in the legal minimum wage forced them to pay a 25 percent higher hourly wage to the teenagers they employ. It simply is not true that it takes a fixed number of workers to operate the franchise; there are many margins on which adjustments might be made that would reduce the number of employees. One is hours of operation. At a low wage rate, it might be profitable to open during less busy times of the day, but not at a higher wage rate. Another is quality of service. Quick service can be offered at peak times by having surplus employees during slack times; when wage rates rise, economies can be achieved by reducing that surplus and making customers wait a bit longer during peak periods. Of course, that will raise the effective price to customers and so turn some away, but no sensible business firm wants to serve customers regardless of the cost of doing so. There are all sorts of ways to economize on labor of any particular kind, ways that an outsider won't be able to think of. Some of them will be ways to economize that the owners didn't think of either until a rise in their labor costs gives them a strong incentive to think harder and longer.

It's true but largely irrelevant that the present federal legal minimum wage won't provide a weekly income sufficient to support a family at the level to which most Americans are accustomed. For one thing, many wage earners don't have families to support or are not the principal source of support for the families to whose income they contribute. Nearly one-half of those employed at the minimum wage are members of families with incomes above the U.S. average. More crucially, if $200 a week isn't an adequate income, nothing per week is even less adequate. A large increase in the legal minimum wage would produce more income for some, but it would mean less income for a substantial number who could not obtain employment at any significantly higher wage.

It's important to look at the actual numbers when talking about the probable effects of an increase in the legal minimum wage and also at who is exempted. If the minimum is raised to \$5.75 an hour at a time when fast-food franchises are offering \$6.00 to starting employees, and if exemptions are written into the law for agricultural workers, employees who receive income from tips, and trainees, the increase would probably have few observable effects. Battles over the minimum wage do sometimes seem to be mostly opportunities for people with different political views to call each other insulting names.

Who Pays the Tax?

What effects can we predict from higher taxes on cigarettes? Here the elasticity of demand for cigarettes is the crucial consideration. Most studies show that the demand is quite inelastic in the current price range, so higher taxes will do more to raise revenue for the taxing authority than they will do to improve Americans' health. But as ever-higher taxes continue to raise the price of cigarettes, total expenditure on them becomes a larger item in the budgets of smokers, who are therefore likely to become more sensitive to further price increases. At some high enough level of taxation, the demand is almost certain to become quite price sensitive and therefore elastic. When that happens, further tax increases will reduce the revenue from the tax. The twin goals of deterring smoking and raising revenue by boosting cigarette taxes are not fully compatible.

Are there any general principles that will enable us to predict how taxes on the purchase or sale of a good will affect its price? Does it matter whether the government requires the supplier or the demander to remit the tax? Figure 6–3 gives you additional practice in working with demand and supply graphs while presenting the basic logic of tax incidence, or who actually pays the tax. Economists like to use agricultural commodities in presenting such analyses because there are typically so many different demanders and suppliers that strategic calculations don't muddy the picture. (We'll get into strategic calculations and all that beginning with Chapter 9.) Figure 6–3 presents a demand curve and a supply curve for soybean oil. The market-clearing price, as you can see, is 20 cents per pound. Then the government levies a tax on all soybean oil sold, requiring sellers to remit 5 cents for each pound they sell. What will subsequently happen to the price?

Step one is to show the effect of the tax on the supply curve. Since the marginal opportunity cost of selling soybean oil is now 5 cents higher, we shift the supply curve up vertically by 5 cents all along its length. Where will this new supply curve intersect the demand curve? Because the quantities demanded and supplied will now be equal at a price of 24 cents per pound, this will become the new market-clearing price. The quantity bought and sold will fall from 4.0 to 3.5 billion pounds per time period.

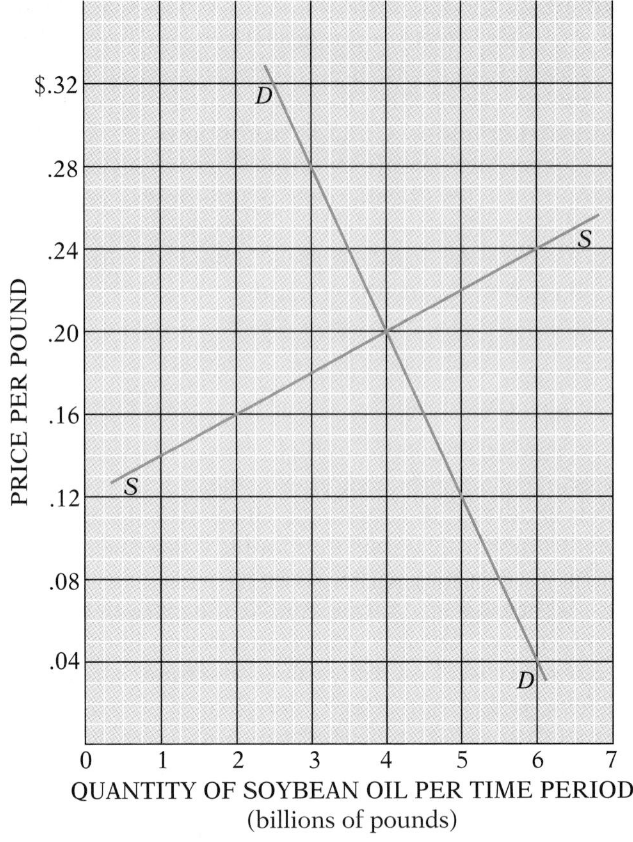

Figure 6–3 **Supply and demand for soybean oil**

So who will pay the tax? Demanders will now be paying 24 cents where they previously paid only 20 cents, and suppliers will receive a net price of 19 cents instead of the pretax 20 cents. So demanders will pay 80 percent of the tax and suppliers the remaining 20 percent, despite the fact that the tax was levied on the suppliers.

For administrative reasons, sales taxes are almost always imposed on suppliers. Tax payment and collection would be a far more costly matter in practice and tax evasion would be much more common if the government relied on demanders to pay sales taxes. Just for practice, however, we'll take a look at what would have happened had the government required the purchasers of soybean oil to pay the tax of 5 cents per pound.

We would now show the effect of the tax as a downward vertical shift of the demand curve. Think about why this is so. The demand curve shows the quantities demanders plan to purchase at various prices. If the tax requires them to pay 5 cents more per pound, they will want to purchase any given quantity only at a price 5 cents lower than they were willing to pay before the tax. So the demand curve moves down by 5 cents at every quantity.

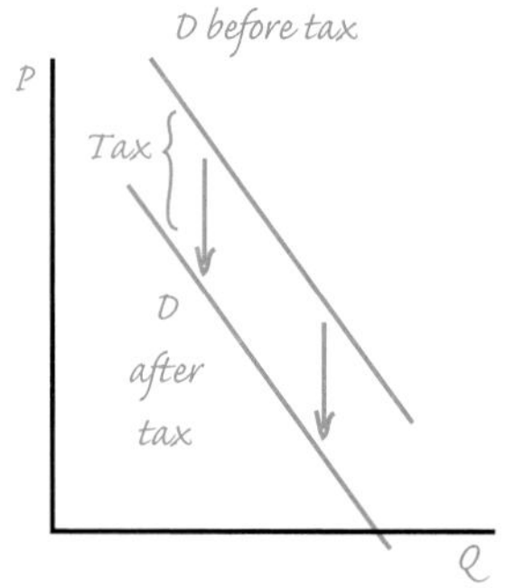

The new, tax-adjusted demand curve intersects the supply curve at a price of 19 cents. This will therefore be the new market-clearing price. Suppliers will be paid 19 cents per pound, just as they were when they had to remit the tax, and demanders will pay 24 cents per pound—19 cents to the suppliers and 5 cents to the tax collector for each pound purchased. Again demanders will pay 80 percent of the tax and suppliers will pay the remaining 20 percent.

Why did the incidence of the tax turn out to be 80 versus 20 percent? The relative elasticities of demand and supply determined the outcome. Between the quantities of 3.5 billion and 4.0 billion, the price elasticity of demand is 0.73, a relatively inelastic demand, whereas the price elasticity of supply is 2.6, a relatively elastic supply. The less elastic or responsive buyers or sellers are to the price change induced by a tax, the more of that tax they will naturally have to pay.

You might want to ask yourself, after working through all of this, who ultimately pays the taxes that the federal and state governments levy on the profits of corporations. If you can use this analysis of tax incidence to come up with a clear and persuasive answer to that question, you know more than the authors of the textbook. It's as impossible to make a corporation pay a tax as it is to make a package of cigarettes or a barrel of soybean oil pay a tax. *Taxes are paid by people*. Which of them finally pays the taxes levied on corporate profits? Do the taxes raise the prices of the goods the corporations sell? Do they lower the wages of the people the corporations hire? Do they reduce the incomes of the people who own the corporations? The transactions that finally produce corporate profits are so many and so diverse that no one really has a good idea of who ultimately pays the taxes on corporate profits. That could be seen as a good reason to abolish the tax or as a good political reason to retain it.

Any particular tax, whether imposed on sellers or buyers of a good or service, drives a wedge into the supply and demand process. Regardless of who must remit the tax, a taxed activity reduces *both* the sellers' and buyers' abilities to engage in that activity, to enjoy further opportunities for mutually beneficial exchange. That is one reason why there's a tax on cigarettes and alcohol, of course. But sales taxes on groceries, toiletries, books and magazines, clothing, and innumerable other goods have the same effect.

High-Priced Sports, Low-Priced Poetry: Who's to Blame?

When the owners of professional football teams announce in the summer that ticket prices will be raised in the fall, they like to blame the increase on rising costs, and especially on the higher wages that must be paid to the players. Are they telling us the truth? Not altogether. Why do the players receive such high wages? It can't be that their work is so dangerous and grueling, because it was just as dangerous and grueling in the days when players received only a few thousand dollars for the season. It's the demand, the willingness of many people to pay high prices to watch, that has made football players such valuable resources. The more ardently professional football fans yearn for opportunities to view their heroes in the flesh, the more money they will find themselves paying for tickets to the games. Soccer players in the United States receive far less, not because they work less hard or because "soccer costs less," but because soccer isn't that popular in the United States. There's nowhere near the same demand.

No wonder that the Cubs organization might announce that it will have to increase ticket prices after striking a new multimillion-dollar contract with Sammy Sosa. The owners might point the finger at Sosa, but Sosa brings many, many fans into the ballpark. *It's the fans' willingness to pay* to see Sosa—reflected by the strong if not growing demand for Cubs tickets—that allows, and offers the incentive for, owners to bid up the wages and therefore retain players like Sosa. Economists seem more willing to point the finger at the true source of the cost increase.

Most poets aren't rich. They barely get by. Are ticket prices so low because the cost of producing a poetry reading is low, or because the demand for poetry reading is low? The latter. Maya Angelou, on the other hand, is a rich poet. She often fills the house across college campuses and in other venues, earning several thousand dollars for a single appearance. Join your college platform personalities committee and see for yourself. Her fees are stiff. So are the ticket prices. If you conclude that her high fees *cause* high ticket prices, you've erred in the economic way of thinking. The *high demand* for Maya Angelou appearances allows for the high ticket prices. It is a *much more scarce* good than, say, a Peter Boettke poetry reading ever will be (that's emphatically not his comparative advantage!), and this translates into the high fee that Maya Angelou can capture.

Supply and demand.

Do Costs Determine Prices?

The last set of examples actually points toward an important and altogether misunderstood topic, worthy of further consideration.

When sellers announce a price increase to the public, they like to say that the increase was compelled by rising costs. The business press publishes frequent announcements of this kind, and it's rare indeed when the announcement fails to include an expression of deep regret that higher *costs* have made it necessary to raise prices. Probably no sellers in history have ever announced that they were raising their prices because of

"Higher pork prices have forced us to raise our sandwich prices. Sorry."

increases in *demand* for their product—they resist pointing their finger at their customers. It's not good business!

So in our everyday experience we hear and see all around us the claim that higher costs lead to higher prices. But *costs always depend not only on supply but on demand, too*. Economists have been rightly skeptical of the "commonsense" wisdom for a long time. It's not good economics! Consider Kenneth Boulding's insight over five decades ago:

> There is no law which says that because a commodity has cost $40 per ton its price must be $40 per ton. If a man builds a house at the South Pole at a cost of a million dollars, the mere fact that it cost a million dollars would not enable him to receive that much for it. But there is, nevertheless, a close relationship between costs of production and price. The price of a commodity depends on its demand and supply curves, and the position of its supply curve depends on its costs of production.

By "law" Boulding means, of course, a universal economic law or principle, rather than a legal rule. Noneconomists seem to believe that higher prices are universally explained by higher costs of production. It just isn't so. Let's back up Boulding's example with another simple one; then we'll continue on to somewhat more complex examples.

The Dropouts Release Their First CD

The Dropouts are a hypothetical punk band. The Dropouts paid $20,000 for their studio recording time and another $2,000 for copying and packaging their first 1,000 CDs. With a boxload of fresh CDs in hand, they discuss how much to charge.

Spike is the first to speak up. "Twenty-two thousand divided by one thousand equals twenty dollars. We should charge twenty dollars—we're not in it for the *money* anyways," he confidently reports.

Needle corrects him. "Twenty-two thousand divided by one thousand is twenty-one thousand dollars. I mean, *twenty-two* dollars."

Shaft asks, "But what about the cost of our instruments and equipment? We gotta add that, too."

"But those are, uh, sunk costs, man. We bought those instruments five years ago," Needle retorts. The others are unsure where *that* came from.

After quite some time they all agree to go with Needle's suggestion and charge $22 per CD. They hit the road and in between sets try to sell their CDs for $22 apiece. But in a market where CDs normally sell for, say, $15 each, who's willing to pay an extra seven bucks for *this* band? A couple of parents, a brother, three cousins, a few drunks at the shows. The Dropouts are left holding 988 CDs.

Another lesson on sunk cost!

In fact, the band is worthy of its name—the members will drop out of the business if they continue this line of reasoning. They thought the cost of production determines the price they can charge. They weren't thinking at all about the *demand*—people's willingness to pay! Moreover, they weren't even looking at the appropriate costs. Needle was right—the costs of the instruments were sunk (outside the portion that could be recovered if they sold their equipment). *But so, too, were the costs of the studio time, copying, and packaging of the CDs once the shipment was in their hands.* Better now to charge $8, $6, or even perhaps $2 than maintain the $22 price and sell nothing. Like our examples back in Chapter 4, chalk the whole experience up once again as a lesson in life.

"There's Gold in Them Thar Hills!" So What?

One of the authors lives less than 20 miles from the Ropes gold mine. It had operated a century ago and also for a brief period during the 1980s. Today it is shut down. It's not because the mine ran out of gold. Everybody in the area *knows* there's gold in that mine. So why did the owners voluntarily shut it down? Because the market price of gold dictated it. And market prices are established by supply *and* demand processes. Suppose, if somebody decides to reopen, the cost of mining would be $600 per ounce. Owners of the mine can't, however, insist on $600 per ounce when today's price of gold is about $400 an ounce. They might claim they *deserve* it after all their hard and dangerous work, but their gold would be no different from anybody else's. Were the overall demand for gold to surge considerably in the future, driving gold prices back up and beyond the highs of the 1980s, perhaps someday the Ropes Mine will be reopened. But with the foreseeable low market price for gold, economizers look elsewhere for other potentially profitable ventures. The Ropes is simply too costly to reopen and maintain.

Monetary calculation: opening the mine is not expected to be profitable.

Even Butchers Don't Have the Guts

Suppose there is a sudden and unexpected increase in the demand for beef. Although it is occurring throughout the country, any single butcher will observe an increase only in his *own* sales. His beef products will sell out more rapidly than expected, and he'd begin to dip into his inventories to satisfy his customers. The butcher's inventories are a mere cushion for transient changes in demand. As his inventories become depleted, he'll simply phone other middlemen—the meatpackers and distributors—and increase his order of beef. But because customer demand has increased in the *overall* market, not only he but thousands of other butchers will also be placing larger-than-expected beef orders. That, of course,

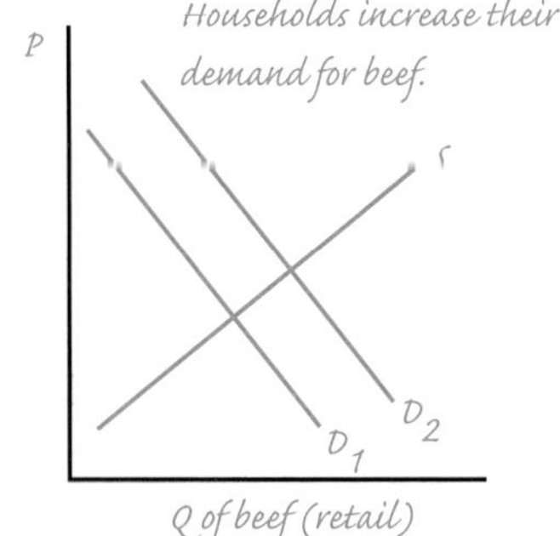

puts a strain on the meatpackers' inventories. Meatpackers, in turn, will try to order more cattle for slaughter.

And there's the binding constraint. We expect the supply of *final* beef products to be relatively elastic—responsive to small changes in price. A butcher can chop more or less beef at will. But new cattle can't be raised overnight; the supply of cattle is *inelastic* in the short run. The increased demand for cattle will therefore lead to competition among meatpackers, who must bid up the market price of cattle. The packers will consequently inform the butchers that they were able to obtain beef, but only at the higher cost. The butcher who wishes to obtain more beef will therefore have to pay the higher price.

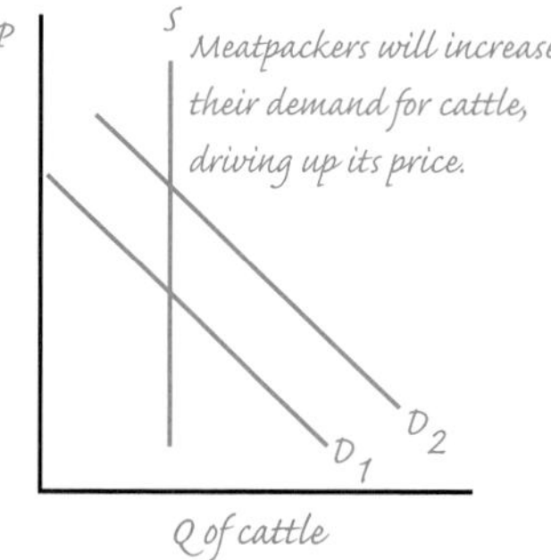

What will the butcher do? To him, the cost of beef has risen. He will charge his customers a higher price for his beef products, all the time apologizing, "They raised my cost, so unfortunately I have to charge you a higher price." Of course, the "they" in this case is not really the meatpackers. Who was ultimately responsible for those higher costs? The people on the other side of the butcher's counter—the customers.

Why Does It Cost So Much to Change Bedpans?

Why are hospitalization costs forever on the increase? Under a system in which patients' payments for medical service are exactly the same whether they enter the hospital or receive only outpatient care, patients are much more likely to enter the hospital. That's a direct invitation to people to increase the demand for scarce hospital services, and it quite predictably produces a rising level of room charges. The care is usually better in the hospital than outside it, and physicians can more easily monitor patients' progress in the hospital. On top of that, insurance often covers the full cost of hospital care but pays only a part of outpatient care.

Hospital administration also demonstrates that sunk costs do have their uses. Suppose a particular hospital adds a 200-bed wing and purchases a lot of sophisticated new laboratory equipment. Once these steps have been taken, the costs associated with them are sunk costs. But that doesn't mean they can't be useful to the hospital's administrators. If the government and private insurance companies have agreed to make payments to the hospital based on the hospital's cost of providing service to patients, and if the hospital gets to decide what counts as cost, every dollar of those sunk costs will be used. The sunk costs will be "spread over" each patient, according to whatever formula enables the hospital to recover them as quickly as possible without unduly antagonizing those who must pay.

Cost *to whom?* Benefit *to whom?* That's always the best way to pose the question of costs and benefits if you want to find out why some policy is being followed. If the benefits from a hospital's ownership of all the most modern equipment accrue largely to its medical staff, if the cost of not pleasing the medical staff falls primarily on the hospital's administrators, and if the cost of acquiring that equipment is borne entirely and uncomplainingly by government, insurance companies, or philanthropists, then hospital administrators will purchase expensive equipment even if it is rarely used—and the cost of hospital-care services will soar.

Employers who pay the premiums have begun in recent years to put pressure on insurers to control costs, and insurers have responded by putting pressure on physicians to economize in their provision of medical care. Insurers have also experimented with paying hospitals a fixed fee for particular services rather than just reimbursing the hospitals for whatever costs they claim to have incurred. While this gives the providers of medical care incentives to economize, their efforts to economize sometimes upset patients. The problem of guaranteeing adequate health care to everyone without inflating costs to an intolerable extent will be with us for a long time to come. The beginning of wisdom in this area is the recognition that *demand affects costs and that some method of rationing medical-care services will unavoidably be used because, at a zero out-of-pocket cost to patients, the quantity demanded is far greater than any quantity that is likely to be supplied.*

More, Please, Since It's Free

Recall our urban traffic example from Chapter 1. After using that example several times to illustrate social cooperation, we pointed out something you already knew: Urban traffic is not always a smoothly coordinated process. Traffic congestion now rates with high crime rates and poor schools in the average American's list of serious social problems, problems that government ought to do something to correct. Why have urban roadways become increasingly congested over the past few decades? A common answer is the population increase. But the larger population *also* uses movie theaters, butcher shops, private tennis courts, and paintball facilities. Why aren't *those* institutions also congested?

Congestion is another word for *shortage.* We can have a shortage of any good we choose if we keep the price low enough. Those who want more roadways built to end traffic congestion are saying that we should supply as much road space as people want to use at a zero price. That's close to absurd. The marginal cost of adding roadways is not zero, and in urban areas it is quite high. Why should we incur large additional costs for the sake of small additional benefits? The benefits are not small, you say? But how can we tell without using the market? The willingness of customers to pay tells private producers what costs are worth incurring for the sake of satisfying consumer demand. The willingness of motorists to rant and rave about congestion tells legislators next

Traffic congestion = a shortage of roadways. We can experience a shortage of anything if we keep the price of using it low enough.

to nothing about what costs are worth incurring to provide more urban and suburban roadways.

The question is whether urban motorists value the elimination of congestion highly enough to pay the money it would take to eliminate it. It is certain that they do *not* if we're thinking about building enough roadways to handle all the driving people want to do when the money price of using the roadways is zero. But if we decided to test motorists' willingness to pay by charging tolls, we would quickly discover that the amount of road and street space that Americans "need and want" is far less than they've been proclaiming. The quantity demanded would decrease as the price rose. People would use their cars only when good substitutes were not available, thereby freeing up the roadways for one another. They might all be better off (even though they would grumble about paying tolls) because they would all be keeping the roadways open for highly valued uses by not cluttering them with uses that have a low marginal value.

As long as government owns the roadways and, in response to political pressure, makes them available for use at a zero price, we'll have congestion. That congestion won't disappear if we build new subways and light rail systems. The best evidence is the fact that they have not done so anywhere they've been tried. Traffic expands to congest the urban roadways built to eliminate the congestion, and public transportation does not essentially change that picture. As long, that is, as we continue to give away scarce urban street space for nothing.

Costs and Ownership

Property rights and incentives.

Property rights matter. Everyone who has been in the armed forces knows horror stories about the inefficient ways the military makes use of its personnel. A highly skilled accountant is put to work painting barracks, and the commissary books are kept by someone who counts on his fingers. The stories are probably exaggerated—somewhat. Nonetheless, we have grounds for predicting that personnel will tend to be used in such wasteful ways in the military more often than in civilian life. Why? Because, in civilian life, those who employ people are usually compelled to pay them their opportunity cost. When you have to pay accountants the wages of accountants, you don't have them paint barracks—at least not if you're an employer with regard for the profitability of your enterprise. On the other hand, what is the cost to a sergeant of assigning a highly skilled recruit to a task that requires no skill at all? If the sergeant happens to resent the recruit for his air of superiority, real or imagined, then transferring him to a job more suited to his abilities might actually entail the sacrifice of a valuable opportunity for the sergeant—the opportunity to humiliate someone he dislikes. Everyone economizes, but not everyone shares the same objectives.

Resources tend to be employed thoughtlessly and carelessly when users do not themselves have to pay the full opportunity cost or the value of the resources in their next-best use. (If you believe "thoughtlessly and carelessly" is too strong, would you settle for "differently"?) Users are most often compelled to pay the opportunity cost of resources when those resources are clearly and definitely owned by someone. A man who is drafted does not "own his own labor," because the law has deprived him of the power to decide where and for whom and on what terms he will work. And so he can't insist on receiving his opportunity cost when Uncle Sam beckons—as he can when Home Depot wants his services. The point also applies, of course, to nonhuman resources. If no one owns a resource, there is no one to insist that potential users of the resource pay the value of the opportunities sacrificed by their use. The resource will consequently tend to be underpriced. And underpriced resources tend to be used with little care or thought for the consequences.

All of this is fully applicable to a socialist society in which resources are allocated by government planners. To economic planners in the former Soviet Union, the cost of building a railway from Lubny to Mirgorod was the value of whatever could otherwise have been done with the resources. But if government officials have the power to obtain valuable resources without having to bid for them, how will they discover the value of the resources in alternative uses? Recall the remarkable workers who could install spokes in bicycle wheels while standing on their heads and whistling "Dixie." In the absence of circus owners willing to bid for their services, how would central planners ever find out that they were too valuable to be assigned to bicycle production?

Lack of monetary calculation.

A distinguishing characteristic of different economic systems is the way in which they assign costs to alternative actions. Where resources are privately owned, competing bids and offers generate prices that approximate opportunity costs to resource owners. Where resources are not clearly owned by anyone, this process cannot operate. What takes its place? Who determines the relative value of this railway line and that one, or of using steel for railroad tracks versus using it to build trucks, or of improving transportation versus improving the quality of what is transported, or of more and better consumer goods versus additional leisure? In the absence of the information that the demand and supply process creates, the economic planners are almost compelled to impose their own private and arbitrary evaluations on the alternatives before them.

Some method of assigning realistic indexes of value to alternative opportunities, marginal benefits as well as marginal costs, must be used in any economic system if its decision makers are not to operate blindly. Supply and demand, or the market process of competing bids and offers, creates such indexes by placing price tags on available resources. Wherever the rules of the game do not clearly assign to particular persons rights to control and exchange specific resources, the supply and demand process will not generate realistic indexes of scarcity to guide allocation and coordinate activity.

An Appendix: FRAMING ECONOMIC QUESTIONS CORRECTLY

Here's a classic brainteaser for you to consider. Three guys go to a motel and get a room. The total charge is $30, and each guy pays $10. After they go to their room, the desk clerk realizes he overcharged them. He forgot about the special rate of $25 tonight. The clerk can't leave his desk, so he contacts the maid, gives her five $1 bills, and asks her to go to the room and reimburse the three guys. On her way, the maid wonders how she can divide $5 among three people. She decides, since they aren't aware of the overcharge anyway, to give them $3 back and secretly pocket the remaining $2. No one will be any the wiser.

Now for the brainteaser: Each guy paid, in effect, $9: 3 times 9 equals 27. And the maid pocketed $2, for a total of $29. But the three guys originally paid $30, not $29. *Where did the other dollar go?*

Close your book. Don't read any further until you've tried to figure out the answer! If you can't figure it out after 15 or 20 minutes, reopen the book and continue to read on. (We shall admit here that it took one of the authors about 20 years to come up with the answer!)

Beware of Wrong Questions or Misleading Specifications of the Problem

We know that some teachers say, "There are no wrong questions, only wrong answers." Well, we hate to say it, but those teachers are wrong. The question at the end of the brainteaser is, simply, *the wrong question*. (It's as nonsensical as asking, "What is the weight of the color blue?") It's a question that was intentionally designed to mislead you, because it doesn't originally appear nonsensical at all, given the way the question is framed. And that's what makes this brainteaser so cruel. There is *no* answer to the question "Where did the other dollar go?"

The bill for the room was really $25. The three guys didn't realize that. They *overpaid* by $5. They did eventually receive $3 back from the maid. *Where did the rest of the overpayment go?*

That's the right question. And now you can clearly determine the correct answer. It went into the maid's pocket. It's that simple.

Why mention this brainteaser, which really has nothing to do with economics? Because, whether by ignorance or design, a lot of analysis about everyday economic events is misspecified and thoroughly misleading, not unlike our brainteaser. A large part of the art of the economic way of thinking is the ability to see through the nonsense. We will give you three rather common examples to help you sharpen your skills.

Beware of Data That Appear to Speak for Themselves

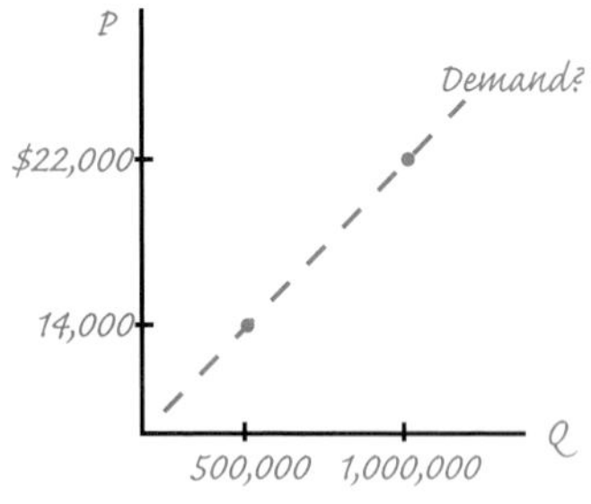

Suppose you were presented with the following data:

	Price of Brand X Minivans	Purchases of Brand X Minivans
1995	$14,000	500,000
2005	$22,000	1,000,000

Let's assume the data for this hypothetical market is true. No tricks there. And with relatively low rates of inflation over the previous 10-year period, the relative price of Brand X minivans has actually increased substantially. Now for our question: What does this data imply about the demand curve for minivans?

Don't be tempted to say that we've asked the wrong question *this* time. It's a perfectly legitimate question. We're interested in your answer.

If you conclude that the demand curve for Brand X minivans is upward-sloping, we accomplished what we hoped to do. Although the question is perfectly legitimate, we framed it with data that provided the *appearance* of an upward-sloping demand curve.

Data never speak for themselves. Indeed, data can't speak at all. As we discussed in Chapter 1, an economist employs a theory in order to interpret and make sense out of the data. Our principles of supply and demand are a big part of our theory. Does the law of demand allow for upward-sloping demand curves? No. (Heck, it doesn't even acknowledge vertical demand curves.) Demand curves always and everywhere slope downward.

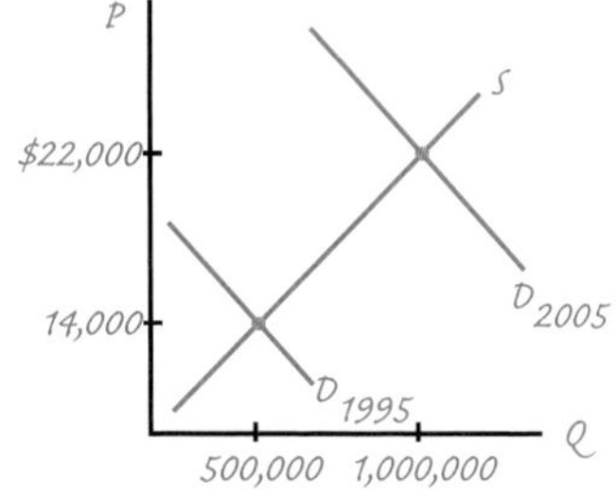

Always keeping that in mind, how might you start to explain the increases in purchases and the higher price of minivans? *The overall demand for Brand X minivans has increased between 1995 and 2005*, thereby explaining at least part of the increase in the market price. (Higher personal incomes, larger families, and big advertising campaigns help explain the increase in demand during that period.) That's a much better start to answering the question, compared to the conclusion that the data imply that the demand curve must slope upward.

Beware of Academic Scribblers and Would-Be Economists

Often, the problem is not limited to letting data somehow speak for themselves. Read almost any newspaper in the country and eventually you will come across a statement as nonsensical as this one:

> The recent freeze continues to play havoc in the orange market. Our growers will experience even worse problems in the

> coming weeks. Some futures traders correctly predicted that the lower supply would increase orange prices. But they left something out. Higher prices will reduce the demand for oranges, which is only more bad news for growers. Falling demand will quickly lead to lower prices. A rather dismal situation for our growers. They have fewer oranges to sell and will soon face falling prices. Markets are unforgiving. A double whammy that most growers would be lucky to survive.

We hope you noticed the reporter's misleading way of making the market appear as an "unforgiving" person. We can forgive him for that. It's the rest of his analysis that is really troubling, because it's framed using familiar economics concepts like supply and demand, and it's written with confidence and conviction.

The fall in supply *does* lead to a rise in price. The rise in price, however, does *not* imply a fall in demand for oranges as the reporter said. Other things remaining constant, it reduces the *quantity demanded*. That reduces the temporary shortage in the orange market. By mistaking a decrease in quantity demanded with a decrease in overall demand, however, the reporter's own predictions are as likely to hold up as a house of cards in a hailstorm. (An especially sharp student, recalling our discussion in Chapter 3, might argue that other things aren't constant. If people expect higher orange prices in the future, overall demand might actually *increase* as households attempt to buy more now before the price rises further.)

Always be on guard for confusions between changes in supply and demand with changes in quantity supplied and quantity demanded. Believe it or not, the more you look for them in newspapers and financial publications, the more you will find them. (We even placed a couple in the questions at the end of the last chapter. If you haven't noticed them, perhaps now is a good time to give them a look.)

The Graphic Case of Growing and Permanent Shortages

Often the most effective way to present an economic argument is by using graphs. We use several throughout this textbook. In this chapter alone we've used graphs to understand and predict the consequences of rent controls and tax incidence, for example. Newspapers rarely employ graphs, but policy institutes and think tanks use them quite often. Consider the one in Figure 6–4.

It appears to be a graph depicting a supply curve and a demand curve for oil from 1950 to 2050. The two curves intersect at the year 2010. It shows that the United States has enjoyed surpluses of oil for over 50 years, but will soon face growing and permanent shortages of oil after 2010. The think tank that produced this graph offers many recommendations on how we must enact

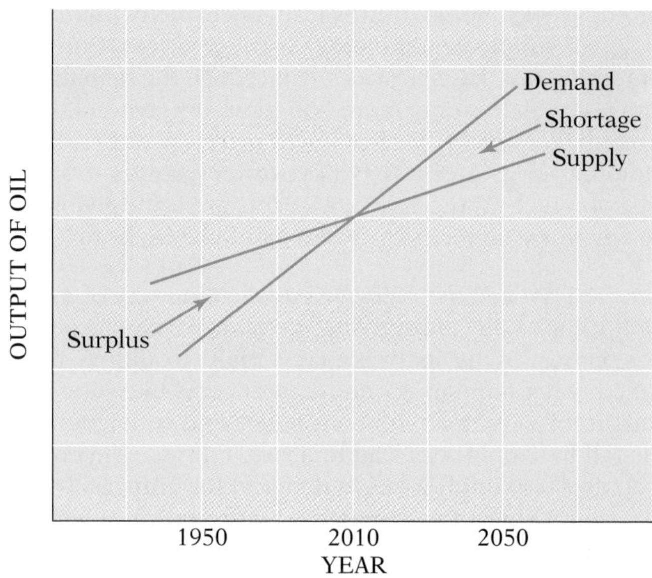

Figure 6–4 **False supply and demand curves for oil**

policies at the federal and international levels to conserve oil and thereby ward off this growing market crisis.

But notice the graph offers no information regarding the *price* of oil. Although the analyst labels one curve "supply" and another "demand," *these really aren't supply and demand curves at all.* We've been tricked! Supply curves illustrate a relationship between price and quantity supplied; demand curves illustrate a relationship between price and quantity demanded. *These* curves illustrate no such relationship.

The "surplus" and "shortage" in the graph are equally misleading. *A surplus is defined as quantity supplied exceeding quantity demanded at a given price*, not "supply" exceeding "demand" at a given point in time. And market prices, of course, would fall during a surplus. *A shortage is defined as quantity demanded exceeding quantity supplied at a given price*, not "demand" exceeding "supply" at a given point in time. And market prices would rise during a shortage.

The graph fails to account for the principles of supply and demand in the market process. It acknowledges no role for the price-adjustment process. Were the demand for oil to increase faster than the supply through time, its market price would increase to reflect its increased marginal value and marginal cost. A growing and permanent shortage wouldn't occur. Instead, the increased price would lead users to *economize* oil.

We continued our theme that the rules of the game affect supply and demand conditions by shaping incentives.

Incentives change, for example, when price controls are implemented into an otherwise free market process. When a price control is effective, it unintentionally generates market discoordination.

A price ceiling is a legally mandated maximum price. Whether a price ceiling is placed on gasoline or on a very different good, such as rent on apartment units, it creates a shortage. Price competition will tend to be substituted for nonprice or nonmonetary competition. The legally mandated lower price does not eliminate or even reduce the scarcity of the good under the control.

A price floor, such as an agricultural price support or a minimum wage on unskilled labor, is a legally mandated minimum price. If effective, the price floor unintentionally generates a surplus. With agricultural commodities, that surplus is typically purchased by the government, representing a transfer of wealth from consumers (in the form of higher prices) and from taxpayers (in the form of a higher tax burden to pay for the government support programs). In the case of the minimum wage, the surplus comes in the form of unemployed workers, who are not bought (like agricultural goods) by the government itself. While those who maintain or find jobs at the minimum wage are better off (compared to what they would have earned at the free market wage), those who are unemployed are simply out of luck.

Prohibition on alcohol and drugs drives market processes underground. Those with a comparative advantage in crime are successors in the competitive process.

Things, places, or organizations don't pay taxes. People do. A taxed activity tends to reduce further opportunities for people to participate in that activity.

There is no economic law that says costs of production determine price. It is wrong to suppose that we can choose between basing prices on costs or letting them be set by demand and supply, because the demand and supply process determines all costs.

By altering relative costs in response to changing conditions, the demand and supply process sets prices that reflect the relative scarcities of goods and indicates how they can be used most economically.

Prices that reflect changing relative scarcities coordinate the activities of people in a commercial society.

When resources are not privately owned or the rules of the game governing their use are unclear, cooperative activity in a commercial society becomes more difficult.

Many different people use economic terms and concepts in ill-informed or misleading ways. Debunking their stories is part of the art of the economist.

QUESTIONS FOR DISCUSSION

1. Do price controls keep the wealthy from obtaining more than the poor? One reason that local governments sometimes impose rent controls is precisely to prevent money prices from rationing scarce residential space. Do the controls succeed in doing this? How has it happened, do you suppose, that most of New York City's rent-controlled apartments are occupied by relatively wealthy people?
2. The rent-control ordinances that cities sometimes enact usually try to restrict rent increases to the amount of the owners' cost increases. Use the analysis of this chapter in thinking about the following questions.
   (a) What is the cost to a landlord of renting an apartment to you for $500 if someone else is willing to pay $600? What is the benefit of renting to you?
   (b) What effect will a rent-control ordinance have on the cost to landlords of letting an apartment unit stand idle or of using it themselves or of allowing relatives to live in it rent-free?
   (c) What concept of cost do you think supporters of rent controls have in mind when they speak of basing maximum rents on landlords' costs?
   (d) Mortgage payments reflect the cost of purchasing a building and hence can usually be included as legitimate costs when landlords operating under a rent-control law request rent increases. What determines the cost to a potential landlord of purchasing an apartment building?
   (e) The costs of purchasing fuel for heating purposes can always be included as legitimate costs when landlords request rent increases. What determines fuel prices?
   (f) Suppose a landlord rents space in a nearby parking lot and makes it available to his tenants. If the demand for parking space in the area rises, he will probably have to pay more to rent parking spaces. Why would a rent-control commission be more likely to grant the landlord's request for a rent increase based on the increased demand for parking than for one based on the increased demand for rental housing itself?
3. The city of Seattle owns a marina and rents space to boat owners. When city officials decided to set rental rates that would yield a 5 percent profit on the estimated cost of replacing the facility, they said this would call for an approximate doubling of mooring fees over the next three years.
   (a) What does the estimated cost of replacing the facility have to do with the cost of renting out mooring space?
   (b) The most important part of the facility is the ocean water that fills Puget Sound, on which the marina was constructed. Should the estimated cost of replacing the ocean be included in the price? (If you argue that it should *not* be included because the ocean is a free gift of nature, go back and check your answer to question 9 at the end of Chapter 4.)
   (c) At the time they announced their intention to raise the fees, city officials estimated the waiting time for a space at 17 to 20 years. What does this have to do with the cost of renting out mooring space?

4. Alcohol is illegal in the dorms at ACME College. Why are students more likely to sneak in a couple bottles of, say, tequila rather than cases of beer, even though most would rather drink beer than tequila?
5. In the United States today the largest denomination note is the $500 bill. The $1,000, $5,000, and $10,000 bills no longer circulate as money. Can you explain why authorities abolished larger-denomination notes as part of their effort to fight organized crime?
6. In the movie *The Godfather*, Vito Corleone (the Godfather himself) had several scarce talents, from organizing his "family" to stabbing and killing others. Why, then, did he tend to specialize exclusively in overseeing the family and employ others to take on the other jobs?
7. What is the relationship between costs and prices? The four parts of this question ask you to analyze some specific cases.
   (a) It costs a lot of money to build and equip a halibut fishing boat. Is that why halibut is so expensive to purchase? What is the relationship between the price of halibut and the cost of a fully equipped halibut fishing boat?
   (b) Do people in poorer neighborhoods pay more for groceries because grocers must charge more to cover the high costs associated with higher crime rates? What is the relationship between the price of groceries and the cost of insurance in high-crime areas?
   (c) Does the U.S. government offer price supports to farmers who grow certain crops because the cost of growing those crops is high? Or is the cost of growing certain crops high because the government offers price supports to farmers?
   (d) Are hand-carved redwood flamingos that sell for $150 valuable because they take so many hours to carve? Or do people spend many hours carving redwood flamingos because they are valuable? Does the value of an object ever depend on what people know about how it was produced? Would a flamingo be more valuable if people thought it had been carved by Pope John XXIII than if they thought you had carved it?
8. A severe hurricane passing through a populated area will blow out a lot of windows and thereby cause a huge increase in demand for the services of window makers. If window makers respond by raising their hourly rates, the cost to homeowners of having their windows repaired will rise. But does a hurricane raise the cost to *window makers* of repairing windows? Or are window makers who raise their rates merely taking unfair advantage of the situation? The following questions might help you think the issue through.
   (a) Why are window makers able to raise their prices?
   (b) Who is likely to put the most pressure on window makers to raise their prices?
   (c) In what ways will window makers experience rising marginal opportunity costs?
   (d) Why might window makers be reluctant to raise their prices?
   (e) What might a window maker do to raise prices without angering people in the community?

(f) In what ways will rising prices make more window maker services available to people in the community?

9. Elderly Instruments is a national mail-order business that sells all kinds of musical instruments, from acoustic and electric guitars to banjos and mandolins. On the inside page of its catalog is written: "We take pride in providing you with unusual and hard-to-find musical merchandise. But because of its specialized nature—much of it handmade and in limited supply—the price and availability of items in this catalog are subject to change without notice. We will raise our prices to you only if the price we pay has gone up." Elderly offers a line of high-quality Gibson mandolins, cherished by bluegrass players throughout the country. Gibson employs a small team of very specialized and talented craftsmen to produce its top-of-the-line models. Suppose the recent rise in the popularity of bluegrass music creates an unexpected increase in the demand for these Gibson mandolins at Elderly and at music shops across the United States. Can you explain the supply and demand processes at work that will eventually lead music shops such as Elderly to say, "Sorry, the costs of Gibson mandolins has increased. We regret that we are forced to raise our price"?

10. Your grandmother heard you were studying economics and decided to make use of your knowledge. She is selling her house and wants to know what price to ask for her well-kept house in a growing neighborhood. You need more information: What did it cost her? She says it cost $15,000 forty years ago. With these givens, advise her on her asking price.

11. Daniel Kahneman, Jack L. Knetsch, and Richard Thaler have done research on the notions of fairness that people apply to market transactions. One of their articles, titled "Fairness as a Constraint on Profit Seeking: Entitlements in the Market," reports the results of a public opinion survey designed to determine the rules of fairness people use in evaluating actions by business firms. Here is one hypothetical situation that was described in the survey:

> A grocery store has several months' supply of peanut butter in stock, which it has on the shelves and in the storeroom. The owner hears that the wholesale price of peanut butter has increased and immediately raises the price on the current stock of peanut butter.

Of the 147 respondents surveyed, only 21 percent thought this was acceptable behavior while 79 percent deemed it unfair.

(a) The wholesale price of peanut butter in stock is a sunk cost. Is it relevant to pricing decisions for a seller who shares the majority view on fairness in pricing?

(b) How could it be relevant to a seller who personally holds the minority view but also knows that his customers will find out what he has done if he raises the price on "old" stock?

(c) The economic way of thinking does not usually distinguish a sum of money *paid out* from a sum of money *not received*: Both are equally costs. The majority of the public apparently does distinguish, because it holds that sellers may raise their prices to cover higher wholesale cost payments but may not do so merely because consumers are willing to pay the higher prices. Can you defend the popular distinction, or do you think it is simply the product of failure to understand what's going on?

12. Physicians who have borrowed extensively to finance their medical educations often enter practice with large debts that they must begin repaying.

    (a) What differences would you expect to observe in the fees set by three young physicians just setting up practice if one financed his education by borrowing and must now make payments of $9,600 per year for 15 years, another had her entire education paid for by her parents, and the third went all the way through on government-provided scholarships and grants?
    (b) Evaluate the argument, put forward by the business manager of a medical school, that the government could lower our doctor bills by paying for the entire education of physicians, thus making it unnecessary for physicians to recover the costs of their education (plus interest) by raising their fees.
    (c) The author of the preceding argument asserted that "you and I" will have to cover the cost of the doctors' loan repayments in our fees because these payments "are a legitimate cost of doing business." What difference does it make whether particular payments are or are not "a legitimate cost of doing business"? Suppose all physicians practicing in an area had to pay $5,000 a year to the local crime syndicate as protection money. Would these payments be "a legitimate cost of doing business"? Would they affect doctors' fees?

13. Is it possible to provide health care without rationing? In 1948 every household in Britain received a leaflet stating that the new National Health Service would "provide you with all medical, dental and nursing care. Everyone—rich or poor, man, woman, or child—can use it or any part of it. There are no charges, except for a few special items."

    (a) This pioneering system of health-care provision, which celebrated its fiftieth anniversary in 1998, was based on the assumption that the quantity of health care that would be demanded at a zero price is finite. This assumption has been disproved in Britain and all the countries that subsequently initiated similar systems and found themselves confronted by shortages of health-care services. How would a shortage show itself in such a situation?
    (b) If health care is made available to everyone at a zero money price, and at this price the quantity demanded exceeds the quantity supplied, how will health care be rationed?
    (c) What system of rationing would you recommend?

14. The textbook claims that when people do not have to pay anything to use valuable resources, such as urban roadway space, they will continue using them until their value diminishes to zero. That often strikes people who have not yet become thoroughly familiar with the marginal way of

thinking as wrong. Why would people choose to act in a way that caused the value of an activity—the value to themselves—to become zero? Their confusion arises from failure to realize that it is *marginal* value that diminishes to zero and that this is very different from *total* or *average* value. Suppose you love chocolate chip cookies. It's 10 o'clock in the morning, you're quite hungry, and someone comes by selling freshly baked chocolate chip cookies. You peer into your psyche and discover your demand for chocolate chip cookies. You won't pay more than $3 for a cookie, and you don't want to eat more than four under any circumstances. (We rule out the possibility of storing them for eating later.) Table 6–1 shows your demand schedule:

Table 6–1

Price	Cookies Demanded per Day
$3.00	1
1.50	2
0.40	3
0.10	4
0.00	4

(a) How many will you eat per day if the price is zero?
(b) How much total value, measured in dollars per day, will you thereby obtain?
(c) What will be the average value of the cookies to you, measured in dollars per cookie?
(d) What will be the marginal value of cookies to you, measured in dollars per cookie, when they're free to you?

15. Figure 6–5 portrays a supply curve of physicians' services and a demand curve for those services. The market-clearing fee is $30.
    (a) To what position will the demand curve shift if the government agrees to pay the entire fee charged by physicians? What will consequently happen to the market-clearing price? (*Hint*: What quantity will people demand at a zero price?)
    (b) What will happen to the demand curve and to the market-clearing price if the government commits itself to pay one-half of physicians' fees? (*Hint*: When the fee *charged* is $30, what is the fee *paid* by consumers? What quantity will they want to purchase at this price?)
    (c) What will be the market-clearing price if the government pays 80 percent of the fee charged by physicians?
16. Mastering the economic way of thinking means learning to reason in terms of supply and demand. Here are additional questions on which you can practice. Your answers are less important than the reasoning with which you arrive at those answers. You should probably begin in each case by sketching a small supply and demand graph. Then ask yourself whether the event described would affect the supply curve or the demand curve, in which direction the curve would move, and what

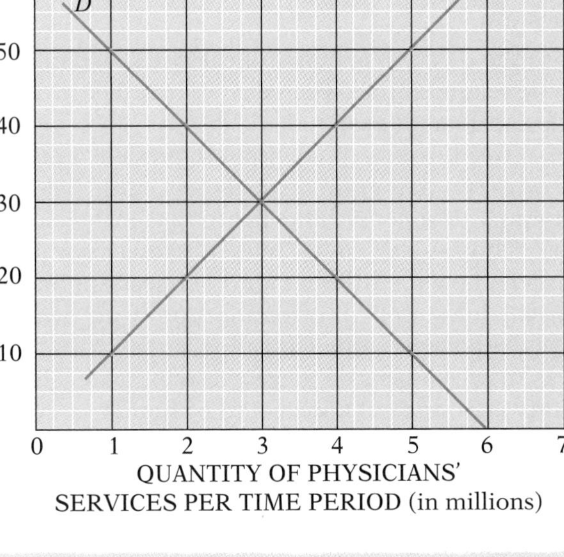

Figure 6–5 **Demand and supply for physicians' services**

effect that would have on the price and the quantity exchanged. Don't be content merely to conclude that the price will rise or the price will fall. Would you expect a large or a small change in price or in the quantity exchanged? You will usually have to supply some information from your own experience. Keep in mind that the answer will often depend on the length of time you are allowing for adjustments to occur. Are you predicting a very short-run effect or are you thinking about the long-run effect?

(a) Suppose scientists discover that eating soybeans prevents cancer and heart disease.
   (i) What effect would you predict on the price of soybeans?
   (ii) What effect would you predict on the price of *feed corn* (which can usually be grown on land suitable for growing soybeans)?

(b) What effect would you expect each of the following to have (or to *have* had) on the market for domestically grown cotton?
   (i) Nylon is invented.
   (ii) The cotton gin is invented.
   (iii) The boll weevil becomes extinct.
   (iv) Foreign cotton growers bring in an exceptionally large harvest.

(c) Suppose that all of the states adopt a serious no-fault rule to cover automobile accidents, so that it becomes impossible to sue for damages after an accident.
   (i) What effect would you predict on the cost of hiring a lawyer to draw up a will?

(ii) If only *one state* moves to no-fault, what effect would you predict on the cost of hiring lawyers to draw up wills in *that state?* Would you expect a larger or smaller effect than in the preceding question?

(d) Suppose the dental hygienists of the country persuade everyone to floss at least three times each day. What effect would you predict on the price of dental floss?

(e) If it takes five times as much grain to provide a nourishing diet to people who run that grain through beef cattle before eating it than it takes to provide a nourishing diet to those who eat the grain directly, do those who eat beef cause hunger among poor people in the world?

(f) Here is a somewhat different kind of question, one for which you obviously can't supply information from your own experience. Suppose you discover that consumers are currently purchasing 20 times as many widgets as they were purchasing 10 years ago. Would you expect the price of a widget to be higher or lower today than it was 10 years ago? Under what circumstances would you expect it to be higher? Under what circumstances would you expect it to be lower?

(g) What effect would you predict on the price of rental housing in an area if several major new employers set up operations in the area?

(h) If the city council passes an ordinance requiring all apartment owners in a particularly congested area to provide one off-street parking place for each apartment that they rent out, what effect would you predict on the level of rents in that area and on the number of apartment units being rented?

(i) If the city council did not require provision of parking spaces but simply prohibited all on-street parking on the streets in this congested area, what effect would you predict on the level of rents in the area and on the number of apartment units being rented?

(j) What effect would you predict on the price of gasoline if automobile manufacturers succeeded in doubling the number of miles that drivers can obtain per gallon?

17. Many fight to get the minimum wage increased above $5.35 per hour.

(a) Do you think unskilled workers as a whole—and perhaps even society as a whole—would be better off if the minimum wage were increased to $6.00 per hour?

(b) Protesters of the World Trade Organization carried signs calling for a $10 an hour minimum wage. Would that increase the incomes of the working poor in general?

(c) Why settle for $10 an hour? Suppose instead they insist on a $50 an hour minimum wage? Wouldn't almost everybody be richer?

(d) Unions often call for higher minimum wages, even though unions represent *skilled* workers and therefore do not directly benefit from a minimum-wage increase. Recalling from Chapter 5 how an increase in the price of a substitute good will tend to raise the demand for the good in question, can you make an argument that wages for union members will tend to increase when the minimum wage for unskilled, nonunion labor is increased?

(e) In his book *The State Against Blacks*, economist Walter Williams observes the following:

> Youth unemployment, even during relatively prosperous times, ranges from two to three times that of the general labor force. Black youth unemployment, nationally for more than a decade, had ranged from two to three times the unemployment rate for white youths. In some metropolitan areas it is reported that black youth unemployment exceeds 60 percent!

Why is youth unemployment, and especially black youth unemployment, so high? Williams argues it's a direct effect of minimum-wage legislation. Can you construct the argument?

Profit and Loss

7

"*P*erhaps no term or concept in economic discussion is used with a more bewildering variety of well-established meanings than *profit*." That sentence was written 75 years ago by Frank Knight, a distinguished student of the subject, to introduce an encyclopedia article on profit. The situation has not changed greatly since then.

The most common definition of profit is simply *total revenue minus total cost.* That's almost everyone's intuitive definition of the term and that's how we've used it until now. A synonym would be *net revenue*. When the owner of a business firm has paid all the costs, what is left over is profit, or net revenue. That seems simple and clear enough. So why did Knight find the use of the term bewildering? To understand the concept of profit, it would be worthwhile to briefly consider the meaning of wages, rents, and interest.

Wage, Rent, and Interest: Incomes Established in Advance by Contract

Is anybody confused over the meaning of a market wage? Most of us already know what a wage is—it's the payment to people for their labor service, typically established by a contractual agreement between a firm owner and a labor supplier. Nobody would say a worker's wage is also "profit." The laborer *knows in advance* what the wage will be if he remains on the job. That's the point of the contract. Conversely, the employer will know what must be paid to workers under the current contract. A great deal of uncertainty has been removed by this contractual agreement. (Of course, nothing is certain in the end—the firm might have to lay off people in the future, for example. Or a worker might quit the job for a better prospect elsewhere.)

The same holds true for rents. You and your landlord have reached an agreement, and signed a lease, establishing the terms of trade. The landlord leases you the apartment for a predetermined price, in this case, rent. You've agreed to this monthly obligation. The landlord's rent is just that—rent, not "profit." Again, a great deal of uncertainty has been diminished by the rental contract (but let's face it, nothing is ever certain—you might skip town without paying your last three month's rent as you relocate to your new job).

Wage, rental, and credit contracts reduce uncertainty for workers, leasers, and lenders.

Interest is also established contractually, like a wage or rent. The moneylender's interest return is not "profit." It is a return that is already determined in advance. The credit contract sets the conditions for principal plus interest payments in advance.

Put simply, wage represents the payment to labor, rent represents payment to landlords and others who lease their property, such as tools and machinery, and an interest rate represents payment to lenders of financial capital. Wage, rent, and interest are three important forms of earned *income* in a market economy. Moreover, the wage *rate*, rental *rate*, and interest *rate* represent a *price: a price for labor services, a price for rental property, a price for credit.* Those prices are established by supply and demand conditions in the labor, rental property, and credit markets, as we've seen in earlier chapters.

In this chapter we are more concerned with some historical—and contemporary!—confusion over the meaning of *profit.* We shall clearly define what economists mean by the term *profit* and then discuss the roles that monetary calculation and entrepreneurial profit seeking play in coordinating the plans of buyers and sellers.

Profit: Income That Can Be Positive or Negative

Profit is the fourth form of earned income in a market economy, but it is something very different from wage, rent, or interest income. *Profit* is generally defined as "total revenue minus total cost." It's the *residual*, or the difference, between revenues and costs. It's what's left over once all the relevant costs have been subtracted from the revenues. (Sometimes it is referred to as *net revenue*.) Moreover, profit can be positive or negative. A negative profit is also called a *loss*. Compare that to the other forms of earned income: nominal wages, rents, or interest will not be negative (as long as people live up to their contractual agreements). Profits, however, can be. Unlike the wage earner, who will get paid for labor services, the entrepreneur seeking profits can never be sure that personal effort will in fact be profitable. The entrepreneur may instead be punished with a loss, no matter how hard the effort or how honorable and sincere the commitments made. We will have much to say about the entrepreneur and uncertainty in short order. For now let's concentrate on how profit is measured and calculated.

The search for profit, on the other hand, means accepting greater uncertainty.

Calculating Profit: What Should Be Included in Costs?

Total revenue minus total cost. Seems simple enough so far. But the problems begin with that word *cost*. Recall, in the economic way of thinking, "cost" means the next-best foregone opportunity. We have been using the word *cost* in this way all the way up until now, and we have no intention to change it. Monetary expenses do not capture the total costs of production, at least not from the opportunity-cost perspective. This becomes clearest in the case of owner-operated businesses.

Part of the cost of doing business is the owners' own labor, even when they write no weekly payroll check to themselves. Surely the payroll checks written to hired laborers will be accounted for in the calculations of cost. But the value of the opportunities that the owner sacrifices by operating a business won't appear in the accounting calculation, even though it, too, is clearly a cost. Presumably the small business owner's labor is valued elsewhere by other businesses. The owners sacrifice the next-best job opportunity to be their own boss. If a woman gives up the opportunity to earn a wage of $30,000 a year at ACME Community College to run her own business, that foregone wage does not represent an accounting cost—an expense—but it does represent a cost to her. It might not appear anywhere on her accounting ledger, but it will remain in her mind and influence her choices. She surely knows what sacrifices *she* makes to operate her business.

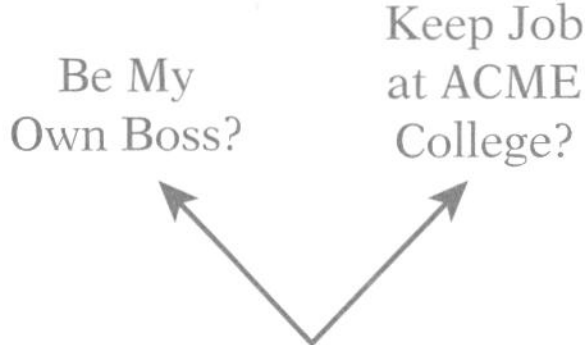

Many people associate profit with capital and think of profit as the income earned by the owner of capital. The term *capital* in economics means *produced goods that are used to produce future goods*. Machinery is the standard example. But the income that the owner of capital earns by allowing property to be used in a business operation is a rent on capital, similar to what you pay when you go to a tool rental shop and borrow a floor sander. As such, it's another cost of production, and hence not profit at all. The fact that the owner of the business happens also to own the capital employed in the business makes no more difference than the fact that the owner of the business happens also to own the labor employed in the business. The income forgone by not using the capital or the labor in its best alternative use is an opportunity cost, and hence it's not profit.

The rental value of machinery is not profit. It's a cost.

Buildings used for productive purposes are just as much capital as the machinery used. And the rent foregone is a real cost of production when the owner of the business owns the building in which it's housed, in the same way that it's a cost of production when the building is leased from someone else.

The rental value of land and buildings is not profit. It's a cost.

So payments for the use of capital are not profit and neither are payments for the use of land or buildings. What about

Payments made to obtain current purchasing power are not profit. They're a cost.

payments for the use of money, or what we commonly call interest? Strictly speaking, we don't pay for the use of money, as we discussed in Chapter 5. When a business firm pays interest, it is paying for the use of purchasing power. A firm might want to substitute the payment of interest for the payment of a rent on capital. It wants to use a particular machine or building, let's say, but can't obtain what it wants on suitable terms, so it decides to buy its own. For that it needs purchasing power. If the owner of the business withdraws the purchasing power from prior savings, the owner foregoes the interest that those savings would otherwise own, incurring a clear opportunity cost. If there are no savings, the owner must borrow to obtain the purchasing power required and pay interest on the amount borrowed. In either case, interest is a cost, and hence not profit.

Comparing Economic Profit and Accounting Profit

The key issue, then, is what shall be included in the total costs of production? Accountants measure the *explicit* costs of production—typically the expenses that are incurred to produce a good or service. In the economic way of thinking, however, the expenses don't capture the *total* costs of production. In addition to the expenses, the notion of economic profit includes the explicit and *implicit* costs of production—the value of *all* the scarce resources used in the production process. *What could I earn elsewhere with the resources I own and commit to my business?* Economic profit takes this into consideration; accounting profit doesn't. Business owners are concerned not only with accounting profits but with economic profits, too.

Let's further consider Ann Trepreneur, the woman who earns $30,000 a year as a secretary. Suppose she also owns a small building that she rents for $6,000 per year, and she has $23,000 in a certificate of deposit that earns 10 percent ($2,300) per year. These payments come from *contracts* that Ann has entered. They represent flows of earned income, which reduce uncertainty in her life.

Now suppose Ann quits her job to become her own boss. She opens up a pizzeria and works full time. She uses her own building and cashes out her $23,000 CD, and also borrows an additional $20,000 (at 10 percent annual interest) for hired labor, equipment purchases and rentals, payments for ingredients, and so on for the first year. There are no guarantees that Ann's pizzeria will prosper. She *has,* however, sacrificed those flows of income. She has become, in part, an entrepreneur who is willing to take the gamble. She wishes to prosper in her new business.

Suppose Ann's total revenues are $85,000 after one year. What is her profit? Well, that depends on what will be included in the "total costs" of her business operation. The following calculation illustrates Ann's *accounting* profit:

Accounting profit = *TR* − *TC* (all explicit costs)
= $85,000 − $45,000 ($43,000 for hired labor, ingredients, equipment, etc., plus $2000 for interest on the loan)
= $40,000

Accounting profit: Total Revenue – Total Explicit Cost

So far so good. But Ann *also* realizes that

- Her own labor is not a free good. She had previously earned $30,000 as a secretary, her "next-best" full-time job opportunity. That's the market wage value of Ann's labor.
- Her own building is not a free good. She had previously earned $6,000 as a landlord on that building. That's the market rental value of the "next-best" opportunity of the building.
- Her own financial capital is not a free good. She had previously earned $2,300 as a simple "capitalist." That's the market interest that she knows can be earned on her own capital.

That is, Ann Trepreneur realizes that her own resources (labor, building, and financial capital) are not free goods. They, too, are scarce—like the other resources Ann employed to make pizzas and run the pizzeria. Ann's *forgone* wage ($30,000), *forgone* rent ($6,000), and *forgone* interest ($2,300) are very real opportunity costs *for her*. These added together ($38,300) represent Ann's *implicit costs*—something that does not necessarily show up on her accounting ledger, because they don't show up as monetary expenses. Nevertheless the implicit costs represent the value of Ann's scarce resources.

The entrepreneur's resources are not free goods. They're scarce!

So then just what is Ann's *economic* profit? Consider the following calculation:

Economic profit = *TR* − *TC* (all explicit *plus* implicit costs)
= $85,000 − ($45,000 + $38,300)
= $85,000 − $83,300
= $1,700

Economic profit: Total Revenue—Total Explicit and Implicit Costs

Notice the difference between the accounting profit and the economic profit. The $1,700 *economic profit* is the return to Ann's *entrepreneurial* skills. It's what's left over *after* Ann has paid the market value of all resources (labor, equipment, ingredients, capital)—*including her own*. It's what Ann enjoys as a profit-seeking, risk-taking entrepreneur. The presence of economic profit might further encourage Ann to continue the entrepreneurial gamble.

Don't get us wrong. Economists do not claim that accountants incorrectly calculate a firm's profits or losses. We *do* claim that the accounting measure does not fully capture (account for!) all the opportunity costs of production. And we *also* claim that business owners—such as Ann—will look not only at their accounting calculations of profit when deciding what to do next with their property rights. Like any other decision maker, business owners will also consider the opportunity costs of their choices as well.

Because there are no guarantees in the pizzeria business, Ann could have suffered an *economic loss*. For example, if she had earned revenues of only $50,000 after the first year (and an accounting profit of $5,000), what is the return on Ann's entrepreneurial skills? In other words, what is her economic profit? (Note that her total costs are still the same.)

$$TR - TC = \$50{,}000 - \$83{,}300 = -\$33{,}300.$$

The expected amount of the residual influences entrepreneurial decisions.

As an entrepreneur, Ann would face a $33,300 economic loss. In this case, she would not enjoy the "reward" of being an entrepreneur. Although Ann would show a $5,000 accounting profit ($50,000 – $45,000), she would have been punished as an entrepreneur. That might encourage Ann to seriously consider revising her plans, *and that's why economists say economic profits (and losses) matter!*

Uncertainty: A Necessary Condition for Profit

Business decisions are influenced by the presence (or absence) of economic profit. The economic profit calculation includes not only a firm's payments to others for commodities and services used—the monetary expenses that show up on the firm's accounting ledger—but also the implicit payments for use of any goods—labor, land, capital, prior savings—that the owner firm itself supplies. When we include all these opportunity costs in our calculations of total costs, there seems to be no reason why any firm would have to earn revenues in excess of costs. Firms could make zero profits and continue in business. They could even be considered successful firms and be able to borrow new funds for expansion—as long as their revenues were adequate to cover all their costs.

A "good deal" that is a "sure thing" won't continue to be a good deal after others learn about it.

In fact, if there were some way for a firm to get into a line of business that *guaranteed* more in revenue than it entailed in cost, wouldn't so many people move into that line of business that competition would reduce the difference between revenue and cost to zero? The certainty of a return greater than this would surely attract new business firms. Their entry would increase output, reduce the price of the product consistently with the law of demand, and thus reduce the gap between total revenue and total cost. The gap might simultaneously be reduced from the other direction as the new entrants increased the demand and raised the cost for the specific resources used in turning out the product. Only when the gap between expected total revenue and expected total cost had disappeared, or when expected profits had been reduced to zero, would there no longer be any incentive for new firms to enter.

In the actual, continually changing, and always uncertain world, it doesn't work that way. People see profits being made in particular lines of business but they aren't sure how to go about cutting themselves in on those profits. In a world of scarce information, the existence of such profits might not even be widely known. And so *profits do exist and continue to exist* without being reduced to zero by competition. But this happens *because of uncertainty*, in the absence of which everything relevant to profit making would be generally known, all opportunities for profit-making fully exploited, and profits everywhere consequently equal to zero.

The same argument applies to *losses.* A firm suffers a loss if its total revenues fall short of its total (opportunity) costs. No one would embark on a business enterprise knowing that the total revenue was going to fall short of the total cost. They go into business hoping, or expecting, profits. But the future is uncertain, events don't always work out as people hope they will, decisions are made and actions taken that prove to be mistakes, and so losses do occur. Nominal wages, rents, or interest will never be negative as long as individuals live up to their contracts and agreements. *An entrepreneur's profit, on the other hand, can indeed be negative, even if all contracts and agreements have been met.*

Because there would be no profits or losses in a world without uncertainty, we conclude that *profit (or loss) is the consequence of uncertainty.* Profit is thus not a payment that has to be made to obtain some resource or another. *Profit is a residual;* it is what's left over out of revenue when all costs have been met; it is the result of predicting the future more accurately than others have predicted it and then acting on that prediction.

The Entrepreneur

The argument of the preceding sections may have left the impression that people make profits simply by forecasting better than others, so that profits are nothing but the consequences of successful speculation. That would be highly misleading. The far more important part of profit making is its active and creative side. People don't just sit around and bet on the outcome of other people's activity. They try—or at least some of them do—to organize things differently. They start up things like pizzerias, hotels, new technology, and Internet commerce sites. Their incentive is the belief that a particular reorganization will return revenues greater than its cost. The term for such people is *entrepreneur.* This is why we called Ann an entrepreneur in the preceding example.

The English equivalent is *undertaker*, a nicely descriptive term whose use we have unfortunately lost by surrendering it completely to undertakers of funerals. Entrepreneurs are people who undertake to reorganize a segment of the social world. What makes them the undertakers or entrepreneurs rather than mere participants is that they accept responsibility for the outcome. They say in effect to all the others whose cooperation is required for their project, "I'll take the profit or loss." Entrepreneurs claim the residual, what is left over after all prior agreements (typically, contracts) have been honored. They choose to put themselves in this position because they think they can "pull it off." They have confidence in their own insight, foresight, and organizational ability. What Adam Smith called a commercial society and what most people rather misleadingly call a capitalist society is also sometimes referred to as an enterprise society. Those who choose to call it by that name are emphasizing the crucial role of the entrepreneur.

The entrepreneur is the residual claimant.

The Entrepreneur as Residual Claimant

A good way to understand the role of the entrepreneur and the function of residual claimancy is by asking, "Who gets to be boss?" How do the many people whose cooperation is essential to the production of particular goods manage to agree on who is in charge of each particular operation? Those are important issues to settle, because the opinions and the interests of people are bound to conflict at many points. Down at the gizmo plant on East Industrial Avenue, Achilles maintains that six rivets are more than enough, while Hector insists that anything fewer than nine means shabby work. Nine rivets would make a sturdier gizmo but also one that's more costly to manufacture. A sturdier gizmo will attract more customers, but a higher price to cover the higher marginal cost will repel some customers. Hector believes that he should be allowed to decide because he has an engineering degree, but Achilles has contempt for college degrees and points to his own years of on-the-job experience. Their disagreement could be a completely honest difference of opinion, but it might also be colored by the fact that Hector is the riveter and hopes for overtime, or that Achilles is the riveter and wants to reduce his workload. Who makes the final decision? More to the point, who decides who gets to make the final decision?

Willingness to be the residual claimant confers the authority to decide.

The basic answer is *the residual claimant*. If you want to be boss, you must become the residual claimant. You do that essentially by purchasing the consent of everyone else on the team. You make a deal with them. "What are your terms?" The entrepreneur promises to meet those terms. That promise must be believed, of course. To persuade others to give up their next-best opportunities and to suppress their misgivings, disagreements, or dislikes and go along with what the entrepreneur decides, the entrepreneur must offer credible guarantees.

Where Does the Buck Stop?

When you were browsing the other day in a clothing store downtown, you saw some attractive sweaters on sale at a very low price, and you bought one that especially caught your eye. When you got it home, however, you found it was just a little too small. So you returned it to the store, only to discover that you had overlooked something. The huge sign right next to the sweaters says, "ALL SALES FINAL. NO REFUNDS, NO EXCHANGES."

The clerk is very sorry, but she can't exchange it or give you a refund. You are quite upset and point out that you spend a lot of money in this store. The clerk is even sorrier, but she just isn't allowed to do it. When you persist and become a little testy, she says, "I'll let you speak to my supervisor."

The supervisor is extremely apologetic, too, but tells you that the prices were set so low because the store wanted to clear these sweaters out; that's why they put up the big sign stating that all sales were final, and it's a store policy to allow no returns on items sold at super-discount prices. You are now quite angry, and when you say that you spend hundreds of dollars in this store every year, the supervisor relents; she says she will allow you to exchange the sweater for a larger one. Unfortunately, there are no larger sweaters left except for two in a ghastly color. The supervisor smiles weakly and says there is simply no way she can give you a refund except by taking it out of her own pocket, because the computer won't allow refunds on super-discount sales. "It's store policy, and I can't do anything about it," she says in a pleading tone.

"It's a *rotten* policy," you respond. "Let me talk to the owner." Why do you want to talk to the owner? Because that is where the buck stops. It doesn't stop with "store policy," because someone *sets* store policies. If this policy is just part of a larger policy, someone set that larger policy. You want the policy altered. That means you have to reach the person ultimately responsible. You want to argue that the few dollars the store will make by refusing you a refund are not worth all the dollars the store will lose by sending you home infuriated. The person with whom you want to argue is the person with an incentive to take account of *all* costs and *all* benefits to the enterprise. That will be the residual claimant.

The residual claimant is the only party with an incentive to take into account everything relevant to costs and revenues.

"Let me talk to the owner" constitutes an appeal from partial perspectives to the overall perspective. You want to speak with the person who has an incentive to consider *everything* relevant to the business, predict *all* future effects, and construct a balance of *overall* gains and losses—*and* who has the authority to *decide*. Only the residual claimant matches that description.

Not-for-Profit Institutions

Residual claimants are crucial actors in any society characterized by extensive specialization and exchange. Institutions that do not have residual claimants do not, by and large, function as effectively as institutions that do. Consider buyers' queues, for example. Standing in line to buy, as we pointed out in Chapter 6, is a deadweight cost, because it's a burden on the buyer that is not also a benefit to the seller. Because that burden is a real cost to the buyer, it reduces the quantity demanded. How many times have you turned away and gone somewhere else because the line was too long? Why, then, doesn't the seller take steps to reduce the length of the line? It might be because the expected marginal cost of shortening the line exceeds the expected marginal revenue to the enterprise. But it also might be because there is no residual claimant on the scene. There is no one with the incentive to estimate all costs and all benefits and the authority to act appropriately.

That is why we *expect* long lines at the post office but not at the grocery store. It's not that no one at the post office cares. Postal employees are probably just as caring or noncaring on average as the checkout people in grocery stores. The difference arises from the fact that policies are set for the grocery store by a residual claimant, someone with an incentive to estimate the costs to the enterprise of long lines and the costs to the enterprise of a reserve supply of checkers and the authority to act as those comparative costs decree. There is no residual claimant in the post office branch or in the postal service as a whole.

Not-for-profit institutions by definition have no residual claimants. That is why they so often behave in such clumsy ways. If you want an example, try the college or university you are attending. Colleges and universities do a lot of "stupid" things because there is no one with the incentive to compare the cost of continuing current policies with the cost of eliminating them *plus* the authority to act appropriately. The word *stupid* has to go in quotation marks because the policies of colleges and universities are not really the product of stupidity. They are the product of social institutions without residual claimants and therefore without intelligent command centers.

A standard example of "stupidity," one familiar to almost everyone who has ever worked in a nonprofit institution, is the rush by each department manager to spend every dime in the budget before the budget period ends. Why not? "If we don't spend it, we'll lose it." A department that ends the budget year with $1,000 still left in the travel account loses an opportunity to send two people on a round-trip junket. The recapture of that money by the institution would make an additional $1,000 available to purchase essential supplies in another department. But the value of the junket to the head of the first department, while small, is still greater than the value *to that manager* of the extra supplies now available to another department in whose welfare the manager of the first department has not the slightest interest.

Who has the incentive and authority in such a case to estimate the relative benefits to the institution as a whole of the junket and the extra supplies and to allocate that $1,000 accordingly? College and university administrators know that waste is occurring, just as do administrators in other nonprofit institutions, including the gigantic institutions of government. But in the absence of a residual claimant, incentives to change these situations do not confront people who have the authority to change them. The buck stops nowhere.

Universities have no residual claimant.

Entrepreneurship and the Market Process

So far we have focused on some simple examples of entrepreneurship, and compared the incentives of the entrepreneur-as-residual-claimant to that of nonprofit business operators. It is now time to discuss the critical role entrepreneurship plays in *coordinating* plans in a market process. Entrepreneurial activity is the driving force within market processes.

In the economic way of thinking, entrepreneurial activity takes three forms: arbitrage, innovation, and imitation. Let's consider them one-by-one.

First, entrepreneurs engage in *arbitrage*. They seek out profit opportunities by attempting to *buy goods at a low price and sell them at a higher price*. Suppose, for example, that syrup currently sells for $4 per pint in Maine, and $9 per pint in New Jersey. (Those prices would be formed, as we learned in Chapter 5, by the competitive supply and demand conditions in those two regional markets.) Potentially, a profit opportunity exists. You can purchase truckloads of syrup in Maine and sell them to consumers in New Jersey. You estimate that you could transport the syrup to New Jersey at a cost of 50 cents a pint (which includes the rental of the trucks, the value of your time, and other opportunity costs you incur). Of course, you would most likely have to bid up the price of syrup in Maine. Your entry and your attempt to buy thousands of pints of syrup in Maine's regional market would lead to a new market-clearing price of, say, $6 per pint. Your actions have increased the demand curve for syrup in Maine, but consumers in Maine would tend to purchase less syrup for the breakfast table (their *quantity demanded* decreases in light of the higher price). Your sales in New Jersey would tend to affect the market-clearing price there, too—your activity would increase the supply curve of syrup in New Jersey. Consumers' plans were previously fulfilled at the $9 price. To encourage them to purchase more syrup (to increase their *quantity demanded*), you would have to sell your surplus syrup at a lower price to clear the market. Say, $7 per pint.

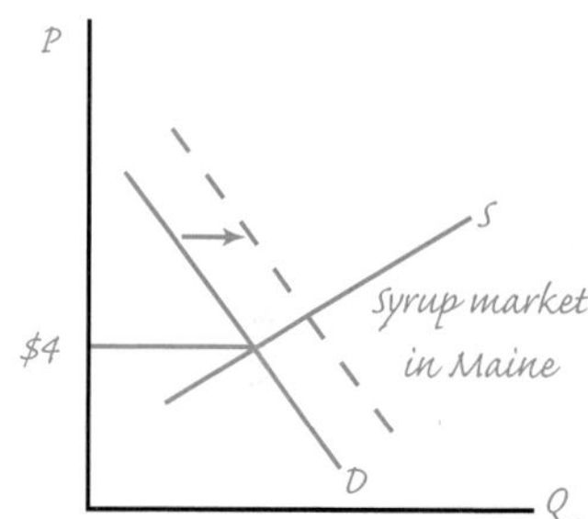

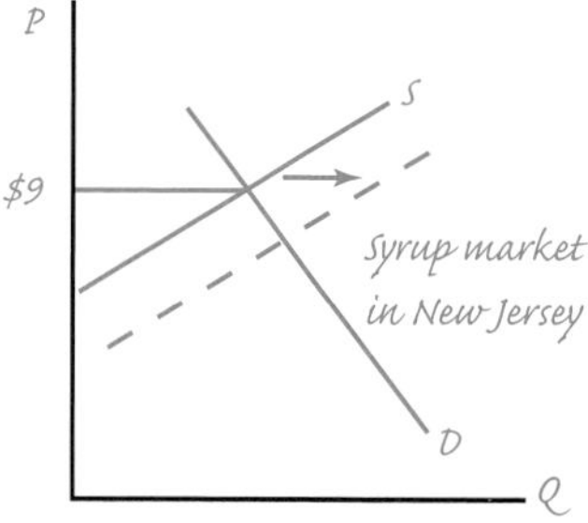

You've earned an economic profit of 50 cents per pint. You bought low ($6 per pint), incurred the transaction cost (50 cents per pint), and then sold the syrup in New Jersey at $7 per pint. You indeed seized what appeared to be a profit opportunity. Your judgment and foresight were correct.

Remember that the economic way of thinking looks at choices and both the intended and unintended consequences of choices. Fortunately, you got what you intended—you enjoyed a profit. What's the unintended consequence of this activity? It generates useful information and furthers plan coordination. *Entrepreneurship tends to correct for errors in the market process.* Literally thousands if not millions of other people were not aware that New Jersey consumers could obtain syrup at a lower price. That includes the typical household in New Jersey. They paid $7 per pint when others were buying the same product at $4 per pint. Also, sellers in Maine were asking $4 per pint when others elsewhere were paying $7 per pint. These price differentials (accounting for transaction costs) are a sign of genuine errors being made by those buyers and sellers. *If they only knew!* They all have the economic freedom to buy and sell syrup as they see fit. But it's the entrepreneur who discovers the opportunity to bid up the asking price in Maine *and* provide cheaper syrup to New Jersey consumers. The entrepreneur's alertness to the potential economic profit provided the incentive to search for that opportunity. The entrepreneur only intended to make a profit; the unintended result is the new information provided by the entrepreneur's arbitrage activity. Moreover, similar to our discussion of middlemen in Chapter 2, entrepreneurial arbitrage further integrates local markets into a national market. This doesn't emerge through a National Syrup Production and Distribution Board, but through the arbitraging practices of profit-seeking entrepreneurs. Buying low in some regions tends to increase prices there, and selling high in other regions tends to decrease prices there. The unintended result of arbitrage is a *converging of market prices*—taking into account transaction costs—across regions.

Error detection

Arbitrage activity tends to reallocate goods, shifting them from lower-valued uses to higher-valued uses. Our discussions of speculation can also be further understood as a particular act of entrepreneurial arbitrage. Speculators attempt to buy at what they believe to be a relatively low price today and sell for what they believe will be a relatively high price in the future, which, as we have seen, tends to transfer goods through time.

Second, entrepreneurs engage in *innovation*. Entrepreneurial innovators are trailblazers, always on the lookout for better ways to satisfy consumer demand, whether it be through improved quality, durability, service, or price of the goods and services they sell. Innovations may range from introducing new technologies (personal computers, palm pilots, DVD players) to new organizational strategies (standardized chain stores such as Wal-Mart and Target, Internet auction sites such as eBay). Entrepreneurs—in their search for economic profit—seek less costly ways of combining scarce resources into something valued more highly by consumers. They discover *new* cost structures, *more efficient* ways of producing and delivering scarce goods and services.

In a sense, entrepreneurial innovation (and, as we shall soon see, imitation) entails an element of arbitrage. Consider the introduction of the DVD player. The innovators found new ways of combining skilled and unskilled human labor, wires, plastic, silicon chips and other resources—essentially buying them at relatively low prices and—after their innovative recombination—selling the final product at relatively higher prices, and enjoying the profit in between.

Third, entrepreneurs engage in the *imitation* of previous trailblazing entrepreneurs. Ford introduced the assembly line for mass car production. Other entrepreneurs quickly got the message, and found that they, too, could reduce their costs of producing cars by following Ford's lead. Apple produced the household-friendly Macintosh computer. This, too, was an innovative feat of tremendous influence. IBM soon imitated—*learned from*—Apple's success to create their own personal computer. Within a short period of time dozens of other imitators followed, producing their own IBM "clones." Unintentionally, a whole new industry was born, better serving consumer wants and demands. New knowledge is created. Most people found, thanks to entrepreneurial innovation and imitation, that a personal automobile is more efficient than a traditional horse and buggy; that a personal computer is more efficient than the traditional typewriter. We witness this by their willingness to purchase property rights to those items and discard or refrain from purchasing the others.

Mere Luck?

But not every entrepreneur enjoys economic profits. In fact, Frank Knight suggested that entrepreneurs as a class may have negative profits. Many of Ford's competitors went out of business; there are far fewer producers of IBM "clones" today compared to 15 years ago. And look what happened to the typewriter and 8-track tape producers. Arbitragers and speculators also face uncertainty and can stand to lose millions. When they lose huge sums, it makes the evening news. After all, we should never forget that the market economy is a profit *and loss* economy (hence the title of this chapter)—economic profit and loss can only emerge in a world of uncertainty.

That voice from the back of the room has been patient with us for too long. He interjects: "Entrepreneurs who enjoy profits are merely lucky, and those who suffer losses are just unlucky. The only information they create is: he was lucky, she was unlucky. And their luck can change tomorrow. How is any of that useful information?" No doubt *some* profits and losses, at any given time, are due to mere accident and chance. Nobody denies that fact. But if luck were the chief source of entrepreneurial profit, we couldn't possibly expect market processes to become more integrated and coordinated through space and time—facts that we *do* observe in the real world. The economic way of thinking emerged, with Adam Smith and others, to try to explain and understand those real-world facts. Orderly market processes (like orderly traffic patterns) would fail to appear if people's plans—including entrepreneurial plans—could be accomplished only out of pure luck—supplies and demands could not possibly be expected to become better coordinated in the markets for insulin, corn, guitars, gasoline, health care, and the others we've discussed in the previous seven chapters. We would instead observe only chaos. There would be no working commercial society left for us to explain.

Profit and Loss as Coordinating Signals: The Role of Monetary Calculation

Markets create information and incentives to act on that information.

The tendency for people to better coordinate their production and consumption plans in commercial society—that is, the tendency for markets to clear—rests on something more fundamental than pure luck or accident. *Markets create information*. People, by freely exchanging their property rights, are guided by, and learn from, the price signals that emerge in the market process. Successful entrepreneurs have a comparative advantage in spotting profitable differences in those price signals—they seek out opportunities to buy low and sell high. Entrepreneurs use market prices to judge the expected costs of their activities, and the expected revenues. That is, market prices are a key to estimating whether a particular business endeavor—whether it's just another new pizzeria or a revolutionary technological innovation—will combine scarce resources in a more efficient and profitable manner or inefficient and unprofitable manner. Very few, if any, busses are made out of gold, although manufacturers are free to use gold if they wish. Why? They expect, using the price information that is available to them, that gold busses—though rare and unique—would be terribly unprofitable. Why, then, would they put *their* wealth on the line?

Institutions and rules of the game matter! Monetary calculation can take place only in a system based upon private property rights, market exchange, and the use of money. Ludwig von Mises, the Austrian economist, put it this way:

> The system of economic calculation in monetary terms is conditioned by certain social institutions. It can operate only in an institutional setting of the division of labor and private ownership of the means of production in which goods and services of all orders are bought and sold against a generally used medium of exchange, i.e., money.

> Monetary calculation is the main vehicle of planning and acting in the social setting of a society of free enterprise directed and controlled by the market and its prices. It developed in this frame and was gradually perfected with the improvement of the market mechanism and with the expansion of the scope of things which are negotiated on markets against money. It was economic calculation that assigned to measurement, number, and reckoning the role they play in our quantitative and computing civilization.

Expected vs. realized profit

In this way, the everyday entrepreneur's calculation of expected profit provides useful information to decide whether or not to engage in arbitrage or launch a new enterprise. The entrepreneur's *realized* profit or loss will further inform about the accuracy of entrepreneurial foresight. The expectation of enjoying the residual—the economic profit—provides the incentive to act entrepreneurially. The entrepreneur, by earning the profit, obtains more wealth. But equally important, entrepreneurs who misjudge profit potentials, and who actually confront an economic loss, destroy their wealth. Such entrepreneurs suffer the penalty of using resources ineffectively. Those scarce resources will be reallocated to others who believe they can find more profitable, and effective, uses. The owners of 8-track tape factories learned the hard way that, although they are still free to produce 8-tracks, consumers don't value them as highly anymore and to continue in that business would further reduce the owners' wealth. By exercising their option to exit the market—to quit manufacturing those products—the land, labor, and other scarce resources were made available to produce things of greater value than the 8-track tapes.

varieties of speculation

The dictionary defines speculation as "trading in the hope of profit from changes in the market price." That's too narrow a definition, but it will do to get us started. The most celebrated (or more accurately, the most vilified) speculator is the "bear" of Wall Street, who "sells short"—that is, sells for future delivery shares of stock the speculator does not own at the time of sale. Bears believe that the stock will go down in price, so that when the time comes for delivery of the shares, they can be purchased at a low price and sold at the previously agreed-upon higher price.

A more important speculator is the commodity speculator, who may trade in such items as wheat, soybeans, hogs, lumber, sugar, cocoa, or copper. (You can find a long list of the most important commodities markets in the *Wall Street Journal.*) This kind of speculator buys and sells "futures." These are agreements to deliver or to accept, at some specified date in the future, amounts of a commodity at a price determined now.

A less-publicized speculator is you yourself. You are buying education now, partly in the hope that it will increase the value of the labor services you'll be selling in the future. But the future is uncertain, so the actual price of your services could turn out to be too low to justify your present investment. Nevertheless, you've decided to take the chance and accept the challenge. Another familiar speculator is the consumer who reads that the price of sugar is expected to rise and responds by loading the pantry with a two-year supply. If the price of sugar rises far enough, those sugar hoarders gain. If it does not, they lose; their wealth has been tied up in sugar, cluttering the pantry shelves and blocking the opportunity to purchase more valuable assets.

The motorist who fills the gas tank at the sight of a sign advertising gasoline at 2 cents a gallon less than the usual price is speculating; the price may be 4 cents lower two blocks ahead. The motorist who drives on an almost empty tank in hope of lower prices up ahead is a notorious speculator. And the motorists who continually "top" their tanks when gasoline supplies are rumored to be short are surely speculators.

But many people, while failing to notice that they themselves are often speculators, heap blame on the "profiteers" who allegedly "take advantage" of special situations and innocent people in pursuit of profit. Are speculators really the enemies of the people they are so often alleged to be? It is often said that speculators exploit natural disasters by driving up prices before the disaster occurs. And sometimes the expected disaster never even materializes. That is true. But it is only one small and misleading part of the truth.

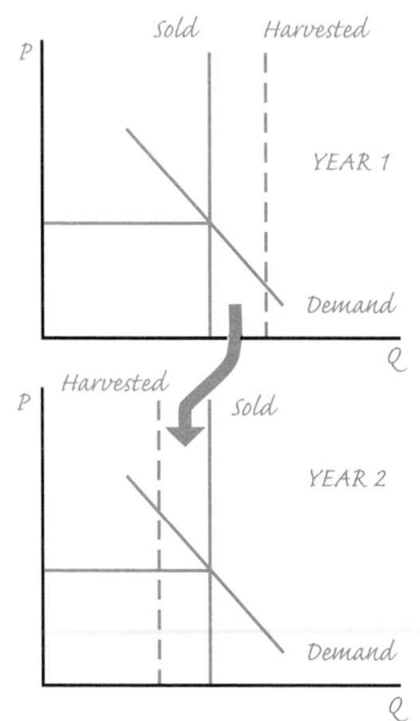

Storage in good year for sale in bad year stabilizes the price.

Consequences of Entrepreneurial Speculation

Suppose evidence begins to accumulate in early summer that corn-leaf blight is spreading to major corn-producing areas of the Midwest. A significant percentage of the year's corn crop could be wiped out as a result. People who think this is likely to occur will consequently expect a higher price for corn in the autumn. This expectation will induce some people to pull some corn out of current consumption in order to carry it over to the fall when, they believe, the price will be higher. That is speculation.

Many different parties engage in such speculation: Farmers substitute other livestock feed for corn in order to maintain their corn stocks at a higher level, either to avoid having to buy corn later at a higher price or to be able to sell it then at the higher price; industrial users increase their inventories now while the price is relatively low; and traders who might not know a bushel of corn from a peck of soybeans try to make a profit from buying cheap now and selling dear later. There are well-organized commodity markets to facilitate this kind of transaction, in which people can buy or sell "futures." The effect of all these activities is to reduce the quantity of corn currently available in the market; the price consequently rises. And just as the critic protested, it rises before the disaster occurs.

But that is only part of the picture. These speculative activities cause corn to be transported *over time* from a period of relative abundance to one of greater scarcity. The price in the fall, when the blight is expected to have its effects, will therefore be lower than it otherwise would be. Speculators thus even out the flow of commodities into consumption and diminish price fluctuations over time. Because price fluctuations create risks for those who grow or use corn, speculators are actually reducing risk to others. More accurately, they are purchasing risk, in hope of a profit, from others less willing to take risk and willing to pay something in the form of reduced expected returns to avoid it. That is the speculator's comparative advantage. (Those who choose to sell in order to reduce their own risk and sell it to others are called *hedgers*.)

Commodity Speculators and Futures Markets

Adam Smith once compared those who speculate on the future price of grain to the prudent captain of a sailing ship, who puts the crew on short rations the moment he discovers there is not enough food on board to last through the voyage. Grain speculators, Smith argued, reduce the suffering that poor harvests cause by inducing consumers to start economizing early. That is still one of the most important achievements of professional commodity speculators. We can see just how it works by looking at speculation on crude-oil futures.

The New York Mercantile Exchange maintains a market in futures contracts for *light sweet*, the most popular grade of crude petroleum (the authors don't know if the oil really tastes sweet, but we accept the label). Each contract calls for the delivery or acceptance in a specified future month of 1,000 barrels of crude oil at a price agreed upon now. This market is used both by oil producers who want to insure themselves against the consequences of a possible future decline in the price of their product and by oil consumers who want to insure themselves against the adverse consequences of a rise in the price of oil.

For example, airline officials looking forward to a booming summer business might start worrying in May about a summer increase in fuel costs that could wipe out all the profits they are hoping to make. The airlines can take out insurance—that is, reduce their risk—against that eventuality by purchasing, in May, crude-oil futures for each of the coming summer months. If the airline buys August futures in May for $16.50, the price at which they are trading in May, it *hedges* against any August increases in fuel costs. A 10 percent increase in the price of jet fuel, caused by an increase in oil prices, will cut into the airline's profits by raising its operating costs. But this reduction in profits will be offset by a 10 percent increase in the price of the August contracts that the airline purchased in May, because the price of the futures contracts will change to match the price of the actual commodity as the date approaches for which the contracts have been made. It all works out *as if* the seller of the futures contract delivers oil to the buyer in August at the agreed-upon price of $16.50 and the buyer of the contract then sells that oil at the August price of $18.15, a price 10 percent higher than the price that had been generally anticipated back in May.

We all face an uncertain future. Prices could rise or fall, or even remain unchanged. *Futures markets allow people to allocate their risks and deal with uncertainty as they best see fit.* Those who wish to reduce their risk (economists call them "risk avoiders") have the option to hedge. Those who wish to increase their exposure to risk (economists call them "risk takers") have the option to speculate.

A farmer who sells September corn futures when he plants in May is hedging. A corn chip maker hedges by buying corn futures.

Hedging reduces risk. The airline gives up the extra profits it could make if the price of petroleum products fell in order to avoid the loss it would sustain if the price of petroleum products rose. Oil producers, on the other hand, would hedge in May by selling August futures. The producers thereby lock in the May price of August futures for as many barrels as their contracts cover. They are insuring against a fall in price just as the airlines were insuring against a rise in price. If the producers sell August futures in May for $16.50 and the price in August turns out to be 10 percent higher than anticipated, they will make more profit than they had expected on all the oil they sell in August; but part of this will be offset by the loss sustained on those futures contracts, which will have risen to $18.15, requiring them (in effect) to buy oil at $18.15 a barrel and resell it at the contracted price of $16.50. The goal of the hedging operation, of course, was for the producers to insure against the losses they would sustain if the price of the product fell between May and August. They forego the profit that results from a price increase in order to insure against the loss they would suffer from a price decline.

What is the role of the professional speculator in all this? Speculators widen the market, to begin with. They make sure that those who want to buy or sell futures can find people on the other side of the market ready to do business with them. Suppose lots of oil consumers begin worrying about a future increase in oil prices and consequently try to buy oil futures. There is no reason to believe that oil producers will be willing to sell all the contracts that consumers wish to purchase. But when a shortage of sellers develops, the price of the contracts starts to rise, and that attracts the professional speculators. These are people who have specialized in acquiring information about the commodity whose futures they agree to trade. They step in and deliberately take on risk because they believe that their special knowledge enables them to predict the future course of prices better than others. *Speculators accept the risk—at a mutually agreed-upon price—that the hedgers seek to avoid.* That is what economists mean when they say that futures markets offer the opportunity for people to allocate risks.

Speculators do much more, however, than just help out hedgers. Professional oil speculators have a keen eye for anything that might affect the supply of or demand for oil and thereby alter its price, such as new discoveries, military hostilities, revolutions, conflict among the members of the Organization of Petroleum Exporting Countries, newfound harmony among the members of OPEC, severe storms in offshore oil-producing areas, political changes that might affect governments' energy policies, recessions in industrialized economies that reduce the demand for oil, shifts in attitudes toward the environment—anything at all. When they believe that oil is going to become more scarce, they buy oil futures. That begins to raise the price of futures. As other people notice that futures prices are rising, they conclude that those who are in the best position to know have put their money on a higher price in the future and they adjust their own actions accordingly. That helps all the rest of us.

Those who are holding large inventories of crude oil, for example, will reduce their current sales in order to have more for future sales, when the price is expected to be higher, so that the quantity currently supplied will decrease. Those who plan to buy in the future will try to accelerate their purchases in order to beat the predicted price increases, and the current demand will increase. The result of this current reduction in quantity supplied and current increase in demand—triggered, remember, by the increase in the price of futures that the speculators caused—will be a *current* increase in the price of oil. The predicted future increase will become an increase *right now*. And that price increase will enlist everyone who uses petroleum products in the cause of conservation, including the millions of people who don't even know where to find futures prices in the daily newspaper. The final users of petroleum products will respond to the increase in the current price by beginning now to economize on consumption.

Is that good or bad? Suppose that the speculators' actions were based on predictions of military hostilities in the Middle East that will seriously disrupt the flow of oil into world markets. Which is better? That we have no advance warning, do nothing to prepare, and make all our adjustments when the disruption actually occurs? Or that we receive advance warning, start economizing now, and have more oil on hand to tide us over when the disruption hits?

It is hard to see how the first scenario could be better than the second. Unless, of course, the speculators are wrong—which is certainly possible. If they are wrong then their actions will cause the price of oil and its products to rise in anticipation of a disaster that never occurs. We will have economized when there was no reason to do so. And the petroleum products we saved through our efforts will be on hand to drive future prices down below what they would otherwise have been. Speculators who are wrong *cause* price fluctuations by themselves disrupting the balance of supply and demand.

But they are correct far more often than they're wrong. It's their business to be correct—*their* wealth is on the line—and they won't be in the business for long if they are often wrong. Moreover, when they *are* wrong, they are quick to learn and to alter their behavior; otherwise they will be weeded out of the futures market (or, as happened to Dan Akroyd's character in the movie *The Great Outdoors*, they'll be stuck wearing yellow runner's jackets, fetching coffee for the professional speculators on the exchange floors). They are not like people who don't have to pay the price of their own mistakes and so can go on holding stubbornly to a prediction after every sensible and impartial person can see that it has been refuted.

Futures markets provide clues about the future prices of scarce goods.

Professional speculators are our distant early warning system. They enable us to avoid crises by giving us better information and the incentive to act on it. Their buying and selling of futures contracts provides us with continuously adjusted predictions of what prices will be in the future, thereby enabling all of us to make better decisions in the present. Like middlemen, speculators are a valuable resource. If political hostility sometimes threatens to turn them into an endangered species, better understanding of futures markets and the functions of speculators can help to preserve them.

Prophets and Losses

All this assumes, however, that the speculators are correct in their anticipations. What if an unusually large crop appears instead? The blight does not materialize and the weather turns out to be superb for growing corn. Then the speculators are transporting corn from a period of lesser to a period of greater abundance and thereby magnifying price fluctuations. This is clearly an unfortunate reallocation of resources, involving as it does the giving up now of some high-valued corn for the sake of obtaining later an equal amount of low-valued corn. That doesn't help anyone.

But neither is it profitable for the speculators! They will sustain losses where they had hoped for gains. We should not expect them, consequently, to behave in this fashion *except as a result of ignorance*. Are speculators likely to be ignorant? Speculators do make mistakes. (Why would they otherwise be called speculators?) But living as we do in an uncertain world, we have no option but to act in the presence of uncertainty. We can't escape uncertainty and the consequences of ignorance by refusing to act or to anticipate the future. And if we think we know more than the speculators, we can counter them at a profit by betting against them. It is revealing to note that those who criticize speculators for misreading the future rarely give effective expression to their own supposedly greater insight by entering the market against them. Hindsight, of course, is always in huge supply—and the price is appropriately low.

Speculators provide information for all to see. They are another important source of the information that is created in market processes. Their offers to buy and sell express their judgments concerning the future in relation to the present. The prices generated by their activities are, like all prices, indexes of value: information for decision makers on present and future opportunity costs. This information is at least as important to those who always try to reduce risk as it is to those who like to gamble. It is true that the information they provide is "bad" information whenever the speculators are wrong. But harping on this is again a case of comparing a poor situation with a better but unattainable situation. If we think we can read the future better than the speculators, we are free to express our convictions with money, profit from our insight, and benefit other people in the process. The free market allows us that option.

Meanwhile, those whose ordinary business activities involve them in the use of commodities that are speculatively traded do make effective use of the information generated by the speculators. Farmers consult the prices predicted in the markets for futures contracts on the commodity exchanges in order to make their plans and so do industrial users. And those who use goods not ordinarily thought of as speculative commodities also take advantage of the information generated by speculators. For we all use prices as information, and prices reflect competing bids and offers inevitably based to a large extent on a (speculative!) reading of the future. Natural disasters such as droughts, crop diseases, and unseasonable frosts have surprisingly small effects on the price and availability of grain, fruit, and vegetables in the United States. The credit for that must largely go to speculators, whose foresight acts as an effective buffer between the vagaries of nature and the sturdy dependability of grocers.

Middlemen coordinate markets across different regions; speculators coordinate markets through time.

In summary, while *middlemen* tend to coordinate market exchanges across *regions*, integrating local markets into a highly complex national and global economic system, *speculators* tend—whether they fully realize it or not—to coordinate market exchanges through *time*. They tend to bring quantity supplied closer to quantity demanded. Not only current supply and demand plans but those of the foreseeable future as well. Entrepreneurial middlemen and speculators, pursuing what they believe is their comparative advantage, are "merely" striving to make a profit. The economic way of thinking steps outside the box of "mere profiteering," however, and analyzes the opportunities they create that both inform people and provide them the opportunity to allocate their risks. These specialists efficiently provide important sources of scarce information to the rest of us whose comparative advantages lie elsewhere.

Beware of Experts

The key, then, to a robust and efficient market process is straightforward but remarkably underappreciated. It is *open entry and exit*. Open entry and exit allows those people who believe they have a comparative advantage in entrepreneurial activity (such as arbitrage, innovation) to *enter* markets and trade as they see fit. If their judgment is correct, they will earn profits—and those realized profits will inform *other* entrepreneurs to also enter and imitate the successful. Consumer demands would be served more efficiently as a result. But, equally important, these rules of the game allow those people who once had—or simply thought they had—a comparative advantage in entrepreneurship to *exit* the market if they face economic losses and wish to seek opportunities elsewhere. Those losses detect errors in misjudging the value of scarce resources, too.

Open entry and exit help us discover our comparative advantage.

Comparative advantage can and often does change over time as perceived costs and benefits of one's area of specialization change. Our emphasis on the role of entrepreneurship is not intended to exalt "the entrepreneur" into a special social status devoid of criticism. We emphasize the *role* of entrepreneurial activity in facilitating and better coordinating market exchange. What's important is to acknowledge the effects of the *rules of the game*—open entry and exit—that allow for individuals to pursue entrepreneurial activity if they so wish. Certainly economists are in no privileged position to pick which people will be—or continue to be—successful entrepreneurs in the future. Nor can government officials. None of us have that kind of information. Participants in commercial society rely, instead, on the open market process to provide that information, in the form of expected and realized profit and loss calculations, and its effect on personal wealth.

If that sounds a little too abstract, consider the following judgments and predictions, made by experts and authorities in their respective fields:

- "Heavier-than-air flying machines are impossible." (Lord Kelvin, President of the Royal Society, 1895).
- "Drill for oil? You mean drill into the ground to try and find oil? You're crazy!" (response from drillers who Edwin L. Drake tried to employ for his oil-drilling project in 1859).
- "Everything that can be invented has been invented." (Charles H. Duell, Commissioner of the U.S. Office of Patents, 1899).

- "We don't like their sound, and guitar music is on the way out." (Decca Recording Company's rejection of the Beatles, 1962).
- "Computers in the future may weigh no more than 1.5 tons." (*Popular Mechanics* magazine, 1949. Actually, they were correct!)
- "I think there is a world market for maybe five computers." (Thomas Watson, Chairman of IBM, 1943).
- "There is no reason anyone would want a computer in their home." (Ken Olson, President, Chairman & Founder of Digital Equipment Corporation, 1977).
- "640K ought to be enough for anybody." (Bill Gates, 1981).

Open entry allows these claims to be tested. It allows potential pioneers to test the judgments of previous pioneers and other authorities, to act on what *they* perceive as profitable, wealth-generating opportunities, to discover comparative advantages, and to increase options for the consumer.

Entrepreneurship is society's source of change. Entrepreneurs are the people who perceive gaps between what is and what might be and opportunities to profit from closing those gaps. They acquire control over the resources they must employ to close the gaps by hiring resources from other owners. Those owners surrender control over the resources they own in return for the entrepreneur's payment. The sum of these payments, and the estimated value of the entrepreneur's opportunity costs, is the entrepreneur's total cost. The difference between these costs and the total revenue from the entrepreneur's project is the entrepreneur's profit—or loss, if the entrepreneur's perception was mistaken. Open markets allow for different individuals to act on the knowledge available to them to form expectations and pursue what they believe are profitable, wealth-generating projects. Closed markets—legally barring potential entrepreneurs from entering—stifle competition and limit the knowledge-generating and plan-coordinating features of the market process. Decisions as to who should be allowed to enter, who has what kind of comparative advantage, who can most efficiently serve the consumer will be determined by the limited information and expectations of individual lawmakers and bureaucrats, whose personal wealth is most likely not on the line.

A society that prohibits profit undermines responsibility.

Restrictions on Competition

Often entrepreneurs (or the people they employ) will seek to legally restrict the market in order to preserve *their own* profit (and wage) opportunities. Nobody hates increased competition more than the already-established enterprises. When associations of physicians, plumbers, farmers, airline pilots, nursing home operators, or automobile manufacturers urge the government to restrict competition in their trade, what are they after? They are

"We're not in favor of free competition. We want fair competition!"

trying to reduce uncertainty, at least for themselves, by preventing price cutting and keeping out competitors. If they succeed in their efforts, don't they secure for themselves something close to a guaranteed profit? And a guarantee is at the opposite pole from uncertainty. Let's take a closer look to see whether restrictions on the ability to compete really do give rise to something we can call a *guaranteed profit*.

Suppose that you accidentally—with no investment of time, effort, or other resources—discover the way to build a better mousetrap. You snagged the blueprints, let's say, while out fishing. Recognizing the value of your find, you immediately obtain a patent from the government and make plans to go into production. Because the world will beat a path to the door of anyone who builds a better mousetrap, and because the patent prohibits any competitor from duplicating your product for 20 years, you are going to become rich. It's a virtual certainty. And the first year's results confirm your happy prediction: Net revenue is $100,000. You can confidently expect another $100,000 for each of the remaining years. It looks like an annual *and fairly certain* profit of $100,000. But let's pursue the story further.

What is the source of this "profit"? It's your patent, of course, which prevents competition from eroding the difference between your total revenue and your total costs. But have you accurately calculated the cost of producing these superior mousetraps?

Competition on Other Fronts

If ownership of the patent generates a virtually certain $100,000 per year for you in net revenue, wouldn't its ownership generate just as much income for somebody else? In fact, wouldn't the patent be even more valuable—generate more than $100,000 annually—in the hands of someone who had specialized in mousetraps and knew more than you about their production and distribution? So some of those who beat a path to your door when you build a better mousetrap are going to be established mousetrap manufacturers who want to purchase or rent your patent. You will consequently discover that the cost to you of continuing as the exclusive producer of these superior mousetraps has gone up by the value of the opportunity you spurn if you decline to sell or lease your patent.

Suppose a long-established maker of mousetraps offers to buy your patent for $1.5 million. How might the firm arrive at such a figure? It could estimate that your patent will produce at least a $200,000 annual increase in its net revenue. If the going rate of return on relatively risk-free investments, such as U.S. government bonds, is currently 7 percent, your patent is a good investment at a purchase price of $1.5 million; it promises to yield more than 13 percent per year. Of course, the firm would prefer to get that patent for less. At a price of $1.2 million, $200,000 becomes a 16.67 percent annual return on investment. But there are other mousetrap manufacturers—16.67 percent is too good a deal for them to pass by—and so the winning bid rises to $1.5 million. That's the process by which the market price of your patent would be determined.

What does all this do to your annual "profit" of $100,000? It wipes it out entirely and turns your "profit" into an actual loss. Do you see why and how? When competition among mousetrap makers sets a price of $1.5 million on your patent, the cost to you of continuing to manufacture mousetraps increases by at least $105,000 per year, which is the income you will forego if you decide not to sell your patent and invest the proceeds in government bonds at 7 percent per year. What has happened is this: When the word got out that ownership of your patent was a virtual guarantee of profit—an annual revenue greater than cost—potential owners began bidding for the patent. Their bids transformed your "profit" into a cost of production: the value of the opportunity you forego by not selling.

When uncertainty disappears profits get transformed into costs of production by competitive bidding.

What about the firm that buys your patent? Will it make a profit afterwards? It might. If events turn out as the firm has hoped and its net revenue does increase by $200,000 a year, acquisition of the patent will prove to have been a smart move. Of course, over half of that $200,000 will be a cost of production: the income foregone by investing $1.5 million in the patent rather than in government bonds. The remaining revenue could be viewed as a genuine profit, the result of prior uncertainty about the actual value of the patent to the acquiring firm, a return to the firm's entrepreneurial initiatives in obtaining and employing your patent.

Notice, though, that the process of competition just described will resume once the profit becomes relatively "certain." Other firms might renew the bidding for the patent, raising its price above $1.5 million. Should the patent be worth more than $1.5 million *only to this firm*, that would suggest this firm controls some unique complementary resources—a marketing manager, perhaps, with a special talent for designing ads that arouse a frantic fear of mice. In that case, the price of the complementary resources will be bid up as other firms discover what's going on and try to obtain these "profitable" resources for their own use. If the firm is forced to pay the marketing manager a higher salary to stay on, a part of the "profit" will turn into an addition to its wage and salary costs. You can watch this happening in all sorts of places once you have learned what to look for.

Competition for the Key Resource

When the government tries to increase the income of wheat farmers by guaranteeing them a higher price for their product, land suitable for wheat production becomes more valuable, and its price

Price supports for wheat raise the cost of growing wheat.

rises. Tenant farmers subsequently have to pay more for the land they rent and farmers who try to buy land must pay more to get it. The increased "profit" for wheat farmers at which the government policy was aimed generates, as soon as the policy becomes known, an increase in the cost of producing wheat, through a rise in the cost of using land. The beneficiaries will be those who owned land suitable for growing wheat before it became generally known that the government was going to raise the support price of wheat. The profits from the increase in the support price for wheat will go to those lucky enough or foresighted enough to have had the relevant property rights at the appropriate time.

Licenses to restrict an activity raise the cost of engaging in that activity.

When taxicab operators secure legislation restricting the number of cabs that are licensed to operate in a city, ownership of a license becomes more valuable. Competition for the licenses then bids up their price until the cost of operating a cab—including the opportunity cost of acquiring or of retaining ownership of the license—is equal to the revenue from its operation. That does not mean taxicab operators don't get any benefit from their lobbying campaign. Those who owned licenses before the legal restrictions were generally anticipated do benefit from an increase in the value of their licenses. That increase is their profit, and it's what they were hoping for when they launched their lobbying efforts, when they became political entrepreneurs. But after the lobbying efforts have succeeded it will cost more to operate a cab, because each cab operator will now have to own a costly license in order to do so.

The right to broadcast on a VHF television channel in a large city is a very valuable property right. If the Federal Communications Commission were to assign these rights to the highest bidder, the government would receive a tidy sum and the "profit" from use of the channel would become a cost of doing business to the broadcaster. In fact, however, the FCC has always assigned the right to use a particular channel, without charge, on the basis of obscure criteria having to do with the merit of competing applicants and the promises they make regarding future public service. As a result, applicants compete by hiring lawyers, accountants, and assorted public-relations specialists to influence the FCC's assignment. In this case, the critical resource that creates a "profit" is the FCC's decision, and competition among entrepreneurs consequently aims at acquiring control of that decision. The "profit" from receipt of the channel is transformed along the way into the cost of exerting political influence.

Competition and Property Rights

Profits and losses arise from uncertainty and cannot exist in the absence of uncertainty. Where everything relevant to the making of a profit is known for certain, competition to obtain the profit will eliminate it, either by reducing revenue or by raising cost. There's nothing very surprising about that conclusion; it follows logically from the way we have defined cost and profit. What matters, and what this chapter was intended to clarify, are the forms that competition and entrepreneurial activity take in response to the lure of a possible profit and the social consequences that emerge.

Will the pursuit of profit lead people to produce better mousetraps or to prevent others from selling better mousetraps in their territory? Will it yield more wheat or higher-priced wheat land? Better taxi service or an increase in the cost of licenses? Lower prices for consumers or higher incomes for the owners of critical resources? Exploration or retrenchment? Innovations in technology or in social organization? A wider range of choices or more restrictions on choice? The answers will depend on the rules of the game and the system of property rights that they create.

An Appendix: *DISCOUNTING AND PRESENT VALUES*

Recall from Chapter 5 that the prevailing annual interest rate reflects the greater value that people assign to goods now over goods one year from now. It therefore follows that the value of goods expected to be received a year from now must be discounted by the rate of interest to determine their *present value*. The process of discounting to determine the present value of future goods plays a large part in economic decision making, including the calculation of expected future profit or loss. Mastering this process will equip you to understand better some of the analysis in subsequent chapters and will acquaint you with procedures widely employed in the business and financial world.

Suppose that Ivy College offers the parents of entering students a Tuition Stabilization Plan. Tuition, currently at $4,000, is almost sure to rise each year, the college points out, because of rising costs. Ivy even announces in advance its intention to increase the annual tuition charge by $400 in each of the next three years. But parents who subscribe to the TSP receive a special deal. They pay $16,000 in September of the first year and nothing thereafter. In effect, says Ivy's multicolored brochure, parents who sign up for TSP save $2,400 on the cost of their child's education. Ivy may go so far as to call it a 15 percent saving.

But is $16,000 paid now really less than $4,000 now plus $4,400 one year from now, $4,800 two years from now, and $5,200 three years from now? The last three amounts are amounts due in the future, and future dollars, like any other future goods, must be discounted if we want to assess their present value. What discount rate should we use? The best answer is provided by the opportunity cost to the parents of lending money to Ivy College, because that is in effect what they are doing. They are lending Ivy money by paying the tuition before it is due. Thus $4,000 of the sophomore year tuition is lent for one year, $4,000 of the junior year tuition is lent for two years, and $4,000 of the senior year tuition is lent for three years. What's the alternative opportunity for those amounts?

What a Present Amount Grows to

Suppose the parents sell stock to obtain the money, and their stock investments ordinarily earn an annual return, in dividends plus increased market price, of 12 percent a year. This implies that the opportunity cost of lending \$4,000 to Ivy College for one year is \$480. That's \$480 expended to avoid \$400 in increased tuition—not an attractive arrangement. The junior year loan is an even poorer investment: \$4,000 grows in two years, at 12 percent, to \$4,000 × 1.12 × 1.12 or \$5,017.60. The phenomenon of compound interest is at work, and it makes the three-year loan even less appealing. To avoid the \$1,200 in additional tuition due for the senior year, the parents give up \$1,619.71 that they might otherwise have earned from the ownership of stock, because \$4,000 × 1.12^3 is \$5,619.71.

Present Value of Future Amounts

We've assessed Ivy's proposal by calculating what a dollar now will grow to, at the appropriate rate of return, in one year, in two years, and in three years. We can reach the same conclusion by working in the other direction. What is the present value of the \$4,400 that will be due in one year? That amounts to asking: What present sum would grow to \$4,400 in one year if invested at 12 percent? The answer is \$4,400 divided by 1.12, or \$3,928.57, which means that in prepaying the sophomore year tuition the parents give up \$4,000 now to save about \$70 less than that in present value. The \$4,800 that would be due in two years has a present value of \$4,800 divided by (1.12 × 1.12), or \$3,826.53, which is \$175 less than what the parents actually pay. The \$5,200, when divided by 1.12^3, turns out to have a present value of only \$3,701.26.

People who make these computations in the course of their everyday business decisions use tables that enable them to calculate quickly the sum to which a present amount will grow or the present value of future amounts. Three such tables are provided on the succeeding pages. You can use the first two, Tables 7–1 and 7–2, to check the conclusions just presented, which is a subtle way of suggesting that you practice with the tables until you're able to obtain the results we have presented. One more problem will be presented to introduce you to the third table, Table 7–3.

Present Value of Annuities

What should a maker of mousetraps be willing to pay for a patent that is expected to produce an addition to net revenue of \$200,000 per year for the next 17 years? It is certainly less than 17 times \$200,000, or \$3.4 million. If U.S. government bonds are available

Table 7–1 **Amount to Which $1 Will Grow in the Designated Number of Years When Compounded Annually at Various Interest Rates**

Year	1%	2%	3%	4%	5%	6%	7%	8%	9%	10%	12%	15%	Year
1	1.0100	1.0200	1.0300	1.0400	1.0500	1.0600	1.0700	1.0800	1.0900	1.1000	1.1200	1.1500	1
2	1.0201	1.0404	1.0609	1.0816	1.1025	1.1236	1.1449	1.1664	1.1881	1.2100	1.2544	1.3225	2
3	1.0303	1.0612	1.0927	1.1249	1.1576	1.1910	1.2250	1.2597	1.2950	1.3310	1.4049	1.5209	3
4	1.0406	1.0824	1.1255	1.1699	1.2155	1.2625	1.3108	1.3605	1.4116	1.4641	1.5735	1.7490	4
5	1.0510	1.1041	1.1593	1.2167	1.2763	1.3382	1.4026	1.4693	1.5386	1.6105	1.7623	2.0114	5
6	1.0615	1.1262	1.1941	1.2653	1.3401	1.4185	1.5007	1.5869	1.6771	1.7716	1.9738	2.3131	6
7	1.0721	1.1487	1.2299	1.3159	1.4071	1.5036	1.6058	1.7138	1.8280	1.9487	2.2107	2.6600	7
8	1.0829	1.1717	1.2668	1.3686	1.4775	1.5938	1.7182	1.8509	1.9926	2.1436	2.4760	3.0590	8
9	1.0937	1.1951	1.3048	1.4233	1.5513	1.6895	1.8385	1.9990	2.1719	2.3579	2.7731	3.5179	9
10	1.1046	1.2190	1.3439	1.4802	1.6289	1.7908	1.9672	2.1589	2.3674	2.5937	3.1058	4.0456	10
11	1.1157	1.2434	1.3842	1.5395	1.7103	1.8983	2.1049	2.3316	2.5804	2.8531	3.4785	4.6524	11
12	1.1268	1.2682	1.4258	1.6010	1.7959	2.0122	2.2522	2.5182	2.8127	3.1384	3.8960	5.3503	12
13	1.1381	1.2936	1.4685	1.6651	1.8856	2.1329	2.4098	2.7196	3.0658	3.4523	4.3635	6.1528	13
14	1.1495	1.3195	1.5126	1.7317	1.9799	2.2609	2.5785	2.9372	3.3417	3.7975	4.8871	7.0757	14
15	1.1610	1.3459	1.5580	1.8009	2.0789	2.3966	2.7590	3.1722	3.6425	4.1772	5.4736	8.1371	15
16	1.1726	1.3728	1.6047	1.8730	2.1829	2.5404	2.9522	3.4259	3.9073	4.5950	6.1304	9.3576	16
17	1.1843	1.4002	1.6528	1.9479	2.2920	2.6928	3.1588	3.7000	4.3276	5.0545	6.8660	10.7613	17
18	1.1961	1.4282	1.7024	2.0258	2.4066	2.8543	3.3799	3.9960	4.7171	5.5599	7.6900	12.3755	18
19	1.2081	1.4568	1.7535	2.1068	2.5270	3.0256	3.6165	4.3157	5.1417	6.1159	8.6128	14.2318	19
20	1.2202	1.4859	1.8061	2.1911	2.6533	3.2071	3.8697	4.6610	5.6044	6.7275	9.6463	16.3665	20
21	1.2324	1.5157	1.8603	2.2788	2.7860	3.3996	4.1406	5.0338	6.1088	7.4002	10.8038	18.8215	21
22	1.2447	1.5460	1.9161	2.3699	2.9253	3.6035	4.4304	5.4365	6.6586	8.1403	12.1003	21.6447	22
23	1.2572	1.5769	1.9736	2.4647	3.0715	3.8197	4.7405	5.8715	7.2579	8.9543	13.5523	24.8915	23
24	1.2697	1.6084	2.0328	2.5633	3.2251	4.0489	5.0724	6.3412	7.9111	9.8497	15.1786	28.6252	24
25	1.2824	1.6406	2.0938	2.6658	3.3864	4.2919	5.4274	6.8485	8.6231	10.8347	17.0001	32.9190	25
26	1.2953	1.6734	2.1566	2.7725	3.5557	4.5494	5.8074	7.3964	9.3992	11.9182	19.0401	37.8568	26
27	1.3082	1.7069	2.2213	2.8834	3.7335	4.8223	6.1239	7.9881	10.2451	13.1100	21.3249	43.5353	27
28	1.3213	1.7410	2.2879	2.9987	3.9201	5.1117	6.6488	8.6271	11.1671	14.4210	23.8839	50.0656	28
29	1.3345	1.7758	2.3566	3.1187	4.1161	5.4184	7.1143	9.3173	12.1722	15.8631	26.7499	57.5755	29
30	1.3478	1.8114	2.4273	3.2434	4.3219	5.7435	7.6123	10.0627	13.2677	17.4494	29.9599	66.2118	30

Table 7–2 **Present Value of $1 at the End of the Designated Number of Years When Compounded Annually at Various Interest Rates**

Year	1%	2%	3%	4%	5%	6%	7%	8%	9%	10%	12%	15%	Year
1	0.9901	0.9804	0.9709	0.9615	0.9524	0.9434	0.9346	0.9259	0.9174	0.9091	0.8929	0.8696	1
2	0.9803	0.9612	0.9426	0.9246	0.9070	0.8900	0.8734	0.8573	0.8417	0.8264	0.7972	0.7561	2
3	0.9706	0.9423	0.9151	0.8890	0.8638	0.8396	0.8163	0.7938	0.7722	0.7513	0.7118	0.6575	3
4	0.9610	0.9238	0.8885	0.8548	0.8227	0.7921	0.7629	0.7350	0.7084	0.6830	0.6355	0.5718	4
5	0.9515	0.9057	0.8626	0.8219	0.7835	0.7473	0.7130	0.6806	0.6499	0.6209	0.5674	0.4972	5
6	0.9420	0.8880	0.8375	0.7903	0.7462	0.7050	0.6663	0.6302	0.5963	0.5645	0.5066	0.4323	6
7	0.9327	0.8706	0.8131	0.7599	0.7107	0.6651	0.6227	0.5835	0.5470	0.5132	0.4523	0.3759	7
8	0.9235	0.8535	0.7894	0.7307	0.6768	0.6274	0.5820	0.5403	0.5019	0.4665	0.4039	0.3269	8
9	0.9143	0.8368	0.7664	0.7026	0.6446	0.5919	0.5439	0.5002	0.4604	0.4241	0.3606	0.2843	9
10	0.9053	0.8203	0.7441	0.6756	0.6139	0.5584	0.5083	0.4632	0.4224	0.3855	0.3220	0.2472	10
11	0.8963	0.8043	0.7224	0.6496	0.5847	0.5268	0.4751	0.4289	0.3875	0.3505	0.2875	0.2149	11
12	0.8874	0.7885	0.7014	0.6246	0.5568	0.4970	0.4440	0.3971	0.3555	0.3186	0.2567	0.1869	12
13	0.8787	0.7730	0.6810	0.6006	0.5303	0.4668	0.4150	0.3677	0.3262	0.2897	0.2292	0.1625	13
14	0.8700	0.7579	0.6611	0.5775	0.5051	0.4423	0.3878	0.3405	0.2992	0.2633	0.2046	0.1413	14
15	0.8613	0.7430	0.6419	0.5553	0.4810	0.4173	0.3624	0.3152	0.2745	0.2394	0.1827	0.1229	15
16	0.8528	0.7284	0.6232	0.5339	0.4581	0.3936	0.3387	0.2919	0.2519	0.2176	0.1631	0.1069	16
17	0.8444	0.7142	0.6050	0.5134	0.4363	0.3714	0.3166	0.2703	0.2311	0.1978	0.1456	0.0929	17
18	0.8360	0.7002	0.5874	0.4936	0.4155	0.3503	0.2959	0.2502	0.2120	0.1799	0.1300	0.0808	18
19	0.8277	0.6864	0.5703	0.4746	0.3957	0.3305	0.2765	0.2317	0.1945	0.1635	0.1161	0.0703	19
20	0.8195	0.6730	0.5537	0.4564	0.3769	0.3118	0.2584	0.2145	0.1784	0.1486	0.1037	0.0611	20
21	0.8114	0.6598	0.5375	0.4388	0.3589	0.2942	0.2415	0.1987	0.1637	0.1351	0.0926	0.0531	21
22	0.8034	0.6468	0.5219	0.4220	0.3418	0.2775	0.2257	0.1839	0.1502	0.1228	0.0826	0.0462	22
23	0.7954	0.6342	0.5067	0.4057	0.3256	0.2618	0.2109	0.1703	0.1378	0.1117	0.0738	0.0402	23
24	0.7876	0.6217	0.4919	0.3901	0.3101	0.2470	0.1971	0.1577	0.1264	0.1015	0.0659	0.0349	24
25	0.7798	0.6095	0.4776	0.3751	0.2953	0.2330	0.1842	0.1460	0.1160	0.0923	0.0588	0.0304	25
26	0.7720	0.5976	0.4637	0.3607	0.2812	0.2198	0.1722	0.1352	0.1064	0.0839	0.0525	0.0264	26
27	0.7644	0.5859	0.4502	0.3468	0.2678	0.2074	0.1609	0.1252	0.0976	0.0763	0.0469	0.0230	27
28	0.7568	0.5744	0.4371	0.3335	0.2551	0.1956	0.1504	0.1159	0.0895	0.0693	0.0419	0.0200	28
29	0.7493	0.5631	0.4243	0.3207	0.2429	0.1846	0.1406	0.1073	0.0822	0.0630	0.0374	0.0174	29
30	0.7419	0.5521	0.4120	0.3083	0.2314	0.1741	0.1314	0.0994	0.0754	0.0573	0.0334	0.0151	30

Table 7–3 **Annuity Table: Present Value of $1 Received at the End of Each Year for the Designated Number of Years When Compounded Annually at Various Interest Rates**

Year	1%	2%	3%	4%	5%	6%	7%	8%	9%	10%	12%	15%	Year
1	0.9901	0.9804	0.9709	0.9615	0.9524	0.9434	0.9346	0.9259	0.9174	0.9091	0.8929	0.8696	1
2	1.9704	1.9416	1.9135	1.8861	1.8594	1.8334	1.8080	1.7833	1.7591	1.7355	1.6901	1.6257	2
3	2.9410	2.8839	2.8286	2.7751	2.7232	2.6730	2.6243	2.5771	2.5313	2.4869	2.4018	2.2832	3
4	3.9020	3.8077	3.7171	3.6299	3.5460	3.4651	3.3872	3.3121	3.2397	3.1699	3.0373	2.8550	4
5	4.8534	4.7135	4.5797	4.4518	4.3295	4.2124	4.1002	3.9927	3.8897	3.7908	3.6048	3.3522	5
6	5.7955	5.6014	5.4172	5.2421	5.0757	4.9173	4.7665	4.6229	4.4859	4.3553	4.1114	3.7845	6
7	6.7282	6.4720	6.2303	6.0021	5.7864	5.5824	5.3893	5.2064	5.0330	4.8684	4.5638	4.1604	7
8	7.6517	7.3255	7.0197	6.7327	6.4632	6.2098	5.9713	5.7466	5.5348	5.3349	4.9676	4.4873	8
9	8.5660	8.1622	7.7861	7.4353	7.1078	6.8017	6.5152	6.2469	5.9952	5.7590	5.3282	4.7716	9
10	9.4713	8.9826	8.5302	8.1109	7.7217	7.3601	7.0236	6.7101	6.4177	6.1446	5.6502	5.0188	10
11	10.3676	9.7868	9.2526	8.7605	8.3064	7.8869	7.4987	7.1390	6.8052	6.4951	5.9377	5.2337	11
12	11.2551	10.5753	9.9540	9.3851	8.8633	8.3838	7.9427	7.5361	7.1607	6.8137	6.1944	5.4206	12
13	12.1337	11.3484	10.6350	9.9856	9.3936	8.8527	8.3577	7.9038	7.4869	7.1034	6.4235	5.5831	13
14	13.0037	12.1062	11.2961	10.5631	9.8986	9.2950	8.7455	8.2442	7.7862	7.3667	6.6282	5.7245	14
15	13.8651	12.8493	11.9379	11.1184	10.3797	9.7122	9.1079	8.5595	8.0607	7.6061	6.8109	5.8474	15
16	14.7179	13.5777	12.5611	11.6523	10.8378	10.1059	9.4466	8.8514	8.3126	7.8237	6.9740	5.9542	16
17	15.5623	14.2919	13.1661	12.1657	11.2741	10.4773	9.7632	9.1216	8.5436	8.0216	7.1196	6.0472	17
18	16.3983	14.9920	13.7535	12.6593	11.6896	10.8276	10.0591	9.3719	8.7556	8.2014	7.2497	6.1280	18
19	17.2260	15.6785	14.3238	13.1339	12.0853	11.1581	10.3356	9.6036	8.9501	8.3649	7.3658	6.1982	19
20	18.0456	16.3514	14.8775	13.5903	12.4622	11.4699	10.5940	9.8181	9.1285	8.5136	7.4694	6.2593	20
21	18.8570	17.0112	15.4150	14.0292	12.8212	11.7641	10.8355	10.0168	9.2922	8.6487	7.5620	6.3125	21
22	19.6604	17.6580	15.9369	14.4511	13.1630	12.0416	11.0612	10.2007	9.4424	8.7715	7.6446	6.3587	22
23	20.4558	18.2922	16.4436	14.8568	13.4886	12.3034	11.2722	10.3711	9.5802	8.8832	7.7184	6.3988	23
24	21.2434	18.9139	16.9355	15.2470	13.7986	12.5504	11.4693	10.5288	9.7066	8.9847	7.7843	6.4338	24
25	22.0232	19.5235	17.4131	15.6221	14.0939	12.7834	11.6536	10.6748	9.8226	9.0770	7.8431	6.4641	25
26	22.7952	20.1210	17.8768	15.9828	14.3752	13.0032	11.8258	10.8100	9.9290	9.1609	7.8957	6.4906	26
27	23.5596	20.7069	18.3270	16.3296	14.6430	13.2105	11.9867	10.9352	10.0266	9.2372	7.9426	6.5135	27
28	24.3164	21.2813	18.7641	16.6631	14.8981	13.4062	12.1371	11.0511	10.1161	9.3066	7.9844	6.5335	28
29	25.0658	21.8444	19.1885	16.9837	15.1411	13.5907	12.2777	11.1584	10.1983	9.3696	8.0218	6.5509	29
30	25.8077	22.3965	19.6004	17.2920	15.3725	13.7648	12.4090	11.2578	10.2737	9.4269	8.0552	6.5660	30

that pay 7 percent per year, $3.4 million invested in these low-risk assets will yield $238,000 a year, which is a considerably higher return on a much less risky investment. Moreover, that $238,000 will continue indefinitely while the $200,000 will end after 17 years. So the mousetrap maker clearly won't be willing to pay $3.4 million for the patent.

The maximum that the firm will be willing to pay is the present value of $200,000 expected to be received at the end of each of the next 17 years. (We assume that all the income becomes available at the end of the year to simplify our calculations.) We could calculate that by summing the first 17 amounts in the appropriate column of Table 7–2 and multiplying by $200,000. Table 7–3 saves us that effort. The row for 17 years shows the present value of $1 received at the end of *each* of the next 17 years at various interest rates.

But what discount rate should we choose? If a less risky investment, like government bonds, pays 7 percent, then we wouldn't want to choose a rate lower than 10 percent. On the other hand, that 7 percent rate on government bonds is the return on a *fixed dollar* amount. It is therefore a nominal, not a real, rate of return: a return expressed in dollars that can change in value rather than a return expressed in real purchasing power. If the value of the dollar were to fall 4 percent each year, which is to say, if inflation occurred at a 4 percent annual rate, then the real return from a nominal interest rate of 7 percent would be only 3 percent.

The net revenue from manufacturing mousetraps can reasonably be expected to vary right along with the rate of inflation. If the price of everything doubles, the net revenue from mousetrap manufacturing ought to double, too—if other things are equal, as we're assuming. In that case, we would be taking into account twice of the effects of inflation if we discounted the expected net revenue from acquiring the patent at a rate incorporating expectations of inflation. We should therefore ignore the potential effects of inflation upon future income and discount at a rate of 3 or even 4 percent.

Except that now we have left out the risk factor. The appropriate discount rate will be one that takes account of the patent purchaser's subjective estimate of the risks entailed in the purchase. Will the patent stand up to legal challenges? Will someone else invent an even better mousetrap? Will new technologies for the eradication of mice turn mousetraps into museum relics? The more uncertain the expected income whose present value we want to determine, the higher the rate at which we will want to discount it.

It all sounds pretty risky. So let's add 6 percent for risk to a 3 percent real interest rate and discount at 9 percent. What is the present value of $200,000 to be received at the end of each of the next 17 years when discounted at 9 percent? Table 7–3 says that $1 for 17 years has a present value of $8.5436. The present value of a $200,000 annuity (an annuity is an annual amount) is therefore $1,708,720.

One last question: What happens to the present value of the patent if we assume it can be renewed upon expiration for an additional 13 years? If we discount at 9 percent, $200,000 for each of the next 30 years is $2,054,740. Notice that this is only $346,000 more than the value of a 17-year income stream. That shouldn't surprise you. A dollar that isn't due until 18 years from now has a present value of only 21 cents when discounted at 9 percent. And a dollar in 30 years has a present value of only 7.5 cents. (Consult Table 7–2.)

Once Over Lightly

Profit is defined as total revenue minus total cost. Accounting profit includes only the explicit costs (such as expenses) when determining total cost. Economic profit can be usefully defined as total revenue minus total cost if we include *all* opportunity costs in our calculation of total cost.

Profit arises from uncertainty. In the absence of uncertainty, any differences between expected total revenue and expected total cost would be competed away and profits would become zero.

The possibility of an economic profit encourages entrepreneurial activity. Entrepreneurs undertake to reorganize some part of the social world in the belief that the reorganization will create benefits greater than its costs. The entrepreneurs profit is the residual: whatever is left over after paying all those whose cooperation had to be secured in order to complete the entrepreneur's project. The system of residual claimancy facilitates social cooperation by enabling people to agree among themselves on who will take responsibility for each aspect of a common project.

A system of private property rights, market exchange, and money gives rise to monetary calculation: the ability to use market prices as signals to evaluate the potential profitability of one's actions. It allows entrepreneurs to calculate the expected effects of their decisions.

Entrepreneurship itself takes three forms: arbitrage, innovation, and imitation. Entrepreneurial innovation and imitation are essentially sophisticated versions of arbitrage: attempts to buy scarce resources at a perceived low price and recombine and sell them at a perceived higher price.

The entrepreneur's profits disappear when "the truth gets out." Once the entrepreneur's activity has shown how a profit can be made, the revenue available to the entrepreneur or any imitator will decline. If scarcity of a key resource prevents others from imitating the entrepreneur, competition for that resource will raise its price until expected total cost equals expected total revenue.

Uncertainty is a fact of life. Everyone who makes a decision in the absence of complete information about the future consequences of all available opportunities is a speculator. So everyone is a "speculator" in a world of uncertainty.

Professional speculators—those who feel they have a comparative advantage in taking risks—coordinate markets through time.

Futures markets provide people the opportunity to allocate their exposure to risk. Hedgers reduce their exposure by entering into a futures contract with speculators, who seek to increase their exposure to risk.

People who think they know more than others about the relationship between present and future scarcities will want to buy in one time period for sale in the other. If they are correct, they will make a profit on their superior insight and also transport goods through time from periods of lesser to periods of greater scarcity. If they're wrong in their predictions, they will perversely move goods from periods of greater to periods of lesser scarcity and suffer the penalty of a personal loss on their transactions.

The forms that competition takes in any society are determined by the relevant rules of the game, or by the property rights that assign the ability to allocate resources and to appropriate the benefits from their use.

QUESTIONS FOR DISCUSSION

1. Chuck Waggin owns and operates a small tax-accounting firm, which he runs out of the basement of his home.
   - (a) The basement was just wasted space until Chuck turned it into an office for his business. He says his firm is more profitable than most tax-accounting businesses because he doesn't have to pay any rent. Do you agree that rent is not a cost of production for Chuck?
   - (b) Chuck recently turned down an offer to go to work for a larger firm at a salary of $45,000 a year. Chuck's personal income from his business runs about $35,000 a year. Would you say that Chuck's firm is profitable?
   - (c) Chuck says he likes being his own boss and that he would be willing to sacrifice at least $25,000 a year in income to avoid working for someone else. Does that information change your answer to part (b)?
   - (d) Chuck recently invested $10,000 of his savings in an office computer. How would you include the effects of this investment in his costs?
   - (e) Chuck could have earned 12 percent per year on his savings had he not used them to buy the computer. If he had not had these savings, he still would have bought the computer, using a loan from the bank at 18 percent annual interest to finance the purchase. Is the opportunity cost of owning the computer really less for Chuck because he had savings of his own from which to buy it? If Chuck had been required to pay 18 percent interest to the bank rather than giving up 12 percent interest, for what would the additional 6 percent have been a payment? Does Chuck reduce his costs by financing the computer purchase himself?

2. Some people consider the spring herring run near Sitka, Alaska, the most profitable fishing opportunity in the world. Fishing boats have occasionally netted $500,000 worth of herring in a three-hour season. It is not the herring so much as their eggs, called roe, that the fishermen are after, because of the enormous Japanese demand. The basic question: Is it really possible to earn enormous profits by fishing for a few hours in the ocean off Sitka?

   (a) In order to protect the spawning herring from overexploitation, the state limits the season to a few hours and a small area and allows only licensed boats to participate. The number of permits has been 52 since 1978. Anyone who wants to participate must purchase a license from a current holder. The price is about $300,000. Why? What determines the going price of a license? How does this affect the profitability of herring fishing?
   (b) Boat captains hire airplane spotters to increase the likelihood that they will catch some herring during the three-hour season. Spotting is a dangerous occupation with several dozen planes crisscrossing a small area, and pilots can sometimes command $30,000 as herring spotters. Why are boat captains willing to pay such an extraordinary fee?
   (c) If a licensed boat's fishing gear malfunctions, the captain may rent a bystander's boat for as much as $100,000. Why would anyone pay such an exorbitant rental fee? Why would there be any fully equipped bystanders in the area in the first place?
   (d) A licensed boat may catch as much as $500,000 worth of herring. Or it may catch nothing. Estimate the annual loss of a licensed captain whose boat catches nothing.
   (e) The crew's wages depend on their boat's success. Are they entrepreneurs? Are their wages really wages? Or are they profits (or losses!)?
   (f) If a captain who has agreed to pay each of five crewmen 10 percent of the catch and to pay his airplane spotter 20 percent hauls in $100,000 worth of herring, has he earned a profit?

3. The text argues that if an activity is known to be profitable, more people will go into that activity and the profits will disappear. Does that apply to the selling of cocaine?

   (a) The costs of selling cocaine include the risk of being arrested and imprisoned. Why is a ten-year sentence not twice as strong a deterrent as a five-year sentence? Why does one chance in five of being imprisoned for ten years translate into *less* than two years' imprisonment? Is a cocaine seller likely to use a high or a low discount rate in deciding on the subjective cost of possible imprisonment? Why is the threat of imprisonment more effective in deterring some people than others?
   (b) Another cost of selling is the risk of being killed by competitors. This cost will be much lower for some people than for others. Characterize a person for whom this cost will be relatively low.
   (c) For whom is the selling of cocaine profitable?

4. About half of all new restaurants fail within a year, and 85 percent close within five years. What do these figures indicate about the profitability of the restaurant business? Why do so many entrepreneurs nonetheless start up new restaurants every year?
5. "Everybody knows" that laborers receive wages and only owners receive profits. But is it true?
   (a) If employees agree to continue working for an employer who is currently unable to pay them, because they don't want the firm to fail, are they working for wages or for profits?
   (b) If you agree to loan your lawnmower to someone who wants to start a lawncare business, on condition that he pay you $2 each time he borrows it, are you a capitalist? Is your $2 properly called profit? Would your answers differ if he agreed to pay you 20 percent of his gross receipts?
6. The governments of poor countries often display what some call an "edifice complex": They enthusiastically build new roads, dams, and other structures but then don't keep them in adequate repair.
   (a) Can you explain this phenomenon using the concept of the residual claimant?
   (b) What attitude would the private owner of a road take toward maintenance?
7. Are entrepreneurs necessarily capitalists?
   (a) The text defines the entrepreneur as the one who assumes responsibility by guaranteeing all others a fixed amount for their cooperation. When and why do others trust the entrepreneur's guarantee? If this question seems abstract, ask yourself whether you will work hard for someone when you don't expect to see your first paycheck until you have worked three weeks. When and why will you *not* trust an employer in this way?
   (b) Who besides employees typically receive guarantees from the entrepreneur that they must trust if they are to do business with the entrepreneur? What is the basis for their confidence in the entrepreneur's promises?
   (c) Why do employees ever agree to let the employer have all the profits?
   (d) Why do employers ever agree to guarantee the employee a certain wage, no matter how badly things turn out?
8. Suppose that you are leaving tomorrow for a two-week combined business and vacation trip to a distant location. You'll be traveling by plane.
   (a) In what way are you speculating as you pack your suitcase?
   (b) On which side would you be more inclined to err—taking too many clothes and having to haul heavy suitcases around, or taking too few and finding yourself without an item you want?
   (c) Would your answer to the previous question differ according to whether you were planning to be in a large city or a remote resort?
   (d) Suppose you take only a single pair of dress shoes and accidentally spill ink on one of them just before an important business meeting. You dash out quickly and buy a new pair of shoes. Explain how the shoe seller's willingness to take a risk reduced your risk in taking only a single pair of dress shoes.

9. In an article on hoarding in the United States in which a number of social scientists were quoted, a sociologist said that gasoline hoarding was not rational but rather a result of Americans' emotional stake in their cars. A historian said hoarding was an absolutely typical American trait. Some attributed hoarding to a "shortage psychosis," and others spoke of "panic buying." Another sociologist said that strong leadership was required to stop such "competitive behavior."

   (a) How could we decide whether hoarding is irrational, psychotic, a national character trait, a product of emotion and panic, *or* an intelligent response to uncertainty?
   (b) What is the difference between hoarding and maintaining an appropriate level of inventory?
   (c) Why do both business firms and households maintain inventories? How do they decide on the proper level of inventories for particular goods?

10. Are you speculating when you buy fire insurance on your home? Could you save money by getting together with your friends to form an insurance cooperative, thereby eliminating the necessity of paying something to a middleman (the insurance company)? What kinds of useful information do insurance companies provide?
11. Perhaps you are familiar with the story of Joseph in the Book of Genesis. Joseph had an inspired interpretation of the Pharaoh's dream: Egypt will enjoy seven years of abundant crops, he told the Pharaoh, followed by seven years of severe famine that would sweep across all of Egypt. Joseph advised the Pharaoh to collect one-fifth of the grain crop during the abundant years and hoard it under guard, to be held as a reserve against the impending seven years of famine. The Pharaoh was so impressed with this insight that he appointed Joseph to discharge the plan. He did so, and during the famine, Joseph reopened the granaries and sold it to the Egyptians.

    Compare Joseph's actions to those of modern-day speculators who predict a greater scarcity of grain in the future.

   (a) What was Joseph intentionally trying to accomplish?
   (b) What do professional speculators intentionally try to accomplish?
   (c) What effect did Joseph's actions have on the supply curve of grain when he hoarded it and kept it under guard?
   (d) What effect do professional speculators have on the current supply of grain when they enter contracts that promise to sell grain only in the future?
   (e) What effect did Joseph's actions have on the supply of grain during the famine period?
   (f) What effect do professional speculators have on the supply of grain in the future period?
   (g) Are the outcomes substantially different?
   (h) Finally, what was the source of Joseph's information, and what is the source of the professional speculators' information?

12. The news media report that a severe frost has done extensive damage to the Florida orange crop and that frozen orange juice will soon be in very short supply. How would you evaluate each of the following actions?

Choose one of the options: completely fair, probably fair, probably unfair, totally unfair.

(a) Local grocer raises the price on all frozen orange juice in the store as soon as she hears the news.
(b) Homemaker rushes to the store and buys a three-month supply of frozen orange juice as soon as she hears the news.
(c) Orange grower whose crop was not touched by the frost raises the price for all his oranges as soon as he hears the news.
(d) Orange grower whose crop was severely damaged raises the price for all of her remaining oranges as soon as she hears the news.
(e) Orange juice processors rush to purchase as many oranges as they can as soon as they hear the news.

Are all your answers consistent?

13. You decide in May that the coming summer's corn crop will be much larger and the fall corn price consequently much lower than most people expect.
    (a) To act on your beliefs, should you buy or should you sell December corn futures? (*Futures* are contracts to buy or sell at a future date at a price established now.)
    (b) If a substantial number of knowledgeable people come to share your opinion about the size of this summer's crop, what will happen to the price of December corn futures?
    (c) What information will this change in the price of corn futures convey to current holders and users of corn?
    (d) How will this information affect their decisions about holding corn for future sale or use?
    (e) How will these decisions, based on the information provided by the change in the price of December corn futures, affect June consumption?
    (f) Can speculators carry a bumper crop *backward in time* from a period of lesser to a period of greater scarcity?
14. Worldwatch Institute regularly predicts an increased scarcity of grain worldwide in the coming year and warns that the world is about to run out of food.
    (a) How could you use the commodity futures page in the newspaper to evaluate this prediction?
    (b) If professional speculators disagree with the forecasts of the Worldwatch Institute, in whose forecasts would you have more confidence? Why?
    (c) Do you think that the people at Worldwatch Institute buy wheat futures at the time they issue their forecasts? *Should* they?
15. You ask your college for permission to set up a lemonade stand at the annual spring commencement, and the college grants permission. After paying your bills for materials (lemons, sugar, cups, and so forth), you clear $250 for an afternoon's work.
    (a) Did you make a $250 profit?
    (b) Are you likely to be given the lemonade concession again next year? What difference does it make whether or not word gets around about how much you cleared?

(c) If the college next year auctions off the franchise, how much would you be willing to bid? Who will then get the profit from the lemonade stand?

16. Before 1980, the Interstate Commerce Commission rarely granted new permits to trucking firms to haul goods interstate, and operating rights were often extremely valuable. They were listed as assets on the books of trucking companies and made up a significant part of the purchase price whenever such companies were sold.
    (a) What factors established the market value of such operating rights?
    (b) When the Motor Carrier Act of 1980 took effect, allowing much easier entry into interstate trucking, the market value of operating rights fell. Why?
    (c) Was this fall a loss?
    (d) Losses as well as profits are the consequence of uncertainty. What was the uncertainty that produced this loss for trucking companies in 1980?
    (e) What would have happened to the value of operating rights in the 1970s if everyone had known 10 years in advance that Congress was going to ease restrictions on entry into interstate trucking after 1980?
    (f) The Motor Carrier Act of 1980 was a change in the rules of the game. Which were the principal property rights affected, and with what consequences?
17. The U.S. Department of Agriculture used to control hops production by assigning each established hops grower a specific share of the total amount of hops that could be sold. Those who wanted to go into the business of growing hops had to purchase or lease allotments from existing growers, at a considerable price. The Agriculture Department, in announcing its decision to terminate the system, objected to the fact that new growers had to pay for an allotment that had been given to the original growers at no charge. Does the Agriculture Department's objection make any sense? If the allotments had *not* acquired any market value, what would this imply about the original decision to restrict hops production?
18. The following paragraph is condensed from a long letter to the editor of a metropolitan newspaper:

    > If you want to make money real fast, buy a mobile home park. You can raise the rents to your heart's content, because the tenants usually can't afford to move. And even if they could, there is usually no place to go, since there aren't enough mobile home parks to take care of all the people who own mobile homes.

    (a) If the situation is as dire for owners of mobile homes as the letter writer says, what will already have happened to the purchase price of mobile home parks? Do owners of such parks make huge profits from renting space to mobile home owners?
    (b) If existing mobile home parks can be operated very profitably or sold for very high prices, why don't entrepreneurs create more such parks?

(c) If the city responds to the complaint of this letter writer and others by putting price controls on the rental rates mobile home parks may charge, what will happen to the price of mobile homes currently occupying rent-controlled sites?

19. Can those who own the stock of a large business corporation prevent the managers from pursuing their own interests rather than the interests of the shareholders? How can they effectively monitor the managers' behavior and persuade the corporation's board of directors to discharge executives whose goal is power, privileges, and "perks" for themselves rather than net revenue for the owners? Can't the managers generally use their positions and the corporation's resources to nominate and secure the election of directors who will be partial to management rather than guardians of the shareholders' interests? (The question that follows continues this line of inquiry, but in a different direction.)

20. Can those who own the stock of a large business corporation prevent the managers from pursuing their own interests rather than the interests of the shareholders?

    (a) What happens to the price of a corporation's stock when it is managed for the benefit of the managers rather than the shareholders?
    (b) What would happen to the stock price if some individual or group gained voting control over the board of directors and replaced the management with people willing and able to pursue maximum net revenue for shareholders?
    (c) How do these facts create incentives for some people to invest resources in monitoring managers' behavior?
    (d) How does the prospect of what managers like to call "a hostile takeover" restrain the behavior of managers? Toward whom is a hostile takeover hostile? Toward whom is it friendly?
    (e) Are those who specialize in corporate takeovers entrepreneurs?

21. Are the profits of entrepreneurs obtained through coercion or through persuasion? (Definition of terms: *coercion*—inducing people to cooperate by threatening to reduce their options; *persuasion*—inducing people to cooperate by promising to expand their options.) If you don't know how to answer the question, try thinking about the adequacy in this context of the proposed definitions for coercion and persuasion.

22. The state lottery claims that its grand prize is $1 million. The lucky winner will receive $50,000 upon presentation of the winning ticket plus $50,000 at the end of each of the next 19 years. Is that really a $1 million prize? What is it actually worth? Will you want to use a real or a nominal interest rate to discount these future amounts? Why? Suppose the 19 future payments were all to be adjusted for any intervening changes in the value of money. What interest rate would you use then to calculate the present value of the "$1 million" prize? What effect does the decision to "index" future payments to changes in the value of money have on the present value of the prize?

23. "Save it," somebody says. "Don't sell it. It's not worth much now, but in 20 years it will probably be worth five times as much." Should you save it or sell it? What will $1 now be worth in 20 years if invested at the rate of interest currently obtainable from relatively risk-free loans?

24. Take a look at the yellow pages in your local phonebook. Can you provide a list of five entrepreneurial firms in each of the following categories, and provide reasons for your placement? Do some of the firms fall into more than one category?

   (a) Firms that primarily engage in arbitrage activity
   (b) Firms that primarily engage in innovative activity
   (c) Firms that primarily engage in entrepreneurial imitation

Competition and Monopoly

8

When we say that prices are set by supply and demand, we're employing a metaphor. If we wanted to be realistic, we would have to say that sellers set the majority of prices, buyers set most of the rest, and a few are set by negotiations between sellers and buyers. Sometimes government agencies decree minimum or maximum prices, but that still leaves sellers and buyers free to set prices somewhere within the limits that the law allows.

How much freedom do sellers and buyers have when they set their prices? We have already learned that substitutes abound so we know that sellers do not have complete control in dictating the terms of exchange. However, it is also not the case that they have no control whatsoever—every product is unique to some extent in some dimension of good characteristics such as quality or location. So we find ourselves in the market caught in situations described as either seller's markets or buyer's markets. We like to buy in a buyer's market and sell in a seller's market, though normally we don't have control over which market we buy and sell in to the extent we would like. Those conditions are largely given to us.

Market transactions are an *activity*. Because scarcity is a logical condition, not a material one, we must choose. We cannot go to the ballgame and watch television at the same time. In making our choices, as we have discussed, we ration or prioritize. In our interactions with others this means we *compete*. We cannot escape competing, though competition can take many different forms.

Who Qualifies as a Monopolist?

In order to understand better the meaning of competition, we will—paradoxically—begin with the word that is usually taken to mean the opposite, *monopoly*. The word *monopoly* is the product of two Greek words meaning "one seller." Are there any monopolists in that strict sense of the word? Try to think of something that is sold exclusively by one seller.

"Monopoly" literally means "one seller."

Before the advent of cellular phones, local telephone service seemed a good example. But was it an accurate example even then? There were many independent sellers of telephone service in the United States, as a matter of fact, even before the breakup of AT&T in 1984. Still, that may be beside the point. For any given buyer there was typically one seller, because telephone companies usually enjoyed exclusive selling privileges in particular areas. On the other hand, buyers don't have to live in a given area; they can move to another franchise area if they prefer the product there. Back comes a justifiably impatient snort: "That's irrelevant." But it's not completely irrelevant. Moving your residence may be a prohibitively expensive way to shift your telephone patronage, and it's hard to imagine people actually moving just because they resent the local phone company. But that *is* a way of obtaining a substitute product. And by its absurdity, our example calls attention to the crux of the problem: the availability of substitutes.

Suppose we redefine the commodity sold by telephone companies and call it "communication services." There would be nothing intrinsically misleading about that. After all, that is why anyone wants a telephone: to obtain communication services. But if this is the product being sold, the telephone company never was a monopolist, but rather a seller in competition with Western Union, the post office, various messenger and delivery services, loud shouting, fast running, and all sorts of computer communication techniques. The point of all this is simply that, if we define the commodity broadly enough, not a single commodity in the country is sold by a monopolist.

Now let's look at the other side of the coin. Suppose we define the commodity very narrowly. If telegrams are not the same thing as telephone calls, neither is a gallon of milk at the little store next door the same thing as a gallon of milk three blocks away at the supermarket. If you have no car, are rocking a screaming baby who won't stop until fed, and have no one to leave the baby with, the milk three blocks away is a vividly different commodity from the milk at the store next door. Ask any parent of a small baby. Thus, we are forced to conclude that, when the commodity is defined narrowly enough, every seller is a monopolist, because no two sellers will ever be offering completely identical products.

If those examples haven't persuaded you yet, let's take a very simple one: Consider, for example, McDonald's. Certainly it is a huge fast-food chain, but is it a monopoly—is it a *sole seller* of a good or service? Professor OnThe Onehand says no: He declares, as an incontestable fact, that there are many substitutes for McDonald's food—think of all the other fast-food chains in the economy—Wendy's, Burger King, White Castle, Taco Bell, Pizza Hut, the thousands of Chinese food carryouts, and so on. If we define the good that McDonald's produces as "fast food," then the list of substitutes for *McDonald's fast food* is huge. Surely McDonald's is not a single seller of fast food.

But Professor OnThe Otherhand claims, using the very same definition of monopoly, that McDonald's is indeed a monopolist. How can that be? Suppose we narrow the definition of the good that McDonald's produces to the "Big Mac." It is an incontestable fact that *McDonald's is the sole seller of Big Macs*. Therefore, McDonald's can be called a monopoly. Both of our hypothetical economists are using the term *monopoly* in the same way, but reaching very different conclusions because they have very different notions of the particular good that the firm is selling, and the market that the firm operates within. (Try it for yourself: Consider Hallmark greeting cards. Can you argue both sides—that it is a monopoly *and* that it is not a monopoly?)

With that definition, everybody and nobody is a monopolist!

The word *monopoly* is extraordinarily ambiguous. For everyone or no one is a sole seller depending on how we define the commodity being sold. Furthermore, there is no satisfactory way to decide in all cases just how broadly or narrowly the concept of a commodity ought to be defined. Most households purchase almost all of their electricity from a single seller, usually known as the electric company. *Almost* all of it? If they use any battery-powered equipment, they are obtaining some of their electricity from suppliers other than the local electric company. Do they buy any of their power from the local gas company? The gas company doesn't sell *electrical* power, but gas and electricity are substitutes for many household purposes. So what is the commodity here? Electricity? Electricity obtained from power lines? Power? If we decide it's electricity obtained from power lines, should we distinguish between the electricity coming in through the wires currently in place and the electricity that would be coming in if some competing company supplied it? Is there an alternative supplier? Increasingly there is, or at least there could be. So who qualifies as a *sole* seller? Imagine public policy founded on such a definition of monopoly.

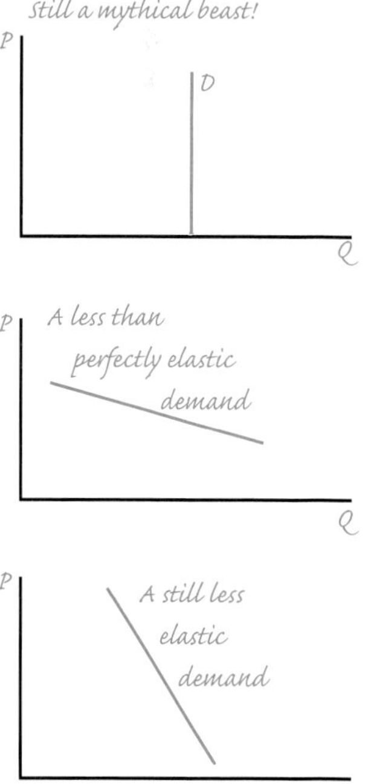

Alternatives, Elasticity, and Market Power

Let's try another approach. What would be so bad about a single seller? If we find a case where there really is only one seller of a good, then those with a demand for the good will have no alternatives. No one wants to be without alternatives. The poorer our alternatives, the weaker our position and the more easily we can be taken advantage of.

But we learned in Chapter 3 that there are always some alternatives. There is a substitute for anything, even the services of the local electrical utility. After all, no one really needs electricity; humans got along without it for thousands of years. On the other hand, electricity is an extremely valuable convenience for households and business firms. The concept from economics that suggests itself is price elasticity of demand. No seller is a monopolist in the strictest sense of the word because there is no such thing as a *perfectly* inelastic demand. No seller has any buyer totally over the barrel. On the other hand, very few sellers of anything face perfectly elastic demand curves. Anything less than complete elasticity means that sellers will retain some business when they raise their price, which in turn implies that sellers have at least a morsel of market power. Where is the line between a morsel and monopoly?

There is no clear line of demarcation unless we decide to draw one arbitrarily. Elasticities of demand reflect the availability of substitutes; other things remaining equal, the more good substitutes there are for anything, the more elastic will be the demand for it. Market power is thus seen to be a matter of degree and to be inversely related to elasticity of demand. Defined in this way, the term *market power* has a meaning that we can talk about and use. But we have not yet found a useful definition for the word *monopoly*.

Privileges and Restrictions

Let's try yet another approach. In the early nineteenth century there was often no distinction made in the United States between a monopoly and a corporation. The reason was that corporations had always been created by special governmental acts. They received, whether from Crown and Parliament before the Revolution or from state and national legislatures afterward, special "patents," as they were called: official documents granting rights and privileges not available to others. Corporate charters were therefore called "grants of monopoly" because they gave to one party a power that was withheld from others. The East India Company was such a "monopoly," and the special privilege of selling tea in the colonies, given to it in 1773, helped bring on the American Revolution.

Here is another and quite different meaning of monopoly, one related to acts of the state. If the state allows some to engage in an activity but prosecutes others for doing so, or if it taxes or restricts some sellers but not others, or if it grants protection or assistance to some while compelling others to make their own way unaided, the state is creating exclusive privileges. This meaning for the word *monopoly* has contemporary relevance as well as historical significance.

Many business organizations operate with monopoly grants of this kind. In the name of all sorts of commendable-sounding goals—public safety, fair competition, stability, national security, efficiency—governments at all levels have imposed restrictions on entry into various industries or trades. The beneficiaries of these restrictions always include the parties who can escape them. These parties will rarely admit that they enjoy a grant of monopoly power. But the effect of the restrictions nonetheless is to prevent some from competing who would otherwise do so.

We could, if we wished, use the word *monopolist* to describe any individual or organization operating with the advantage of special privileges granted by the government. The trouble is that most people no longer use the word in this way. By such a definition, the postal service is a monopolist, as are most public utilities, many liquor stores, morticians, and crop dusters; the American Medical Association, state bar associations, and labor unions; farmers with acreage allotments, licensed barbers, and most taxicab firms. The list is long indeed. And so, unlike most other economics textbook authors, we are going to take the heroic step of dropping the word *monopoly* from our working vocabulary. Its meanings are too many and too vague. " 'When I use a word,' Humpty Dumpty said in a rather scornful tone, 'it means just what I choose it to mean—neither more nor less.' " *Monopoly* is a favorite of contemporary Humpty Dumpties. And that's why we are not going to employ it. We shall try to use alternative terms that are more likely to communicate the precise situation we have in mind.

Historical definition of monopoly.

Price Takers and Price Searchers

Let's go back now to the questions with which this chapter began: Who actually sets prices and how much freedom do they have?

It's a free country, as they say, and businesses are usually free to set their own prices. The USX Corporation (formerly United States Steel) has substantial discretion when it prints its price lists, and a wheat farmer from Kansas can feel quite safe from the threat of prosecution if he decides to offer his crop at $6.00 per bushel. But there is obviously an important difference that helps explain why USX hires people to decide what its prices should be and wheat farmers do not. The difference, we shall nonetheless insist, is a difference of degree, not kind.

Take the case of the wheat farmer first. If he consults the financial pages of his newspaper or tunes in for the noonday market reports, he will find that number-two ordinary hard Kansas City wheat opened at $3.48¾ a bushel. That news may disappoint or delight him, but there is almost nothing he can do to change it. If he decides that the price is an excellent one and sells his entire crop for immediate delivery, the market will feel scarcely a ripple. Even if he is one of the biggest wheat farmers in the state, he is still such a small part of the total number of those offering to buy or sell wheat that he cannot affect the price. The difference between what the closing price will be if he sells all his crop and what it will be if he sells only half of it will not be as much as ¼ cent.

Price	Quantity demanded (of that farmer's wheat)
$3.50	None at all
$3.48	All he has
$3.46	All he has

(when the market price is $3.48 3/4)

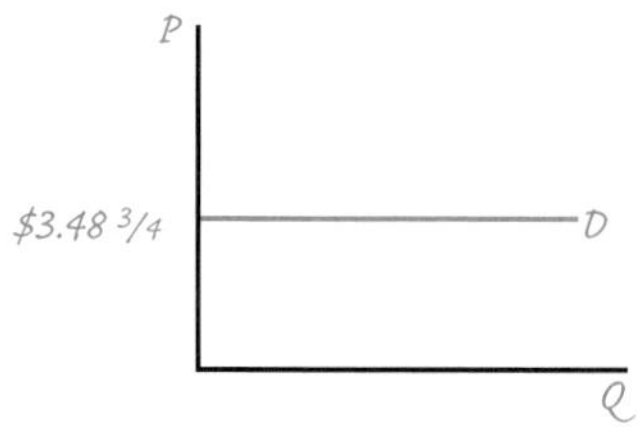

A perfectly elastic demand curve

Economists therefore call the wheat farmer a *price taker*. He cannot affect the price by his own actions. The price at the local grain elevator is determined by the actions of many buyers and sellers all over the country. If the farmer exercises his legal right to put a price tag on his wheat as little as 2 cents higher than the market decrees, he will sell no wheat. And since he can sell all the wheat he has at the going price, he has no incentive to offer to sell any wheat at less than the going price. Price takers face perfectly elastic demand curves, or what for all practical purposes amount to perfectly elastic demand curves. The demand curves are horizontal at the going price.

Most sellers are not in this position. They can raise their prices, if they choose, without losing all their sales. And, unlike the farmer, they can't always sell everything they're capable of producing without lowering their prices. At higher prices they will sell less; at lower prices they will be able to sell more. They must choose a price or set of prices. Economists therefore call them *price searchers*. Torn between the desire for higher prices and the desire for larger sales, they must search out the price or set of prices most advantageous to them.

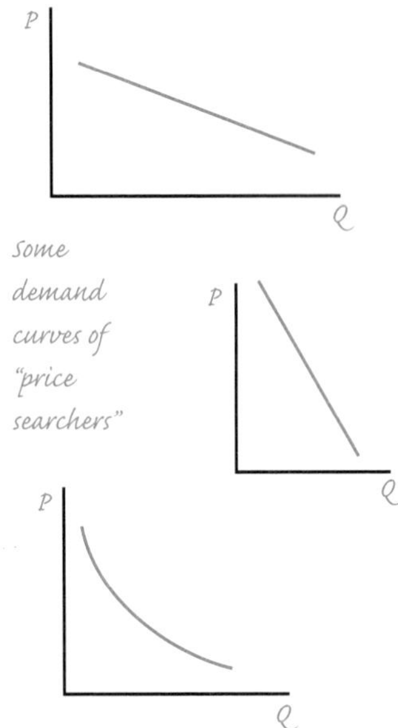

Some demand curves of "price searchers"

Price searchers include USX, the trustees of a private university weighing a tuition increase, the proprietor of a local grocery store, and the little boy selling lemonade on a hot afternoon. There is a long tradition in economics of referring to all price searchers as monopolists. But this is a technical use of the word that is confusing to everyone except professional economists. Because the little boy selling lemonade does not face a perfectly elastic demand curve, he is not a price taker but a price searcher. It seems silly to anyone not steeped in the history of economics to call him a monopolist. So we shall not do it. The term *price searcher* captures the situation in which we're interested. Price searchers all have some market power, but it is a matter of degree inversely related to the elasticity of the demand the seller faces.

Price Takers' Markets and "Optimal" Resource Allocation

Economists applied the disapproving term *monopolist* to what we shall call *price searcher* in large part because they wanted to emphasize the different consequences of these two types of price setting. Markets in which all buyers and sellers were price takers were graced with the approving term *competitive markets*. We want to point out the advantages they saw in price takers' markets without adopting the misleading monopolistic–competitive distinction, which erroneously implies that price searchers face no competition. To do so we shall use the graph of Figure 8–1, which shows the demand and supply curves for house painters during a particular summer in the town of Pratte Falls.

The number of house-painting hours that will be demanded and supplied depends on the price per hour of house painters'

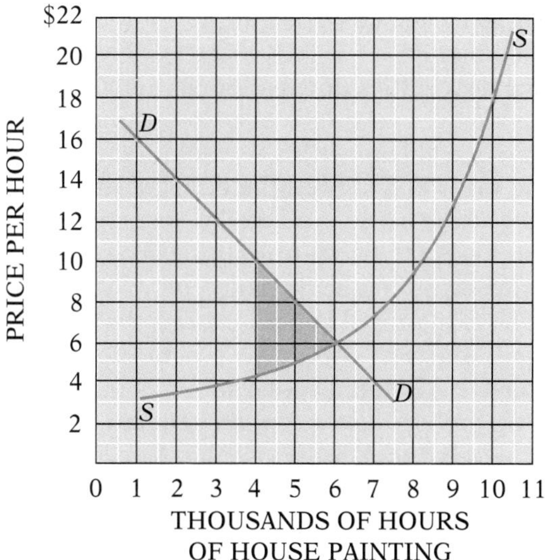

Figure 8–1 **Demand and supply curves for house painting in Pratte Falls**

services. Because people's skills in this area differ considerably, we shall simplify our exposition by assuming that each hour of service shown on the horizontal axis has been adjusted for quality. If Porter is only 40 percent as productive in an hour as the average Pratte Falls painter, he will take 2½ hours to supply "1 hour" of the good shown on the graph. Wagner, who is three times as good as the average, supplies "1 hour" of house painting every 20 minutes.

The first point to remember is that supply curves are marginal opportunity-cost curves. The curve labeled *SS* in Figure 8–1 shows the value of all the opportunities given up as Pratte Fallers provide progressively larger amounts of house-painting services. The people who contribute to the lower-left portions of the curve are people with large comparative advantages in house painting, because they are either extremely adept painters or extraordinarily inept at everything else. The upper-right portion of the curve, including sections not even shown, depicts the supply responses of those who would have to give up a lucrative law practice to paint, who are subject to attacks of dizziness at heights above seven feet, or who for any other reason must sacrifice a highly valued opportunity in order to supply an hour of house painting. Keep in mind that the marginal-cost curve of any single individual will also eventually slope upward to the right. The value of the opportunities forgone as one devotes more and more time to any particular activity is bound to increase as that activity crowds out alternative activities, simply because people sacrifice their least-valued opportunities first and give up more highly valued opportunities only in response to a stronger inducement.[1]

If the price now settles down at $6 an hour, so that 6,000 hours of the good are exchanged over the summer, the heart of many economists will leap with a special kind of joy. Why? Because at the price of $6, given the demand and supply curves, no unit of the good is being produced whose marginal opportunity cost, as represented by the supply curve, exceeds its marginal benefit, as represented by the demand curve. Moreover, every unit of the good whose marginal benefit exceeds its marginal cost is being produced. And how could we do better than that? Economists have traditionally gone so far as to call such an arrangement an *optimal allocation of resources*. *Optimal* means best, which is surely excessive praise; but let's look a little more closely to see exactly what's happening here.

Suppose that the people supplying those 6,000 hours at $6 an hour decide that they deserve larger incomes and somehow persuade the town council to pass a law setting $10 an hour as the minimum price for an hour of house-painting services. We'll suppose further that the law is effectively enforced. What will happen? Only 4,000 hours will now be demanded. And because that's all that can be sold, that's all that will *actually* be supplied, even though, as the graph shows, painters will *want* to supply about twice that amount at a price of $10.

Establishment and enforcement of the $10 price will make some people better off and others worse off. Note that some of those who are worse off may be former house painters forced into less desirable occupations by the legislated price increase. Economists have no satisfactory way of balancing one person's gain against another person's loss to decide whether net social well-being will go up or down as the result of such a change. About all they can really do is point out that the Pratte Falls law prevents mutually advantageous exchange. The area under the demand curve between 4,000 and 6,000 hours represents the dollar value of what demanders are willing to give up to obtain those units of the good. The area under the supply curve represents the dollar value of what suppliers are willing to give up to provide those units of service. The difference between the two areas, shaded in Figure 8–1, is a potential gain from trade that the

[1] This hypothetical example also illustrates the fundamental similarity of supply and demand. The people who are willing to pay up to $20 per hour to have someone else paint their houses, and who thereby create that portion of the demand curve below $20, may well be among the people who create the supply curve at prices above $20. Example: "I'll pay up to $20 per hour to get my house painted this summer. But if I have to pay more than that, I'll do it myself." Such a person, who stops demanding and starts supplying to himself at some high enough price may, even at a higher price, also begin supplying to others. (If you ask nicely enough, even Boettke and Prychitko might consider painting your house for, say, $250 an hour each, plus travel, meals, and accommodations. At current prices, however, it is obviously not our comparative advantage to be house painters!)

ordinance effectively removes by prohibiting any exchanges at less than $10 an hour.

What does all this have to do with price takers' markets and their superiority, in traditional economic analysis, over price searchers' markets? It comes to this: Prices that are fixed above marginal cost rule out some mutually advantageous exchange opportunities. In price takers' markets, there are so many sellers that no one of them has the power to set and keep the price above marginal cost. In price searchers' markets, they do.

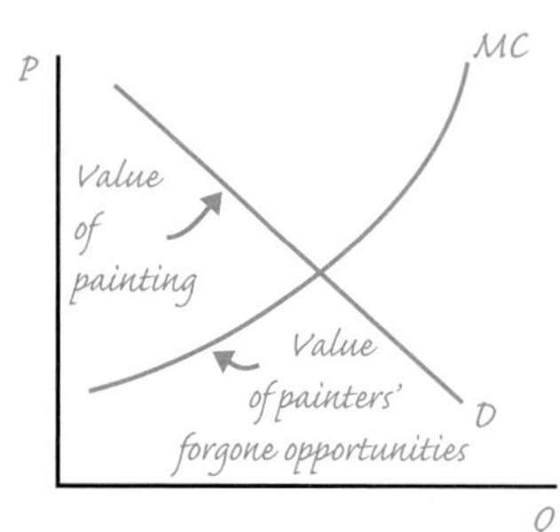

How serious that problem is and how high the costs of correcting it might be are two of the questions that will run through the rest of this chapter and in Chapter 10.

Competition as a Process

When we use the term *competition* in everyday language we more often than not mean it to refer to an activity that individuals engage in. Tiger Woods is fiercely competitive in the sense that he combines his genetic endowment with hard work and forged mental toughness to compete against and defeat his opponents in golf tournaments. Michael Jordan's career in the NBA has been distinguished by his competitive drive to excel on an individual and team level. His goal, as is the goal of all great sports figures, has been to win and win overwhelmingly. It is this itch to compete that has forced Michael Jordan to return from retirement once again and test himself against the best basketball players in the world. It was no different for Ted Turner when he revolutionized television news or Bill Gates when he lowered our costs of using computers through software innovations.

Many economists attribute a slightly different meaning to the word *competition*. For them, the economic notion of competition represents a state of affairs. A competitive market is said to exist when these conditions are present:

Characteristics of "perfect competition."

- There is a large number of buyers and sellers so nobody possesses market power.
- Market participants possess full and complete information of alternatives.
- Sellers produce a homogenous product.
- There is costless mobility of resources.
- Economic actors are price takers.

When all these conditions exist, economists call this "perfect competition." The logic of perfect competition results in a hypothetical optimal allocation of resources and zero economic profits.

This basic model has been very useful to economists for close to a century. But its use has not been without serious costs to our economic understanding. The development of this model has obscured the institutional framework that underlies a functioning economic system (which we examine in Chapter 11). It has overlooked the dynamic and multifaceted nature of exchange behavior on the market (as we discussed in Chapter 7). And it has ignored the entrepreneurial adjustment process that is at the center of the robust nature of market economies and the source of their vibrancy that is the engine of economic growth and prosperity in the modern world (the subject of Chapter 20). Ludwig von Mises (whom we quoted in Chapter 7) was well aware of that adjustment process in his emphasis on the calculative properties of the market economy. The notion of perfect competition has unfortunately overlooked the entrepreneur, whom Mises' own student, Israel Kirzner, further describes as being the "driving force" of real-world markets:

Perfect competition ignores the role of entrepreneurship.

> To claim that, at any given instant, all conceivably relevant available opportunities have been instantaneously grasped, is to fly in the face of what we know about real-world economic systems. It is one thing to postulate rapid equilibrating processes as imposing systemic order upon markets; it is quite another thing (in the absence of any theory about equilibrative processes!) to treat the world as at all times already in the attained state of equilibrium.

In Kirzner's view, which your authors share, the entrepreneur "operates to *change* price/output data. In this way . . . the entrepreneurial role drives the ever-changing process of the market."

The model of the "perfectly competitive" economy, which has no special focus on entrepreneurship, was used by economists to explain the supply-demand coordination proposition we explored in Chapter 5. There is a general interconnectedness to economic activity that is often forgotten in less developed depictions of the economic system. The fact that a revolution in Chile will be immediately registered in the price of copper in the futures market in New York City is one of the most essential points of sophisticated economic theory. A functioning market economy provides incentives and information for economic actors to coordinate their plans with one another to realize the mutually beneficial gains from exchange. Under the conditions of "perfect competition," however, the market accomplishes this coordination task *perfectly* so that no further gains from exchange exist and all least-cost technologies are being employed in production. Furthermore, the logic underlying the proposition that a profit opportunity known to all will be realized by none provides us with a clear example of the economic way of thinking.

Just to illustrate the power of this proposition, consider what you witness on a regular visit to the checkout counter at your local supermarket. As you prepare to check out you look for the shortest line in which to stand. But so do all your fellow shoppers. If the line two registers to the left of you is moving faster, those in the back of the line will move over. They will seize that opportunity to get on the faster line and in so doing increase the number of people in that line, thus slowing down the checkout process on that line. The *movement* of shoppers—a *readjustment process*—has reduced the length of the original line and increased the length of the shorter line and in the limit pushed the situation to where all checkout lines are equivalent in waiting time.

What is true for shopping lines is also true for toll lines on highways and stock tips on the stock market. Sound economic theory is grounded in this logic. Unfortunately, the model of perfect competition tends to obscure the active process by which this result tends to emerge. By assumption, the model focuses on that state of affairs that occurs *after* all this activity has taken place, *after* all the readjustments have been successfully accomplished. There is a prereconciliation of economic plans in the model, not an explanation of how economic actors engage in exchange and production activity to realize the gains from exchange, which if pursued to its logical limit would exhaust all potential gains. Over 200 years ago Adam Smith talked about haggling on the market, but modern theory focuses on the conditions that would result to *eliminate* the possibility for any further haggling. It is our opinion that this has been a major intellectual error that has led to confusion in both economic theory and public policy.

Perfect competition ignores the plan-adjustment process that characterizes real-world market activity.

Once Over Lightly

The word *monopoly* means literally one seller. But whether any seller is the only seller depends on how narrowly or broadly we define the product. Under a sufficiently broad definition, there are innumerable sellers of every product. Under a sufficiently narrow definition, however, every seller's product differs from every other's, and all sellers are monopolists. The word *monopoly* is therefore inherently ambiguous and will not be used in subsequent chapters.

The antisocial connotations of the word *monopoly* stem from the belief that the customers of a sole seller have no alternatives and are therefore at the mercy of the seller. Because there are in fact alternatives to every course of action and substitutes for every good, no seller ever has unlimited power over buyers. Market power is always a matter of degree.

The concept of price elasticity of demand provides a useful way of thinking and talking about the degree of market power. Demand elasticities, which can vary between zero and infinity, reflect the availability of substitutes. The more good alternatives buyers have, the more elastic are the demand curves sellers face and the more limited is the power of sellers to establish terms of sale strongly advantageous to themselves.

In the early years of the United States, a monopoly usually meant an organization to which the government had granted some exclusive privilege. The monopolist was often the only legal seller. Although this meaning of the term is no longer common, it does have contemporary relevance because federal, state, and local governments are extensively involved in the granting of special privileges that restrict competition.

A useful distinction to make in trying to understand how prices are established is the distinction between *price takers* and *price searchers*. Price takers must accept the price decreed by the market. Buyers have such excellent substitutes for the product that any attempt to raise the price or otherwise shift the terms of sale will leave the seller with no customers at all. The price searcher, on the other hand, can sell different quantities at different prices and must therefore search for the most advantageous price.

QUESTIONS FOR DISCUSSION

1. List some commodities or services that are sold by only one seller. Then list some of the close substitutes for these goods. How much market power is possessed by the single sellers you listed?
2. Does a firm have a monopoly if it publishes the only morning newspaper in a particular city? If it publishes the only daily newspaper, morning or afternoon? If it publishes the only daily newspaper and owns the only television channel in the city? What are the various goods that a daily newspaper supplies? With what other goods does it compete?
3. Electric utilities are usually given exclusive franchises by the government to sell electricity in a particular area. Are they in competition with sellers of anything else? Do they compete for sales in any way with electric utility companies franchised to operate in other areas? Is a company that manufactures electrical appliances in competition with electric utilities? If you think not, remember that there are many margins on which competition can occur. Suppose the appliance manufacturer is looking for ways to increase the energy efficiency of its products. Doesn't that bring it into competition with electric utilities?
4. Is the U.S. Postal Service a monopoly?
   (a) With whom does the Postal Service compete in its first-class mail service (for correspondence)? Its second-class mail service (for publishers of newspapers and magazines)? Its third-class mail service (for advertisers)? Its parcel service? Its express mail service (guaranteed next-day delivery)?
   (b) If the Postal Service has the power to set its prices without regard to supply and demand, why does it so often operate at a loss? Why doesn't it raise its prices and eliminate those troublesome losses?
   (c) When the Postal Service raised the first-class postage rate in 2000 by about 8 percent, from 32 cents to 34 cents, do you think its revenue from first-class mail also rose by 8 percent? What would an 8 percent

increase in revenue have implied about the elasticity of demand for first-class mail service?

5. The good that the public school systems in American cities supply is one that many persons are required by law to consume. Moreover, competing suppliers, because they are denied the right to finance their activities through taxation, must ordinarily charge much higher prices than the public schools charge. Are public school systems monopolists?
6. It is illegal to market certain agricultural commodities, such as tobacco, unless the product was grown on land that the federal government has licensed for the growing of these commodities. Does this mean tobacco farmers are monopolists? Are they price takers or are they price searchers?
7. If monopolies are undesirable, as almost everyone seems to assume, why do governments so often try to protect particular sellers against the competition that additional entrants to the industry would provide?
   (a) Why does the U.S. government prohibit people from competing with the Postal Service in the delivery of first-class mail?
   (b) Why do cities almost always impose stringent restrictions on those who would like to provide a transportation service to compete directly with the city-owned or -licensed urban bus service?
8. Is the college you're attending a price searcher? How much freedom does it have in setting the tuition rate you will pay? Might a freshman about to enroll answer differently than someone about to enter the senior year? Does your college enjoy any special grants of legal privilege?
9. Adam Smith wrote the following in *The Wealth of Nations*: "The price of monopoly is upon every occasion the highest which can be got . . . the highest which can be squeezed out of the buyers, or which, it is supposed, they will consent to give." Does this assertion have any clear and defensible meaning, or must we conclude that even the founder of economics sometimes reasoned carelessly?
10. Suppose that while digging in your backyard to plant peonies you strike oil. Your gusher is capable of producing up to 20 barrels of oil per day. How much incentive will you have to restrict daily output in order to keep your price from falling? Why does the oil minister in Saudi Arabia think more about restricting production than you do?
11. A newspaper headline proclaims: "Oil Price Data Imply Gouging During Cold Snap." If prices for home heating oil rise during a prolonged period of winter cold, does this prove that those who sell heating oil have a great deal of market power?
12. The graph on the left in Figure 8–2 portrays the market demand for U.S.-grown wheat (*D*) and the aggregated marginal cost curves of U.S. wheat growers (*S*) in a given year.
   (a) Draw the demand for the wheat of Ferdinand Elizer, a South Dakota wheat farmer, on the right-hand graph.
   (b) How would the demand curve faced by Ferd Elizer shift if the government offered all wheat farmers a subsidy of $1.50 per bushel?
   (c) What would Ferd Elizer's demand curve look like if the government imposed a tax on wheat, requiring farmers to remit $1.00 for every bushel they sell?

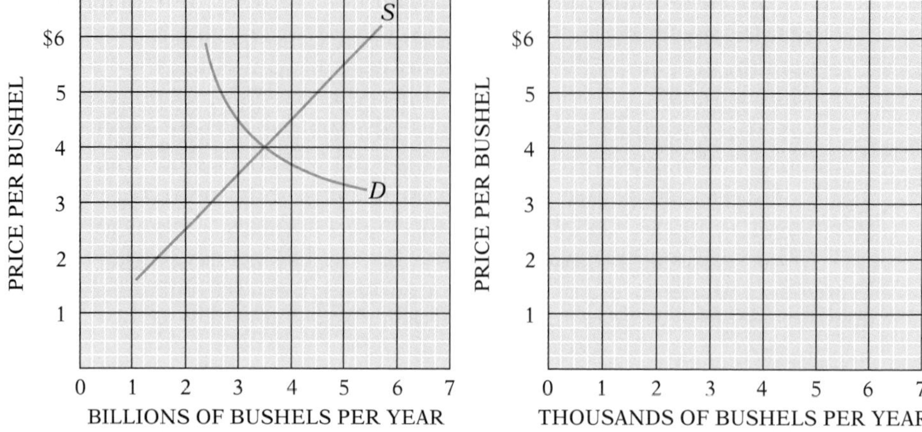

Figure 8–2 **Market demand and the demand facing one producer**

13. Market power is not the only kind of power that business firms might have and exercise. Neither market power nor any of these other types of power is necessarily correlated closely with the size of business firms. You might want to think about the nature, sources, and consequences of some of the powers listed here and how they are linked (or not linked) with market power. Power:
    (a) As capability, the ability to achieve desired results
    (b) To influence the outcome of elections
    (c) To influence legislation
    (d) To influence regulatory agencies of government
    (e) To manipulate people through advertising
    (f) To pollute the environment or to reduce pollution
    (g) To pursue sexist and racist hiring policies or to institute affirmative action programs
    (h) To intervene in the affairs of other nations
    (i) To shape the basic attitudes and beliefs of people

    What about the power that we sometimes assume others must have simply because we ourselves feel power*less*? Is it true that someone always has power to cause or to prevent undesirable events?
14. Congress has authorized the Federal Communications Commission to monitor the content of radio and television broadcasts and to revoke the licenses of stations that do not adequately serve the public interest. No member of Congress would seriously contemplate exercising such supervision over newspapers, especially in view of the clear prohibition contained in the U.S. Constitution's Bill of Rights. Two justifications are usually offered whenever anyone questions this control over broadcasters' freedom of expression. One is that Congress may regulate radio and television stations because the airwaves belong to the public. The other is that broadcasting frequencies are naturally scarce and that broadcasters must be prevented from abusing the power given to them by control of a scarce natural resource.

(a) Why do the airwaves belong to the public? Can you think of a fair and effective way for the public to relinquish its ownership so that Congress would no longer be obliged to control broadcast content?
(b) There are over 1,500 television stations and more than 10,000 radio stations currently broadcasting in the United States. Over 95 percent of U.S. households receive at least five television signals, and cable has enormously expanded these options. Dozens of radio stations are available in major urban areas, and where they are not, it is not because of any scarcity of spectrum space. How much power does the natural scarcity of broadcasting frequencies actually give to broadcasters?
(c) Can you think of any reason why members of Congress would want to argue that radio and television broadcasters have a monopoly?

Price Searching

9

How do price searchers find what they're looking for, and what happens when they find it? We're going to argue in this chapter that price searchers estimate marginal costs and marginal revenues and then try to set prices that will enable them to sell all those units of their product—and only those units—for which marginal revenue is expected to be greater than marginal cost. Firms are seeking profits, consumers are seeking deals, and a bargaining process results whereby marginal costs are led through the competitive process to be equated with marginal revenue. The equating of marginal cost with marginal revenue is the result of the competitive market process, not an assumption of actor behavior prior to that process. Does that sound complicated? It's just the logic of the process for maximizing net revenue, or total revenue minus total cost. But is it the procedure business firms actually use? It sounds much too theoretical, like something an economist might dream up but few real-world sellers would even recognize.

Net revenue defined: Total revenue minus total cost

The Popular Theory of Price Setting

It certainly is not the way most people assume that prices get set. The everyday explanation is a simple cost-plus-markup theory: Business firms calculate their unit costs and add on a percentage markup. A large number of price searchers will themselves describe their price-setting practices in terms of the cost-plus-markup theory. Their testimony deserves to be taken seriously, but it isn't conclusive evidence. A lot of people cannot correctly describe a process in which they themselves regularly and successfully engage. Most people who ride bicycles, for example, don't know how they keep the bicycle balanced. And if asked to think about it, they'll conclude that they keep the bicycle from tipping by leaning or shifting their weight slightly each time the bicycle inclines in one direction. If that were the way they actually balanced, they wouldn't make it to the end of the block. In reality, they balance primarily by steering, not leaning; they turn the front wheel imperceptibly and allow centrifugal force to counter any tendency to tip. That's what keeps them going straight. And, when asked how they *turn* the bike, most would probably say they turn the front wheel, when, in fact, they *lean* in order to get the bike to turn. (Otherwise how could somebody turn a bike when riding no-handed?) But the fact that they don't "know" what they're doing doesn't keep them from doing it. Although they can balance successfully only by winding along a series of curves whose precise curvature will be inversely proportional to the square of the speed at which they're proceeding, many mathematical illiterates are skillful cyclists.

Why are percentage markups so much greater in furniture stores than in grocery stores?

There are excellent reasons for doubting the cost-plus-markup theory. One is that it tells us nothing about the size of the markup. Why choose a 25 rather than a 50 percent markup? Why do different firms mark up their prices by different percentages? Why will the same firm vary its percentage markup at different times, on different products, when selling to different parties, and even, sometimes, when selling different quantities to a single person? Why do sellers sometimes set their prices *below* their average unit cost?

Why do furniture stores ever declare bankruptcy if their percentage markups are so large?

Moreover, if firms can always mark up their prices proportionately when their costs rise, why don't they raise their prices *before* their costs rise? Why are they satisfied with a smaller net revenue when they could be earning more? That doesn't square with the perennial complaints of many price setters that they aren't making adequate profits. We all know, too, that firms are sometimes forced out of business by rising costs. That couldn't happen if every firm were able to mark up its prices to cover any increase in costs.

The popular cost-plus-markup theory is obviously inadequate. It just doesn't explain the phenomena with which we're all familiar. We'll return to the question of why so many people, including price searchers themselves, nevertheless hold to the theory. But we can't do that until we've gone through the economist's explanation of the price-searching process.

Introducing Ed Sike

Simple cases are best for illuminating basic principles. We're going to examine the imaginary case of Ed Sike, a sophomore who is supporting himself at Ivy College by working as special-events manager for the College Student Association. One of Ed's tasks is to run a Friday night feature-film series that is open to the college community, and a large part of that job is setting ticket prices.

Let's suppose that Ed has to pay the following bills each time he shows a movie:

Film rental	$1,800
Auditorium rental	250
Operator	50
Ticket takers	100
Total:	$2,200

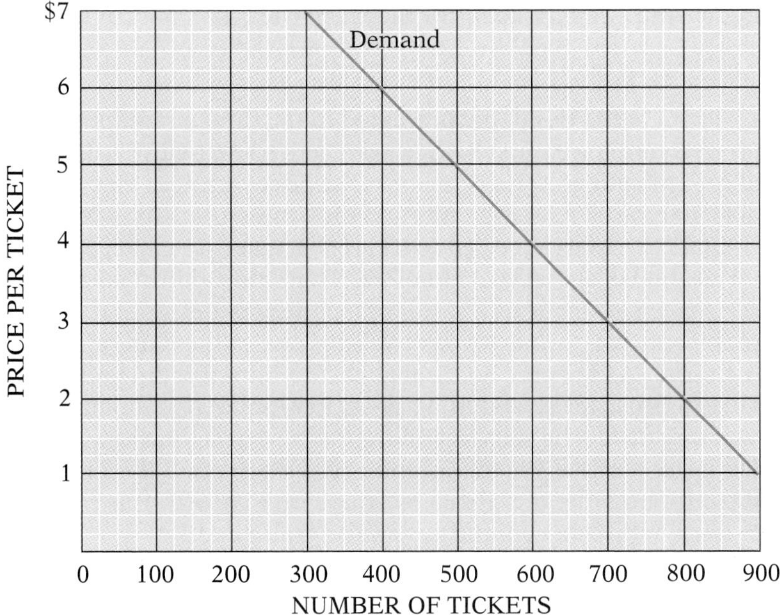

Figure 9–1 **Weekly demand for tickets to films**

Ed's budget receives all the revenue from ticket sales. The auditorium seats 700 people. And Ed has somehow discovered the precise demand for the films he shows. (We'll relax that heroic assumption later on.) The demand, which (quite remarkably) does not change from film to film, is graphed in Figure 9–1. Given this information, what will Ed want to charge for tickets?

We can't answer that question until we know Ed's objectives. If his aim is to fill all the seats without having to turn anyone away, $3 would be the best price to set. That's the price at which the quantity of tickets demanded would equal the number of seats available in the auditorium. One possible objection to a $3 price, however, is that each film showing would lose money. Total costs would be $2,200, but total revenue would be only $2,100.

That isn't necessarily a compelling objection. The student association may be willing to subsidize the films, perhaps because someone thinks movies make an important contribution to liberal education. If Ed doesn't have to cover costs out of ticket revenue, all sorts of possibilities open up. For example, he might set the price at $2.50. That would cause the quantity demanded to exceed the quantity supplied, but it might also make Ed a very popular man on campus—someone who can get you tickets to a Friday night film even though the film is already "sold out."

Price	Quantity Demanded	Total Revenue	Net Revenue
$3.00	700	$2100	–$100
2.50	750	$1875*	–$325

*Remember – there are only 700 seats.

Let's assume for now that Ed not only has to get enough revenue from ticket sales to cover all costs but that he's under orders to earn as much net revenue from the series as he can. Under these circumstances, what price will Ed want to charge for a ticket?

The Basic Rule for Maximizing Net Revenue

To maximize net revenue, set a price that will enable you to sell all those units, but only those units, for which marginal revenue is expected to be greater than marginal cost.

Look again at the basic rule presented in the first paragraph of this chapter, the rule we said all price searchers try to follow if their goal is to maximize net revenue: Set the price or prices that will enable you to sell all those units and only those units for which marginal revenue is expected to be greater than marginal cost.

Marginal cost you've met before. That's the additional cost a seller expects to incur as a result of a contemplated action. In this case the action is *selling another ticket*. Look at the data on Ed Sike's costs. What is the additional cost to him of selling another ticket? Because all $2,200 of his costs have to be paid no matter how many tickets he sells, the marginal cost of selling another ticket is zero, under the assumptions we've adopted. If you wanted to draw the marginal cost curve on Figure 9–1, it would be a horizontal line running across the graph at $0.

The Concept of Marginal Revenue

But what's marginal revenue? *Marginal revenue is the additional revenue expected from an action under consideration*. For Ed Sike, marginal revenue is the extra revenue received from selling one more ticket.

Price	Quantity Demanded	Total Revenue
$7	300	$2100
$6	400	$2400
$5	500	$2500
$4	600	$2400
$3	700	$2100

If you look at the demand curve in Figure 9–1, you can see at a glance that Ed Sike's net revenue is going to depend on the price he decides to set. At $3 total revenue would be $2,100, and so net revenue would be *minus* $100. At $6 net revenue would be $200: $2,400 in total revenue minus $2,200 in costs. It would also be $200 if the ticket price were set at $4. At what price would net revenue be maximized, given the data with which we're working?

The answer is $5. If the price is set at $5, then 500 tickets will be sold. Total revenue will be $2,500, and net revenue will be $300. Ed can't do any better than that.

How do we know? One way to find the answer is to try out every possible price. A better way, because it clarifies the logic of the process we're trying to explain, is to locate the quantity at which marginal revenue equals marginal cost and then find the price at which exactly that quantity can be sold.

The logic is simple. Each of the first 500 tickets that Ed sells adds more to his revenue than it adds to his costs. (Remember that in this particular case it adds *nothing* to his costs; marginal cost is zero no matter how many tickets are being sold.) But each ticket sold beyond 500 adds more to costs than to revenue. It adds nothing to costs, but it adds *less than nothing* to total revenue, because marginal revenue becomes negative after 500 tickets have been sold.

Why Marginal Revenue Is Less Than Price

It seems at first that this can't be correct. Because Ed is still taking in money for each ticket he sells beyond 500, the additional revenue from selling another ticket, or marginal revenue, looks as if it ought to be positive. But that appearance is in fact false. It ignores something very important. In order to sell additional tickets, Ed has to lower the price. And when he does so, he lowers the price not only to the additional customers he's trying to capture with the price decrease but also to all those customers who would have purchased tickets at the higher price. The additional revenue he gains from the new customers is offset by revenue lost, or given up, from the old customers. After he has sold 500 tickets, the revenue lost becomes greater than the revenue gained, and so marginal revenue becomes negative.

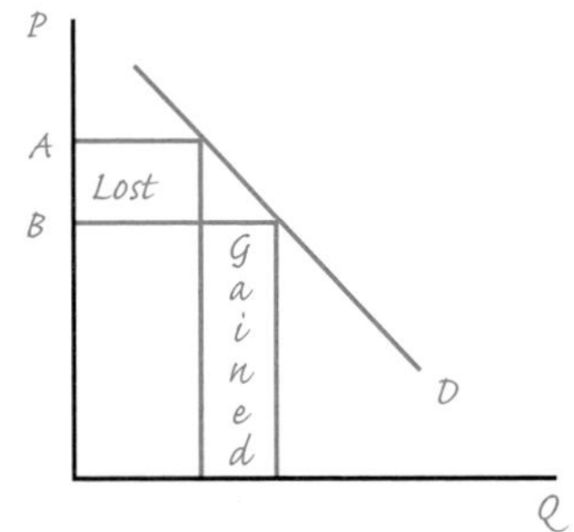

Lowering the price from A to B gains some revenue from additional sales but also loses some revenue because all buyers now pay the lower price.

Let's check it out by looking carefully at the graph. Suppose Ed set the price at $5. At that price he would sell 500 tickets, and total revenue would be $2,500. What would happen if he decided to sell 550 tickets? To do so, he would have to lower the price to $4.50. That would bring him an additional $4.50 from each of the 50 "new" customers, for a total of $225 extra. But it would cost him 50 cents *not* paid now by each of the 500 "old" customers who were willing to pay $5.00 until Ed offered to sell them tickets at $4.50: 500 times 50 cents is $250. That more than offsets the $225 gained. Ed Sike actually reduced his total revenue by $25 when he decided to expand his ticket sales from 500 to 550. Marginal revenue is *negative* over this range.

We can be even more precise. Because the additional revenue from the 50 additional tickets sold is minus $25, we can say that marginal revenue per ticket is minus 50 cents when Ed tries to expand sales from 500 to 550. To show that on Figure 9–1, we can plot marginal revenue as minus 50 cents at 525 tickets, the midpoint between 500 and 550.

Check your understanding of the basic idea by asking what happens when Ed expands his sales from 450 to 500 tickets. The demand curve shows he could sell 450 tickets for $5.50 each. To sell 500 tickets, he must lower the price to $5.00. So his total revenue will be $2,475 when he sells 450 tickets and $2,500 when he sells 500 tickets. The additional or marginal revenue is 50 cents per extra ticket sold when Ed expands his sales from 450 to 500 tickets. We would therefore plot plus 50 cents as the marginal revenue at 475 tickets.

If we connected these two points with a straight line, the resulting marginal-revenue curve would intersect the marginal-cost curve at precisely 500 tickets. Consequently, we can say that if Ed is content to sell fewer than 500 tickets, he sacrifices potential net revenue by failing to sell some tickets for which marginal revenue is greater than marginal cost. If he sells more than 500 tickets, Ed sacrifices potential net revenue by selling some tickets for which marginal revenue is less than marginal cost. He therefore maximizes net revenue by selling exactly 500 tickets: the quantity at which marginal revenue equals marginal cost. And the demand curve tells us that 500 tickets can be sold by setting the ticket price at $5.

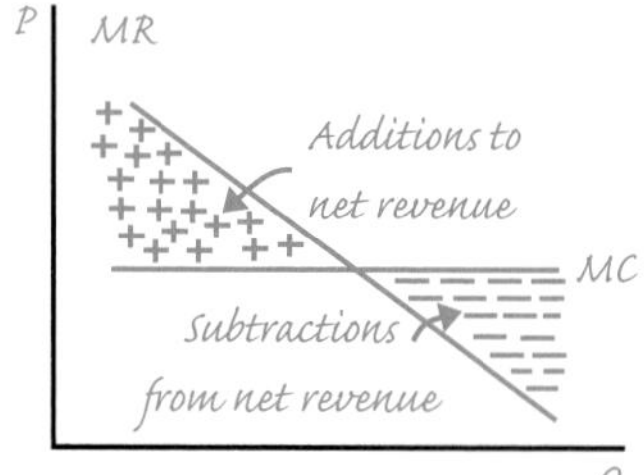

Setting Marginal Revenue to Equal Marginal Cost

You can be sure you've grasped the idea if you're able to figure out what would happen if the film distributor changed the rental fee from a flat $1,800 to $800 plus $2 for every ticket sold.

The key difference is that Ed's marginal costs would now rise from zero to $2. Each additional ticket sold would now add $2 to total cost; the marginal-cost curve would be a horizontal line at $2. Because, to maximize net revenue, Ed must sell all those tickets for which marginal revenue is greater than marginal cost, and no tickets for which marginal cost is greater than marginal revenue, Ed wants to find the price and quantity at which marginal revenue will exactly equal $2.

The marginal-revenue curve has been drawn in Figure 9–2. This curve shows by how much the sale of one additional ticket increases total revenue at the various volumes possible. Marginal revenue is $4 when 300 tickets are being sold and falls rapidly as sales increase, becoming negative after 500 tickets are sold. We now see at once that, given the film distributor's new policy, Ed

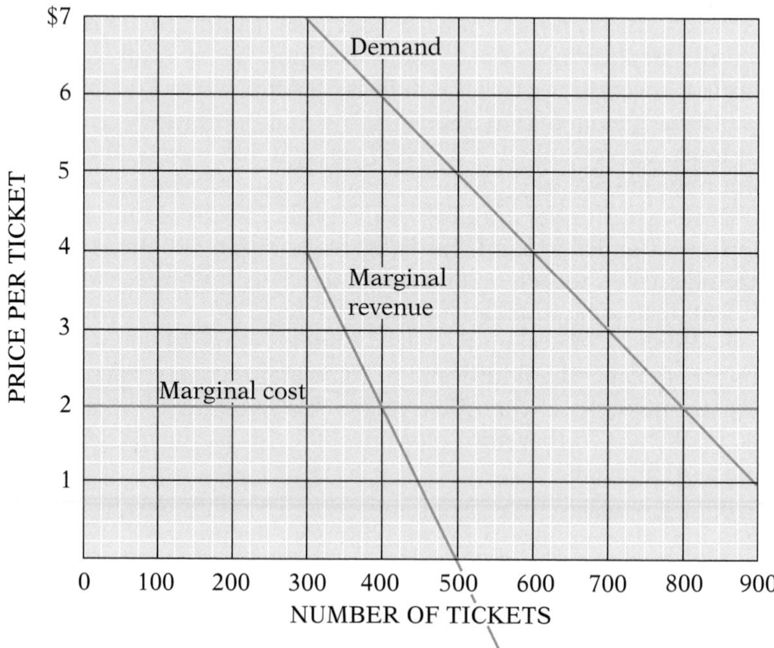

Figure 9–2 **Weekly demand for tickets to films and marginal cost of selling tickets**

will want to sell 400 tickets. This is the quantity that equates marginal revenue and marginal cost. To sell 400 tickets, Ed should set the price at $6. It turns out that Ed does somewhat better under the film distributor's new policy than he did under the old one. Total revenue is now $2,400 and total cost is $2,000, for a net revenue of $400.

What About Those Empty Seats?

Under both the old and the new policy, seats were "going to waste." That phrase is in quotation marks because waste, you should recall from Chapter 2, is an evaluative concept. What constitutes waste from the point of view of moviegoers may be efficiency from the point of view of exhibitors like Ed. Still, there does seem to be something wasteful about this situation from everyone's perspective. There are people who want to see the movies, who are willing to pay Ed an amount greater than his marginal cost if he will let them in, but to whom Ed nonetheless denies admission. Movie fans are missing an opportunity for which they're willing to pay the marginal cost, and Ed isn't getting any revenue from those empty seats for which people are willing to pay more than his marginal cost. There seems to be a substantial gain from exchange that isn't being realized.

Situations like this are quite common. At almost any major league baseball game there will be empty seats inside the stadium and people outside the stadium who would be happy to pay the team owner for the chance to sit in them. Because letting in another spectator adds nothing to the cost of playing the game, the owner would gain extra net revenue from each additional fan admitted at any ticket price greater than zero. But this will be the case only if the owner can reduce the ticket price to the "new" customers without also reducing the price to those who are willing to pay more to see the game.

The Price Discriminator's Dilemma

There's the catch. It is in fact efficient (from his point of view) for Ed to leave 200 or 300 seats empty, as long as the cost of discriminating among potential ticket buyers is greater than the additional revenue that can be gained through discrimination. Let's see what this means.

Suppose Ed is paying a flat $1,800 rental fee, charging $5, selling 500 tickets, and earning $300 per week. One Friday night he looks over the house and says to himself: "I could increase my net revenue by filling those 200 empty seats. All I'd have to do is lower the price to $3, but only for those who won't attend if I charge them more than that. I'd get an extra $600 each week, and 200 additional people could enjoy these fine movies."

A brilliant idea? The following week Ed hangs up a new sign at the campus ticket outlet: "$5 per ticket," it says; and then it adds in smaller print: "$3 for those unwilling to pay more." What's going to happen? Almost all the ticket buyers will pay $3, because they're all "unwilling to pay more" if they can get their tickets for $3. Ed will end up with only $2,100 in revenue and a loss of $100 from that week's program. It wasn't such a brilliant idea after all.

The flaw, however, was more in the execution than in the idea itself. What Ed must do if he wants to eliminate the "waste" of empty seats and lost revenue is find a sufficiently low-cost procedure for distinguishing among potential buyers. He has to be able to offer low prices to those who otherwise won't buy, without making those low prices available to customers who are willing to purchase tickets at higher prices. Ed might be able to pick up a few hints from the Ivy College administration.

The College as Price Searcher

College administrators often talk about the high costs of providing an education and the need for philanthropic contributions to make up that 50 percent or so of the cost not covered by tuition. Have you ever wondered why it is, then, that privately owned colleges grant tuition scholarships to needy students? If colleges are so poor that they must ask for charity, why do they simultaneously *dispense* charity? The answer is that they don't in fact dispense charity. Tuition scholarships for needy students are a successful attempt to do what Ed Sike failed to do.

Figure 9–3 is the demand for admission to Ivy College as estimated by the college administration. We shall assume that the marginal cost of enrolling another student is zero. That isn't accurate, but it's realistic enough for our purposes and it doesn't affect the logic of the argument in any event. Ivy College, though a not-for-profit institution, still wants to find the tuition rate that will maximize its receipts.

If Ivy restricts itself to a uniform price for all, it will set the tuition at $3,000 per year, enroll 3,000 students (the enrollment at which marginal revenue equals marginal cost), and gross $9,000,000. But some students whom it would be profitable to enroll are excluded by this tuition rate, and some students who would have been willing to pay more are admitted for only $3,000. Ivy's administrators wish they could charge what each student is willing to pay. If they could find out the maximum each student (or the student's parents) would pay rather than be denied admission to Ivy, they could set the annual tuition at $6,000 and then give scholarships (price rebates) to each student. The scholarship would equal the difference between $6,000 and the maximum each student is willing to pay.

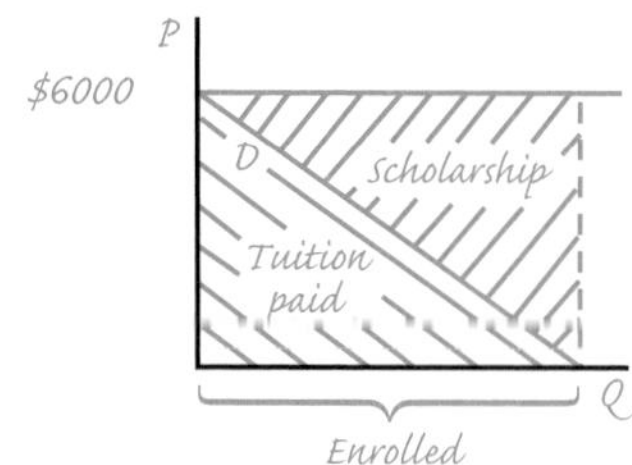

The problem is how to get information on willingness to pay. Students or their parents will not reveal the full value to themselves

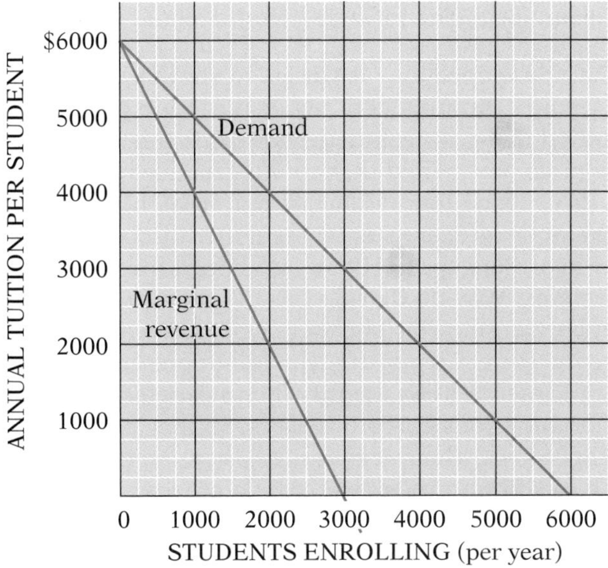

Figure 9–3 **Demand curve for enrollment at Ivy College**

Note: There is a simple gimmick you can use to quickly obtain the marginal-revenue curve corresponding to any straight-line demand curve. Draw perpendiculars to the price axis from the demand curve; bisect the perpendiculars; extend a straight line through these midpoints. The marginal revenue corresponding to any point on the demand curve will then be the point on this line (the marginal-revenue curve) directly below the point on the demand curve in which you're interested. Thus at a quantity of 1,500 students, marginal revenue is $3,000 and price is $4,500.

of attending Ivy if they know that candor will cause them to pay a higher price. But if willingness to pay is correlated with wealth, a partial solution lies at hand. Ivy announces that scholarships are available to needy students. Need must be established by filling out a statement on family wealth and income. Families will complete the forms in order to qualify for scholarship aid and will thereby provide the college with information it can use to discriminate. If the correlation were perfect between income and willingness to pay, and if families filled out the forms honestly, Ivy could discriminate with precision and increase its gross receipts to $18,000,000 (the area under the entire demand curve). Marginal revenue would be equal to price despite the fact that Ivy is a price searcher.

Be careful about condemning Ivy College! Notice some of the consequences of this discriminatory pricing policy. First of all, Ivy earns more income. If you approve of Ivy, why begrudge it a larger income from tuition? Is it better for philanthropists and taxpayers to cover Ivy's annual deficit than for students (or their parents) to do so through being charged the maximum they're willing to pay? Notice, too, that under a perfectly discriminating system of tuition charges, 3,000 students who would otherwise be turned away are enabled to enroll at Ivy. They aren't complaining.

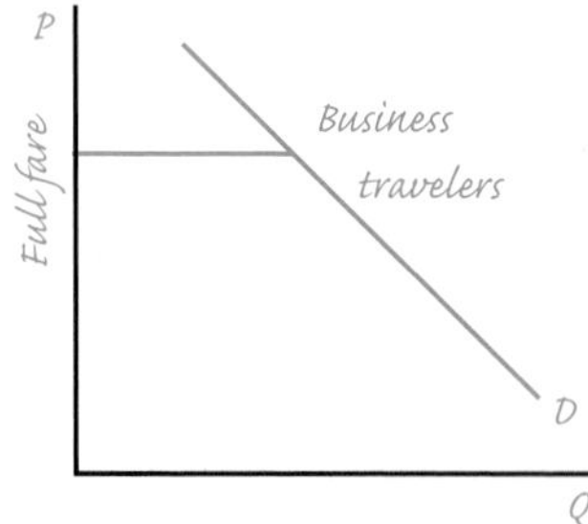

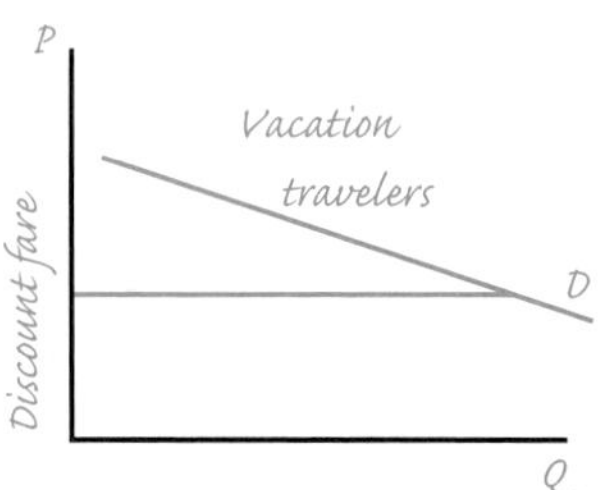

Some Strategies for Price Discrimination

Sellers have developed a wide variety of strategies for doing what Ivy College does through its tuition scholarship program. The goal is to find low-cost techniques for distinguishing high-price from low-price buyers and then to offer reduced prices exclusively to those who otherwise won't purchase the product.

For example, grocery stores often offer discounts to customers who present special coupons clipped from newspaper advertisements. Why do they do this? The discounts are designed to attract bargain-hunting shoppers who otherwise wouldn't patronize the store. Customers who fail to present coupons at the checkout counter thereby identify themselves as people who aren't price-conscious bargain seekers. So they pay higher prices.

If airlines lower their ticket prices, they can fill some empty seats with vacation travelers who would otherwise go by car. But the airlines don't want to lower their prices for business travelers who are willing to pay high fares to save time and for whom the cost of travel is a tax-deductible expense anyway. How can the airlines distinguish these two classes of travelers and give discounts only to those who won't fly without them? One way is to confine the discount prices to those who buy round-trip tickets far in advance and stay more than a week or over a weekend. Business travelers usually can't afford to stay away that long and frequently have to travel on short notice. It's far from an infallible way to discriminate, but it's a low-cost system and it works surprisingly well.

Discount prices are commonly offered for all kinds of entertainment events to children, students, and senior citizens. Is this an act of generosity on the part of those who sponsor the events? It's more likely that they want to attract some additional business from groups that are more sensitive to prices, but without lowering the price to everyone. Potential customers with more elastic demands for the good are prime targets for special price reductions, *if* the seller has a low-cost way to identify the people with more elastic demand curves *and* can prevent them from reselling to people with less elastic demand curves.

Ed Sike Finds a Way

Let's return to the case of Ed Sike. Suppose his data on the demand for tickets enable him to distinguish the student demand from the staff and faculty demand. In Figure 9–4 we've drawn two demand curves to show these separate student and staff–faculty demands for tickets to the Friday film series. (If you add the curves together—summing the quantities demanded by each group at various prices—you'll get the demand curve presented in Figure 9–1.) Our question is this: Can Ed, knowing these separate demand curves, increase his net revenue by setting different prices for students and for staff or faculty?

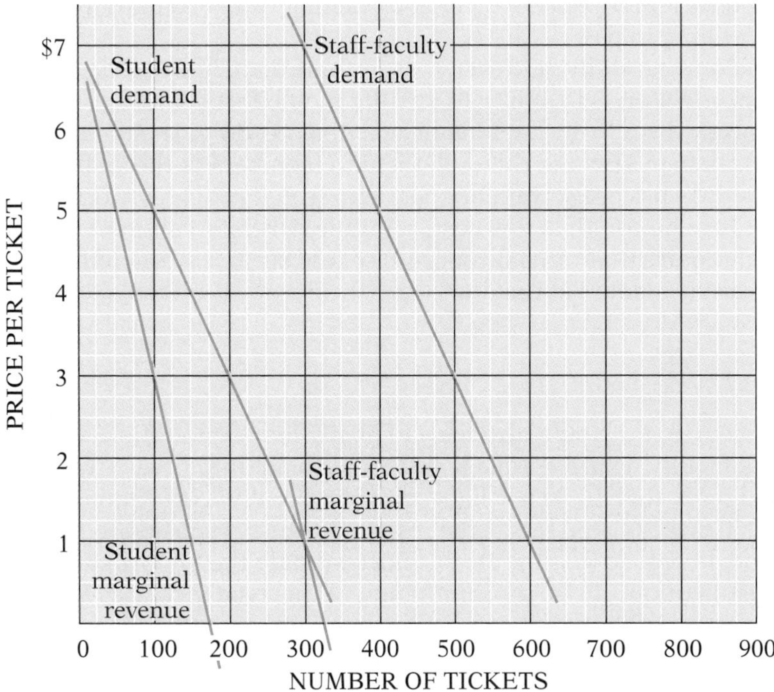

Figure 9–4 **Weekly demand for tickets**

Intuition suggests it might work. The typical student doesn't have a lot of income and so tends to pay attention to prices. Staff and faculty members who want to see the films are less likely to change their minds because of a modest price increase. It might be that Ed could do better by lowering the price he charges students and raising the price to staff and faculty.

Recall that when marginal cost was zero, Ed maximized net revenue by charging $5 per ticket and selling 500 tickets. Now he wants to set marginal revenue equal to marginal cost *for each group separately*.

Marginal revenue from sales to the students equals zero (marginal cost) at 175 tickets. To sell 175 tickets to students, Ed should charge them $3.50.

Marginal revenue from sales to staff and faculty equals zero at 325 tickets. To sell that number to staff and faculty, Ed should charge them $6.50.

He'll still be selling 500 tickets. But his total revenue will now be $2,725 rather than $2,500, and his net revenue will increase from $300 to $525.

Why did it work? It worked because the student demand for tickets was much more elastic than was the staff and faculty demand at the common price of $5. By lowering the price to the students, who are more responsive to price changes, and raising the price to staff and faculty members, who are less responsive,

Ed does a more effective job of extracting from each group what it's willing to pay.

Note carefully, however, that the entire scheme is crucially dependent on Ed's ability to identify members of each group and prevent them from reselling tickets. It won't do to let students buy tickets for $3.50 and then sell them to members of the staff or faculty. Ed's price-discrimination system would probably work because he could, at low cost, print the tickets in different colors and require that official college ID cards be shown when the tickets are presented at the door.

Resentment and Rationale

Three conditions for successful price discrimination: The seller must be able to (1) distinguish buyers with different elasticities of demand, (2) prevent low-price buyers from reselling to high-price buyers, and (3) control resentment.

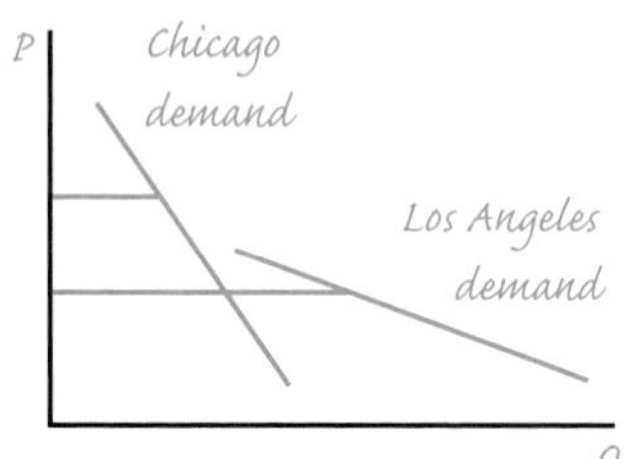

Of course, Ed would also have to justify his "exploitation" of staff and faculty. That's not likely to be a problem in this case. He could say that $6.50 is what each ticket "really" costs and that the $3.50 price to students is the result of a special subsidy to promote liberal education. Don't underestimate the importance of "justification." Price discrimination of this type increases Ed's net revenue and doesn't compel anyone to pay more than he or she is willing to pay. But it can arouse fierce indignation on the part of those who aren't offered the discount prices.

As an example, consider the bitter complaints of all those cross-country air travelers who found a few years ago that they had to pay more per mile than people flying between Los Angeles and New York. Why should a round-trip ticket from Chicago to New York, for example, cost more than a similar ticket from Los Angeles to New York when Chicago is so much closer to New York? The explanation was the fierce competition among the numerous carriers operating between the nation's two largest cities. This competition created excellent substitutes for any one airline's tickets, made the demand curve that each airline faced very elastic, and kept prices close to marginal cost. To Chicago–New York travelers, however, it looked as if they were subsidizing Los Angeles–New York passengers, and they didn't like it.

Lunch and Dinner Prices

Everything we've been talking about is nicely illustrated in the common restaurant practice of charging more for the same food in the evening than at lunch.

Why do restaurants catering to both a luncheon and a dinner trade mark up their prices so much more on dinners than on lunches? The theory we've presented looks for the answer in different elasticities of demand. Lunch customers as a class are much more responsive to price increases or decreases than are dinner customers. A 10 percent increase in the price of a luncheon entrée will often lose the restaurant more customers than would a 30 percent increase in the price of the same item on the dinner menu. There are several reasons for this.

One is the fact that lunch customers eat out so much more frequently. People who buy lunch five times a week have many opportunities to gather information on relative prices. And because 50 cents less or more adds up over the course of a month, they have a strong incentive to shop around for the best deal, to stick to it when they think they've found it, and to shift when something better comes along. A dinner out, by contrast, is a much more rare event for most people; they have, as a consequence, less opportunity and less incentive to gather information on relative prices.

Another major reason for the lower price elasticity of demand among dinner patrons is the fact that what they pay for their food is typically only a fraction of what they are paying for the entire event or experience of "dinner out." A couple going out for dinner may pay $10 for a baby-sitter, $3 for parking, and $15 for cocktails or wine. If they pay $14 each for their dinners, the food is only half of their costs for the evening. And so a 40 percent hike in the menu price comes through to them as only a 20 percent increase in the cost of their evening out.

We should therefore expect to see restaurant managers following low-markup policies at lunch and high-markup policies at dinner. To reduce the chance of indignation and resentment, they will do a little more than merely raise the price of the London broil from $8 at lunch to $14 at dinner. They will also offer the dinner patron both soup and salad (the luncheon customers must choose one or the other) and perhaps include coffee in the price of the dinner (but not the lunch). A $6 increase is thus "justified" by an increase in marginal food cost of perhaps 40 cents. The real reason for the different markups, however, is found in the different elasticities of demand characteristic of luncheon and dinner patrons.

Those who automatically condemn all instances of price discrimination might want to take a broader look at the practice. Successful discrimination increases the wealth of sellers, of course; that's why they do it. But it also increases the wealth or well-being of those buyers who can obtain, as a result of price discrimination, goods that would not otherwise be available to them. Price discrimination eliminates some of the "waste" that occurs when A and B cannot arrange a transaction despite the fact that A wants what B has to offer and is more than willing to pay B's cost of supplying it.

You can legitimately view price discrimination as a form of cooperation between sellers and buyers, cooperation that occurs only, however, when the transaction costs are sufficiently low. In the case of price discrimination, those costs are principally the costs of distinguishing among different demanders, preventing them from exchanging among themselves, and controlling any resentment that might prompt potential buyers to take their business somewhere else. If it were not for transaction costs, we would observe far more price discrimination than we actually do.

Cost-Plus-Markup Reconsidered

So how do price searchers find what they're looking for? By (1) estimating the marginal cost and marginal revenue, (2) determining the level of output that will enable them to sell all those units of output and only those units for which marginal revenue is greater than marginal cost, and (3) setting their price or prices so that they can just manage to sell the output produced. That sounds complicated, and it is. The logic is simple enough. But the estimates of marginal cost and especially the estimates of demand and marginal revenue are hard to make accurately. That's why price searchers are called "searchers." And why they could sometimes be called price "gropers." Again, the point to stress is that equating marginal cost and marginal revenue is the outcome of the competitive market process, not a behavioral assumption we are imposing on economic actors independent of the market process.

The complexity and uncertainty of the price searcher's task help explain the popularity of the cost-plus-markup theory. Every search has to begin somewhere. Why not begin with the wholesale cost of an item plus a percentage markup adequate to cover overhead costs and yield a reasonable profit? If costs increase, why not assume that competitors' costs have also increased and try passing the higher cost on to customers? Why not begin with the assumption that the future will be like the past and that the procedures that have previously yielded good results will continue to do so? In that case, one would try to increase prices roughly in proportion to any cost increases experienced, and one would expect eventually to be forced by competition to lower one's prices roughly in proportion to any lowering of costs.

The cost-plus-markup procedure is in general a rule of thumb for price searchers, offering a place from which to begin looking, a first approximation in the continuing search for an elusive and shifting target. But price searchers engage in cost-plus-markup pricing only as a search technique and only until they discover they are making a mistake. The marginal-cost/marginal-revenue analysis of this chapter explains how price searchers recognize mistakes and what criteria they use in moving from rules of thumb and first approximations toward the most profitable pricing policy.

Once Over Lightly

Price searchers are looking for pricing structures that will enable them to sell all units for which marginal revenue exceeds marginal cost.

The popularity of the cost-plus-markup theory of pricing rests on its usefulness as a search technique and the fact that people often cannot correctly explain processes in which they regularly and successfully engage.

A crucial factor for the price searcher is the ability or inability to discriminate: to charge high prices for units that are in high demand and low prices for units that would not otherwise be purchased, without allowing the sales at lower prices to "spoil the market" for high-price sales.

A rule for successful price searching often quoted by economists is this: Set marginal revenue equal to marginal cost. This means: Continue selling as long as the additional revenue from a sale exceeds the additional cost. Skillful price searchers are people who know this rule (even when they don't fully realize they're using it) and who also have a knack for distinguishing the relevant marginal possibilities. The possibilities are endless, which helps to make price theory a fascinating exploration for people with a penchant for puzzle solving.

Sellers in the real world don't have precisely defined demand curves from which they can derive marginal-revenue curves to compare with marginal-cost curves. Working with such curves is nonetheless good exercise for a student who wants to begin thinking systematically about the ways in which competition affects the choices people make and the choices they confront.

QUESTIONS FOR DISCUSSION

1. The rule for maximizing net revenue (total revenue minus total cost) is: Take any action if, but only if, the expected marginal revenue exceeds the expected marginal cost. What is marginal revenue? How is it related to demand? You can test your grasp of this key concept by examining the case of Maureen Supplize, who runs a yacht dealership. She has five potential customers, and she knows how much each would be willing to pay for one of her yachts.

J. P. Morgan	$13 million
J. D. Rockefeller	11 million
J. R. Ewing	9 million
J. C. Penney	7 million
J. P. Kennedy	5 million

   (a) Fill in the blanks in the second column to complete the demand schedule implied by these data.
   (b) Fill in the blanks in the third column to show Maureen's total receipts from yacht sales at the various prices listed.
   (c) Fill in the blanks in the fourth column to show the extra revenue obtained by Maureen from each additional yacht she manages to sell when she lowers her selling price.
   (d) How many yachts will she want to sell if her goal is to maximize *total* revenue? (Don't start thinking yet about selling to different people at different prices. We'll take that up later. Assume for now that she can't get away with charging one buyer more than another.) What price will she want to set?

				Under Perfect Price Discrimination	
Price of Yacht	Quantity Demanded	Total Revenue	Marginal Revenue	Marginal Revenue	Total Revenue
$13 million	_____	$_____	$_____	$_____	$_____
11	_____	_____	_____	_____	_____
9	_____	_____	_____	_____	_____
7	_____	_____	_____	_____	_____
5	_____	_____	_____	_____	_____

(e) Now assume that her goal is to maximize *net* revenue and that the marginal cost to her of selling a yacht is $6 million. In other words, each additional yacht she sells adds $6 million to her total costs. How many yachts will she now want to sell? What price will she want to set?

(f) If you have proceeded correctly, you should now be able to experience something of Maureen's frustration. Ewing and Penney are both willing to pay more for a yacht than it costs Maureen to sell one to them. Yet she can't sell to either without reducing her net revenue. Why?

(g) Suppose now that none of her customers is acquainted with any of the others and that she can consequently get away with charging each one the maximum he is willing to pay. Under such an arrangement, which we shall call "perfect" price discrimination, what is Maureen's marginal-revenue schedule? Fill in the blanks in the fifth column.

(h) How many yachts will Maureen now want to sell?

(i) Fill in her *total* revenue schedule under "perfect" price discrimination.

2. "A price searcher should set marginal revenue as far above marginal cost as possible." Explain why this statement is wrong. What is being erroneously assumed by someone who thinks that net receipts will be zero at an output where marginal revenue equals marginal cost?

3. Locate the most profitable uniform price for sellers to set in each of the situations graphed in Figure 9–5 and the quantity they will want to produce and sell. Then shade the area that represents the addition to net income from that pricing policy. What will happen to net income in each case if the price is raised? If it's lowered? (*Caution*: What happens if a seller whose marginal-revenue curve is the same as the demand curve raises the price?)

4. The marginal-cost curves of the Anchorage Aardvark Breeding Company and the Houston Aardvark Breeding Company are identical, but the demand curves they face differ, as shown in Figure 9–6.

   (a) What price will each firm want to set?

   (b) Suppose something happens to raise marginal cost for each firm to $20 while nothing else changes. What price will each now set?

   (c) What is the relationship between elasticity of demand and the profit-maximizing percentage markup?

5. Have you ever wondered why otherwise identical books usually sell for so much more in hardcover than in softcover editions? Surely it doesn't cost that much more to attach a hard cover when it's all being done on an assembly-line basis! This question tries to construct a plausible

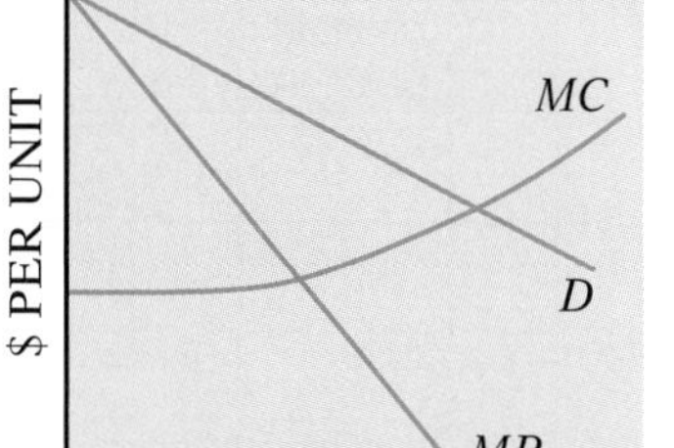

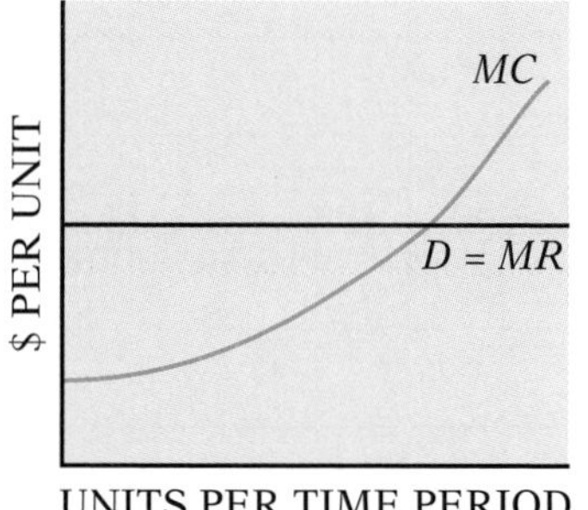

Figure 9–5 **Finding the most profitable selling price**

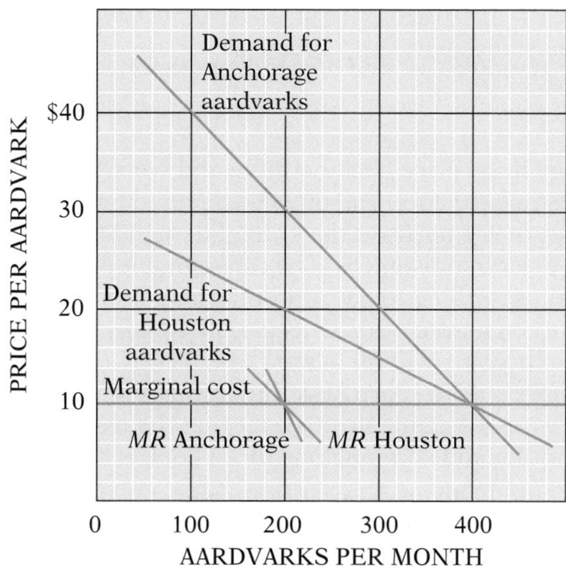

Figure 9–6 **Marginal cost and demand curves for two companies**

explanation and to give you practice in working with the concepts of marginal cost and marginal revenue.

Some potential purchasers of a new book will be eager to obtain it as soon as it's published and will be willing to pay a high price to do so. Those who want to give the book as a present may be willing to pay a high price to demonstrate their generosity and may appreciate having a hard cover on the book as a sign of its quality. Still other potential purchasers—libraries are the clearest example—want hardcover books because they stand up better to heavy use; these purchasers are willing to pay a substantially higher price for a book to avoid the considerable expense of having to bind it themselves between hard covers. Libraries also will want to purchase a popular book right after it has been published in order to satisfy their eager patrons. There are also many potential purchasers, however, who want to read the book, would be willing

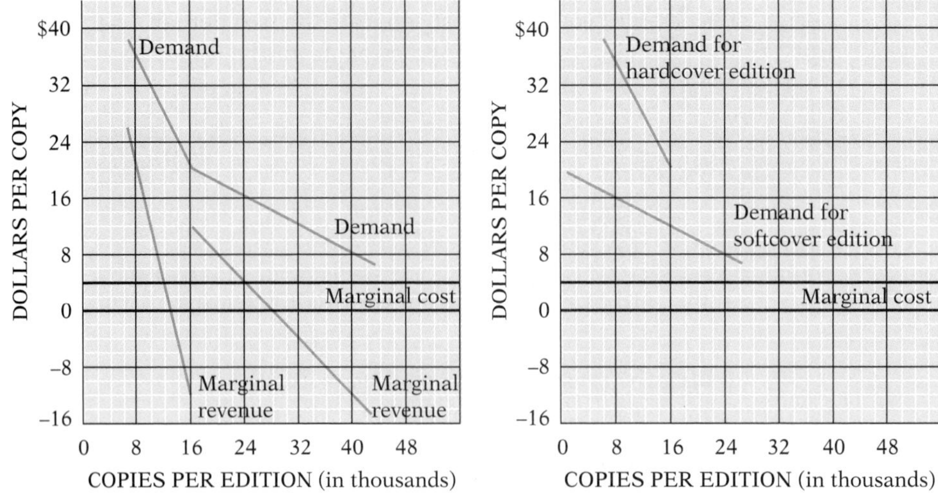

Figure 9–7 **Marginal cost and demand curves for a book publisher**

to buy a copy if the price isn't too high, and who don't very much care whether it is in hard cover or soft. The demand curve on the left-hand graph in Figure 9–7 portrays the kind of demand for the book that might emerge in such circumstances. The top segment of the demand curve is created by those willing to pay a premium to obtain the book quickly or to get it between hard covers. Once the price falls below $20, "general readers" also become willing to purchase a copy. (The demand curve would not have such a sharp kink, but straight lines are easier to work with than curves.) Assume throughout that the marginal cost to the publisher of printing and shipping one more book is $4.

(a) What would be the most profitable price for the publisher to set for the book? The marginal-revenue curves that correspond to each segment of the demand curve have been drawn for you, using the gimmick explained in Figure 9–3.

(b) The most profitable price is the price that enables the publisher to sell all those copies but only those copies for which marginal revenue is greater than marginal cost. The problem in this case is that in order to sell the units from 16,000 to 24,000, for which marginal revenue exceeds marginal cost, the publisher must also sell the units between 12,000 and 16,000, for which marginal revenue is less than marginal cost. Which is the more profitable place to stop? Should the publisher set the price at $28 and sell 12,000, or set the price at $16 and sell 24,000?

(c) Suppose the publisher puts a hard cover on the book when it's first published, then waits six or eight months before bringing the book out in a paperback edition at a lower price. What prices should it set for each edition? A reasonable approach would be to assume that all prospective purchasers at prices above $20 either are not willing to wait or want the hardcover edition, while those below $20 are willing to wait and to accept the paperback edition. To calculate the prices to set for each edition, you must first separate the two demand curves. Cut the lower section of the demand curve from the upper section and drag it to the left so that it begins at the price axis; it will then show the quantity of softcover books that will be demanded at various prices when the paperback edition is published. This has been done for you on the right-hand graph in Figure 9–7. Draw the marginal-revenue curve for each demand curve, find out where marginal revenue crosses marginal cost in each market, and set the appropriate prices.

6. Many firms use a technique called *target pricing* in trying to decide what prices to set for new products they're introducing. The target price is a price that enables the firm to recover a certain percentage of the product's development and production costs. What, in addition to costs, must the seller know in order to calculate the return a particular price will yield? If earnings from the sale of the product turn out to fall short of the target, should the firm raise the price? If earnings exceed the firm's expectations, should it lower the price?
7. How should the British and French manufacturers of the Concorde supersonic commercial airliner take account of the plane's development costs in determining the prices to charge airline companies? Should they suspend production if they can't obtain a price that will cover development costs?
8. When the university's athletic director announces that football ticket prices are being raised for next year, he is likely to say this unfortunate step has been made necessary by rising costs—perhaps the rising cost of the women's sports program. How does the cost of the women's sports program affect the marginal cost of selling a football ticket? If you are unable to think of any answer to that question, ask yourself how the prospect of a winning season affects the cost of selling a football ticket. Which plays a larger role in determining the most profitable price at which to sell football tickets: the athletic department's budget for women's sports or an excellent team?
9. On the day of home football games, the university raises the price of parking on some of its lots from $1.50 to $10.00 per vehicle. This is done, according to the Committee on Transportation, so that regular parking users do not subsidize the cost of providing parking for football fans. Would regular users be subsidizing football parkers if the rate stayed at $1.50 on football Saturdays?
10. Are advertising costs capable of affecting the net-revenue-maximizing price for the product advertised?
    (a) Do beer drinkers have to pay more for the beer they drink because the brewery pays a huge sum of money to advertise it on national television?
    (b) When a breakfast-food company pays a celebrity athlete a million dollars for the right to put his picture on the cereal box, will this lead to an increase in the price of the cereal?
11. Can an oil company raise the price of its gasoline to cover the costs of a huge oil spill for which it is liable? What would happen if Exxon, for example, raised the refinery price of gasoline at a time when other refiners were not raising their prices?
12. Do small convenience stores charge higher prices (on average) than large supermarkets charge because the small stores have higher overhead

costs per unit of sales? How can a seller induce customers to pay a higher price for a product than they would have to pay elsewhere?

13. When Missouri began assessing commercial property for tax purposes at a higher percentage of "fair market value" than residential property, apartment buildings of five or more units were classified as commercial property. Property taxes on such buildings consequently increased sharply, while taxes on apartment buildings with four units or fewer did not change.
    (a) Would you expect this change to increase the rents paid by people living in large apartment buildings relative to the rents paid by tenants in buildings with fewer than five units? Does the tax increase affect either the marginal cost to the landlord of renting or the demand for apartments on the part of tenants?
    (b) What effect do you think this tax change will have on the average size of apartment units in existing buildings? What effect will it have on the average size of apartment buildings constructed in the future?
    (c) What effect would you predict from this change in assessment methods on the rental rates tenants will pay?
    (d) The president of the St. Louis Apartment Association was quoted as saying that no apartment owners would pay those tax increases, but rather would pass them along in the form of rent increases. If owners can raise rents in this fashion after property taxes rise, why don't they raise them *before* the taxes rise and thus increase their income? If owners can pass on tax increases, why did some Missouri apartment owners go to the expense of filing a suit to overturn the reassessment?
14. Why do camera retailers so often sell the cameras themselves at prices very close to their own wholesale cost, while marking up the price of accessories (carrying cases, lens cleaner, filters, and so on) by 100 percent or more?
15. Some theaters presenting live drama have begun experimenting with "pay-what-you-can" pricing for certain performances. A theater in San Diego adopted this policy for one Saturday matinee per production. Normal ticket prices run from $18 to $28. Payments for the special matinees ranged from 25 cents to $18.
    (a) How do these theaters prevent *everyone* from taking advantage of the lower prices?
    (b) Why would anyone pay $18 for a ticket that he or she could have purchased for 25 cents?
    (c) Do you believe that people will really pay what they *can* under such a system? Do you think that wealthier people will on average pay more than poorer people?
    (d) Many theaters sell steeply discounted tickets on the day of the performance. How do they keep all their patrons from waiting until the day of the performance to purchase tickets?
16. New York City has an ordinance requiring retailers to post prices for items they sell. When the Department of Consumer Affairs began to enforce the ordinance against art galleries, many gallery owners protested vehemently. Why?

17. A newspaper story reported what it called "a mystery." Representatives of the manufacturer and the regional distributor of Head skis tried to buy the entire stock of their own skis being offered for sale at very low prices by a chain of discount stores. At one store the purchasers immediately went outside and broke all the skis in the store parking lot. Can you explain this mystery?

    Does the following information provide any clues? The manager of a sporting goods store that regularly carries Head skis said the action was an attempt by the distributor to get defective skis off the market. An executive with the discount store said the skis were not defective but were a standard production model originally destined for shipment out of the country. What were the manufacturer and distributor trying to do and what went wrong?
18. Advice columnist Ann Landers in her column has several times attacked a practice engaged in by some clothing retailers. They will slash or tear items they have been unable to sell and throw them away rather than give them to employees or low-income people. Ann was puzzled by this behavior. The only plausible explanation she could think of was one suggested by a Nebraska reader: Stores are trying to protect themselves against people who will obtain such merchandise at no charge and then bring it back to the store for credit. Can you give her an alternative explanation?
19. The discussion of lunch and dinner prices at the end of the chapter may be leaving out something important. Dinner patrons almost always take more time to eat than do lunch patrons. Doesn't this raise the cost of providing dinner? Under what circumstances would it *not* raise the cost? If lingering over a meal is costly to restaurants, they will presumably try to prevent or limit it. How might they do this without irritating customers? Will restaurants ever want to *encourage* lingering? How might they do this?
20. You want to sell at auction an antique dining-room suite. There are three people who want it, and they're willing to pay $8,000, $6,000, and $4,000, respectively. Your reservation price (the price above which the bidding must go before you sell) is $5,000. No one in the room has any information about the value of the suite to anyone else.
    (a) At about what price will the suite be sold?
    (b) Suppose you run a Dutch auction. The auctioneer announces a price well above what anyone would be willing to pay and then gradually lowers the price until a bid is received. At about what price will the suite be sold?
    (c) Why do stores sometimes add to their advertisements: "Available only while supplies last"?
21. You and your fiancée are shopping for wedding rings. After showing you a sample of his wares, the jeweler asks, "What price did you have in mind?"
    (a) Why does he ask this question?
    (b) If you tell him you don't plan to spend more than $200 on each ring, are you helping him find the rings to sell you or the price to charge for the rings you prefer?
    (c) What might be a good technique for finding out the lowest price at which the jeweler is willing to sell the rings you like?

Competition and Government Policy

10

Will economic competition disappear unless the government has an active program to preserve it? Or does competition preserve itself, even in the face of diligent efforts by the government to restrict it?

Is the government promoting competition when it prevents larger, more productive, or perhaps more unscrupulous firms from driving other firms out of business? Or does the protection of competitors entail the suppression of competition?

When the government prohibits mergers, is it preventing competitors from eliminating rivals? Or is it stifling the development of more competitive and effective organizational forms?

If particular sellers face so little competition that they can charge prices far above cost, can government protect consumers from exploitation by regulating prices?

What do we mean by competition, and how are we to decide whether the economy or some sector of it is adequately competitive? Is competition in an industry to be measured by the number of competitors, by the practices in which they engage, or by the behavior of prices, costs, and profits and the industry's record with respect to innovation?

These questions will not be answered conclusively in this chapter. But we hope that when you've finished thinking about the sources and consequences of competition as well as the origins and effects of government policies, you will have a better sense of what the issues are.

The Pressures of Competition

All sellers facing demand curves that are less than perfectly elastic—tilted downward to the right rather than horizontal—will maximize net revenue by restricting sales or output and keeping the selling price above marginal cost. (Unless they can practice "perfect" price discrimination.) How and why that occurs was the theme of the preceding two chapters.

One problem from the seller's viewpoint with prices higher than marginal cost is that such prices are a standing invitation to competition. If a piece of apple pie that costs the cafeteria owner 50 cents is selling for $1.50, the owner is likely to insist that the $1.00 difference isn't profit; it's only a contribution toward meeting all the other costs of running the cafeteria: labor, taxes, rent, equipment maintenance, breakage, theft, and so on. That may be completely true. Nonetheless, each additional piece of pie that is sold for $1.50 contributes a net $1.00 toward the owner's wealth. If the same is true for all the other cafés and cafeterias in town, each owner will be earnestly wishing that more hungry people would abandon the other eating places and buy their apple pie from him or her.

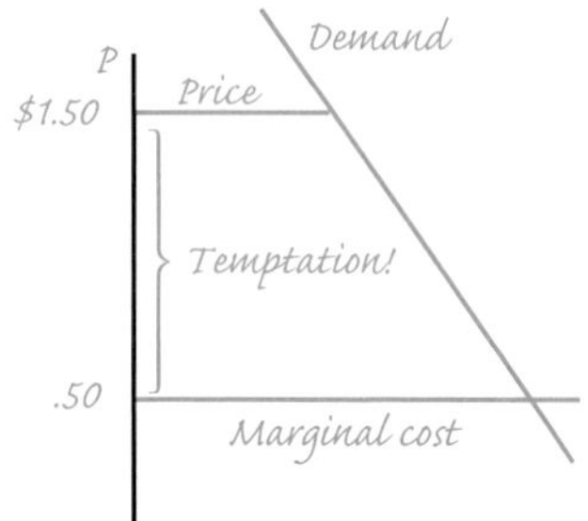

Wishes like this often prompt action. Pie prices might be slightly reduced after 3 P.M. to induce some afternoon coffee-break customers to allow themselves a little treat. Or a sign could be put up after 3 P.M. announcing free coffee with pie purchases. There are dangers inherent in this strategy. Some lunch customers may simply postpone their dessert at noon and have it at 3 P.M. when it's cheaper. And competing restaurants may undermine the promotional effort by offering their own inducements, so that instead of capturing additional customers each owner ends up selling only as much pie as previously but at lower prices.

We assumed in the last chapter that Ed Sike and some of the other sellers whose policies we were examining somehow knew exactly what the demand was for their product. That assumption was useful in enabling us to present the logic of the simple price-searching process. In reality, of course, sellers must usually probe for information on the demand for their product and try to stimulate and maintain it by advertising and by offering reliable service. Moreover, when there are several sellers of a product in the market, each seller's demand curve is going to depend on the policies, including the price policies, of those competing sellers. The demand for Ed Sike's film series will shift downward to the left if neighboring theaters show better movies or cut their prices, or if sororities and fraternities pick Friday nights to sponsor parties, or if the college basketball team plays home games on Friday nights and hits a winning streak.

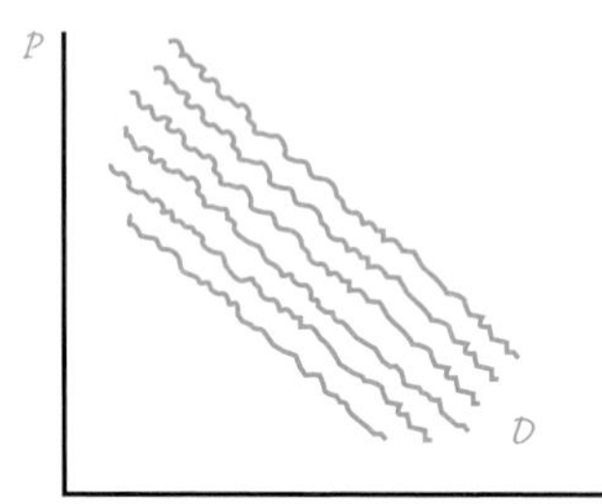

Demand curve as seller perceives it

The price that any one cafeteria in the downtown area sets for apple pie will affect the demand (curve or schedule) for apple pie at other restaurants. Because each of the restaurants will be using estimates of its own demand to set prices that will, in turn, affect the demand all other restaurants encounter, we have a situation more closely resembling chess or poker than a technical maximization problem. The best price for anyone to set *next* may depend on the price set *last*, as in a game of chess. The neat little world of Chapter 9, with its clearly defined curves, becomes blurry. Unfortunately from an analytic standpoint, though perhaps fortunately from an aesthetic one, the real world is not as neatly outlined as the pages in a coloring book.

controlling competition

Then why don't sellers agree not to compete, or to compete less, or to share the market among themselves in some mutually satisfactory way? Even Adam Smith wrote in *The Wealth of Nations* that "People of the same trade seldom meet together, even for merriment and diversion, but the conversation ends in a conspiracy against the public, or in some contrivance to raise prices." So the answer is that sellers would very much like to restrict competition among themselves and often try, but it isn't as easy as it might seem at first. Just as transaction costs often prevent suppliers and demanders from cooperating effectively, so they frequently prevent suppliers from getting together to take advantage of demanders. To begin with, agreements between competing sellers to maintain prices and share markets are usually unenforceable in court and are, moreover, illegal under the laws of many states and under federal law where it is applicable. That fact alone substantially raises the transaction costs of arranging an agreement not to compete. In addition, it's very difficult to devise agreements that everyone will accept, that will cover all the major possibilities, and that can be enforced without the aid of the courts. The incentives to compete are so persistent that soon one or another party will find an excuse to circumvent the agreement or, lacking an acceptable excuse, will circumvent it secretly. On top of all this, successful collusion by the members of a cartel will attract the attention of outsiders, who will begin trying to enter the business in order to enjoy some of the profits that collusion has created.

Cartels consequently reveal a fragility that often surprises people who don't realize on how many margins competition can occur. To be successful in increasing the wealth of its members, a cartel must solve two problems. It must first prevent competition among its own members from dissipating the profits of collusion, whether through a fall in actual selling prices or a rise in selling costs. And then the cartel must find some way to keep new competitors from spoiling the whole operation by trying to enter the act.

A cartel's two problems: prevent members from competing and prevent new firms from entering.

That is why price searchers and even price takers yearn so ardently for *legal restrictions* on competition. They seek to alter the property rights of themselves as well as *others*—namely, the rights of their potential competitors. They seek to *restrict entry.* But as you might recall from Chapter 7's discussion of profit and loss, open entry and exit are the *key* that unleashes entrepreneurial activity and the discovery of comparative advantage.

Sellers are sometimes extraordinarily imaginative in devising reasons why the government ought to outlaw price-cutting or prevent new sellers from entering the market. Here are a few actual items culled from a number of newspapers, with identities sometimes altered slightly to protect the guilty. It's a very good idea to ask in each case exactly who stands to gain and who is most likely to lose.

- The Washington, D.C. Medical Society launched a major lobbying campaign over the weekend against proposed legislation that would encourage granting of hospital privileges to qualified nurse midwives, psychologists, podiatrists, and other nonphysician health professionals. The medical society envisioned erosion of standards, speculating in its newsletter that "pretty soon a boy scout with a rusty knife will be permitted to perform brain surgery."
- All plumbers must spend a minimum of 140 hours a year for five years learning higher mathematics, physics, hydraulics, and isometric drawing.
- Woolen makers are arguing that because woolen worsted fabric is essential to national defense, the government should impose quotas on imports from abroad.
- The deregulation of cosmetologists and barbers would put consumers in our state at the mercy of professionally uneducated and governmentally unregulated hairdressers and barbers. This is extremely irresponsible, because hairdressers today utilize extremely hazardous acids and alkalines in the course of their everyday work.
- The prominent owner of a local television sales and service center said today that he welcomed the state's investigation of the television repair business and he demanded regulation of the industry. "We must eliminate janitors, firefighters, messengers, and similar amateurs who defraud the public by providing poor-quality services at cut-rate prices," he argued.
- The Senate Public Health Committee yesterday rejected a bill to allow use of multiple offices and trade names in the diagnosis of eye problems and fitting glasses. Single-office optometrists contend that optometrists who have private offices are in effect employed by their patients. If optometrists work under a trade name, their boss is their company.
- The owner of the Piney Woods Nursing Home and secretary of the State Association of Licensed Nursing Homes accused the state health department last night of approving new nursing-home construction without proper investigation of the need for additional facilities or the qualifications of the applicants. "Unqualified people, including speculators from other parts of the country, are hoping to reap big profits," he said. "A great surplus of beds will bring about cutthroat competition, which means nursing homes will have to curtail many needed services, resulting in lower standards detrimental to patients and the community."
- Some state officials are so adamant that dogs' teeth should be cleaned only by licensed veterinarians that they sent in an undercover pooch a couple of months ago to break up what they considered an illegal dog-tooth-cleaning operation. The executive director of the state's Board of

> Examiners in Veterinary Medicine said that groomers who invade a dog's gums are practicing medicine and might cause the dog unnecessary pain. (Do you think people with their hand in a dog's mouth are likely to cause the dog unnecessary pain?)

The Ambivalence of Government Policies

An old proverb wisely asserts that the wolf should not be sent to guard the sheep. Should the government be relied on to preserve competition in the economy? The history of government intervention in economic life reveals a pattern of concern for the special interests of competitors at least as strong as concern for competition. And the two are not identical, even though our rhetoric so often and easily uses them interchangeably.

concern for competition is not the same as concern for competitors.

The cases just cited show government taking or being urged to take a variety of actions designed to prevent potential sellers from offering more favorable terms or more attractive opportunities to buyers. These actions constitute restrictions on competition, regardless of the arguments used to defend them. The ultimate effect of a particular restriction on competition might be to preserve competition, by protecting a substantial number of competitors who would otherwise be forced out of business. But whether or not that is the long-term effect in certain cases, it is important to begin any evaluation of government policy toward competition by acknowledging one principle: *A law that restricts competitors restricts competition.*

One very common justification for such laws is that they preserve competition by preventing "predatory" practices.

Selling Below Cost

Do you agree with the following paragraph?

> In order to preserve our competitive economic system, we need laws that prohibit unfair practices such as sales below cost. Large firms can often afford to sell products below cost until their rivals are driven out of business. If they are not restrained by law, we could easily wind up with an economy dominated by just a few huge corporations.

Most Americans apparently accept this argument. Our laws, at the federal, state, and local level, abound with provisions designed to prevent or inhibit price-cutting. Many states have statutes prohibiting sales below cost, statutes that usually go by some such name as Unfair Practices Act. And regulatory commissions, ostensibly created to hold down the prices that may be charged by public utilities, often wind up enforcing minimum rather than maximum rates. This was true, for example, of the grandfather of all such commissions in the United States, the Interstate Commerce Commission (created by Congress in 1887).

It's fairly obvious why some business firms would approve that kind of legislation: They want protection against competition. But why do consumers and the general public go along? The public seems to have accepted the argument that price-cutting can create "monopolies" by driving competitors out of business. And monopolies, of course, are considered bad. The paragraph with which this section began states the essential argument. How valid is it? Is it possible to construct a defensible case for laws that prohibit "sales below cost"? A lot of questions should immediately arise in your mind.

What Is the Appropriate Cost?

What is the cost below which prices should not be set? Does anyone actually sell below cost? Consider the case of Ms. Profetta Seeker, proprietor of the Thrifty Supermarket, who orders 1,000 pounds of ripe bananas. She gets them for 5 cents a pound, because the produce distributor is eager to move them before they become too ripe. Profetta advertises a weekend special on bananas: 10 cents a pound. But Monday morning finds her with 500 pounds of bananas, now beginning to turn brown. How low can Profetta cut her price without selling below cost? The answer is *not* 5 cents a pound. Most of that is *sunk* cost and hence no longer a cost at all. If Profetta will have to pay someone to haul the unsold bananas away on Tuesday morning, her cost on Monday could be less than zero. In that case, it might be to her advantage to give the bananas away. If a zero price is to her advantage, how can it be "below cost"? Below *what* cost? (By the way, did Profetta *buy* the bananas below cost?)

Or suppose Profetta bought a truckload of coffee: 1,000 one-pound cans for $750. It was an unknown brand on which a local distributor offered her an attractive price. But it turns out that her customers aren't interested. She cuts the price down to 80 cents a pound, but still can't move it successfully. Four weeks after her purchase she still has 987 cans of coffee cluttering her shelves and storage room. If she now cuts the price below 75 cents, is she selling below cost? She is not. She has no intention of replacing the cans she sells so each sale is that many additional cents in the till and one less can in the way. The relevant cost of a pound of coffee could well be zero. The relevant cost is, of course, the marginal cost.

Let's try a different kind of example and then return to Profetta Seeker. It might make sense to estimate the cost of producing a steer, but does it make any sense to estimate separately the cost of producing hindquarters and forequarters? Should the price of steaks, which come from the hindquarters of a beef carcass, cover the cost of producing the hindquarters, leaving it to pot-roast prices to cover the cost of the forequarters from which they derive? The question is nonsensical. Unless it is possible to produce hindquarters separately from forequarters, one cannot speak of the cost of producing one and the cost of producing the other. Hindquarters and forequarters, or steaks and pot roasts, are joint products with joint costs. There is no way to determine the specific costs of joint products or to allocate joint costs "correctly."

Back to Profetta Seeker. Can we legitimately segregate the costs of each item sold in her grocery store? Think of her frozen-food items, for example. How much of the cost of owning and operating the freezer case should be allocated to vegetables, how much to Chinese dinners, and how much to orange juice? It's true that she could not carry frozen cauliflower without a freezer case. But if she finds it profitable to own and operate a freezer case just for the sake of the frozen juices she can sell, and if she then has some extra room in which she decides to display boxes of frozen cauliflower, it might make sense for her to assign *none* of the freezer cost to the cauliflower.

A successful businesswoman (or businessman) is not concerned with questions of cost allocation that have no relevance to decision making. She knows that production—and a merchant is a producer just as certainly as is a manufacturer—is usually a process with joint products and joint costs. The businesswoman is interested in the additional costs associated with a decision and the additional revenue to be expected from it, not in such meaningless problems as the allocation of joint costs to particular items for sale. If there is room for a magazine rack near the checkout counter, the question is: How much will its installation *add* to total costs and how much will it *add* to total revenue? If the latter is larger, the rack makes sense, and the magazines sold need not have a price that covers utilities, rent, depreciation on cash registers, *or even the wholesale prices of the magazines*.

Below cost? Cost to whom? Cost of doing what?

Mark well the italicized phrase. It may be profitable to sell a morning newspaper for 25 cents even if it costs 50 cents to obtain it from the distributor. Why? Because availability of the newspaper may bring in new customers who add to net revenue—the profit—through the purchases of other items. Profetta Seeker is interested not in the net revenue on any *one* item she sells, but in the difference between total revenue and total costs. Hardware stores that sell odd-lot bolts, screws, and nuts lose money on each sale but (or so their owners hope) more than make it up through the goodwill they thereby create. Even Ann Trepreneur—our pizzeria owner from Chapter 7—provides napkins, crushed red pepper, parmesan cheese, water, and toothpicks for "free" to her customers, regardless of the quantity of pizza they eat. (Her competitors at the Chinese restaurant down the street go so far as to offer piping hot tea for no charge.) She's not concerned with "making money" on every single item she provides to her customers. She's concerned with the overall *profit* of the pizzeria, the difference between *total* revenues and *total* costs.

"Predators" and Competition

There would be little point in stressing all this were it not for the popular mythology of "selling below cost." Our argument suggests that many allegations of sales below cost are based on an arbitrary assignment of sunk costs or joint costs. Business firms often complain about below-cost sales, of course, but that is because they dislike competition and want government to protect them from its rigors by prohibiting price-cutting.

But aren't there dangers to competition in allowing firms to cut prices as low as they wish? It is odd, but not really surprising, how often people identify the protection of competitors with the preservation of competition. In reality they are more like opposites. Competitors are usually protected by laws inhibiting competition, laws that benefit privileged producers by restricting consumers and nonprivileged producers. The hobgoblin hauled out to justify this is "predatory price-cutting" backed up by a "long purse."

Protecting competitors is not the same thing as preserving competition.

Predatory price-cutting means reducing prices below cost in order to drive a rival out of business or prevent new rivals from emerging *with the intention of raising prices afterward to recoup all losses*. It is supposedly a favorite tactic of larger firms that can stand prolonged losses, or temporary losses on some lines, because of their larger financial resources—the so-called long purse. Economic theory does not deny the possibility of predatory price-cutting. But it does raise a long list of skeptical questions, headed by all the questions we have been discussing regarding the proper definition of an item's cost.

How long will it take for such a policy to accomplish its end? The longer it takes, the larger will be the short-run losses accepted by the predator firm and, consequently, the larger must be the long-term benefits if the policy is to justify itself.

What will happen to the physical assets and human resources of the firms forced out of business? That's an important question, because if those assets remain in existence, what is to prevent someone from bringing them back into production when the predator firm raises its prices to reap the rewards of its villainy? And if this occurs, how can the firm hope to benefit from its predatory policy? On the other hand, the human resources may scatter into alternative employments and be costly to reassemble.

Is it likely that the predatory firm will be able to destroy enough of its rivals to secure the degree of market power that it must have to make the long-run profits justify the short-run losses? Charges of predatory pricing have most frequently been leveled against large discount houses, drug chains, and grocery supermarkets. But these sellers are not pitted exclusively against small independent competitors: They must tangle with other large discount houses, other drug chains, and other supermarkets. Perhaps a grocery chain could cut its prices far enough and keep them low long enough to drive Profetta Seeker out of business, but that wouldn't work on other chains. And it isn't Profetta Seeker who keeps grocery chain executives awake at night.

We are not denying the possibility of predatory pricing in business. Well-documented examples are hard to find, but it is surely possible. Minimum-price laws, however, offer the *certainty* of higher prices in order to eliminate the *possibility* of higher prices: a case of accepting a known and certain evil as a way of avoiding an uncertain evil of unknown dimensions. That may or may not be a good social bargain. But because it is so often advocated by business firms that clearly stand to gain from it, we should at least approach their arguments skeptically.

Regulating Prices

But what about sellers who face so little competition that they can earn large profits by charging prices far above their costs? Suppliers of electricity or telephone services are standard examples. Where such firms are investor owned, should the government protect consumers from exploitation by regulating the prices they may charge?

How will regulators determine the costs of running the enterprise?

How should the regulators choose the proper price to set in such cases? By looking at costs, of course. Prices should be set to enable the firms to cover their costs and earn a reasonable profit. But as you surely know by this time, costs are not mere facts of nature. They are the consequences of managerial decisions. And if the managers of an enterprise know that their prices will be adjusted to take account of any change in costs, what incentives will they have to lower costs or to keep them down? They could choose instead to surround themselves with thick office carpets and company jets and to inflate salaries, build monuments, and enjoy a quiet life. What incentive will they have to innovate? Why take risks in such an environment?

Who will guard the guardians?

Regulators would consequently have to examine continually the decisions of managers. To do so effectively, they would have to learn as much about the firm as the actual managers know. That means in effect that every regulated firm would have two sets of managers. Does that make sense? Wouldn't the second set of managers tend over time to adopt the perspective of the first set, from whom they would almost inevitably be obtaining most of their information? Who then will regulate the regulators? The history of regulated industries reveals a disturbing tendency for the members of regulatory commissions to be "captured" by those whom they are supposed to regulate, not through bribery or corruption, but simply because regulators quite naturally acquire an interest over time in the well-being of the industries for which they are responsible.

Banking institutions in the United States were closely regulated by governments before 1980. They were also protected against competitors by government restrictions on entry. And so *were customers better served with or without regulation:*

- *in banking?*
- *in airline travel?*
- *in telephone service?*

they opened at 10, closed at 3, and provided none of the numerous services that we have come to take for granted since 1980, from cash machines through telephone transfers to much longer hours of operation.

Before 1978, the government regulated commercial airline prices and restricted entry into the industry. Although service was much more luxurious in the days of regulation, it was luxurious for far fewer passengers. The airlines charged the high prices that the government mandated and competed for the relatively few customers available at those prices by offering such amenities as empty seats across which to spread out and quality food and drink with attractive young flight attendants to serve their overwhelmingly male passengers.

When competition began to displace regulation in the telephone industry in the 1980s, all sorts of new services started to appear. An industry that had been reliable but static and unimaginative suddenly discovered innumerable ways to make the telephone do things for us that we hadn't even known we wanted done.

The standard argument for government regulation of prices is that government *must* regulate where competition *cannot*, or else consumers will be at the mercy of greedy sellers. This argument often kept us from asking whether competition really was unable to constrain the behavior of firms in traditionally regulated industries. We took for granted that competition could not be effective in transportation, communication, financial services, utilities, and other industries and so never put that assumption to a test. The movement toward deregulation of the past two decades or so has not settled all the issues, but it has unquestionably showed us that there are more margins on which competition can occur than we formerly suspected and that competition has some distinct advantages over government commissions as a method of restraining market power.

"Antitrust" Policy

We shall see in Chapter 13 why it is that governments so often intervene in ways that harm consumers by *reducing* competition, despite the fact that consumers and competition always win easily in the rhetorical battles. But local and state governments and especially the federal government also have adopted specific policies to *promote* competition, policies that are ordinarily justified on the ground that competition is an effective coordinator of economic activity but requires some government maintenance if it is to be adequately preserved. The assessment of these laws, their applications, and their consequences forms an interesting study in history and judicial interpretation as well as economic analysis. All we shall try to do here, however, is raise a few fundamental questions.

The most important such law is the Sherman Act, often called the Sherman Antitrust Act, enacted by Congress with almost no debate or opposition in 1890. (The name reflects the attempts of nineteenth-century businessmen to use legal trusteeships as a device to prevent competition.) Its sweeping language has caused some to call it the constitution of the competitive system. It forbids all contracts, combinations, or conspiracies in restraint of interstate trade and all attempts to monopolize any part of interstate trade. The language is so sweeping, in fact, that it was bound to be qualified in its application. After all, any two partners entering into business together could be deemed to have combined with the intention of making trade more difficult for their competitors and thus gaining an ever-larger share of trade for themselves. The federal courts consequently came to hold that combinations or other attempts to monopolize had to be "unreasonable" or major threats to public welfare before they could be prohibited under the Sherman Act.

Interpretations and Applications

To help the courts in their efforts to apply the policies of the Sherman Act, Congress has passed additional legislation such as the Clayton Act and the Federal Trade Commission Act, both of which became law in 1914. The latter act created the Federal Trade Commission as a supposedly expert body and authorized it to promote competition by prohibiting a wide range of "unfair" practices. A principal provision of the Clayton Act (and subsequent amendments) aims specifically at the question of mergers, prohibiting all mergers that might "substantially" lessen competition. But difficult and important questions remain unresolved.

When does a merger substantially lessen competition? And do mergers ever increase competition? Suppose two steel firms want to merge. This would be a *horizontal merger*. At first glance we would be inclined to say that the merger will substantially lessen competition in an industry already made up of a relatively few very large firms. But suppose they sell in different geographic areas? Suppose they each specialize in a different line of steel products? Suppose each is on the edge of failure and that the merger will lead to economies that may enable both to survive?

Horizontal merger: two oil refiners

A great deal of dispute surrounds so-called *conglomerate mergers*: mergers between firms producing widely divergent goods. Does the acquisition of a car rental firm by an electrical machinery manufacturer enable the rental firm to compete more effectively against Hertz and Avis? Does it lead to special arrangements between the machinery manufacturer, its suppliers, and the rental firm that tie up a portion of the car rental business and thus reduce competition? Do conglomerate mergers lead to concentrations of financial power that are dangerous and undesirable regardless of their effects on competition?

Conglomerate merger: an oil refiner and a steelmaker

Vertical merger: an oil refiner and a chain of gasoline retailers

What about *vertical mergers*, mergers between firms that previously existed in a supplier—buyer relationship, as when a supermarket chain acquires a food processor? Is this more likely to increase efficiency or to reduce competition by depriving other food processors of opportunities to sell?

What constitutes an illegally unfair trade practice? Is it unfair for a large firm to demand discounts from its suppliers? Is it unfair for suppliers to offer discounts to some purchasers but not to others? What about the whole question of advertising? Do large firms have unfair advantages in advertising, advantages that advertising increases? Must advertising be truthful in order to be fair? Of course it must, almost by definition. But what is the truth, the whole truth, and nothing but the truth? Anyone who thinks about this issue seriously or for very long is forced to admit that the regulation of "deceptive" advertising by the Federal Trade Commission inevitably involves the commission in complex questions of purpose and effect and in a large number of judgments that appear quite arbitrary.

And always we return to the root problem: Restrictions on competitors will reduce their ability to compete. Competition is essentially the offering of additional opportunities, and additional opportunities mean a wider range of choices and hence greater wealth. But the manner in which a firm expands the set of opportunities it offers may diminish, over a shorter or a longer period, the set of opportunities other firms are able to offer. Under what circumstances do we want the government to restrict one firm's competitive efforts for the sake of the larger or long-run competitive situation? It is extremely important to take note of the fact that the most effective pressures on government policies stem not from consumer but from producer interests. And those policies will too often be shaped by the desire of producers to protect themselves against the rigors of the competitive life.

Vertical Restraints: Competitive or Anticompetitive

Current controversies over vertical restraints on competition illustrate many of the opposing arguments and conflicting interests that complicate antitrust policy. From 1937 to 1976, federal legislation exempted from the Sherman Act state-endorsed price-fixing agreements between manufacturers and retailers. Congress had no sooner rescinded this exemption, making such agreements automatically illegal once again, than the courts started to carve out exceptions to the principle that manufacturers may not try to control competition at the retail level. Congress subsequently responded by trying to prohibit altogether what it had once encouraged. Legislation has been repeatedly introduced that would sharply curtail the power of manufacturers to control the behavior of those who distribute their products.

Is there any way that consumers could benefit from a manufacturer's refusal to sell to a retailer who reduced the resale price

Why would a manufacturer want retailers to charge more (and consequently sell less)?

Why would a manufacturer want fewer retailers selling its products?

below some recommended minimum, or from a decision to limit the number of retail outlets that will be allowed to carry the manufacturer's product in a given geographic area? It would seem that such actions could only produce higher prices and poorer-quality service for consumers. That conclusion becomes much less certain, however, when we ask why any manufacturer might want to prevent price discounting by retailers or to hold down the number of stores carrying its product.

Manufacturers sometimes conclude that they will be unable to market their product successfully unless consumers are provided with a substantial range of pre- and postsale services, such as information on ways the product can be utilized profitably, continuing instruction on operating procedures, or fast and dependable maintenance service. Retailers will want to supply these services only if they can increase their own net revenue by doing so, that is, if supplying these services will increase their sales by more than enough to cover the cost of the service.

Such services will not be supplied, and hence the manufacturer's product cannot be successfully marketed, whenever retailers are able to "free ride" on the services provided by other retailers. Consider the case of personal computers. These products could not have been introduced into offices and homes as quickly as they were if selling effort had not been accompanied by a whole lot of instructional effort. Instructional effort was selling effort, perhaps the most effective kind of selling effort. And there's the catch. Retailers who incurred the cost of teaching people how to make effective use of one type of personal computer could easily be undermined by competing retailers who provided no instructional services but catered to the demand that others had created.

Manufacturers who set minimum resale prices or limit the number of outlets in an area may be trying to protect cooperating distributors from free-riding distributors. Their interest would be in marketing their product effectively, not in reducing competition. Of course, the manufacturer's actions *would* limit competition if we defined competition in some "perfectly competitive" sense. But in the absence of such actions there might be even less competition, as the product could not be effectively marketed at all.

Should manufacturers be allowed to restrict competition at the retail level, then, as part of a reasonable effort to market their product? The courts have been allowing such activities in recent years, on a case-by-case basis, looking at the context, intent, and probable effects of the "vertical" restrictions. That has not made everyone happy. Distributors who were cut off or otherwise disciplined by manufacturers have complained to Congress, and some members of Congress have responded with bills that would severely limit the rights of manufacturers in this area. Proponents of such bills argue that they want to enhance competition. Opponents reply that the effect will be to reduce competition by seriously curtailing the power of manufacturers and distributors to devise and agree upon effective marketing procedures.

The Range of Opinion

Is the whole body of "antitrust" law perhaps more of a hindrance than a help to competition? There are some who come to that conclusion. There are others—heavily concentrated, it often seems, in the economics profession—who would retain the Sherman Act and the antimerger provisions of the Clayton Act and junk the rest. Some of these defenders claim that the Sherman and Clayton acts have made important contributions to the maintenance of a competitive economy. Others claim that they could make a much larger contribution if they were seriously enforced. But still others view them at best as harmless rhetoric, at worse as weapons that, in the hands of ignorant political appointees, may do a lot of damage to the economy. As Judge Robert Bork explained in his book *The Antitrust Paradox*: "A determined attempt to remake the American economy into a replica of the textbook model of competition would have roughly the same effect on national wealth as several dozen strategically placed nuclear explosions."

"Antitrust" policy is certainly full of contradictions, of cases where the right hand is doing what the left hand is undoing. State laws rarely promote competition; more often they promote the interests of the competitor protectors rather than the competition protectors. Federal enforcement of the Sherman Act and the antimerger provisions of the Clayton Act often seems to strain at gnats while swallowing camels. Firms unable to compete effectively by offering their customers lower prices and better quality sometimes file complaints under the antitrust laws to see if they can persuade the courts to raise the prices or reduce the quality of their competitors' offerings. On the other hand, the existence of the Sherman Act, with its ringing denunciation of price-fixing conspiracies, may have retarded the development in this country of the cartel arrangements that have so often appeared in Western Europe and Japan. The economist George Stigler once suggested that "the ghost of Senator Sherman is an ex officio member of the board of directors of every large company." While that statement will never meet the minimum criteria for empirical scientific truths, good history is still a long way from being a pure science.

Toward Evaluation

The conclusions that we shall offer at the end are far more modest than the questions with which we began.

Restrictions on potential competitors reduce the range and diminish the availability of substitute goods and allow sellers more room to increase their own wealth by denying opportunities to others. Competition is a process, not a state of affairs. To put it another way, competition can be recognized only in motion pictures, not in still photographs. The fact, for example, that the price of some good is exactly the same, no matter from which seller you buy, establishes absolutely nothing about whether the industry producing that good is adequately competitive. The important question is how those prices all came to be identical. It happens with surprising frequency that even public figures, who ought to know better, will infer an absence of competition from the uniformity of price. The quickest antidote to this error is the recollection that wheat farmers all charge the same price.

The other observation is that an inadequate situation must be compared with more desirable situations that are actually attainable. It is a mistake to contrast a less-than-ideal situation with an ideal-but-unattainable situation. There are also costs involved in changing market structures and business practices. They include not only the costs of an investigation, prosecution, court order, and compliance under antitrust statutes. They also include the costs of mistakes and of the increased uncertainty that shifting policies create for business planning. Only if these marginal costs are less than the marginal benefits can one maintain that we would be "better off" if we took legal action to reduce the market power of price searchers, to prevent business mergers, or to prohibit practices that might eventually lessen competition.

Once Over Lightly

A gap between the price of a good and the marginal cost of making it available is a source of potential advantage to someone. Competition occurs in the economy as people locate such differentials and try to exploit them by filling that gap with additional goods.

Competition takes more forms than we can list and usually more forms than competitors can anticipate and head off.

Because competition tends to transfer the gains for providing a good to purchasers and to other suppliers, firms frequently try to obtain government assistance in excluding competitors, often displaying remarkable ingenuity and stunning sophistry.

Firms often charge that their competitors, whether domestic or foreign, are "selling below cost" and call for the government to prevent such "predatory" practices. Most such charges make sense only if they include some expenses in per-unit cost that are irrelevant to the particular decisions under attack. They make a different kind of sense when we remember that sellers characteristically prefer less competition.

Government regulation of pricing and other business practices has often blocked the development of competition that might otherwise have arisen and done a more effective job of inducing firms to serve the interests of consumers.

The notion that government is the Defender of Competition Against Rapacious Monopolists is probably more a hope than a reality. Federal, state, and local governments have created and preserved numerous positions of special privilege whose effect is to restrict competition and reduce the options available to consumers.

An adequate, balanced, and complete evaluation of the substantial body of statutes, commission decrees, and judicial holdings that makes up federal antitrust policy has not yet been published.

Competition is a process in which competitors engage. We obviously cannot have competition without competitors. It does not seem as obvious to people that we also cannot have competition if we prohibit competitors from taking actions intended to increase their share of the market.

QUESTIONS FOR DISCUSSION

1. Soon after the government deregulated airline pricing, a major airline began asking in-flight passengers to complete a lengthy "Passenger Survey." A cover note from the senior vice president for marketing said that passengers who completed the survey would be helping the airline provide "the best possible service." Questions were asked about the purpose of this trip, frequency of flying, type of fare paid, what would have been done had no discount fare been available, how the ticket was purchased, and income of the traveler. What was the airline trying to do?
2. How would you account for the fact that although some observers claim competition is declining in the American economy, every business firm insists that it faces strenuous competition?
3. Consult the technical definition of *oligopoly*: competition among the few. Are commercial airlines oligopolists by that definition? Are the owners of the gasoline stations in a small town oligopolists? Name some other sellers who are and are not oligopolists by that definition.
4. The attempt by sellers to make their product more attractive to consumers is sometimes called *product differentiation*.
   (a) Is product differentiation a wasteful process, imposing costs on sellers that are greater than the benefits conferred on buyers? Think of cases where it probably is wasteful in this sense and other cases where it is not.
   (b) Evaluate the following argument: "New practices initiated by sellers to differentiate their products are liable to be wasteful from the social point of view because they are liable to entail high marginal costs and low marginal benefits. But this only means that producers have already made use of the low-cost/high-benefit techniques of product differentiation; it does not show that the whole process of product differentiation is wasteful."
5. Why must an effective price-fixing agreement between sellers include such restrictions on sales as output limitations or geographic divisions of sales territory?
6. This problem is designed to help you appreciate the joys and tribulations of cartels. Let D in Figure 10–1 be the demand for oil and MC be the sum of the marginal-cost curves of all oil producers. Ignore for now the line labeled H.
   (a) If oil producers are price takers because there are thousands of them and they have no effective cartel, why will the price of oil move toward \$9 per barrel? What will occur if the price is much above or below \$9?

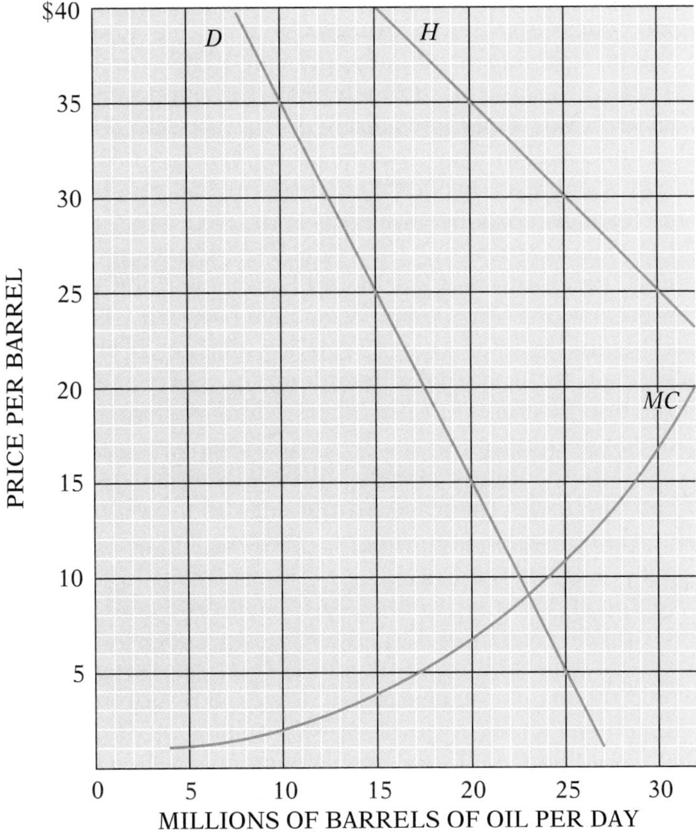

Figure 10–1 **Market demand for oil and combined marginal cost curves of producers**

(b) Now assume that one party acquires control over all producing oil wells and hence the power to control the price by controlling output. How many millions of barrels per day (mb/d) will be produced if the goal is to maximize net revenue? What price will be set?

(c) Change the preceding assumption slightly. The oil wells remain under the ownership and control of the thousands of original owners, but each owner agrees to sell only at the price determined by the Organizer of Prices to Exploit Consumers (OPEC). This is an agent hired by the oil producer to determine and announce the price for oil that will be most advantageous to oil producers collectively. OPEC announces that the price shall be $29 per barrel. What must occur if this price is to hold?

(d) Why will the individual oil producers want to sell individually a quantity of oil that sums in aggregate to far more than 13 mb/d?

(e) How can OPEC prevent output from expanding way beyond 13 mb/d and thereby bringing down the price of oil? If OPEC assigns production quotas to each individual oil producer, how can it make sure that all the producers will be satisfied that their quotas are "fair"? How can it make sure that individual producers don't exceed their quotas?

(f) Is the demand curve for oil that obtains when oil has long been selling at $9 per barrel and is expected to remain at about that level likely to remain unchanged when the price of oil rises to $29 per barrel and is expected to stay at that much higher level for a number of years? What sort of developments are likely to *shift the demand* over time? What effect will this have on the oil producers who created OPEC?

(g) A serious threat to the wealth of the OPEC oil producers is likely to come from *new* producers who are attracted into the industry by OPEC's success in raising the price of oil. In the case of the real-world OPEC (Organization of Petroleum Exporting Countries), the 13 member nations saw their sales decline between 1980 and 1985 from over 30 mb/d to fewer than 15 mb/d, with some of the difference reflecting a reduced total demand but most of it a result of increased production by non-OPEC members. Suppose that *H* had been the demand for OPEC oil when the cartel began operating. Compare the price, output, and total revenue of OPEC's members when the demand is *H* with the price, output, and total revenue when the demand is *D*—even assuming no "cheating" by cartel members.

7. Cartels tend to break down in the absence of support from a government that is willing and able to penalize cartel members who violate the cartel's agreements. Why? Isn't it in the interest of each cartel member to abide by any agreement that aims at maximizing the net revenue of the cartel? Why would the members have to be compelled by government to adhere to the agreement? One way to see why cartels break down is to ask yourself what would happen if four people played the following game.

> Each player holds two cards, one marked L and the other S. When a signal is given, the players simultaneously play one or the other of their cards and are then awarded monetary prizes that vary according to the pattern of cards played.
>
> If the pattern is 4 S cards, each player receives $5.
>
> If the pattern is 3 S cards and 1 L card, those who played S lose $5 and the player who played L wins $15.
>
> If the pattern is 2 S cards and 2 L cards, those who played S lose $10 and those who played L win $10.
>
> If the pattern is 1 S and 3 L, the player who played S loses $5 and those who played L win $5.
>
> If all play the L card, all lose $5.

(a) What do you think will occur, assuming that each player acts freely and independently and tries to maximize his or her winnings?

(b) Why will it be difficult for the players to avoid losing rather than winning money in the absence of an "enforcer" who punishes anyone who plays the L card?

(c) Now suppose that the four "players" are actually four independent producers that dominate an industry and that "playing the L card" means deciding to produce a *large* quantity of output, while "playing the S card" means deciding to produce a *small* quantity of output. Look again at the payoffs. Think of them now as the profits that would accrue to the producers depending on (i) whether they individually decided to restrict their output for the sake of a higher price and (ii) what the other producers decided. Why does a producer always make a larger profit by choosing a large output, regardless of what others choose?

(d) What procedures might be available to the members of the industry that would induce every producer in the industry to choose the small output and thus maximize the profit accruing to the industry as a whole?

8. The analysis in the preceding two questions raises an interesting issue: Why did the Organization of Petroleum Exporting Countries succeed so well for so long in raising the world price of oil? A major part of any answer is contained in the concept of the marginal cost of producing and selling oil. The cost of extracting oil from an established field can be very low indeed, so low as to be almost negligible. But the relevant marginal cost is the cost of extracting and *selling*. In the 1970s, many respected parties were predicting that, because the demand for petroleum products was highly inelastic and the world's reserves were quickly running out, the price per barrel might rise by the end of the century as high as $1,000 a barrel. How do expectations of such dramatically higher future prices affect the opportunity cost of selling oil currently? How would such expectations solve OPEC's "cheating" problem? Why did those extravagant expectations, so common in the 1970s, disappear by the mid-1980s?
9. The legislature of a large state considered a bill that would require all grocery stores and drugstores selling package liquor to provide separate entrances to their liquor departments. It was maintained by supporters of the bill that this was necessary to prevent minors from entering the liquor department. Who do you think lobbied for this bill? Why?
10. A study pointed out that 73 percent of the professions licensed by a populous midwestern state required entrants to have "good character." Why? How can good character be determined? Who is best able to determine whether morticians' characters are sufficiently blameless to entitle them to a license?
11. While a state legislature was debating a bill that would allow optometrists to administer certain eyedrops during eye exams, 50 ophthalmologists descended on the capitol to lobby against the bill. The chairman of the state Academy of Ophthalmology told a reporter: "There is no economic advantage one way or the other." The ophthalmologists' sole concern was that, if the bill became law, "more people will be harmed through inappropriate use of drugs." Do you believe that 50 medical specialists all took a day off from their practices to lobby the legislature exclusively out of concern for the public's health?
12. The Washington State Utilities and Transportation Commission periodically launches a crackdown on unlicensed movers of household goods.

    (a) The commission's enforcement chief said the crackdowns occur because of consumer complaints about damaged goods and price manipulation and because authorized carriers are complaining about growing competition from unlicensed movers. Which set of complaints do you suppose put the most pressure on the commission? How many consumers do you think know about the existence of the State's Utilities and Transportation Commission? How many licensed movers probably know about the commission?

    (b) State officials have said that the legislature set strict requirements for entry into the moving industry in the 1930s because legislators were concerned that "unregulated, cutthroat competition would lead to a deterioration in service, safety problems, overly intensive competition in urban areas and a lack of service in rural areas." Do you agree that these problems are likely to arise in the absence of regulation? Does competition *usually* lead to a deterioration in service? When is competition "cutthroat" and "overly intensive"? If you ask this last question of people already in the moving industry, how are they likely to respond?

(c) There is a "stringent public convenience and necessity test" for any new firm seeking a mover's permit, which places on the applicant firm the burden of proving that its services are needed. Can that be proved?

(d) The transportation director for the state commission is on record as believing that there are currently "more licensed movers than is necessary—as far as service rather than rates are concerned." What is the relationship between high rates and sufficient service?

(e) What does the fact that there are dozens of unlicensed movers operating in the state indicate about the transportation director's claim?

13. After 25 years, the U.S. Justice Department agreed to drop a consent decree that it had extracted from Safeway, under which Safeway had been prohibited from selling at prices below its cost of acquiring grocery products or at "unreasonably low prices" that might be above cost. The decree stemmed from a government suit that had accused Safeway of selling below cost in an effort to monopolize the market for retail food in Texas and New Mexico.

    (a) How likely is it that Safeway or anyone else would be able to monopolize the market for retail food in two states?

    (b) The alleged attempt to monopolize led Safeway to reduce prices to customers. Who do you suppose complained to the Justice Department about Safeway's behavior?

    (c) What is the appropriate way to determine the cost of specific grocery items? Is a retailer selling paper bags below cost when it makes them available to customers at no charge? Is the retailer cross-subsidizing paper bags?

14. Three elements that must be present for a firm to be engaged in predatory pricing are pricing (a) below cost, (b) in order to eliminate rivals, and (c) with the intention of raising prices afterward to recoup. What factors would make the last step of the process difficult to complete? Under what kinds of circumstances would it be relatively easy? Can you cite any actual examples?

15. The Staggers Rail Act of 1980 substantially reduced the power of the Interstate Commerce Commission to control the rates that railroads charge shippers.

    (a) The president of the National Coal Association has denounced the system of "letting the railroads charge what the traffic will bear" and has called for renewed rate regulation. Many other shippers, however, applaud the extensive deregulation of the railroads. Why might the coal industry favor rate regulation while most shippers oppose it?

    (b) One study of the price elasticity of demand for rail transport of grain in the Corn Belt states calculated an elasticity coefficient of 3.75. What is the nature of the competition that makes the demand elasticity so high?

(c) If the railroads, barge lines, and trucking firms of this country were allowed to set their rates free from government regulation, what do you think would follow: "gouging of customers" (higher prices) or "ruinous price-cutting" (lower prices)? Does this happen in other areas of the economy where prices are not regulated by commissions—for example, in the grocery or automobile industry?

16. What is the difference between reducing prices to attract more customers and reducing prices in order to monopolize?

17. When the government regulates the maximum prices that firms may charge in some industry, it usually does so on the grounds that competition cannot adequately regulate prices because the nature of the industry will not allow for enough firms to make competition effective. It usually accompanies price regulation with protection of the regulated firm against the entry of new firms. The cable television industry is a good example.
    (a) Suppose that a cable television firm has been granted an exclusive franchise to serve a specified section of some large city. On what margins will the firm have to compete?
    (b) What can the firm do to increase its net revenue if regulators will not allow it to raise its prices?
    (c) There is no standard product known as "cable television service." Regulators who set maximum prices must, therefore, specify with some precision the exact product being sold. Why will that be difficult in the case of cable television?
    (d) Is it true that cable television companies must be granted exclusive franchises because it would be too costly to construct more than one set of wires to serve an area? Are there other ways to bring cable TV service to an area besides constructing a new set of wires?
    (e) Who besides the cable TV company might benefit from a system under which cities grant exclusive franchises?

18. Is it legitimate for government to prevent independent business firms from agreeing among themselves not to sell below a certain price? If you have no misgivings about the legitimacy of this legal restraint, ask yourself whether it is also acceptable for government to prevent business firms from agreeing among themselves not to purchase above a certain price. What about extending the prohibition to customers? Why should it be legal for customers to do what business firms may not do? What about employees who agree not to work below a certain wage? Can you reconcile what appears to be legislative discrimination against business firms with the principle that all citizens ought to be equal before the law?

19. The Federal Trade Commission staff has sought unsuccessfully to secure approval for "no-fault" antitrust cases. The government would not have to prove, under this approach, that a large firm had acted anticompetitively, but only that the firm in fact commands a dominant share of the market. Would this promote or retard competition?

20. Think about this assertion once put forward by the economist M. A. Adelman: "A useful if not very precise index of the strength of competition . . . is the resentment of unsuccessful competitors." How would you evaluate the argument by other firms in the computer software industry that Microsoft engages in unfair competition?

11 The Distribution of Income

Have you ever reflected on the fact that we all obtain our incomes by inducing other people to provide them? We also produce some goods for ourselves directly, of course, and there may even be a few hermits in the country who never use money and never have to depend on other people's cooperation. Except for counterfeiters, however, we all get our money incomes from other people. As Adam Smith put it in *The Wealth of Nations*: "It is not from the benevolence of the butcher, the brewer, or the baker that we expect our dinner, but from their regard to their own interest. We address ourselves, not to their humanity, but to their self-love, and never talk of our necessities but of their advantages."

We persuade them to hire us, to buy from us, to lend to us, or simply to recognize that our status entitles us to income. The last technique is the one employed by children to extract income from their parents, by retired people to get Social Security benefits, by people who qualify for unemployment compensation, and by the lucky holders of winning lottery tickets, to mention just a few. Another way to put it is that we supply what other people are willing to pay for. In short, the distribution of income results from supply and demand.

Suppliers and Demanders

We took this roundabout route to get to that very orthodox conclusion in order to underline the fact that income isn't really distributed—regardless of what the title of this chapter asserts. No one actually distributes income in our society in the sense of parceling it out. People's incomes are the outcome of many interacting decisions, decisions ultimately made by different individuals on the basis of the benefits and the costs they expect from their decisions.

We cannot treat distribution separately from the process of exchange and production. In dealing with our children we may divide a fixed piece of pie by having one child cut and the other choose, but this is not applicable to economic life where the "pie" is not fixed and simply waiting to be cut. The economic pie is continually being made within the process of exchange and production, and the way we slice up that pie will impact the way the pie is being made. In fact, one of the most important points to emphasize in political economy is that policy choices are never about particular distributions, but always about the rules of the game, which engender a pattern of exchange and production. It is this process of exchange and production that we have studied throughout the various chapters, and the same principles of economic coordination apply to the question of distribution.

Individuals aren't free to decide just anything they please, of course. Few of us can decide to obtain $300,000 per year by getting others to watch us play basketball. People make *constrained* choices. But they do choose. Income is not a fact of nature. Unlike height and (natural) hair color, choice can change it. Income may be more like place of residence. Although few of us can choose to live anywhere, most of us have substantial discretion about where we're going to live, whether Iowa or California, city or suburb, apartment or house. The decisions of other people, from relatives through employers to housing developers, interact with our own preferences to determine the relative costs and advantages of living in one place or another. Places of residence, like incomes, are the outcome of millions of interrelated decisions.

Those decisions, it should be noted, can even be unfair—and often are. Racial prejudices limit people's options with respect both to choosing a residence and to securing money income. Suppliers and demanders sometimes perpetrate frauds. People are the victims of poor schooling or destructive environments that limit their options in later life. Sometimes what matters is who you know rather than what you can do. Thus the claim that income accrues to people as a result of supply and demand is not an endorsement of existing income patterns but a way of thinking about the subject.

Economic theory explains the distribution of income as the product of the supply of and demand for *productive services*. The word *productive* means no more than *demanded*; an activity is productive if it enables people to obtain something for which they're willing to pay. All sorts of thoroughly disreputable persons (you may provide your own list) are thus suppliers of productive services. Nor does the word *service* necessarily mean that effort has been expended. A man who lives entirely on his inheritance is supplying a productive service, in our sense of the term, by giving up some command over current resources. No one would dream of commending him for effort, because he makes none. But a playboy heir who lives off dividends still contributes to current production by the activity of not consuming his capital. The relevant fact for economic analysis is not the merit of the playboy, but the demand for the resources whose ownership provides him with regular income.

The demand for productive services will generate no income for a person who owns no resources capable of supplying those services. The distribution of income among individuals or families depends fundamentally, therefore, on the ownership of productive resources. Sometimes this is expressed by saying that the distribution of income depends on the prior distribution of wealth. That's an acceptable restatement, as long as we don't define wealth too narrowly. The trouble is that most empirical studies of personal wealth holdings, as well as the ordinary connotation of the word, restrict wealth to such assets as cash, bank accounts, stocks, bonds, and real estate. However, most of the income that Americans receive annually does not derive from ownership of wealth in these forms but rather from the ownership of *human capital*.

Capital and Human Resources

When economists use the term *capital*, they usually mean *produced means of production*, or *produced goods that can be used to produce future goods*. Machinery is capital, as are industrial and commercial buildings. But so are the *knowledge and skills that people accumulate through education, training, or experience that enable them to supply valuable productive services to others*. Only when we include *human capital* in our definition of wealth is it at all adequate to say that the distribution of income depends on the distribution of wealth.

Total employee compensation dwarfs corporate profits in the government's annual calculations of the national income; "compensation of employees" typically sums to about 15 times the total of dividends plus retained corporation earnings. This does not mean that factory operatives and office workers take home the bulk of the nation's income. The human services that produce most of the nation's income include the services of physicians, corporate executives, athletes, actors, and rock stars as well as teachers, typists, and technicians. The point is that, contrary to popular belief, inequality in the distribution of income in the United States today arises primarily from unequal abilities to supply valuable human services. Human capital has to be included in our definition of wealth because most income is earned in the United States by supplying the services of human resources.

Most of the income Americans receive derives from ownership of human capital.

Human Capital and Investment

Is it misleading, though, to refer to these resources as *capital*? Capital means *produced resources*. To what extent are the abilities that enable people to command high incomes *produced* rather than inherited or just stumbled upon? It seems impossible to generalize safely or usefully in response to this question. Perhaps

People add to their stock of human capital by investing in their personal skills.

human capabilities would therefore be a more satisfactory term than *human capital*.

On the other hand, the implication that these capabilities are *produced* does call attention to a fact of some importance. People can and do choose to acquire additional capabilities in the expectation of earning additional income. They invest in themselves by going to school, acquiring special job training, practicing certain skills, or otherwise adding to the value of the services they can supply to others. It makes sense to refer to such investments in oneself as the acquisition of human capital. The value of a tax accountant's services doesn't depend on the extent to which skills were acquired rather than inherited. But it does depend on the level of those skills, and that level can usually be raised through diligent effort. The expectation of an increased income from the sale of their services induces tax accountants to pore over tedious tax-court rulings when they would rather be playing golf. Pride and a sense of craftsmanship may also be at work. But the prospect of a greater income exercises a constant and steady pressure on people to acquire capabilities that will permit them to supply more valuable services to others. Incentives do make a difference.

Property Rights and Income

The productive resources that generate income are owned by many different people, individually and jointly, through partnerships, corporations, and informal arrangements. The owners acquired these resources by many different means, most of which we can never hope to untangle in retrospect. The resources themselves have an enormous variety of forms, running all the way from ideas and skills to turret lathes and fertile fields. Do not assume, however, that the people who own productive resources are the ones who happen to have possession or who have the title deed in their safe-deposit box. Property rights depend on the reigning rules of the game, not on mere physical facts.

Suppose you "own" your driveway but are unable to prevent people from parking on the street in a way that blocks your entrance. Because you can't expect to park in it yourself or to receive income from renting the space to others, you don't have an effective property right and consequently don't actually own a parking space. Perhaps what you own is a shuffleboard court or a splendid place to play hopscotch.

Or consider the case of a woman who has been expertly trained as a physician but can't obtain a license to practice because she was educated in a foreign country. She owns a human resource of limited value; the only services she can supply will be to her own family and friends.

The owner of an apartment building under rent controls may be unable to set rents high enough to cover taxes and maintenance. In that case, he doesn't actually own the units. The services that the units provide are appropriated by the tenants occupying the apartments, who are thus the effective owners. The proof of the nominal owner's actual nonownership in such a case would be his inability to sell the units at any price and his willingness simply to abandon them by surrendering legal ownership to the taxing authorities.

Federal law says that the airwaves belong to the public. But the Federal Communications Commission allows the owners of television stations to use assigned channels at no charge. Because the owners of the stations can appropriate the income from supplying television services, they are the actual owners of the channels. A proof of this will be their ability to sell the physical plant and facilities at a price many times greater than the cost of the facilities' reproduction—*if* the purchaser can expect to obtain, along with the station, the right to use the assigned channel.

The mayor of a city doesn't legally own any of the city's facilities. But if she can expect to enjoy the benefits supplied by a spacious office, a large staff, motorcycle escorts for her limousine, and a place at the head table for just about any banquet she chooses to attend, her wealth is much greater than it seems. She cannot sell these property rights, it's true; so they're limited in that respect. But *all* property rights are limited in one respect or another. The ability to sell is an important part of property rights, but it is only one stick in a larger bundle, and its absence limits but doesn't eliminate property rights.

Ownership is a bundle of sticks. Some sticks may be missing from the bundle.

Actual, Legal, and Moral Rights

A useful distinction that can often help us agree on what we're talking about is the distinction between actual, legal, and moral property rights. It is people's *actual* rights that govern their expectations and consequently determine how they will behave. If the city council decrees that dog owners must keep their pets on a leash while they are in city parks and clean up all mementos that the dogs leave behind, the council thereby grants city residents the *legal* right to stroll barefoot through the parks without fear or trembling. If the police cannot enforce the ordinance, however, and many dog owners simply ignore it, residents' actual rights will diverge from their legal rights. What park users see as their actual rights will determine whether or not they take off their shoes. If they leave their shoes on while indignantly insisting that they "have a right" to a park free of dog feces, they are asserting a *moral* right, a right that they believe they *ought* to enjoy. Because rights are social facts, they depend on acceptance by others of the

Rights:

- *actual*
- *legal*
- *moral*

appropriate obligations. Until dog owners accept the obligation to monitor their pets' behavior—either to avoid legal penalties or to show consideration for others—park users will not enjoy the actual right to frolic fearlessly and will consequently keep their shoes on while strolling in the park.

Expectations and Investment

Every decision about the use of resources is based finally on the expectations of the decision maker. Families and individuals decide whether to consume or to invest their income by assessing the relative values of the benefits they expect to receive from each option. And they choose among alternative investments by considering not only the expected rates of return but also the confidence with which those returns can be expected. People who fear confiscation of their investments will opt for investments that are difficult to confiscate, even though they promise a lower return than more vulnerable investment projects. Dictators who suspect their control is slipping shift into Swiss bank accounts, and ethnic minorities encountering native hostility invest in jewelry or other readily portable wealth. The most readily portable form of wealth is human capital, which may explain why throughout the world prospering ethnic minorities have so often obtained unusually high levels of education. Of course, even human capital can be confiscated; people who are barred from practicing a profession for which they were trained have effectively been deprived of the human resource that training created.

When you reflect on the fact that the returns from investment decisions are *future* returns, you realize that a person's rate of time preference also affects consumption or investment decisions. Someone who discounts future events at a high rate will be present oriented, will prefer consumption to investment, and will thereby choose in effect to receive a lower income in future years. On the other hand, people who discount at a low rate will be more willing to give up present consumption for the sake of greater consumption in the future and will consequently invest more heavily while they're young, thereby securing for themselves a higher expected income in later years. The interesting implication of all this is that people choose, to some extent, their lifetime income profiles.

A further implication is that we can't always tell from a simple comparison of two people's current incomes which of them has the higher income. A promising student in the last year of medical school probably has a large *negative* income. But would we really want to say that the student is poorer than someone the same age who is earning $20,000 a year from a semiskilled job? The relevant comparison is *lifetime* incomes. That was the comparison relevant to the medical student's decision to become a physician, and it's probably the more relevant comparison for anyone who wants to evaluate the equity of a particular income distribution. The effects of lifetime incomes are not as immediately visible, of course, as the effects of current incomes. That's probably why we continue to exaggerate the poverty of many people who are students and the wealth of many who were students long ago. The two errors don't necessarily cancel out, however. If public policy responds to these opposite exaggerations by transferring income from the older to the younger group, it lowers the expected rate of return and hence the amount of investment that will occur during people's younger years.

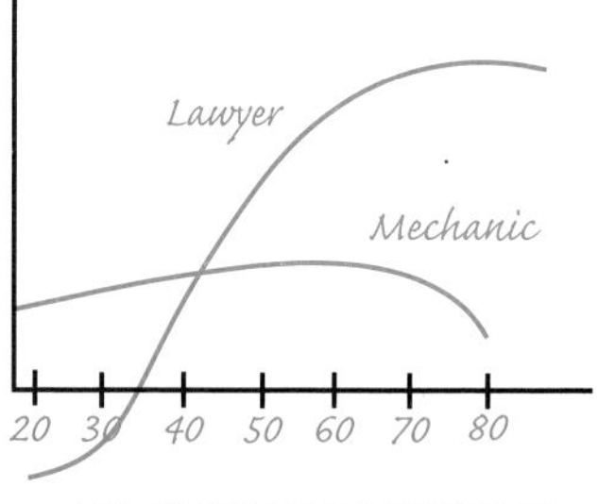

People or Machines?

The strange notion that the demand for labor services of any type is completely inelastic with respect to the wage rate also seems to underlie the widespread belief (or fear) that machines "destroy" jobs because they are so much more productive than people. But what could it mean to say that machines are "more productive" than people? Employers aren't interested in mere physical or technical capabilities; they're interested in the relation between marginal revenues and marginal costs. A machine is more efficient than a person and hence will be substituted for a person only if the marginal revenue from the machine's use *relative to its marginal cost* is greater than the ratio for a person. That implies, among other things, that wage rates play an important part in shaping the speed and direction of technological change in the economy.

Automatic elevators didn't replace elevator operators in the United States merely because of improvements in technology. Time, money, and energy were spent to develop automatic elevators—and building owners subsequently installed them—because of benefit–cost estimates they made, not because automatic elevators were new and shiny. In some other society where the wage rates (opportunity costs) of elevator operators are quite low, elevators run by trained operators could still be more efficient than automatic elevators.

Technological innovations release labor resources from some employments and make them available for others. The automatic or self-service elevator made it possible for people who were formerly employed in transporting passengers up and down to do something else, to make some other and additional contribution to our total output of commodities and services. At the same time, the reallocation of labor in response to changed circumstances does lead to a loss of wealth for some people. A rising demand for labor attracted some elevator operators into more remunerative employments and pulled up the wages of the rest; automatic elevators were in part a response to this situation. But as they were introduced, some elevator operators found themselves pushed rather than pulled: deprived of their present jobs and compelled to accept less desirable alternatives, rather than attracted away from their present positions by better opportunities. Such people suffered, at least temporarily, a loss of wealth. They were forced to incur the cost of searching for new employment, and they were not guaranteed that the new job would be better than the old. Resistance to technological change and fear of automation are therefore quite understandable. Even college professors have been known to speak harshly about the introduction of such technological innovations as videotaped lectures, computerized courses, and education through the Internet.

The Derived Demand for Productive Services

Another factor that may help conceal the downward-sloping character of the demand curve for productive services is the derived nature of that demand. The demand for productive services is derived from the demand for the goods they produce. When firms announce that they're expanding their hiring or laying some workers off, they almost never attribute the decision to a change in wage rates. Instead, they credit (or blame) the demand for their product: "Sales have increased beyond our expectations" or "Inventories of finished goods have grown to unacceptable levels because of disappointing sales." Thus the quantity of services demanded at any time from carpenters or automobile assemblers will seem to depend on conditions in the housing or automobile market, rather than on the wages of carpenters or automobile assemblers. But they actually depend on both. The prices of houses and of automobiles and the way they are produced have been influenced by the wage rates that had to be paid to obtain the services of carpenters and of automobile assemblers. In the case of carpenters, fewer new houses are purchased, and hence fewer carpenters are employed, insofar as the cost of obtaining carpenters' services has raised the price of new construction. Moreover, houses are increasingly constructed in ways that economize on carpenters' services, with less elaborate woodwork, for example, and with factory-built cabinets.

This discussion of the demand for productive services has emphasized the demand as a *constraint*: The income that owners of productive resources can obtain by supplying the services of the resources they own is limited by the demand for these services. The corollary also deserves emphasis: The income that resource owners can receive is *created* by the demand for the services of those resources. Any sheik who owns an oil well provides a vivid illustration. Whether a country that each year produces about a thousand barrels of oil per inhabitant is fabulously wealthy or almost desperately poor depends on the demand for the services of a thick and flammable liquid hydrocarbon that seemed both ugly and useless when it was first discovered. In the absence of that demand, the Organization of Petroleum Exporting Countries (OPEC) would have had less influence over world affairs during the 1970s than the Audubon Society. But given the enormous demand that had developed in this century for the services of petroleum, OPEC became a household word.

Who Competes Against Whom?

When owners of productive resources form organizations such as OPEC in an effort to increase their incomes, they often argue that their association will enable them to compete more effectively against the buyers of whatever service they're supplying. Whether we call this argument confused or devious depends on how we want to assess the motives of those who make it. The plain fact is that buyers don't compete against sellers. Buyers compete against one another to obtain what sellers are supplying. Sellers compete against sellers to obtain the custom of buyers. We learned that way back in Chapter 5. The competition that OPEC was designed to eliminate was competition among the petroleum-exporting countries. OPEC succeeded insofar as it was able to restrict production, and it lost control of prices and income when it could no longer keep production down.

Buyers may try to play the same game. We can refer at this point to an example used earlier: the agreement among owners of professional sports teams not to compete for the services of athletes. To make this agreement effective, they had to assign the exclusive right to each athlete's services to a single owner. This is the purpose of the "draft," as developed by owners' associations in major professional sports. When buyers present this kind of unified position, organization on the part of sellers may be an effective way of countering their power. But the objective of the sellers' association in such circumstances would be to *reactivate competition* among the buyers or to *reduce competition* among the sellers and could not be described correctly as an attempt to compete more effectively against the buyers.

Buyers prefer that sellers have 12 players on the field rather than 11, because buyers don't compete against sellers.

Unions and Competition

In the case of labor unions, the basic federal statute regulating union organization and collective bargaining makes the mistake of asserting in its preamble that unorganized workers need unions to help them compete against corporations. But workers compete against workers, corporate employers against corporate employers. And this is the competition that affects wage rates.

Employers can't pay their workers whatever wage their callous hearts suggest for the same reason that Aramco was never able to buy oil from Saudi Arabia for whatever price it chose. Workers have alternative opportunities in the form of other employers, and Saudi Arabia always had alternative opportunities in the form of other refiners. The services of workers are valuable to employers, so they're willing to bid for them, even though that may raise the going wage. The services of crude oil are valuable to refiners, so they too are willing to bid, raising its price above $3 a barrel in 1972 before OPEC learned how to restrict production, above $30 a barrel when OPEC mastered the art, and keeping it for a while above $20 a barrel even when OPEC began to disintegrate in the 1980s. It then hit record highs (above $41 a barrel) in 2004.

Similarly, workers cannot successfully insist on the wage they think they deserve if other workers are willing to supply very similar services at lower wage rates. Workers compete against other workers, and unions are in part attempts to control *this* competition. The implication is that unions improve the position of the members they represent by finding ways to restrict competition from those who are not members of the union. They may do this directly, for example, by securing contracts with employers that make union membership a prior condition of employment and then limiting membership. Or they may do it indirectly. Just as a legal minimum wage excludes some people from employment opportunities, so a high wage secured by union contract (perhaps under the threat of a strike or total withdrawal of labor services) excludes those who would be willing to work for less.

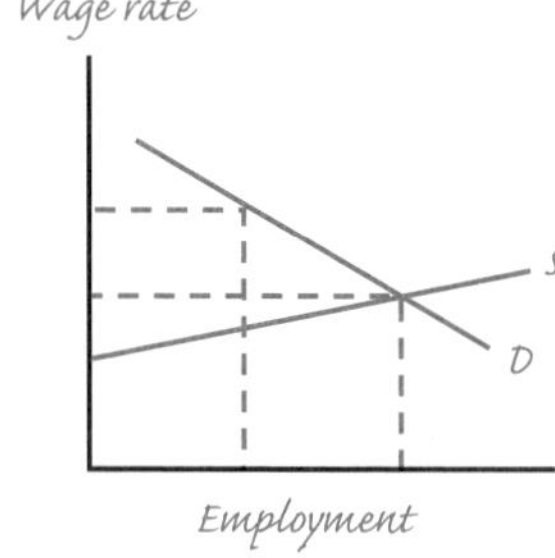

The belief that unions arose in the United States to counter the power of large corporations is unsupported by history. Unions first became powerful in this country in industries characterized by small-scale firms: construction, printing, textiles, and mining. The railroads are an exception that supports the rule: It was special legislation that enabled unions to become powerful in the railroad industry. The unions that today bargain with the large corporations in steel, automobiles, and electrical machinery were originally missionary projects of the unions that bargained mostly with small employers.

Poverty and Inequality

Employment opportunities are eliminated by enforcement of high wages.

Income cannot be greater than output. Monetary or nominal incomes can grow as fast as those who create the society's money are willing to allow. But no one is better off with an income of twice as many dollars or pesos or francs if each dollar, peso, or franc purchases half as much food, clothing, shelter, and other real goods as before. To increase the real incomes of the members of society, it is necessary to increase the production of real goods.

It is possible, however, to increase the incomes of *some* members of society without an increase in real output by reducing the incomes of others. This can be done in order to reduce inequality or to reduce poverty. Those are not identical goals even though they are often spoken of as if they were. The percentage of the population in poverty, however measured, can be and has been greatly reduced in the United States in the twentieth century, but often without any significant reduction in inequality.

Reducing poverty is not the same as reducing inequality. They may or may not go together.

There are many ways to summarize the data on income inequality that the Bureau of the Census gathers. One of the most common is the quintile (by fifths) distribution of family income. Table 11–1 shows the percentage of total family income received in 2000 and in five earlier years by the 20 percent of families with the lowest incomes, by the second-lowest fifth, and so on up to the 20 percent who received the highest incomes. If family income were equally distributed, each fifth would receive 20 percent of the total. That obviously isn't the case. The percentage received by the highest 5 percent is also shown in Table 11-1.

Two characteristics of these numbers stand out. One is the remarkably small change in the pattern of family income distribution in the United States over the past half century, despite progressive income taxes and vastly expanded government programs for transferring income to low-income families and individuals. The other is the gains made by the top quintile since 1980 and the losses sustained by the bottom quintiles. Some of the apparent stability of the percentages since 1950 is illusory. To begin with, these percentages refer to income before the payment of personal taxes. The data also takes no account of *in-kind transfers*. They do reflect *money transfers*. Thus, they include income from private

Table 11–1 **Money Income of Families—Percentage of Aggregate Income Received by Each Fifth and Highest 5 Percent**

	1950	1960	1970	1980	1990	2000
Lowest fifth	4.5	4.8	5.4	5.3	4.6	4.3
Second fifth	12.0	12.2	12.2	11.6	10.8	9.8
Middle fifth	17.4	17.8	17.6	17.6	16.6	15.5
Fourth fifth	23.4	24.0	23.8	24.4	23.8	22.8
Highest fifth	42.7	41.3	40.9	41.1	44.3	47.4
Highest 5%	17.3	15.9	15.6	14.6	17.4	20.8

Source: U.S. Bureau of the Census Historical Income Tables—Families, Table F-2: www.census.gov/hhes/income/histinc/index.html.

pensions, veterans' benefits, Social Security benefits, the program of what used to be called Aid to Families with Dependent Children and is now called Temporary Assistance to Needy Families, and all other welfare assistance—*when paid in money*. But they don't include the value of such in-kind transfers as medical assistance, rent subsidies, or food stamps—all of which are real income even though they don't involve the exchange of money. Nor are the data adjusted to take account of differing family sizes. The top quintile contains about 30 percent more persons than the lowest quintile.[1] When these adjustments are made, the share of lower-income groups rises and that of upper-income groups falls.

The point we want to emphasize now, however, is that poverty has been substantially reduced over this period despite only modest reductions in inequality. Table 11–2 shows, for selected years, the percentage of all families in the United States with incomes below the *poverty line*. The poverty line is the amount of income that households of various sizes presumably require to live decently, which government officials calculate as three times the income required to purchase an adequate diet. The poverty threshold is adjusted each year to take account of the changing value of money. The Census Bureau does not publish this series for years before 1959. But if it did, the earlier decline in poverty would be far more dramatic than what is shown in Table 11–2. A Department of Health and Human Services study by Gordon Fisher estimated the poverty rate for individuals in 1948 at 33 percent. Attempts to estimate poverty rates in the United States for years before World War II place them between 60 and 70 percent.[2]

What brought the poverty rate down so dramatically was economic growth. When total output increases at an annual compounded rate of 3 percent, which was the average growth rate in the United States during the first half of the century, total income will more than quadruple over the course of 50 years. If the poverty line is fixed in absolute terms and adjusted only for price-level changes, a huge decline in poverty will occur even with no change in the pattern of inequality.

Is poverty a low income? Or an income significantly lower than the average income?

But is it appropriate to set the poverty line in absolute terms? It is somewhat odd, to say the least, to suppose that more than half of the population in the wealthiest country in the world was living in poverty in the early decades of the twentieth century. Most people think of poverty in relative terms. Polls repeatedly

[1]It is also important to know that families in the top quintile supply four times as many weeks of work as families in the bottom quintile.

[2]The estimates are from *The Twentieth Century Record of Inequality and Poverty in the United States*, by Robert D. Plotnick, Eugene Smolensky, Eirik Evenhouse, and Siobhan Reilly (New York: Academic Press, 1975), none of whom should be held responsible for the extensive uses that this discussion makes of their excellent survey.

Table 11–2 **Percentage of Families with Incomes Below the Poverty Line**

Year	Percentage
2000	11.3
1990	10.7
1980	10.3
1970	10.1
1965	13.9
1960	18.1

Source: U.S. Bureau of the Census Historical Poverty Tables—Families, Table 13: www.census.gov/hhes/income/histinc/index.html.

Table 11–3 **Family Mean Incomes in 2000**

Age of Householder	Mean Income
15 to 24 years	$36,626
25 to 34 years	56,229
35 to 44 years	70,813
45 to 54 years	82,369
55 to 64 years	74,007
65 years and over	45,713

Source: U.S. Bureau of the Census Historical Income Tables, Table F-11: www.census.gov/hhes/income/histinc/index.html.

show that when asked how much income a family needs in order to live decently, most Americans will state a figure somewhere around one-half the median income of their community. By this standard, a significant decrease in poverty necessarily entails a reduction in inequality. What do we really mean, however, by income inequality? When looking at data such as those in Table 11–1, we are inclined to assume without thinking about it that the families in the second or fourth quintile in a current year are the same families (or an earlier generation of the same families) who occupied those fifths in some preceding year. This isn't necessarily the case. In fact, it's quite unlikely to be the case for one simple reason: The relative income position of a family depends very much on the age of the family's principal earner.

The data of Table 11–3 illustrate what we're talking about. They show the average (mean) income of all households in 2000 by the age of the householder. (Embarrassed by its use of the term *head*, the bureau has substituted the term *householder*, defined as the owner of the residence or, in the case of joint ownership, the person whose name appears first on the survey form.) The table demonstrates unmistakably that a substantial amount of the inequality that shows up in a still picture would disappear if we were able to take a moving picture—that is, to compare the incomes of households over the lifetimes of the householders.

Why Inequality Is Increasing

If we want to inquire why inequality has been increasing since 1980 (actually since about 1974), we should begin by recalling that at least 80 percent of family income in the United States comes in the form of employee compensation. If we want to explain any increase in the inequality of incomes, therefore, we should look first at changes in the structure of wages and at changes in supply and demand conditions that produced these structural changes.

Inequality, education, and skills

A trend over the past few decades toward increased inequality in wages accelerated in the 1980s and 1990s. On the supply side, we have experienced slower increases in the number of college graduates than in the number of high school graduates entering the labor force. Other things remaining equal, that will tend to widen the gap between the average wages of college and high school graduates and thus increase wage inequality. On the demand side, several important changes have been occurring. The manufacturing sector has been shrinking as the service sector of the economy has grown in size. Because wages in manufacturing tend to be less unequal than wages in other sectors, the decline in the relative size of the manufacturing sector has increased inequality. In addition, the most rapidly growing industries in the economy have been ones that traditionally employ college graduates. The predictable result of all this has been an increase in the difference between the wages of skilled and extensively educated workers and the wages of those with fewer skills and less education.

Redistributing Income

Interest in issues of this sort usually grows out of a belief that too much inequality in the distribution of income is undesirable. Note again that this is something quite different from a belief that *poverty* is undesirable. Poverty can accompany close equality in a society, as it has often done and continues to do in many countries, just as enormous inequality can exist side-by-side with very little poverty. Few people pause to think their way carefully through the questions of why inequality (as against poverty) is undesirable, how much inequality is acceptable, or why inequality in monetary income should be of so much more concern than inequalities of other kinds.

Regardless of how these important questions are answered, programs to reduce the income inequality among U.S. families and individuals will run up against a fundamental difficulty: Because income isn't really distributed by anyone, it can't actually be redistributed. No one is in a position to apportion shares of the social product. The most that even government can do is alter the rules of the game in the hope of securing a preferable outcome. What happens next will never be exactly what was intended and may be something altogether different.

The simplest and most direct way to reduce income inequality would appear to be a program of taxes on high incomes and cash transfers to people with low incomes. But nothing about economic systems is ever as simple and direct as it seems at first glance. To raise taxes on high incomes, the government must change the rules that relate taxes owed to particular kinds of income received. When it does so, people don't merely pay the higher taxes; they also try to adjust their behavior to minimize the impact of the new rules. Some of these adjustments will be legal tax avoidance; others may be illegal tax evasion; but they all combine to drive a wedge between what was intended when the rules were rewritten and what actually emerges. The revenue that results from the tax increase will be less, and may be much less, than what was hoped for.

Taxes and subsidies alter incentives and so alter behavior.

In order to supplement the incomes of poor people, government must write new rules controlling eligibility for grants. These rule revisions will also have undesired effects as people adjust their behavior to fit the new criteria. Once again the adjustments will be both legal and illegal; but their combined effect can be substantial, because there are so many margins along which adjustments can be made. The number of people classified as poor may actually increase as a result of efforts to reduce poverty.

Consider the hypothetical but unfortunately not implausible case of a single-parent family with three small children. Suppose the mother is currently receiving $400 a month in cash grants, food stamps worth $100 per month, and subsidized medical care for herself and the children worth $50 a month. Then she obtains a job offer promising $1,000 per month. Will she take the job and go off welfare? Would she be better off if she did so? Her income from welfare is not taxed, but she will have to pay Social Security and income taxes on her earnings. She will also have to secure day care for the children, buy some additional clothing, and incur transportation expenses if she takes the job. Moreover, she will lose her monthly cash grant and her family's eligibility for food stamps and Medicaid. When she adds up all these costs of taking the job, she may find that her earnings are going to be taxed at a marginal rate of 90 percent or more.

Plug in some plausible numbers and check the results for yourself. If the income and Social Security taxes plus day care, transportation, and clothing expenses take $350 a month from

Marginal tax rate: the percentage of additional income taken by the tax collector

her paycheck, and the loss of welfare reduces her monthly income by $550, she would be giving up $900 in order to earn $1000. That amounts to a 90 percent marginal tax rate, or a 90 percent tax on additions to her welfare income—which isn't terribly attractive. No one could accuse a mother in such a situation of laziness or irresponsibility if she decided to turn down the job offer, stay on welfare, and care for her children.

People with yachts are wealthy; people who scrounge through trash barrels and garbage cans are poor. But if we write new rules that obligate every yacht owner to contribute $10,000 a year to a fund for trash and garbage scroungers and grant each scrounger a right to $2,000 a year from the fund, the number of recorded yacht owners will rapidly decline and the number of people claiming to be scroungers will show a remarkable increase. That may be an overly dramatic way to summarize the problem, but it makes the essential point. A large society such as the United States cannot allocate tasks and benefits to its citizens the way that loving parents do it in a family: on the basis of abilities and needs. Tasks and benefits will inevitably be allocated in response to people's pursuit of their own interests under the perceived rules of the game. What government can achieve by way of income redistribution is pretty well confined to what can be achieved by changing the rules. That will almost certainly turn out to be something less satisfactory than what was hoped for when the rules were changed.

Changing Rules and Social Cooperation

It might be thought that the solution is to change the rules again when the initial change doesn't yield the desired results and to keep on modifying the rules until the target has been attained. But who has the knowledge that would be required to choose these fine adjustments? Even if the knowledge were available, would anyone have the power to put the adjusted rules into effect in a democratic society? Most important of all, what happens to the complex cooperative processes on which a highly specialized economic system depends when the society is subjected to continuous changes in the rules of the game?

People invest, make sacrifices, and otherwise commit themselves in the belief that established property rights will be respected, that the rules will *not* be changed "in the middle of the game." A rule that says the rules can be changed at any time would destroy the foundation for most social cooperation. Property rights must be reasonably clear and stable if people are to plan for the future and to take long-run consequences into account. It's also worth observing that when expectations are regularly frustrated by unanticipated changes in the rules of the game, participants stop playing the ordinary game and shift their attention to the game that matters: making the rules.

Once Over Lightly

The distribution of income is the result of the supply of and demand for productive services.

The production of productive resources is investment, or the creation of capital. One very important form of capital is human capital, or productive capabilities generated by investment and embodied in human beings. The production of human capital is an important consideration, because monetary income is primarily earned in the United States, even by the wealthy, through supplying the services of human resources.

The amount and nature of the investment that will occur in a society depend on established and accepted property rights, because property rights determine what consequences people can expect from the actions that are open to them.

Lower rates of time preference encourage investment over consumption. Greater uncertainty about future returns from investment will prompt the discounting of future income at higher rates and consequently will lead to less investment.

The demand for productive services of any kind will not be perfectly inelastic. A greater quantity will be demanded at lower prices and a lesser quantity at higher prices, because there are substitutes for any productive service.

Potential users of productive services decide on the amount they will demand by comparing the marginal-benefit/marginal-cost ratios of alternative procedures for achieving their purposes.

The demand for productive services, and hence their price, is partly dependent on the demand for the goods they produce. But the price of productive services also affects the cost of producing particular goods, their prices, the quantities demanded, and thus the demand for those productive services.

Suppliers of productive services don't compete against buyers of those services. Suppliers compete against other suppliers, buyers against other buyers. The quest for higher incomes produces attempts to suppress competition, because what a seller can obtain and what a buyer must pay will depend on the alternative opportunities that competitors are providing.

While economic growth in the United States dramatically reduced the percentage of the population living in poverty through the first three-quarters of the twentieth century, the poverty rate has pretty much stabilized and even increased somewhat during the last quarter of the century. The last quarter of the century has also been marked by small but steady increases in income inequality. The principal causes appear to be greater increases in the supply of less skilled and less schooled workers along with greater increases in the demand for more highly skilled and more extensively schooled workers.

Social cooperation on any extensive scale requires relatively stable property rights because it presupposes the ability to predict the consequences of decisions.

QUESTIONS FOR DISCUSSION

1. *Income* is a flow of receipts per unit of time: $240 per week or $30,000 a year. *Wealth* is a stock of assets: cash, shares of stock, buildings, tools, skills, and so on. How are income and wealth related?
   (a) If you own an annuity that will pay you a $10,000 income for each of the next 20 years, what is the present value of that annuity? How much does the annuity contribute to your wealth?
   (b) Suppose you own 100 shares of stock in a promising new company that has not yet begun to pay dividends and probably won't do so for several years. The stock is currently exchanging on the New York Stock Exchange for $50 a share. What is your wealth from ownership of this stock? If you wanted to convert this wealth into income, how could you do so? About how much income could you obtain without reducing the amount of your wealth?
   (c) Why would the stock referred to in part (b) be bought for $50 a share if the company isn't expected to pay any dividends for several years?
   (d) A privately owned automobile is wealth. Does it yield income to its owner? In what form?
   (e) What determines the market value of a house and thus its contribution to the wealth of the owner? Do the expected benefits from living in the house (income) determine the value of the house (wealth)? Or does the price of the house determine the income received by living in it? Suppose someone happens to detest the house that he owns and occupies because it has such distracting views of the bay and the mountains from every window. Would this idiosyncratic attitude reduce his income from living in the house? Would it reduce his wealth from owning the house? What behavior would this inconsistency between his income and his wealth probably induce?
   (f) Is an engineering degree wealth? What determines the value of such a degree? How could an engineer with a freshly minted degree who is just beginning her first job convert some of her wealth into current income in order to buy furniture for her apartment?
   (g) A successful and popular physician decides to retire and "sell his practice." What is he actually selling? What will determine its value to a buyer?
   (h) Is the expectation of future retirement benefits a part of one's wealth? Is the expectation of Social Security benefits a major part of the wealth of someone 65 years of age?

2. In a widely publicized case in California, the ex-wife of a doctor sued to obtain half the value of his medical degree, on the grounds that she had helped put him through medical school and was entitled to half of everything they owned under California's community property law.
   (a) The attorney for the doctor insisted that education was not property and so could not be shared because it had no value at the time it was acquired. If the doctor had dropped dead upon receiving his diploma, his wife would not have gotten one cent, the attorney claimed. Do you agree?
   (b) Suppose the couple had owned a house, which burned down at the time of their divorce. What steps do people take to protect themselves against the accidental destruction or other loss of valuable physical assets? What steps do young physicians usually take to assure their families a large income even if the physician drops dead?
   (c) The wife's attorneys asked for $250,000 as her share of the value of her ex-husband's medical training. Suppose the medical degree could be conservatively expected to add $30,000 per year for 30 years to what the doctor would have earned without the degree. Because this amount will presumably rise with any inflation that occurs over the period, a real rather than nominal interest rate should be used to calculate its present value. Would you support the ex-wife's attorneys in their estimate of what she was entitled to? What is one-half the present value of a $30,000 annuity for 30 years when discounted at 4 percent?
   (d) The doctor said: "I don't think she is entitled to half of my future." His ex-wife said: "I should get a return on my investment in the partnership." The couple separated after 10 years of marriage, during which she worked as an accountant while he completed medical school, an internship, and a residency. How would you decide the issue?
   (e) A New York Supreme Court judge ruled that when a former professional football star quit his job with the New York Jets, he wasted a marital asset and thus owed his former wife a share of his lost earnings. The player had quit six games into the season because, he said, he wanted to spend more time with his fiancée. If he had retired on the advice of a physician, he probably would not have been charged with squandering marital assets. But the judge apparently decided that he behaved irresponsibly in choosing to retire for the reason he gave. A family law attorney commented as follows on the judge's decision: "I thought Lincoln freed the slaves 150 years ago." How would you evaluate the decision? Is it possible to award a portion of a person's human capital to an ex-spouse without violating the Thirteenth Amendment's prohibition of involuntary servitude?
3. Who owns national parks? The government? The people? Park Service officials in the Interior Department? What are the implications of a sign that reads: "U.S. Government Property: No Trespassing"?
4. A Santa Monica apartment owner decided to tear down his six-unit apartment building rather than operate under rent controls.

The city refused him permission to tear down the building, however, claiming that its interest in preserving rental housing took precedence over his right to demolish his property. The California Supreme Court sustained Santa Monica's refusal to allow the demolition. Who owns the building? Sort out the actual, legal, and moral property rights in this case.

5. "Entitlement programs" of the federal government are defined as "programs that provide benefit payments for individuals whose eligibility is determined by law." Because the criteria for eligibility are established by existing law, expenditures are not controlled by the process of congressional appropriation.

   (a) Would you say that the beneficiaries of entitlement programs receive income because of certain property rights?
   (b) The criteria for some entitlement programs are outside the range of the beneficiaries' choice: Payments based on age are an example as are veterans' benefits. Other programs use criteria that persons can more or less choose to satisfy. Would you expect the law of demand to affect the rate at which expenditures increase in this second category?

6. Teachers began encountering serious job shortages in recent years after many years of rising demand for their services. An intensified interest in unionization followed. What can unionization accomplish for teachers in a highly unfavorable job market? Who is likely to benefit? Who will be harmed?
7. Under a closed-shop arrangement, employers may hire only workers who are already union members. Under a union-shop arrangement, employers may hire whomever they please but the employees must then join the union. What different effects would you expect these alternative arrangements to have on wages? On employment? On discrimination by the union against members of minority races? Why?
8. Do the relative salaries of humanities professors and football coaches at major state universities reflect the relative value of football and humanities? Do they reflect the number of years that professors and coaches must spend acquiring an education? The number of hours they work? The difficulty or unpleasantness of their work? Why do the football coaches usually receive salaries that are so much higher?
9. In what sense do relative prices reflect relative value? Here is a question to help you think about it. Suppose that the average wage of a hairdresser is twice the average wage of a child-care worker, and that prompts the following comment: "By paying hairdressers twice as much as child-care workers, this society is saying that people who cater to human vanity are twice as valuable as people who care for our children." Is that true in the situation summarized in Figure 11–1? D_{hd} portrays the demand for hairdressers and D_{ccw} the demand for child-care workers. S_{hd} portrays the supply of qualified hairdressers and S_{ccw} the supply of qualified child-care workers. The market-clearing wage is $10 for hairdressers and $5 for child-care workers.

   (a) In what sense precisely is a hairdresser worth twice as much as a child-care worker in this society?

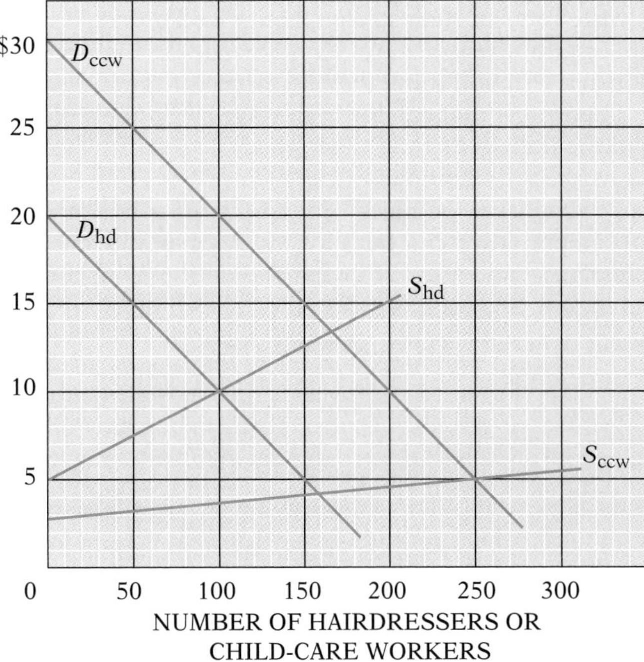

Figure 11–1 **Demand and supply for services of hairdressers and child-care workers**

(b) The demand for child-care workers seems to be considerably greater than the demand for hairdressers. Why then do hairdressers command twice as high a wage?

(c) Do the *supply* curves tell us anything about the relative value people place on styling hair versus caring for children? If the social esteem attached to a particular job increases, what effect will this have on the supply of qualified people willing to work at that job? What effect will that have in turn on the market-clearing wage rate for the job?

(d) Use the information provided on the graph to make an argument that this society in fact places more than twice as much value on the services of child-care workers than it places on the services of hairdressers.

10. Employers and unions sometimes negotiate two-tier contracts, under which current employees are paid according to a high wage scale but new employees accept a much lower scale.

(a) How might such an arrangement initially benefit each of the following four parties: employers, current employees, union leaders, and new employees?

(b) For which of these four groups would such a two-tier contract tend to become less satisfactory as time went by?

11. Do high wage rates in such strongly unionized industries as steel and automobiles pull up the general level of wages in nonunionized, lower-wage industries? If you think they do, what is the process by which this occurs? If contracts that call for high wages reduce employment opportunities in the industries that must pay these wages, where do the excluded workers find employment?
12. A letter to a magazine wonders "How [we will] cope with the growing number of unemployed put out of work by corporate capital-intensive high technology," and asks: "To what end do these corporate methodologies actually impoverish more than they enrich most of us?"
    (a) Can you help the writer find an answer?
    (b) The percentage of Americans 16 and over and not in the armed forces who were employed through the year averaged 57.4 percent in 1970, 59.2 percent in 1980, 62.7 percent in 1990, and 63.8 percent in 1997. Does this trend support the letter writer's argument?
13. Recall our discussion of the impact of a federally mandated minimum wage in Chapter 6. How would each of the following groups be affected by a large increase in the legal minimum wage?
    (a) Unionized workers
    (b) Teenagers
    (c) Unskilled workers
14. "Comparable worth" is the name of a movement that began in the 1980s to determine the worth of different jobs and then to adjust relative wage rates to the relative worth of those jobs. The movement gains most of its support from the belief that women are unfairly discriminated against in the labor market. The jobs at which some of them work (e.g., secretaries and nurses) are widely and unfairly regarded as "women's jobs" and so are allegedly paid less than their "comparable worth." The comparison is with jobs traditionally held by men.
    (a) Can a job have an inherent worth? Can you think of any situation where the worth of a job is not its value to some particular party in a specific situation?
    (b) Imagine a medical clinic with 20 medical doctors, 1 nurse, and 1 laboratory technician. Is it plausible to suppose that an additional nurse or lab technician could have more worth to the clinic in such a situation than an additional doctor?
    (c) The worth or value that influences decisions is always *marginal* worth or value. Why is a secretary worth more to the economics department if it employs only one than if it employs eight? Describe a situation in which the worth of a secretary to the economics department would likely be greater than the worth of an economist fully armed with a Ph.D.
    (d) Why will an employer who follows the maximizing rule of Chapter 9—do more if marginal revenue exceeds marginal cost, less if marginal cost exceeds marginal revenue—want to pay employees a wage equal to their marginal worth? What would be implied by the assertion that an employer was paying employees less than their marginal worth?
15. What happens when buyers are not price takers, but price searchers? Suppose you receive $6.25 per 100 for distributing advertising flyers

door to door. You have a very large territory so that your business is limited only by your ability to hire help. Your potential help consists exclusively of the teenagers in your neighborhood, each of whom can distribute 100 flyers per hour. They are all willing to work one hour for you, but each insists upon a different minimum wage. Here are their minimum demands:

Alan	$3.00
Betty	3.50
Chuck	4.00
Donna	4.50
Elmer	5.00
Frances	5.50
George	6.00
Hepzibah	6.50

How many of these workers do you want to hire if your goal is to maximize your net revenue and *all employees must be paid at the same wage rate*?

(a) What is your marginal revenue from hiring an additional worker?
(b) What is your marginal cost from hiring an additional worker when you hire Alan? When you hire Betty? When you hire Chuck? Which is the last worker you can hire if you want to keep marginal cost from exceeding marginal revenue?
(c) Suppose a large hospital is in a similar position with respect to nurses. It can hire all the nurses it is likely to want, but it must offer a higher wage to attract additional nurses. Some will work for very little, others for a bit more, and so on, up to those who will work only if they can obtain a very high wage. Why might such a hospital find itself facing what it perceives as a chronic shortage of nurses? How might it respond? (*Hint*: What do sellers attempt to do when additional sales would "spoil" their market?)

16. Should high school history and English teachers be paid as much as science and math teachers?
    (a) Suppose that a school district pays all high school teachers with the same years of experience the same salary, regardless of teaching field, and that this produces a surplus of history and English teachers and a shortage of science and math teachers. Would this create a case for salary differentials?
    (b) How could the problem of concurrent surplus and shortage be solved without paying science and math teachers more than history and English teachers?
    (c) Why has the policy of identical wages in fact produced shortages of science and math teachers along with surpluses of history and English teachers in many school districts? What factors have contributed on the demand side? On the supply side?
17. According to the American Medical Association, physicians in family practice have experienced a decline in their average incomes in recent years while medical specialists' incomes were rising. Surgical specialists

have been doing best of all, and their average incomes are now about twice what generalists earn.

(a) Much of this difference in income arises from long-established differences in the fees paid by insurers for various medical services. The American Society of Internal Medicine claims that insurers' fee schedules are unfair. How would you decide on the validity of such a claim? What is a fair way to determine the relative worth of a successful surgical procedure against that of an accurate diagnosis followed by an effective prescription?
(b) Surgeons justify their higher incomes by claiming that they spend four more years in school than do general practitioners. Do four additional years in school justify higher fees because it's costly to attend school, or because those extra years in school improve knowledge and skill levels?

18. In each of the cases described here, an increase in the family's monetary income puts all members of the original family into families with lower incomes. Explain how this occurs. Does it imply that the individuals involved are worse off? What important questions does it raise about the interpretation of family-income data?
   (a) An elderly couple living with their married son receives an increase in Social Security benefits that permits the couple to obtain their own apartment.
   (b) Two married people who fight constantly and stay together only because they can't afford to maintain two homes, separate with great relief when both receive promotions and raises, each taking one of the children.
   (c) The husband of an orthopedic surgeon quits his job to stay home, tend the house, and give the children better care when his wife's practice begins to earn a very large income.
19. How should in-kind transfers be treated in calculating the incomes of people on welfare?
   (a) Does it make sense to count the monetary value of food stamps, rent subsidies, and free school lunches in the income of a family on welfare?
   (b) How would this lead to an overstatement of their income? (*Hint*: Would you rather have a shopping cart full of items that someone else selected or the money equivalent of those items?)
   (c) Medicare benefits are a major contribution to the well-being of many elderly Americans. If an elderly person receives a $5,000 operation, should we calculate that person's income as $5,000 higher?
20. The claim is often made—and also often ridiculed—that taxes on income reduce people's incentives to earn income.
   (a) If you were required to pay the government 50 percent of all money income you earn during the summer, would you choose to work more or fewer hours than if your income were not subject to tax? Would you look for ways to raise your income without raising your money income or taxable income?
   (b) How does a 50 percent marginal tax rate (additional taxes divided by additional income) affect the cost to a physician of building her own home rather than hiring a contractor?

(c) An unmarried woman with three preschool children has no earned income but is receiving $400 a month in cash welfare assistance, plus food stamps worth $200 a month and government-financed medical care worth $100 a month. She is offered a job that will pay $1,000 a month. If she takes the job, she will no longer be eligible for any of the cash or in-kind assistance. What is the marginal tax rate to which her earnings are subject? Would you take the job in her situation?

Externalities and Conflicting Rights

12

According to the economic way of thinking, individuals choose their courses of action by weighing the expected marginal benefits of any decision against its expected marginal costs. Benefits and costs for other people will not affect the decision unless the benefits and costs for others *matter to the actor*. That turns out to be extremely important for the understanding of a wide range of social problems.

Externalities, Negative and Positive

Denny is the very model of a courteous driver, partly because he values his own safety, but mostly because his heart just overflows with kindness and consideration. Yet Denny hits the road each weekday morning at about 7:45 with no regard whatsoever for all the drivers whom he slows down by doing so. Unlike the others, he's not even heading to work. He's retired and is on his way for another round of golf. The hardship he puts on other commuters doesn't affect his decision because they don't enter into his calculations. He has actually never thought about them. Traffic engineers can figure out the additional time that each of the motorists who are behind Denny at 7:45 will have to spend on the road because Denny added slightly to the congestion; and when they multiply this time delay by the number of motorists on the road at that hour, it sums to a significant figure. Denny, the soul of sweetness and courtesy, is dumping a lot of cost on his companions in the commute. Because *he does not take this cost into account in making his decisions*, economists call it an *external cost* of Denny's action, or a *negative externality*. A less fancy term is *spillover cost*.

One additional minute for each of 1,200 motorists is 20 extra hours of travel time.

Denny would be distressed to find out that he is generating negative externalities but absolutely delighted to learn that he often generates *positive externalities*. These are *benefits from an action that the decision maker does not take into account*. Suppose this summer Denny paints his garage a gleaming

Does a teenager's radio create negative or positive externalities when played loudly at the beach?

magenta, which he himself rather dislikes, but he does so because his neighbor loves magenta (and you remember the kind of person Denny is). Denny knows that his neighbor derives benefit from the new paint job—that's why he considers doing it—and so his neighbor's benefit is not an externality. What Denny does *not* know is that many passersby will also derive great joy and laughter from seeing his magenta garage for the first time. This benefit is a positive externality because Denny did not take it into account when deciding what color to paint the garage. Unfortunately, there are also people in the neighborhood who will avert their eyes when passing Denny's place because the sight of that magenta garage irritates them. Denny's paint job, as it turns out, generates both positive and negative externalities.

Chapter 12 will focus on negative externalities. Some of the interesting problems that positive externalities create will be taken up in Chapter 13.

Perfection Is Unattainable

The beginning of all wisdom on this topic is a clear recognition that negative externalities cannot be completely eliminated. To see why not, let's consider the case of Roger, a stay-at-home dad who lives in a pleasant suburban neighborhood and goes for a short morning ride on his motorcycle before his wife heads out for work. (Is Roger unemployed? We'll save *that* question for Chapter 16.) When he innocently starts up the cycle at 6:30 each weekday morning, he wakes up eight neighbors, who individually curse his cycle and roll over for another hour of sleep. Each of them, if they thought about it, would be willing to pay up to $5 a week to be rid of that morning motorcycle noise. And Roger, if he thought about it, would be willing to push his motorcycle out of earshot before starting it up for a payment as low as $15 a week. In other words, the neighbors would be willing to pay $40 to get rid of the noise, and Roger would be willing to accommodate them for $15. But they probably won't make a deal, because the transaction costs are too high.

Transaction costs, you recall from Chapter 5, are the costs of arranging contracts or transaction agreements between demanders and suppliers. Transaction costs rule out a lot of wealth-enhancing exchanges that would otherwise occur. Although the neighbors and Roger would all be better off if each neighbor gave Roger $3 a week to push his motorcycle out of earshot before cranking it up, the total cost of gathering the required information, collecting the payments, and enforcing the agreement would be larger than the potential benefit. So nothing happens and the externality persists.

It doesn't necessarily take a monetary payment to eliminate an externality. Roger might hear through the grapevine (grapevines often reduce transaction costs) that his 6:30 departure irritates some of his neighbors and decide on his own to push the cycle to

Internalizing externalities

the end of the block before starting it up. He would be deciding that he dislikes offending his neighbors more than he dislikes pushing the motorcycle. But first he has to find out that he is generating an externality. When he finds out, he "internalizes the externality," which means he takes it into account—and then chooses to alter his behavior.

Roger doesn't have to be such a nice guy. He might push the cycle to the end of the block because some angry neighbor taped an anonymous note on the cycle seat threatening unspecified damage to the cycle if Roger continued cranking it up before 7:30. That also internalizes the externality. Another possibility is that someone calls the police, who then inform Roger that a suburban ordinance prohibits the operation of motorcycles in residential areas before 7:30 on weekday mornings. In this case, it's the visit from the police officer that internalizes the externality for Roger.

In an urban, industrialized society, in which people interact daily with thousands of others, negative externalities will multiply rapidly. Civil people learn to ignore most of the negative externalities that others inflict on them and try to be sensitive to the unintended costs that their own actions impose on others. The first step toward containing the problems created by negative externalities is to cultivate the civic virtues of empathy, courtesy, humility, and tolerance. Civilization will simply be impossible among a people who don't possess substantial amounts of these virtues. If people insist on obtaining absolutely everything to which they think they have a right, civilization will give way to warfare. How to cultivate or renew these virtues where they have withered is a question far beyond the scope of this book. We would do well to remember, however, that all the other procedures that we're going to discuss for dealing with problems created by externalities presuppose these virtues to some extent.

Negotiation

Our everyday garden-variety procedure for minimizing the social problems that negative externalities create is negotiation. We strike bargains with one another. People consent to bear the cost associated with the production of particular goods because other people who want those goods offer compensation that makes it worth their while. That's why baggage handlers don't complain about jet noise or automobile mechanics about the grease on their clothes, and why the owner of a dog kennel will cheerfully let other people's dogs perform the same act that arouses an urban law fancier to fury.

"Work it out for yourselves" is sound advice. Because people differ so widely in their tastes, talents, and other circumstances, they will often be able to negotiate an exchange of costs that makes everyone involved better off than before. Moreover, the necessity of working it out for themselves encourages cooperation among those who are in the best position to know the possibilities.

Negotiation produces mutual gains from exchange.

When people aren't required to negotiate, they often adopt positions that are costly to others. For example, they demand legislation that would prohibit smoking in restaurants, rather than ask for a table where no smoke will reach. And they point indignantly to minute traces of tobacco smoke in the air, while ignoring the dangerous emissions that they themselves put into the atmosphere by driving to the restaurant.

We would probably have a much greater respect for negotiation as a social procedure for reducing externality problems if we learned to recognize the myriad ways in which we actually use it. People who hate the noise and dirt of the city move to outlying areas. People who detest the culture of suburbia live in small towns. People who despise the isolation of rural life choose to live in the city. The hard-of-hearing get residential real estate bargains under airport approach lanes. Surfboard riders seek out companions and thereby voluntarily segregate themselves from swimmers who hate to dodge surfboards. The afternoon nap taker pays $1.59 for a box of earplugs and thereafter lives in peace with the neighboring teenager's mufflerless motorcycle. Not everyone is completely satisfied. But voluntary exchange does reduce the total of costs imposed on reluctant bystanders.

Negotiation cannot be effective, however, unless property rights are adequately defined. Voluntary exchange of any sort works well only when all involved parties agree on who owns what. In some cases, a clarification of property rights may be all that stands in the way of a mutually satisfactory agreement. Suppose, for example, that Smith and Brown (our home brewer of stout from Chapter 2) disagree by two feet on the location of the boundary line dividing their properties. It wouldn't matter much, because both want to plant flowers in the disputed strip, except for the fact that Smith wants to plant zinnias and Brown has her heart set on petunias. Until the question of who has a right to do what is settled, neither one will plant flowers, and both will be living with the inferior alternative of crabgrass. If they then hire a surveyor who proves that Smith in fact owns the disputed strip, flowers can finally bloom. Nor will the flowers necessarily be zinnias! Once it's clearly established that Smith is the owner and hence has the right to decide what will grow in the boundary strip, Brown may be able to purchase that right. Brown's passion for petunias could be so powerful that she offers Smith $25 a year for the right to grow them between their lots. And if Smith prefers petunias *with* $25 to zinnias without $25, the flowers that bloom will be petunias.

Clearly established property rights provide the basis for negotiation.

Reducing Externalities Through Adjudication

In introducing the boundary surveyor, we introduced another important social procedure for reducing externality problems: *adjudication*, by which we mean *a process for deciding who has which rights*. People will not be able to improve their positions through the exchange of rights if they aren't sure what rights anyone has to begin with. Adequately defined property rights are not a sufficient condition for successful negotiations, but they do seem to be a necessary condition.

Property rights that might once have been clearly and adequately defined can become vague and uncertain when surrounding circumstances change. The development of low-cost photocopying techniques, to take one example, created an enormous amount of uncertainty about what copyright holders could realistically expect to sell in view of the new capability that photocopy machines gave to every possessor of a book. When evolving circumstances make previously compatible property rights incompatible, adjudication is one way of settling the conflict.

Adjudication clarifies property rights.

We are using the term *adjudication* to refer specifically to the kind of resolution that the surveyor provided: a resolution that *discovers* who has which rights. The surveyor answered the question of ownership by investigating, not by choosing. If Smith and Brown had agreed to flip a coin, they would have relied on a procedure that does not discover but rather *creates* property rights. The distinction between the discovery and the creation of property rights is an important one, because *discovery or adjudication aims at maintaining the continuity of expectations*. At the end of Chapter 11 we emphasized the importance of stable expectations in securing effective cooperation among the members of a society. When expectations change radically, supply and demand decisions also change radically. That in turn alters in unpredicted ways the relative costs and benefits of all kinds of actions and so induces additional changes in supply and demand. In short, if no one knows what to expect, no one knows what to do or what others will do. The result is chaos. Stable expectations are another of those realities whose importance we haven't learned to recognize because we don't notice how society is working when it's working well.

The Case of the Complaining Homeowner

We can use the flights of commercial airliners to bring out the importance of adjudication, or the discovery rather than creation of rights, in resolving disputes over externalities. Consider the case of Regretta Sigh (Profetta Seeker's married sister) who owns a house 10 miles from a major airport but directly under the principal approach route. She may decide one morning—when her sleep has been interrupted by commercial jets—that she deserves compensation. The airport or the airlines ought to pay her something, she decides, for depriving her of the opportunity to use her bedroom as a place of rest and renewal. She is the victim of an externality. So she files suit demanding compensation.

Ought she to get it? Is she *likely* to get it? Assume that Regretta bought the house before the airport was even thought about, so that no one can say she knew the situation when she bought and has already received her compensation in the form of a lower purchase price. *Should* she be compensated? The trouble is that there are thousands of homeowners with equally valid claims. If one receives compensation, all ought to receive compensation. But if all receive compensation, a heavy cost will be imposed on the airport and the airlines and eventually on airline passengers, either through reduced service or higher prices.

At first glance, that might seem fair enough. Higher prices will compel airline passengers to pay the costs of the noise that is created as a by-product of their travel. But now a new problem forces itself on our attention. Externalities run throughout society. Shall we correct for them *all*? Shall homeowners receive compensation for the automobile traffic that goes past, the dandelions that their neighbors let go to seed, the passing gifts of dog walkers and their pets, the noise of the neighborhood children, the sound of power mowers, the spreading chestnut tree next door that blocks their view, or the loss of the shade if their neighbor cuts down the spreading chestnut tree because it blocks *his* view? When we are through with homeowners, we would have to start ordering the compensation of pedestrians, many of whom suffer from the same sorts of uncompensated costs that afflict homeowners. Perhaps we could, in the final stages of our effort to make the world perfect, impose fines on especially dull people in order to compensate those whom they bore.

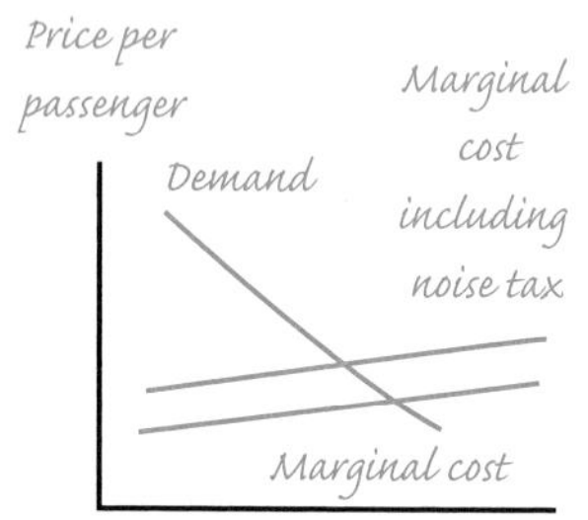

We just can't do that. There are too many spillovers; the appropriate compensations would be too difficult to determine. Even the direction in which compensation ought to be paid will often be unclear. Wouldn't it be just as much in order, for example, to levy fines on inattentive people to compensate the bores whose sensitivities they offend? Who says bores are worse than boors?

The Importance of Precedents

We are ready for the question: *Should* Regretta Sigh, the troubled homeowner 10 miles from the airport, be compensated by airline passengers for the inconvenience she suffers as a result of the flights from which they benefit? Our answer: It would be extraordinarily difficult and probably impossible to do so in a way that was both practical and fair.

We originally asked *two* questions, however. The second question asked whether homeowners in such circumstances were *likely* to receive compensation. The answer to this question is almost certainly *no*. The courts would attempt to decide the issue by *discovering* what rights the contending parties have, and homeowners would end up with very little to show on their behalf. The

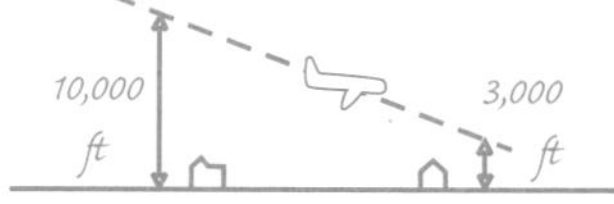

ruling consideration would almost surely be that both homeowners and those in the business of providing airline transportation have proceeded for a long time on the expectation that no such compensation must be paid. *These expectations indicate the respective property rights of homeowners and airlines*. We could even "prove" that homeowners 10 miles from the airport don't have a legal right to be compensated for the noise simply by showing that the market price of homes under the approach route would jump sharply if the court decision held in favor of the homeowner. This would be an *unexpected event* that would create profits for homeowners and losses for holders of airline stock. The appearance of these unexpected changes in values would be conclusive evidence that the affected parties did not believe such compensation was owed and that the court decision had consequently *created* property rights that had not existed previously.

There's a qualification to this conclusion that further establishes the point we're making. If a judge held for the homeowner in such a case, the price of affected houses might rise very little, because prospective home buyers would probably be advised that the judge had erred and was likely to be reversed on appeal. The concept of error is instructive. There can be no error when the decision *creates* the rights. Error is possible only when the decision seeks to *discover* what the rights are that actually prevail and therefore ought to govern the outcome of the case.

Adjudication, or the attempt to resolve conflicting claims by seeking to discover existing rights, always tries to avoid unexpected decisions or outcomes. It tries to settle disagreements over property rights by supporting and reinforcing the *expectations that are most widely and confidently held*. Adjudication is thus an effort to maintain the continuity of expectations in the presence of changing circumstances. And stable expectations, we remind you once more, are the foundation of effective cooperation in any large, complex society.

The Problem of Radical Change

Adjudication is an evolutionary approach to the problems created by negative externalities. But sometimes changes don't occur at an evolutionary pace. When we're overtaken by events so novel that established principles and practices furnish little guidance in dealing with them, adjudication cannot work very well. Technological innovations often force rapid changes on us in a wide variety of situations. Snowmobiles, pesticides, radar-assisted whaling ships, antibiotics, and nuclear reactors are just a few of the many examples that could be cited from recent years. When technological innovation radically multiplies negative externalities, new rules may be required to resolve the problems.

The demand for new definitions of property rights has also been created by rising incomes. Not too many years ago

Americans seemed to have had a working consensus that the social advantages from allowing the atmosphere to be used as an industrial dump were greater than the disadvantages. Our laws and customs decreed that the atmosphere belonged to everyone and therefore to no one, so factory owners were free to use it unthinkingly as a receptacle for industrial wastes. People could move away from factories or purchase residential space near the factories at a low price if they preferred that savings to the delights of clean air. Meanwhile, factories held their costs down by discharging wastes into the atmosphere, and this meant a greater availability of the goods that factories produced. But the situation has changed. The goods that factories produce are now available in much larger quantities, and many people have begun to place a lower marginal value on them. When we begin to place a higher marginal value on blue skies and clean air, we start to think of them as our right. We start to claim a property right in these environmental goods and demand that others stop putting them to uses that are incompatible with our ability to enjoy them. That requires new rules, not just an application of the old rules to new situations.

Reducing Externalities Through Legislation

Legislation clarifies property rights by creating them.

We call the creation of new rules *legislation*. The line between adjudication and legislation is not as clear in practice as all this pretends. But the distinction is important in principle, because legislation creates changes in prevailing property rights, and changing the rules of the game always raises the question of fairness and often compels major adjustments in behavior. The challenge for a society is to legislate in ways that avoid gross injustices and that minimize the cost of achieving the objectives. We shall focus on the second of those criteria, not because it's more important, but because economic theory has more to say about minimizing costs than about maximizing justice.

As you have probably noticed by now, many of the social problems that we refer to as "pollution" can be usefully analyzed as the product of negative externalities. People don't dirty the air or water because they prefer to live with dirty air and water, but as an unintended consequence of some other activity in which they want to engage, such as using their car or producing goods for sale. They ignore the spillover costs because they don't seem to matter. Motorists driving back and forth to work do dirty their own air, but not by enough to notice, whereas taking the bus would be (in their judgment) a huge inconvenience. They overlook the fact that they are also dirtying the air of thousands of other people and that a lot of dribbles of dirt too small to make any noticeable difference add up to a huge amount of dirt, which makes a great deal of difference. Nonetheless, each contributor to the problem acts as if the personal benefit from driving exceeds in value the tiny additional cost that this act imposes on everyone in the community. The final result can be disastrous. The solution, it would seem, is to internalize those externalities through new legislation.

using "command and control" to reduce pollution is a flawed approach.

The legislation of physical restrictions is a popular approach to the problem of pollution. "Command and control," it's called. After some date, no one is allowed to discharge more than so many particles of this or that into the air or the water system. This approach will almost certainly fail to minimize the cost per unit of pollution reduction. It ignores the variety of ways in which a given objective can usually be achieved and, therefore, offers few incentives to people to search for and implement the least costly alternative. We're going to use a very simplified example to illustrate some principles of pollution control that deserve to be better understood.

Minimizing costs

Suppose that all the "yuck" that fouls the air over the city of Arcadia comes from three sources: Factory A, Factory B, and Factory C. Table 12–1 shows the quantities of yuck put into the air monthly by each factory and the monthly cost to each factory of reducing its emissions of yuck. Now let's suppose that the Environmental Protection Agency (EPA) decides that, because yuck is ugly and damaging to the lungs, the 90,000 units of yuck should be reduced to 45,000 per month. Why not reduce them to zero, you might ask? Because the EPA has determined that the cost of reducing emissions to zero would exceed the benefits. Perhaps a little yuck harms no one's lungs and isn't even visible. We'll pass over the process by which the EPA arrives at that conclusion and simply assume that the decision was made on the basis of the best available scientific information and with a due regard to the overall interests of the people of Arcadia. We want to ask about the best way to achieve the target.

A: $1 × 0 = $0
B: $2 × 15,000 = $30,000
C: $3 × 30,000 = $90,000

There are several ways to do it. The EPA could prohibit any factory from emitting more than 15,000 units of yuck per month. That would compel Factory B to reduce its emissions by 15,000 at a monthly cost of $30,000 and Factory C to reduce its emissions by 30,000 at a monthly cost of $90,000, for a total cost of

Table 12–1 **Yuck in Arcadia**

	Units of Yuck Emitted Monthly	Cost of Reducing Emissions, per Unit
Factory A	15,000	$1
Factory B	30,000	2
Factory C	45,000	3

A: $1 × 7,500 = $7,500
B: $2 × 15,000 = $30,000
C: $3 × 22,500 = $67,500

A: $1 × 15,000 = $15,000
B: $2 × 15,000 = $30,000
C: $3 × 15,000 = $45,000

A: $1 × 15,000 = $15,000
B: $2 × 30,000 = $60,000
C: $3 × 0 = $0

$120,000. Alternatively, the EPA could order each factory to reduce its emissions by half. Factory A would then pay $7,500 to reduce its emissions by 7,500; Factory B would pay $30,000 to reduce its emissions by 15,000; and Factory C would pay $67,500 to reduce its emissions by 22,500. The total cost would be $105,000, a less costly way to reach the goal. A still less costly approach would have the EPA ordering each factory to reduce its emissions by 15,000. Then Factory A would pay $15,000 to eliminate all 15,000 units of its emissions; Factory B would pay $30,000 to eliminate half of its emissions; and Factory C would pay $45,000 to reduce its emissions by one-third. This approach would enable Arcadia to reach the goal at a total cost of only $90,000.

As you can see, the total cost goes steadily down as more of the burden of reducing yuck emissions is placed on Factory A, which can reduce emissions for $1 per unit, and less on Factory C, which can reduce them only at a cost of $3 per unit. So if our goal is to get emissions down to the tolerable level of 45,000 at the lowest cost, why not impose the responsibility entirely on Factory A and Factory B? If the EPA allowed Factory C to go on doing what it is currently doing while requiring Factories A and B to reduce their emissions entirely, the total cost of achieving the target would fall to $75,000.

Why not? Well, the unfairness of it all might be a very good reason not to impose all the costs on A and B while allowing C to escape completely. Minimizing costs isn't the only consideration, after all, when government officials are trying to achieve some objective; fairness is also an important criterion for the evaluation of government decisions. It would seem, on the face of it, that the smaller polluters in Arcadia would be punished for being able to reduce their emissions at a lower cost than the biggest polluter can do it. Would the EPA be likely to choose this approach?

Another Approach: Taxing Emissions

Let's defer that question and examine the problem further. Suppose that the EPA doesn't actually know how much it will cost per unit to reduce pollution from each source. That's much more plausible than our original assumption, for several reasons. The polluters themselves will be in the best position to know the actual costs, but they will also have an incentive to exaggerate their costs in pleadings before the EPA or the public. Moreover, exaggeration will not be wholly dishonest, because one never knows for certain the costs of something that hasn't yet been tried, and it's just ordinary prudence to estimate them high, especially if higher estimates mean the costs are less likely to be imposed. Finally, though costs can usually be reduced through research and experiment, no one can predict the results that research and experiment will produce. What is the least costly solution when the EPA is faced with this kind of information scarcity?

The EPA would gain the applause of many economists if it responded to this situation by imposing a tax per unit of emissions and then allowing each party to respond as it thought best. If you're willing to grant that pollution is a spillover cost, a cost not borne by its producer, then placing a tax on polluting activities makes good sense. If the tax per unit of pollutant can somehow be set equal to the spillover cost per unit, the creator and presumed beneficiary of the costs is made to bear them. If that makes the polluting activity too costly to continue, it will cease, as it should if its costs are greater than its benefits. If the benefits still outweigh the costs when the tax is being paid, the polluting activity will continue, though at a lesser rate because it's now more costly. But in that case the tax revenue will be available to compensate—to buy the consent of—those on whom the spillover costs are falling.

Suppose that the EPA refrained from telling any of the factories how much they had to reduce their emissions and simply required them to pay a tax of $2.01 for each unit of yuck emitted monthly. That would treat each factory alike, which seems fair. How would the factories respond? Factory A would find it cheaper to eliminate all its emissions rather than pay the tax. So would Factory B. Factory C, on the other hand, would find it more advantageous to pay the tax and continue emitting 45,000 units of yuck per month. So the total cost of cutting yuck emissions in half would be $75,000 and all factories would be treated alike. Notice that the $90,450 in taxes that Factory C would pay under this proposal would be a transfer of wealth to the rest of society rather than a net cost. Factories A and B would be paying all the costs of the pollution-reduction program, while Factory C would be compensating the community for the right to continue emitting 45,000 units of yuck each month.

A: $2.01 > cost
B: $2.01 > cost
C: $2.01 < cost

The task for the EPA is to compare the marginal costs of reducing the emissions with the marginal benefits. The use of taxes enables the EPA to acquire information about these costs and benefits by observing what happens when variously estimated pollution costs are assessed against the polluters. It's an approach that lends itself to learning by experimentation. And obtaining reliable information about costs and benefits is essential to any program of environmental protection that is concerned with human well-being.

Licenses to Pollute?

Let's go back now to a question that we asked but deferred answering. After comparing the costs of different ways of reducing air pollution, we asked whether the EPA was likely in such a situation to choose the least costly approach. We put off answering in order to argue that physical directives of any sort—the "command and control" method—were generally inferior to taxes as a way of controlling pollution. By taxing emissions, we enlist the aid of the price system in solving our problem. But the tax approach isn't popular with the public for a reason that would also make it difficult for the EPA to issue the least costly set of physical directives. Taxes on pollution have acquired the derogatory label of "licenses to pollute," which sounds a lot like official permission to commit crimes.

This begs an important question, however. While we may want to regard some polluting acts as so inherently undesirable that they ought to be prohibited altogether, we clearly do not want to take this attitude toward most of what we now call pollution. The polluting activities in which people engage are commonly activities that generate benefits, sometimes very large benefits, for other people as well as for themselves. To condone these activities is to condone pollution, whether we want to admit it or not. The very word *pollution* probably misleads us here. Historically, the term has had a strong moral connotation, as any good dictionary will point out. In classical literature, a polluting act corrupted the whole community. A "license to pollute" in such a context is like a license to commit immoral or criminal acts. But surely no one wants to say that homeowners who turn on their furnaces and thereby put "pollutants" into the air are behaving in an immoral or criminal manner. Most pollution should be viewed as a cost, not a crime, and should therefore be "licensed" if the cost is less than the properly calculated value of the benefits associated with it.

Efficiency and Fairness

Some people also object to taxes on pollutants because they regard such taxes as fundamentally unfair. They supposedly place the whole burden of reducing pollution on the poor while allowing the rich to go right on fouling the environment. Choosing the people who must reduce their pollution on the basis of the cost to them of doing so, which is required by the least-cost solution, also seems arbitrary and unjust to many people. An important part of any reply to those who raise the fairness issue, however, is to show that the *efficient* solution can be achieved while settling the *fairness* issue in different ways. In other words, we don't necessarily commit ourselves to place the costs on any particular parties when we select the most efficient solution. The Arcadia case can again provide our illustration.

Suppose that the EPA for some reason wants to impose the entire cost of pollution reduction on Factory C—perhaps because Factory C can best afford it, or because it is the heaviest polluter, or because it was the last factory to set up in Arcadia. Whatever

Emissions trading

the reason, all the EPA need do is tell managers of Factory C that they must reduce emissions into the Arcadian air by 45,000 or pay $2.01 for every unit by which they fall short of that goal. The managers of Factory C will then look for the least costly way to lower emissions by 45,000 units. If the managers possess the information in Table 12–1, they will offer Factory A $15,000 plus a few hundred dollars to eliminate all its emissions and offer Factory B $60,000 plus a little to do the same. Factory C will thus reduce the level of emissions to the target level. But rather than pay $135,000 to do the job themselves, the managers of C will pay a total of $75,000 to A and B to perform the task on their behalf.

Pollution reduction is a lot like any other useful activity in that some are more efficient at it than others. Just as we gain from having our food, toys, and cosmetics produced by those with a comparative advantage in their production, so we gain by having additional clean air produced by those with the greatest comparative advantage at the job. But comparative advantages are exploited through exchange. That's why the tax approach to pollution reduction is in general superior to an approach that assigns physical restrictions to particular firms. The tax approach tries to alter relative money costs to reflect new decisions about who has which rights. But it then leaves all parties free to trade on the basis of their own comparative advantages and to secure the new social goals in the most efficient manner.

The Bubble Concept

The Environmental Protection Agency took a large step in the direction suggested by this analysis in 1979 when it issued new regulations to permit and encourage trade-offs among air-pollution sources. Rather than set rigid limits on allowable emissions from each smokestack, enforcement agencies would permit factories to exceed the limits at one point if they could make it up at another point. They could pretend that there was a giant bubble over the entire factory (hence the name for this approach—the bubble concept) and control total emissions into the bubble. Under this policy, firms could lower the cost of achieving a target level of air quality by allowing emissions to rise wherever their control was especially costly and making it up where emissions could be reduced at lower cost.

This approach was challenged in court by environmental groups, who claimed that it allowed additional pollution to occur in areas where air quality was already not in compliance with EPA standards. A firm should not be allowed to belch obnoxious substances from smokestack A just because it had reduced the emissions from smokestack B. If the emissions from B could be reduced at low cost, the environmentalists argued, then they should be reduced. But the emissions from A should not be allowed to increase. The environmentalist argument implicitly assumes that there is only one good: clean air.

The Supreme Court rejected this argument in 1984, thereby opening the way for existing plants and factories to expand in areas with air-quality problems (without worsening the air quality) and encouraging the EPA to go one step further. If firms and plants were to be allowed to make internal trade-offs in the interest of efficiency, or achieving given goals at the lowest possible cost, why couldn't such trade-offs also be allowed *between* firms? If an electrical utility wanted to build a new generating plant to satisfy its customers' demands, it might be able to do so without worsening air quality by persuading some other firm to reduce its emissions by the amount that the utility was going to expand emissions. In effect, firms would be allowed to buy and sell "rights to pollute."

That did not sit well at all with more ardent environmentalists, who argued that no one owned a "right to pollute" and therefore no one else could buy it. The premise is questionable, however. Firms do in fact have rights to discharge obnoxious substances into the air, as proved by the fact that they do it openly and are not fined. They have both actual and legal "rights to pollute." By accepting and clarifying those rights, the EPA allowed a market in such rights to evolve, which meant in turn that firms could purchase their pollution-control programs from other firms that had a comparative advantage in pollution control. If the EPA allows the purchasing firm to use only some percentage of the rights purchased—to use 100, for example, it has to purchase 130—it can enlist the expanded bubble concept in the service of progressively cleaner air. Note, too, that those who want the air to be even cleaner than the EPA requires may be able, under this system, to buy up "pollution rights" and retire them.

The system won't work, however, unless the rights are clearly defined and can be counted on. No individual or group will be willing to buy up rights in order to retire them if the regulatory authorities can respond by creating new rights to replace the ones retired. Nor will firms be willing to pay money to purchase rights if they believe they can get the same rights from the regulatory authorities with just a little lobbying. And firms are much more likely to invest resources in discovering and devising ways to reduce their emissions below what they are legally entitled to emit if they know that they can sell the results to someone else.

Cleaning up the air is an especially difficult environmental challenge. The sources of air pollution are numerous and hard to monitor. And the costs of cleaning up the air, in benefits forgone, will often be much higher than we are inclined to suppose when we're thinking exclusively about factories (where other people work) and conveniently forgetting about our own chimneys, automobile exhaust pipes, backyard barbecues, and household sprays. The enormous benefits from cleaner air coupled with the high costs of attaining it ought to make us appreciate any system that can give us more of what we want at a lower cost.

Rights and the Social Problem of Pollution

We don't want to conclude this chapter with an endorsement of efficiency, because inefficiency is not the fundamental problem. Pollution is a major social and political concern at this time because people disagree about rights. More people are beginning to say: "You are obtaining your benefits by imposing this cost on me (or us), but you have no *moral* right to do that and so should have no *legal* right." Disagreements of this sort can be extremely difficult to resolve. The economic way of thinking suggests a few principles that might be of considerable help as we embark on the task.

The first is that the demand is never completely inelastic for any good, not even for the good of clean air. We must decide how much we want, preferably with a clear-eyed recognition that more can be obtained only by giving up ever larger amounts of other goods that we also want.

The second is that we should leave people as much freedom as we can to choose their own ways of adapting. If our goal is to reduce the burning of fossil fuels, for example, we want to let people choose the means that reduce the cost to themselves. We should avoid "command and control," which typically raises the cost of achieving any objective and, by raising the cost, also increases resistance to the objective itself. Using the price system lowers costs. Letting people exchange also lowers costs.

Finally, we should keep in mind the importance of stable property rights. When people know what the rules are and can count on them not to be changed arbitrarily, transaction costs go down and effective cooperation increases.

Traffic Congestion as an Externality

But sometimes our obsession with rights blinds us to the real world, as in the case of traffic congestion. Traffic congestion is consistently ranked by Americans as one of the most pressing problems of urban life. It's a puzzling sort of social problem, when you think about it, because the people who complain about it are the very same people who create it. When you understand the concept of externalities, however, the puzzle evaporates. Congestion is a negative externality, which is to say that it's a cost generated by people who don't take it into account when making their decisions. They take into account only the costs that *other* drivers create.

What would happen if we induced drivers to internalize the externalities of traffic congestion? If we could find a way to turn the costs of congestion back upon the motorists who created them, what would happen? They would drive only when the marginal benefits of driving exceeded the marginal costs. Everyone does that now, of course; but under our current practices those costs do not include the costs imposed on other people. If motorists had to pay the marginal congestion costs that their decision to drive imposed on others as well as the costs to themselves, they would choose to drive less. They would drive only when the marginal benefit to themselves was greater than the sum of the marginal costs to everyone in the society. All motorists could be better off! The streets would no longer be congested. Drivers would get where they're going without becoming bogged down in traffic. Drivers would choose substitutes for those car trips with less marginal value and thereby lower the cost for everyone of making trips with greater marginal value. And the quality of the substitutes would almost surely increase. Car pools would become easier to form; buses would move more swiftly through the now uncongested streets and would run more frequently in response to the increased demand. How wonderful it would be—if only there were some some way to internalize the externalities!

Driving without having to pay a toll is best for each of us but very costly for all of us.

There *is* a way. It's called *pricing*. Economists call it *congestion pricing*. Almost everyone else calls it tolls for driving and doesn't want to hear anything more about it. "I pay for the roads with my gasoline taxes; I don't want to pay again with a toll." But gasoline taxes pay the cost of constructing the roads, not the cost of using them. It's the ignored cost of using them that generates the congestion about which everyone complains. We experience traffic congestion because the government, which owns the roads, allows everyone to use them without payment of a fee. If we were all required to pay fees based on the costs our driving imposes on others, we could eliminate congestion.

Technology now exists through which motorists can be charged prices finely adjusted to the level of congestion (the external costs). Moreover, it can all be done automatically without anyone having to stop and pay a toll. Bills can be sent at the end of the month. The technology is not used because people are so hostile to the very idea of tolls; they assume they have a right to drive free of charge on the streets for which their taxes paid. They think that a toll would just take money from their pockets and don't realize that a well-managed system of congestion pricing could create benefits of greater value to them than the costs they would have to pay in the form of tolls. It's another case where the pricing of a scarce good, in this case urban street space, can reduce deadweight costs and thereby make all parties better off.

Once Over Lightly

The actions that people take often impose costs on others that the actors do not take into account. Economists refer to these as spillover costs or negative externalities.

Negative externalities multiply rapidly in urban, industrialized societies. Even where the spillover costs of particular actions are greater than the benefits to the actors, transaction costs will frequently prevent people from negotiating more satisfactory arrangements.

Negotiation is the standard procedure used by members of a society to secure the cooperation and consent of others without imposing unwelcome costs on one another. Clearly defined property rights make negotiations easier by lowering transaction costs.

Conflicting claims of right can often be resolved by examining established principles and practices. Adjudication in this manner preserves the continuity of people's expectations. Unclear property rights and arbitrary changes in these rights make social cooperation more difficult by making it harder for anyone to plan with confidence.

Rapid or radical social change may make it so difficult to resolve conflicting claims of right through adjudication that legislation is called for. Legislation entails the creation of new rules to establish and define what people may do with the resources at their command.

New rules will produce lower-cost resolutions of such negative externality problems as "pollution" if the rules make it easier for people to exchange rights and obligations. Taxes on undesired spillover costs and systems for trading "pollution rights" provide appropriate incentives to polluters and facilitate low-cost arrangements to reduce pollution. So-called command and control approaches, by contrast, pay far less attention than do market-oriented systems to the information and incentive problems that challenge any policy aimed at reducing pollution.

QUESTIONS FOR DISCUSSION

1. Officials in River Edge, New Jersey, passed an ordinance making it illegal for residents to park vehicles with commercial license plates or with signs on the doors in their driveways overnight.
   (a) Were the parkers generating negative externalities?
   (b) Why did those who disliked seeing such vehicles in their neighborhood choose to push for a new ordinance rather than talk directly to the owners of the vehicles?
   (c) The ordinance made some people better off and some worse off. How can we know whether the benefits of the ordinance exceeded its costs?
2. Which of the following actions generate negative externalities that *also create social problems*?
   (a) Tossing peanut shells on the sidewalk
   (b) Tossing peanut shells on the floor at a major league baseball game
   (c) Dropping a candy wrapper on the sidewalk
   (d) Dropping confetti from an office building during a downtown parade

(e) Setting off loud firecrackers on Independence Day
(f) Producing a fireworks display on Independence Day

3. Why do people sometimes disturb others by talking during movies? Do the talkers and those whom they disturb agree about the rights one acquires when purchasing a movie ticket? How could the owners of movie theaters resolve this conflict? Why don't they do so?
4. What are the property-rights claims that are in conflict in each of the cases described here? How would you prefer that they be resolved (assuming that you are an impartial observer)?

(a) Owners of motorcycles want to remove their mufflers to obtain more efficient engine performance, but the law limits the noise that any motorcycle may emit.
(b) A group wants to prohibit billboards along rural highways, but farmers claim they have a right to erect any kind of sign they want on their own property.
(c) A Missouri state legislator introduces a bill making it a crime to blow your nose in a loud or offensive manner in a restaurant.
(d) A Connecticut state legislator proposes a bill that would ban the throwing of rice at weddings on the grounds that uncooked rice is unhealthful for birds.
(e) Restaurant owners want to exclude people whose dress doesn't satisfy certain standards. (Should this be legal?)
(f) People who never bathe want to use city buses. People who never brush or comb their hair want to sit and stroll in public parks. (Should the unwashed be barred from the buses? The unkempt banned from the parks?)

5. A large mulberry tree in your neighbor's yard provides you with welcome shade but gives her only a lot of inedible and messy mulberries. She wants to cut the tree down.

(a) Does she have the legal right to do so?
(b) You say to her: "I know you hate those messy mulberries, but not nearly as much as I would hate losing the shade." Can you prove your statement? If you can't prove that you value continued shade more than she values a clean yard, can you induce *her* to place a higher value on *her* benefits from leaving the tree than on *her* benefits from cutting it down? (*Hint*: How do you induce the sewer cleaner to decide he would rather clear your sewer line on a Sunday afternoon than watch his favorite football team?)
(c) An alternative route for you is to challenge her legal right to cut down the tree. You might try to have the tree declared a historic landmark, or go to court to demand that she file an environmental impact statement before being allowed to remove the tree. What is the danger to you in this tactic? (*Hint*: If you think you may be prevented in the future from exercising a right you now possess, will you wait to see what becomes of your right or will you exercise it while you still clearly have it?)

6. Two children are quarreling about who gets to choose the program that will be watched on the family's single television set. This is a case of conflicting property rights.

(a) Should the parents tell them to work it out for themselves? Under what circumstances is this likely to produce a satisfactory resolution of the conflict?
(b) How do poorly defined property rights make it more difficult in such a case to achieve a satisfactory resolution through negotiation?
(c) Show how the parents might contribute to a resolution of the conflict first by offering adjudication, then by providing legislation.

7. According to a poll conducted by the *Wall Street Journal* and NBC News, eight out of ten Americans say that they are "environmentalists." Do their buying and consumption practices support that claim?

(a) Sixty-seven percent of those polled said they would be willing to pay 15 to 20 cents a gallon more for gasoline that causes much less pollution than the current blends. One major refiner responded that it had developed such a blend, but it wasn't selling. Would you say that members of the 67 percent who do not purchase a less polluting blend when it becomes available are not sincere in claiming to be environmentalists?
(b) When asked whether they would favor a 25-cent addition to the gasoline tax to encourage less driving and more conservation, 69 percent of those polled opposed the tax and only 27 percent supported it. Can you reconcile this position with the claim of two-thirds of those polled that they are environmentalists?
(c) Eighty-five percent of those polled wanted the government to require cars to be more fuel efficient and less polluting even if that made them more expensive, although only 51 percent were willing to see cars made "smaller and less safe" in order to protect the environment. Can you provide a plausible explanation for these combinations of attitudes?

8. The sign on the beach reads "$25 fine for littering." A beach user nonetheless tosses his used soda bottles on the sand rather than walk to the distant trash barrel. He knows that the beach patrol has seen him and will issue a citation, but he is very wealthy and so places a very low marginal value on money and a very high marginal value on time. Would you call him a litterer if he is willing to pay the fine? Or has he purchased the right to use the sand as a waste receptacle?

9. Surveys by the Michigan Highway Department showed that beverage-container litter decreased 82 percent and total litter decreased 32 percent when the state adopted a mandatory-deposit law for beer and soft-drink containers. According to one estimate of the effect of the law on prices, Michigan consumers were paying an extra $300 million per year for beer and soft drinks as a result of the law.

(a) If these figures are correct, is this mandatory-deposit law "cost-effective" in your judgment? How could you decide?
(b) Suppose we knew that Michigan citizens actually value the reduction in litter at more than $300 million per year. Would this demonstrate the cost-effectiveness of the mandatory-deposit law?
(c) How many people could be hired full-time to walk around picking up litter for $300 million per year? Assume that litter lifters receive $5 an hour, which works out to $10,000 a year for 50 weeks of 40 hours

each. Do you think such an army of full-time litter lifters could reduce total litter by considerably more than 32 percent?

10. Bombast City allows motor vehicles to be operated without mufflers if they carry a current noise license, which costs $20 per month. In Tranquil Heights it is illegal to operate a motor vehicle without a muffler, and the fine for violation is $100. Motorists who choose to violate the Tranquil Heights ordinance are caught and fined about once every five months. In other words, Bombast City permits noisy vehicles upon payment of a fee and Tranquil Heights prohibits them and fines violators. The fee and the fine are monetarily equivalent when we multiply the fine by the probability of 0.2 that it will have to be paid in any month.

    (a) Given this monetary equivalence, what is the difference between the approaches of Bombast City and Tranquil Heights to the problem of mufflers and noisy motor vehicles?
    (b) It's clear that people who drive without mufflers in Bombast City are licensed to make noise. Do the people who drive without mufflers in Tranquil Heights acquire a license when they pay their fines? Would the legislators of Tranquil Heights agree that payment of the fine authorizes one to drive without a muffler?
    (c) One difference between "you may make noise if you pay" and "you may not make noise and you'll pay if you do" is that in the latter case but not the former the party who makes noise does something that the society condemns as wrong. Does this fact exercise its own effect on behavior? How do societies usually respond when individuals *persist* in behavior that has been legally condemned as *wrong*? Does the penalty remain constant, as it does in the case of a fee for permitted behavior?
    (d) Does this distinction aid us in understanding what lies behind some of the objections to pollution fees? When people protest that fees based on emissions into the air or water constitute a "license to pollute," are they perhaps objecting to the law's *authorization* of the emissions? Do they want the emitters to bear moral blame as well as higher monetary costs? Why might people who are intensely interested in cleaner air or water want the issue to be a moral one?
    (e) When would it be desirable to treat discharges into the air or the water as costs imposed on others that will be allowed upon payment of a fee, and when would it be better to treat them as crimes punishable by fines?

11. History books often lament the destruction of the great herds of bison that roamed the western prairies before the arrival of nonnative hunters.

    (a) Why were so many people willing to shoot these animals and leave their meat and hide to rot? Wasn't this highly wasteful? Why did so many apparently place such a high value on a moment of sport as to kill these animals for no other reason than the excitement of it?
    (b) Who bore the costs when a hunter shot a bison or "buffalo" from the window of a passing train?
    (c) Was the near extinction of the buffalo an irreversible act? Or could we bring those huge herds of buffalo back within a few years if the proper incentives existed?

(d) What animal has replaced the buffalo on the western prairies? Why do the numerous vast herds of cattle that cover the country not suffer the fate of the buffalo? What do you think would happen to the relative size of cattle and buffalo herds if Americans lost their taste for beef and acquired an intense love of buffalo meat?

12. What difference does ownership make? Go way back and take a look at question 9 at the end of Chapter 1. Then try to answer these questions:

    (a) What response would you predict from the Sierra Club if an oil company requested a permit to extract natural gas from a wilderness area owned by the federal government?
    (b) What difference do you think it would make to the Sierra Club's decision if the oil company were willing to pay an enormous royalty to the federal government because there was a great deal of natural gas available in that wilderness area?
    (c) What difference do you think it would make if the oil company promised to extract the natural gas in ways that had a very small impact on the environment?
    (d) What difference do you think it would make if the wilderness area, instead of belonging to the federal government, was the property of the Sierra Club?
    (e) Why do you suppose the Audubon Society allows three oil companies to extract natural gas from its 26,800-acre Rainey Wildlife Sanctuary in Louisiana?
    (f) The oil companies in the Rainey Sanctuary pay almost a million dollars per year in royalties to the Audubon Society. Do you think this arrangement promotes the purposes of the Audubon Society? Do you think it promotes the well-being of natural-gas consumers? (The instructive story of the Rainey Sanctuary was told by economists John Baden and Richard Stroup in the July 1981 issue of *Reason* magazine.)
    (g) Is it rational for the Audubon Society to allow extraction of natural gas from its own land while opposing it elsewhere?

13. Do we need laws to prevent cropland erosion? Does cropland erosion create negative externalities?

    (a) How will farming practices that cause soil erosion affect the present value of farmland?
    (b) How will an owner of farmland who wants to maximize the present value of the land decide whether or not to adopt particular soil conservation measures?
    (c) Why will a tenant farmer ordinarily adopt fewer and less effective soil conservation techniques than an owner?
    (d) Why would landowners ever permit farm tenants to reduce the present value of the land through practices that raise current yields but increase the vulnerability of the land to erosion?
    (e) What are some of the consequences of soil erosion that impose costs on people other than landowners? Will even an owner-operator take these costs fully into account in making decisions about whether and how to plow and plant land that is particularly subject to wind or water erosion?

(f) Suppose that people who are farming their own land have trouble earning enough income to pay their mortgages and begin to fear that they will lose ownership of the land to lending institutions. How will this fear affect their decisions about the trade-off between increased yields and reduced soil erosion?
(g) A Montana farmer buys hundreds of thousands of acres of grazing land from longtime ranch operators, then plows up the land and plants wheat. Why did the ranchers sell? Why did the purchasing farmer convert the land from livestock to wheat production? If the farmer knew he would be required to compensate residents of the county for the dust storms that will result when the land is shifted from livestock to wheat, might he find raising livestock more profitable than growing wheat?
(h) Should farmers whose practices aggravate the problem of dust storms be required to compensate others for the additional dust they put into the air? How could such a compensation system be administered?

14. Here is a multiple-choice question for you to think about. The buildings and grounds at Ivy College are far more littered than the buildings and grounds at the Ivyville Shopping Mall because: (1) students are slobs by nature; (2) more people use the Ivy College campus than use the shopping mall; (3) customers at the shopping mall have less opportunity to litter because they don't smoke or purchase take-out food; (4) customers at the mall have less incentive to litter because they are proud to be "Ivyville Mallers" and so take good care of their "campus;" (5) there are people at the mall but not on the Ivy College campus who expect to receive substantial financial benefits from keeping the buildings and grounds litter-free.
15. When you bought your house, only 5 commercial planes passed over it daily, on average. That number has grown slowly and almost imperceptibly over the intervening years and now numbers 150. Is the change from 5 to 150 a drastic or radical change? Is your situation with 150 planes flying over your house each day more tolerable because the number increased slowly and imperceptibly? Would you be more likely to receive compensation of some sort if the changes had occurred over a very short period of time? Does the fact that we can't tell which straw broke the camel's back mean that the addition of more straw to the camel's burden was not the cause of its broken back?
16. Many large urban airports have established programs for buying out those homeowners most seriously affected by airport noise.

(a) Do people who own houses directly under an approach route and within 5,000 feet of the runway deserve compensation for the noise made by planes landing or taking off? If you think they do, ask yourself where you will draw the line. What about people whose homes are 15,000 feet from the beginning of the runway or who live very close to but not quite under the approach route?
(b) If the owner is renting the house out, should it be the owner or the tenants who receive compensation? Why?
(c) Are *current* owners the appropriate people to compensate? Wasn't a current owner compensated in the purchase price if the house was bought within the past few years?

(d) What difference does it make in your answer to the previous question whether it was generally believed when the house changed hands that the airport would buy out those homeowners most severely affected by the noise?

17. If airlines are required to pay landing fees that are adjusted to take account of the level of particular aircrafts' noise emissions, the time of day or night when they land, and the density of the residential population in the vicinity of the airport, how will airlines take steps to reduce the impact of their operations on homeowners who live near airports?

    (a) A government agency calculated for each of 23 airports the decline in the annual rental value of surrounding property due to noise and divided this total by the number of takeoffs and landings during the year. The highest average was $196.67 for New York's La Guardia; the lowest was the Portland, Oregon, airport, with a cost of $0.82 per takeoff or landing. This means that each takeoff or landing imposed a combined cost of almost $200 on La Guardia's neighbors, but less than a dollar on all those living around the Portland airport. Will airlines find it in their interest to use some airports more than they now do and others less if their landing and takeoff fees are increased by these amounts?

    (b) Will airlines be more likely to install retrofitted noise-control gear or buy new and quieter planes if they must pay higher fees for noisier aircraft? Respond to the argument that "no airline is going to scrap an expensive plane just to save a few $400 airport surcharges." Is this critic of surcharges thinking marginally?

    (c) How would such a system of surcharges induce airlines to fly their noisier planes to Portland and their quieter ones to New York City, or to use Dulles Airport rather than National when flying into Washington, D.C.? (Dulles, which is far out in the Virginia countryside, showed a cost of $5.64 per operation in the study.)

18. How stringently should ozone be controlled? Federal legislation has set the ozone standard at a level that would prevent any adverse health effects on people who exercise in an area with high ozone concentrations.

    (a) Is there any scientific way to decide whether the benefits from a stringent ozone standard are greater than its costs?

    (b) According to a *New York Times* article, 51 percent of the annual emissions of volatile organic compounds that produce ozone at ground level come from the operation of motor vehicles. So we could protect our health either by prohibiting so much driving or by exercising less in those urban areas where, on a few days in the year, ozone levels exceed the standard. Which is the more efficient way to protect our health?

    (c) Suppose that industrial solvents create 4 percent of certain harmful emissions and household solvents create 5 percent of them. If we pass legislation to reduce the use of solvents, is the legislation more likely to restrict industrial or household use? Would a restriction on industrial use show that people are more important than profits?

19. A Tacoma, Washington electrical utility purchased from a manufacturing firm, for $265,000, the right to add 60 tons of "particulate matter" to the

air each year. The manufacturer had reduced its annual emissions by 69 tons a few years earlier through modernizing its plant. The representative of an environmental organization objected that the practice of selling rights to pollute simply meant that "as soon as one air polluter drops out of the ring, there will be a ready substitute."

(a) What benefits of the system does this criticism ignore?
(b) The utility used the credits to renovate and operate a generating plant that would burn garbage as well as other fuels, thus reducing solid-waste disposal problems. Is it better for the environment to bury or to incinerate garbage?

20. Suppose that government environmental agencies decide exactly how much of each kind of industrial pollutant they will allow within a given airshed and sell the rights to discharge these quantities of pollutants to the highest bidder.

    (a) Which firms would offer the highest bids?
    (b) How could citizens interested in cleaner air than the environmental agency had ordered use this system to obtain what they want?

21. "Taxes can't control pollution. They'll just drive the little firms out of business while the big firms, who can afford to pay, go right on polluting." Do you agree?

22. Here is a paragraph from a letter to the *Wall Street Journal* written by the chairman of the House Subcommittee on Health and the Environment:

    > The cheapest and best way to clean air is to make sure that new industrial facilities are built clean. It is far easier to build a new coke oven or blast furnace clean than to try to retrofit an old facility with pollution controls. Just as replacing old, dirty cars with new, clean cars will lessen automotive pollution, so too will turning over America's capital stock clean the air.

    A law that requires new cars or new industrial facilities to be "clean" raises the cost of producing new cars or new facilities and hence their price. How will that encourage longer use of old and "dirty" cars and facilities? Show how a law could result in dirtier air by setting excessively stringent and costly controls on new cars or industrial facilities.

23. Assume that the graph in Figure 12–1 shows how much it costs per year per car to reduce undesirable automobile emissions by various percentages through mandatory exhaust-control devices.

    (a) Why does the curve rise slowly at first and increase more rapidly as emission levels decline? Is this a peculiar characteristic of automobile exhaust-control systems, or is it a more general relationship?
    (b) Does this curve tell us how much emissions ought to be reduced? Does it provide any guidance at all to those who make public policy in this area?
    (c) If you think of this curve as the marginal cost of supplying cleaner air, what kind of data would you want in order to construct the demand for cleaner air? What would be the significance of the intersection between these two curves?

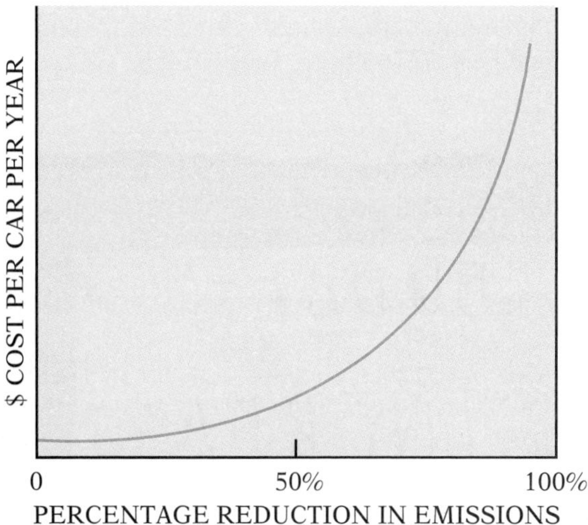

Figure 12–1 **Costs of reducing automobile emissions**

(d) Suppose you want to find out how much people in your area value cleaner air. So you commission a survey in which people are asked how much they would be *willing to pay* in order to obtain various levels of reduction in the amount of noxious automobile emissions in their community. Can you generally count on them to tell the truth? Remember that they know they won't be held to their valuation—that is, they won't actually be required to pay what they say they would be willing to pay. What are the major sources of bias in such a survey procedure?

(e) Suppose that your survey is done for the government and that the people whom you ask know they will actually be required to pay an annual tax equal to the amount they say they are willing to pay for whatever level of reductions is finally decided on and enforced. What sort of bias will this introduce into your measurement of the community demand for cleaner air?

24. Where is the best place to dispose of solid waste? The most common answer is NIMBY—Not In My Back Yard.

    (a) How does a city discriminate unfairly against some people whenever it chooses a new waste disposal site?

    (b) What makes people willing to let others dispose of solid waste in their "backyard"?

    (c) What would happen if a city "awarded" its new waste disposal site to the community that was most willing to accept it? How might such willingness be obtained and measured?

BUDGET
1939
NO. INCREASE
IN PRICE
OF
TOBACCO OR
CIGARETTES
YET
20 for 1/-
DIGGER
CAPSTAN
GOLD FLAKE
10 for 6d
50 for 2/5
PLAIN OR CORK-TIPPED
WILLS'S CAPSTAN MEDIUM
DAVIES'S
Sweet Memories
GOLD MEDAL MIXTURE
LLOYDS' SKIPPER MEDIUM

Markets and Government

13

The issue of externalities—negative and positive—is often cast in the language of *market failure*. The idea is that the market process fails to achieve some *optimal* standard. It also suggests that government corrective action can propel the market system *closer* to some hypothetical optimum. Good-intentioned people (including economists) often *assume* that government officials will have the information *and* the incentive to improve real-world economic coordination problems. But there is the possibility that government policy might make matters worse. James M. Buchanan, a Nobel laureate in economics, has often said, "Economists who analyze market failure have a moral obligation to also analyze *government failure*." Your two coauthors got that message loud and clear as former students of Professor Buchanan. This chapter continues the exploration of externalities, now with a specific focus on positive externalities. We shall delve into this material while keeping Buchanan's professional ethic in mind.

The focus of this chapter addresses key questions in constitutional political economy: What shall we leave to the market and what are appropriate tasks for government? It's difficult to answer that question unless we know what we mean by the *market* and by *government*. To choose intelligently, we must know what the options are, and the choice between market and government is by no means as clear as our public-policy debates often make it seem.

Private Versus Public?

Most of the standard contrasts between the market system and government don't hold up very well under close examination. To begin with, the market is usually characterized as the *private* sector, with government agencies and officials occupying the *public* sector. But what can this possibly mean? It surely doesn't mean that actions taken in the market don't affect the public or are of exclusively private concern. Nor can it seriously mean that consumers and the managers of business firms pursue private interests whereas everyone who works for government pursues the public interest. The senator who claims that "the public interest" guides all his decisions is in fact guided by a personal interpretation of the public interest, filtered through all sorts of private interests: reelection, influence with colleagues, relations with the press, popular image, and place in the history books. Senators *may* be less interested than business executives in maximizing their private monetary income, but they're probably more interested on average in acquiring personal prestige and power.

The same kind of analysis applies to any employee of a government agency, whether it's a high appointed official on a regulatory commission or someone just starting a job at the lowest civil-service rank. However lofty, noble, or impartial the stated objectives of a government agency, its day-to-day activities will be the consequence of decisions made by ordinary mortals, subject to the pull and push of incentives remarkably similar to those that operate in the private sector. Moreover, in recent years a special devotion to "the public interest" has been claimed for themselves by many executives in leading business corporations, eager to persuade us that the ultimate touchstone for their policies is not the maximization of net revenue, but the fulfillment of their social responsibilities. We would be well advised to discount all the rhetoric about public versus private interests and to look for the incentives that actually shape the decisions that people make.

Competition and Individualism

Some other common contrasts between the market and the government also grow more indistinct the longer we look at them. The market sector is often called the *competitive* sector. But there is competition in government, too, as every election year demonstrates. Within any government agency, competition for promotion exists among employees. Competition also occurs between government agencies vying for a larger share of appropriations. The two major political parties are continually competing. The executive branch competes with the legislative, members of Congress compete for committee assignments, even district court judges compete with one another in the hope of an eventual appointment to a higher court. Do Supreme Court justices holding appointments for life at the pinnacle of their profession compete for reputation among editorial writers and law school professors?

Sometimes we're told that *individualism* is the distinguishing characteristic of the market sector. But what constitutes "individualism"? Many of those who enter the market sector go to work for large corporations right after leaving school and continue as employees until retirement. Is there any significant difference between working in Baltimore as an employee of the Social Security Administration and working in Hartford as an employee of an insurance company? When Britain experimented after World War II with nationalizing, denationalizing, and renationalizing its steel industry, most of the employees (and lots of other people, too) had trouble discerning any difference. Some of the characters who frequent the halls of Congress seem far more individualistic (or at least more idiosyncratic) than the people who pass through the corridors of business.

Economic Theory and Government Action

The economic way of thinking attempts to explain the workings of society on the assumption that all participants want to advance their own interests and try to do so in a rational way. The marginal-cost/marginal-revenue rule that we introduced explicitly in Chapter 9, but have in fact been using throughout the book, is merely a formal expression of these assumptions: The way to advance one's interests is to expand each activity whose marginal revenue exceeds its marginal cost and to contract any activity whose marginal cost is greater than its marginal revenue. The economist does not assume, as we've pointed out before, that money or material goods are the only costs and revenues (or benefits) that consumers and producers care about, or that the interests people pursue are necessarily narrow and selfish ones. Economic theory can throw light on the social consequences of every kind of human interest. Why shouldn't that apply to the human purposes and the social processes that control the course of government activities?

Our answer is that it *does* apply. The principles of social interaction that guide production of *Time* or *Newsweek* are not so different from those that guide production of the *Federal Reserve Bulletin* as people commonly suppose. Governments as well as privately owned firms produce commodities and services. Governments, too, can do that only by obtaining productive resources whose opportunity cost is the value of what they would have produced in their next most valuable employment. Governments as well as privately owned firms therefore must bid for the resources they want and offer the owners of those resources adequate incentives. You'll want to note (we'll come back to it) that the government can use negative as well as positive incentives: The threat of imprisonment, for example, may be a major incentive as some people decide what portion of their income to offer the Internal Revenue Service each spring. United Way can't use that inducement. Governments even face the problem of marketing their output and of price searching, though monetary prices play a much smaller role in the distribution of government products.

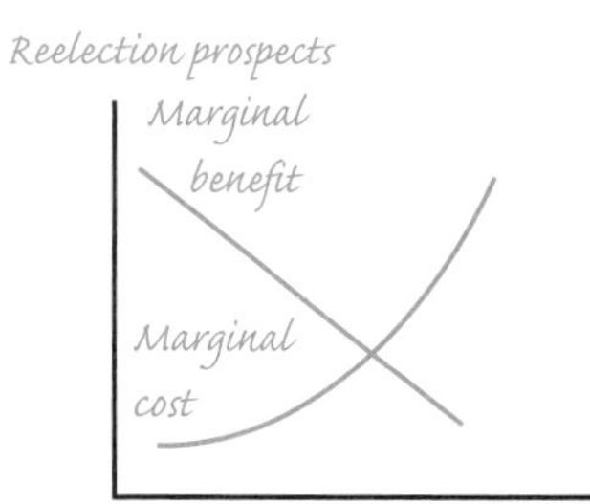

But there can be no doubt that demand curves exist for government-provided goods and that, because these goods are characteristically scarce, they must be rationed by means of some discriminatory criteria. And the people with a demand for government goods will consequently compete to satisfy those criteria, to pay the established price. The main advantage of looking at government in this way is that it counters the tendency to think of government as a *deus ex machina*: a heaven-sent power that can resolve difficulties as magically as a playwright does in the final act of every farce. It makes our expectations of government more realistic. It encourages us to ask about the conditions that enable government to act effectively in any given circumstance and not just to suppose that government always gets what it wants or catches what it chases. This way of looking at government also reminds us that the immediately preceding sentence was misleading in its suggestion that government is an "it"; for *government is many different people interacting on the basis of prevailing property rights.*

If you're wondering what property rights have to do with the behavior of government, you may have forgotten momentarily that economists use the concept of property rights to describe the rules of the game. Every participant in the processes of government, from voters through civil-service employees to the president, has certain expectations about what voters or civil servants or the president can and may do. Those expectations reflect *property rights*. Maybe it would help if we substituted for *property rights* the phrase *what people think they can get away with*. Unfortunately, that has connotations of conniving and unethical behavior that we don't intend at all. But the phrase does convey the force of the property-rights concept; the actions that people take will depend on their expectations about the consequences of those actions, on the anticipated marginal benefits and marginal costs to themselves of the decisions they're weighing. That's as true in the Senate Office Building as it is on the floor of the New York Stock Exchange. The key to understanding each of those worlds is a grasp of the very different property rights of senators and of stockholders.

The Right to Use Coercion

There is one significant difference between government and nongovernment that doesn't grow indistinct or disappear as we inspect it more carefully. *Government possesses a generally conceded and exclusive right to coerce adults*. The right is *generally* conceded, but not universally; thoroughgoing anarchists don't grant it, and neither do those who accept government in principle but reject as illegitimate the authority of the particular government under which they live. It's an *exclusive* right because, as we say, "people don't have the right to take the law into their own hands";

everyone is supposed to appeal to officers of government (police, judges, legislators) when coercion seems called for. And it's the right to coerce *adults* that uniquely distinguishes government, because parents are generally conceded the right to coerce children under certain circumstances.

What does it mean to coerce? *To coerce means to induce cooperation by threatening to violently reduce people's options*. Coercion should be contrasted with the other way of obtaining cooperation from people, which is persuasion. *To persuade means to induce cooperation by promising to expand people's options*. In a few cases we may not be able to agree whether particular actions constitute coercion or persuasion. These cases will often turn out to involve real or alleged deception, so that our disagreement turns on the issue of what people actually thought their options were when they were induced by others to cooperate. Or we might be disagreeing about the rights that we think people *ought* to have. But this definition will usually allow us to distinguish coercive from noncoercive efforts to influence the behavior of others. It is only to government that we grant the right to secure cooperation by threatening to withdraw options, to reduce people's freedom, to take away some of their rights.

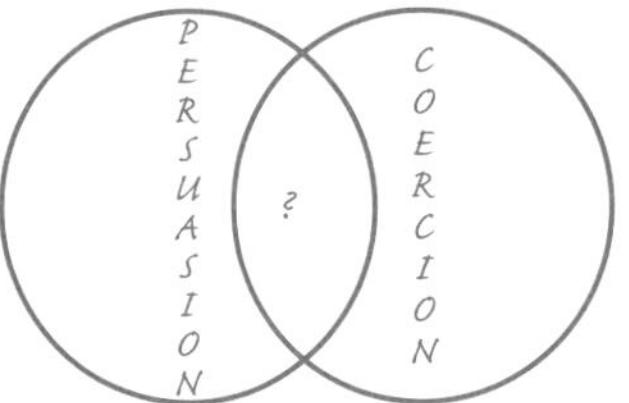

Coercion has a bad reputation, because most of us believe (or think we believe) that people should generally be allowed to do what they want to do. In addition, coercion implies authority, and many of us react with automatic hostility to claims of authority. But the traffic laws that tell us we must drive on the right and stop when the light turns red simultaneously coerce us and expand our freedom. The reason they expand our freedom is that they also coerce others. We all get where we're going faster and more safely because we accept the coercion of traffic laws. This is the traditional defense of government and its right to coerce: We may all be able to achieve greater freedom and expanded options if we all accept some limitations on our freedom and some reduction in our options.

Is Government Necessary?

But do we have to use coercion? Couldn't we get equally good results by relying on voluntary cooperation? We have seen throughout this book that voluntary exchange is the principal mechanism of coordination in our society. Why couldn't voluntary exchange become the *only* means through which we induce cooperation? By asking this question seriously and pushing for an answer, we can gain some additional insights into the capabilities and limitations of the various ways in which we try to get things done.

One way to get at the issue is to ask what would happen if there were no government at all in our society. What problems would arise? Would important tasks cease to be performed? Couldn't people resolve those problems and accomplish those tasks either through individual action or by forming voluntary associations? A good example with which to begin sorting out the issues is the case of police protection. Would there be no police if there were no government? That can't be the case, because private police forces exist at the present time. But these forces supplement a basic, given level of government police protection, providing additional protection for those who want it and are willing to pay for it. Could we obtain that basic protection in the absence of government?

Excluding Nonpayers

Why not? If there were no government, people who wanted police protection could simply purchase it from private security agencies—much as those people do who aren't satisfied with the service that government provides now. Wouldn't that system be more fair than the one we actually have? People with lots of property to protect and little time, inclination, or ability to protect it themselves would have to pay for the service. Those who own little property or are in a good position to guard it themselves wouldn't have to pay taxes for police protection that doesn't really benefit them. We make people pay for their own food, rather than providing it out of tax revenues, in part because we know that people want vastly different quantities and qualities. Why not use the same system for police protection?

The correct answer is *not* that police protection is a "basic necessity"; food is even more basic and necessary. The difference is that food can be supplied exclusively to those who pay for it and denied entirely to those who refuse to pay. And that's not altogether the case with police protection. The patrol officers whom my neighbors hire to guard their houses provide a measure of security also to my house, as a spillover benefit, when they patrol our street. Potential burglars won't realize that I haven't subscribed to the neighborhood security service and that they're consequently safe from apprehension if they break into my house. In fact, the burglars may *not* be altogether safe if they do that. The patrol officers might decide that they can most effectively protect their customers' property by arresting *all* the burglars they discover, regardless of whose property is being burglarized. That gives me protection for which I didn't pay.

In much the same way, firefighters hired to protect my neighbors' houses might choose to put out a grass fire in my yard or a blaze in my attic just to keep it from spreading to their customers' property. And when they extinguish fires on their customers' property, they diminish the chance that the property of adjacent nonsubscribers will catch fire. In both cases, someone who doesn't pay nonetheless acquires a benefit from production of the good. The key feature is the inability of the producers—the police officers or the firefighters—to exclude nonpayers.

The Free-Rider Problem

When people can obtain a good whether they pay for it or not, they have less incentive to pay. They're tempted to become *free riders: people who accept benefits without paying their share of the cost of providing those benefits*. But if no one has an incentive to pay the costs, no one will have an incentive to provide the benefits. As a result, goods won't be produced, despite the fact that everyone values them more than the cost of producing them.

Who will have the incentive to supply a good if people can obtain it without paying for it?

The free-rider concept describes one of the most frustrating problems in the study of social organization. It especially frustrates those who don't understand why the problem exists and who therefore keep insisting that it *ought* to go away: "We can lick the energy problem if each of us will only . . . ." "There would be no litter on our highways if each of us would only . . . ." "If each of us studies the issues and goes to the polls on election day . . . ." "If every nation would only renounce forever the use of force as a means of resolving international disagreements . . . ." Those who plead so plaintively in all these and dozens of similar cases recognize correctly that we could all gain "if each of us would only." They are frustrated by the persistent failure of people to do what would clearly and by everyone's admission make them all better off.

The free-rider problem frustrates economists, too, because economists encounter so much resistance when they try to persuade people that *each will not do what is in the interest of all unless it is in the interest of each*. People's actions are guided by the costs they expect to bear and the benefits they expect to receive *as a result of those actions*. If the benefits accruing to Serena Dippity will be exactly the same for all practical purposes whether or not she takes a particular action, but she will incur significant costs by taking it, she will not take the action. If Serena is noble and generous, she will derive a great deal of benefit from helping others while thinking lightly of the sacrifices she makes to do so and will, consequently, take some actions other, less noble and less generous persons will not take. That must be stressed, because the free-rider concept definitely does not assert that people are completely selfish or that altruism plays no part in social life. Quite to the contrary, no society could continue to exist in which people were *completely* selfish. We asserted in Chapter 12—and will remind you again here—that some amount of genuine concern for the well-being of others is essential if any social cooperation at all is to occur. Neither markets nor governments could exist among people with no ability to empathize, to internalize at least some of what others experience.

If all wheat farmers . . . . What would you predict?

Positive Externalities and Free Riders

In stressing the significance of the free-rider concept, the economist is insisting only that people have *limited* concepts of self-interest, that they do not by and large entertain the inner feelings of others, especially more distant others, with as much vividness and force as they experience costs and benefits that impinge on them more directly. The economist who calls attention to the free-rider problem is saying that positive externalities exist as well as negative ones and that these externalities encourage people to behave as free riders. *Positive externalities are benefits that decision makers do not take into account when making their decisions*. Positive externalities raise this question: Will anyone have an adequate incentive to create those benefits, or will everyone wait and hope to receive them as a spillover benefit from the actions of others?

Positive externalities or spillover benefits are probably even more widespread in modern societies than are spillover costs, the negative externalities that give rise to complaints about pollution. Homeowners who maintain beautiful lawns produce spillover benefits for neighbors and passersby. People with engaging smiles distribute spillover benefits to everyone they encounter. Citizens who take the trouble to inform themselves on community issues improve the quality of public decisions and thereby benefit everyone. Moreover, ordinary producers and sellers regularly and as a matter of course provide benefits to customers considerably greater than what the customers are required to pay for them. Eliminating all spillover benefits would be as absurdly impossible as eliminating all negative externalities. Nonetheless, spillover benefits and the free-riding tendencies they encourage do create some serious social problems. Coercion through the agency of government is one way of dealing with these problems.

The amount of mutually advantageous exchange that occurs in a society is limited by transaction costs.

Remember that exchange always entails transaction costs. Demander and supplier must find each other, agree on what they're willing to offer and want to receive, and make reasonably sure that they're actually getting what they expected to get. Sellers in particular must incur transaction costs to be sure that nonpayers don't obtain the goods that they're supplying. Long-established business operations keep down transaction costs by reducing them to routine, thereby enabling all parties to derive larger net benefits from exchange. When transaction costs are so high, however, that they exceed the benefits from exchange, exchange won't occur and the potential benefits will be lost. *Government can be viewed as an institution for reducing transaction costs through the use of coercion*.

Law and Order

Let's take a look at some traditional functions of government to see how much this approach explains. We begin with the problem of "law and order." We can now summarize the argument of the last few pages: High transaction costs make it difficult to exclude nonpayers from the spillover benefits of police patrols. To prevent free riders from destroying the incentive to supply police protection, government employs coercion. It supplies the service to everyone and pays for it with involuntary contributions called taxes.

A judicial system for resolving disputes that arise between citizens could perhaps be created through voluntary efforts somewhat more easily than a police force, as is suggested by the existence of numerous arbitration systems financed by voluntary efforts. But everyone benefits when the people occupying a common territory are all subject to the same system of laws and judicial rulings. Uniform and consistently enforced rules that are binding on all, whether or not they consent, make it much easier for everyone to plan with confidence. And the ability to plan confidently is what distinguishes a cooperating society from a chaotic mob. Because a system of laws and courts confers substantial benefits on people whether or not they choose to help pay for it and to be bound by it, societies use coercion to create and operate systems of justice.

National Defense

How can a supplier of national defense make it available exclusively to those who have paid their defense subscription fee?

National defense is a traditional function of government, and it provides the classic example of a benefit that can't be provided, except at prohibitive cost, exclusively to those who pay for it. Because free-rider problems would make it practically impossible to rely on voluntary contributions to finance a system of national defense, societies resort to coercion, collecting the funds through taxation.

Note carefully, however, because the point is easily overlooked, that government does not have to rely entirely on coercion to produce the good called national defense. And no government does. The taxes used to finance a military force are coercive levies. But when the funds are used to hire people for the armed forces and to purchase equipment from suppliers, government is relying on persuasion and voluntary cooperation, just as it does in supplying police officers and judges. This raises an interesting question. Why will a government sometimes use coercion to achieve its objectives when it would appear that persuasion would work just as well or even better? Why will a government choose to draft people into the armed forces (and onto juries) rather than rely on volunteers? Most people who work for government are persuaded, not compelled to do so. Why are some coerced? The dangers to which military personnel are subject cannot be the whole answer, because people are attracted into far more dangerous occupations without conscription. We'll suggest an explanation a little further on.

Roads and Schools

What about roads? Would we enjoy an adequate system of streets and highways if we didn't use coercion to finance them? Be careful;

an adequate system doesn't necessarily mean the quantity and quality we now have. Roads are oversupplied if the benefits from particular additions are less than the costs of making those additions, and that can surely occur. But is there any reason to expect a systematic undersupply of streets and highways if their provision is left entirely to voluntary efforts? The transaction costs could be rather staggering if all streets and highways were owned and operated by people who had to rely entirely on tolls for the collection of revenue. The benefits, moreover, don't accrue exclusively to those who drive. People who live along a dusty gravel road receive benefits from the paving of that road even if they never drive. The experience of those who have built roads in remote areas or in private developments without using coercion suggests both that it can be done and that the costs of securing cooperation by exclusively voluntary means can be quite high.

What is the case for using coercion to finance education? The argument here is that people will acquire education only up to the point at which the marginal cost to themselves equals the marginal benefit to themselves. But education supposedly generates substantial positive externalities, benefits that accrue to people other than the person acquiring the education. Thus, everyone in a democracy benefits when citizens learn to read and to think more clearly. Because we don't take account of the spillover benefits to others in deciding how much education to obtain, we obtain less than the optimal amount. By using taxes to subsidize education, the government lowers its cost to potential students and induces them to acquire more than they otherwise would. The question arises, as it does with roads, whether the use of coercion to prevent undersupply does not lead in practice to oversupply. We'll return to that question.

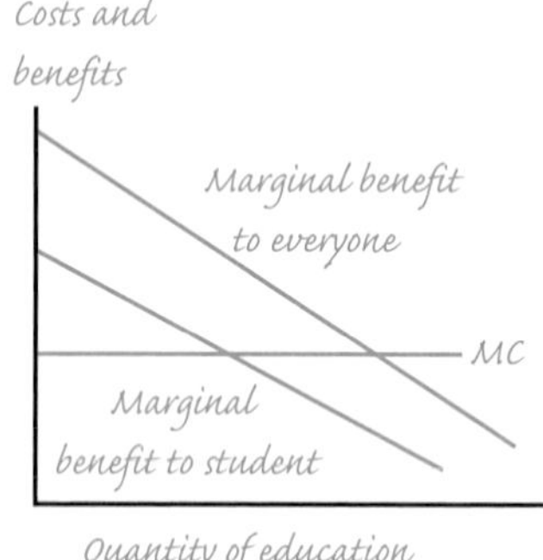

Income Redistribution

Another important category of government action is the provision of special benefits—money grants, food stamps, medical care, housing subsidies, and a variety of social services—to impoverished or disabled people. Why does this kind of activity require the use of coercion? Why don't we leave it to voluntary philanthropy, rather than compel people to contribute through the tax system? One part of the answer is that charity is subject to the free-rider problem. Assume that all citizens are charitably disposed and want to see more income made available to especially poor and unfortunate people. Although some citizens derive direct satisfaction from contributing to a charitable cause, most would prefer that problems be solved and suffering be relieved at a minimum cost to themselves. They want to see poor people helped, but they also want to see others do the helping. And so they tend to behave like free riders. They hold back somewhat on their contributions in the hope that others will contribute enough to take care of the problem. But with everyone waiting for others to contribute, contributions fall short of the amount that everyone would prefer to see raised. Under such circumstances taxation can make people want to contribute more by assuring them that others are also doing their share.

The Regulation of Voluntary Exchange

What about the extensive list of government activities that fall under the category of regulation? Why do federal, state, and local governments regulate so many of the activities of citizens, using coercion to control the terms on which people are allowed to engage in voluntary exchange? Putting it in just that way—using coercion to control voluntary exchange—may prompt us to think a little harder and longer about all the things that government does in the name of regulation.

Part of the answer is the widely held belief that the powerful and unscrupulous will take unfair advantage of the weak and the innocent unless the government regulates certain kinds of voluntary exchange. This is the parentalistic argument,[1] which no doubt has some merit but which has also often been abused by special interests precisely to take unfair advantage of the weak and the innocent. Transaction costs provide another part of the answer. It would be very costly for all of us to carry our own scales to check the accuracy of the ones that butchers use and our own gallon cans to be sure the gasoline pumps aren't cheating us. When physicians must be licensed and new drugs approved by the Food and Drug Administration before they can be marketed, buyers are spared the cost of evaluating goods whose quality most of them would be unable to assess for themselves, except at prohibitive costs. By compelling sellers to obtain certification, government agencies can enable us all to make satisfactory exchanges at lower cost. A substantial amount of government regulation can be viewed as coercion designed to reduce the cost of acquiring information.

The glaring flaw in this defense of regulation, however, is that it fails to account for the enthusiasm with which sellers so often support regulation. Those who have studied the matter know very well that the demand for government regulation of sellers more often originates with the sellers than with their customers. We saw in Chapter 10 why this occurs: Sellers are eager to restrict competition, and government regulation in the name of consumer protection is a technique of proved effectiveness for eliminating competition. But why do the victims cooperate? Why does government employ coercion to promote special interests when it's

[1]Most people would say *paternalistic*, but *parentalistic* is a more accurate and less sexist term.

supposed to be the responsibility of government to promote the public interest?

Government and the Public Interest

The basic answer suggested by economic theory brings us back in a surprising way to the problem with which we began this chapter. The coercive actions taken by government to compensate for the limitations inherent in purely voluntary cooperation are themselves subject to the same limitations. The reason for this is that coercion itself depends on voluntary cooperation. Persuasion always precedes coercion, because government will not act until particular people have been persuaded to act. Government is not the genie in Aladdin's lamp. Government is people interacting, paying attention to the expected costs and benefits of the alternatives that they perceive. The disconcerting part of all this is that the problems created by transaction costs, positive externalities, and free riders are particularly acute in the political life of democracies.

A surprising number of people assume without thinking about it that "government acts in the public interest." But does it really? Does it always do so? Why do we think so? Do citizens become more virtuous when they move from the line in the supermarket to the line at the polling place? Do people's characters change when they give up a post in industry or academia to take a position with the government? Suppose we define the public interest as what everyone would want if everyone were adequately informed and impartial. Does economic theory have anything useful to say about the likelihood that government actions will proceed from adequate information and an impartial viewpoint?

Those whose decisions make up the sum of government actions will pay attention to the information actually available to them and the incentives that actually confront them. Economic theory predicts that this information and these incentives will tend to be both limited and biased.

Information and Democratic Governments

Rational ignorance exists when it's not worthwhile to learn.

We can begin with citizen voters. None of us knows enough to cast an adequately informed vote. To persuade yourself that this is so, conduct a little mental experiment. Suppose you know that your vote, whether on a candidate or a ballot position, will determine the outcome of the election; your vote and your vote alone will decide the question. How much information will you gather before casting that crucial vote? A lot would depend, of course, on the importance of the office or the issue. But you would surely invest far more time and energy in acquiring information than you do when you're just one voter among 50 thousand or 50 million. As it is, most citizens, including intelligent, well-read, and public-spirited citizens, step into the polling place on election day equipped only with a lot of prejudices, a few hunches, some poorly tested bits of information, and vast areas of total ignorance. We do this because it's rational to do so! Given the actual importance of our one vote in 50 thousand or 50 million, it would be an almost unconscionable waste of time for us to learn enough to cast an adequately informed vote. The issue is not simply one of selfishness or lack of dedication to the well-being of society. A voter who wanted to make a personal sacrifice for the good of the commonwealth could do far more per hour, per dollar, or per calorie in social-service volunteer work than by gathering enough information to cast an adequately informed vote.

"But if everybody thought that way," goes the standard objection, "democracy wouldn't work." This objection is another instance of the argument that the free-rider phenomenon doesn't exist because the world would be a more satisfactory place if it did not exist. Those who are committed to democracy had better concern themselves with ways to make it work when citizen voters are uninformed and misinformed and not pretend that voters have knowledge they obviously don't have.

Some defenders of democracy aren't overly discouraged by the incompetence of citizen voters. They rely on elected representatives to acquire the information that must be available if decisions are to be made in the public interest. Their confidence has a reasonable foundation in reality. Because the vote of each legislator has a far greater probability of affecting the outcome, because legislators can use the information they acquire to influence others in significant ways, because legislators are provided with staff and other information-gathering resources, because many people will have a strong interest in making relevant information available to legislators, because legislators' votes are monitored and must be defended—for all these reasons, elected representatives are far more likely to be adequately informed about the issues on which they vote than are ordinary citizens.

The Interests of Elected Officials

But even if we can assume that legislators' votes are adequately informed, are we entitled to assume that they will be votes in the public interest? Are elected representatives impartial? Another way of asking the same question is to ask whether they will always vote in the way that the information available to them tells them they ought to vote. Economic theory assumes that people act in their own interest, not that they act in the public interest. Sometimes it will be in a legislator's interest to pursue

Paying $2,000 one year from now for $1,000 in benefits right now is worthwhile to someone who wouldn't otherwise be around one year from now.

the public interest. But finding ways to produce such harmony is the major issue in the design of political institutions; we can't simply *assume* this advantageous concord without asking whether the institutions under which we live are likely to produce it. Because an interest in reelection is a common and healthy interest among most elected officials, we'll focus our analysis on this one particular private interest. Is an interest in being reelected likely to lead elected officials to vote and act in the public interest?

Let's begin by noticing how it limits their planning horizons. Elected officials can't afford to look too far ahead. Results must be available by the next election or the incumbent could be replaced by someone who offers better promises. We shall see in the last part of this book how an emphasis on the short run makes it difficult for governments to deal effectively with recessions and inflations. But the same will be true for any policies. Elected officials will tend to discount heavily the value of all future costs that aren't expected until after the next election and to crowd into the period before the election as many benefits as they possibly can. Their interest in reelection will thus keep them from fully using their own superior knowledge about the consequences of particular policies.

In listing some of the reasons why legislators are likely to be well informed, we mentioned two that also explain why legislators will not always vote in the way that their information tells them they ought to vote. These were the last two reasons cited: Many people have a strong interest in making relevant information available to legislators, and legislators' votes are monitored and must be defended. The problem is that the interest in providing information (or lobbying) and in holding legislators accountable for their actions is concentrated in special-interest groups. The positive externalities associated with the political process make this almost inevitable. Some of the clearest examples of this process at work are the grants that the federal government makes to local governments to finance local projects that would not be undertaken without those grants. They would not be undertaken because the benefits that would accrue would be less than the costs that would be incurred. Why does the federal government subsidize such projects and thus secure the completion of projects that cannot pass a benefit–cost analysis?

Suppose the city of Metropole examines the feasibility of constructing a light-rail system, which it does not currently have. It hires traffic engineers, civil engineers, demographers, urban planners, economists, and other experts to estimate the dollar costs of constructing the system and the dollar benefits to residents of the city and its suburbs. And suppose they conclude that the direct costs of construction will be twice as high as all the future benefits (tangible and intangible, probable and improbable, real and merely imaginable) when all costs and benefits have been discounted at appropriate rates. That ought to be the end of the matter. But there's a good chance it won't be. Lots of local special interests want that light-rail system to be constructed. First and foremost are all the people in the construction business. Right behind them come all the citizens who never outgrew their childhood love of trains, followed closely by all the local boosters who want Metropole to be more like New York and Chicago and believe that a world-class city requires a system of commuter trains. The major newspapers of Metropole are almost certain to line up behind such a glorious project with so much potential for contributing to the growth of the area and especially the growth of advertisers. Finally, but crucially, come the local politicians: not only city and county officials but also the area's representatives in Congress and the state's two senators, who would all very much like to be known as people who can bring home the bacon.

The politicians will go to work in Washington, D.C., in search of a federal grant that will cover 60 percent of the construction costs and thereby push the project over the threshold for local voters. And why should taxpayers of the United States pay 60 percent of the cost of constructing a project that cannot pass a benefit–cost test? Because most of them won't be watching! The few extra dollars that taxpayers in Los Angeles and everywhere else will have to pay to finance a boondoggle in Metropole won't matter enough even to stir their curiosity. And so legislators from Los Angeles and California can be persuaded by legislators from Metropole to vote for Metropole's light-rail system, with the implicit understanding that the Metropole politicians will support a Los Angeles boondoggle when LA's turn comes around. The system generates large benefits for local politicians who will be closely watched and generously supported in their bids for reelection by the construction industry, the railroad romantics, the local boosters, and the Metropole daily newspapers.

Legislators pay more attention to those who are themselves paying attention.

Concentrated Benefits, Dispersed Costs

The *process* is always the same. The few who have much to gain invest vast resources in trying to influence the political process. The many with more to gain in total but less to gain individually invest almost nothing. *The logic of the situation within democratic political processes is to concentrate benefits on the well-organized and well-informed few who gain the most and disperse the costs on the unorganized and ill-informed mass who have little to gain individually*. Legislators respond to this sort of pressure, because a substantial number of them find that doing so serves their interest in being reelected. It seems rather futile to fault them for this, because an *ex*-legislator with untarnished principles is a less effective public servant than an intelligent and honest legislator who has bent a few principles to survive and fight another day.

The fault lies with the positive externalities that prompt most of us to behave like free riders, hoping that someone else will assume the costs of lobbying for the measures from which we would all benefit. Nevertheless, the demonstration by modern political economists of the tendency within democratic governments to concentrate benefits and disperse costs within policymaking has been one of the most important contributions to our intellectual understanding of why good politics is not necessarily good economics.

Positive Externalities and Government Policies

Our conclusion should come as no surprise. Government policies will tend to be dominated by special interests. Government will lean toward actions that harm many people just a little bit, rather than actions that displease a few people very much. Government policies will be guided not so much by the public interest as by an endless succession of extremely partial interests. This is why consumer interests win the oratorical contests, but producer interests control policy. The interests of producers are simply more concentrated, more sharply focused. Producers know that their action or inaction can make a significant difference to their own welfare, so it's in their interest to act. But no individual consumer can expect more than a small benefit from political action, so none of them has an incentive to accept the costs.

Is this why the use of coercion to prevent an undersupply of roads often leads to an oversupply? The taxpayers' general interest in economy doesn't fare well when it goes head to head with a small group's intense interest in having a road or building a road. The same analysis applies to schooling. Those who produce schooling (our own vested interest, let it be noted) can make life difficult for legislators who try to save taxpayers money by reducing expenditures on education or research. Here is an explanation for the otherwise puzzling behavior of legislatures that approve larger and larger expenditures even when every member favors reduced expenditures. There is no way to cut a budget without cutting specific projects. With every special interest organized to make certain that the cuts occur in someone else's project, expenditures cannot be reduced.

Why did we long have a military draft in this country, and what is the probability that Congress will restore it? Military conscription extends the use of coercion into areas where persuasion is quite capable of securing the cooperation we want (at least in peacetime). The draft probably persisted as long as it did because the military establishment had a strong and sharply focused interest in maintaining a ready flow of personnel for the armed forces, whereas most of those who were adversely affected by the draft had a stronger incentive to find a personal escape route than to attack the whole system. It is interesting to note how many current advocates of reinstating the draft, especially since 9/11 and the war in Iraq, are now talking about *universal* conscription of young people for short-term service of some kind. Will this tactic (assuming that it is a tactic) increase the number of those who are opposed to the draft? Or will it reduce the expected cost to each draftee below that critical point at which he or she would be willing to do political battle to prevent reestablishment of the draft?

What can we say about government actions to relieve poverty? We can predict that legislators will be slow to replace in-kind transfers with money transfers. Farmers benefit from the food-stamp program, the building trades benefit from housing subsidies, the medical care industry expands with health care assistance, teachers benefit from educational subsidies for the poor, and social workers know that giving money to the poor will never be as advantageous as hiring more members of the "helping professions." The political influence of these groups makes it easier for legislatures to support in-kind transfers to the poor than to support money transfers. There may be other and better grounds for rejecting money transfers, but this alternative would get more respectful attention in Congress if money were produced and sold by a money industry.

How Do People Identify the Public Interest?

None of this implies that farmers, hospital administrators, or social workers have no regard for the public interest. It implies only that they all have *some* regard for their own interests. And even those who work for government agencies charged specifically to protect the public interest define it with reference to their own special interests.

Consider, for example, a member of the Food and Drug Administration (FDA), responsible for preventing the introduction of new drugs without adequate testing. What is adequate testing? It's testing that makes sure we know all the side effects of a new drug before we allow it on the market. But we can *never* be sure. All we can do is acquire additional information and thus reduce the risk that someone will be killed or seriously harmed by an unanticipated side effect. How far should we reduce the risk? Not *too* far, because there are costs as well as benefits attached to additional testing. A major cost will be the lives lost and the suffering not relieved because the drug isn't available while it's being tested.

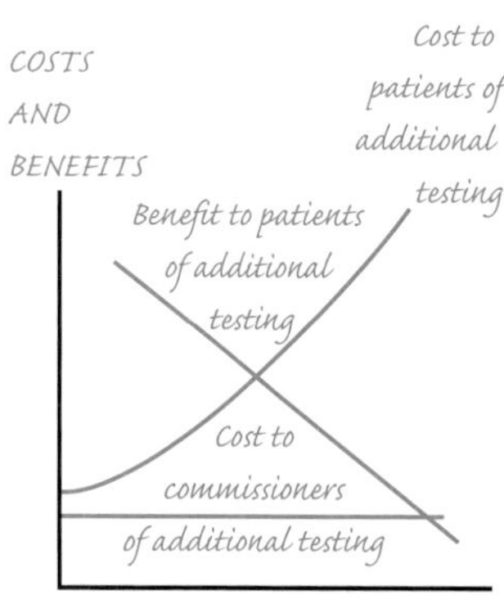

How will an FDA commissioner evaluate these two costs: the lives lost through premature introduction and the lives lost through excessive delay in introduction of new drugs? People will blame the FDA if an approved drug turns out to have disastrous side effects, and they will applaud the FDA if it refuses to approve a drug that subsequently turns out to have disastrous side effects in other countries. But almost no one will condemn the FDA for lives lost or suffering endured while a drug that eventually proves to be highly successful is being tested. FDA commissioners will consequently find it in the public interest to test drugs beyond the point at which the marginal benefit to patients equals the marginal cost to patients.

The Prisoners' Dilemma

An interesting concept that illuminates the central feature in many of the problems we've been discussing is the prisoners' dilemma, a name that reflects the original exposition of the dilemma through a story about two prisoners and a clever prosecutor.

Let's suppose that every citizen urgently desires Good Government and would gladly give up two hours of leisure per week to secure it. Those two hours would be spent, let's say, investigating current issues, discussing policy questions with other citizens, and monitoring the actions of legislators. If all or almost all citizens contribute those two hours per week, Good Government is assured. Will we get Good Government? Because, by assumption, every citizen sincerely desires Good Government and is willing to make the required sacrifice to obtain it, it would seem that we ought to. Nonetheless, we probably will not.

Here is the dilemma. Each citizen knows that his or her decision will not affect the outcome. If I spend two hours Doing My Duty but none of my fellow citizens do theirs, my efforts will be wasted. I will be just one informed voice and vote lost in a hundred million uninformed voices and votes. I will have given up two hours of bowling (or whatever is my most valued forgone opportunity) to accomplish exactly nothing. On the other hand, if I decide just to do my own thing while all my fellow citizens are Doing Their Duty, I will get all the advantages of Good Government plus two hours of recreation at the alleys as a bonus. And so my *dominant strategy* is to go bowling. I will always be better off if I bowl than if I Do My Duty, because I cannot through my own decision affect anything except whether my time gets spent in tedious politicking or in joyous bowling.

Unfortunately, choosing recreation over duty will be the dominant strategy for everyone else, too, with the consequence that we will not get Good Government even though everyone wants it and is willing to contribute his or her share of what is required to obtain it. We can summarize all this in the diagram

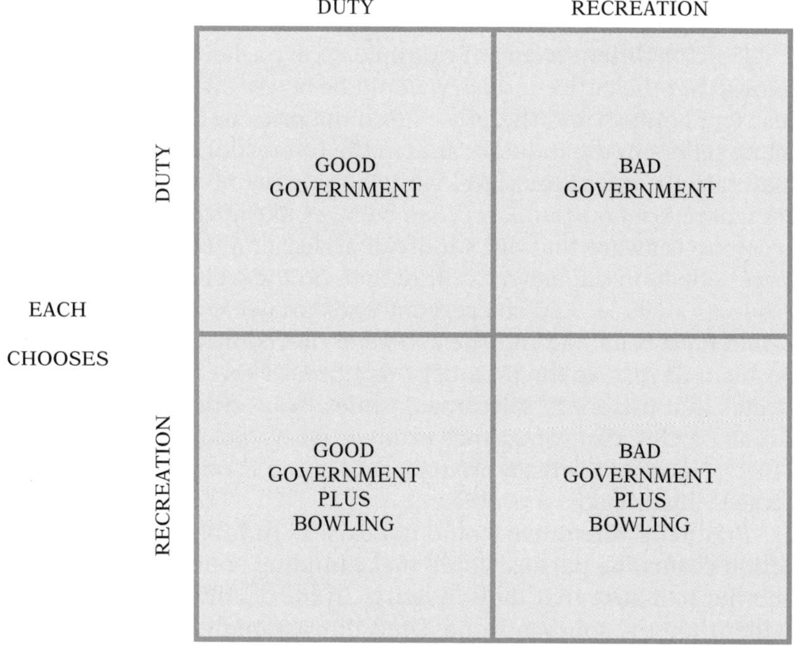

Figure 13–1 **A prisoners' dilemma**

of Figure 13–1. Each citizen follows the dominant strategy in choosing Duty or Recreation, with the results portrayed. The society ends up in the southeast square despite the fact that every single member prefers the northwest square. That's the dilemma.

There are four possible payoffs for each individual who chooses. The one who must give up bowling to Do His Duty will always be better off by choosing Recreation over Duty, because by so doing he obtains the good of Bowling. The choices of others determine whether he gets Good or Bad Government. But each of the others faces the same situation. So all choose Recreation and all end up with Bad Government, despite the fact that all would be willing to give up the equivalent of Bowling to obtain Good Government.

Dilemmas of this sort are fairly common. Everyone in the city wants clean air, for example, and would be willing to reduce driving to obtain it. But since no *one's* decision can measurably affect the quality of the air, everyone chooses to continue driving, and the city's air becomes unbreatheable. Everyone would be better off if all drivers chose a substitute for driving alone when the substitute was available at only a small extra cost. Acceptance of the small extra cost would reward everyone with the large benefit of uncrowded streets. But what is in the interest of all drivers is not in the interest of each driver at the time each driver has to make a decision.

Here's a different sort of example. Every seller in an industry knows that the entire industry would be better off if each seller restricted output and thereby caused the price to rise. But with many sellers in the industry, it is in the interest of each seller to maintain the old output level while hoping (vainly) that other sellers will restrict output. Everyone behaves like a free rider because everyone is aware that one's individual decision has a much larger effect on one's own welfare than on the welfare of the group as a whole. And so everyone ends up worse off than each would have been had they been able to overcome the free-rider problem or resolve the prisoners' dilemma. This example demonstrates that prisoners' dilemmas, while always frustrating to the acting parties, can sometimes produce desirable consequences for others. In other words, a prisoners' dilemma is not always the same thing as a social problem.

Prisoners' dilemmas would not exist in the absence of transaction costs. The parties would make binding contracts with one another to assure that they ended up in the northwest square rather than the southeast one. One contract might specify that the bowling fan forfeits three hours in the lanes if he fails to put in a faithful two hours per week Doing His Duty. It thereby becomes in his interest to Do His Duty, and in everyone else's interest to Do Their Duty, because they are all constrained by similar contracts; and so the society enjoys life in the northwest square. As you realize, however, it would be much too costly to devise, write, negotiate, record, monitor, and enforce such contracts. (Who can tell for sure whether the bowler is putting in a faithful two hours or just going through the motions?) Transaction costs thereby prevent us from doing what we all want to do.

We work at the problem, however, in an infinite variety of interesting ways. It would take another book to describe all the formal and informal institutions that evolve in a society as people try in their varied social exchanges to control the negative effects of prisoners' dilemmas. We use smiles, frowns, customs, conventions, formal and informal contracts, deposits, and even constitutions. You can very usefully think of the Constitution of the United States as an institution that functions to control prisoners' dilemmas, by constraining the private interests of people who claim to be serving the public interest.

The Limits of Political Institutions

If all this is unsettling to those for whom it is an article of faith that the government takes care of the public interest, it may be time to question this article of faith. Perhaps it stems from the habit of equating "government" with "nation" and extending to the former the reverence felt for the latter. Or it may be a result of our belief that government is the last resort and therefore must be an effective resort, because we don't like to admit to any unsolvable problems. There's a popular bit of deductive reasoning that also leads toward this conclusion. It asserts that all social problems are the result of human behavior, that human behavior can be altered by law, and that government makes the laws, from which the argument concludes that government can solve all social problems. Alexis de Tocqueville offered a more realistic view in *Democracy in America* (Volume I, Part I, Chapter VIII): "There is no country in which everything can be provided for by the laws or in which political institutions can prove a substitute for common sense and public morality."

Once Over Lightly

Economic theory assumes that the actions of government follow from the decisions of citizens and government officials who are paying attention to the marginal costs and marginal benefits to themselves of alternative courses of action.

The distinguishing characteristic of government is its generally conceded and exclusive right to use coercion. To coerce means to induce cooperation by threatening to reduce people's options. Voluntary cooperation relies exclusively on persuasion, which secures desired behavior by promising additional options.

Coercion is useful to the members of a society because it can sometimes secure the production of goods that everyone values at more than the cost of supplying them, but which would not be supplied through purely voluntary cooperation. A supply failure of this sort is likely to occur when there is no low-cost way of confining supply of a good to those who pay for it or of preventing demanders from becoming free riders.

Coercion may be able to secure the supply of such goods by lowering transaction costs. The traditional activities of government turn out on examination to be largely actions aimed at reducing transaction costs and overcoming free-rider problems.

The coercive activities of government presuppose voluntary cooperation. Persuasion precedes coercion because, in the last analysis, citizens and government officials must be persuaded to employ coercion in particular ways. This implies that the limits on the effectiveness of voluntary cooperation that justify coercive action by government are limitations also on the effectiveness of the government's coercive action.

Positive externalities thoroughly permeate the political process in a democratic government. They make it unlikely that citizen voters will be adequately informed or that elected or appointed officials will consistently act in the way that the information available to them tells them they ought to act.

QUESTIONS FOR DISCUSSION

1. A letter to the *Wall Street Journal* attacking a proposal to privatize the nation's air traffic control system concluded as follows:

   > A business exists to maximize economic return. A government exists to maximize public benefit. No amount of imagined gain in efficiency will offset the loss of public control of either the town stoplight or the nation's air traffic system.

   (a) What does it mean to say that business exists to maximize economic return and government exists to maximize public benefit? Is this a statement of intentions (whose?) or of outcomes?
   (b) Can a business ordinarily earn a large economic return if it does not provide substantial public benefits?
   (c) How can we measure the public benefits flowing from the air traffic control system if users of the system are required to pay the costs of providing those benefits? How can we measure them if users are *not* required to pay but all costs are instead financed from taxes?
   (d) The author of the letter quoted described himself as president of the Aircraft Owners and Pilots Association. Does this suggest to you any reason for his opposition to privatizing air traffic control?
2. In what general, systematic way do the interests pursued by officials in government differ from the interests pursued by people in the private sector? Consider the following cases:
   (a) The president of a state-owned university and the president of a privately-owned university
   (b) A member of the U.S. House of Representatives who aspires to a seat in the Senate and a traveling sales representative for a large business corporation who wants a job as sales manager at one of the firm's plants
   (c) A prominent political figure who wants to become president of the United States and a prominent actor who wants to receive an Academy Award
   (d) An urban police officer and a uniformed guard employed by a private security firm
   (e) A grant-awarding official in the Small Business Administration and a loan officer in a bank
3. In each of the following examples, what are the significant differences between government-owned and non-government-owned enterprises? Why do you think the government owns the enterprises mentioned? What different forms does competition take in the case of government-owned

enterprises? In what different ways do they operate because of their government ownership?

(a) Investor-owned utilities and utilities owned by states or municipalities
(b) State colleges and private colleges
(c) City-owned intraurban bus companies and interurban bus companies such as Greyhound and Trailways
(d) Forest Service campgrounds and privately owned campgrounds
(e) Public libraries and private bookstores

4. A frequent argument in support of government-produced goods is that they are vital to social welfare and therefore their provision cannot safely be left to the "whims" of the marketplace. Does this explain why parks and libraries are usually municipal services, whereas food and medical care are usually secured through the market? Can you suggest a better explanation to account for these cases?
5. Advocates of government regulation often make their case by attacking "unrestrained" or "unbridled" competition. Is competition ever "unrestrained"? What were some of the important restraints on competition that operated in the U.S. economy in the nineteenth century when, according to some accounts, competition was "unrestrained"?
6. Critics of government regulation often try to make a case for the "free" market. Are markets ever completely free? Free from what? Is a market "unfree" if participants operate under laws that prohibit the use of dishonest weights and measures? Laws that prohibit misleading advertising? That prohibit price increases that have not been approved by a government agency? Where do you draw the line between free markets and unfree or regulated markets? Why do you draw it where you do?
7. The text warns about the dangers in speaking of government as an "it" that can be manipulated, like a tool, to do whatever we want done. Isn't it also misleading to use the word *we* the way it's used in the preceding sentence? Who are the "we" who want government to do this or that? Everyone? The majority? All informed and public-spirited citizens? Those who share my interests and my understanding of the situation? What do people mean when they say, "We must use government to control the effects of selfishness and greed"? Who is supposed to control whom in this vision of the way society works?
8. A growing number of Americans are currently living in tightly controlled communities of condominiums, co-ops, or even single-family homes. These communities are usually governed by elected associations of homeowners that establish and enforce rules designed to protect property values. Some students of such residential communities argue that, because they are private governments with the power to collect taxes, provide services, and regulate behavior, they should be subject to the Constitution's restraints on government action.

   (a) Do the governors of such associations use coercion or do they use persuasion to induce residents not to post signs, erect satellite dish antennas, park pickup trucks on the streets, or neglect their lawns and gardens?

(b) Defenders of such associations argue that compliance with the rules is voluntary because residents consent to obey the rules before they purchase. Do you agree? What if the governing association enacts a new rule to which a particular homeowner strongly objects? Is that homeowner's compliance still voluntary?

(c) One critic of such associations argues that consent is not voluntary because such common-property developments are often the most affordable housing available and that people therefore have little choice about living in them. He points to the fact that these developments are the fastest-growing form of new housing in the United States in order to argue that they are private governments and should be subject to the constitutional protections that constrain regular governments. Do you agree?

9. Does either persuasion or coercion enjoy any inherent advantages over the other as a way of inducing cooperation?

   (a) People who are cooperating because they have been persuaded usually want to maintain the relationship. Those who have been coerced will typically be looking for ways to sever the relationship. What does this imply about the level of transaction costs that will be associated with cooperative endeavors in each case?

   (b) Coercion can be used to deny people the opportunity to engage in voluntary cooperation. Does this occur? Why should anyone want to use coercion to prevent others from cooperating on a voluntary basis?

10. Adam Smith assigned to the sovereign or commonwealth the duty of erecting and maintaining those public institutions and those public works, which, though they may be in the highest degree advantageous to a great society, are, however, of such a nature, that the profit could never repay the expense to any individual or small number of individuals, and which it therefore cannot be expected that any individual or small number of individuals should erect or maintain (*The Wealth of Nations*, Book V, Chapter I).

   (a) How does this description of the goods that government should supply differ from the text's description of goods subject to the free-rider problem?

   (b) Smith discusses four public institutions or works that at least partially satisfy his criterion: those "for the defense of the society . . . , for the administration of justice . . . , for facilitating the commerce of the society, and those for promoting the instruction of the people." How does Smith's assignment compare with the duties generally assigned to governments today? Is there any major duty of government that Smith overlooks?

11. Should the members of a volunteer fire department refuse to put out a fire in the home of someone who has refused to contribute to the fire-fighting service? (Assume that no property of subscribers is in danger.) What damage would they be doing by putting out the fire?

12. Is the free-rider phenomenon always a *problem*? Doesn't it sometimes prevent people from cooperating to take advantage of others? Why do cartels generally break down unless they can enlist the support of government with its coercive powers?

13. Most automobile drivers probably exceed the legal speed limits somewhat when they think they can get away with it. Does this imply that they would vote for higher speed limits if given a chance?
14. Here is the opening sentence of a newspaper editorial lamenting the tiny turnout for a public hearing on improving the high schools in a large U.S. city: "Given the number of people who complain about public education, it's amazing how few attend meetings to tell the schools how to do better." Is it really surprising that many complain but few attend meetings?
    (a) What is the cost of complaining? What is the cost of attending a meeting?
    (b) What is the probability that a concerned citizen who spends an evening at a public hearing will actually be able to influence policies in a large urban school district?
    (c) The relative benefit–cost ratios of complaining and attending would seem to provide an adequate explanation for the facts lamented by the newspaper editorialist. But how can we explain the behavior of "activists," those few people who seem always willing to turn out for meetings on even the most inopportune occasions? Are there satisfactions other than that of actually affecting public policy that people can obtain through political participation?
15. Each of the 10 families on a suburban block is likely to have its own power lawn mower. Why don't families more often share a single lawn mower? Try to enumerate the principal transaction costs that stand in the way of such a cooperative arrangement.
16. It's difficult for entertainers to supply their services exclusively to those television viewers who are willing to pay for the entertainment.
    (a) How do entertainers nonetheless manage to secure payment for providing their services to television viewers? Think through the way in which the free-rider problem is handled in radio and television broadcasting. To whom do entertainers sell their services? Through what sequence of transactions do viewers receive the entertainment? How is the free-rider problem handled at each stage?
    (b) Some homeowners today try to get cable television programs without subscribing by picking up the signal from satellites, using their own receiving dishes. How does the use of scramblers and decoders by pay-television companies illustrate the acceptance of transaction costs to eliminate free riders?
17. Why do our courts require citizens who have been selected for jury duty to serve whether they want to or not? Couldn't courts obtain as many jurors as they require on a voluntary basis if they raised the fee for jury duty? Why don't we raise the fee, staff juries with volunteers, and stop imposing the heavy costs of jury duty on so many people who must abandon other valuable activities to do their "jury duty"? How do you suppose the composition of juries would be affected by such a move to a system of all-volunteer jurors? Is it legitimate to use coercion in this case, because serving on a jury is every citizen's duty? If so, why don't we fine people who don't vote? Isn't voting a citizen's duty? Even better, why not fine people who fail a rigorous current affairs test or do not vote? That way we would coerce citizens into casting an informed vote. Or would we?

18. Would you agree that the U.S. Constitution *describes the property rights* of the president, members of Congress, and Supreme Court justices?
    (a) Why does the Constitution prohibit Congress from lowering the salaries of the president or of federal judges during their terms of office?
    (b) Are we likely to be governed better or worse during a president's first term than during the second? (The Constitution prohibits a third term.)
    (c) Would you expect more statesmanlike decisions from members of the House of Representatives, who must stand for reelection every two years, or from justices of the Supreme Court, who are appointed for life?
    (d) Would you expect more statesmanlike decisions from the U.S. Congress if all members were subject to term limits?
19. "If You're Paying, I'll Have Top Sirloin." That was the title of an editorial-page essay by economist Russell Roberts in the *Wall Street Journal*. Roberts used a familiar example to capture neatly the essence of the free-rider dilemma as it applies to congressional spending.
    (a) Suppose that you regularly turn down dessert and an extra drink when you're having lunch alone because these two items would add \$4 to the cost of your \$6 lunch and they aren't worth that much to you. But now suppose you're having lunch with three friends and you have all agreed to split the bill evenly. What will dessert and an extra drink cost you in the second case? Why might you decide in the second case to enjoy dessert and that extra drink?
    (b) Suppose you restrain yourself when ordering even though you know the bill will be split evenly because you don't want to take advantage of your friends. How effective would that restraint be on your ordering if you were going to split the bill evenly with all 100 people eating in the restaurant? What would be the monetary cost to you in this case of ordering the dessert and extra drink?
    (c) If you thoroughly enjoy steak and lobster, by far the most expensive item on the menu, would you be much less inclined to order it if you were paying your own bill than if you were splitting evenly the total bill of *all 100 people* in the restaurant?
    (d) Use Russell Roberts' analogy to explain why Congress so often appropriates money for local projects whose expected benefits, measured in monetary terms, fall far short of their expected monetary costs.
20. How can we retain the advantages of democratic government but reduce the problems caused by prisoners' dilemmas? Here is a radical proposal for reflection and discussion.

    Abolish all congressional staff. Create a one-house legislature with 600 members who serve six-year terms and cannot succeed themselves. Select 100 new legislators each year. Grant automatic eligibility for selection to every citizen who is 25 years of age or older and who has either worked four years *or* earned a high school diploma. Pay each legislator generously and grant each one equally generous lifetime retirement benefits that begin after their six-year term has ended. Then call them to the service of their country *through a lottery*.

(a) Would this system be democratic?
(b) What information and incentives would shape the outcome of the legislative process under this system?
(c) Would this system produce better or worse government than we now have?

TESTI
DEP

14

The Overall Performance of Economic Systems

In the course of using economic theory to explain how commercial societies function, we have paid very little attention to the overall performance of the U.S. economy. That is about to change. We now turn to a *macroeconomic analysis*, which focuses on the performance of the overall economy, as opposed to examining the supply–demand conditions within any particular market or industry. This is the stuff that often makes the evening news. Is the economy "strong," or is it "weak"? Is it growing, or is it falling into a recession? Will the future bring us inflation, deflation, or relatively stable prices? What's happening to the unemployment rate in America? Will the Federal Reserve raise or lower interest rates? What's the status of the federal government's budget? Is it balanced, in a surplus, or in deficit? Should taxes be raised or lowered? What impact will that have on overall economic conditions? What is the present administration doing to improve the economy? Who has the better plan, Democrats or Republicans?

These are all macroeconomic questions, and a source of seemingly endless debate among newspaper columnists, political figures, ax grinders, radio talk-show personalities, and everyday coffee shop pontificators. Everybody seems to have an opinion. We can begin to clear up the muddle by further developing the economic way of thinking on these grand, economy-wide issues in the remaining chapters. In this chapter we shall focus on the most widely used (and, literally, "grossest") indicator of overall economic performance, gross domestic product.

Gross Domestic Product

Gross domestic product is the market value of final goods and services produced within a country in a particular period of time.

GDP is a flow of current production.

Typically, analysts and policymakers are concerned with yearly measurements of GDP, but they also make quarterly estimates as well. The goal is to estimate the overall *flow* of current production within a nation, and the income that it generates, through time. Some might say it's like taking the "pulse" of the economy. But we have to be very careful with our metaphors here, for the economy is nothing like a cardiovascular system. Remember from Chapter 5: The market is not a person, place, or thing. It is a process of competing bids and offers, a process of individuals trying to work things out in the face of scarcity and uncertainty. Even in light of all the complexity of a modern economic system, with millions of decisions being made by the minute, most economists are confident that the GDP concept gives us some guide as to how well the economy is performing in total. (We shall reserve our discussion of the limits of GDP accounting in this chapter's appendix.)

• Uses market prices to measure market values

Take a good look at that definition. GDP uses *market values* in its measure of economic activity, but just what are market values? How do we measure, for example, the market value of goods as different as a pack of ramen noodles, a gallon of gasoline, or an hour's worth of plumber's services? Answer: We look at their prices formed on the market. As we already know, prices are expressed in a common denominator: units of money. They provide us information about the relative value (and scarcity) of goods and services. Therefore the market value of ramen noodles is 20 cents, a gallon of gasoline about $2.00, and for the plumber perhaps $80 per hour. Of course, as the market prices of these goods change, so, too, do their market values.

• Focuses on final goods (and services)

GDP focuses on *final goods*, as opposed to intermediate goods. A *final good* is something that is purchased by an ultimate user, whether or not that user is in a household, business, or government bureau. It is a good that is purchased without the goal of reselling it or further processing or manufacturing it into another sellable good. Compare that against an *intermediate good*, which is any good that is purchased in order to be resold or to be further processed and manufactured. Consider, for example, corn. Is it a final or intermediate good? Well, that depends! When you purchase ears of corn from the local grocery, it's a final good. You plan to eat it. But think about the grocer's purchases. He bought corn and placed it on the shelves *in order to sell it to somebody like you*. (In fact, the grocer is engaged in arbitrage. He buys corn low and hopes to sell it at a higher price.) At *that* stage in the exchange of corn in the economy, the grocer's purchase of corn represents the purchase of an intermediate good. The same can be said for, say, Kellogg's, which might be buying tons of corn (perhaps hedging through futures contracts!) in order to reprocess it into corn flakes. Here, the corn is an intermediate good. So, too, is the box of cornflakes that Kellogg's produces, because that will be sold to a grocer, who in turn hopes to sell it to somebody else. The box of cornflakes becomes a final good when it's been purchased by the final demander.

Students often interpret the word *final* as "finished." Don't fall into that temptation! Yes, the boxes of cornflakes are "finished" goods once packaged at the Kellogg's facility. Yes, the local grocer is therefore buying a finished good. But those finished goods are not yet *final* goods because they were purchased by the grocer with the plan to sell them yet again.

Finally (or should we say lastly), GDP is a measure of economic performance that takes place *within a country* during the course of a year. The GDP of the United States measures the market value of final goods and services produced *within the United States itself, regardless of the nationality or citizenship of the people owning or producing those goods*. If Kellogg's were to be bought out by foreign investors, yet still maintained its cereal operations in Battle Creek, Michigan, then those boxes of cornflakes that you buy would still represent a contribution to economic performance within the United States, and their value would be added to U.S. GDP. Consider a different example. The U.S. brewer, Anheuser-Busch, produces beer within the United States and within China as well. Its production within the United States contributes to U.S. GDP. But Americans employed at an Anheuser-Busch plant within China do not directly contribute to U.S. GDP. That's part of *China's* GDP.

GDP or GNP?

GDP: performance of the domestic economy; GNP: performance of the nation's citizens

To satisfy the inquisitive student, we can compare GDP to the notion of *gross national product*, or GNP. GNP is defined as *the market value of final goods and services produced by permanent citizens of a country in a particular period of time*. The GNP of the United States would measure the total economic performance of U.S. citizens *regardless of where they happen to be producing*. Of course, most U.S. citizens reside here at home. But many also produce goods and services abroad (which includes Iraq these days). The production of beer by U.S. citizens working for Anheuser-Busch in China contributes to U.S. GNP. Those productive contributions by Americans in China would not, however, add to *China's* GNP.

GNP used to be the most common measure in national income accounting to determine macroeconomic performance. Since 1991, however, national income accountants and policymakers have switched their focus to the GDP measure (for reasons that even your authors feel are too dull to be worth discussing). The quantitative differences between the two measures are not, in fact, all that great. (The difference between U.S. GDP and U.S. GNP is less than 0.1%.) Because GDP has become the national income accounting convention, we shall simply stick with that as we proceed.

GDP as Total Income Created in the Domestic Economy

You might have noticed that we emphasize *purchases* of final goods. Your *purchase* of the cereal, versus the grocer's *purchase*. Indeed, one way to think about and conceptually measure GDP is by adding up the dollar value of all the purchases—the expenditures—on final goods and services. In the U.S. economy, that amounted to more than 10 trillion dollars in 2004. That means individuals within households, businesses, and government bureaus (including the net difference between foreign purchases of U.S. exports and American purchases of foreign imports) spent over 10 trillion dollars on final goods and services. But note that *a purchase always involves a sale*. Jones's purchase of a $10 apple pie creates $10 worth of *income* for all those engaged in the production of that pie. The total of 10 trillion dollars spent on final goods and services in 2004 created 10 trillion dollars worth of *income* to those involved in all the stages of production of those goods and services in the domestic economy, income in the form of wages, rent, interest, and profit.

Your purchase is my sale.

We therefore also consider GDP to be a measure of *national income* created in the domestic economy. The dollar expenditures on final goods will flow back to the resource providers in the form of wages, rents, interest, and profits (but let's never forget, profit can be positive or negative!). Recall our pizzeria owner from Chapter 7. When customers spent a total of $85,000 at Ann Trepreneur's pizzeria last year, GDP would in principle rise by that amount, as those expenditures represent purchases of final goods and services. But those same expenditures *also* represent incomes to those involved with the pizzeria. They provide the means for Ann to employ workers, purchase ingredients, and pay back debts plus interest. Whatever is left over in the form of *accounting* profit is left as an income for Ann herself. In that example, all *other* resource providers received $45,000 in income, and Ann Trepreneur received the remaining $40,000.

Production generates income. Therefore GDP is also a measure of total income of all producers in the domestic economy.

The value of the national output must necessarily equal the value of the national income, when properly calculated, because every dollar paid for output becomes income for someone. An apparent exception would be the amount of tax, such as sales tax, paid on a purchase. But this is income, too; it's income for government, which uses it to pay for the resources that government employs in the process of producing goods.

GDP Is Not a Measure of All Purchases in the Economy

"I'm a bit confused," says a tentative voice, from the front of the room this time. "It seems that GDP is a measure of *all* expenditures in the economy, not just the purchases of *final* goods and services. After all, each and every person's income was paid by somebody, right? So why can't we add *all* expenditures together, regardless of whether or not they are spent on final or intermediate goods?"

Let's be careful here. GDP *is* a measure of all the *income* created within the economy, but not all the *expenditures*. We *exclude* expenditures on intermediate goods, but why? Because the expenditures on *final* goods and services *already accounts* for the value added through all the intermediate stages of production and delivery. If we included *all* expenditures, we would be victims of double counting.

National income accountants exclude expenditures on intermediate goods to avoid the double-counting problem.

We can demonstrate this with a very simple example. (Suppose the following activities all occur during the course of this year.) A logger cuts down an oak tree and sells the logs to a sawmill owner for $50. That represents an expenditure on an intermediate good, as the sawmill owner will further process the logs into oak boards. The sawmill owner does just that and sells the boards to a woodworker for $75. The woodworker purchases the cut boards in order to further process those materials into an oak bookcase, so that expenditure, too, represents a purchase of an intermediate good. The woodworker then builds the bookcase and sells it to a furniture retailer for, say, $250. The oak bookcase is "finished," but it is still considered an *intermediate* good at this point, because the retailer buys it with the goal of further resale (he's engaged in arbitrage—the act of buying low and, he hopes, selling high). Suppose the retailer finally sells the bookcase to you for $400. *That* $400 now represents an expenditure on a *final* good. Let's put this sequence of exchanges in Table 14–1:

Table 14–1

Producer	Begins with	Ends with	Value Added
Logger	One oak tree	$50 (cut and sold to sawmill)	$50
Sawmill Owner	$50 cut oak tree	$75 (milled boards, sold to woodworker)	$25
Woodworker	$75 oak boards	$250 (built oak bookcase, sold to retailer)	$175
Retailer	$250 oak bookcase	$400 (sold bookcase to you)	$150
		(Total expenditures = $775)	(Total value added = $400)

The activities of the logger, sawmill owner, woodworker, and retailer represent property-rights exchanges of *intermediate goods*. In each case, the good in question was purchased with the intention of further processing and/or resale. GDP is the dollar value of *expenditures* on *final* goods and services only. And here's why. In this example, that expenditure is $400—the price *you* paid for the new bookcase—so GDP would increase by $400. Notice what would happen if, instead, we added together *all* the expenditures in this sequence, as our student suggested. That would add up to $775. But did people in the economy really produce something with a market value of $775? No, not at all. Their activities ultimately fit together to produce a new oak bookcase valued at $400. If we added *every* expenditure, we would engage in double counting and mistakenly overstate the actual performance of the economy.

GDP as Total Value Added

Now take a look at the last column, labeled "value added." This represents the net income enjoyed by each of the producers. Consider, for example, that of the sawmill owner. He starts with $50 worth of oak logs and *increases their market value* by cutting the logs into something that others find more useful—oak boards. By selling them for $75 to the woodworker, the sawmill owner has *added value* to that physical material. Moreover, that $25 value added represents the *net income* enjoyed by the sawmill owner. The woodworker adds value by converting the boards into a bookcase. His $175 value added represents net income for him. Notice that the retailer buys the bookcase for $250 and sells it for $400. Although he hasn't physically produced anything new, he, too, has added value to that bookcase. He has found a *customer* and arranged for the delivery (recall from Chapter 2, information is a scarce good and transaction costs tend to be positive!). His net income would amount to $150 in this simplified example.

Gross domestic product = value added by all producers = total income of all producers = total purchases of newly produced final goods

Here's another interesting part of the analysis: When we sum together all these values added (the net incomes) across all the stages of production and exchange, it equals $400. This is *exactly* the expenditure you made when you purchased the bookcase! *Your $400 expenditure on the final good represents the completion of a process that generated $400 in total value added among the participants in all the exchanges that eventually provided you with ownership rights to that bookcase.* So there are actually *three* ways to interpret, and to conceptually measure, GDP: expenditures on final goods and services, total income generated in the economy, and total value added in the economy.

Is Value Added Always Positive?

"Just a second," says the student once again. "I now think I understand how GDP represents total income. Wages, rents, interest, and even profits. But in your example, everybody enjoys some profit. Nobody lost money. The values added are all *positive*. But in the real world a business might actually *lose* money. Suffer a loss instead of making a profit. You wrote that back in the chapter on profit and loss, and I think you just mentioned it a little while ago. So how are *losses* accounted for in GDP?"

Great question. In fact, we did assume that all these people enjoyed positive accounting profits. So let's pursue this just a bit further by considering Table 14–2:

Table 14–2

Producer	Begins with	Ends with	Value Added
Logger	One oak tree	$50 (cut and sold to sawmill)	$50
Sawmill Owner	$50 cut oak tree	$75 (milled boards, sold to woodworker)	$25
Woodworker	$75 oak boards	$250 (built oak bookcase, sold to retailer)	$175
Retailer	$250 oak bookcase	$200 (sold bookcase to you)	−$50
		Total value added =	$200

Here we make the retailer the victim of uncertainty and the associated loss. He buys the bookcase for $250, and of course hopes to sell it for $400 (as in the original example). But let's suppose he was too optimistic and the customers aren't interested in paying *that* price. He puts it on sale for $350, then $300, then $250. No takers. He finally marks it down, regrettably, to $200, and sells it. *Using our expenditures approach, GDP rises by $200—the market value of the final good*. Now take a look at the value-added column. The logger, sawmill owner, and the woodworker all enjoyed a positive value added (and, therefore, positive net incomes), as before. The retailer, however, suffers a $50 *loss* for his efforts. He paid $250 for a bookcase and eventually sold it for $200. His value added is actually a negative amount, *minus* $50. Still, if we sum up *these* values added, we get $200, which, *once again*, is *exactly* the market value of the final good.

Because nominal wages, rents, and interest will be positive, but profit might be positive *or* negative (the result of uncertainty faced by the entrepreneur), we should add all these amounts. In the case of accounting losses, those negative dollar amounts are also "added" *as negative amounts* to the total. So losses, indeed, are accounted for. After all, they are some sign of the performance of the overall economy, too. "Only *accounting* profits and losses?," our student now persists. "What about *economic* profit and losses?" The student got us there! We shall save *that* question for the appendix. It's instead time to tie together a few remaining loose ends.

Loose Ends: Unsold Inventories and Used Goods

You might consider the following question. How are *unsold goods* accounted for in the GDP calculation? For example, say all the activities from the logger to the retailer are accomplished this year. However, the retailer buys the oak bookcase in September but doesn't sell it until February of *next year*. Let's even assume he sells it—next year—for $400. (Back to Table 14–1.) How would we account for this?

Using the income or total value-added approach, we can clearly see that GDP rises this year by $250—the value added by the first three stages. After all, the logger, sawmill owner, and woodworker *were* contributing to the economy's overall economic performance. The retailer is adding to this year's performance too, by making the bookcase currently available to customers. The problem is, the retailer hasn't earned anything—yet. It would be a mistake to say that GDP rises by $400 *next year*, when the bookcase is finally bought, because, in fact, the economy did not produce that $400 worth of output or income next February. Most of that activity was performed *this* year. Cases like this might be a headache for the national income accountants who compute GDP. They simplify things by classifying the retailer's unsold bookcase as part of *gross business inventory investment*. That bookcase is surely a part of the retailer's inventory. And the national income accountants will treat it as being "purchased" by the retailer with a market value of $400—using the retailer's good-faith estimate of the value of his unsold inventory. The economy did produce that bookcase this year with an estimated market value of $400, it's just that it hasn't been purchased yet by the final consumer. Officially, GDP will go up another $400 this year.

inventory investment

Now, were the retailer to successfully sell it next February for $400 , then there's nothing the accountants have to do to this year's GDP. Their estimate was correct. Suppose, instead, the retailer were only able to sell it for, say, $300 next February. Then this year's GDP would have to be revised when that new data comes in. National income accountants had estimated gross inventory investment at $400—and therefore added $400 to this year's GDP. In fact, however, they find that the market value was really only $300. They overestimated it (as did the retailer) by $100. So they would have to go back (in theory) and *reduce* their estimate of this year's GDP by $100. They would do the same for, say, any unsold vehicles produced by the Ford Motor Company this year, but sold next year, or farm inventories created this summer but sold next spring. National income accountants would rely upon estimated market values of the unsold inventory and revise the GDP statistic in light of the actual market values at the time of future purchase. (Now you know one of the reasons why the TV news anchorperson gives us *revised* GDP numbers for the preceeding year.)

Another issue we should get out of the way relates to used goods. Consider the Wee Rob U auto dealer in town. Suppose he buys a 1995 Olds for $500 on Monday and sells it to somebody later that week for $1,800. And the "only" thing he did was place a "for sale" sign on it. Recall that GDP is a measure of *current* output and income. Should GDP increase this year by $1,800? Well, did the economy produce an $1,800 car this year? No. That car was produced in 1994 and was properly accounted for back then. (One of the great marketing schemes of the automakers is to produce a car in year n but give it an $n + 1$ model year.) Did the economy produce *anything* new this year? Yes! The used-car dealer performed a *service*. A service is always fresh and current. He lowered the transaction costs for used-car shoppers *and* for used-car owners who wish to sell. What's the market value of his service? In this case, $1,300. He paid $500 for the car and sold it for $1,800. He added value to that car by performing a *service* as an arbitraging middleman. GDP would increase *not* by the market value of the used car itself, but by the $1,300 market value of the service provided by the seller.

Sellers of used goods are productive, too!

Aggregate Fluctuations

Let's begin to put this GDP concept to work. Historically, the aggregate output and hence the aggregate income of nations, especially in developed commercial societies, display sizable fluctuations over time. For example, from 1929 to 1933, the gross domestic product of the United States, adjusted for changes in the price level, declined by 30 percent. Because the long-term trend in GDP in the United States has been a 3 percent *increase* each year, GDP in 1933 was more than 40 percent less than it could reasonably have been expected to be in 1929. That's more than merely inconvenient. Moreover, the resulting decline in personal income was not evenly distributed across the population. A decline in GDP means a decline in the production of goods and entails layoffs for some workers. Some individual and family incomes fell by a lot more than 30 percent over the course of those four years. In 1929, 3.2 percent of the labor force was counted as unemployed; but in 1933, that had grown to 24.9 percent. In 1933, approximately one in every four workers was unemployed, and many more were working shorter hours than they would have preferred.

In order to make the point that fluctuations in total output and income are significant, we have deliberately chosen the worst recession in the history of the United States. Most declines in GDP are neither as long nor as deep as the decline from 1929 to 1933, a decline that produced the Great Depression of the 1930s. The sharpest decline experienced by the United States since the

1930s occurred in 1974, when GDP (adjusted for price changes) fell by 6.6 percent from the last quarter of 1973 to the first quarter of 1975. Most people could easily survive, though perhaps not without some grumbling, a 6 or 7 percent reduction in their annual income. But because reductions of this sort are not distributed equally, some people's incomes fell by a much greater percentage than the aggregate national income fell. The recession of 1974–1975 raised the unemployment rate from 4.9 percent in 1973 to 8.9 percent in May 1975. The most troubling consequence, in the public mind, of reductions in gross domestic product are the increased levels of unemployment that always follow them.

Inflation

The economic systems of commercial societies are subject to another kind of aggregate fluctuation in addition to fluctuations in gross domestic product. They also experience changes in the value of their unit of account, the monetary unit in terms of which the relative values of goods are expressed. That's why, in the preceding section, when referring to changes in the gross domestic product, we had to point out twice that GDP had been adjusted for price changes. What we really meant was that GDP had been adjusted for changes in the value of money.

We cannot use unadjusted changes in the gross domestic product to measure changes in the total output of goods because GDP is the product of prices as well as quantities. In 1970, popular writers on economics celebrated the arrival in the United States of the "trillion-dollar economy," because in 1970 the gross domestic product rose for the first time above $1 trillion. It took only eight additional years, however, for the GDP to climb above $2 trillion, and three years after that it had reached $3 trillion. This was not the result of spectacular economic growth, but of unprecedented peacetime declines in the value of money. The Bureau of Economic Analysis therefore "deflates" the numbers on gross domestic product to calculate what GDP would have been from year to year if prices had not changed. The bureau chooses a recent year as the reference year and calculates what the value of total output would have been in each year had the prices of the reference year been charged. It calls these numbers the *real* gross domestic product, as distinct from the merely *nominal* gross domestic product. *Real gross domestic product is the value of all final goods produced in a year stated in unchanging prices*, specifically, the prices that held in whatever year is being used as the base year. It is our most comprehensive measure of changes in the rate at which goods are being produced.

The process of calculating the real gross domestic product yields an implicit indicator of changes in the overall or average price level, called the *GDP deflator*. It is simply the nominal GDP divided by the real GDP, multiplied by 100 to give us an index number. Although the GDP deflator is our most comprehensive measure of changes in the purchasing power of money, it is not the best-known measure. That distinction belongs to the Consumer Price Index, a measure of changes in the money price of all the goods that enter into the budgets of typical urban consumers. The Bureau of Labor Statistics surveys consumer prices each month and publishes the results toward the end of the succeeding month. The GDP deflator, by contrast, is much more difficult to calculate and appears only at quarterly intervals and after a lengthy time lag. So while the GDP deflator is more comprehensive, the Consumer Price Index is more timely. It's the index that makes the front page of newspapers each month, especially whenever there is substantial public concern about inflation.

(Nominal GDP/real GDP) × 100 = GDP deflator

But why should the public be concerned about inflation? Some readers might think that's a stupid question. Isn't inflation a rise in the cost of living? And anything that makes it more costly for people to live is obviously a matter for concern. But inflation is not a rise in the cost of living, and we have been careful not to suggest that it is. *Inflation is basically a fall in the value or purchasing power of money*. Looking at it in another way, we can say that inflation is a rise in the *money* price of goods. You may even, if you wish, speak of inflation as a rise in the money cost of living. But the key word is *money*. A $2 hamburger this year really costs no more than a $1 hamburger last year if the cost of obtaining a dollar has been cut in half since last year.

Inflation does not raise the cost of living.

If inflation does not actually raise the cost of living, why is it a problem? Why does everyone worry so much about it? *The problems that inflation creates are caused almost entirely by uncertainty*. It is not the fact that the value of money is falling that creates problems, but the fact that the future value of money cannot be *predicted*. Inflation *distorts the signals that are provided through market prices*. A high but steady rate of inflation on which everyone could confidently depend would cause fewer problems than a lower but less predictable rate of inflation.

Inflation does create uncertainty.

Deflation, which is *a rise in the value or purchasing power of money*, is just as much of a problem for society as is inflation, insofar as it also introduces uncertainty into the calculations of planners. The same is even true of *disinflation*, something experienced in the United States in 1982 and 1983. *Disinflation is a slowing down of the inflation rate*; it also creates serious difficulties for those who fail to anticipate it correctly when making long-term plans.

The Difficulties of Monetary Calculation

Inflation, deflation, and disinflation, especially when any of it is unanticipated, makes monetary calculation more difficult. It *changes in the purchasing power of money make it more difficult to calculate the expected consequences of our financial activities.*

makes household budget planning, saving and investment decisions, wage and salary agreements, and the entrepreneurial calculation of profit and loss much more complicated and confusing, if not, at some point, impossible. F. A. Hayek, a Nobel laureate (and an astute theorist about the way relative price signals help coordinate the plans of individuals), put it this way:

> The point we must constantly keep in mind is that *all* economic adjustment is made necessary by unforeseen changes; the whole point of employing the price mechanism is to inform individuals that what they have been doing or can do is now in greater or lesser demand, for some reason that is no responsibility of theirs.
>
> [T]he methods of accounting on which all business decisions rest make sense only so long as the value of money is tolerably stable. With prices rising at an accelerating rate, the techniques of capital and cost accounting that provide the basis for all business planning would soon lose all meaning. Real costs, profits, or income would soon cease to be ascertainable by any conventional or generally acceptable method.
>
> Inflation thus can never be more than a temporary fillip, and even this beneficial effect can last only as long as somebody continues to be cheated and the expectations of some people unnecessarily disappointed. Its stimulus is due to the errors it produces. It is particularly dangerous because the harmful effects of even small doses of inflation can be staved off only by larger doses of inflation.

The importance of all this will become clearer when we start to discuss the causes of aggregate fluctuations along with some of the remedies that have been proposed for reducing them.

Recession and Inflation Since 1960

Table 14–3 presents, for the United States, nominal gross domestic product, real gross domestic product, and the GDP deflator for each year from 1960 to 2004, along with the percentage changes from the preceding year for the latter two measures. These percentage changes are then graphed in Figure 14–1 to provide a visual portrayal of aggregate output and price fluctuations.

Recession: a slowing down or actual decline in the rate of real GDP growth

The recessions sustained by the U.S. economy over this period show up fairly clearly in the fourth column of Table 14–3, as prolonged slowdowns or actual declines in the rate of real GDP growth. They aren't completely clear, because the National Bureau of Economic Research, the private research organization that officially decides when a downturn is a recession, has no

Table 14–3 **Gross Domestic Product (in billions of dollars) and the Price Level, 1960 to 2003 (minor inconsistencies are due to errors introduced by rounding)**

Year	Nominal GDP	Real GDP (2000 $s)	% Change from Previous Year	GDP Deflator	% Change from Previous Year
1960	526	2502	2.5	21.0	1.4
1961	545	2560	2.3	21.3	1.1
1962	586	2715	6.1	21.6	1.4
1963	618	2834	4.4	21.8	1.1
1964	664	2999	5.8	22.1	1.5
1965	719	3191	6.4	22.5	1.8
1966	788	3399	6.5	23.2	2.8
1967	833	3485	2.5	23.9	3.1
1968	910	3653	4.8	24.9	4.3
1969	985	3765	3.1	26.2	5.0
1970	1039	3772	0.2	27.5	5.3
1971	1127	3899	3.4	28.9	5.0
1972	1238	4105	5.3	30.2	4.3
1973	1383	4342	5.8	31.9	5.6
1974	1500	4320	−0.5	34.7	9.0
1975	1638	4311	−0.2	38.0	9.5
1976	1825	4541	5.3	40.2	5.8
1977	2031	4751	4.6	42.8	6.4
1978	2295	5015	5.6	45.8	7.0
1979	2563	5173	3.2	49.6	8.3
1980	2790	5162	−0.2	54.1	9.1
1981	3128	5292	2.5	59.1	9.4
1982	3255	5189	−1.9	62.7	6.1
1983	3537	5424	4.5	65.2	3.9
1984	3933	5814	7.2	67.7	3.8
1985	4220	6054	4.1	69.7	3.0
1986	4463	6264	3.5	71.3	2.2
1987	4740	6475	3.4	73.2	2.7
1988	5104	6743	4.1	75.7	3.4
1989	5484	6981	3.5	78.6	3.8
1990	5803	7113	1.9	81.6	3.9
1991	5996	7101	−0.2	84.5	3.5
1992	6338	7337	3.3	86.4	2.3
1993	6657	7533	2.7	88.4	2.3
1994	7072	7836	4.0	90.3	2.1
1995	7398	8032	2.5	92.1	2.0
1996	7817	8329	3.7	93.9	1.9
1997	8304	8704	4.5	95.4	1.7
1998	8747	9067	4.2	96.5	1.1
1999	9268	9470	4.4	97.9	1.4
2000	9817	9817	3.7	100.0	2.2
2001	10101	9867	0.5	102.4	2.4
2002	10481	10083	2.2	103.9	1.5
2003	10988	10398	3.1	105.7	1.7

Source: Bureau of Economic Analysis, U.S. Department of Commerce

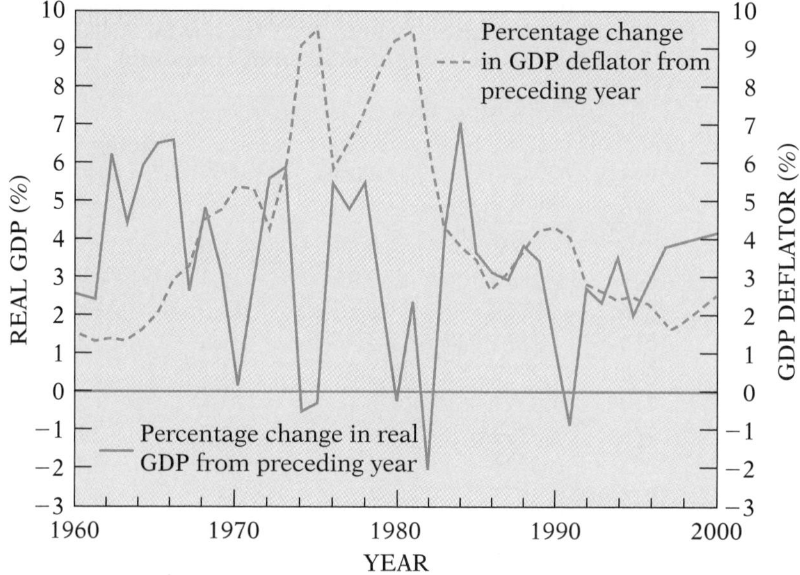

Figure 14–1 **Fluctuations in U.S. output and price level**

hard criteria for infallibly distinguishing a recession from something slightly less serious. There were officially designated recessions in each of the years in which real GDP declined or barely grew—1970, 1974–1975, 1980, 1982, and 1991—but the National Bureau also decided that a recession occurred in 1960 and that the 1991 recession began in 1990. All this becomes more graphic in Figure 14–1.

The last column in Table 14–3 shows that inflation also became a more serious problem in the 1970s and early 1980s than it had been in the preceding decades. When looking at Figure 14–1, be careful not to read a decline in the curve as deflation. The line portraying the GDP deflator would have to drop below zero to show actual deflation, or a fall in the price level. The decline from 1981 to 1986 was disinflation, not deflation. Inflation averaged about 2.5 percent per year in the 1960s. From 1970 to 1981, however, it ran at an average annual rate above 7.5 percent. The years 1974 and 1975 are especially disturbing. A severe recession in those years produced sharply higher unemployment rates while at the same time the price level was shooting up at percentage rates unknown in the United States except in conjunction with major wars. The word began to spread in the 1970s, aided powerfully by television and newspaper commentators, that an unprecedented malady had seized the economy, one that economists were powerless to explain: recession combined with inflation. This is called *stagflation*: a stagnating economy with inflation.

stagflation: simultaneous recession and inflation

Those rumors were incorrect. Inflation had occurred previously during recessions, most recently in the recessions of 1958 and 1960—though the inflation in those years had been considerably less rapid. Nor were economists completely at a loss for an explanation. On the other hand, some oversimplified notions about the causes of recession and inflation, notions that economists had helped create, were very definitely called into question by the experiences of the 1970s. The severe recession of 1974–1975, occurring at a time when prices were rising at almost a 10 percent annual rate, made it abundantly clear that recession and inflation were not simple "opposites."

What Causes Aggregate Fluctuations?

What causes the sharp fluctuations revealed in Table 14–3 in the rate at which aggregate production increases? What could make the real gross domestic product grow at an annual rate of 9 percent in the second quarter of 1978, decline at an annual rate of 9.5 percent in the second quarter of 1980, and then increase once more in the first quarter of 1981 at an annual rate of 9 percent? Why has the GDP deflator, our most comprehensive measure of the overall price level, risen in every year since 1960? Why does it rise at such varying rates?

One answer is: Why not? Change and chance characterize the social universe. Production and prices are bound to be affected by the shocks of wars, new discoveries, revolutions, or natural disasters. It is stability, not fluctuations, that would require explanation. A look at the data for almost any commodity we might name will not reveal stability over time in either output levels or prices. Why then should we expect stability in aggregate output or in the average of all prices?

That argument is pertinent but not altogether satisfactory. Large changes in production and price levels for individual goods—agricultural commodities, automobiles, personal computers, movie admissions—are easier to understand than are large changes in overall production and the average level of money prices. A lot of changes and chances that shift the demand or the supply for individual goods ought to cancel each other out, in accordance with "the law of large numbers." Why doesn't this law produce a much more steady rate of growth in real GDP and a more stable price level?

Part of the explanation is that economic systems transmit viruses. A setback or an unexpected bit of good fortune in one sector of the economy generates setbacks or good fortune for other sectors with which it is linked. A bad month for automobile sales, for example, triggered by a spell of unusually cold and snowy weather, could lead to production cutbacks and layoffs in automobile assembly plants, which might in turn produce reduced orders at steel plants that specialize in sheet metal and reduced business for the stores and shops that cater heavily to assembly plant workers, resulting eventually in layoffs in steel plants and retail establishments and thus setting off further ripple effects.

Economists have developed a variety of models and metaphors to describe the ways in which relatively small initial disturbances might be transmitted through the economic system to produce large aggregate effects. Many of them rely on some kind of circular-flow mechanism to show how an economic system can transform small events into the boom-and-bust patterns that have been known to characterize market-coordinated economic systems for at least 200 years. Because everyone's spending becomes income for someone else and income in turn determines how much people will be able to spend, the decision to spend a little more or a little less, prompted perhaps by a slight change in the public's confidence about the future, can produce a spiraling effect.

Total income necessarily equals total output.

As national income and product accounting reminds us, the total income available for the purchase of newly produced goods is always and necessarily equal to the price paid for those goods. This is an important truth—at least to begin with. It counters the strange but widespread and persistent fear that total output might increase too fast for total demand to keep up, so that the economic system collapses as a result of overproduction. Total income is always going to increase at precisely the same rate as total output, for the simple reason that they are the same phenomenon viewed from opposite sides. That can be granted, however, without conceding that total *demand* will necessarily equal total output. What if people choose not to spend some of their income? Won't the decision to save a portion of the income received reduce aggregate demand below the level of total output? And might this not cause overproduction and economic collapse?

But total demand can be less than total output.

The answer depends on what people do with the income they save. Except in the rare and unimportant case of misers and similar cranks, people invest what they save. That at least was the consensus view of the great majority of economists up until the 1930s. People don't tuck their savings under their mattresses or into their cookie jars. They put their savings to work. If they themselves don't purchase capital goods with the income they save, then they purchase financial assets of some kind (bonds, stocks, savings accounts) and thereby turn their savings over to someone else who is going to purchase capital goods. Adam Smith put the doctrine concisely when he said, "What is annually saved is as regularly consumed as what is annually spent, and nearly in the same time too; but it is consumed by a different set of people."

Smith thought that people would have to be "perfectly crazy" (his term) not to invest everything they chose to save, at least where there was "tolerable security." The fear of overproduction or underconsumption was therefore groundless. In the opinion of Smith and most of his successors in the nineteenth century, worrying that aggregate demand might be insufficient was evidence that one had not understood the basic working of economic systems. Overproduction was not a problem; the challenge was to increase production so that people might be supplied with more of the "necessaries and conveniences" of life. Government's job in the economic system was not to stimulate demand but to preserve incentives, principally by maintaining the security of property. If this were done, people's natural desire to better their condition would lead them to produce, to save, to invest, and thereby to promote a continually rising rate of output. Consumption—the demand side—would take care of itself.

The Great Depression laid this optimistic belief firmly to rest. In the eyes of many politicians and intellectuals it became obvious in the 1930s that aggregate demand did not always "take care of itself." The result was the rise of new economic theories and policies concerned with the care and nurture of aggregate demand. These theories flourished for many years, until experiences of the 1970s and 1980s revealed some of their more glaring limitations. In a striking reversal of the general rule that scientific knowledge progresses, economists today are probably less sure that they understand what causes aggregate fluctuations and how to cure them than they were a generation ago.

Where do we go from here? We shall begin by turning to another widely used indicator of what's occurring throughout the overall economic system, the rate of unemployment. That is the subject of Chapter 15. We shall then turn to the role that money and banking play in our complex, commercial society.

An Appendix: *LIMITATIONS OF NATIONAL INCOME ACCOUNTING*

GDP attempts to measure economic performace, period.

National income accountants compute GDP to measure macroeconomic performance. It is emphatically *not* a measure of "societal welfare" or national "well-being," or "overall satisfaction." A sustained rise in real GDP (economic growth) does not necessarily mean people are typically happier than before, or feel better about themselves, or have found more meaning in their lives, or are one step closer to finding God. Nor does a decrease in real GDP necessarily imply that people are less happy about their lives, and so on. GDP is strictly meant to get some sense of *economic performance*. And it does so only imperfectly. Economists realize that GDP systematically ignores several kinds of productive activities that contribute to economic performance. We shall discuss only a few of them to give you a feel for some of the issues at stake.

GDP ignores all nonmarket forms of production. Recall that GDP is measured using market *prices* of final goods and services. Likewise, it can be computed by summing up all the *incomes paid in money* to all the resource providers in the domestic economy. And, of course, in a modern commercial society a great deal of our activities are accomplished through the purchase and sale of property rights. But certainly not *all* of our productive activities are exchanged for money in markets, even though those activities, too, *contribute to the production of wealth*. Consider, for example, these two cases. The Brown family hires the services of a daily housekeeper/nanny to maintain the house and baby-sit the children. They pay the housekeeper/nanny $300 per week for her services. Across the street at the Jones household, Mrs. Jones is a stay-at-home mom and maintains the house and watches over the children. Mrs. Jones might (or might not) have some control over her husband's take-home pay, but she herself is not *paid* in money for her efforts. Their activities are scarce goods in *both* households. But only Brown's hiring of the housekeeper/nanny will affect GDP. It will rise by $15,600 this year ($300 times 52 weeks). Mrs. Jones's efforts go unnoticed in the GDP accounts. She provides the same services, but in a nonmarket setting. Her contribution to the family (*and* to the overall economy) is therefore ignored by GDP accounting. Likewise, if a mechanic replaces the starter on your car, GDP will increase by both the price of the new starter (say, $100) *and* the price of his service (say, $40 for his half-hour of labor). If, on the other hand, your boyfriend buys a new starter and replaces it himself because he loves you, GDP increases only by the price of the $100 starter. *His* labor goes unrecorded; he offered it in a nonmarket context. The official GDP statistic would therefore tend to *underestimate* the actual performance of the overall economy by excluding nonmarket production within that economy.

Paying a counselor for advice increases GDP, but seeking advice from a friend does not.

GDP ignores illegal (black market) production. Suppose the nanny is instead working illegally, in the underground market. Her service, though indeed market-based, and paid in money, would not be recorded in the GDP measure. Now, one reason why GDP overlooks illegal production is clear and simple: Who in their right mind is likely to *report* illegally acquired income? How many drug dealers do so? How many pimps and prostitutes do so? (In Nevada, where prostitution is legal, they *do* report their income, and that does get included in GDP; in all other states where it is illegal, the incomes from their productive services go unreported.) As a general rule, GDP accounting ignores *all* illegal production. Yet, and without a doubt, illegal production *is* a part of a nation's overall economic performance. Once again, then, the GDP measure would tend to underestimate actual performance by excluding all illegal economic activity.

National income accountants' rule: Ignore all illegal exchanges.

GDP ignores economic value added. Here's an instance which, in itself, would lead GDP to *overestimate* actual economic performance. In our discussions of value added in this chapter, we measured it strictly in the *accounting* sense. That is, we focused exclusively on *accounting profit* as opposed to *economic profit*. But remember we made a big fuss about the difference between accounting and economic profit back in Chapter 7. And your authors remain firm that there's an important conceptual difference between the two. We would hate to forget about that, *especially* now that we are trying to examine the overall economy. What *really* matters to the entrepreneur is the economic profit, because economic profit appraises the *opportunity costs of the entrepreneur's resources* contributed to the firm. That's also why economic profit is such an important concept in the economic way of thinking. From the economist's point of view, *the entrepreneurial search for economic profit is the driving force of the market process*. Economic profit opportunities help explain the innovative changes that rumble throughout the economic system.

Economic profit will typically be *less* than accounting profit. But, for purposes of GDP measurement, *only* accounting profits are used to measure the performance of the economy. GDP accountants can't possibly determine all the implicit or opportunity costs of all the entrepreneurs across the United States. No accountant or economist can do that. Instead, for better or worse, they rely upon the official accounting profits that are reported by proprietors and corporations, even if those accounting profits are really generating economic *losses*. In this sense, national income accounting of total "profit" income generated in the economy should be taken with a good grain of salt. By essentially assuming that entrepreneur-owned resources are *free* goods, the profit aggregate in the GDP accounts must be systematically overestimated.

National income accountants have no way to measure and aggregate economic profits and losses.

The Dangers of Aggregation: A Methodological Reflection

Trying to obtain a clear measure of the overall performance of an economy is a rather difficult task. At best, it is imperfect. Often, it is not very meaningful. By way of conclusion, let's consider the broader problem of macroeconomic analysis: its emphasis on statistical aggregates.

Let's start with a completely noneconomic example. Suppose climatologists were to obtain a measure of the *total* (let's call it *aggregate*) U.S. rainfall. Even if they obtained the exact quantity (say, in inches per year), what does that really tell us? Suppose they could show that total rainfall is 3% greater this year over last year. Can we conclude from the *aggregate data* that those specific locales that could have used more rain—or less rain, depending on the circumstances—actually got it? Looking at the *aggregate* measure in and of itself probably won't lead those in the farming communities, for example, to make significant changes to their plans. They will look, instead, to the levels of rainfall that affect their *specific circumstances of time and place*. The central Iowa corn farmer seeks information that will affect *his* local circumstances. Aggregate rainfall in the United States provides him with little useful information. Would that aggregate amount help the good people at the Department of Agriculture? It's unclear just how it might.

Now, as far as we know, very few people carefully follow *aggregate* U.S. rainfall amounts. Many people, however, including economists and policymakers, do follow the quarterly GDP measures. GDP is an aggregate concept. It is a measure of the *total output (or total income)* produced in the overall domestic economy. One of the temptations of macroeconomic theory is to study the economy by focusing largely (if not exclusively) on the relationships between the aggregate variables themselves: GDP, the "price level," the unemployment rate, and so on. But this is quite a problem, for it makes it appear that—somehow—the *aggregates* are interacting with one another. Policymakers trying to improve the economy might then be tempted merely *to get the aggregates right*. But recall what we've emphasized from the very beginning of this textbook. The economy is *always and everywhere* composed of *individuals*. Only individuals choose. Individuals act and interact. Individuals attempt to coordinate their plans through the market process. Individuals seek and create wealth. A heavy focus on the interactions among clusters of *data*—the aggregates themselves—might make us lose sight of the specific pieces of information, and often heterogeneous information at that, that individual decision makers themselves use to coordinate their everyday plans and projects. Even Kenneth Boulding, an early proponent of macroeconomic analysis (and professor of your two coauthors), offered his misgivings as far back as 1948:

Losing sight of the individual trees by focusing only on the forest

> In macroeconomic discussion . . . it is easy to forget that the aggregates or averages under discussion are in fact made up of innumerable individual items, and that changes in their internal structure or composition may be more significant in the interpretation of some particular problem than the changes in the aggregate itself. This fact explains why the supply and demand analysis becomes less and less useful the larger the aggregates considered.

Boulding's last sentence is particularly troubling. Most macroeconomists from the 1950s through the 1970s implicitly responded with "well, so much for supply and demand analysis." They believed that supply and demand theory, and the basic conception of the individual decision maker—call it *micro*economics—was inherently limited and couldn't explain overall economic phenomena. Macroeconomics at that time became further focused on aggregate analysis and placed the individual chooser in the scrapheap of macroeconomic thought—useful only for micro but not for macroeconomic theory. Since the 1980s, however, more and more macroeconomists have come to argue that *aggregate analysis* itself is limited. They've sought to improve the theory by rediscovering the value of supply and demand analysis and the formation of relative market prices, and price expectations, in their search for the "microfoundations of macroeconomics." So far the search has offered mixed results. Time will tell if it leads to a fundamental change in macroeconomic thinking.

Once Over Lightly

The most common measure of a nation's output or income is gross domestic product, which is the market value of all final goods and services produced within a country in the course of a year.

It is possible to measure gross domestic product in three ways, all of which would yield the same total if no errors were made in counting: (1) the total purchases of final goods and services by households, business firms, and government, plus the purchases of foreigners in excess of what the foreigners sold in return; (2) the total income received, in the form of wages and salaries, interest, rent, and profits, by those who contributed the resources used to produce the year's total output; (3) the value added by each producer in the course of contributing to the year's total output of final goods. When unsold goods are counted as additions to inventory and added to the total purchases of business firms, the sum of household, business, government, and (net) foreign expenditures on final goods must add up exactly to the total value of the goods produced.

A question might arise about unsold goods. They are part of the year's output, but because they aren't sold, they don't seem to generate income for anyone. This is handled in the accounts by assuming that the business firm that produced the goods also bought them. It surely had to pay to get them produced. And while it may not have intended to buy them itself, goods produced and not sold are indeed added, however reluctantly, to the inventories of the firm that produced them.

Services in the economy are fresh. They're part of the economy's current performance. GDP therefore includes the market values of services, even from those who arbitrage used goods, such as used-auto sellers or antique dealers.

Inflation is a sustained fall in the purchasing power of money, which is the same thing as saying a rise in the money price of goods. It is not a rise in the "cost of living," particularly with the economist's notion of opportunity cost.

Deflation is a sustained rise in the purchasing power of money, or fall in the money price of goods.

Disinflation is a fall (slowing down) of the rate of inflation.

All three—inflation, deflation, and disinflation—create serious distortions in market price signals and lead to problems for those engaged in monetary calculation, budgets, and long-term planning.

Real gross domestic product measures a nation's total output or income in dollars of constant purchasing power. Nominal gross domestic product, or GDP in current dollars, divided by real gross domestic product yields what is called the GDP deflator, which functions as a measure of inflation or of the changing value of money.

Economic growth entails a sustained increase in real GDP. A recession, on the other hand, is traditionally determined by an actual decrease in real GDP over two consecutive quarters or (more recently) a slowing down of the rate of economic growth.

In all commercial societies, the rate of increase in real gross domestic product (the rate of economic growth) fluctuates over time, generating "booms and busts" whose causes and cures are not well understood, or at least not sufficiently well understood at this time to enable government policymakers to bring them under complete control.

Finally, the measurement of GDP (called national income accounting) has a number of limitations, as does aggregate analysis as a whole. GDP systematically ignores many activities that contribute to a nation's overall economic performance, including nonmarket production, illegal or black market production, and the pursuit of economic (as opposed to merely accounting) profit.

QUESTIONS FOR DISCUSSION

1. What is the difference between a final good and an intermediate good? What's the difference between a "finished" good and a final good?
2. Consider the following situations:
   (a) An American citizen is hired to work on a pipeline in Iraq. How does this affect U.S. GDP? How does it affect Iraqi GDP?
   (b) A professor from France is hired this year to teach French at Ivy College in the United States. What happens to U.S. GDP? What happens to the GDP of France?
   (c) "Americans pay $30 billion a year in health care costs associated with smoking?" How would those expenditures affect GDP?
3. "Measuring the wealth or well-being of the people in a country by their money incomes is much more defensible than the critics suppose. Whatever makes for well-being, money will help you get it. Money may not buy happiness, but it's better than whatever is in second place." Do you agree or disagree?
4. Consider this simplified sequence: A farmer starts with a unit of wheat and sells it to a miller for 20 cents. The miller grinds it into flour and

sells it to a baker for 50 cents. The baker converts all the flour into a loaf of bread and sells it to a grocer for $1.00. The grocer then sells that bread to a customer for $1.35. How much does GDP increase? What is the total value added by all these stages of production?

5. If it could be shown that a rising GDP is associated with a rising level of anxiety, tension, and conflict in the population, would you favor deducting these psychological costs to obtain the true value of gross domestic product? How would you do so? How would you place a dollar value on increased anxiety?
6. List some ways in which increased inefficiency could cause GDP to rise. How many goods contributing to the total GDP can you list whose rising output clearly reflects reduced welfare?
7. At the end of 1991, the Bureau of Economic Analysis fell in line with the standard practice in most other countries and changed its comprehensive measure of national income and output from gross national product to gross domestic product. To obtain the GDP from the GNP, one subtracts income received from the rest of the world and adds income paid to the rest of the world. For example, an American owns stock in a British corporation and receives dividends. Although this is a part of American income, it was not generated in the United States and really should not be counted as a part of domestic U.S. product. So it is subtracted from total U.S. income to obtain the gross domestic product. Meanwhile, of course, income payments to foreigners who have invested in the United States, which are excluded from the gross national product, must be included in the gross domestic product, because they are the income counterpart to goods produced in the United States.

   In every year between 1960 and 1976, U.S. GNP was larger than GDP. In every year from 1983 to 1998, GDP was larger than GNP. What does this imply? Should it be a matter for concern?
8. Does a junk dealer contribute to GDP? What about a fine-antique dealer? How? Why?
9. Suppose IBM produces 10,000 Thinkpads in December of 2005, with an estimated market value of $2,000 each. None of those are sold until some time in the spring of 2006.

   (a) How much would GDP increase in 2005?
   (b) How much would GDP increase in 2006?
   (c) Suppose IBM decides to actually raise their price at the beginning of 2006 and successfully sells all of them for $2,100 each in 2006. How does this affect 2005 GDP?
10. To be certain that you understand the relationship between nominal GDP, real GDP, and the GDP deflator, fill in the following table:

Year	Nominal GDP	Real GDP	GDP Deflator
1	$4,400 billion	$4,000 billion	__________
2	$5,600 billion	__________	140
3	__________	$4,400 billion	160

11. If you are suspicious of the textbook's claim that inflation is not a rise in the cost of living but merely a fall in the value of money, ask yourself how inflation could occur in a society that did not use money but relied exclusively on barter. What form would inflation take in such a society? How would you recognize it?
12. If public-opinion surveys show that the majority of Americans regard inflation as a more serious threat than unemployment:
    (a) Does this imply that the majority of Americans would rather be unemployed in a period of stable prices than employed in a time of rising prices?
    (b) If the management of a firm allowed employees to vote on whether the firm should lay off 10 percent of the employees or reduce wage rates by 5 percent, how do you think they would vote? Do you think the outcome of the vote would depend on whether the employees knew in advance exactly who would be laid off?
13. Some people claim that recessions are caused by excessive saving on the part of the public. When people decide to save more, they are deciding to buy less. Won't that cause some goods to go unsold? And won't that cause producers to reduce their levels of output, laying people off and thus reducing their incomes, causing these people to buy less, thus setting off a downward spiral? How would you evaluate the claim that those who spend lavishly create prosperity while those who save bring on recessions?
14. Would you favor including the services of homemakers in the calculation of gross domestic product? What arguments could be given for doing so? Are there any good reasons for continuing to exclude these services from the calculation of GDP? Do you think the exclusion reflects sexist attitudes and that if more men were homemakers, the Bureau of Economic Analysis would change its ways? Why doesn't the bureau count the value of a husband's work as a backyard barbecue chef, when it does count the very same sort of work done for pay by someone in a barbecued-rib outlet?
15. Many small family-owned "cash" businesses try to avoid taxes by concealing a portion of their revenues. And they simply don't report their total earnings when it comes time to file taxes. If this is a common practice, how would it affect the GDP figures, particularly in its national income measurement?
16. As the production and use of marijuana for medical purposes becomes legally recognized in Canada, how will those activities affect Canadian GDP? How will continued illegal uses of marijuana (for nonmedical reasons) affect Canadian GDP?
17. Recall back in Chapter 2, Brown swapped some of her stout for some of Jones's lager beer. Both enjoyed more wealth as a result. They were able to enjoy a larger combination of those two beers by specializing and exchanging.
    (a) Do you agree that this is an "economic activity" on their behalf? That is, their acts of specialization and exchange are part of the overall economic system?

(b) Do you agree with the national income accountants that the activity should *not* be considered when computing the GDP figures, even though those figures are attempting to estimate the real performance of the overall economy?

(c) If you *disagree* with the national income accountants, then answer this question: How do you propose that they measure and include that activity? Considering this new question, how do you feel about your initial answer to part (b)?

Employment and Unemployment

15

The most troubling consequence of recessions, in the minds of most Americans, is the rising levels of unemployment associated with them. So we're going to spend a chapter looking at the phenomenon of unemployment and especially its relationship to recessions. But before we can do that, we have to decide what we mean by unemployment.

Unemployment and Nonemployment

Approximately half of the people currently living in the United States are not employed. They are neither earning a wage by working for someone else nor working for themselves in a business that they own. But it would be ridiculous to suggest that 50 percent of the U.S. population is *unemployed*. Almost a quarter of the population is under 16 years of age and about one-eighth is over 65. Moreover, many of those between 16 and 65 are quite fully employed, although not in the sense just described; they are raising children and caring for a household. There is clearly an important difference between being unemployed in any sense that might trouble us and simply not being employed.

There is some amount of unemployment that everyone seems to take for granted and no one worries about. How much is that? What is an acceptable unemployment rate? In the year 1944, 1.2 percent of the labor force in the United States was officially classified as unemployed, at a time when one-sixth of the entire labor force was in the armed forces and people were being urged to leave school to take jobs, to come out of retirement, and to work six- or seven-day weeks. No one who lived through those labor-hungry years would believe that 1.2 percent of the labor force could not find jobs in 1944.

How can we distinguish problem unemployment from nonproblem unemployment? In some circles, it is still common practice to duck the whole question by saying that unemployment becomes a problem when it rises above the level of purely "frictional" unemployment, with frictional unemployment defined as the amount of unemployment that poses no problem because it represents ordinary labor-market turnover. This might be a satisfactory procedure if we had reason to believe that ordinary labor-market turnover was some identifiable constant over time. Quite to the contrary, however, we have excellent reasons for supposing that ordinary labor-market turnover is a *variable*, rather than a constant, and that it changes in response to factors that have shifted substantially in recent years.

So how shall we distinguish those who are *unemployed* from those who are merely *not employed*? The extreme cases are easy to distinguish. Some people would do almost anything to find satisfactory employment, whereas there is almost nothing that would persuade others to accept a job. But did you spot the fudge factors in that sentence? People who would describe themselves as "desperate" for work will nonetheless decline *some* job opportunities in the hope of finding something better. And very few of those who say they "absolutely" don't want a job would decline *every* offer that might come their way. People who say they "can't find a job" mean they can't find a job at which they're willing to work. Those who say they "don't want to work" mean that they don't want to work at any job they can find. In some cases, the difference between those two situations isn't going to be discernible to an outside observer.

Employed, Not Employed, and Unemployed

The outside observers on whom we depend to make this distinction for us are some carefully trained employees of the U.S. government. The official data on U.S. unemployment are published by the Bureau of Labor Statistics (BLS), an agency in the U.S. Department of Labor. The source of the data is the *Current Population Survey*, a sample survey of households that the Bureau of the Census conducts on behalf of the BLS. The sample consists of about 60,000 households, selected to represent the entire population and interviewed monthly. (The data are not derived, contrary to what many people think, from claims for unemployment compensation.)

Total population
– under 16 or institutionalized
= noninstitutionalized population
– not in the labor force
= labor force
– employed
= unemployed

In order to be included at all in the BLS report, a person must first be in the *noninstitutional population. This is the total of those who are 16 years of age or older and not residing in an institution*, such as a prison or a hospital. Those who are not yet 16 just aren't counted, no matter how hard they work or how desperately they would like to have a job. But those over 65 are counted. Each person in the noninstitutional population is then classified as either employed, unemployed, or not in the labor force. Deciding who is employed presents no serious problems. But what is the distinction between someone who is *unemployed* and someone who is "not in the labor force" and therefore merely *not employed*? The BLS has developed precise criteria for distinguishing between these two groups and measures the size of each with considerable confidence. Measurement is not the problem. The problem is the significance of the distinction, especially in light of the highly diverse and changing costs to particular people of being "not in the labor force" or being officially unemployed.

Let's look more closely. To be classified in the household survey as unemployed, an individual must (1) be in the noninstitutional population, (2) have been without employment during the survey week, (3) have made specific efforts to find employment sometime during the preceding four weeks, and (4) be presently available for work. (Persons who are on layoff but have been told they will be recalled within six months or who are waiting to start a new job within 30 days are counted as unemployed without meeting the third criterion, which requires that they be actively looking for employment.) The unemployed divided by the labor force yields the official unemployment rate, which makes the newspapers and the newscasts when the BLS publishes it each month.[1]

Details of this sort don't make very exciting reading. But it is crucial that we know what people must do or not do in order to meet the BLS criteria for being unemployed. There is simply no way to understand the nature, causes, or significance of unemployment unless we know something about the cost of being unemployed to those who make choices that then lead to their being unemployed.

Labor-Market Decisions

The concept of choice is important, because economic theory tries to explain *all* behavior as the consequence of choice—under constraints, of course. Insofar as people have no discernible or significant amount of choice in a situation, economic theory has little that is useful to say about their behavior. In assuming that unemployment results from the choices people make, we are not assuming that everyone has good choices, much less that unemployed people enjoy their condition. To choose simply means to select the best available alternative, on the basis of one's expectations regarding relative costs and benefits. The economic way of thinking urges us to explain changes in social phenomena,

[1]Data on the number of people employed or unemployed in any quarter or month are *seasonally adjusted* by the BLS. This means that they have been corrected to eliminate the effects of variations caused entirely by seasonal factors—the closing of schools in June, extra hiring in December, major holidays, and so on. Seasonal adjustment lets us detect trends that would otherwise be concealed or exaggerated by purely seasonal fluctuations. For a complete discussion of the overall statistical methodology used in estimating unemployment in the United States, visit www.bls.gov.

Noninstitutional population . . .

including changes in unemployment rates, as consequences of changes in the costs and benefits that employers and employees perceive.

The BLS definition makes quite clear the specific choices that produce the status called "unemployed": (1) a decision to look actively for employment and (2) a decision not to accept any of the employment opportunities available. Both clearly are choices people make. The first decision stands at the fork that leads either to being unemployed or to being out of the labor force. The second decision marks the fork that leads to employment or to continued unemployment. For large numbers of people, the anticipated benefits and costs of decisions at those forks have changed considerably in recent years. As a result, particular unemployment rates don't mean what they meant 50 or even 15 years ago.

Unemployment Rates and Employment Rates

Table 15–1 summarizes labor force activity in the United States from 1950 through 2000. The unemployment rates for each year appear after "Number Unemployed" in the column headed "Percentage of Labor Force." If you run your eye down that column, you will notice that the unemployment rate rises and falls. The sudden increases usually mark the appearance of recessions, and the subsequent (and slower) declines in the rate reflect recovery from the recessions. We'll return to that relationship.

Unemployment rate = number unemployed / labor force

The table shows something else that Figure 15–1 displays even more clearly: an apparent inconsistency between the unemployment rate and the employment rate. The two are not opposites or mirror images of each other. The employment rate compares employment with population. It shows that a higher percentage of working-age Americans were actually employed in 1982, when the unemployment rate was 9.7 percent, than had been employed in 1953, when the unemployment rate was only 2.9 percent. The basic reason for this surprising fact is that many more people *wanted* to work in 1982 than in 1953. The labor force participation rate, shown in the fourth column as Percentage of Noninstitutional Population in Labor Force, has risen substantially in recent decades. The principal cause, as you might suspect, was the decision of so many more women to enter the labor force. There was actually a decline in the rate of labor force participation by males during this period, but the flow of females into the labor force more than made up for it. Whereas 377 of every 1,000 employed civilians in the United States were female in 1970, 467 of every 1,000 were female in June 2001. If people had known in 1968, when the labor force participation rate was slightly less than 60 percent, that in 30 years more than 67 percent of the noninstitutional population would be in the labor

$$\text{Employment rate} = \frac{\text{Number employed}}{\text{Noninstitutionalized population}}$$

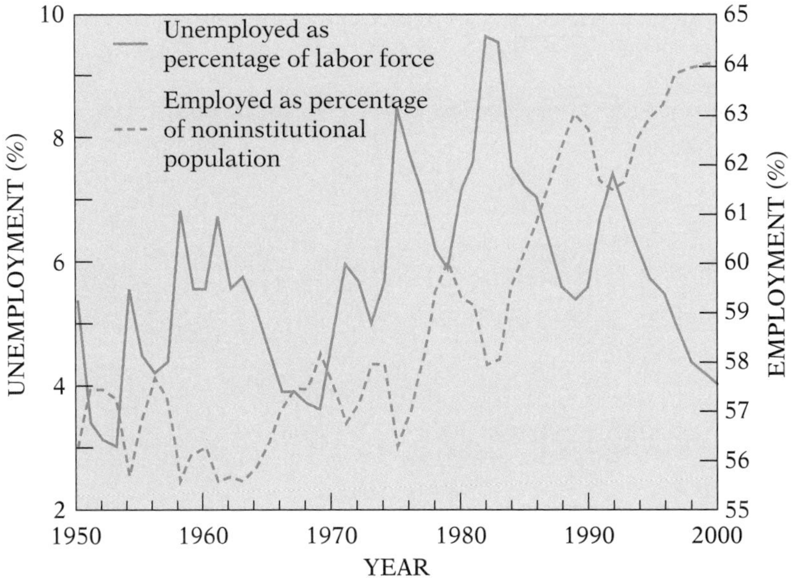

Figure 15–1 **Unemployment and employment in the United States**

force, most of them would probably have predicted an extremely high unemployment rate for 2001. There is no way, they would have insisted, that the economic system can create that many new jobs, especially when the tendency is for machines to replace people everywhere.

At the end of the Napoleonic wars, bands of English workmen, known as Luddites, went around smashing machinery in the belief that machines caused unemployment. For some people they do, at least in the short run. If you were a telephone switchboard operator 75 years ago, the invention and deployment of automatic switching machinery may have taken away your job. But the telephone system now in operation in the United States could never have evolved if automatic switching machinery had not been installed, because most of the labor force in the United States would have to be working for telephone companies if we were using the system the way we do today but under the old technology. Machines do replace people, but the people who are replaced usually go on to do something else, and almost everyone enjoys the larger output that results from increased productivity. Luddite-like movements recur periodically; but although the demands (plural) for workers are changing constantly, the introduction of machinery seems still to be creating more jobs than it's destroying. As long as our wants for producible goods remain unsatisfied, we should not run out of useful tasks for people to perform. A rise in the unemployment rate reflects not a growing scarcity of jobs, but rather a change in the expected costs and benefits of looking for and accepting employment.

Table 15–1 **Employment Status of the Noninstitutional Population 16 Years and Over, 1950 through 2003 (numbers in thousands)**

Year	Civilian Noninstitutional Population	Civilian Labor Force	Percentage of Noninstitutional Population in Labor Force	Civilian Employment	Number Unemployed	Percentage of Labor Force	Not in Labor Force	Employed as Percentage of Noninstitutional Population
1950	104,995	62,208	59.2	58,918	3,288	5.3	42,787	56.1
1951	104,621	62,017	59.3	59,961	2,055	3.3	42,604	57.3
1952	105,231	62,138	59.0	60,250	1,883	3.0	43,093	57.3
1953	107,056	63,015	58.9	61,179	1,834	2.9	44,041	57.1
1954	108,321	63,643	58.8	60,109	3,532	5.5	44,678	55.5
1955	109,683	65,023	59.3	62,170	2,852	4.4	44,660	56.7
1956	110,954	66,552	60.0	63,799	2,750	4.1	44,402	57.1
1957	112,265	66,929	59.6	64,071	2,859	4.3	45,336	57.1
1958	113,727	67,639	59.5	63,036	4,602	6.8	46,088	55.4
1959	115,329	68,369	59.3	64,630	3,740	5.5	46,960	56.0
1960	117,245	69,628	59.4	65,778	3,852	5.5	47,617	56.1
1961	118,771	70,459	59.3	65,746	4,714	6.7	48,312	55.4
1962	120,153	70,614	58.8	66,702	3,911	5.5	49,539	55.5
1963	122,416	71,833	58.7	67,762	4,070	5.7	50,583	55.4
1964	124,485	73,091	58.7	69,305	3,786	5.2	51,394	55.7
1965	126,513	74,455	58.9	71,088	3,366	4.5	52,058	56.2
1966	128,058	75,770	59.2	72,895	2,875	3.8	52,288	56.9
1967	129,874	77,347	59.6	74,372	2,975	3.8	52,527	57.3
1968	132,028	78,837	59.6	75,920	2,817	3.6	53,291	57.3
1969	134,335	80,734	60.1	77,902	2,832	3.5	53,602	58.0
1970	137,085	82,771	60.4	78,678	4,093	4.9	54,315	57.4
1971	140,216	84,382	60.2	79,367	5,016	5.9	55,834	56.6
1972	144,126	87,034	60.4	82,153	4,882	5.6	57,091	57.0
1973	147,096	89,429	60.8	85,064	4,365	4.9	57,667	57.8
1974	150,120	91,949	61.3	86,794	5,156	5.6	58,171	57.8
1975	153,153	193,775	61.2	185,846	7,929	8.5	59,377	56.1

Year	Civilian Noninstitutional Population	Civilian Labor Force	Percentage of Noninstitutional Population in Labor Force	Civilian Employment	Number Unemployed	Percentage of Labor Force	Not in Labor Force	Employed as Percentage of Noninstitutional Population
1976	156,150	196,158	61.6	188,752	7,406	7.7	59,991	56.8
1977	159,033	199,009	62.3	192,017	6,991	7.1	60,025	57.9
1978	161,910	102,251	63.2	196,048	6,202	6.1	59,659	59.3
1979	164,863	104,962	63.7	198,824	6,137	5.8	59,900	59.9
1980	167,745	106,940	63.8	199,303	7,637	7.1	60,806	59.2
1981	170,130	108,670	63.9	100,397	8,273	7.6	61,460	59.0
1982	172,271	110,204	64.0	199,526	10,678	9.7	62,067	57.8
1983	174,215	111,550	64.0	100,834	10,717	9.6	62,665	57.9
1984	176,383	113,544	64.4	105,005	8,539	7.5	62,839	59.5
1985	178,206	115,461	64.8	107,150	8,312	7.2	62,744	60.1
1986	180,587	117,834	65.3	109,597	8,237	7.0	62,752	60.7
1987	182,753	119,865	65.6	112,440	7,425	6.2	62,888	61.5
1988	184,613	121,669	65.9	114,968	6,701	5.5	62,944	62.3
1989	186,393	123,869	66.5	117,342	6,528	5.3	62,523	63.0
1990	188,049	124,787	66.4	117,914	6,874	5.5	63,262	62.7
1991	189,765	125,303	66.0	116,877	8,426	6.7	64,462	61.6
1992	191,576	126,982	66.3	117,598	9,384	7.4	64,593	61.4
1993	193,550	128,040	66.2	119,306	8,734	6.8	65,509	61.6
1994	196,814	131,056	66.6	123,060	7,996	6.1	65,758	62.5
1995	198,584	132,304	66.6	124,900	7,404	5.6	66,280	62.9
1996	200,591	133,943	66.8	126,708	7,236	5.4	66,647	63.2
1997	203,133	136,297	67.1	129,558	6,739	4.9	66,837	63.8
1998	205,220	137,673	67.1	131,463	6,210	4.5	67,547	64.1
1999	207,753	139,368	67.1	133,488	5,880	4.2	68,385	64.3
2000	212,577	142,583	67.1	136,891	5,692	4.0	69,994	64.4
2001	215,092	143,734	66.8	136,933	6,801	4.7	71,359	63.7
2002	217,570	144,863	66.6	136,485	8,378	5.8	72,707	62.7
2003	221,168	146,510	66.2	137,736	8,774	6.0	74,658	62.3

Source: Bureau of Labor Statistics, *Employment and Earnings;* www.bls.gov/news.release/empsit.toc.htm

Costs and Decisions

Recall our discussion in the appendix to Chapter 14. We must be careful with aggregated data. Both the cost of taking a job and the cost of not taking one will differ considerably from one person to another, depending on such factors as skill, experience, age, family responsibilities, other sources of income, and even the values and attitudes of those whose opinions the person respects.

Consider the situation of teenagers living with their families. They often want jobs and may actively seek them in ways that qualify them for inclusion in the ranks of the officially unemployed. But if they're currently attending school, they are "presently available" for a very limited number of jobs. If they're on summer vacation, employers won't want to hire them for jobs that require a lot of training, so they aren't really "available" for these jobs either. If they're out of high school but trying to make up their minds about college, they'll be reluctant to accept any job that requires a commitment. Moreover, the job opportunities available to them will tend to be relatively unattractive, because employers don't want to pay much to teenagers, who tend to be unskilled and who quit before the employer has recovered the cost of training them. But someone receiving free room and board from parents can afford to search for a long time or to quit a job that proves unsatisfactory and start looking again. Any job will begin to seem unsatisfactory to teenagers who discover that they must work while their friends are partying. When we put all this together, we see that the cost of taking and keeping a job is high for most teenagers and that the cost of continuing to look is relatively low. Should we be either surprised or disturbed, then, to discover that the unemployment rate among people 16 to 19 years old is often three times the unemployment rate among the general population?

Because lost income is usually the main cost of being unemployed, anything that promises to maintain people's income while they're not working is likely to increase the unemployment rate. If we offer unemployment insurance to more workers, extend the duration of benefits, and generally loosen the criteria for eligibility, this won't induce people with well-paid and highly satisfying jobs to get themselves fired so they can start drawing unemployment compensation. At the margin, however, more generous unemployment benefits do make people less determined to hang on to current jobs and less eager to accept new ones, thus raising the unemployment rate. A rise in the number of multiearner families will have the same kind of effect. When we consider the impact of income and Social Security taxes on earnings plus all the other costs associated with working, the financial incentive for a second earner to find a new job when an old one has been lost diminishes dramatically. It will sometimes even be negative until eligibility for unemployment compensation has been exhausted.

Remember, too, that economic decisions depend on expectations. People enter the labor force because they expect to find satisfactory employment. If for some reason the expectations of many labor force entrants are unrealistically high, the result will be an increase in the unemployment rate. Suppose, for example, that more opportunities open up in the business world for women who want to enter management. These improved prospects will induce more women to enter or remain in the labor force. It's quite possible that the expectation of more and better career opportunities for women could pull so many additional women into the labor force that the female unemployment rate would actually rise. Unemployment would remain high until expectations adjusted to reality—or reality caught up with expectations.

Similarly, if recent college graduates or freshly minted lawyers hold exaggerated views about the value of their degrees in the labor market, the unemployment rate among them will rise. Steelworkers who are accustomed to wage rates about double the average of the wages usually paid in manufacturing will be slow to accept employment at lower wages when the steel companies for which they've been working go out of business. They aren't very different from homeowners who refuse to believe that the house they are trying to sell won't move at the price they're asking. "For sale" signs consequently multiply and stay up longer in a declining real estate market.

Unemployment and Recessions

Figure 15–2 shows the relationship between recessions and unemployment. The unemployment rate rises sharply soon after the onset of a recession. It then declines when the recovery begins, but always much more slowly than it rose. After the recession of 1949 (not shown in Figure 15–2), the exceptionally strong recovery, fueled in large part by the Korean War, lowered unemployment from 5.9 percent in 1949 to 2.9 percent by 1953. The recession of 1954 boosted it back up to 5.5 percent, from which it slowly declined until another recession, beginning in the last quarter of 1957, hiked it to 6.8 percent. The unemployment rate had little time to fall before the recession of 1960–1961 raised it once more. The long expansion after 1961 gradually lowered the unemployment rate to 3.5 percent in 1969, after which the recession of 1970–1971 bumped it up to 5.9 percent.

The recovery after 1971 never got the unemployment rate below 4.9 percent, and the recovery after the deep recession of 1974–1975 failed to push the rate below 5.8 percent. By the middle of the 1980s, students of the U.S. labor market had generally come to the conclusion that the "natural" rate of unemployment for the United States was close to 6 percent. The "natural" rate is sometimes defined as the lowest rate to which unemployment

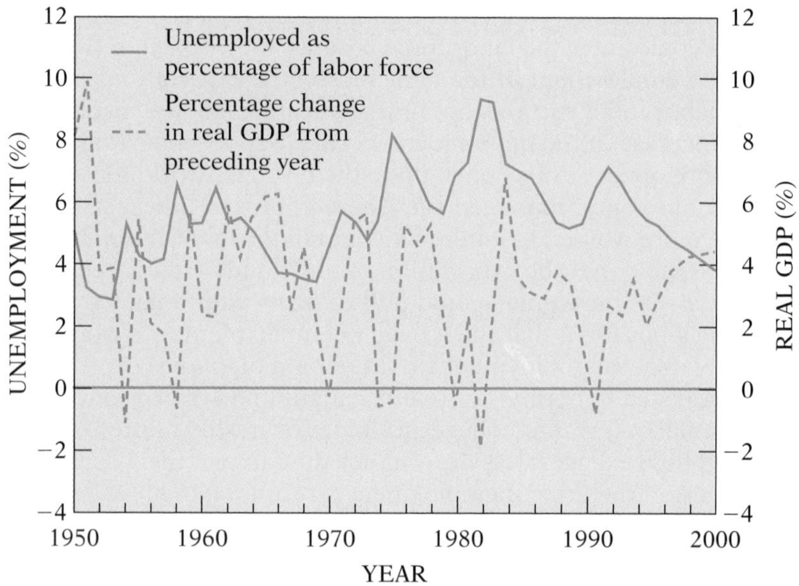

Figure 15–2 **Recessions and unemployment in the United States**

could fall without accelerating the inflation rate. At other times, it is more loosely described as a kind of equilibrium rate, the rate that would be established in the absence of destabilizing shocks, or the rate that reflects people's considered preferences between labor force participation and nonparticipation and between accepting employment and searching for something better. When the unemployment rate fell below 6 percent in 1988 and all the way down to 5 percent in March of 1989, numerous authorities predicted an imminent rise in the inflation rate.

The inflation rate did rise slightly from 1989 to 1991. But the expansion after 1991 pushed the unemployment rate steadily downward until it hit a low of 4.3 percent in April and May 1998, all without rekindling inflation. There was at least as much fear of deflation as of inflation on the part of economic prognosticators in the last half of 1998. Since 1998, unemployment rates have remained rather steady, rising only slightly to the June 2001 level of 4.5 percent. Throughout this period of low unemployment, a low inflation environment continues.

Why Does Unemployment Persist?

Why does unemployment rise so sharply in a recession and then persist somewhat stubbornly long after the recession has ended and a recovery has begun? The former question probably doesn't need much of an answer. When the demand for what a firm is selling declines unexpectedly and unsold inventories begin to mount, the firm will restrict production and look for ways to trim costs. Because labor costs generally make up a sizable part of firms' marginal costs, layoffs and a rise in the unemployment rate are only to be expected once a recession gets going.

But why doesn't the unemployment rate return to its prerecession level when the economic recovery has brought the level of output back to what it was before the recession began? One obvious reason is that it takes longer to hire employees than to lay them off. Those who were laid off during the recession will not all sit home waiting for the phone call that summons them back to work. Most will search for other jobs and many will end up accepting alternative employment. So a firm that wants to expand employment again in the recovery will have to search for and train some new employees. Many firms will be reluctant to do that until they are fairly sure that the recovery is genuine. They will be more inclined to provide overtime employment for existing personnel than to add new names to their employee roster. Some firms will learn during a recession how to get more done with fewer employees. Long expansions encourage firms to hire more people than necessary and perhaps to become a bit careless about using resources efficiently. Recessions in turn create strong incentives to reduce "waste" and to economize on as many margins as possible. The learning that occurs during a recession doesn't disappear when the recession ends, so that some of the employees who were laid off during the recession will not be rehired or replaced after the recession has ended.

The supply and demand model introduced in Chapter 5 suggests another question: Why don't workers looking for jobs offer to work for a lower wage? *Unemployment represents a surplus of labor*: The quantity supplied is greater than the quantity demanded. A lower wage would presumably reduce the quantity supplied and increase the quantity demanded until the market-clearing wage was reached. If a worker's marginal productivity exceeds the wage offered, the worker will always be able to find employment. On the other hand, if the wage rate exceeds the marginal product of that employee, it will be hard to find a job unless the wage rate is adjusted downward. If an employer offers a wage below the value of the worker's marginal product to that firm, other employers will find it in their interest to compete for that employee and thus put an upward pressure on that employee's wage rate. The market for labor, in this picture, operates the same way that all other markets operate. Adjustments by employers (buyers) and employees (sellers) in the labor market will tend to equate the value of the marginal product with the wage rate and clear the market.

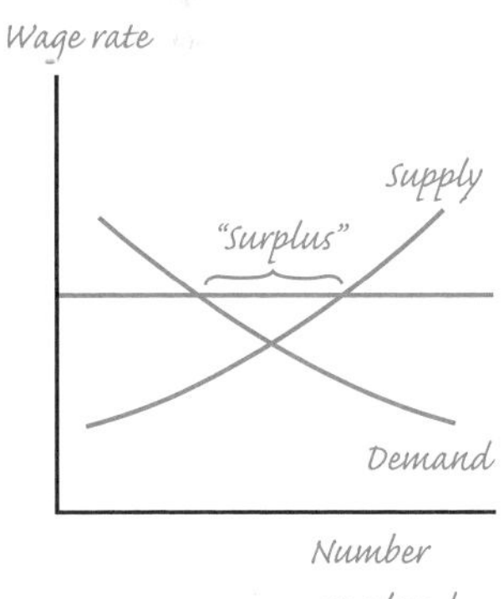

But the market for labor does not always work in the same way as the market for agricultural commodities. There are good reasons to suppose that a surplus of labor might result in the labor market, for the simple reason that many employers will want to pay a wage (an "efficiency wage") somewhat higher than the market would require. Why would they choose to do that—apart from any sense of generosity that might move them? If they pay a wage that exactly clears the market, then their employees can expect to find a new job just as good as the one they now have should they leave their present job, voluntarily or involuntarily. That means employees will have weak incentives to live with slights and disappointments and strong incentives to exaggerate the advantages of working somewhere else. The result will be a high turnover rate, which is expensive for employers whenever the cost of training new workers is more than trivial. Even if employers are motivated exclusively by concern for the bottom line, they want their employees to think of their present job as something better than they are likely to find elsewhere.

That conviction on the part of employees also reduces what is called "shirking." Ask yourself these questions: Why shouldn't an employee do only what is required and nothing more? Put out only as much effort as the employer can monitor? Goof off, steal, and even sabotage the firm when there is little chance of being detected? One reason would be the employee's sense of moral responsibility. But that sense weakens quickly when employees believe, with or without good reason, that they aren't being treated fairly. Quite apart from reasons of conscience, a strong reason not to behave in any of these ways is the belief that being discharged would be costly. And a discharge is costly whenever workers are being paid more than their opportunity cost. So we see once again that pure concern for net revenue will induce many employers to offer a wage appreciably above the wage that clears the market.

When a recession strikes and firms' demand for labor declines along with the demand for the product they are selling, employers have strong reasons to reduce employment rather than wages. Employees seldom respond kindly to wage reductions. If they are not unionized already, employees are likely to think more seriously about becoming unionized when their pay envelope suddenly shrinks. If they are working under a union contract, the contract will probably prohibit reductions without the union's consent, a consent the union is unlikely to give, even if persuaded that a wage reduction will preserve employment opportunities, because the union leaders are far more likely to be blamed for the reduced wages than applauded for the saved jobs. Moreover, workers who are laid off permanently may cease to be members of the union, whereas all those whose wages are reduced continue to be voting members of the union. The employer will come to similar conclusions for analogous reasons. A workforce made up of 90 satisfied employees could very well be more productive than one made up of 100 disgruntled employees who have sustained a 10 percent reduction in their take-home pay.

How much pressure on wage rates do unemployed workers exert? Marx and others have argued that a reserve army of the unemployed outside the factory gates enables employers to press wages down within the factory. Whatever may have been the case in the nineteenth century, that claim seems dubious under standard conditions in the industrialized nations today. Employers are far more attentive to those already on the payroll—the insiders—than to those outsiders who would like to get on the payroll. That would probably be true even if the outsiders had some effective way to communicate their willingness to work for less and employers had persuasive reasons to believe the communication. But neither condition is likely to be met. The implication is that wage rates will rise during a recovery and thereby retard somewhat the rate at which employment expands.

The consequence of all this is a persistent surplus of labor: The quantity supplied will regularly be greater than the quantity demanded. The almost universal experience of workers confirms this implication of our various hypotheses. The number of potential employees looking for work is almost always perceived to be much larger than the number of jobs that employers are trying to fill. There exists, in other words, a chronic shortage of jobs and a chronic surplus of job seekers.

The Phillips Curve

In 1958, an economist named A. W. Phillips published a study titled "The Relationship between Unemployment and the Rate of Change of Money Wage Rates in the United Kingdom, 1861–1957" and gave birth to an idea that quickly grew up to become the "Phillips curve." Phillips showed that there was a stable relationship during the period he studied between the unemployment rate and the rate at which the average money wage increased. Unemployment was greater when money wage rates were increasing more slowly and fell in periods when money wage rates were rising rapidly. That seems thoroughly plausible. During periods of high demand for labor, employers will tend to bid up wage rates to obtain and keep the employees they want. In periods of high unemployment, employers will not have to bid so energetically for labor, and wage rates will increase less rapidly.

But the argument was soon extended to suggest that unemployment might be reduced by generating an inflationary rate of increase in money wages through expansionary monetary and fiscal policies that caused all prices to rise. The Phillips curve of this latter argument purports to show that there is a general tradeoff between inflation and unemployment, so that less of one can be obtained by accepting more of the other. The conclusion does not follow either from A. W. Phillips's data or from reflection on the causes of inflation and unemployment. And the notion that government policymakers can reduce the rate of unemployment by deliberately causing inflation is an extremely hazardous one.

It is probably true that prices and wages will be more likely to drift upward when the economy is close to "full" employment. The economic system always contains a great deal of internal movement: Some industries grow, others decline, firms rise and fall, new production techniques are introduced, the composition of demand changes, people enter and leave the labor force. Resources must therefore be attracted continuously into particular employments through the offer of acceptable employment terms. But employers and employees don't have perfect information. They must search for what they want and incur the costs of that search.

In a period of low unemployment, the cost of finding a new job will, on the average, be lower for employees than during a period of high unemployment. Employees will therefore be more ready to give up a job when they think the wage is unsatisfactory and begin searching for another. So employers will find it difficult to reduce wages. Search costs for employers are higher in periods of low unemployment. And so employers will offer higher wages than they might otherwise be willing to offer in order to avoid making an extensive and costly search for the new employees they want and to reduce the risk of losing present employees, who would be expensive to replace. The same argument applies to prices in product markets. When the economy is operating close to capacity, it may be difficult to obtain additional supplies in a timely manner, and buyers may consequently be willing to offer higher prices rather than search for alternative sources of supply. In a period of high unemployment and substantial excess capacity, sellers will be shaving prices, because buyers are harder to find.

The identical conclusion emerges whichever way we look at it. "Full" employment fosters an upward creep in prices and wages; periods of substantial unemployment and excess capacity encourage a downward drift in prices and wages.

The basic argument asserts that the direction of drift in price and wage movements is a response to tightness or slackness in markets. In other words, the level of employment is the cause and price-wage movement the effect. But we can't assume that because full employment causes inflation, inflation will bring about full employment. When there's a big crowd at the basketball game, the gymnasium temperature rises because of body heat; but the athletic department can't make a crowd come to watch a losing basketball team by overheating the gymnasium.

Reducing Unemployment by Illusion: Inflation and the Misdirection of Labor

Nonetheless, the policy of deliberately stepping up inflation probably would lower the unemployment rate—temporarily. People in the labor force are unemployed because they don't find the job opportunities of which they're aware sufficiently attractive. A policy of deliberate inflation makes job opportunities seem more attractive by raising the money wage rate offers of employers. And this is how inflation might reduce unemployment. But the higher wage rate offers are only seemingly more attractive. As long as potential employees don't realize that the job opportunities they're now accepting are in reality no better than the opportunities they previously rejected, employment will indeed rise. But it will subsequently fall back down to its previous level when employees discover what's happening: that inflation is creating the illusion of more attractive wage offers. No permanent reduction in unemployment will have occurred, but the economy will be undergoing more rapid inflation.

We've quoted from F. A. Hayek on the signal-distorting effects of inflation in the previous chapter. Here's another quote, with reference to inflation's impact on the labor market:

> The chief conclusion . . . is that the longer the inflation lasts, the larger will be the number of workers whose jobs depend on the *continuation* of the inflation, often even on a continuing *acceleration* of the rate of inflation—not because they would not have found employment without the inflation, but because they were drawn by the inflation into *temporarily* attractive jobs, which after a slowing down or cessation of the inflation, will again disappear.

A "well-behaved" Phillips curve: United States, 1954–1969

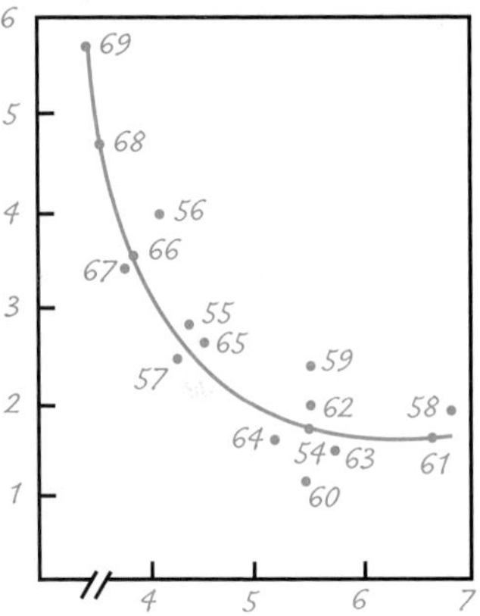

A deliberate policy of pursuing lower unemployment by accepting a higher rate of inflation calls, then, for continuously increasing the inflation rate *so that workers always expect less than the actual rate of inflation*. In that way they can be made to overestimate continuously the real value of the money wages they're being offered. Or else the policy assumes that employees pay exclusive attention to money wage rates, never to real wage rates. This is a superficially plausible assumption, because we know that few employees consult the most recent changes in the Consumer Price Index before deciding whether a wage offer is adequate. They look at *money* wage rates, *nominal* wage rates. But they also learn after a while that their wages buy less and adjust their perception of the wage rate's real value.

Policy cannot be constructed, especially in a relatively free and democratic society, on the assumption that workers can be permanently fooled. People do learn from experience, and even if they themselves are not paying close attention, others are likely to inform them eventually. The simultaneous existence of high unemployment with very rapid inflation in the United States in the 1970s seems to be evidence that people learned quickly how to distinguish real from merely nominal wage increases. When employees begin to take continued inflation for granted, they no longer suffer from the illusion that money wages and real wages are the same thing.

But suppose a government tried this approach, discovered that a policy of deliberate inflation couldn't actually lower unemployment, and decided to abandon the policy. Suppose the government had been causing inflation by applying fiscal and monetary stimulus and then decided to ease up. After a lag of some length, total spending would presumably stop increasing so rapidly and producers would be unable to sell at the prices they had anticipated. Inventories would begin to mount, production would be curtailed, and unemployment would rise. Eventually, sellers would learn not to expect such a rapid rise in prices and would adjust downward the prices they ask and the prices they offer to pay for inputs. Sales would then revive, inventories would decline, production would start up again, and unemployment would (slowly) fall. But that won't all happen within a week or even a month. The higher unemployment that might well result from an attempt to slow down the rate of inflation would be temporary, but temporary can be a long time for those who are laid off.

A "not-so-well-behaved" Phillips curve: U.S., 1970–1981

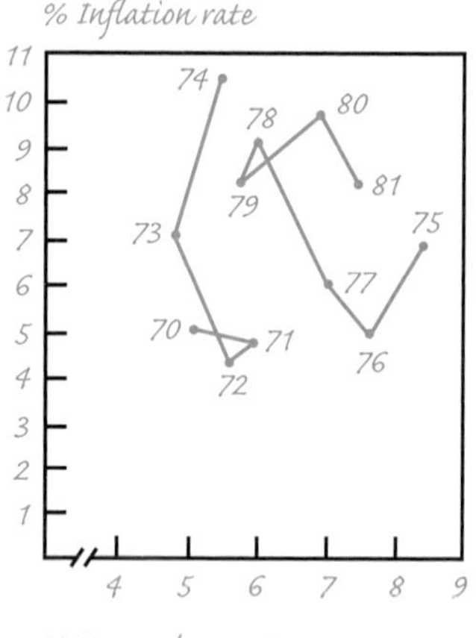

What it all comes to is that if the prevailing rate of unemployment is close to the "natural" rate of unemployment, government policies designed to raise output and lower unemployment by increasing aggregate demand will work only if they succeed in creating erroneous expectations on the part of the public. That probably occurred in the latter half of the 1960s. Expansionary fiscal and monetary policies raised output and lowered unemployment, because the public did not know what was happening and consistently underestimated the rate at which costs and prices were going to rise as a result of current policies. But eventually people figured out what was happening and adjusted both their expectations and their behavior. In the 1970s and early 1980s, even more expansionary aggregate-demand policies produced even more rapid inflation, but accompanied this time by high rates of unemployment. Once the public caught on, expansionary aggregate-demand policies produced little more than a faster rate of inflation.

Labor-Market Policies

There is a great deal of debate, among economists as well as politicians and the general public, about what government can and should do to hold down or reduce the rate of unemployment. Much of the disagreement stems from the simple fact that we really don't know what the consequences of some policies are likely to be. Another cause of disagreement is that government policies rarely, if ever, have only the consequences intended.

A strong consensus supports the view that government can keep the unemployment rate down insofar as it can prevent or reduce those fluctuations in the rate of economic growth that we know as the business cycle. The issues in dispute are the ability and even the willingness (as we shall see in Chapter 20) of government officials to stabilize the rate of economic growth.

A strong consensus also supports the position that government can lower the unemployment rate through appropriate labor-market policies. There is considerably less consensus on what those policies ought to be. Everyone favors training programs that succeed in equipping people who have lost their jobs with relevant skills that enable them to find new jobs. Unfortunately, programs that succeed in doing this on any large scale, that actually manage to place in new jobs a lot of people who would otherwise have remained unemployed, are as rare as they are commendable.

It's logical to assume that government could lower the unemployment rate by abolishing unemployment compensation. That would raise every laid-off worker's cost of looking for a new job and so shorten the period of search. You may construct your own political and ethical arguments against such a step. An economic argument against it is that searching too briefly is as wasteful of valuable resources as searching too long.

Because unemployment, and especially the unemployment created by recessions, is in large part a consequence of mistaken expectations, the government could reduce the unemployment rate by improving the quality of the information available to economic decision makers. But is that much different from saying that we could increase the high school graduation rate by improving the quality of high school education? Perhaps it is different—at least if shifting and unpredictable government policies are themselves a major source of the uncertainty that confronts economic decision makers. Even then we are left with the question of how to prevent a government that is responsive to the next election from pursuing shifting and unpredictable policies.

What we are calling *labor-market policies* differ widely among nations. And so do unemployment rates, even after they have been adjusted to take account of the different ways in which they are calculated. The unemployment rate in Spain in 1994, calculated in roughly the way that we do it in the United States, was 24 percent. Part of that was the result of a recession in 1991 and 1992. But most of it was a result of government policies that, for example, discouraged Spanish employers from hiring new workers by making it almost impossible to lay anyone off. The labor-market policies that currently protect the high wages, lengthy vacations, and generous benefits of employed workers in Germany and France seem to be highly valued by voters in these countries. If everyone could agree on the extent to which the stubbornly high unemployment rates in both countries are a consequence of these policies, which without question reduce the quantity of labor demanded by German and French employers, it might be possible to have a constructive discussion of the benefits and costs of such policies. But few important economic controversies can be clearly settled, a claim that will not surprise you once you realize that any issue that can be clearly settled will cease to generate important controversy.

Once Over Lightly

Many of those who are *not employed* are not in the labor force and therefore not *unemployed*.

The distinction between those who are not in the labor force because they do not want any available job and those who are in the labor force but unemployed because they cannot find a job they are willing to accept is not always crystal clear.

The Bureau of Labor Statistics counts as unemployed all those who are not currently employed *and* are actively seeking employment or waiting to begin or return to a job. Both the decision to enter the labor force and the decision not to accept particular job offers will depend on people's estimates of the relative advantages of alternative opportunities.

Different unemployment rates for different population groups do not merely reflect differences in the demand for the labor services of the people in those groups. They also reflect variations in the cost to different people of searching for, accepting, and retaining employment.

Unemployment rates in the United States became generally higher after 1970 in comparison with unemployment rates in the 1950s and 1960s. But labor-force participation rates and employment rates also rose to record-high levels after 1970. Higher unemployment rates coupled with rising employment rates suggest that the expected benefits and costs both of entering the labor force and of remaining unemployed have been changing in recent years for many members of the noninstitutional population.

Labor markets differ from commodity markets in important respects, including some that cause the quantity of labor supplied to be chronically greater than the quantity demanded, principally because many employers have strong incentives to offer wage rates higher than the rates that would clear the market.

Economic conditions that create rising prices and falling rates of unemployment have created the dubious belief that the unemployment rate can be lowered by policies that increase the rate of inflation. Whatever positive effect inflation has on employment will disappear when workers recognize that they have mistaken a mere decline in the value of money for higher real wage rates.

Although all economists would probably agree that the labor-market policies of governments can make national unemployment rates higher or lower, there is little agreement on particular policies that would in fact lower unemployment rates and that are politically acceptable.

QUESTIONS FOR DISCUSSION

1. Should the imaginary individuals who made each of the following statements be classified as unemployed or as not in the labor force?
   (a) "I quit my job and I'm going to remain unemployed until I find a job that pays $1,000 for 10 hours of work a week."
   (b) "I was laid off last month. I had a great job as marketing consultant to a franchising chain. They paid me $1,000 a week for about 10 hours of work. I'm going to keep looking until I find another job like that one."
   (c) "I decided I could no longer be a part of a system based on violence and exploitation, so I quit my job. I'm looking now for an engineer's position that doesn't require me to support the military-industrial complex."
   (d) "When they laid me off, I figured I could easily find another job just as good. But now I don't care. I'll take any job at all that pays what I used to get."
   (e) "I've been out of work for six months, and I'm pretty desperate. I'll do anything that's legal to get food for my family. But I have an invalid wife and five small children, so I can't take any job that pays less than $500 a week."
   (f) "I could get any one of a dozen jobs tomorrow. But I don't want to. I'm eligible for three more months of unemployment compensation, so I'm just going to take it easy until the checks run out. Oh, if something really good turned up, I'd take it, of course."
   (g) "I could get any one of a dozen jobs tomorrow. But I don't want to. I'm eligible for three more months of unemployment compensation, so I'm just going to spend my time really looking. I'm going to use those three months to find the very best job I can possibly get."
2. Unemployment did not exist by definition in the old Soviet Union, where any unemployment at all was held to be inconsistent with socialism. It was not just a matter of definition, however. There were so many jobs relative to workers that *Pravda*, the Communist Party newspaper, urged the passage of laws that would prohibit job quitting without adequate cause and would subject able-bodied workers to arrest if they were out of work for more than two weeks. How do you suppose the Soviet Union maintained a surplus of jobs while the United States always seems to have had a surplus of workers?
3. Jones is a tool-and-die maker earning $30 an hour. He is suddenly laid off.
   (a) He frequents employment agencies, reads want ads, and follows up leads on tool-and-die–making jobs for two weeks. Is he unemployed during this time, as the BLS measures unemployment?
   (b) At the end of two weeks, he is offered a job driving a bread truck that pays $9 an hour. He turns it down. Is he unemployed?
   (c) He receives an offer of a job as a tool-and-die maker in a city 125 miles away. He turns it down because his teenage children don't want to change high schools. Is he unemployed?
   (d) After three months of searching, Jones becomes discouraged and quits looking. Is he unemployed?

4. In April 1998, the official unemployment rate in the United States fell to 4.3 percent, the lowest level it had attained since February 1970. Test your understanding of the definitions used by the Bureau of Labor Statistics in reporting the data gathered in its monthly household surveys by filling in the blank spaces in the following table. The figures refer to thousands of persons and are seasonally adjusted data for June 2004.

Noninstitutional population	223,196
Employment	139,031
Not in the labor force	75,916
Labor force	____
Unemployed	____
Unemployment rate	____
Employment rate	____
Labor force participation rate	____

5. The textbook points to the greatly increased rate at which women entered the labor force in the United States as the principal cause of the marked rise in the rate of labor force participation over the last 25 years. To what factors would you attribute the decision of so many more women to enter the labor force?
6. Return to Figure 15–1 and look carefully at the patterns that have been traced since 1970 by the unemployment and the employment rates. When one rises, the other falls, which is, of course, what we would expect. But the successive peaks in each rate were both rising until the unemployment rate peaked in 1992 well below its 1982–1983 peak.
   (a) What might have caused this trend toward rising unemployment peaks? Note that not only were the unemployment peaks reached during successive recessions rising (until the pattern was broken in 1992); the lowest level of unemployment reached following each recession was also rising after 1969. You might also want to take note of the fact that a similar pattern was traced from 1950 to 1963.
   (b) While the employment rate seems to be continuing the upward march begun in the 1970s, the unemployment rate now appears to be trending downward—as it began doing in 1964. Can you think of a good explanation for such a break in the trend of the unemployment rate?
   (c) Does Figure 15–1 support or contradict the notion that there is such a thing as a "natural" rate of unemployment?
7. Can there be "overfull" employment?
   (a) Suppose that the vacancy rate of apartments in a large city is less than 1 percent. What undesirable consequences might be associated with such a full level of apartment employment? Would you enjoy moving to a city with such a low vacancy rate?
   (b) If you are driving on only 80 percent of the automobile tires you own, is the spare tire unemployed? Would you like to be driving with your tires at "full employment"? Across the Great Salt Lake Desert?
8. The textbook urges you to use aggregated data cautiously. The unemployment rate of 5.6 percent in June 2004 was the rate for the population

as a whole. Here are the unemployment rates for the same month for various subgroups. Can you draw any interesting conclusions from them? (These are also aggregated data!)

White	5.0%
White males (20 and over)	5.0
White females (20 and over)	5.0
Whites 16 to 19 years old	14.8
Black	10.1
Hispanic origin	6.7
16- to 19-year-olds	16.8
Black 16- to 19-year-olds	32.6
Less than high school diploma	8.8
High school diploma, no college	5.1
Some college, no bachelor's degree	4.2
College graduate	2.7

Source: Bureau of Labor Statistics, *Employment and Earnings*; www.bls.gov.

9. How long are people unemployed? The following data show what portion of those unemployed in June 2004 were unemployed for various lengths of time.

Unemployed less than 5 weeks	33%
Unemployed 5 to 14 weeks	29.5
Unemployed more than 15 weeks	37.6
Unemployed more than 27 weeks	21.6
Average (mean) duration of unemployment	19.9 weeks
Median duration of unemployment	10.8 weeks

Source: Bureau of Labor Statistics, *Employment and Earnings*; www.bls.gov.

The data show that most of those who become unemployed find employment again in fewer than 15 weeks. But more than a third of those unemployed have been looking for work for longer than that. Why would unemployed people in a period of strong employer demand for workers such as prevailed in the summer of 2004 be unable to find a job within 15 weeks?

10. A man is laid off from his job and goes to work for himself (becomes self-employed) "producing" information about alternative job opportunities. How long he will remain self-employed in this way depends on his "productivity" (i.e., whether he is generating what he considers valuable information) and the opportunity cost of this self-employment (which he'll want to continue as long as his anticipated marginal revenue exceeds anticipated marginal cost). How will the duration of his unemployment be affected by the following?
    (a) He is eligible for unemployment compensation.
    (b) He is married and his wife has a high-paying job.
    (c) He hears persistent rumors that the demand for his skills is picking up.

(d) He's a person who is by nature confident and optimistic.
(e) The job from which he was laid off (because the firm failed, not through any fault of his own) was an excellent one with creative challenge and high pay.

11. According to Polson and Company, a Minneapolis executive-search firm, the higher the salary, the longer it takes for a job seeker to obtain a new position. The rule of thumb is one additional month of searching for every $10,000 in annual compensation. Is a month spent in searching rather than earning income a good investment if it promises a return of $10,000 per year? Assume that this additional $10,000 will run for five years and calculate its present discounted value before attempting to answer the question.
12. How many reasons can you list for employers to choose to pay a wage rate higher than they would have to pay in order to obtain as many workers as they require to staff their operation?
13. Why is the price level likely to be rising more rapidly when the unemployment rate is low than when it is high?
14. Suppose that a corporation opened a factory employing 5,000 workers in a town of 10,000 people. Why would you expect to observe low unemployment, rising wage rates, and rising prices for locally produced goods such as housing and services? What is the causal connection in this case between the town's unemployment rate and changes in prices?
15. In the situation described in the preceding question, would you expect prices to start declining if the factory laid off half its labor force? What difference would it make whether the layoff was thought to be temporary or permanent? How much time would it take for a layoff to start bringing down the prices of housing and services in the town?
16. You decide to live in an apartment when you return to campus in the fall. Everyone tells you that apartments are extremely hard to find, so you arrive on campus to start searching a week before school begins.
    (a) If you find something you like but consider it somewhat overpriced, are you likely to take it or to continue looking?
    (b) Is the owner likely to hold it for you for several days, while you continue your search, without a nonrefundable deposit?
    (c) How would the behavior of tenants and owners be different if recent construction had created a surplus of apartment units near the campus?
17. Can inflation reduce unemployment?
    (a) The help-wanted column of an urban newspaper has been advertising for airport skycaps every day for the past six months. The only job requirements listed are a friendly attitude, a driver's license, and the ability to lift large suitcases. Does the continuous running of this advertisement for six months prove that all the truly unemployed people in the city lack either a friendly attitude, a driver's license, or physical strength?
    (b) How could the firm running this advertisement obtain all the qualified skycaps it wants, plus a pool of substitutes and eager apprentices?
    (c) How might a sudden, rapid surge of inflation provide this firm with all the applicants it wants?

(d) When and why would the firm again find itself forced to advertise in the help-wanted column?

18. The unemployment rate in France has been above 11 percent in every year since 1993 and has climbed close to 13 percent, despite the fact that none of these years were recession years. The socialist government elected in 1997 pledged to adopt labor-market policies that would lower the unemployment rate.

    (a) One measure adopted by the new government calls for reducing the official working week from 39 hours to 35 hours with no reduction in pay. Business firms with more than 20 employees had to shorten the workweek by the year 2000; firms with fewer employees had until 2002. Do you think this will reduce the unemployment rate?

    (b) The government was especially concerned about high youth unemployment, which was above 25 percent. It consequently established a program to create 350,000 new jobs in the public sector (plus an equal number in the private sector, for which employers will receive subsidies). All workers are to be paid the legal minimum wage, which is about 65 percent of the average wage. To avoid displacing existing workers, the government designated 22 new career fields, designed, it said, to fulfill previously unmet needs. These include such positions as mediator in landlord–tenant disputes, keepers of peace and order in subway stations and schoolyards, and receptionists in police stations. Do you think this will reduce the unemployment rate among youth?

    (c) How are private employers likely to view job applicants who list on their résumés, as their most recent job, five years in the public sector positions just mentioned?

The Supply of Money 16

R.A. Radford was a British economist who spent time during World War II in a prisoner of war camp and subsequently published an article about his experiences, "The Economic Organization of a P.O.W. Camp."[1] He describes how the prisoners, taking advantage of the different marginal valuations placed on the rations supplied by their captors plus items from Red Cross parcels and private packages received in the camp, established a lively trading economy. Although German currency did exist in the camp, it circulated only as payment for gambling debts because few articles could be purchased with it from the camp canteen. The principal money or medium of exchange was cigarettes.

Cigarettes as Money

No authority decreed that exchange in the camp should take place by means of money, much less that the money used should be cigarettes. It just happened. Prisoners discovered that they could make themselves better off through trading if they were not confined to barter, selling only to those who had what they themselves wanted and buying only from those willing to accept what they themselves had to offer. But the limitations of barter can be escaped only if some good exists that everyone is willing to accept because they know that everyone else is willing to accept it. Cigarettes were convenient: They were both homogeneous and durable and could be used individually for small transactions or in packages for larger transactions. Because the Red Cross provided regular supplies, they were available in sufficient quantity. And the numerous smokers among the prisoners guaranteed that they would always have value. So cigarettes became by consensus the medium of exchange.

[1]Originally published in the journal *Economica* in November 1945 and often quoted.

But cigarettes have serious drawbacks as money. For one thing, they don't *stay* homogeneous. One cigarette will not be just like another for very long once cigarettes become the medium of exchange. The Red Cross issued pipe tobacco in lieu of cigarettes at the rate of one ounce of tobacco per 25 cigarettes. When it turned out that an ounce of pipe tobacco could be rolled into 30 homemade cigarettes, the prisoners began hand-rolling cigarettes from pipe tobacco. As a result, the percentage of hand-rolled cigarettes in the money supply increased rapidly. When prisoners with machine-made cigarettes started removing some of the tobacco to reroll it, those who sold goods for cigarette money had to inspect the money carefully to be sure it was up to standard. A money whose value is unclear raises transaction costs and reduces trading.

Gresham's Law: Poor-quality money will circulate; Good quality money will be hoarded.

An English financier named Thomas Gresham suggested a rule in the sixteenth century, known ever since as *Gresham's Law*, which states that bad money drives good money out of circulation. If two units of money have the same nominal value but one is in reality more valuable than the other, then the one with lower value will circulate and the one with higher value will be hoarded. Isn't that how you behave? Won't you give the grocery store clerk a torn or tattered one-dollar bill rather than the newer one in your wallet? Won't you try to spend the Canadian quarter in your pocket or change purse before you spend the American quarter? Experience in Radford's prison camp confirmed Gresham's Law, as hand-rolled cigarettes drove machine-made cigarettes out of circulation. Everyone tried to spend their worst money first while holding on to their best money, and soon the only cigarettes in circulation were hand-rolled ones of questionable value. That raised the cost of trading.

Another unfortunate feature of a monetary system employing cigarettes was a chronic tendency toward deflation. When the Red Cross supplies were interrupted for any period of time, the number of cigarettes circulating as money declined because smokers were always burning some of them up, with the result that the value of each remaining cigarette increased. An increase in the value of money is what we mean by deflation. Air raids in the vicinity of the camp would also produce sudden, sharp deflations as anxious smokers increased the rate at which they were reducing the quantity of money in circulation. Money to burn in a literal sense won't be the best money.

The Evolution of Money

Throughout recorded history individuals have been searching for ways to gain greater advantages from trading, and their experiences have repeatedly led them to settle on scarce and attractive metals as the preferred medium of exchange. Copper, bronze, silver, and gold are durable, can be divided into parts and easily reunited again, are limited in supply, and, because of their beauty and durability, are valued for other purposes. A major disadvantage is that someone offered pieces of metal in payment cannot readily determine the true weight and fineness of the metal. But politically powerful persons partially resolved this difficulty when they discovered that they could profit from turning the precious metals into coins. They could accept bars of metal and mint them into coins of a specified weight and fineness while keeping some of the metal for themselves. Their customers were willing to accept this deduction, called *seignorage*, because the minted metal, possessing a precisely known value, was worth more in exchange than unminted metal. The politically powerful person issuing the coins could even get some valuable free advertising by placing his own face on the coins. Milling the edges (putting ridges on the edges) made the coins more acceptable and therefore more valuable, because milling preserved the value of the coins over time by making it more difficult for people to shave metal from the coins that came into their hands before passing them on.

From coins...

Merchants or wealthy people who owned bars of gold or silver started looking for safe places to store them and turned in large numbers to goldsmiths, who had facilities for the secure storage of valuables. The receipts that the goldsmiths issued were perhaps the first form of paper money. Why should a buyer go to the trouble and risk of withdrawing his gold bars from the goldsmith's vault in order to pay a seller, who would then have to incur the cost of returning them to the goldsmith for storage? Why not just hand the seller his receipt?

When commercial banks arose and began accepting deposits of coined money, the bankers quickly saw that they could lend out at interest some fraction of the money deposited with them because only a few of the owners of these deposits would ever come in at one time to withdraw their money. Moreover, why lend borrowers the actual gold or silver coins? Receipts would serve just as well and perhaps even better. This was the origin of most bank notes, the direct ancestors of our current paper money. A bank note was a piece of paper, ornately printed to frustrate counterfeiters, promising to pay to the bearer a specified quantity of metallic money.

... to bank notes

Look at the paper money in your possession and you will discover that it's comprised entirely of bank notes, issued by one of the 12 Federal Reserve banks in the United States. Until these notes were redesigned in the late 1990s, the round seal to the left of the portrait that appears on the note always gave the name of the specific bank that had issued it. The major difference between these bank notes and the ones that made up most of the paper money in the United States (and other nations of the world) until about 150 years ago is that now they tend to be issued exclusively by government-managed banks and they do not promise to pay the holder anything.

The Myth of Fiat Money

The Latin word fiat means "let it be" or "let it become." There are quite a few people today who complain bitterly about the fact that the national government has, or so they allege, turned all our money into mere fiat money. Our paper money isn't real money at all, they say; it's just paper that the government has turned into money by an arbitrary declaration. The old privately issued bank notes were not mere fiat money because they were receipts for silver or gold, and they obtained their value from that "backing." The objectors consider this an abuse of governmental authority, a fraud that has allowed the government to enrich itself by printing money to finance its extravagances in disregard of the fact that the more paper money it prints, the lower the value of the money held by its citizens.

Although this argument is partially correct it obscures a fundamental fact about money. No one, not even a powerful government, can turn something into money merely by fiat. *What makes anything money is that it is in fact accepted and used by people as a medium of exchange*. Federal Reserve notes are money in the United States not because the government says so but because the people of the United States are willing to accept them in payment for the sale of goods and repayment of debts. Governments around the world have discovered that if they print too much of their paper money, their citizens will become reluctant to accept it and something else—often United States Federal Reserve notes—will become the preferred medium of exchange within their borders.

The essential characteristic of money is acceptability.

Government does possess some powers that help it get its paper money accepted and used. It can, for example, promise to accept its own notes in payment of taxes. Anything that can be fully used to pay taxes will automatically acquire a considerable amount of acceptability. The government can also (and some governments do) declare the use of any bank notes other than its own notes to be illegal and impose significant penalties on those whose transactions violate the law. But the fundamental fact remains that acceptability is the necessary and sufficient condition for anything to become a medium of exchange. A small piece of ugly, torn, ink-stained green paper bearing a portrait of Andrew Jackson will be accepted anywhere in the United States because everyone knows that it will be accepted anywhere in the United States.

It sounds circular. Is it really that simple? Here's a little mental experiment for you to consider. Suppose that the owners of McDonald's instructed all their franchise holders to return change to customers in the form of either regular coin and currency or Big Smacks, according to the customers' choice, at the rate of one Big Smack per dollar. Big Smacks would be elaborately printed pieces of paper that holders could later redeem at any McDonald's franchise for one Big Mac. Many customers would choose to take

Big Smacks, because they expect to purchase Big Macs in the future and know that Big Macs cost a good bit more than one dollar. Big Smacks might subsequently come to enjoy a limited circulation outside the McDonald's chain. Suppose you often eat at McDonald's and I owe you five dollars. If I offered you five Big Smacks instead, you might accept them. And what if you then bought five dollars' worth of gasoline on the way home before discovering that you had forgotten your wallet? Might not the station owner be willing to take the five Big Smacks as full payment? And then use them to pay his paper carrier? In such circumstances, Big Smacks would be functioning as a medium of exchange.

The militant foes of government-issued paper money will immediately point out that the Big Smacks are not fiat money because they can be redeemed for something of "real" value. But let your imagination run a little wilder for a moment. Suppose that Big Smacks continued to be issued over the course of many years in ever larger amounts, that McDonald's never once defaulted on its commitment to pay on demand one Big Mac for one Big Smack so that people came to acquire complete confidence in them, and that all this time the purchasing power of the United States dollar was declining. Some people would begin to prefer payment in Big Smacks to payment in dollars because they would expect Big Smacks to hold their value better over time. Some of these would be vegetarians with no intention of ever buying a Big Mac. They might nonetheless be willing to accept Big Smacks because they would know that other people are willing to accept Big Smacks. It's conceivable, isn't it, that over a long enough period of time Big Smacks would come to circulate as the medium of exchange merely because they were accepted by others as the medium of exchange, without reference to the Big Macs that originally provided their "backing"?

How IOUs become money

If you don't find this scenario at all plausible—and it certainly is a highly unlikely development—test your credibility on another bit of fiction. Suppose that you ask to borrow $20 from your friend because you want to purchase a new novel that has just come out. He is willing to make the loan but happens to be short of cash at the moment. So he writes you an IOU and signs his name. You go to the campus bookstore, pick out the book you want, and hand the cashier your friend's IOU. The cashier looks at it, recognizes your friend's signature, rings up the sale, slips the IOU in the till, and hands you your change. The next customer uses a $50 bill to make a $10 purchase. The cashier says, "I only have one $20. Would you accept this?" and shows the customer your friend's IOU. He also recognizes the signature, knows that your friend is a person of both wealth and virtue, and says, "Sure." The IOU could circulate indefinitely, as long as everyone to whom it's presented knows your friend's signature, his character, and his ready availability. If this IOU were durable enough to circulate in the community for many years, it *could* come to be accepted simply because everyone knows that it's accepted by everyone else—even after your friend had long departed! Would your friend have created a piece of fiat money? Not by *mere* fiat! By creating confidence, rather, in the acceptability of the paper money that he had brought into existence.

The Nature of Money Today

All this is intended as a prelude to a true and important assertion: *What we use today as our medium of exchange consists almost entirely of the IOUs of trusted institutions*. What do we use in the United States today as our medium of exchange? Most people who think about money think immediately of those green pieces of paper, called *Federal Reserve notes*, and of coins in various sizes and colors. Economists lump these together and call it the currency component of the money supply. The Federal Reserve notes, by far the larger portion of the currency, are all IOUs—the accountants' term is *liabilities*—of Federal Reserve banks. When the Federal Reserve banks were first established, their notes were accepted because they bore a promise to pay "lawful money" on demand. No one much noticed or cared when those words were taken off the notes, because by that time the notes themselves had become "lawful money."

what we use: bank notes (i.e., cash) plus checkable deposits

Are there any substitutes for cash? Well, as we insisted way back in Chapter 3, there are substitutes for everything, including cash money. In fact, the most widely used medium of exchange is not cash *but checkable deposits: deposits in financial institutions that can be transferred to others through the writing of a check*. The most familiar type of checkable deposit is the money in an ordinary checking account with a commercial or "full-service" bank, which bankers call a demand deposit because it can be withdrawn on demand. These deposits are also IOUs or liabilities, liabilities of the particular banks in which the deposits are held. Your bank *owes* you the money in your checking account. American businesses and households pay for most of their transactions by writing checks, that is, by telling their bank to stop owing them a certain amount of money and to start owing that amount to the party to whom the check is written.

Students often have trouble at first in seeing that checkable deposits really are money in the full sense of the term. They themselves may handle all their transactions by means of currency. When they receive a check, they cash it; that is, they obtain currency for the check and spend the currency. But student habits are in no way typical of the transaction procedures employed by business firms, government units, and households. The overwhelming majority of exchanges, measured in dollar value, employ checkable deposits as the medium of exchange. Purchasers instruct their banks to transfer ownership of a portion of the purchasers' deposit to sellers. They write a check, in other words. Sellers typically deposit the checks rather than cash them, thereby instructing their own banks to collect the ownership whose transfer was ordered by the check writer. No currency at all changes hands. The bank in which the check is deposited makes an entry in its books; the bank on which the check is written makes an equal but opposite entry in its books.

What Federal Reserve notes and checkable deposits have in common, in addition to the fact that they comprise almost all of the medium of exchange in the United States, is that they are basically liabilities of trusted institutions. And why is this so important? Because it begins to indicate the difficulty of controlling the quantity of money in a society. The quantity of the medium of exchange in the society can be expanded by any institution that can persuade people to hold and circulate its liabilities. Private as well as public institutions that are able to do this have the ability to create money.

So How Much Money Is Out There?

The Federal Reserve calculates what is called M1, or the narrowly defined money stock, as the sum of currency in circulation, demand deposits, other checkable deposits, and traveler's checks. Table 16–1 gives you some notion of the magnitude of this sum and how it has changed from year to year. The quantity of money in the economy can and does fluctuate considerably from day to day, so figures are usually expressed as averages over some period of time. The numbers provided here are in billions of dollars and give the averages of daily figures in December of each year. Also shown is the percentage by which the total quantity of money increased or decreased from the preceding year.

If the narrowly defined money supply is officially called M1, one might suspect that there exists a more broadly defined stock of money, perhaps known as M2. And there does indeed. M2 is the sum of M1 plus noncheckable deposits in banks in amounts of less than $100,000 and shares in retail money market mutual funds, which are funds allowing initial investments of less than $50,000. M2 is an attempt to measure the dollar value of assets that the public can easily turn into the medium of exchange, such as through a phone call to a bank.

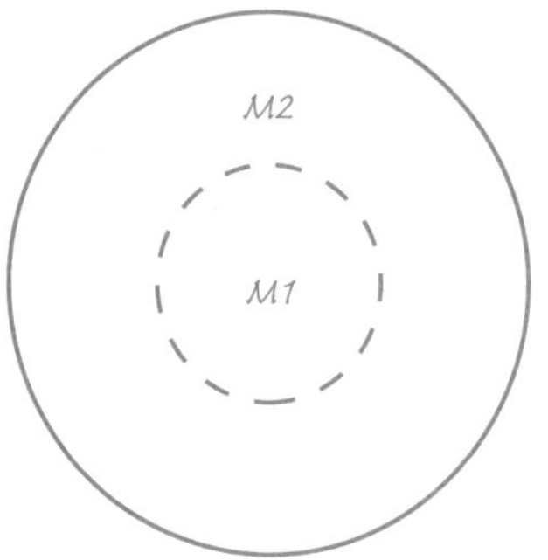

Changes in the size of M2 relative to M1 are the consequence of the public's preferences regarding the form in which it wants to hold its stock of money and moneylike assets. If you transferred the $500 you had borrowed out of your checking account and into a savings account at the bank where you borrowed, M1 would fall by $500. But M2 would be unchanged, because M2 includes everything in M1; the $500 contributes just as much to the total of M2 when it's in a checking account as when it's in a savings account. So bank lending increases M1. The public's desire to hold more or less of its assets in demand deposits or savings deposits will determine the different rates of growth between M1 and M2.

Table 16–1 **M1 in Billions of Dollars (averages of daily figures in December)**

Year	M1	% Change	Year	M1	% Change
1960	141	0.5	1982	475	8.7
1961	145	3.2	1983	521	9.8
1962	148	1.8	1984	552	5.9
1963	153	3.7	1985	620	12.3
1964	160	4.6	1986	724	16.9
1965	168	4.7	1987	750	3.5
1966	172	2.5	1988	787	5.0
1967	183	6.6	1989	794	0.9
1968	197	7.7	1990	826	4.0
1969	204	3.3	1991	897	8.7
1970	214	5.1	1992	1025	14.2
1971	228	6.5	1993	1130	10.2
1972	249	9.2	1994	1151	1.8
1973	263	5.5	1995	1129	−1.9
1974	274	4.3	1996	1083	−4.1
1975	287	4.8	1997	1076	−0.6
1976	306	6.6	1998	1092	1.5
1977	331	8.1	1999	1124	2.9
1978	358	8.2	2000	1091	−2.9
1979	383	6.8	2001	1179	8.1
1980	409	6.8	2002	1217	3.2
1981	437	6.8	2003	1293	6.2

Source: Board of Governors of the Federal Reserve System; www.federalreserve.gov.

Is there an M3? There is indeed. M3 is M2 plus noncheckable deposits of more than $100,000, shares in money market mutual funds that require initial investments of $50,000 or more, dollar-denominated deposits that Americans are holding in foreign branches of U.S. banks or any banks in Canada and the United Kingdom, and repurchase agreements issued by depository institutions. If you haven't gotten all that, it doesn't greatly matter for our purposes.

It may matter very much, however, to those at the Fed who calculate all these Ms and try to figure out exactly what they imply for the future. If the quantity of money demanded by the public is greater than the quantity supplied, or if the quantity supplied is greater than the quantity demanded, the disequilibrium could set off powerful changes that might lead to inflation or to recession. Because M2 and M3 can be converted into M1 quickly and at low cost, officials at the Fed want to keep their eye on all of them and to be continually ready to stimulate bank lending and money creation if that seems appropriate or to slow down bank lending and money creation if that's what the data seem to call for.

The Creation of Money

Banks create money. Literally. But they don't do so by *printing* up more green pieces of paper. Let's see how it happens. Suppose your application for a loan of $500 from the First National Bank is approved. The lending officer will make out a deposit slip in your name for $500, initial it, and hand it to a teller, who will then credit your checking account with an additional $500. Total demand deposits will immediately increase by $500. The money stock will be larger by that amount. Contrary to what most people believe, the bank does not take the $500 it lends you out of someone else's account. That person would surely complain if it did! The bank *created* the $500 it lent you.

But is that $500 *really* money? Let's say you borrowed the money to buy a computer. If you go down to the computer store and write it a check for $500, the employees will allow you to walk out the front door with the computer you wanted. That's persuasive evidence that your deposit really is money. The store's financial officer will then take your check to the store's bank and deposit it, receiving in return a credit for an additional $500 in its own checking account. The store's bank will send the check to the Federal Reserve's check-clearing system. There the store's bank will receive credit for an additional $500 in the amount it keeps on deposit with the Federal Reserve bank of its district, and your bank will have $500 deducted from the account it keeps on deposit there. The Federal Reserve bank will then send the check to your bank, which will cancel the debt it owes you: the $500 it had earlier credited to your account. But the total quantity of money in circulation won't go down when this happens, because that $500 your bank created still exists—in the checking account now of the computer store.

Why was the bank *willing* to create $500 for you? Because you gave the bank your own IOU, a credible promise to pay the bank $500 plus interest at some specified future date. Why was the bank able to create $500 for you? Because people are willing to accept its demand deposit liabilities and use them as a medium of exchange. Commercial banks are the prime example of private institutions that are able to persuade people to hold and circulate their liabilities. That's all it takes to create money.

Commercial banks are able to create money because the public is willing to accept bank liabilities in payment.

Surely it can't be that simple, you say. It seems just like having your own money machine in the basement. We would all like to be able to create money. It's a lot easier than working for it. How is it that banks can get away with it and you can't? And if all this is true, wouldn't the quantity of money in circulation expand and expand until it no longer had any value at all? If the banks have such a good thing going, why should they ever stop?

What Can Be Created Can Be Destroyed

And here's another question: Does anything happen to the quantity of money when you repay the loan? Suppose you have been building up your own stock of money, either as demand deposits in your checking account or as currency in your cookie jar, so that you can pay back the principal plus the interest when it's due. Due day comes and you go down to the bank with the $575 you now owe the bank, in the form of Federal Reserve notes. When you turn it over to the bank, money in circulation drops by $575. Remember that currency counts as money when and only when it's held outside the banking system.

If, as is more likely, you have the $575 in your checking account, you write a check for that amount to the bank. The bank subtracts $575 from your demand deposit balance and the money stock goes down by $575. So money is created when banks make loans, and it's destroyed when customers repay bank loans. Thus the total quantity of money in circulation is going to increase during any period when banks are making new loans at a faster rate than old bank loans are being repaid, and the quantity of money will decrease whenever old bank loans are being repaid faster than new ones are being made.

Credibility and Confidence

In a society where bank lending was not carefully regulated by law, the only limit on a bank's ability to go on creating money indefinitely would be its ability to maintain its credibility. A bank can create money by creating liabilities only so long as people have confidence in those liabilities, that is, so long as they believe the bank will be willing and able to pay its debts when asked to do so. If people who have checking accounts with a particular bank start to doubt that the bank would be able to pay its debts on demand, they will decide to collect those debts. (Remember: Your bank deposit is a liability of the bank, a debt that the bank owes you.) They will rush to the bank and ask to be paid. In what form? In the form of the liabilities of some other institution in which they still have confidence, such as the Federal Reserve banks. Suppose you have exactly $237.28 in your checking account. If you're one of those doubters, you will withdraw the $237.28 by transforming it into Federal Reserve notes plus one quarter and three pennies.

This action on your part will not change the quantity of money in circulation, because the money supply does not include currency and coin that is held within the banking system. When you closed your checking account, the quantity of money held in the form of demand deposits went down by $237.28, while the quantity that takes the form of currency in circulation rose by the same amount. But your action plus the action of all or most of the bank's other depositors, if they have all come to doubt the bank's willingness and ability to pay its debts on demand, will drain from the bank all the currency it's holding in its vaults and compel it to call on the Federal Reserve bank of its district for additional supplies. The Federal Reserve bank will do for your bank just what your bank is doing for you. The Federal Reserve bank will hand over the Federal Reserve notes your bank requests and reduce by an equivalent amount the size of the deposit your bank is holding with the Federal Reserve bank. *Either* your bank's deposit with the Federal Reserve bank will be large enough that your bank can obtain all the Federal Reserve notes it needs to satisfy the demands of its suspicious depositors—in which case they were mistaken, your bank is in fact sound, and the "run" on your bank will end. *Or* it will exhaust its account with the Federal Reserve bank before its depositors have all been satisfied—in which case the depositors' suspicions will be confirmed, the bank will be proved insolvent, and it will be forced out of business.

So what limits an unregulated bank's ability to go on creating money indefinitely is its ability to maintain the confidence of its depositors that it can and will, upon demand, convert its deposit liabilities into some other form of money in which the public has more confidence, in this case, Federal Reserve notes. The more money a bank creates, other things being equal, the less ability it will have to meet its depositors' demands. The reason is simple. The process of creating money creates more liabilities for the bank, unless its depositors pay that money to people who deposit it in other banks—as you did at the computer store. But that's not a better outcome for the bank because, you recall, the Federal Reserve bank "clears" your check by taking money out of your bank's account and placing it in the account of the bank with which the computer store does business. That causes your bank to lose reserves that it could otherwise use to satisfy depositors' demands for currency. Banks that want to earn interest by creating money to lend must therefore maintain a balance between their desire for additional income and their need to retain the confidence of their depositors.

People must remain confident in a particular money or they'll stop accepting it.

Banks Under Regulation: Legal Reserve Requirements

We have described the restraints on bank money creation that would exist in an unregulated banking system in order to clarify the essential nature of the system. But all banking systems in the world today are in fact regulated. The most basic regulation and the one that acts as the fundamental restraint on money creation by banks in the United States is a *legal reserve requirement*. Banks are not allowed to have deposit liabilities in excess of some multiple of their reserves.

Required reserve ratio: the percent of a bank's reserves that must be held in its vaults or on deposit at a Federal Reserve bank

Bankers seek profit opportunities by investing their excess reserves!

The reserve requirement is expressed as a percentage, called the *required reserve ratio*, which serves as an important rule of the banking game. The required reserve ratio states the percent of a bank's total reserves that must be held by the bank in the form of vault cash or deposits on reserve at a district Federal Reserve bank. For example, a required reserve ratio of, say, 25 percent would mean that a bank with $100 million in total checkable deposits must hold $25 million in its vaults. The remaining 75 million serve as the bank's *excess reserves*, which are used by the bank to seek profitable investments, typically in the form of loans. Don't forget that commercial banks are in the business of seeking profit. They plan to borrow at a low rate of interest (for instance, what they pay you in your savings account) and lend at a higher rate of interest (for an auto loan or mortgage, for example), and the *difference* represents potential profit, after, of course, all other bank expenses have been accounted for.

What is the required reserve ratio among commercial banks in the United States? Can you take a guess? 90 percent? 50 percent? Or maybe it's lower, like 25 percent, or even 15 percent? Believe it or not, it typically *averages less than 10 percent*. The required reserve ratio is actually set at different levels depending on the type of reserves on deposit (called *tranches*). For several years now the required reserve ratio for a commercial bank has been set at 0 percent for the first $6.6 million in total checkable deposits, 3 percent for deposits between $6.6 million and $45.4 million, and 10 percent for deposits greater than $45.4 million. Currently, banks face a 0 percent required reserve ratio for reserves in the form of savings deposits.

Checkable Deposits	Req. Res. Ratio
$0 to $6.6 million	0%
$6.6 to $45.4 million	3%
over $45.4 million	10%

Savings Deposits	Req Res. Ratio
any level	0%

Given these different tranches, the required reserve ratio averages around 7–8 percent today. Which means a typical commercial bank with $100 million in total reserves might well be holding $8 million in its vaults and has the blessings of the Federal Reserve to invest the remaining $92 million in (appropriate) profit-seeking activities. The dollars that are held in the vaults of a bank earn no interest. From the individual banker's perspective, therefore, the reserve requirements appear to them as a kind of *tax*. Increasing the required reserve ratio through the different tranches means banks would have lower excess reserves, which would reduce their ability to make loans, impose higher costs, and reduce their potential profitability.

Reserves held in the banker's vault earn no return, and therefore are like a tax on the banker.

The Fed as Monitor and Rule Enforcer

We've been talking about Federal Reserve banks for several pages without properly introducing them. Let's repair that failure now. The Federal Reserve is the central bank of the United States, created by an act of Congress in 1913. Although technically owned by the commercial banks that are its members, the Fed is in practical fact a government agency. Its board of governors in Washington is appointed by the president of the United States, with the advice and consent of the Senate. And the board effectively controls the policies of the 12 banks that make up the system. We *seem* to have 12 central banks, but this is mostly for the sake of appearances, a legacy from the days when much of the country harbored a populist suspicion of Easterners, Wall Streeters, and men in striped pants with cutaway coats. These suspicions were allayed by scattering banks around the country. But the Fed has actually been a single bank (with branches) at least since the legislative changes enacted by Congress in the 1930s. The power of any one of the 12 district banks depends pretty much on the amount of influence it is able to exert on policy formation through its executive officers and research staff.

By virtue of its power to fix legal reserve requirements for banks (within wide limits set by Congress) and its power to expand or contract the dollar volume of reserves, the Fed, as it's commonly known, restrains the lending activities of the commercial banking system and thus the process of money creation. The Fed also decides what may count as legal reserves. Since 1960, it has been the banks' vault cash plus the deposits the commercial banks themselves have at the Federal Reserve bank of their district.

To summarize, then, you were quite correct in suspecting that privately owned banks cannot just go on creating money indefinitely. First, the bank must find people willing to borrow on the terms at which the banks are willing to lend and able to convince the banks that they will repay as they promise. Second, each bank must operate within the constraint imposed by its reserves. That's the constraint that government authorities use in their efforts to exercise control over bank lending and hence over the process of money creation. Every bank is legally required to hold reserves in forms specified by law. A bank may make new loans, and thus create money, only when it has excess reserves—that is, reserves greater than the minimum amount it is legally obligated to hold. And the Fed has the power to increase or decrease the reserves of the banking system or, alternately, to increase or decrease the percentage of their total deposit liabilities that the banks must hold as reserves. *Banks' required reserves act as a constraint on the growth of the quantity of money in circulation*. This seems to have little or nothing to do with the usual concept of a reserve fund, something that can be drawn on in an emergency. Legal reserves do not in fact perform a significant reserve function in this sense today. The reserve requirement is today primarily a limitation imposed by law on the ability of the commercial banking system to expand the money stock.

But isn't it necessary, you might ask, for the banks to hold reserves against the possibility of a "run" by depositors? If a lot of depositors suddenly lost confidence in a bank for some reason and tried to withdraw their deposits in currency, the bank would be unable to honor those withdrawals. It would have to close, making the deposits of all its customers valueless. And if that happened, the loss of confidence might spread to other banks and bring down a large part of the banking system.

There actually hasn't been a financial panic like that in the United States since the 1930s. The reason, however, has little to do with the level of bank reserves. Bank customers no longer rush to withdraw their deposits on every rumor of financial trouble at a bank because their deposits are now insured by the Federal Deposit Insurance Corporation (FDIC). If a bank closes, for whatever reason, its depositors can expect reimbursement from this federal government insurance system within a few days. Some critics argued when the FDIC was created in 1933 that the premiums it charged banks to insure their deposits were far too low, and that the FDIC would go broke trying to pay off depositors when banks closed their doors. But the very existence of the FDIC ended the phenomenon of bank runs; and in the absence of runs, banks no longer failed at the rate they formerly did. The FDIC premiums have thus proved more than adequate.[2] And the institution of the FDIC may well be the single most stabilizing monetary reform enacted in the 1930s.

Substantial credit must also go to improved Federal Reserve procedures since the 1930s. The Fed now understands clearly that it has the responsibility to provide currency to the banking system, without regard to the amounts banks happen to be holding as reserves. Thus, a bank today can meet any demand for currency, however large, by securing additional currency from the Fed. If the bank were to use up its entire reserve balance, the Federal Reserve would simply lend the bank additional reserves, taking as collateral some of the IOUs in the asset portfolio of the borrowing bank. Banks are granted access to this lending privilege whenever they have a legitimate demand for additional reserves, and this has made the whole banking and monetary system more flexible in response to changing conditions as well as more resistant to crises and temporary dislocations.

[2]If it's a good idea for the government to insure depositors in commercial banks against loss, it must be a good idea for the federal government to insure depositors in savings and loan institutions against loss. Right? The trouble with all such insurance is that it gives depositors no incentive to monitor the behavior of the institutions in which they place their deposits. Depositor indifference combined with lax oversight by the regulatory authorities (a lax oversight often prompted by members of Congress seeking to do favors for generous constituents) created enormous losses in the 1990s in the savings and loan industry for which American taxpayers had to pay. "We" agreed to do so when "we" promised that the Federal Savings and Loan Insurance Corporation would cover any losses that depositors in S&Ls might suffer.

The Tools Used by the Fed

Okay, so the Fed sets and enforces the specific legal reserve requirements. But how does the Fed actually go at the job of expanding or contracting the money supply? (We shall save the question of *why* the Fed might strive to manipulate the money supply for Chapter 17.) The most powerful tool and the one that sets the stage for the rest is the authority to establish legal reserve requirements.

The required reserve ratio is used as a given rule of the banking game.

But *changes* in the required reserve ratio are generally viewed by Fed officials as a blunt weapon and could potentially wreak havoc in the banking system. After all, bankers must strive to meet their reserve requirements, so changes in the required reserve ratio could make the business of banking more difficult. The Fed therefore prefers to establish the reserve requirements such that bankers take them as a given rule of the game and uses other means to alter the overall volume of reserves in the banking system. Specifically, it does so by altering the discount rate or engaging in open market operations. In either case, the Fed creates and destroys reserves in the same way that commercial banks create and destroy money: by extending and contracting loans.

The Discount Rate

The Fed can extend a loan to a commercial bank directly. After all, the Fed is known as a "banker's bank," or a "lender of last resort." Should a bank fall short of meeting its reserve requirements or, worse, should a run take place, the Fed is there to provide the liquidity that the bank needs to meet the demands of its depositors. When a bank borrows from the Fed itself, it is charged interest on the loan. That interest rate is called the *discount rate*. It is the rate that the Fed charges banks for short-term loans. It does so by crediting the bank's reserve account and taking in return the bank's IOU or someone else's IOU (e.g., a government bond) that happens to be in the bank's portfolio—just as a commercial bank lends to its customers by creating a deposit balance in return for an IOU.

Discount rate: The interest rate the Fed charges banks for short-term loans

The Fed can, if it wishes, increase or decrease the overall reserves of the banking system, and therefore the overall money supply in the economy, by altering the discount rate. Specifically, if the Fed lowers the discount rate, that would tend to encourage banks to borrow from the Fed itself and expand the amount of credit they make available in the commercial marketplace. On the other hand, the Fed's raising of the discount rate would discourage such activity by making it more costly to borrow directly from the Fed. Increases in the discount rate would tend to reduce the willingness of commercial banks to extend more loans, and therefore it would tend to reduce the overall money supply.

A decrease (increase) in the discount rate could increase (decrease) the nation's money supply.

Banks typically do most of their short-term borrowing from other banks, in the federal funds market.

But the discount rate is probably more of a symbol than a genuine rationing device, because the Fed is selective about the banks to which it will lend. Official Fed policy is to accommodate *special circumstances*, rather than lend to any bank willing to pay the rate, and to behave more like a stern uncle than a profit-seeking lender. The Fed treats commercial bank borrowing as a privilege rather than a right of the banker. Banks instead do most of their short-term borrowing not from the Fed, but from other commercial bankers in what is called the *federal funds market*. (We discuss the Fed's targeting of the *federal funds rate*, which is the interest rate that commercial banks charge one another for short-term loans, in the next chapter.)

Open Market Operations

The Fed rarely changes the required reserve ratio. And it alters the discount rate only infrequently. The most common technique that the Fed uses to manipulate the nation's money supply is the purchase and sale of U.S. government bonds in what are called *open market operations*.

The Fed currently holds a portfolio of already-issued government bonds worth close to half a trillion dollars. When it increases its holdings by purchasing bonds through dealers in government bonds, it writes checks for the amount of the purchases, creating new liabilities that match the bonds it adds to its assets. These checks are deposited in commercial banks. When the banks forward the checks to their Federal Reserve bank, they are credited with additions to their reserve balances.

The Fed tries to indirectly influence other interest rates (especially the federal funds rate) by buying or selling U.S. securities on a large scale.

The news anchorman will announce that "the Fed has lowered interest rates today." And we heard that kind of news frequently between 2000 and 2003. But that way of stating things is somewhat misleading. The *only* interest rate that the Fed directly sets is the discount rate. The Fed, however, can set a *process* in motion that *does* tend to reduce interest rates throughout the economy—on bank-to-bank loans (the federal funds rate) as well as rates for car loans, mortgages, business loans, and so on—through open market operations. If the men and women at the Fed decide that they want to lower interest rates generally, they can do so indirectly by *selling bonds* in mass quantities. The Fed can try to sell, say, $100 billion in U.S. government bonds that it already holds to major securities dealers (which include large commercial banks as well) with whom it already has well-established relations. How does it get those 40 or so dealers to bite? By contacting them all and asking them the prices that they would want in order to sell those securities. The Fed would then match those prices (starting with the lowest, of course) and continue buying until it has purchased $100 billion worth of U.S. government bonds.

The logic here is quite simple. The Fed receives the bonds. And the dealers in total receive 100 billion *dollars*, which they deposit into the commercial banking system. Total reserves in the banking system will now increase by another $100 billion initially, which provides tens of billions of new dollars in the form of excess reserves. And what will bankers do with those excess reserves? Make new loans, to households, businesses, and others. But how will bankers actually encourage the rest of us to take out more loans? By *lowering their interest rates*. (All demand curves slope downward, which includes the demand for credit!) As interest rates decline and more loans are established, the overall money supply would tend to increase. In short, the Fed's purchase of bonds on a mass scale increases commercial bank reserves by that amount. And that enables commercial banks to lower interest rates and extend more loans. The overall impact is an increase in the M1 money supply.

When the Fed buys bonds, banks get dollars. M1 increases and interest rates fall.

The entire process is reversible. In fact, the Fed began to "raise interest rates" in the summer of 2004. To do so, the Fed *withdrew* reserves from the banks by *selling* some of the government bonds already in its asset portfolio to the securities dealers expressing the highest bids to purchase those bonds. For example, when the Fed sells a billion dollars' worth of government bonds, the bonds wind up in the hands of people who pay the bond dealer with a check. The dealer in turn pays the Fed with a check, and the amount of the check is deducted from the reserve account of the bank on which it is drawn. Bonds go to many people and organizations scattered throughout the economy, and a billion dollars flow to the Fed itself, *dollars that are now taken out of circulation in the economy*. This tends to reduce the M1 money supply, because it wipes out a portion of the total reserves of the banking system and compels banks to reduce their liabilities by curtailing their net lending, and raises interest rates throughout the system as a whole.

When the Fed sells bonds, banks get bonds and the Fed gets dollars. M1 decreases and interest rates rise.

But Who Is Really in Charge?

Open market operations, as we said, are the principal working tool of monetary management. A special committee, made up of the seven members of the board of governors and five of the twelve Federal Reserve bank presidents, sits as the Federal Open Market Committee (the FOMC) and continuously determines the direction this management should take. The question of the effectiveness with which the Open Market Committee manages the money supply has long been debated by friends and critics of the Fed, among both economists and politicians.

There are two main questions. One is the determination of policy: Does the Fed set appropriate goals? Does it try to do what it ought to be doing? The other is the execution of policy: Does the Fed do an effective job of achieving the goals it sets for itself? The questions are related, of course, because intelligent policy formulation presupposes a realistic assessment of technical

Incentive and knowledge problems

capabilities. The football coach who orders a passing strategy when his team is two touchdowns behind in the fourth quarter is making a poor policy decision if the quarterback has a rubber arm and all the receivers have butterfingers. Beware of textbook accounts that, like football plays on the blackboard, gloss over problems of execution and assume that the opposition isn't doing any planning of its own.

It's a gross oversimplification to suppose that the Fed has a monetary brake and a monetary accelerator with which it adjusts the money stock as quickly and surely as you slow down and speed up your car in traffic. Monetary management may be more like driving a balky mule train that sometimes won't stop going even when firmly ordered to halt. To make matters worse, there's a bunch of bickering backseat drivers on the wagon, and some of them aren't above shouting their own instructions or even trying to grab the reins from the driver. As we shall see in the chapters ahead, the management of the monetary system can be a difficult and delicate task, and it carries some weighty unintended consequences. But as we shall also see, it is a task of fundamental importance to the overall performance of the economic system.

An Appendix: WHAT ABOUT GOLD?

We've discussed the nature of money and the Fed's ability to manipulate the nation's money supply. But hasn't something important still been left out of all this? What is it that provides *backing* for money? Doesn't money have to have *some* kind of backing? And where does *gold* fit into the picture?

If money were backed by gold, what would the gold itself be backed by?

The conviction that money must have "backing" if it is to have value raises an interesting question. What stands behind the backing to give *it* value? And behind the backing of the backing? But the whole set of questions is misdirected. In economics, value is the consequence of scarcity. And scarcity is the result of demand plus limited availability. It's clear enough when and why there exists a demand for any particular kind of money. The money will be demanded if it can be used to obtain all sorts of other things that people want, which is to say, if it's accepted as a medium of exchange. The other part of the picture, limited availability, is taken care of, more or less effectively, by the monetary managers of the Federal Reserve. No "backing" is required. If this makes you nervous or causes you to doubt the value of your currency or checking account, you can easily shore up your faith by "selling" your money to others. You'll find that they're willing to take it and to give you other valuable assets in exchange.

The critical factor in preserving the value of any kind of money is limited availability plus confidence that the supply will continue to be limited. Nature has made gold relatively rare. It's up to the Fed to keep Federal Reserve notes and checkable deposits relatively rare. But many people have far more confidence in the reliability of nature than in the reliability of central banks and governments.

That's why some people would like to see us return to a genuine gold standard, under which currency could be exchanged for gold at some fixed ratio. It's not because they think that money must have backing, but because they distrust government money managers. If the government were required to maintain the convertibility of checkable deposits into Federal Reserve notes and Federal Reserve notes into gold at predetermined exchange ratios, the limited availability of gold would severely restrict anyone's power to increase the amount of money in circulation.

As a matter of fact, governments are often tempted, especially in wartime, to create additional money as a way of financing expenditures without the painful necessity of openly levying taxes. And they haven't always resisted the temptation. The consequence has usually been inflation, a more concealed but hardly a more equitable way for the government to finance its expenditures. Urging a return to the gold standard would seem to be a counsel of despair, however. A government so irresponsible that it must be reigned in by gold would be most unlikely to adopt a gold standard and even more unlikely to respond to the pressure of such a constraint. It would simply declare an emergency and go off the gold standard when it wanted to. The problem of irresponsible government is a weighty one, but it's hard to believe that the problem could be solved through a return to the gold standard. In any event, because the United States seems unlikely to adopt the gold standard in the near future, we will probably have to be satisfied with making the present system work.

Once Over Lightly

Money is a social institution that increases wealth by lowering costs of exchange, thereby enabling people to specialize more fully in accordance with their own comparative advantages.

An item functions as money in a society when people are willing to accept it in exchange merely because other people will accept it in exchange.

The liabilities of trusted financial institutions make up most of the money used in modern commercial societies: principally paper currency issued by central banks and checkable deposits in commercial banks or other financial institutions.

In the United States today, the narrowly defined stock of money (M1) is the total of currency held outside the banking system plus checkable deposits in financial institutions. But other assets that can be converted into currency or checkable deposits at negligible cost are included in more comprehensive measurements of the money stock, such as the M2 and M3.

Commercial banks add to the society's stock of money by creating deposits for borrowers. The banks are limited in their ability to create additional money by the requirement that their deposits not exceed some multiple of their legally defined reserves.

The managers of the Federal Reserve System have the responsibility for regulating the size of the money stock. The Fed does so by controlling bank lending through its power to set the legal ratio between commercial bank liabilities and reserves and to expand or contract those reserves through loans to commercial banks and through buying and selling government bonds in what are called open market operations.

The idea that money must have material "backing" to have value is not correct. Money must only be acceptable as a medium of exchange to have value. Limited availability and the belief that availability will continue to be limited is a necessary condition for continued acceptability of any functioning medium of exchange.

QUESTIONS FOR DISCUSSION

1. Money gets a lot of attention but tends to have a bad press. Are the authors of the following statements talking about money as we have defined it? Or are they using money as a synonym or symbol for something else? What is that "something else" in each case where you conclude that money is not really the subject of discussion?
   (a) "The love of money is the root of all evil." (Often misquoted as "Money is the root of all evil.")
   (b) "Health is . . . a blessing that money cannot buy."
   (c) "If this be not love, it is madness, and then it is pardonable. Nay, yet a more certain sign than all this: I give thee my money."
   (d) "Wine maketh merry; but money answereth all things."
   (e) "Words are the tokens current and accepted for conceits, as moneys are for values."
   (f) "Money speaks sense in a language all nations understand."
   (g) "Americans are too interested in money."
   (h) "Protecting our natural environment is more important than making money."
2. For almost 2000 years, people on the island of Yap in Micronesia have been using huge circular stones as money. Various people own portions of the stones.
   (a) Because the stones are worthless when broken and also heavy, people leave the larger ones where they are and simply take note of the fact that ownership has changed. How is this similar to paying by check?
   (b) Some of the stones are propped up in rows in village "banks." Suppose that the person who lives next door to the "bank" is entrusted with the responsibility of keeping track of who owns what portion of each stone. How could this person use his position to make loans and thereby expand the quantity of money in Yap?
3. The textbook asserts that an item becomes money in a society when the members of that society become willing to accept it not for its own sake, but because they can exchange it for something else that they want. How does some particular item become acceptable in this sense and therefore money?

   (a) Why did cigarettes quickly become acceptable as a medium of exchange in Radford's prison camp even for people who did not smoke? Can you think of any other item that might have become money in the prison camp if cigarettes had not been available?
   (b) Suppose one of the camp residents had run out of cigarettes but wanted to buy a jar of jam from another camp resident and that the owner of the jam agreed to turn over his jam if the buyer gave him a promissory note for eight cigarettes. How could that promissory note become money within the prison camp?
4. The term *fiat money* is sometimes used to describe paper money that is not backed by gold or anything else and that consequently seems to have value merely because some authority has declared, "Let it become money."
   (a) Is fiat money any less money than gold coins are? What kind of "authority" does it take to turn a "worthless piece of paper" into money?
   (b) Are U.S. dollars money in Canada? Are Canadian dollars money in the United States? Why are U.S. dollars warmly welcomed by retailers in many countries of the world? Can you think of circumstances in which the people of a country would refuse to accept their own national currency in payment but would welcome payments made in U.S. dollars? What does all this indicate about the "authority" of governments that try to create fiat money?
5. Adam Smith complained in *The Wealth of Nations* that many people confused money with wealth. Is this a confusion?
   (a) Doesn't everyone's wealth increase when he or she acquires more money?
   (b) If any one person's wealth increases when he or she acquires more money, doesn't it follow logically that more money for everyone means more wealth for everyone?
   (c) What would happen if the government of India tackled the problem of poverty by printing more rupees and distributing them generously to the poorest people in the country?
6. People usually cannot spend the deposits they hold in commercial-bank savings accounts or savings and loan institutions without first withdrawing the funds—that is, converting them into currency or checkable deposits. But because they're able to do that at almost no cost, these savings deposits are assets that come very close to being money.
   (a) Would you expect total spending in the United States over some period of time to be more closely correlated with M1 or with M2?
   (b) Will your answer change if savings and loan institutions allow customers to pay bills through telephone transfers of their deposits to the accounts of others?
7. At any moment some already-printed Federal Reserve notes will be in (a) the wallets of the public, (b) the vaults and tills of commercial banks, and (c) the vaults of Federal Reserve banks. How does each enter into or otherwise affect the total money supply?
8. How does a withdrawal of currency from checking accounts affect the money stock? How does it affect a bank's reserves? How does this affect

the bank's ability to extend loans? What effect might this withdrawal consequently have on the money stock?

9. Commercial banks create money by extending loans. The bankers themselves don't see their activities as actually "creating" more money, but that is the effect of their lending activity. It's important that *you* as a student of economics see exactly why they can do this and why money is ordinarily not created by the lending activities of other institutions.

   (a) What is the advantage possessed by commercial banks that enables them to create money when they make loans? Credit unions and consumer credit companies do not have this advantage and consequently do not create money when they extend loans to their customers. What do they lack that commercial banks have?
   (b) Would you like to be able to make loans to your friends at will, simply by creating the money you lend them? You could help your friends, increase your popularity, and even earn a little interest if you could learn how to do this. What is the secret?
   (c) Suppose everyone in town knows you, knows your signature, and trusts you completely. When a friend asks to borrow $10, you simply write a note saying, "I'll pay $10 to the holder of this note," sign it, and hand it to the friend. Will the friend be able to spend your note, that is, use it as money? Will the merchant who receives the note be able to spend it in turn, perhaps by giving it out in changing a $20 bill? Will you have succeeded in creating money? Would this differ from a situation in which a check you had written, payable to "Cash," circulated from hand to hand without being deposited?
   (d) The narrowly defined money stock, or M1, is made up of Federal Reserve notes, checkable deposits, and traveler's checks. All of these are liabilities of trusted financial institutions. What does a person or institution have to do to be able to create money?
   (e) At one time in the 1980s, the government of the state of California made plans to begin paying some of its bills with IOUs, because the governor and the legislature were unable to agree on a budget. Could a state IOU function as money? Suppose you were a supplier to the state or someone due a tax refund and you received in the mail an IOU instead of a check. Could you spend it? What might you do if you had to pay the rent and buy groceries and couldn't wait for the governor and legislature to resolve their differences?

10. One way to think about the Fed's ability to change the nation's M1 money supply is by thinking about its effects on the *excess reserves* within the banking system as a whole. In short, anything that *increases* excess reserves will tend to *increase* the money supply; anything that *decreases* excess reserves will tend to *decrease* the money supply. With that in mind, what would tend to happen to excess reserves in the banking system, and the M1 money supply, if the Fed

    (a) lowers the required reserve ratio.
    (b) raises the required reserve ratio.
    (c) buys U.S. securities on a mass scale.
    (d) sells U.S. securities on a mass scale.

11. Why might the Fed find it significantly easier to expand the money stock in a period of prosperity than in a period of recession? What must the Fed be able to do if it wants the quantity of money in the hands of the public to increase?
12. The textbook says that the paper currency in a society does not have to be "backed" by anything else into which it can be converted on demand in order for it to have value and function as a medium of exchange. The only requirement is that people accept it as a medium of exchange.
    (a) Do you think that Federal Reserve notes would ever have acquired acceptability at the time they began to be issued if they had not been redeemable in gold or silver?
    (b) What can governments do to make the paper money they want to issue acceptable to the general public, in addition to promising to exchange it on demand for some other asset that people value?
    (c) What could cause government-issued paper money that is accepted by everyone in the society as a medium of exchange to lose acceptability and to cease thereby to function as money?
13. If it is not essential that money have "backing" of some kind, why do so many people believe otherwise? Would money backed by bricks be preferred to money backed by no commodity at all?

Monetary and Fiscal Policies

17

What difference does it make whether the quantity of money in the hands of the public grows rapidly or slowly? Amid all the disputes and uncertainties surrounding contemporary study of aggregate fluctuations in income, output, and prices, one proposition commands pretty general assent: *An excessive rate of growth in a society's stock of money will cause inflation.* Unfortunately, that statement tells us much less than we would like to know. What constitutes an *excessive* rate of growth? Is there such a thing as an *insufficient* rate of growth? If too much growth causes inflation, does too little growth cause *deflation*? Or does it cause something much more widely feared, namely recession with its accompanying rise in unemployment? And even if we know what the rate of growth in the money supply ought to be to prevent any of these undesirable outcomes, does anyone have the ability to bring it about? Moreover, is controlling the rate of growth in the money supply the only way or the best way or even an effective way to prevent undesirable fluctuations in the aggregate level of economic activity?

The Great Depression

It was the Great Depression of the 1930s that forced these questions upon the attention of economists. For four successive years, beginning in 1929, real output and income in the United States declined. It declined by huge amounts: 9 percent in 1930, 8 percent in 1931, 14 percent in 1932, and another 2 percent in 1933. Compare that record with the performance of the U.S. economy since World War II. On only one occasion has total output declined in two successive years: It fell in 1974 and again in 1975. But the declines were less than 1 percent in each year, almost unnoticeable by the standards of the Great Depression.

Moreover, a full recovery never occurred in the 1930s. In each of the three years after the 1974–75 recession, output increased by about 5 percent per year, quickly making up the ground lost during the recession. But six years after the low point of the Great Depression was finally reached in 1933, total output and income were only 1.5 percent above what they had been in 1929. Because the population was larger in 1939 than in 1929, that tiny increase in output and income over the decade was far below what would have been required just to restore predepression levels of prosperity. The per capita after-tax income of Americans actually fell by 7 percent from 1929 to 1939. (It had fallen by almost 30 percent from 1929 to 1933.) The Great Depression even featured a recession within a depression, as real output and income dropped 4 percent from 1937 to 1938.

The most vivid experience of those who lived through the 1930s was the experience of massive, stubborn unemployment. If we leave out 1930, when unemployment was still growing, the unemployment rates of the 1930s averaged more than 19 percent. That is almost one out of every five members of the labor force. In 1933, at the bottom of the recession, 25 percent of the labor force was officially counted as unemployed.

Why? What happened? Toward the end of the 1930s, many thoughtful people all along the political spectrum were concluding, some regretfully, others gleefully, that capitalism had finally failed. It could work productive wonders, as even Marx and Engels had emphasized, but it could not resolve its "inner contradictions," as Marx and Engels also claimed. It was like the fabled sorcerer's apprentice, they said, who was unable to control the powers that he had summoned up from the underworld. "It is enough to mention," they wrote in *The Communist Manifesto*,

> the commercial crises that by their periodical return put on its trial, each time more threateningly, the existence of the entire bourgeois society. In these crises a great part not only of the existing products, but also of the previously created productive forces, are periodically destroyed. In these crises there breaks out an epidemic that, in all earlier epochs, would have seemed an absurdity—the epidemic of over-production.

The system had broken down, in other words, because it produced *too much*. The failure of an economic system through overproduction still seems like an absurdity.

The Incredible Japanese Economy

All the predictions about the system's imminent collapse proved mistaken, however. Bourgeois or commercial society revived vigorously after World War II and the developed industrial countries of the world entered upon an extended period of remarkable economic growth. In no country was the experience of economic growth more remarkable than in Japan.

To place what follows in perspective, keep in mind that the real gross domestic product of the United States has tended to grow over the long run, when we average boom years, bust years, and ordinary years, at a rate of about 3 percent per year. That's a thoroughly respectable rate of growth; income and output will double in slightly less than a quarter century at that rate. In the 1950s, economic growth in Japan, as measured by the increase in real gross domestic product, occurred at an average rate of about 7 percent per year. That is an impressive growth rate for any single year, but to continue it for a decade is almost unprecedented. But the Japanese economy had been devastated by World War II, and many observers pointed out that percentage growth rates could be quite high even for lengthy periods in a country beginning from a very low level of gross domestic product.

The 1960s thoroughly demolished that explanation for the performance of the Japanese economy. In the decade of the sixties, growth in real gross domestic product averaged 11 percent per year. Think what that means. If your personal income were to increase by 11 percent per year, you would double your income in fewer than seven years. And remember that we're talking about *real* income, about gross domestic product adjusted for changes in the value of money.

The Japanese economy descended from these astronomical growth rates in the 1970s and 1980s, and even experienced negative real growth in 1974, when Japan as well as most of the rest of the industrialized world suffered from huge increases in the price of oil. The average annual growth rate in Japan through these two decades was nonetheless a highly respectable 4.5 percent per year. Even at that "modest" rate, which was, of course, modest only by Japan's own record during the preceding two decades, real output and income will double in 16 years. By the end of the 1980s, less than 50 years after the end of World War II, the Japanese economy had become the second largest in the world, ranking behind only the United States, and the per capita incomes of the Japanese population matched those of people in the wealthiest nations of Western Europe.

What were the Japanese doing right? Everyone was asking that question at the beginning of the 1990s. By the end of the 1990s, however, everyone was asking a different question: What were the Japanese doing *wrong*? In 1992, the Japanese economy slid into a recession from which it seemed unable to emerge. The growth rate fell to 1 percent in 1992, to 0.3 percent in 1993, and 0.7 percent in 1994, rose slightly to 1.4 percent in 1995, spurted to 4.1 percent in 1996, but then fell back to 0.8 percent in 1997 and turned negative in 1998. By the end of the decade, economists were beginning to compare the performance of the Japanese economy in the 1990s with that of the United States in the 1930s and were starting to ask whether anything we had learned during the earlier period might be put to use by Japan to cure its persistent troubles.[1]

What exactly was it we had learned from the experience of the 1930s? Unfortunately, economists were much less certain about that by the end of the century than they had been at the middle of the century. We're going to postpone speculating on the question of why the Japanese economy performed so spectacularly for so many years because our concern here will be with fluctuations rather than with growth. We want to reflect at this stage on the causes of recessions and the cures that might be available.

The absurdity: People are poor because they produce too much!

What Happens in a Recession?

Recession is related to *recede*, which means to withdraw or retreat. A recession is a retreat from earlier rates of growth in the total output of the economy. But would every substantial slowdown in growth have to be a recession? Is perpetual growth the only possible norm?

That implication is avoided when we realize that *the costs of a recession are largely the costs of disappointed expectations.* If a recession were merely a slowdown in the rate of economic growth, recessions would be popular with advocates of zero economic growth and all those who think we should reduce our emphasis on the production of marketable goods. But recessions aren't popular with these groups or anyone else, because they entail *unintended and therefore disruptive slowdowns* in the rate of economic growth. Bare statistics on aggregate output are incapable of revealing disappointed expectations. We may be able to infer widespread disappointment from such statistics, but aggregate data could truly measure a recession only if they could somehow measure the output not produced because events failed to develop in the way that producers expected and counted on. Recessions are the result of frustrated expectations.

Producers' expectations are frustrated every day, of course. But every day some other producers are delighted to discover that events have turned out *better* than they had expected. A recession occurs when, for some reason, the number and depth of the disappointments increase without any compensating increase in the quantity and quality of delightful surprises.

uncertainty in a commercial society

In a commercial society, production is typically undertaken in anticipation of a demand for the product, not in response to someone's specific order. Even when goods are produced to order, production almost always begins before the orders are firm. And

[1]See Benjamin Powell, "Explaining Japan's Recession," *Quarterly Journal of Austrian Economics*, 5(2) 2002: pp. 35–50, for an economic history of the policies that led to Japan's recession and the difficulties the country has had in recovering.

the orders are rarely guaranteed. They can be canceled. Most clothing manufacturers, for example, are not in the position of a personal tailor who doesn't purchase the materials or begin working until he has an order in hand from a specific customer and a deposit to ensure that the customer won't back out of the deal. If all production were "bespoke" work, as they still sometimes call it in England, recessions would be far less frequent or severe. But we would also be far poorer, of course, because the greater uncertainty and more frequent mistakes that are associated with production for the market are associated also with much higher levels of output.

A Cluster of Errors

So recessions are the consequence of accumulated mistakes, the consequence of a *cluster of errors among participants throughout the economy*. Investments are undertaken and goods are produced at costs that are not justified by subsequent demand. *Thousands of entrepreneurs have misread the price signals provided by the market process*. Rather than providing information to better coordinate people's production and consumption plans over time, those price signals were instead leading to *malinvestment* and *discoordination*. What were expected to be profitable investments are eventually exposed as losses.

Entrepreneurial plans change when the mistakes are discovered. Production has to be curtailed, workers must be laid off, and capital, whether in the form of productive equipment or inventories, may have to be liquidated (converted into cash) at a loss. Seen in this way, *recessions are a correction to the prior period's accumulation of mistakes*. But why would mistakes *accumulate* in an economic system? Why wouldn't overly pessimistic decisions roughly cancel out overly optimistic decisions? Why do we observe a tendency at certain times for a *general and widespread* curtailment of production, laying off of workers, and liquidation of capital? In other words, why have so many people—not only entrepreneurs but workers who expected to enjoy continued wage income—been "fooled" all at once?

How could so many people be mistaken?

Let's return to the Great Depression for a moment. Although the Great Depression of the 1930s was worldwide in its scope, the recession that brought it on was deeper and longer in the United States than in most other countries. What was happening to the banking and monetary system during this deep and prolonged contraction of economic activity? From the cyclical peak of economic activity in August of 1929 to the bottom of the decline in March of 1933, the quantity of money in circulation fell by more than one-third. More than 20 percent of the commercial banks in the nation, holding almost 10 percent of the volume of deposits existing at the start of the contraction, suspended operations because they could not meet their financial obligations. In an attempt to salvage the banking system and prevent the destruction of customers' deposits, many states legislated "bank holidays"; all banks were ordered to close their doors temporarily so that panicked depositors could not, by trying to withdraw their deposits, force their banks to fail. The national government declared a one-week banking holiday early in March of 1933 that closed the doors not only of all commercial banks but also of the Federal Reserve banks.

There are at least two things that must be explained about the Great Depression of the 1930s: (1) the cause of the cluster of errors and (2) the length and severity of the depression. These are issues still hotly debated among economists. Our argument is that the cause of the original cluster of errors that led to the Stock Market Crash of 1929 was the expansionary monetary policies of the 1920s, which through credit expansion generated a "boom," which led to the "bust" in 1929.[2]

Monetary Mismanagement, Monetary Miscalculation

Credit expansion lowers the interest rate that businessmen must pay in making their investment decisions and leads them to engage in investment projects that previously at the higher rate would not have been undertaken. Because the credit expansion was fueled not by increased savings, but by money creation, the boom is *unsustainable*. The underlying scarcities of capital goods, and the consumer preferences for the trade-off between current consumption and savings, does not warrant the investment. The "cheap credit" created by an expansion of the money supply and lowering of interest rates makes unprofitable investments *appear* profitable. Businesspeople expand investment—perhaps build larger production facilities, employ more workers, beef up inventories, and so on. They *expect* that these activities will pay off in the future. But once the artificially lowered interest rate (through the Fed's increase of the money supply) unexpectedly begins to

Monetary distortions create systematic monetary miscalculations . . .

[2]See Murray N. Rothbard's *America's Great Depression*, originally published in 1963, for an examination of how the monetary policies of the 1920s distorted production and led to the boom–bust experienced in the U.S. economy. On the monetary contraction of the 1930s, see Milton Friedman and Anna Schwartz's *A Monetary History of the US*, also originally published in 1963. Rothbard's work is the main interpretive work on the Great Depression from an "Austrian" or Mises–Hayek perspective, and the work of Friedman and Schwartz is the foundational work on monetarism. What matters for our discussion is that both of these interpretations of the events of the Great Depression challenge the popular perspective that the Great Depression was caused by the collapse of the self-organizing properties of the market system and instead provide arguments and evidence that the cause, and length and severity, of the Great Depression was a consequence of government policy.

rise—along with the inflationary increase in prices for resources, labor, and so on—businesspeople will find that they've misread the signals of the market. They've miscalculated their expected profits. This is a hard lesson. Rather than enjoying economic profits, they discover the errors of their ways in the form of unexpected higher costs and economic losses. They therefore *reverse course* by canceling some projects and laying off workers.

The recessionary "bust" occurs as the investment projects that were undertaken during the expansionary "boom" reveal themselves to be a mistake. Individual businesses fail all the time, in good times and bad. But during a recessionary "bust" there are *clusters of business failures*. These businesses were led to the error by the manipulation of the money and credit system.[3]

. . . and eventually create clusters of business failures.

The behavior of the monetary system may not be the entire answer but is certainly a large piece in the puzzle. *Money pervades all markets*. Economic calculation of expected profit and loss relies upon the *money prices* of goods and services. If these calculations are instead *systematic miscalculations*—so far off the mark that they accumulate and cluster throughout the economic system—then these errors in calculation can be caused by unexpected changes in the overall supply of money itself, engineered by the central bank. Figure 17–1 depicts this complex sequence of events in a simple graph.

There is no logical reason why the bust need be lengthy and severe. Businesses go broke and labor is dismissed, but the adjustment process, while painful, can be relatively quick. During the Great Depression, however, this process of adjustment was thwarted by government policies that slowed down the process of adjustment or actually set in motion new disturbances. The U.S. economy was beginning to recover in early 1930, but the government passed the Smoot–Hawley tariff in June 1930, which had the effect of closing down our international trade and adversely affecting agriculture and thus the rural banking industry; doubled the income tax in 1932, which distorted consumption, and investment decisions; and implemented a great contraction in the supply of money in the mid-1930s. For these reasons, and others, the U.S. economy lingered in depression throughout the decade—with as much as 25 percent unemployment at its worst depths. Rather than an indictment of the market economy, the Great Depression should be seen as the major lesson in U.S. history on how monetary policy can disturb the coordination process in economic life, both through expansion and contraction of the money supply, as was witnessed in the 1920s and 1930s.

[3]As Roger Garrison has stressed, the monetary theory of the trade cycle developed by Mises and Hayek is not a theory of depression *per se*, but a theory of an unsustainable boom. See Roger Garrison, *Time and Money: The Macroeconomics of Capital Structure* (New York: Routledge, 2001), p. 120.

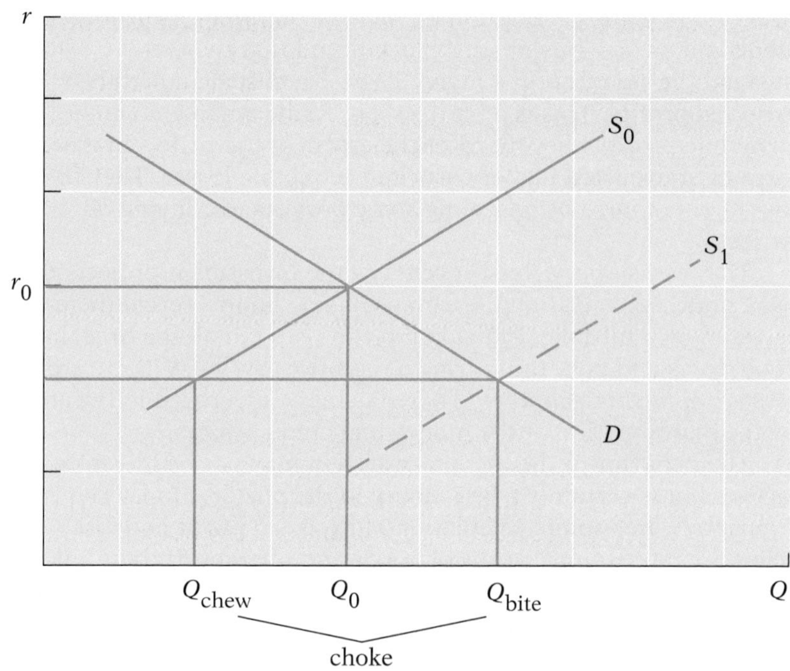

Figure 17–1 **Bite, chew, choke**

Credit expansion by the central bank lowers the market rate of interest below the original rate, leading investors to engage in projects that were previously unprofitable. But this "boom" is not sustainable because real savings have not been increased. The investment "bite" is bigger than the economy's "chew," so the system "chokes."

Monetary Equilibrium

Ideally, the goal of the Fed, as official regulator of the nation's monetary system, is to keep the quantity of money supplied in balance with the quantity of money demanded.[4] From Chapter 1

[4]For a discussion of monetary equilibrium theory, see Steve Horwitz, *Microfoundations and Macroeconomics* (New York: Routledge, 2000), pp. 65–103. Horwitz traces the basic ideas in monetary equilibrium theory from Swedish economists such as Knut Wicksell and Gunnar Myrdal, Austrian economists such as Mises and Hayek, to more contemporary economists such as Leland Yeager and George Selgin. From this perspective, although there may be a variety of causes for macroeconomic coordination problems, the primary reason why coordination problems occur is because of imbalances between the supply and demand for money. Excess supply leads to the set of coordination problems associated with inflation, whereas excess demand will lead to the set of coordination problems associated with deflation. Ideal monetary policy then will minimize the costs associated with inflation and deflation. Selgin has made a strong case that deflation is not costly at all in good times (when productivity is rising), but it is damaging in bad times. Selgin suggests that monetary authorities should adopt a "productivity norm" rather than price-level stability in determining monetary policy. See Selgin, *Less Than Zero: The Case for a Falling Price Level in a Growing Economy* (London: IEA, 1997).

of this book we have stressed the idea of *coordination* as central to the economic system, and thus our presentation of issues that are typically divided as microeconomic and macroeconomic issues seeks to maintain this common emphasis on the coordination of economic activities. In short, the economic way of thinking compels us to realize that although there may in fact be macroeconomic questions, there are in the end only microeconomic answers.

What matters is the *incentives and information* that individuals face, the kind that will lead them to successfully coordinate their actions with others in the market, or to direct them to activities which result in coordination failures. The monetary system is at the center of any advanced economy and the monetary unit is the link in exchange relationships throughout the economy. Money by its nature cannot be "neutral," because it provides the link to all exchange relationships throughout the economy. If the monetary system is out of balance, it cannot help but have an impact on the pattern of exchange and production in an economy.[5] From a *monetary equilibrium* perspective, the goal of monetary policy (the domain of the Fed), should be to strive for monetary neutrality by keeping the quantity of money supplied in balance with the quantity of money demanded. This would generate what is popularly called *price stability*—that is, zero (or very low) levels of inflation or deflation. In other words, it would tend to keep the *purchasing power of money stable*. Equally important, it would not generate the kinds of relative price distortions that cause systematic monetary miscalculation, unsustainable booms and inevitable recessionary busts.

Monetary equilibrium: The amount of money supplied equals the amount demanded, so the value of money remains stable.

The Demand for Money

The concept of a "demand for money" strikes most people as a bit odd when they first hear it. The demand for anything, such as raspberry jam, usually refers to the quantities people will want to purchase during a specified time period at various prices. At higher prices, people will shift toward substitutes for raspberry jam; at lower prices, they'll substitute raspberry jam more

[5]It is important for the reader to keep the distinction between the monetary *unit* and the monetary *system* in mind. The fact that money is nonneutral means that if the monetary system is out of balance, the consequences to the economy can be dire. Therefore a goal of monetary policy is neutrality, so as to minimize the potential damage caused by either excess supply or excess demand of money. This distinction is similar to the distinction between law and the legal system. The law is never neutral in the sense that it rules in favor of one party and against another, but the legal system should strive for as much neutrality as possible. This, of course, is one of the reasons the transition from the rule of man to the rule of law is vital to the development of an economic system, as we will see in later chapters on growth and development.

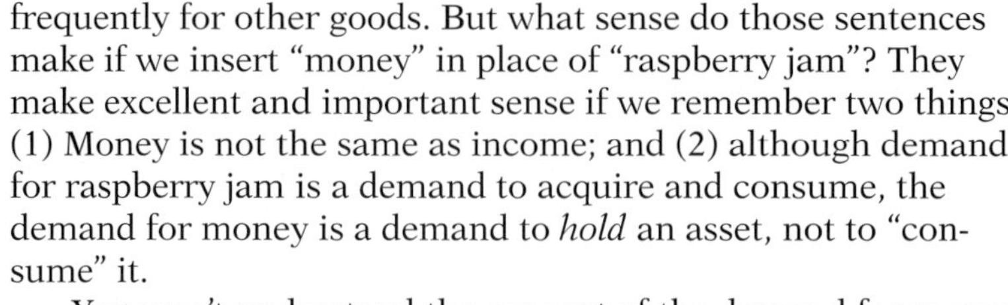
frequently for other goods. But what sense do those sentences make if we insert "money" in place of "raspberry jam"? They make excellent and important sense if we remember two things: (1) Money is not the same as income; and (2) although demand for raspberry jam is a demand to acquire and consume, the demand for money is a demand to *hold* an asset, not to "consume" it.

Income is a flow: an amount per time. Money is a stock: an amount at a time.

You won't understand the concept of the demand for money if you identify money with money income. *Money income is a flow* and so must always be stated with reference to some time period: $8 per hour, $1,600 per month, $24,000 per year. But *money itself is a stock;* it is a certain amount in existence at some time. Because the size of the stock varies from day to day, we can measure it only with respect to some point in time. But it is *at a point* in time that we try to measure the size of a stock; we measure the size of a flow *during a period* of time. Thus, an employee who says, "I'm going in to see the boss this afternoon and demand more money," really means that the employee is going to insist on more money income: a larger flow of money per month. That is *not* what we're talking about here. The amount of money that people hold (as a stock) will usually be related closely to the amount of money income they receive regularly (as a flow). But it's certainly possible for one to go up while the other is going down.

Think it through. How much money, defined as M1, are you currently holding? In other words, what is the sum of your checking account balance and the currency plus coin that you have in your pocket, purse, billfold, and bureau drawer? Whatever it is, what must you do in order to increase or decrease this amount? To decrease it, you must exchange money for other assets (we'll assume you don't lose it or throw it away). These assets could be anything from food for immediate consumption to shares of stock in AT&T. To increase the amount of M1 you're currently holding, you must give up other assets in exchange for currency or an addition to your checking account balance (we'll rule out finding money or stealing it).

Now let's suppose you've been working 20 hours a week for $8 an hour. You've been exchanging 20 hours of your time each week for $160, yielding a money income of $160 per week. Then you decide to spend more time studying, so you cut your work hours to 15 per week and your income to $120 per week. If at the same time you reduce your expenditures by more than $40 per week (you eliminate a lot of recreation activities, let's say, in order to increase your study time), you will be adding to the stock of money you hold, even though your income has decreased. People add to the stock of money they hold, to their money balances, by reducing their expenditures below their income or by exchanging other assets for money. They reduce their money balances by raising their expenditures above their income or exchanging money for other assets.

Why Do People Hold Money Balances?

The demand for money is a demand to hold money.

The demand for money, we said, is a demand to *hold* money, not to consume it. Money isn't unique in this respect. Lots of goods yield services by being held: Fine art, shares of stock, and houses are examples. The demand for all of them should be understood, therefore, as a demand to hold the good in question, not to "use it up." It's clear how paintings, corporate stock, and houses yield services by being held or owned. But isn't it true that money provides a service only when it's spent?

It is *not* true. Money does provide services when it's spent, which is why people want to hold money in the first place. They're looking forward to the enjoyment of what they expect the money to buy them. But money also provides a service while it is being held. If it did not, no one would hold it, because holding money is costly. While holding money, we're sacrificing the valuable current services that other goods would yield us if we bought them with the money: the interest on a government bond, the pleasure of a good movie, a comfortable armchair in which to relax. If present goods are more valuable than future goods, why don't people immediately spend their money income when they receive it and maintain their stock of money balances at zero? They obviously don't do this. And that implies, correctly, that holding money yields a valuable service, a service valuable enough in comparison with the cost of holding money to persuade people to hold those amounts that they do hold.

That service, quite simply, is flexibility. By holding money rather than some other asset, you increase your freedom to maneuver. You make it easier for yourself to buy what you want when you want it, to take advantage of opportunities that you don't know about yet or that aren't available at the moment, or to escape from an unexpected misfortune. Moreover, you make these things possible for yourself without the trouble and expense of first taking a trip to the bank or making a visit to your stockbroker or selling an asset at an unfavorable price. A synonym for flexibility is *liquidity*. An asset that can be exchanged at any time at its full value for any other asset is a completely liquid asset. Money is, by definition, the most liquid asset in a society. The demand for money is a demand for liquidity.

Actual and Preferred Money Balances

The quantity of money supplied necessarily equals the quantity held—but not necessarily the quantity that people want to hold.

Whatever the quantity of money the public *prefers* to hold, the quantity it *actually* holds will be the quantity supplied. This is a simple but important point to keep in mind. The size of the money stock at any time, however measured, is by definition equal to the quantity of money balances the public is holding at that time. But *actual money balances may not be equal to preferred money balances*. If the stock of money increased at a time when the public was satisfied with its current money holdings, some people would find themselves holding larger money balances than they preferred to hold. They would consequently take steps to reduce their money balances back to the preferred level. If the money stock declined when people were holding their preferred amounts of money, they would try to raise their balances back up to the previous level. They would make these adjustments in the way we've already described, by changing the relationship between their incomes and their expenditures, or by changing the composition of their assets—exchanging corporate stock for money, perhaps, or money for government bonds.

The concept of the demand for money implies that when additional money is supplied to a public *already holding the amount it prefers to hold*, the public will attempt to exchange that additional money for other goods. This will increase the aggregate demand for goods other than money, including those newly produced goods that make up the gross domestic product. This increased demand will call forth some combination of higher prices and larger output. Gross domestic product can thus be expected to increase in response to an increase in demand for new goods that was prompted in turn by an increase in the quantity of money supplied to a public already holding its preferred amount of money balances. GDP will continue to rise in this way as long as spending for new goods keeps increasing. And spending will continue to increase as long as people are still holding more money than they want to hold.

Notice that the attempt by individuals to reduce their money holdings by increasing their expenditures adds to the money holdings of others; it doesn't reduce the money stock. The public's attempt to reduce its money balances can't succeed, because all the money that's supplied must be held by someone. What happens instead is that the attempt to reduce actual money balances to the level of preferred money balances causes total income to rise, until the public prefers to hold money balances equal to the quantity that has been supplied.

This way of putting it is a little misleading, because it suggests that people are *coerced* into holding the quantity of money that the monetary authorities, in conjunction with the banking system, supply. That's not true, of course. Remember that the money supply increases when commercial banks increase their loans. More loans mean people who *wanted to borrow* now have the ready money they were looking for. Surely they didn't borrow money and agree to pay interest on it in order to let that money sit idly in their bank accounts. They'll spend it, for whatever they had in mind when they borrowed. Let's suppose it's a couple that borrowed in order to buy new living room furniture. When they make the purchase, they transfer to the owners of the furniture store the amount that the bank had credited to their checking account. What do the furniture retailers do in turn? They don't say: "Drat! Here we were happily holding the quantity of money we preferred to hold. Then that inconsiderate couple stuck us with this extra money. Now we're going to have to waste our time figuring out a way to get rid of it. Do we know anybody we can dump it on?" Rather they say: "Great! We sold a couch and two chairs. Business is good. Our furniture inventory is down, however, so we'd better use this new money to replenish our stock." And so they (joyfully!) pass the money on to their suppliers, who accept it, also joyfully, and repeat the reasoning of the furniture retailers.

How Stable Is the Demand for Money?

The demand for money will change in response to changes in financial practices, such as greater use of credit cards or establishment of telephone transfer systems that make it easy to switch funds from one kind of bank deposit to another. But financial practices usually evolve slowly, so changes in the public's preferences with respect to money balances also occur slowly. All this is consistent with a stable demand for money.

Why the demand for money might change

There are events, however, that can upset this stability. Suppose the monetary authorities announce their intention to pursue rapid, large, and persistent increases in the stock of money. The public will immediately conclude that the purchasing power of money is going to fall substantially and will try to exchange money for other assets. This, of course, will increase the price of those other assets and reduce the value of money, which will reinforce people's anxiety about holding money. The demand for money will fall in the face of immoderate or irresponsible actions by the monetary authorities—or even in anticipation of such actions. Or suppose that the public has been reading warnings that economic troubles elsewhere in the world might spread to the United States. Households may decide to defer large purchases that they were contemplating in order to see what's going to happen. They reason that if a recession starts, prices may decline and they will get what they want for less than they would have to pay if they bought it now. Business firms might reason similarly: "Let's wait and see. We don't want to make an investment that might turn out to be mistaken." Such decisions to reduce expenditures without any prior reduction in income constitute an increase in the demand for money.

What effects on the demand for money would you predict from a large fall in the various indices of stock prices, such as the well-known Dow-Jones index of industrial stock prices? Those who hold substantial amounts of stock would think of themselves as less wealthy than they used to be. And so they might be more reluctant to spend money. They might also be reluctant to put that money they now aren't spending into the stock market, which they fear is going to fall further. As they look around for alternative assets, some of them may decide simply to increase their holding of money balances. And so the demand for money could increase.

The task of the Fed in all such cases is to accommodate the change in the public's demand for money by altering the quantity supplied. Note what might happen if, for example, the Fed fails to increase the quantity of money available when the demand to hold money has increased. Those who want to hold larger money balances will have to obtain them by reducing their expenditures or by selling other assets. Reducing their expenditures will reduce the incomes of others who must then reduce their expenditures in turn just to maintain the level of their own money balances. With no additional money available, this widespread desire to hold more money could set off a downward spending spiral that might culminate in a recession. A deep enough recession would halt the spiral, but only by making people so much worse off financially that they no longer wanted to increase their holdings of money. Selling other assets, such as shares of stock or real estate, in order to increase money balances could cause a severe plunge in asset values if most people are simultaneously pursuing the same objective. By reducing people's wealth in this manner, the fall in asset prices might persuade people to curtail their expenditures with the same eventual results as those just described. If the Fed makes more money available when the public wants to hold more money, it is shielding the economic system to some extent from the pressures that produce fluctuations in output and prices.

If the Fed supplies more money than the public wants to hold or fails to reduce the stock of money in circulation when the demand for money has decreased, it risks setting off inflation. The public probably fears inflation more than it ought to, because it generally fails to distinguish a real increase in the cost of living from a mere decrease in the purchasing power of money. On the other hand, inflation increases uncertainty for economic decision makers and uncertainty is the basic cause of recessions. Moreover, halting inflation once it has begun may itself trigger a recession, so it's best not to let it get started.

Monetary Policy in Practice

Even if you regularly read *The Wall Street Journal* or the business and finance pages of a metropolitan newspaper, there's a good chance that you have never read about the Fed's efforts to increase or decrease the quantity of money in the economy. What you read about instead is the "key interest rate" that the Fed supposedly controls and about whether the next meeting of the Open Market Committee will produce a decision to increase that rate, to decrease it, or to leave it where it is. That "key rate" is the federal funds rate, which is the rate at which commercial banks lend reserves to one another. Recall from the previous

Targeting the federal funds rate

chapter that the Fed cannot *directly* set the federal funds rate in the way that it sets the discount rate, the rate at which it lends money to commercial banks. The federal funds rate is set by supply and demand. But the supply and demand is the supply of and demand for bank reserves, and those the Fed *can* control with a fair amount of precision. So if the Fed decides to lower the federal funds rate by a quarter of 1 percent, it instructs those in charge of its bond trading operations to buy more government bonds. As explained in Chapter 16, this means that the Fed is pumping additional reserves into the banking system. The Fed acquires additional assets, in the form of U.S. government bonds, and takes on new liabilities, in the form of the deposits that commercial banks maintain with the Federal Reserve banks.

The federal funds rate may not fall immediately. And it always bounces around on any single day. The Thursday news report on interest rate movements describing the Wednesday federal funds rate will say something like "8% high, 5.75% low, 6% near closing, 6.5% offered." What this means is that commercial banks that wanted to borrow for overnight use 1 million dollars or more of other banks' excess reserves had to pay on Wednesday as much as 8 percent and as little as 5.75 percent to do so, and that as the market was closing on Wednesday, the last transaction was for 6 percent and someone was asking 6.5 percent. These are the actual figures, by the way, for a day right after the Fed decided to lower its target rate from 5.5 percent to 5.25 percent, which makes it pretty clear that the federal funds rate doesn't immediately do what the Fed says it wants it to do.

Because all the conversation is about interest rates, the question naturally arises whether monetary policy affects economic activity by controlling the money supply or by controlling interest rates. It's hard to decide, because the Fed tries to influence interest rates by procedures that alter bank reserves, hence bank lending, and hence the quantity of money in circulation. Moreover, the additional reserves that are created when the Fed tries to lower the federal funds rate will increase the supply of bank credit and thus put downward pressure on bank lending rates. If businesses and, to a lesser extent, households can borrow more cheaply, they will presumably want to borrow more and spend more. In this way, lowering the federal funds rate could stimulate expenditures quite apart from any change in the quantity of money supplied. But because additional bank lending amounts to the creation of new money, lower interest rates and a larger quantity of money are never cleanly separated. It may even be that the Fed would like to control the quantity of money, realizes it cannot do so with any precision, and targets the federal funds rate as the best way available to hit a target it cannot observe: equality between the quantity of money supplied and the quantity demanded.

When Is Monetary Policy Effective?

For quite a few years after the Great Depression, the dominant opinion among economists seems to have been that although monetary policy might be effective in preventing inflation, it is largely ineffective in countering recession. The favorite analogy of the time was that of a balloon on a string. You can keep a balloon from rising by pulling on its string, but you can't make it rise by pushing on the string.

why monetary policy may be ineffective in a recession

The monetary authorities can increase the excess reserves of the banking system, but they cannot compel the commercial banks to extend loans and thereby turn those reserves into money. Moreover, the creation of a larger money stock will not produce an increase in spending if the public responds simply by building up its money balances. In a recession, most people tend to become more pessimistic and more cautious. Banks scrutinize potential borrowers more rigorously before extending loans and refuse to renew some loans that come due. Borrowers are less eager to apply for loans because short-term profit prospects seem unfavorable. People look for ways to increase their liquidity as a precautionary move. The expectation of declining prices also adds to the public's preferences for holding money rather than assets whose value relative to money is likely to fall. In short, a recession can create a crisis of confidence that worsens the recession by prompting a sharp increase in people's desire to hold larger amounts of ready cash. The monetary authorities may find it difficult to satisfy this desire or to induce people to begin spending their idle balances. In these circumstances, efforts by the central bank to halt a recession or to spur a recovery might very well be like pushing on a string.

The Case for Fiscal Policy

Is there any way in which the central bank or some other agency of government can persuade people to borrow and spend? One way would be to increase the confidence of households and business decision makers. That's why government officials always talk so bravely about the economic future, like to predict an indefinite continuation of current prosperity, and only use the word *recession* in reference to the past. The mere belief that government will take vigorous steps to restore prosperity may be enough to revive confidence, even when no one has any idea what those steps might be. And any threat to raise taxes in the future certainly reduces confidence. Franklin D. Roosevelt's repeated promises in the 1930s to balance the federal budget by raising taxes as soon as conditions would allow it may have been intended to assure the business community of his soundly conservative views. They were interpreted, however, more as threat than promise; the virtues of a balanced budget seemed pale indeed when set against the undoubted virtues of low taxes.

A much more direct way to increase borrowing and spending at a time when fear and timidity rule is for the government itself to borrow and spend. If the government borrows the new reserves that the central bank is creating through its monetary policy and spends the proceeds on worthwhile projects, fiscal policy comes to the aid of a possibly impotent monetary policy. *Fiscal policy is simply budget policy*. As the term is used in this context, it means *using the government budget to bring about desired levels of total spending*.

using fiscal policy to supplement monetary policy

The most influential proponent of fiscal policy in this century was John Maynard Keynes (rhymes with *gains*), a British economist who lived from 1883 to 1946. He enjoyed a brilliant and diversified career as investor, editor, teacher, writer, government servant, and architect of systems for the reconstructing of international finance. But he is chiefly remembered today as the author of a book published at the beginning of 1936, in the midst of the Great Depression, entitled *The General Theory of Employment, Interest and Money. The General Theory*, to give it the abbreviated title by which it's usually known, is by common agreement an obscure and badly organized book. "What *The General Theory* Means" was a topic for innumerable essays and symposia in the years immediately following its publication, evidence that its message was deemed important but that no one quite knew what the essential message was. Regardless of how faithful this was to Keynes's own intentions—and controversy continues to this day about what his intentions were—the essential Keynesian *policy* soon came to be fiscal policy as a corrective to recessions, or what Keynes himself called "loan expenditure." The government takes out loans and spends the money.

Keynes placed less emphasis on changing tax rates. But that is another way to execute fiscal policy. Insofar as total spending depends upon the taxes households and businesses pay or expect to pay, the government may be able to alter spending levels by raising or reducing tax rates. This is less direct than loan expenditure, and its net effects on spending are less predictable.

To many observers, the power of fiscal policy was demonstrated by the "fiscal experiment" of 1940–1944. After a decade of depression caused by low levels of household and business spending and timid government responses, World War II practically compelled the government to run huge budget deficits. Government expenditures shot up much faster than taxes could be raised, and the economy revived spectacularly. Once prosperity had been restored by a massive injection of government spending, private expenditure was able to take up the slack when government expenditures fell sharply again after the war. That, at least, was the story Keynesians began to tell.[6]

The Necessity of Good Timing

No one doubts that the right combination of monetary policy and fiscal policy can alter total spending. But can it reduce aggregate fluctuations? Can it prevent or diminish the severity of recessions and changes in the purchasing power of money? Here is where the doubts begin.

Timing is absolutely crucial if aggregate-demand management is to be an effective stabilizing tool. But good timing proves extraordinarily difficult to achieve when it comes to fiscal or monetary policy, and for several reasons. In the first place, we never know until long afterward whether aggregate demand was rising or falling. The economy doesn't come equipped with a speedometer that tells us how fast it's running at any moment. We find out what GDP is doing during the current quarter only at the end of the quarter. Even then the figures provided by the Bureau of Economic Analysis are highly tentative and subject to sizable revisions as more accurate data become available a month and more after the quarter has ended.

Where are we?

What's worse, even if we could know exactly where we are at any time, that wouldn't be enough. Those who conduct monetary and fiscal policy have to know where we're *going to be*, because

Where will we be?

[6]Abba Lerner, in his *The Economics of Control* (New York: Macmillan, 1946), pp. 302–322, developed the theory of "functional finance" to suggest that the federal government could be used as a tool of public policy to smooth out the business cycle. The basic idea was to use the budget to balance the economy, rather than worrying about balancing the budget. Government would run deficits during bad times, and surpluses during good times, and as a consequence full employment levels of output would be maintained. Keynes's, and then Lerner's, suggestion was a rejection of the fiscal policy religion of balanced budgets that had held sway since Adam Smith. James Buchanan argued vigorously in his book *Public Principles of Public Debt* (Homewood, IL: Irwin, 1958) against this "new" Keynesian theory of public finance and defended the older views of Adam Smith. Buchanan emphasized in his critique the incentives within the political arena for politicians and challenged the idea that the theory of functional finance was practical. Why would it ever be in the electoral interests of a politician to run surpluses in good times? Politicians face incentives, too, and once the constraints to run continual budget deficits are lifted, they would tend to accumulate larger and larger public debt, which is then passed on to future generations, *after* the politicians have left office. Buchanan's criticisms proved to be correct, as the fiscal policies that resulted from the Keynesian revolution led to economic instability in the 1970s. Buchanan's and Richard Wagner's *Democracy in Deficit: The Political Legacy of Lord Keynes* (New York: Academic Press, 1977) documents how Keynesian doctrine resulted in policy failure. In this book, Buchanan and Wagner do not address the *economics* of Keynes as much as they address the underlying *politics* in the Keynesian model. They demonstrate how that underlying politics resulted in ruin because of its lack of appreciation for the basic elements of the theory of public choice (the theory of political decision making highlighted in Chapter 13 of this book).

today's action must aim at compensating for tomorrow's deficiency or excess in aggregate demand. Stabilization policy is necessarily based on forecasting, and short-term economic forecasting, far from being an exact science, isn't even a respectable art.

Particularly troubling is our inability to predict how much time it will take for a monetary or fiscal policy action to have its effects.[7] Estimates of the length of these lags range from a few months to several years, and diligent research efforts designed to nail down the time distribution of the effects haven't produced a workable consensus. The lags may even turn out to vary in ways we can't predict, in which case economists would be trying to measure something that actually has no standard length. There are good reasons for supposing that the time lags between monetary or fiscal policy actions and their effects are not some constant that can be measured and then relied on. The effects of these actions will depend, after all, on how businesses and households read their own uncertain individual futures. Government actions reduce some uncertainties, but they add others; they certainly don't enable people to start planning with complete confidence about what the future holds. Meanwhile, the operating procedures of commercial banks, the payment practices of business firms, the perceptions of households and corporations with respect to the advantages of holding assets in one form or another, international monetary transactions, and even the public's efforts to anticipate the effects of government actions will all play a part in determining the distribution over time of any policy's impact on total spending. These factors will be changing continuously. And they are especially likely to change in response to any improvement in our ability to forecast them! It is a case in which forecasts falsify themselves by altering the stock of information that had to be assumed in order to make the forecast. Here's a simple example: If we knew with confidence the pattern that some stock's market price would take over the coming year, it wouldn't trace that pattern. This is the paradox with which sciences of human behavior must live. Predicting the future changes the future, because the people whose actions create the future read the predictions.

How long is the time lag between action and impact?

The Federal Budget as a Policy Tool

When we turn specifically to fiscal policy, an additional difficulty emerges. There is a touch of comedy in the belief that the federal government can use its budget as a stabilization tool when almost

[7]Milton Friedman is probably the most notable scholar who emphasized the problem of the long and variable lag between (a) recognition of an economic problem, (b) designing appropriate policy to address the problem, (c) implementing that policy, and (d) the policy having the desired effect. His work suggests that proactive policies by the government could be more destabilizing than helpful in addressing economic fluctuations.

all observers agree that Congress no longer has effective control over the budget. The spending programs of the federal government are so many and so complex that no one can even begin to evaluate all of them for the purpose of determining annual appropriations. As a result, next year's budget begins by taking this year's budget for granted and adding on. Once a program gets in, it's almost impossible to dislodge, because its beneficiaries form a knowledgeable and determined lobby for its continuance and no one on Capitol Hill has the time, energy, and interest to accumulate the evidence that could justify its removal.

Fiscal policy is not something under the control of the Council of Economic Advisers. A change in government expenditures or in federal taxes requires action by the House of Representatives and then the Senate, with committee meetings before and often after, and a presidential signature at the end. That takes time—and timing, as we said, is crucial in aggregate-demand management. The discussions will be complicated and prolonged by the fact that even if Congress were to agree quickly on the desirability of a change in expenditures or taxes of a particular amount, it would still have to decide whose taxes will be changed and which expenditures. Conflicting interests will be involved as well as alternative theories about the expansionary or contractionary effects of particular actions. Is it better to cut the taxes of low-income people or to give tax credits for investment? Which will have a greater impact on employment? And are we talking about the long run or the short run? Meanwhile, some members of Congress will certainly decide that an important tax or expenditure bill provides an opportunity to eliminate the capital gains tax, reform the welfare system, bring Medicare spending under control, eliminate agricultural subsidies, or achieve some other objective dear to the heart of important parts of the electorate.

The more in a hurry Congress and the president are, the more likely they are to produce fiscal policy actions that few competent and impartial observers will be able to defend. The imperative of haste tends to enhance the power of those who are willing to enforce their demands by threatening to block any action at all. But due deliberation, the careful assessment of alternatives, and the weighing of the probable short- and long-term outcomes may require so much time that the moment for action passes before any action is taken.

Advocates of stabilization through fiscal policy have long been aware of these difficulties. They know that the protracted discussions that precede any congressional action on taxes and expenditures could easily make fiscal policy unworkable: Action might not be possible until the time for it has passed. They have consequently looked around for ways to speed up the process. One proposal recommended by a few economists and actually urged by President John F. Kennedy was that Congress authorize unilateral action by the president. Appropriations for particular projects could be approved by Congress and then put on the shelf, to be taken off whenever the president and his advisers decided that the stimulus of increased government expenditures was called for. Congress could also authorize the president to increase or decrease tax rates within narrow limits when aggregate demand seemed excessive or inadequate.

If you're wondering why Congress never acted on such a "sensible" recommendation, think for a moment about the political power that presidents would command if they could unilaterally determine the timing of tax decreases and the placement of expenditure projects. Congress isn't likely to grant that kind of power to any president, not even to a trusted president who is a member of the same political party as the majority in both houses of Congress. Some senators and representatives will be deterred by the constitutional principle of a balance of power among the branches of government, some by respect for Lord Acton's maxim that absolute power corrupts absolutely. But all will know that such power in the hands of a president substantially diminishes their own power and influence. The conclusion, therefore, is that fiscal policy *at best* will continue, under most circumstances, to be a stabilization tool that doesn't become available until the appropriate time for its use has passed.

Who can be trusted with uncontrolled power?

Unfinished Business

Japan at the end of the 1990s, suffering from a prolonged slowdown in economic growth, appeared to be in circumstances where fiscal policy *would* work effectively. All forecasters at the beginning of 1998 were predicting a year of negative growth. Was fiscal policy used? Did it have the desired effects?

The Japanese government cut personal taxes in February of 1998 by 2 trillion yen. But consumer spending did not increase appreciably. Japanese consumers, apparently concerned about the state of the economy and their own personal finances, elected to save rather than spend most of the tax cut. The government also increased its spending on public sector projects. But the increase was timid and smaller than originally promised, probably because the government feared the consequences of raising the public debt at a time when it was already twice the size of annual output. It had little effect.

Was monetary policy employed and was it effective? The central bank's official discount rate stood at 0.5% in 1998—it can't get much lower—and the bank pumped large quantities of additional money into the system. But Japan's commercial banks proved reluctant to lend. Their portfolios were full of nonperforming loans, and the liabilities of many banks, including some of the largest, exceeded the value of their assets. Some experts claimed that half of the nation's banks were in such sorry condition in 1998 that they would either have to merge or close their doors. In such circumstances the banks behaved very cautiously, and total bank lending actually declined from the middle of 1997 to the middle of 1998, even though the central bank was trying to expand lending and the money supply. In November 2002, the unemployment rate was 5.5%, tying a post–World War II high, and output continued to fall. From being the darling of would-be economic planners in the 1980s, Japan in the early 2000s was an economy characterized by deflation, public debt, and a risky investment environment. In 2004, it seems that the Japanese economy has been making a strong recovery after the restructuring of its industry in the wake of the "bust" of the 1990s and early 2000s. Firms are now organized in a more cost-effective manner and corporate debt is more aligned with prebubble levels. However, lingering problems with unemployment and low wages have prevented personal consumption from returning to previous levels.

Economists throughout the world were extremely generous with their advice to the Japanese government in the late 1990s and early 2000s. Some went so far as to accuse that government of sacrificing the needs of other East Asian countries by refusing to implement sensible policies, merely to avoid offending powerful domestic political interests. Appropriate policies, if the government could muster the courage to implement them, would allegedly restore aggregate spending in Japan and thereby increase the demand for the exports of neighboring countries, thus pulling them out of the recessions into which many of them fell beginning with the Asian crisis in 1997.

We have said very little so far about political constraints on the policies through which governments influence the overall level of economic activity. That is a major omission that we will now begin to repair. But we have also said very little about the role of international economic relationships in all of this. That is also a serious omission. It's the topic we take up next.

Once Over Lightly

The Great Depression of the 1930s persuaded many observers that market-coordinated economic systems are less stable and their fluctuations less self-correcting than economists had traditionally maintained.

In a world characterized by uncertainty, the responses of economic decision makers to unanticipated events or revised concerns about the future may magnify initial disturbances, producing large cyclical swings in economic activity and even the possibility of sustained economic collapse.

Economic collapse—a recession—is a sign of disappointed expectations. Although many businesses suffer losses in good times and bad, a recession represents a systematic—general and widespread—series of unexpected business losses. Market participants misread the information provided by price signals. Firms engage in monetary calculation of expected profits and losses, and choose their ventures according to what they expect would be most profitable. Instead, over time, they realize losses and change their investment and hiring plans. They reverse course by cutting back output and laying off workers.

Money pervades all markets. Changes in the volume of money affect not only "the price level" but relative prices of scarce goods and services and thereby affect the monetary calculations of expected profits and losses that guide all entrepreneurs in the economy and help them better coordinate their plans with resource providers and demanders for their products.

When monetary miscalculation of expected profits and losses is so widespread so as to represent a cluster of errors throughout the economic system, the likely culprit is an artificial lowering of the interest rate through expansion of the money supply. The "boom" phase of the business cycle created by the temporarily cheaper credit cannot be sustained in the long run and will eventually generate the recessionary bust as plans adjust to the reality of unexpected but realized economic losses.

Such widespread miscalculations and the clusters of errors that they represent would be minimized were the Fed to follow a policy of monetary equilibrium, striving to equate the amount of money supplied in the economy with the amount of money demanded. A stabilizing monetary policy is one that attempts to accommodate changes in the public's demand for money by adjusting the quantity of money supplied.

The mildness of post–World War II recessions and the rapid economic growth experienced by many market-coordinated economic systems persuaded most economists that severe recessions as well as high rates of inflation could be prevented by government policies aimed at countering fluctuations in private expenditures (aggregate demand).

Because the Fed expands or contracts the money supply by expanding or contracting commercial bank reserves, monetary policy today is usually summarized by pointing to changes in the federal funds rate, the interest rate on the lending of reserves among banks, which the Fed explicitly "targets."

In some circumstances, such as a deep and prolonged depression in economic activity, fiscal policy may be a useful or even necessary supplement to monetary policy. An expansionary fiscal policy will be one that increases government expenditures without a matching increase in tax revenues or that cuts taxes without an equivalent reduction in government expenditures.

Timing is crucial in any effective stabilization policy. The time lags that inevitably occur between the appearance and the recognition of a problem, the recognition and the decision to take a particular action, and the action and its ultimate effects combine to make aggregate-demand management less stabilizing in practice than on paper.

Attempts to stabilize aggregate demand through fiscal or monetary policy must entail accurate prediction if they are to be successful. But economic forecasting is an undeveloped art. It is made especially hazardous by the fact that the people whose behavior is to be controlled try to anticipate and adjust for the controls.

The political delays inevitably associated with its use create especially acute timing problems for fiscal policy.

QUESTIONS FOR DISCUSSION

1. What caused the recession that began in the United States in 1929? Why did the decline continue for four years? Why did the decline occur at such a steep rate? Why did real output not regain its 1929 level until 1939? Why did the unemployment rate remain so extraordinarily high throughout the 1930s? Why has no recession or depression of even remotely comparable severity occurred since World War II?
2. How long is the long run? John Maynard Keynes accused his predecessors of ignoring the problem of recessions by assuming that they would correct themselves "in the long run." In a book written some years before *The General Theory*, he observed caustically that in the long run we are all dead.

   (a) Suppose you think there is a 0.25 probability that by trying to remedy a recession the government will in fact make it worse but that it will cure itself "in the long run." How long would you want to wait before accepting the risk of making matters worse?
   (b) How long must a recession continue or a recovery be delayed before we're justified in assuming that recessions are not merely "temporary disturbances"?
3. Do fluctuations in spending for particular goods necessarily cause fluctuations in the output of those goods? Do you think that production rates in the toy industry fluctuate as much as consumer expenditures for toys fluctuate? Under what circumstances can a smooth flow of production be reconciled with variations in expenditure on that output? When are reductions in expenditure most likely to cause production cutbacks and unemployment in a particular firm or industry?
4. Analogies must be used with care. But this one may help you visualize the major relationships between the two flows of income and of expenditures and the stock of money. Imagine a lake formed by a dammed-up river. Let the lake represent the stock of money someone is holding. The river above the lake represents income, and the river below the lake represents expenditures.

   (a) What must be done to raise or to lower the lake level?

   (b) How could the lake level be raised even though the flow above the lake is declining? How could the lake level be lowered even though the flow above the lake is increasing?
   (c) If the dam operator anticipates a late-summer drought and wants to prevent the lake from falling below some desired level, what might be done during the spring?
5. What is the good that people want to obtain more of when they decide to increase the quantity of money they are going to hold?
   (a) What are the major factors you consider in deciding how large you want your stock of money balances to be? What sorts of events would induce you to increase or decrease your preferred stock of money balances?
   (b) What other assets function for you as partial substitutes for money balances?
   (c) What are some of the assets that business firms might choose to hold as partial substitutes for money balances?
   (d) Is a good credit rating an asset that someone might use as a substitute for money balances? Is that what people do when they start off on a trip carrying little currency but a credit card with a large credit limit and a small current balance?
6. Some people think that consumers could stop inflation if they launched a consumer strike against higher prices.
   (a) What would happen to your stock of money balances if, during a period of rapid inflation, you decided to do your part in fighting inflation by reducing your expenditures?
   (b) How likely is it that large numbers of people will choose their preferred level of money balances by neglecting their personal interests and considering instead the contribution they might make to stopping inflation?
   (c) What would happen to the value of your stock of money balances if you did this and inflation continued?
7. Would money function as a medium of exchange if people were unwilling to hold it, even for very short periods of time? Is there any difference between a barter economy and an economy in which people hold no money balances?
8. What effect would you expect each of the following to have on the average size of the checking account balances that a particular business firm or household would want to hold?
   (a) An unusually high rate of expenditures is anticipated in the near future.
   (b) The rate of interest on savings accounts rises.
   (c) Banks offer to provide checking account services at no fee on accounts that maintain a $400 minimum balance during any month.
   (d) Banks pay interest on checking accounts.
   (e) The monetary authorities increase the quantity of money rapidly over an extended period of time and the public begins to anticipate a high rate of inflation.

9. We describe the demand for most goods by referring to prices and the number of units that would be demanded at those prices. But economists describe the demand for money by referring to the price (or cost) of holding money and some percentage of income.

   (a) Why is the quantity demanded expressed as a percentage in the case of money, rather than as a number of units?
   (b) Would you be willing to say that someone's demand for money had not changed if that person held the same quantity of dollars as before that person's money income doubled or the purchasing power of dollars fell 50 percent?

10. Suppose that every household and business firm decided to spend on Tuesday every dollar it was holding.

    (a) What would be the effect on the stock of money balances held on Wednesday by households and business firms?
    (b) What other effects would you predict from such a mass decision to unload money balances?
    (c) Suppose this decision resulted from a sudden conviction that money was going to be worthless by the end of the week. What do you think would happen?
    (d) What might prompt the people in any society to come to the conclusion that their money will shortly be worthless?

11. Anyone who reads extensively in economic history will encounter periodic complaints from merchants about a scarcity of money in the hands of the public.

    (a) What observations by a merchant might prompt such a complaint?
    (b) What might cause a widespread increase in the incidence of such complaints from merchants?
    (c) Why do you suppose it is that so many merchants throughout history have associated an abundance of money with prosperity and a scarcity of it with hard times?
    (d) If more money in the possession of a particular merchant's customers will produce prosperity for that merchant, will more money in everyone's hands produce greater prosperity for all merchants?

12. The following questions all deal with the relationship between interest rates and spending decisions on the part of the public.

    (a) How do higher interest rates affect investment spending?
    (b) How do higher interest rates affect new housing construction?
    (c) "Shall we maintain production and allow our inventories of unsold goods to rise, or should we shut down production until we've managed to sell off most of the finished goods now in the warehouses?" How might the level of interest rates enter into this decision?
    (d) An electric utility postpones construction of a new generating plant because the market price of its bonds is disappointingly low. How does this illustrate the relationship between investment and interest rates?
    (e) A corporation plans to begin a huge capital expansion program using proceeds from a sale of new stock. But common-stock prices decline

and the firm postpones the stock sale and the investment program it was intended to finance. Does that have anything to do with interest rates?

(f) "Higher interest rates don't deter any business firm that has a profitable use for the money. If we can make 30 percent on an investment, we're going to invest whether we can borrow at 3 percent or have to pay 12 percent." Evaluate this statement.

(g) "The higher the interest rate I can get, the more I'm going to invest. Investment increases as interest rates rise." Is that a correct argument?

(h) "Interest rates tend to be higher in booms than in recessions. But investment spending is usually greater in booms than in recessions. This implies that high interest rates encourage investment spending and low interest rates discourage it." Criticize that argument.

13. How independent of each other are monetary policy and fiscal policy?

 (a) Under what circumstances could the federal government run a large budget deficit without thereby producing an increase in the size of the money stock?

 (b) Suppose the Fed determined to run a "tight" monetary policy, allowing no growth in commercial bank reserves, at a time when the federal government was trying to borrow to finance a large budget deficit. What would happen?

 (c) Assuming that interest rates are set by the demand for and supply of loanable funds, under what circumstances could a large increase in federal government borrowing not produce higher interest rates?

 (d) Suppose the Fed tries to prevent the increased government demand for loanable funds from raising interest rates by increasing the supply of loanable funds through an expansion of commercial bank loans. Will this Fed policy succeed in preventing interest rates from rising? At what point will the Fed's expansionary policy step up the inflation rate? How will the expectation of a higher rate of inflation cause interest rates to rise?

 (e) Suppose that the federal government begins to run a large budget deficit at a time when many productive resources are idle—factories are operating far below capacity in most industries and there are surplus supplies of labor in almost every area of the economy. How might the existence of all these idle resources prevent even a very large increase in government borrowing from leading to an increase in interest rates?

14. Evaluate the following assertion: "When aggregate demand is greater than the aggregate capacity of the economy, we get inflation. When it is less, we get recession."

 (a) Do firms ever lay off workers when the average price level is rising?

 (b) Do firms ever raise their prices during a recession?

 (c) How would we know whether the economy was operating at full capacity? Is the aggregate capacity of a single firm ever some definite quantity of output per time period? Think of the college you attend. What would be occurring if it were operating at 100 percent of capacity? Extend the question to an entire industry (e.g., the education industry). Then extend it again to the entire economy.

15. Is aggregate demand inadequate if there is a shortage of automotive mechanics and a surplus of secondary-school teachers? Can substantial unemployment exist at a time when listed job vacancies exceed total unemployment? Why will you find help-wanted ads in newspapers even during recessions?
16. If Congress wants to use fiscal policy to counter recessions, should it cut taxes when the recession is a suspicion, when it's a widespread conviction, or when it's officially announced?
17. Would you favor the proposal, mentioned in the text, to give the president authority to change tax rates or authorize expenditures on his own (within congressionally designated limits) as a way of making fiscal policy more flexible? Why or why not?
18. Transcripts of closed-door deliberations among members of the Federal Reserve Board of Governors, released in January 1996, reveal Federal Reserve Chairman Alan Greenspan saying on October 2, 1990, "The economy has not yet slipped into a recession." The National Bureau of Economic Research subsequently determined that a recession had begun three months earlier. The Fed, however, did not cut interest rates until October 29. How much too late would you estimate this action was? What would have been the best time for the Fed to reduce interest rates in response to a recession that began in July 1990?
19. After summarizing Japan's spectacular economic growth from the 1950s through the 1980s, the text described the dismal record of the Japanese economy in the 1990s. How does this chapter's discussion of monetary and fiscal policy apply to the Japanese experience? Here is some information that you might want to use:

    Japanese producers clearly made a lot of mistakes in the 1980s. They expanded their capacity in many industries well beyond the willingness of domestic or foreign consumers to purchase what they counted on selling. They were encouraged to expand by the policies of Japanese banks, which loaned generously to the large industrial combinations of which they were often an integral part. Japanese households contributed their part by maintaining the high rate of savings that had provided such huge quantities of new capital during the years of rapid economic growth. The Japanese government looked favorably upon the entire process, protecting the domestic markets of favored producers against foreign competition and actively encouraging the expansion of favored industries without much regard for their potential profitability. Shareholders were taught to be patient and to look to the distant future for returns on their investment. All this constituted a recipe for rapid economic growth—for a time. Under favorable circumstances, that might be a long time. But unprofitable investments will lead eventually to costs that exceed revenues. The cozy relationships among government officials, bankers, and the heads of major industrial corporations—what has been called "crony capitalism"—kept overly ambitious projects funded long past the time when they would have been

> curtailed under a system different from that which prevailed in Japan. But eventually, the banks found themselves holding huge amounts of nonperforming loans, and many of even the very largest banks became technically insolvent: Their liabilities were greater than their assets. In such circumstances, banks try not to acquire additional liabilities. So they become reluctant to make new loans.

What would be your policy recommendations?

18

Economic Performance and Political Economy

If all the interrelationships that we've been discussing since Chapter 14 were clearly and confidently understood, so that economists could explain cause and effect as precisely as chemists usually do in their laboratories, government economic policies affecting stabilization and growth might be set in the public interest. But the theories of economists in this area are much less precise and far more subject to debate than are the theories of chemists. That leaves considerable room for policy-makers to talk persuasively about the public interest while actually responding to the pressure of much narrower interests. The net results of such policies seem often to be less stability rather than more and stagnation rather than economic growth.

The Political Setting

Government is not like Aladdin's marvelous genie, who always obeyed commands and always succeeded in accomplishing what he was told to do. The agencies of government are staffed entirely by human beings. In far too many nations of the world, unfortunately, the human beings in control are thieves and thugs whose determination to increase their own power and wealth produces policies that are nothing short of disastrous for their nation and people. But even democratic governments, in which officials are regularly subject to the check of free elections, will not necessarily act in what these officials themselves take to be the public interest. As Chapter 13 tried to show, the policies of governments will tend to reflect the interests of those people who are in the best position to extract benefits for themselves from the political process at low cost. A democratic government may be unable to prevent inflation or to moderate recessions because the people in control of government policies will not find it in their interest to do what they themselves believe ought to be done if fluctuations in the aggregate level of economic activity are to be reduced.[1]

Time horizons are a crucial consideration. Elected officials, with their gaze fixed on the next election, will prefer policies that pay benefits before election day and don't present their costs until after the voters have made their choice. Policies with short-term benefits and long-term costs thus have a strong advantage under the democratic political process. That fact has serious implications for the conduct of stabilization policies that we'll examine in a moment.

Moreover, appointed as well as elected officials in a democracy won't weigh each citizen's interests equally in reaching their decisions. They'll be partial to the pressures and pleadings of those who make their preferences known precisely and who care enough to monitor the decisions that government officials finally make. The squeaky wheel gets the grease. Few sugar consumers know or care very strongly how their legislative representative votes on a bill to raise sugar support prices or exclude sugar imports, but you can be certain that U.S. sugar producers know and care and that your legislator in turn knows and cares who knows and cares—and who does not much care and so isn't paying attention. That also makes it more difficult for governments to adopt and persist in sound economic policies.

Time Horizons and the Sequence of Effects

When we look carefully at the way in which changes in fiscal and monetary policy are likely to affect economic activity, we realize just how important the time horizons of those who are entrusted to construct and implement public policy is for the selection of the economic policies that will in fact be pursued by the government.

Suppose that the government finances an increase in its expenditures by borrowing from commercial banks, thereby increasing the money supply. This will increase the aggregate demand for newly produced goods. We cannot be sure how the resulting effect on GDP will be distributed between larger output and higher prices, but we do have good grounds for believing that any effect

[1]See Richard Wagner, "Economic Manipulation for Political Profit: Macroeconomic Consequences and Constitutional Implications," *Kyklos*, 30 (1977), pp. 395–410, for one of the first discussions to highlight the public-choice problems of macroeconomic policy. Since that time there has been a vast literature that explores the political economy of macroeconomic policy. A representative sampling would include Thomas Willett, ed., *Political Business Cycles: The Political Economy of Money, Inflation and Unemployment* (Durham, NC: Duke University Press, 1988); Torsten Persson and Guido Tabellini, *Political Economy: Explaining Economic Policy* (Cambridge, MA: MIT Press, 2000); Dennis Mueller, *Public Choice III* (New York: Cambridge University Press, 2003); and Charles Rowley and Friedrich Schneider, eds., *The Encyclopedia of Public Choice*, 2 volumes (Boston: Kluwer Academic Publishers, 2004).

on output and employment will appear *before* the effect on prices. Sellers interpret increased sales as an increased *relative* demand for what they are selling and consequently try to expand output. It takes more time for all these efforts to manifest themselves as an increased demand for resources generally and to produce an increase in costs and prices. So the "good stuff" arrives first: a rise in real GDP and a fall in the unemployment rate. The "bad stuff," a higher rate of inflation, is delayed. If politicians are contemplating an imminent election—and in the United States every member of the House of Representatives is on average only one year from the next election—the temptation will be strong to pursue short-run "good stuff" and let someone else worry later about the "bad stuff."

Contractionary policies will also produce their effects on output and employment more quickly than they affect the rate of change in the price level. In this case, however, the "bad stuff" arrives before the "good stuff." Any attempt to lower the rate of inflation by narrowing the government deficit and reducing the growth rate of the money supply will tend to thwart producers' expectations with regard to sales, lead to unsold business inventories, and result in reduced output and employment. The disinflationary impact will be delayed until the reduced demand for resources has had a chance to exert downward pressure on costs and prices. In short, an attempt to slow down the inflation rate by initiating less-expansionary fiscal and monetary policies is very likely to produce a recession before it succeeds in its aim of reducing inflation.

changes in aggregate demand affect output and employment before they affect prices.

This analysis suggests that elected officials will be quick to approve expansionary fiscal and monetary policies, opting for expansion whenever they are in doubt. This course will further commend itself to them because expansionary fiscal and monetary policies would generally be attractive to voters even if they had no effect at all on aggregate demand. Lower taxes and increased expenditures on behalf of interested parties make good campaign material for incumbents. Increased monetary ease tends to lower interest rates, at least temporarily, and that is almost always looked on approvingly by voters.

Contractionary policies, by contrast, inflict pain. Higher taxes and reduced expenditures will antagonize voters, as will any higher interest rates that result from tightening the supply of credit. The ensuing complaints will be listened to attentively by those who are contemplating an imminent election. Those in charge of government policies will be sorely tempted to withdraw the painful medicine and substitute the soothing tonic of expansionary policies.

All this suggests that democratic political processes tend to favor public policies that yield benefits concentrated on well-organized and well-informed interest groups in the short run at the expense of long-run and largely hidden costs that are borne by the unorganized and ill-informed mass of voters. In the macroeconomic realm of public policy, the concentrated benefits and shortsightedness biases will tend to produce jerky aggregate-demand policies that favor fiscal and monetary expansion.[2] When expansionary policies eventually produce an intolerable rate of inflation, the contractionary brakes will be applied. Unless disinflation comes quickly, however, the resulting recession and unemployment will create pressure to let up on the brakes and step once more on the accelerator. Such "go-stop-go" policies make the future more uncertain and result in more mistakes, which are the basic underlying cause of recessions. More frequent and severe recessions along with a rising rate of inflation could easily become the standard pattern in democratically governed societies.

Deficits unlimited

The politics of expenditures and taxes

Governments that must pay attention to popular opinion have long been tempted to spend more than they collect in taxes. You don't have to study economics to learn that it's easier for a legislator to support tax reductions than tax increases and to support enlarged expenditures rather than reduced expenditures. As a result, even if every member of the legislature wanted a budget surplus, a surplus wouldn't necessarily emerge. Although a large majority of voters may want a decrease in government expenditures, they will also want increased expenditures, or at least no reductions, for the tiny part of the total budget that constitutes their own sliver of the pie. And when that particular sliver is being sliced, each little special-interest group lets the legislators know that a cut at this point will have repercussions on campaign contributions and votes. There's no way to reduce the total budget while expanding each individual item in it. That's why government expenditures often rise even when each and every legislator sincerely wants them to decline.

The government of the United States ran a budget deficit in every year from 1970 through 1997, despite the fact that throughout most of this period members of both parties were complaining loudly about the dangers of such deficits. The surplus that finally emerged in 1998 after almost three decades of unrelenting deficits was not produced by any turn toward virtue on Capitol Hill or in the White House, but by the greatly increased tax revenues that a sustained economic expansion generated. Table 18–1 shows the federal budget surplus or deficit in each year from 1940 to 2003. Deficits exceeding one-quarter of a trillion dollars in 1992 and 1993 fell steadily and finally turned into a surplus in 1998, mostly as a result

[2]In the extreme, the tendency is for democratic governments to engage in deficit finance, accumulate public debt, and then monetize that debt, leading to inflation if government is not constrained by rules that bind fiscal and monetary policy. The effort at "tying the government's hands" in fiscal and monetary policy was a major aspect of the public-policy economics of both Milton Friedman (Nobel Prize winner in 1976) and James Buchanan (Nobel Prize winner in 1986). Friedman argued for a monetary rule and Buchanan argued for constitutional rules that called for a balanced budget. They both argued that rules would outperform discretion in generating good economic policy.

Table 18–1 U.S. Federal Government Budget in Current Dollars (dollar amounts in billions)

Year	Surplus or Deficit (–)	Year	Surplus or Deficit (–)
1940	–2.9	1972	–23.4
1941	–4.9	1973	–14.9
1942	–20.5	1974	–6.1
1943	–54.6	1975	–53.2
1944	–47.6	1976	–73.7
1945	–47.6	1977	–53.7
1946	–15.9	1978	–59.2
1947	4.0	1979	–40.7
1948	11.8	1980	–73.8
1949	0.6	1981	–79.0
1950	–3.1	1982	–128.0
1951	6.1	1983	–207.8
1952	–1.5	1984	–185.5
1953	–6.5	1985	–212.3
1954	–1.2	1986	–221.2
1955	–3.0	1987	–149.7
1956	3.9	1988	–155.2
1957	3.4	1989	–152.5
1958	–2.8	1990	–221.2
1959	–12.8	1991	–269.3
1960	0.3	1992	–290.4
1961	–3.3	1993	–255.1
1962	–7.1	1994	–203.2
1963	–4.8	1995	–164.0
1964	–5.9	1996	–107.5
1965	–1.4	1997	–22.0
1966	–3.7	1998	69.2
1967	–8.6	1999	125.6
1968	–25.2	2000	236.4
1969	3.2	2001	127.4
1970	–2.8	2002	–157.8
1971	–23.0	2003	–375.3

Source: http://www.whitehouse.gov/omb/budget/fy2005/pdf/hist.pdf

of healthy increases in government receipts. But those increases occurred without the aid of increases in tax rates. Because the federal government relies heavily for revenue on personal and corporate income taxes, its receipts automatically rise in periods of economic expansion and fall in recessions. A countercyclical fiscal policy, one that tries to dampen expansions and moderate recessions, will be one that produces deficits when gross domestic product falls and surpluses when it rises. But the small surplus of 1998, coming as it did a full seven years after the long expansion of the 1990s had begun and at a time when many analysts were predicting an imminent recession, could hardly have been the product of deliberation and responsible decision by the Clinton administration.

Since 9/11, and during the supposedly conservative administration of President Bush, the United States has returned to deficit financing in earnest, and the budget deficit for 2003 exceeded 300 billion dollars ($375,300,000,000 in current dollars), and as we revise this chapter, the projected deficit for 2004 is over half a trillion dollars ($520,700,000,000 in current dollars).

The other industrialized democracies of the world rarely did a whole lot better during the last decade or so. From 1991 through 1997, each of the following countries ran a government budget deficit in every single year: Canada, Australia, Britain, France, Germany, Italy, Sweden, and Switzerland. More names could be added. The pressures of politics in a democratic society seem to make deficits a way of life for national governments these days, except for rare periods, such as 1998 in the United States, when economic growth caused revenues to expand faster than the legislature could agree on how to spend it and invent plausible justifications for doing so. It's worth noting that the U.S. budget surplus in 1998 would still be a deficit if we excluded the Social Security system; the "surplus" was created by counting funds earmarked for future Social Security benefits.

Why Not Government at All Levels?

If this analysis is to account for chronic government budget deficits, however, it has to explain why state and local governments don't produce such deficits and why national governments did not in peacetime regularly do so before 1970.

First of all, state and local governments differ from national governments in one crucial respect. Only the national government has control over the medium of exchange, the ultimate means for the payment of debts. State and local governments are like you: They can borrow and so can run deficits only if they can convince potential lenders that today's deficit is a temporary shortfall that will be compensated for by a surplus tomorrow. Chronic, persistent deficits on the part of state and local governments are ruled out by the fact that lenders won't extend credit to a government unless they believe the government will be able to repay its debts in full and on time. This fact imposes no constraint on the federal government in the United States, however, because lenders know that the federal government can always *create* the money it needs to meet its obligations. Although money creation of this sort means that lenders will be repaid in dollars of decreased value, it also means that all other holders of dollar-denominated IOUs, not just creditors of the federal government, will be repaid in depreciated currency. Consequently, no one (at least no one who uses dollars as the ordinary medium of exchange) worries about lending to the U.S. government.

Creditors don't worry about lending to the party that controls the means of repayment.

But why did the federal government *not* run chronic peacetime deficits before 1970? And why has it only been within recent years that other industrialized democracies started to make deficits the rule rather than the exception? The answer may be the demise of the once-strong prejudice against government deficits, a prejudice that used to view such deficits as immoral because they demonstrated an irresponsible failure on the part of government to live within its means. Moral convictions that are strongly and widely held do operate as an effective check on legislators, especially when a majority of the legislators themselves adhere to that moral conviction. The old-time "fiscal religion" of the classical economists was summed up by then Governor Franklin Roosevelt, who while campaigning for the presidency in July 1932 stated: "Any government, like any family, can for a year spend a little more than it earns. But you and I know that a continuance of that habit means the poorhouse."

But something changed drastically since Roosevelt uttered those words. Opinion leaders in the United States and other democracies are no longer as firmly persuaded as they once were that deficits are immoral. The public today vaguely "knows" that a budget deficit can be a means for promoting prosperity. The lesson supposedly taught by Keynesian analysis after the Great Depression of the 1930s was that budgets don't have to be balanced from year to year; they need only to be balanced over the course of the business cycle, with surpluses in periods of prosperity making up for deficits in periods of recession. This analysis was widely used by economists in the 1960s and 1970s to argue that deficits were good for the economy and that anyone insisting on a balanced government budget just did not understand "modern economics." Most people are willing to be convinced of something they would like to be true.

Are deficits "immoral" if they are tools of policy?

The trouble with this new doctrine is that its effect is to permit perennial deficits. There is no fiscal period that can be identified with "the course of the business cycle." As a result, the surplus that is supposed to balance the deficit never has to be budgeted; it can always be promised for next year or the year after. With the last effective pressure toward a balanced budget thereby eliminated, the bias of the democratic political process takes over and makes deficits the rule rather than the exception. As the deficit years continue and the national debt increases but the sky does not fall, the conviction that the government's budget really ought to be balanced is bound to lose its hold. Adam Smith and his good friend David Hume looked at the debts of governments in the eighteenth century, debts incurred as the result of wars and quite modest by modern standards, and predicted ruin. Almost no one is alarmed today by public debts much larger than anything Smith or Hume ever encountered. Table 18–2 shows how the U.S. national debt shrank as a percentage of GDP after World War II. To highlight our point about the conflict between "good economics" and "good politics" and how even those who express a strong preference to follow fiscally responsible policies

Table 18–2 **Federal Government Debt as Percentage of GDP (figures are for fiscal years)**

1945	118%
1950	94
1955	69
1960	56
1965	47
1970	38
1975	35
1980	33
1985	44
1990	56
1995	68
1999	62

Source: Bureau of Economic Analysis.

may in the end not pursue those policies because of the incentives in the political arena, it is important to point out that it was a conservative president, Ronald Reagan, who presided over the massive budget deficits that caused the public debt to begin growing rapidly after 1980. Although some somber forecasts of utter ruin were heard at the time the debt ballooned under Reagan, it seems fairly clear close to 25 years later that large deficits and a huge national debt don't *necessarily* make the sky fall, at least not immediately, as long as other factors, such as economic growth, serve to ameliorate the short-run costs of the increasing public debt.[3]

[3]Hyperinflationary periods are, however, often preceded by periods of accumulating public debt. Governments raise revenues to finance expenditures through three sources: (1) taxation, (2) borrowing, and (3) inflation. As we have argued, the incentives for democratically elected officials is strongly biased against the use of tax increases or spending cuts to maintain a balance between expenditures and receipts. Instead, the natural bias is to borrow and then inflate in order to meet the financial obligations in "cheaper" dollars. Milton Friedman was famous for arguing that inflation is everywhere and always a monetary phenomenon and he was right, but we can modify Friedman's dictum slightly, and at the risk of exaggeration, and state that hyperinflations are everywhere and always the consequences of fiscal imbalances. A recent example of how the lack of fiscal discipline eventually threatened the destruction of a monetary system is the crisis in Argentina that befell the country in 2001. The currency board that was in operation made it costly for the government to continue to behave fiscally irresponsibly, and thus Domingo Cavallo moved significantly away from the currency board, leading to the collapse of the Argentina peso and the standard of living of the people in the country. In short, it was not the currency board that failed, but the inability to reign in the fiscal behavior of the government. For a detailed examination of the Argentina crisis, see Kurt Schuler, "Argentina's Economic Crisis: Causes and Cures," *Joint Economic Committee* (June 2003), available at http://www.house.gov/jec/imf/06-13-03long.pdf.

The Political Economy of Monetary Policy

What about monetary policy in all of this? Couldn't the monetary authorities refuse to finance government deficits? Suppose that the Fed allowed the money stock to grow by only 2 or 3 percent per year. What would happen? Could governments run large and continuing budget deficits if their central banks withheld cooperation?

That's an important question because the central bankers in democratic nations are usually not subject to all the political pressures that constrain elected officials. The people who created the Federal Reserve System in the United States in 1913 were aware that popular politics exerts pressure on governments to pursue inflationary policies, so they put control of the monetary system in the hands of an independent agency of the federal government. Members of the Board of Governors are appointed by law for 14-year terms so that they can act independently of Congress and the administration. What would happen if the Fed exercised its statutory independence to the extent of directly opposing the government's fiscal policies?

The Fed would lose in an all-out confrontation, because Congress can, finally, take away the independence that it has granted. On the other hand, Congress would be reluctant to take such dramatic steps or to precipitate a public debate in which members of Congress might be seen as irresponsible advocates of inflation. So the Fed probably could, up to a point, pursue monetary policies designed to constrain government borrowing.

varying degrees of central bank independence

Most German citizens prize very highly the independence of their central bank, largely because they remember or have been taught the disastrous effects of the hyperinflation that Germany experienced in the 1920s, when the central bank turned out new money as fast as it could be printed. That has long imposed a check on tendencies among German legislators to go in for deficit finance. Where central banks enjoy less independence, they are able to impose less constraint on the spendthrift tendencies of their national legislatures.

New Zealand provides an especially interesting case. The spendthrift ways of the democratic political system brought New Zealand to the verge of bankruptcy in 1984. Domestic borrowing by the government of New Zealand, financed by the central bank, was generating a politically unacceptable rate of inflation, and foreign lenders had cut off credit because they doubted the ability of New Zealand to repay except in depreciating New Zealand dollars. Drastic reforms had to be enacted, and they were. The government began saying "No" to every special-interest group and got away with it by pointing to the national emergency that arguably gave it no other option. The government also imposed a contract upon the executive head of the central bank that made limitation of the inflation rate, and, by implication, limitation of growth in the money stock and hence of central bank lending, a condition of keeping his job. You probably didn't notice, but New Zealand was not among the industrial democracies we listed as running government budget deficits in every year from 1991 through 1997. The budget of the New Zealand government was in surplus from 1994 through 1997. Unfortunately, as the economic situation in New Zealand improved, many of the reform measures that led to the economic recovery were reversed once again due to special interest-group pressures.

Although the central bank in the United States is officially an independent agency rather than an arm of the executive branch of government, it is open to doubt whether the Fed would persist for very long in any policy that set it directly in opposition to the goals of elected officials. The reasons are rooted partly in uncertainties about the way in which monetary policy works, partly in the mounting public hostility toward the Fed that such a course would surely nurture, and partly in the bureaucratic conservatism that almost inevitably dominates a central bank. In many nations of the world, the central bank is expected to take its instructions from the government and so enjoys almost no independence.

Discretion and Rules

There is considerable evidence to suggest that the use of discretionary fiscal and monetary policy to stabilize the economy actually increased its instability in the 1970s. This judgment, which cannot be conclusively demonstrated, will be vigorously disputed by those who want to believe that we do possess the knowledge and skills required to achieve milder recessions and greater price stability through aggregate-demand management. The fact that stabilization policy obviously failed in the 1970s won't discourage anyone who thinks it failed only because the right people weren't in charge. But institutions should not be evaluated on the assumption that angels will run them.[4] It is far more likely that

[4]F. A. Hayek (Nobel Prize winner in 1974) argued in an essay written in the 1940s that the classical economists' penchant for favoring rules rather than discretion in public policy can be traced back to Adam Smith and the desire to constrain bad leaders from doing harm when they are in positions of power. "[T]he main point about which there can be little doubt is that Smith's chief concern was not so much with what man might occasionally achieve when he was at his best but that should have as little opportunity as possible to do harm when he was at his worst." Smith's political economy was one, Hayek continued, which did not "depend for its functioning on our finding good men for running it, or on all men becoming better than they now are, but which makes use of men in all their given variety and complexity, sometimes good and sometimes bad, sometimes intelligent and more often stupid." Hayek, "Individualism: True and False," reprinted in *Individualism and Economic Order* (Chicago: University of Chicago Press, 1948), pp. 11–12. Smith's concerns were echoed in the arguments of the Founding Fathers of the United States, such as James Madison in the *Federalist Papers* #51, where he insisted that we must establish governmental institutions that recognize that the task is neither governing angels nor assuming that government is run by angels, and therefore called for the establishment of governmental institutions that would check ambition with ambition. Madison's paradox was that we needed to first empower government so that it would be able to effectively govern but then immediately constrain the government so it could not abuse its power. The contemporary political scientist Barry Weingast has attempted in a series of studies to address Madison's paradox and its relationship to economic policy. See, for example, Barry Weingast, "The Economic Role of Political Institutions," *Journal of Law, Economics and Organization*, 11 (April 1995): pp. 1–31.

government policies will be controlled by politicians than by angels and that monetary and especially fiscal policies will be formulated in the same political context that produces decisions on import tariffs, flood-control projects, highway construction, and the location of military bases.

The alternative to discretionary fiscal and monetary policies is not *no* policy, but rather policies based on firm commitments to published rules. Sometimes this is called *automatic* or *nondiscretionary* fiscal and monetary policy. But there is actually nothing automatic about adhering to clearly enunciated rules, and continuing to do so in the face of strong temptations to relax the rules is certainly a discretionary act. The issue is not whether discretion is better than the absence of discretion. The question, rather, is whether anyone can in fact increase the stability of the economy by deliberately moving the government budget between surplus and deficit and deliberately changing bank reserves or reserve requirements. The skeptics claim that efforts to stabilize in these ways will actually be destabilizing, because no one has the knowledge and other capabilities, technical and political, to manipulate aggregate demand with the necessary precision. A sufficiently graceful elephant could perhaps stabilize a sailboat in rough weather by shifting its weight with delicacy and perfect timing. But the sailing companions of an elephant without these gifts would probably prefer that it remain quietly in the center of the boat.

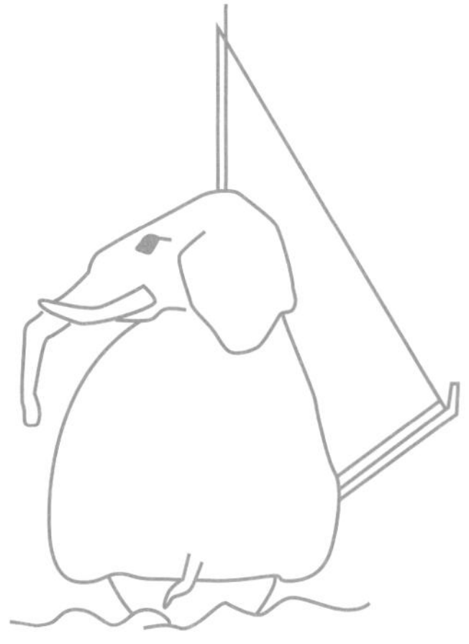

Those economists who believe that fiscal and monetary policies have worsened recessions and increased inflation over the last few decades offer two recommendations. With respect to fiscal policy, they want the level of expenditures determined without reference to any stabilization imperative and tax rates set so as to balance the budget over a normal period. In recessions, tax receipts will then fall and the budget will automatically be in deficit. In a period of boom or when a recovery is well along, tax receipts will be high and will automatically generate a surplus. These recurring deficits and surpluses will function as self-regulating governors, dampening oscillations in the economy, because the government will be reducing net private income and spending when they are unusually high and expanding private income and spending when they are unusually low. Any additional discretionary-policy actions, according to the advocates of automatic policy, are more likely to aggravate than to reduce instability, because discretionary actions are hard to time appropriately and because anticipation of them creates additional uncertainty for private decision makers.

The critics of discretionary-demand management also want monetary policy to enunciate a course and stick to it. They want the Fed to maintain a steady hand on the stock of money, either holding it constant or allowing it to increase by some definite, known, uniform, and moderate rate, perhaps one equal to the long-term average growth rate of real output. There are automatic monetary stabilizers as well as automatic fiscal stabilizers in the economic system. An economic expansion will eventually run against rising interest rates and stricter credit rationing if the monetary managers don't feed the expansion by pumping new reserves into the banking system. And during a period of economic decline, lending terms will tend to improve as the demand for credit slackens, thus encouraging some potential investors. More management than this, as in the case of fiscal policy, is much more likely to increase than to diminish instability—at least according to the critics of discretionary policies.

Who Is at the Controls?

The drive for a constitutional amendment in the United States to require a balanced federal budget rests basically on the belief that political control of the economy must itself be subject to control. That's an important insight. But if such an amendment were to be enacted and ratified, balancing the budget would still be a difficult task. Note that a budget is a prediction, not a command. When Congress draws up a budget, it *expects* some particular amount of revenue and authorizes a particular set of future projects. But the future does not conform exactly to anyone's expectations and sometimes departs from them quite dramatically. Achieving an annual balance between expenditures and receipts, therefore, might well compel sudden and sharp changes in tax rates and expenditure authorizations, which are likely to be *de*stabilizing actions on the part of the federal government. And in the last analysis, it wouldn't prevent Congress and the president from timing and allocating transfer payments, government purchases, or tax-law changes in ways that destabilize the economy but improve the reelection prospects of incumbents.

Although we mustn't expect mortals to be angels, we also mustn't expect miracles from formulas. The Greek physicist Archimedes supposedly said that he could move the earth itself if given one firm spot on which to stand. The thought of such an Archimedean vantage point is alluring to those who worry about economic problems. "There *has* to be a solution. If the economy doesn't work properly, we'll have the government fix it. If the government doesn't work properly, we'll amend the Constitution. If we can't get the Constitution amended, we'll launch a vast educational campaign. If education doesn't work, we'll have the government transform the whole school system." There just isn't any firm spot on which an Archimedes can set his fulcrum and lever society into the proper position.

The functioning of the economy, along with the functioning of government and every other social institution, depends finally on our mutual ability to secure cooperation. We noted on the first page of Chapter 1 how difficult it is for most of us even to recognize the many extraordinary ways in which we successfully cooperate every day. As with an automobile engine, it is only failure that attracts our attention. When the engine is performing well, we don't think about it; we give our attention to the scenery or the road ahead. But because we don't look at our mechanisms of social coordination when they're functioning well, we often fail to discover exactly how they work or how dependent we are on their continued smooth performance. And we often conclude erroneously that some simple bit of tinkering will make them function even better.

Wealthy, industrialized economic systems have always experienced periodic fluctuations in production and employment. Some instability seems to be an inherent characteristic of a free enterprise system in which decisions are decentralized, no one knows what everyone else is doing or will do, and most transactions occur through the medium of money. Some have concluded, with Marx, that this characteristic creates a compelling case for the abolition of free enterprise systems, or what these critics usually call "capitalism." Others join Keynes, who argued that appropriate government intervention can reduce the inherent instability of free enterprise systems to a tolerable level and thus preserve capitalism, whose considerable advantages relative to any feasible alternative make it well worth preserving. Still others argue that instability would be much less than it has been in the past, and therefore politically and socially acceptable, if government simply established a sound system of rules for controlling its own behavior and the behavior of the banking system.

The underlying arguments are very old ones. How smoothly and quickly do prices adjust to changing conditions of demand or supply? How smoothly and quickly do resources move about in response to the new information that changing prices present? Although we can hope that continuing empirical and theoretical inquiry will improve our understanding of these matters, big-picture questions of this sort are notoriously hard to answer to everyone's satisfaction. Fact and fancy, logic and longing get mixed up with each other in the course of such inquiries. Our judgments about what is possible are subtly colored by our visions of what is desirable. We would probably find it easier to agree on how the economy works if we were all agreed on how we *want* the economy to work. In the absence of such a consensus, however, we might just have to go on discussing these issues without ever being certain that we have found the best solutions.

Renewal of the Debate

At the beginning of the 1990s, few people were willing to argue publicly that free enterprise systems, or systems coordinated basically through markets rather than governments, were inferior to systems subject to extensive central planning by governments.

Events, if not arguments, had pretty much silenced them. The collapse of the Soviet version of socialism climaxed a worldwide trend, extending over almost a quarter century, away from government planning and in the direction of leaving more decisions to the market.[5] The editors of a British journal titled *Marxism Today* even closed down their office and ceased publication, as if to say that Marxism is dead today.

The pendulum swings back—

By the end of the 1990s, however, the critics of free enterprise systems were beginning to recover some of their lost confidence, and in 1998 the former editors of *Marxism Today* resurrected their journal for one more issue in order to call attention to what they saw as the failures of world capitalism. Russia, which had so dramatically switched its allegiance from socialism to capitalism at the beginning of the 1990s, was a basket case by the end of the decade, and former communists took over the government. The East Asian nations whose economic growth in the 1970s, 1980s, and early 1990s had created such a persuasive case for capitalism were encountering severe problems toward the end of the 1990s, and experts were predicting that the so-called "Asian Crisis" would soon spread to Brazil, the largest economy in Latin America. In Britain, France, Germany, Italy, and some of the Central and East European nations that had been satellites of the USSR, voters rejected promarket parties and politicians in favor of those with a more socialist orientation or even a communist past.

—but not all the way.

It is easy to exaggerate the significance of all this. The former communists who came to power in the 1990s in Russia, Hungary, Poland, and Italy all disavowed allegiance to past principles and professed no desire to nationalize business firms or "socialize" the economy (whatever that might mean). Among the politicians of the left who triumphed at the polls in Western Europe, all had secured the approval of voters by insisting that they no longer believed in the old principles of socialism but were now advocating a "third way." If the pendulum was swinging back by the end of the 1990s in the direction of less market-oriented policies and more government control of economic activity, the new equilibrium was clearly far more friendly toward private enterprise and market coordination than it had been in the two decades or so following World War II.

[5]This trend and the preceding trend immediately after World War II toward *more* government intervention have been superbly described in a book by Daniel Yergin and Joseph Stanislaw, *The Commanding Heights: The Battle Between Government and the Marketplace That Is Remaking the World* (New York: Simon & Schuster, 1998). In 2002, a television series was produced based on this book and played on PBS stations. An educational Web site was established to provide information on the events and ideas discussed in the series at http://www.pbs.org/wgbh/commandingheights/.

Disagreeing on where the blame lies

Nor was it clear that the "Asian Crisis" represented a failure of free markets. The countries that had been forced to devalue their currencies and that then tumbled into deep recessions had been propping up those currencies at levels that were unrealistically high. Why did so many foreign investors believe that the dollars they were investing in Thailand, Malaysia, or Indonesia would eventually be repaid in bahts, ringgits, or rupiahs that would be worth as many dollars as they were worth when the initial investments were undertaken? Why did they give so little attention to the possibility that the governments of Thailand, Malaysia, and Indonesia would be unable to continue paying dollars in exchange for their respective currencies at the old rate when every sophisticated investor knew that these currencies were not worth what the governments said they were worth? The explanation for what turned out to be grossly imprudent behavior was the belief that some powerful party, whether it was the government of the United States or the International Monetary Fund, was going to guarantee their investments against any loss due to changes in the exchange rate by not allowing such changes to occur. Investors believed that if the governments and central banks of Thailand, Malaysia, and Indonesia exhausted their foreign-exchange reserves in the course of pegging their currencies at too high a level, Someone (the capitalization is deliberate) would step in and take over the task because these governments had guaranteed a fixed exchange rate and governments don't welch on their guarantees.

The investors were wrong. And when a significant number finally came to the conclusion that most of the currencies in Asia were vastly overvalued, propped up by the willingness of overly confident investors to supply dollars and other hard currencies in exuberant amounts, investors started to retreat. But retreats of this sort can quickly turn into routs. The suspicion that Country X will not long be able to continue exchanging its currency for dollars at the high official rate prompts some investors to cash in their investments and get out before the devaluation comes. This drains the foreign-exchange reserves of Country X. As its reserves fall, more investors decide it's time to cash in their chips and the drain accelerates. In a period of just a few days, the demand for dollars and other hard currencies will vastly exceed the ability of Country X to supply them, and, unless the central banks of other nations or the IMF intervenes by providing additional reserves, the peg will collapse and the currency of Country X will fall.

When reality hit foreign investors in Thailand in 1997, the impact alerted investors in Malaysia to the similar situation there and the drama was repeated. Indonesia followed quickly. Foreign investors were suddenly discovering that there was real risk in the high-return loans they were making, and they panicked in large numbers, threatening the stability even of developing nations that had *not* pegged their currencies at unrealistically high levels.

Were the collapse of the pegged exchange rates in one country after another and the losses of foreign investors a failure of free markets? Or was all this the ultimate response of free markets to misguided government policies, policies that had tried to maintain fixed exchange rates in the face of domestic fiscal and monetary actions that were steadily pushing down the purchasing power of domestic currencies? Had the problem been created by flaws in the economic system or by the past habits of the United States and the IMF, who, by previously bailing out foreign investors threatened by a currency devaluation, had taught investors to be indifferent to exchange-rate risks?

Were the severe recessions that followed the devaluations evidence of the inherent instability of capitalism? Or did they merely demonstrate that government policies that encourage overinvestment by pretending to shield investors from risk will inevitably be followed by a withdrawal of investment funds when those governments prove unable to square the circle? The period of overinvestment had set in motion many unsustainable projects whose benefits, realistically assessed, were unlikely to equal their realistically assessed costs. When reality dawned and investment spending dried up, recession ensued and unemployment mounted.

Global capitalism, as it's called, is not simply an economic system. It is an economic *and political* system. And it isn't always easy to decide where the blame should be laid for failures. Most informed observers maintain that the prolonged recession Japan was suffering through in the 1990s resulted in large part from the reluctance of the politicians in charge to close down insolvent banks, which would impose large financial losses on loyal supporters of the party in power. But insolvent banks, trying to save themselves by building up their assets and holding down the growth of their liabilities, are banks that don't lend and consequently make it harder for entrepreneurs to launch new and profitable projects. So the timidity and cronyism of Japanese politicians kept their economy mired in recession.

The rule of law once more

As for Russia, the alleged collapse of its market system in 1998 was no such thing. Russia never did develop a viable market system after the disintegration of communism in 1991. We pointed out in Chapter 4 that a successful movement from central planning to market systems in the former communist countries would require the creation or re-creation of important institutions that had evolved spontaneously in most commercial societies. In the absence of well-defined property rights and the rule of law, markets will not work satisfactorily.[6] Poland, Hungary, the

[6]Again, Adam Smith pointed this out in *The Wealth of Nations* when he argued that "Commerce and manufacturing can seldom flourish long in any state which does not enjoy a regular administration of justice, in which the people do

Czech Republic, and Slovenia have been making a successful transition largely because they did manage to establish a set of generally agreed-upon "rules of the game." China has been proceeding with considerable success, at least if success is measured by economic growth, in its own determined if sometimes inconsistent way. But the republics of the former USSR have signally failed for the most part to create the basic institutions that would enable a market system to function fairly and satisfactorily. The rules of the game by which Russia's managers mostly operate today are overwhelmingly opportunistic, oriented to the very short run, and quite unlikely to extract anything remotely resembling the public interest from the interplay of private interests. The invisible hand to which Adam Smith had referred never came to Russia. Perhaps the 70-plus years in which civil society in the USSR was systematically subjected to political society created a vacuum too great to be overcome once the legitimacy of the political order had dissolved. The official control of the Communist Party for so many years over every aspect of social life may have sterilized or even poisoned the very soil from which new institutions must grow.[7]

What Lies Ahead?

This chapter began with a confession of sorts. Economists today are not in command of the clear and precise knowledge about the overall operation of economic systems that would enable us to prescribe sure remedies for instability or stagnation. But even if we did, the remedies could not be effective unless they were accepted by those with the power to implement them. And the incentives of politicians, not only in tyrannical governments but also in democratic ones, will not always induce them to do what they themselves believe ought to be done to promote steady economic growth and reasonable price stability.

not feel themselves secure in the possession of their property, in which the faith of contracts is not supported by the law, and in which the authority of the state is not supposed to be regularly employed in enforcing the payment of debts from all those who are able to pay. Commerce and manufacturing, in short, can seldom flourish in any state in which there is not a certain degree of confidence in the justice of government." *The Wealth of Nations* (Chicago: University of Chicago Press, 1976[1776]), Vol. 2, p. 445.

[7]For a contrary position, see Andrei Shleifer and Daniel Treisman, "A Normal Country," *Foreign Affairs* (April/May 2004). Shleifer and Treisman argue that the transformation evident in Russia over the past 15 years has been extraordinary and that Russia is now a typical middle-income country, which includes an economic system that is overpoliticized and prone to oscillations between autocracy and democracy. This may be a disappointment for those who hoped for more from Russia, conclude Shleifer and Treisman, but from the perspective of the task of transforming an "evil empire" that just 15 years ago was described as threatening in a menacing manner people at home and abroad, the achievement is remarkable and admirable.

So what lies ahead in the twenty-first century? Economists are not famous for their superior forecasts. Adam Smith, for example, was certain that business corporations had no real future because they separated ownership from actual control, and those who managed them would inevitably use their discretion to enrich themselves rather than to increase the value of the corporations and the wealth of their rightful owners. Thomas Robert Malthus predicted at the end of the eighteenth century that real incomes could never rise because population would inevitably increase to gobble up any increase in per capita income. Karl Marx predicted 150 years ago that the inevitable collapse of capitalism was just around the corner. One of the most able of the late nineteenth-century economists, William Stanley Jevons, predicted that industrial expansion would soon have to slow down because the world was running out of coal. And in the 1970s, some economists predicted that the price of oil would be close to $1,000 per barrel by the end of the century.

Perhaps no one knows what lies ahead. The economic way of thinking does a good job of explaining why things happened as they did and of making minor predictions of the sort "If this occurs, then that will almost surely follow." Its capacity to make large or long-term forecasts, however, is decidedly limited. Economic theory, you may recall from Chapter 1, assumes that all social phenomena emerge from the *choices* individuals make. People's freedom to choose has a disconcerting way of falsifying predictions. One implication of the economic way of thinking might be that neither economists nor anyone else can predict the future. We might just be compelled to go on observing, reflecting, and discussing without ever expecting any final answers. There are far worse fates.

Once Over Lightly

Government stabilization policies are controlled not by impartial—much less omniscient—experts, but by political processes. Those who make policy do so in the light of their own interests and in response to the incentives they perceive.

Stabilization policies in a democratic society are significantly affected by the relatively short time horizons of government officials, who will be under pressure to ignore the long run costs of programs that produce short-run benefits.

An unanticipated change in the rate of growth of aggregate demand will affect output and employment before it affects costs and prices. The benefits therefore precede the costs when policy takes an expansionary turn, but the costs precede the benefits when policy turns contractionary. Political officials looking toward imminent elections will consequently find expansionary policies in their interest and contractionary policies contrary to their interest. This will tend to produce go-stop-go policies with an inflationary bias.

The democratic political process also tends to produce chronic budget deficits on the part of national governments, because national governments usually control the means of payment and can consequently always borrow successfully in their own country. In the absence of any overriding imperative to achieve a long-run budget balance, democratic political processes may produce an indefinite sequence of budget deficits. These deficits in turn put pressure on the monetary authorities to expand the money supply.

Government might make its greatest contribution to economic stability by trying to do less. Government policies that were more stable and predictable would introduce less uncertainty into the economic system.

The argument between advocates of discretionary stabilization policy and those who want policy to be governed by fixed rules known in advance turns largely on the issue of how equitably and efficiently markets work.

Prominent economic failures at the end of the 1990s in countries widely believed to have capitalist or market-dominated economic systems renewed the debate over the proper roles of government and of markets in the control of economic activities.

QUESTIONS FOR DISCUSSION

1. A joke that economists, who are actually not always devoid of a sense of humor, like to tell on themselves says that if all the economists in the world were laid end to end, they would reach—no conclusion. President Harry S. Truman is said to have longed for a one-armed economist, because all the economists who advised him were inclined to say, "On the one hand, . . . but on the other hand. . . ." Perhaps these two characteristics are related.
   (a) Can you think of a single economic policy not now in effect that you would like to see adopted that does *not* entail some possible or even probable consequence that you would *not* like to see come about?
   (b) "The policy may not work, but we ought to try it anyway because we have to do *something*." How probable is it that the person making such a statement believes rather strongly that the policy *will* work and that people who are against the policy believe strongly that it will not work?
   (c) A standard way of assessing alternative policies is to predict and assess their probable consequences. Is there any definite limit to the number of consequences of a particular social policy?

(d) Someone says, "This problem will work itself out. Government intervention is not required." Does it matter *how long* the problem takes to "work itself out"? Do you think proponents and opponents of the policy are likely to agree on how long this will be, even if they agree that it will eventually "work itself out"?

2. Unanticipated changes in the growth rate of aggregate demand tend to affect production and employment *before* they affect prices.
   (a) Can you summarize the argument explaining why this occurs?
   (b) Why does this give elected officials an incentive both to approve expansionary policies and not to persist in contractionary policies?
   (c) Why would a president serving a second term and hence ineligible for reelection still be under pressure to pursue policies with quick benefits and deferred costs? Who would apply the pressure?
3. Suppose that every member of Congress genuinely believes that government expenditures are excessive and ought to be reduced by at least 10 percent. Why would this not be sufficient to assure a 10 percent reduction?
4. Suppose a member of Congress votes against a bill to allocate $100 million in taxpayers' money to an irrigation canal that will provide about $10 million in benefits to a few hundred ranchers. Why might this action cause the legislator a net loss in both votes and campaign contributions?
5. Why do so many members of Congress believe that the federal government should subsidize local projects, such as improvements in bus or subway systems in major cities?
   (a) Who would benefit from construction of a subway system in a large city?
   (b) Can you think of a *public-interest* argument for having taxpayers across the country pay for a local subway system?
   (c) If you knew that your taxes were going to go up $10 a year in order to finance a subway in some distant city, would you write a letter of protest to your legislator?
   (d) If your city was being considered for a large federal grant to subsidize an improvement in the local public transportation system, would you expect your local government officials to go to Washington and lobby actively for it? Would you expect your congressional representatives to support it? Would you form a more favorable opinion of local officials and congressional representatives if your city proved successful in its grant application?
6. If you favor reduced government expenditures, do you also favor reducing government financial assistance to college students?
7. New York City teetered on the edge of bankruptcy some years ago because it had accumulated large debts through deficit spending and seemed unable either to raise taxes or to cut expenditures sufficiently to balance its budget. Lenders refused to extend additional credit unless the federal government guaranteed that it would pay New York City's debts in the event of a default.

(a) How did New York City get into such a situation?
(b) Of what use to lenders was a federal government guarantee when the federal government was at the time running much larger deficits than New York City and had even poorer prospects for balancing its budget?
(c) What consequences would you predict if the federal government committed itself to paying off all creditors who might otherwise be hurt through the financial default of municipal or state governments?

8. In every year throughout the 1970s, the 1980s, and the first half of the 1990s, the combined budgets of state and local governments showed a surplus, whereas the federal government budget was in deficit. How would you account for this dramatic difference?
9. Voters who don't want their taxes increased impose obvious constraints on any democratic government's ability to raise additional revenue, but there are other constraints as well.

(a) How can people legally avoid a state income or sales tax?
(b) Voters don't seem to be terribly hostile toward increased taxes on business. Why can't state and local governments collect all the revenue they want simply by raising taxes on businesses?
(c) Why don't these constraints bind the federal government as effectively as they bind state and local governments?

10. When a state or city government starts borrowing to finance current expenditures (as distinct from capital expenditures for highways, schools, public buildings, and the like), its bond rating usually falls. A lower bond rating indicates a riskier investment.

(a) Why does the bond rating fall?
(b) What will happen to the price of bonds whose rating is lowered?
(c) What does this do to the cost of borrowing?
(d) How does this constrain state and local governments from borrowing to finance current expenditures?
(e) What must a state or local government do if it is determined not to borrow to finance current expenditures?
(f) Why doesn't any of this happen to the federal government when it finances current expenditures through borrowing rather than taxation?

11. When a corporation successfully sells additional bonds or a new issue of common stock, it goes deeply into debt.

(a) Is this evidence that the corporation is failing or that it's succeeding?
(b) How well or poorly does an analogy from the area of business indebtedness apply to questions of government indebtedness?
(c) Suppose the government borrows to construct a dam. How is such borrowing similar to or different from business borrowing for investment?

12. Do you think that people who "live beyond their means" display a character flaw? What about a government that fails to confine its expenditures to the amount of its tax receipts?
13. Suppose the Treasury borrowed $20 billion in September of the presidential election year in order to increase the benefits to be paid on

October 1 to recipients of Social Security benefits, welfare grants, and unemployment compensation. What would be the effects on the money supply? On consumer spending in October? On the unemployment rate? On the price level? On the election? When would you expect these various effects?

14. The Federal Reserve was created to be an independent agency of the federal government—independent, that is, of the immediate political pressures that are felt by elected officials and appointed officials whom the elected officials can demote or discharge.
    (a) Is it "undemocratic" to have an organization as powerful as the Fed that isn't answerable to the voters?
    (b) If Fed officials had to answer to elected officials, would that make them answerable to the voters?
    (c) Under which of these three circumstances do you think it is most likely and under which do you think it is least likely that monetary policy would promote the public interest: the present system, a system under which presidents could dismiss Fed officials the way they can now dismiss cabinet members, or a referendum system under which the Fed's policies would have to be periodically approved by a majority vote of the electorate?
15. How independent is the independent Fed? Fed officials and Treasury officials regularly cooperate to smooth the financing and refinancing activities of the federal government as it borrows the vast sums required to cover current deficits and refund the huge national debt.
    (a) Don't people who work cooperatively usually come to see their problems in similar or at least compatible ways? Isn't the Fed more likely to conclude that a particular monetary policy is the best policy if it also happens to ease the financing problems of the Treasury?
    (b) The Treasury would like to keep down the costs of its borrowing and refunding. How could the Fed help achieve this laudable objective?
    (c) If the Fed tries to provide enough reserves to the banking system to make sure that borrowing costs don't rise during large Treasury borrowing operations, what must it do? Why might a succession of such cooperative moves by the Fed eventually cause interest rates and Treasury borrowing costs to rise steeply?
16. Would you expect to find a relationship between an informed person's attitude toward attempts at fine-tuning and his or her reactions to the following judgments? Explain why.
    (a) "Fiscal and monetary managers have better information than business decision makers because they have access to statistical data on the overall performance of the economy and don't have to concern themselves with details."
    (b) "The government must establish procedures for national economic planning if we are to avoid the kinds of problems experienced in the 1930s and again in the 1970s and that Asian countries experienced in the 1990s."

(c) "The market does not work as it used to. Competition no longer sets prices or allocates resources in the U.S. economy. Most of that is done by organized interest groups with substantial market power."

(d) "The U.S. economy displays an absurd social imbalance. Privately purchased goods are produced in abundance while public sector goods such as education must be content with the leavings."

National Policies and International Exchange

19

Adam Smith was no admirer of the people who keep track of a nation's exports and imports. He thought their activities lent themselves to "absurd speculations," and he ridiculed those who measured national prosperity by the excess of a nation's exports over its imports. Balance-of-payments accounting nonetheless provides a useful, even if potentially misleading, way to think about the effects of international transactions on national economies. You can usually avoid being misled if you keep one simple truth in mind: *The balance of payments always balances*. Let's see why that's so and what it implies.

Accounting for International Transactions

In a simplified summary of a nation's balance of payments, all transactions can be assigned to one of four categories: exchange of merchandise, exchange of services, exchange of IOUs, and unilateral transfers.

Exchange of merchandise is self-explanatory. *Exchange of services* may be less clear. The services exchanged internationally include transportation services, insurance services, financial services, and the many kinds of services that tourists purchase when traveling abroad. But the most important service that people in one country provide to people in another is the service of capital goods. Investors are providing a very valuable service when they make capital available to other countries. For this service they receive investment income in return, and income from foreign investments is the largest part of the "services" item in the balance of payments. It is so important that the Bureau of Economic Analysis classifies it separately from all other services, as investment income receipts and investment income payments.

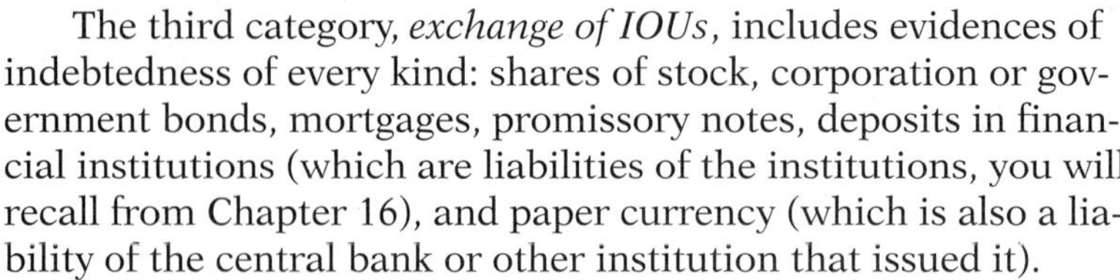

The third category, *exchange of IOUs*, includes evidences of indebtedness of every kind: shares of stock, corporation or government bonds, mortgages, promissory notes, deposits in financial institutions (which are liabilities of the institutions, you will recall from Chapter 16), and paper currency (which is also a liability of the central bank or other institution that issued it).

People exchange
- *merchandise*
- *services*
- *IOUs*
- *grants*

Unilateral transfers is a fancy term for one-way transactions: payments for nothing at all, such as gifts (including government-financed foreign aid), or for services rendered in some earlier period, such as pension benefits. Transactions in each category produce either payments into or payments out of the nation. Exports generate payments into a nation and so are put in the credits column. Imports and other transactions that generate payments out of the nation are assigned to the debits column. Thus, when General Motors sells an American-made Buick to a Briton, payment is made to someone in the United States and the transaction is recorded as a credit item in the U.S. balance of payments. If a British museum sells a Turner painting to an American collector, the American makes a payment abroad and the transaction is a debit in the U.S. balance of payments. The United States gave up a Buick and Britain lost a Turner, but the balance of payments looks at payments, not at the goods for which the payments are made. So those transactions are credit items respectively in the U.S. and British balance of payments. This should put you on guard. A nation that decided to sell all its art treasures to foreigners would be accumulating credits on its balance of payments as it denuded its museums and galleries. *Credit* is clearly not a synonym for *good thing*.

If the data gatherers who construct the balance of payments had a complete and accurate record of every international transaction, the sum of the items in the credits column would exactly equal the sum of the items in the debits column. Because the records are far from complete, the sums are never equal. The record keepers rise to each occasion. They add the difference to the smaller total, label it "statistical discrepancy," and thereby *compel* credits to equal debits.

Why Credits Must Equal Debits

Every exchange entails a balancing transaction.

Credits must always exactly equal debits because every international transaction necessarily entails another transaction that precisely offsets it. The case of a simple gift probably shows the process most clearly. Suppose that Dr. Hugh R. Sick, who resides and works in New York, decides to give $100 to his old friend back in London, Eliza Doolittle. Eliza once told Doctor Sick that the balance of payments always balances, but he did not believe it for a moment, and now he wants to vindicate his skepticism while simultaneously demonstrating his affection and esteem for Eliza. "This is a pure gift," he trumpets triumphantly as he drops his $100 check into the envelope and addresses it to Eliza. "I'm getting nothing in return. So debits will rise by $100 while credits will not change. I shall have unbalanced the balance of payments!"

But Hugh is mistaken. Although the gift is a debit, the check that Eliza acquires is a financial claim on his New York bank. When Eliza holds the check in the air and says, "Hah hah hah, Hugh," she is the proud owner of an American IOU: $100 of demand deposits in a New York bank. Hugh overlooked the fact that in making his gift to Eliza he enabled foreigners to increase by $100 the amount of U.S. IOUs that they hold. As long as Eliza keeps the check, she is a foreigner with an investment in the United States. This $100 increase in foreign investment exactly balances the $100 unilateral transfer that Hugh R. Sick thought had unbalanced the balance of payments.

When Eliza goes to her bank to cash the check and obtain British pounds for it, her bank becomes the owner of the IOU. When the bank sells that deposit to a British importer, the importer owns the IOU. When he in turn uses the $100 to pay for merchandise imported from the United States, foreigners reduce their holdings of U.S. IOUs, creating a debit in the U.S. balance of payments. The balancing item for this debit will be the $100 worth of merchandise that was exported to England, which necessitated a payment into the United States and so counts as a credit item in the U.S. balance of payments.

The easiest way to understand how the balance of payments remains in continuous balance is to focus on the international exchange of IOUs. If everyone in the United States—households, business firms, and government—imports merchandise and services over some period of time whose value is greater than the value of merchandise and services exported during this time, and if the difference is not made up by unilateral transfers, then Americans must owe the difference to foreigners. That means Americans have exported IOUs to foreigners, which amounts to saying that foreigners have increased their investments in the United States by the exact amount required to close the gap.

Equilibrium and Disequilibrium

If there cannot be a surplus or a deficit in a nation's balance of payments, what is bothering all those people who worry aloud about "the trade deficit" and warn that disaster is imminent if we don't reduce the deficit? Would their anxieties disappear if they learned that credits always equal debits? Probably not. They may be worried about something else, something that should properly be called a *disequilibrium* in the balance of payments.

A disequilibrium in economic theory is a discrepancy between what is happening and what people want to happen, between reality and intention. A disequilibrium price for wheat, for example, doesn't show up as a difference between actual sales and purchases, which are necessarily identical, but as a difference between the *intentions*—the *plans*—of sellers and purchasers. The quantity that farmers plan to sell is greater or less than the quantity that consumers plan to buy. Another example would be the gap analyzed in Chapter 17 between the quantity of money supplied and the quantity of money demanded. The quantity of money actually held by the public has to be the same as the quantity supplied by the monetary system. But the public can want to hold more or less. When that's the case, a monetary disequilibrium exists.

A disequilibrium implies that something will change.

The implication of a disequilibrium is that matters will not continue the way they are; adjustments are going to occur, because some relevant parties are not realizing their intentions. The price of wheat will rise, for example, because consumers are unable to buy as much as they want to buy and they are going to bid the price up. Or durable goods inventories are going to begin increasing because the public wants to hold larger money balances than it's currently holding, and that means people will be postponing durable goods purchases.

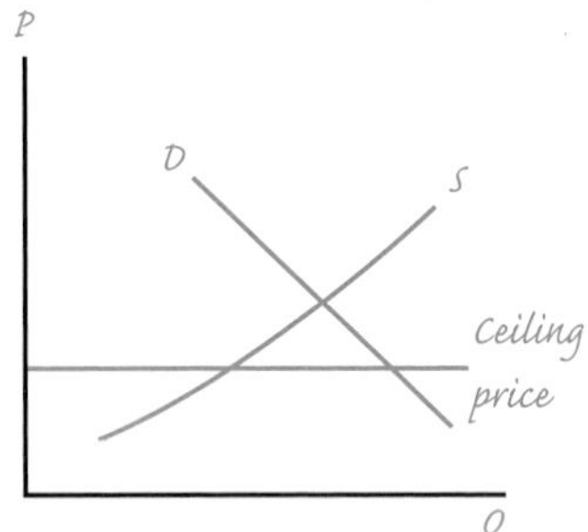

The quantity demanders want to purchase is greater than the quantity suppliers want to sell.

It follows from all this that we cannot use the concept of equilibrium or disequilibrium unless we can specify the intentions that are currently being frustrated. Those who worry or complain about disequilibrium in the balance of payments rarely identify the people who are not succeeding in carrying out their plans. That shouldn't surprise us. The concept of a balance-of-payments disequilibrium is so extraordinarily ambiguous that we might be better off if we discarded the notion altogether. There are just too many intentions of too many different kinds entering into the aggregate of international transactions for anyone to assert that intended credits are larger or smaller than intended debits—which is the meaning of a disequilibrium. In general, the larger the universe to which we try to apply the equilibrium concept, the more vague and uncertain is its meaning—and the more likely it is to obscure rather than clarify the problems at which we're looking.

To claim that the U.S. balance of payments is in disequilibrium is really to claim that something unsustainable is occurring because people aren't able to do what they want to do. But from whose point of view is this claim made? Didn't the importers want to purchase whatever they purchased? Didn't banks want to lend whatever they lent? Didn't governments, corporations, or individuals want to offer the gifts or grants they sent abroad? Who were the people for whom the results of international trade turned out to be inconsistent with what they had intended? A simple little question should always be addressed to anyone who claims that the balance of payments is in disequilibrium: "How do you know that?" The answer, if followed up properly, will tell you what is worrying the speaker.

The Ambiguities of International Disequilibrium

Suppose we find some people who are concerned about the U.S. trade balance and we ask exactly what is disturbing them. If they are well informed, they may point to the fact that since 1976, the United States has each year imported more merchandise, in value terms, than it exported. The proper reply is to ask why they ignore exports of services and IOUs. Merchandise, services, and IOUs are *all* valuable to the people who receive them. They want them. They give up other goods of value to get them. What is there to worry about?

Our worried friends may point in reply to the fact that since 1983, U.S. imports of merchandise *and services* have been greater than our exports of merchandise and services and that we haven't made up the difference through unilateral transfers. (Except for 1991, when Saudi Arabia and others were compensating the United States for its expenditures in the Gulf War, we have run net debits in unilateral transfers for as long as the records go back.) But once again we must ask why this should be an occasion for concern. It means that Americans in the aggregate are borrowing more from foreigners than foreigners are borrowing from Americans. It does not imply a disequilibrium.

Does foreign investment in the United States imply that the U.S. economy is weak? Or that it is strong?

Is it nonetheless reason to worry? A great deal of concern, verging occasionally on hysteria, has frequently erupted in recent years over the huge deficits in the U.S. balance on merchandise trade. The merchandise deficit was not being made up by the balance on services and transfers, with the inevitable consequence that foreigners were increasing substantially their holdings of U.S. IOUs. A lot of people reacted to this with panic, as if foreigners were in a position to foreclose on our mortgage and eager to do so. That's absurd. Lenders don't foreclose when the borrowers are keeping up their payments. Foreigners have been eagerly investing in the IOUs of Americans because they regard investments in the United States as a better deal than the other investments they could make. They like our prospects, so they want to own our IOUs. They are happy to be our creditors because they expect it to be profitable for themselves. It is only possible for foreigners to invest more in the United States than Americans invest abroad if the United States runs a deficit in the total of all the other items in the balance of payments. It is not true that foreigners are lending to us *because* we're buying more from them than we're selling to them. Put another way, it is just as true that we're buying more from foreigners than we're selling to them *because* foreigners want to extend loans to us.

Perhaps our hypothetical worriers are concerned about all the interest we will have to pay on those loans. But "we" won't be paying the interest. That will be the obligation of those who did the borrowing. If they were sensible folk, they borrowed intelligently, after calculating that the benefits of the loans would probably exceed the interest costs. If our worrywarts think they were foolish borrowers, how did they come by this insight? People certainly do borrow foolishly at times. But lenders usually monitor this fairly well.

It's worth noticing that many of the outstanding loans foreigners have made to the United States are loans for which no one pays any interest. Federal Reserve notes are liabilities that pay no interest to the holder but that many foreigners nonetheless choose to hold because they have confidence in the future value of U.S. currency and want to use it in transactions. They must buy that currency from us by offering valuable assets in return, whether merchandise, services, or income-earning financial assets. If we refused to import more than we export, foreigners would be unable to acquire the dollars they want and consequently unable to provide us with interest-free loans. It seems foolish for Americans to worry about such generosity on the part of foreigners and to try to thwart it by restricting imports.

Disequilibrium as a Disguised Policy Judgment

We have probably gotten very close to the basic anxiety afflicting many of those who began to fret in the 1980s about the U.S. balance of payments. They were worried about the spendthrift ways of Americans as consumers and taxpayers. The sum of what we are currently willing to save and to pay in taxes seems to be considerably less than the sum of what we want to spend on investment projects and government programs. Our growing foreign indebtedness is evidence, according to these people, of our shortsightedness, our selfishness, our self-indulgence, our want of self-discipline, and lack of the ability to govern ourselves.

All that might conceivably be true. But none of it constitutes a disequilibrium in the balance of payments. The balance of payments is equilibrating nicely to our shortsightedness, selfishness, and so on. The balance of payments reflects our situation; it does not cause it. If we are in fact suffering from some sort of national malaise, we will not find any remedy in the balance of payments. The eagerness of foreigners to invest in the United States in the 1980s and 1990s was in fact an enormous advantage to us. With the federal government running huge budget deficits before 1998, someone had to come up with a lot of loanable funds. Foreigners did what American households and business firms were unwilling to do: save enough to finance the federal budget deficits. Without their assistance, interest rates would have been higher and the U.S. capital stock would have grown more slowly.

On the other hand, if foreigners stopped lending to us so liberally, we would begin to feel some of the consequences of our alleged vices. And maybe we would reform our ways! But if you and I decided to live beyond our means, would it be appropriate for us to blame the people who were willing to lend us the money to do so? A substantial amount of the informed concern in the 1980s and 1990s about the deficit on merchandise and services in the U.S. balance of payments seems to have been a disguised concern about the federal government's persistent budget deficits and the low saving rate of U.S. households. But using the concept of international disequilibrium to disguise domestic policy judgments has some unfortunate policy consequences of its own. It muddies discussion, of course, and makes it that much harder to deal responsibly with domestic policy problems. It also opens the door to all those special interests that would welcome a "public-interest" justification for special-interest policies. If patriotism is the last refuge of scoundrels, as Samuel Johnson suggested, the balance of payments is very often the last refuge of pretending patriots.

The alleged balance-of-payments deficit has been used to justify tariffs and quotas on imports, restrictions on the relocation of manufacturing plants, subsidies to questionable research and development projects, exemptions from the antitrust laws, threats against foreign governments, dubious taxpayer loans to exporters, and a long list of other government favors to special interests. Some of these might be wise and prudent policies. If they are, however, they ought to be defended openly and clearly, not advocated in the name of a nonexistent balance-of-payments problem.

But Will It Go on Forever?

A claim of disequilibrium, if it's not a disguised policy judgment, is a prediction that things are going to change. The price of wheat will rise, durable goods inventories will increase, and so on. What is being predicted by someone who contends that a nation's foreign trade is in disequilibrium? What is it that cannot be expected to continue as it is?

This is an excellent question with which to pester anyone still determined to employ the concept of disequilibrium when talking about problems of international trade. Those who are worried about the current U.S. "disequilibrium" would most likely point to the willingness of foreigners to increase their holdings of American IOUs. "They won't go on lending to us forever." That may not be true, because there is no definite limit to the ability of borrowers in the United States to pay a satisfactory return to their creditors. But what if it *were* true, as it surely is for smaller, less prosperous, and less stable nations of the world?

When lenders decide that potential borrowers may be in over their heads, they request repayment or withdraw further credit or demand better collateral or scrutinize projects more carefully or insist on a higher rate of interest. Whenever U.S. borrowers start to make foreign lenders nervous, foreign lenders will behave in ways that make it harder for Americans to borrow. There is no single response that all lenders will make simultaneously and consequently no reason to expect a crisis. Excessive borrowing creates its own corrective—at least in a nation like the United States, with a well-established international reputation for paying its debts. The situation, however, is quite different for those smaller, less prosperous, and less stable nations mentioned in the preceding paragraph. But before we can examine their problems, we have to understand foreign-exchange rates.

Foreign-Exchange Rates and Purchasing Power Parity

Foreign-exchange rates, most simply, are relative prices that tie together sets of relative prices. The existing exchange rate between two currencies at any time will roughly express the relative purchasing power of the two currencies. If it takes 67 cents to buy a German mark but only 0.67 cents to buy a Japanese yen, you can assume, as a first approximation, that 1 dollar, 1.5 marks, and 150 yen will all buy roughly the same amount of goods in the United States, Germany, and Japan, respectively. Thus exchange rates, to begin with, adjust toward creating *purchasing power parity* among national currencies.

Purchasing power parity: One cup of coffee costs $1 in Tucson, 1.5 marks in Tubingen, and 150 yen in Tokyo.

The simplest way to see why this is so is to think about what will happen if it's *not* so. If 1 dollar exchanges for 150 yen, but 150 yen buys appreciably more goods in Japan than 1 dollar buys in the United States, then dollar holders will want to buy yen with dollars in order to get more for their money. That increased demand for yen on the part of dollar holders will not be matched by an increased supply of yen, because yen holders will not be willing to give up 150 yen in return for just 1 dollar. The dollar price of the yen will consequently rise. Dollar holders will have to start offering 1.05 dollars to obtain 150 yen. Viewing the same event from the other side, yen holders will now be able to purchase 1 dollar for about 143 yen.

Purchasing power parity is only a first approximation, however, when we seek to find out why national currencies exchange for one another at the rates they do. To begin with, exchange rates can never exactly equate the purchasing power of two currencies because no two currencies will ever purchase exactly the same array of goods. Some goods, such as a vacation near Mt. Fujiyama, just aren't available for purchase with dollars in the United States or with marks in Germany. Moreover, exchange rates are more responsive to the relative prices of internationally traded goods (farm commodities, machinery, petroleum, automobiles) than to the relative prices of those goods that are rarely exported or imported (housing, haircuts).

More important, however, foreign-exchange rates won't express the *current* purchasing power of currencies when their relative purchasing power is expected to change. A belief that Canada will experience more rapid inflation than the United States in the coming year is a belief that the Canadian dollar will lose more value than the U.S. dollar during the year ahead. That belief will increase the present demand for U.S. dollars, relative to the demand for Canadian dollars, and cause the current value of the U.S. dollar to rise relative to the value of the Canadian dollar. One result is that, until Canadian prices actually rise by as much as people expect, tourists who visit Canada with U.S. dollars will find food and lodging delightfully inexpensive. Canadians who visit the United States, on the other hand, will find food and lodging south of the border unusually hard on the pocketbook.

The expectation that an asset will increase in value causes its value to increase now.

The global economy is in continuous change. Constantly changing conditions and shifting expectations cause foreign-exchange rates to move up and down in ways that make international transactions riskier than they would otherwise be. Uncertainty of this kind makes it more difficult for producers to anticipate future demands for their products; even when they don't sell for export, they may have to compete with imported products whose prices relative to their own can change suddenly and substantially due to an exchange-rate movement. Foreign investors keep an especially nervous eye on foreign-exchange rates. An American who makes a one-year loan that will be repaid in French francs could end up taking a loss on the transaction if the value of the French franc unexpectedly falls during the year. So exchange-rate fluctuations provide an additional uncertainty for producers and investors to worry about, especially in an increasingly globalized economic system. Costly mistakes are consequently made more often, and recessions, which are ultimately rooted in mistaken predictions, tend to become more frequent and more severe. Wouldn't it be far better if exchange rates were fixed and stable?

The Bretton Woods System

It was largely in order to create a system of stable foreign-exchange rates that the Western nations established the International Monetary Fund (IMF) after World War II. The IMF was supposed to assist any member nation whose currency was tending to depreciate and to advise on devaluation when it appeared that existing exchange rates seriously overstated the currency's value. With varying rates of economic growth from country to country and different rates of domestic inflation, exchange rates might have to be altered occasionally. But the objective of the Bretton Woods System (named after the town in New Hampshire where the international monetary agreements were negotiated in 1944) was *fixed* exchange rates. Under the system, each nation was supposed to buy and sell its currency in order to keep it pegged at the officially established rate of exchange with the U.S. dollar, the benchmark currency for the world. The dollar, in turn, was pegged to gold. Out of all this, it was hoped, would emerge greater certainty and a steady expansion of wealth-creating international trade.

The system wasn't a failure. International trade did expand under the Bretton Woods System, at roughly twice the rate of increase in world GDP. And the advantages of international specialization contributed substantially to rising levels of real income. But an international monetary system with fixed exchange rates is difficult to maintain among governments pursuing divergent domestic policies. Those policies inevitably produced different patterns of growth in industrial and agricultural production, different movements in the structure of relative prices between countries, different rates of inflation, and consequently large fluctuations in the international demand for different countries' currencies. To prevent depreciation or appreciation under these circumstances, governments were often required to intervene heavily and continuously in the foreign-exchange markets.

A government must sell its currency for other currencies to prevent its rise in value (appreciation).

The governments whose currency was tending to appreciate had to buy foreign currencies. The central bank of West Germany, to take the most prominent example, bought foreign currencies with its own currency, the deutsche mark, in order to keep the foreign-exchange value of the deutsche mark from rising. This entailed putting more deutsche marks into circulation in West Germany, which lowered their value, that is, caused domestic inflation. The Germans, carrying vivid memories of hyperinflation from the 1920s and the enormous damage it did to the economy, the society, and the political order, were determined to prevent inflation. But noninflationary monetary policy was impossible to pursue for a central bank required to keep its currency from rising in the foreign-exchange markets. The deutsche mark tended to appreciate because it was undervalued at the fixed exchange rate, and it was undervalued precisely because the West German government and central bank had been doing a better job than were other governments and central banks of holding down the rate of domestic inflation. What it all came to was that countries that controlled inflation through domestic policies were put under international pressure to accelerate their rate of inflation.

Governments whose currency was tending to depreciate, usually because of higher-than-average actual or expected inflation rates, were required under the Bretton Woods System to purchase their own currency to keep its price from falling. But purchase it *with what*? With the currencies of other nations, of course, and especially with U.S. dollars. But their currency was depreciating precisely because the quantity of dollars and other currencies being supplied fell short continually of the quantity demanded. Where was the central bank to obtain the dollars with which to buy its own currency and thus keep its price up?

Enter the IMF. The IMF could lend foreign-exchange reserves to the central bank that wanted to halt and reverse a decline in the foreign-exchange value of its currency. But obviously this could only be a stopgap measure. Without a change in the domestic policies that were producing the pressure for depreciation, devaluation was inevitable. Those domestic policies characteristically consisted of government expenditures in excess of tax revenues, financed through the creation of new money, with inflation as the eventual result. When the IMF extended loans, therefore, it was always with the proviso that the government reduce its budget deficit and slow down its creation of new money. But this was often empty counsel. The domestic pressures that were creating the budget deficits weren't going to disappear because the International Monetary Fund said that deficits were naughty.

Fixed or Floating Exchange Rates?

In the early 1970s, the United States essentially abandoned its efforts to keep the dollar's value fixed in terms of gold, and other countries more or less reluctantly gave up their commitments to maintain a fixed rate of exchange between their currencies and the dollar. Exchange rates were turned loose and were allowed to *float*, as the jargon has it, in response to the changing expectations of suppliers and demanders. Some experts immediately announced the breakdown of the international monetary system and the onset of a world monetary crisis. Central bankers around the world called for emergency conferences to create a new system that would restore order before the flow of trade and exchange broke down in chaos.

Outside academic circles, and especially among the economists working for central banks, floating exchange rates were regarded as unworkable if desirable and undesirable if workable. They would increase uncertainty for foreign traders and investors, it was argued. But they would also create additional uncertainty for domestic producers and investors, because a change in exchange rates could quickly and radically change the potential profitability of industries producing import-competitive goods, as well as goods that might be exported. Moreover, governments weren't likely to remain passive when a sudden depreciation in the currency of a major trading country led to an unexpected surge of imports or threatened established export markets. Governments would far more likely retaliate with trade and investment controls or with deliberate devaluations of their own currencies, all of which could quickly lead to a breakdown of international exchange.

Nonetheless, the advocates of floating rates generally had their way in the seventies, eighties, and nineties, although this was usually more by default than by design. Conflicting national interests simply prevented governments from agreeing on the structure of a new fixed exchange-rate system. Most countries did not allow their currencies to float freely, but tried to keep them in some loose relationship with another major currency or set of currencies. A variety of limited international agreements were created to reduce fluctuations in exchange rates, at least among countries that traded extensively with each other. And some small nations whose international trade was predominantly with a much larger economy tried to maintain a rigidly fixed rate of exchange between their currency and the currency of the dominant trading partner. The system that evolved after the breakdown of the fixed exchange-rate system had its faults and its localized crises, but it worked, for the most part. Floating exchange rates did not turn out to be the disaster that the central bankers forecasted. The global volume of international trade increased more than twice as fast as global GDP after 1975.

Nobody Knows

But the existing international system is rickety, and the so-called "Asian Crisis" that began in 1997 put the spotlight on some of its serious flaws. The context was set by the excellent growth records in the 1990s of various East Asian countries. Investment by foreigners contributed to this growth, and the growth encouraged additional lending of capital by foreign banks and other investors.

Foreigners who lend money to countries such as Thailand, Malaysia, or Indonesia want to be paid back eventually in their own currencies. An American bank that lends 10 million dollars for a project in Indonesia will therefore agree to accept rupiahs, the Indonesian currency, in payment of interest and repayment of principal only if it expects rupiahs to maintain their value relative to dollars over the period of the loan, *or* the agreed-upon interest rate makes up for any expected decline in the relative value of the rupiah. The interest rate charged on foreign loans denominated in the local currency will incorporate the expected rate of the local currency's depreciation—just as nominal interest rates *within* one country reflect the expected rate of decline in the value of the money that will be used to repay the loan. If foreign investors decide that the interest rate on loans denominated in rupiahs does not adequately compensate for the risk of rupiah depreciation, they will no longer want to lend to Indonesia and will, if they can, withdraw short-term credit already extended.

Nominal interest rates include the expected decline in the value of the currency.

So a government and its central bank will want to assure foreign investors that they need not fear depreciation. The best way to reduce that fear is to prop their currency up whenever it shows signs of slipping, by purchasing their own currency with dollars or other "hard currencies" (currencies that everyone expects to maintain their value). But if the currency is in fact overvalued, as determined by the considered judgment of those who use rupiahs in international transactions, the quantity of it demanded will continually fall short of the quantity supplied, the central bank will continually have to buy its own currency with hard currencies, and eventually the bank is going to run out of hard currency.

What happens then? There are several possibilities. One is for the central bank to abandon its price-fixing operations and let its currency fall to the market-clearing level. That will inflict losses on foreign investors, however, and raise the price of imports because it will now take more domestic currency to purchase a unit of foreign currency. Another possibility is to raise interest rates. If the interest rate is high enough to compensate for the risk of exchange-rate depreciation, foreigners will want to buy the domestic currency rather than sell it and it will stop depreciating. High interest rates, however, will raise the cost of obtaining capital and put a brake on economic growth.

A third option is to borrow from the International Monetary Fund. But as we have already pointed out, that can be only a stopgap measure. Something must be done to reverse the underlying tendency toward depreciation. The IMF will make its assistance conditional upon the willingness of the supplicant country to adopt reforms that IMF officials believe have the potential of halting the decline in the foreign-exchange value of the country's currency. Because currencies depreciate when investors expect their relative value to decline, because investors come to hold this expectation when the money supply is increasing too rapidly, because persistent and excessive increases in the money supply are the result of printing money to finance government deficits, and because these deficits are the consequence of the government's spending more than it collects in taxes—for all these reasons the reforms for which the IMF calls will be largely reforms aimed at reducing government expenditures relative to taxes. And so the IMF may agree to lend the country foreign exchange with which to prop up its currency only if the country agrees to raise interest rates to a painful level, to eliminate popular but expensive subsidies, and to increase taxes. Whatever the IMF recommends will be unwelcome advice. Had it been welcome advice, the advisee would already have adopted it.

The Trouble We've Seen

Now let us suppose that the advice is not accepted, or it's implemented too slowly, so that the IMF assistance is delayed. Foreign investors, increasingly nervous, may stop extending credit to the country and may try to withdraw credit already extended. If a movement in that direction begins, it can accelerate rapidly, because everyone wants to be first in line to get their money out of a country when they suspect that the country does not have the reserves that will enable it to meet its obligations. The phenomenon is similar to the runs on banks that were so common in the United States in the early 1930s and before. Fear of a collapse in a currency's value causes that currency's value to collapse, because everyone who is able to do so tries to sell the currency and financial assets denominated in that currency for something else.

The desire to sell before the price falls causes the price to fall.

The resulting "capital flight" may prompt the government of the affected country to choose option one as the easiest and indeed the most "natural" way out. Let demand and supply take over. Let the currency fall to whatever level the market process chooses. The problem is suddenly solved, at least for the short run. Popular expenditures don't have to be cut, unpopular taxes don't have to be levied, popular subsidies and special-interest protections can be maintained, and interest rates don't have to be raised. Foreign lenders will be furious, of course; they will feel betrayed, and they will vow never again to lend to the country that treated their interests with such contemptuous disregard. But that is a problem for the long run. The short-run problem is solved, and governments dependent upon popularity can't afford to take too much of a long-term view.

The collapse of the exchange rate in one country will prompt foreign investors to reappraise their investments in other countries in what seem to be similar situations. When the Thai baht falls, the Indonesian rupiah may not be far behind. The collapse of the rupiah may cause a capital flight from Malaysia so that the ringgit falls next. How long will the South Korean won be secure? Or the Philippine peso? The Taiwan dollar? Investors may start looking farther away in this world suddenly grown more risky and begin to question the stability of the Brazilian real. Even countries that peg their currency firmly to the dollar, such as Argentina, will come under increasing suspicion. To maintain that peg, the Argentine central bank must command a supply of dollars sufficient to meet the demand of all those who want to sell the peso for dollars. How long will its stock of foreign-exchange reserves hold out in the face of fear on the part of foreign investors around the world who suddenly begin looking for less risky investments rather than higher return on their investments? In order to attract the dollars it needs, will the Argentine central bank have to raise interest rates, with all the adverse consequences that such a move entails for the level of domestic economic activity?

Which should take priority for government officials? The interests of foreign investors or the health of their own economy? The choice would be an easier one if the two weren't so closely related. The withdrawal of foreign investment has severe consequences in the long run, but it will also have major consequences in the short run for countries whose economic growth has depended so heavily on continuing infusions of foreign capital. Major development projects may have to be suspended and workers laid off when the funds to finance them suddenly dry up. Moreover, devaluation means that imports of consumer goods as well as producer goods will suddenly become much more expensive and no longer within the means of people who had become dependent on them.

The case for a common currency

The advocates of fixed foreign-exchange rates and the advocates of floating rates are *both* correct. The ideal system is one of fixed exchange rates. Try to imagine what would happen if the dollar had a different and constantly changing value in each of the 50 American states. Do you see how many additional costs and how much new uncertainty that would create for business firms? Our national wealth is in large part a consequence of the extensive specialization that we have been able to practice because low-cost, low-uncertainty trade was possible throughout our vast territory. Fixed exchange rates between the states—the dollar of a Maine film fan always exchanges for exactly one dollar of California-produced films, and everyone can confidently count on it—plays an enormous, even if unappreciated, part in facilitating that specialization and trade.

Fixed rates are the ideal system with ideal governments.

But the advocates of floating exchange rates are correct, too. The states of the United States are unlike the nations of the world in two critical ways: They are prohibited by the national constitution from restricting the free movement of merchandise, services, financial assets, and people across borders, and they do not have the ability to run independent monetary policies. The governments of our states consequently lack the power to create the conditions that would permit dollars in Alabama or Alaska to change in value relative to the dollars used in Hawaii and New Hampshire. The governments of nation-states do have those powers as well as political incentives to use them in ways that are almost inevitably going to cause the purchasing power of their currencies to change at divergent rates. Trying to maintain fixed exchange rates in a world of radically diverse national economic policies can easily do more harm than good. It will encourage and sometimes even require governments to interfere with international trade, as the only way in which they can reconcile politically opportune domestic policies with predetermined foreign-exchange rates.

The governments of Germany and France have long been working toward the reduction of barriers to the international movement of people and goods in Western Europe, and they have looked upon the reduction or removal of these barriers as a major step toward a political and economic integration that would both reduce the threat of any future war and enhance efficiency throughout Europe. A major step toward that goal was to be a common currency for Europe. On January 1, 1999, the euro became the common currency of the 11 nations in the European Monetary Union that both wanted to join and met the criteria for joining. Those criteria basically required every nation that wanted to be a part of the new European currency to show that it had been able to keep government spending within sight of government revenue. The hope of those who champion the euro is that it will eventually replace the German mark, the French franc, the Italian lira, and all the other different national currencies that now serve to complicate international exchange within Europe.

But governments that surrender their national currencies thereby surrender a powerful tool for placating their electorates. To put it most simply and bluntly: A government without its own currency is limited in its ability to finance the programs that the voters might demand as a condition for maintaining that government in power. Even the French, who for two decades regularly asserted their determination to lead the way toward economic integration for Western Europe, lost much of their ardor as the date for introduction of the euro approached and they began to see how difficult it would be to persist with a number of politically popular policies under a common European currency.

Fixed exchange rates limit the policy options of national governments.

One can wish the euro well and still wonder what is going to happen when a member of the currency union experiences a recession that does not affect the other nations. With no currency of its own, it cannot shift to an easier monetary policy. With no power to finance a deficit by creating additional money, it may have to pay very high interest rates to finance an expansionary fiscal policy. It will not be able to protect the jobs of its workers by tightening restrictions on imports. It may very well be a good thing that it is prevented from pursuing any of these policies. But what methods of adjustment are left to it? Will its unemployed workers move to other countries where jobs are more plentiful? Europeans do not move as readily as Americans, and they will be especially reluctant to move to a place with a different language and culture. How will these European citizens respond when they discover that by joining the euro their governments have surrendered the power to pursue policies that may or may not be wise in the long run but that have always been popular? The euro will be an interesting experiment.

Private Interests, National Interests, Public Interests

It sometimes happens that we become so absorbed in our search for solutions that we forget what the problem was. Is it our goal that consumers, investors, producers, tourists, and bagpipe players—people, in short—be enabled to cooperate more freely across the barriers that national boundaries raise? Or is that the problem—namely, that people are engaging in international transactions that interfere with the goals of national governments?

It is certainly possible that the interests of the larger public might require some restrictions on international exchange. But a thoughtful person will wonder why the national interest seems so regularly to require that more be given away than is received in return, that jobs be preferred to goods, that efficient producers be hobbled to prevent them from using their advantage to the detriment of less efficient producers, and that in general people be prevented from increasing their wealth by exchanging freely. The skeptic should be pardoned for concluding that the public interest may be something quite different from the national interest, at least as the national interest is usually defined by those who shape international economic policy.

The principle of comparative advantage explained in Chapter 2 received its first explicit statement in the early nineteenth century as an explanation of the gains to be obtained from international trade. But the principle has never fared well in the area where it originated. "Everyone knows" that imports hurt domestic firms and destroy jobs, whereas exports generate profits for domestic producers and create additional jobs. Policies aimed at restricting imports and subsidizing exports have consequently had a strong political appeal for centuries, and never more so than when a recession is cutting into sales and adding to the level of unemployment. The argument that imports destroy jobs has the seductive appeal of a half-truth. When Americans buy Japanese cars, they don't buy as many domestically made cars. An increase in car imports can therefore lead to production cutbacks and layoffs in the domestic car industry. So the owners and employees of car-manufacturing firms have an obvious interest in restricting imports. And when they go to Congress to request taxes or quotas on car imports, they have a handy slogan with which to claim that such protection is good for the country: It protects American jobs. But the argument is misleading.

In the first place, jobs are created by the production of export goods as well as by the production of goods that compete with imports. And American firms can't continue indefinitely to sell abroad if foreigners aren't allowed to sell in the United States. Trade is ultimately a two-way street. Moreover, jobs should not automatically be treated as goods. Some jobs no doubt are intrinsically satisfying and worth doing for themselves without regard to the commodities or services that result. But that's certainly rare. The justification for jobs generally is the income they provide for workers and the corresponding benefit to others in the form of useful goods. The "protect American jobs" argument ignores the gains in real income that come from specialization. If the Japanese can make better cars and sell them at lower prices than American manufacturers can, why should American consumers be compelled to purchase from American manufacturers? If American car manufacturers cannot produce cars as efficiently as the Japanese can, why shouldn't they go out of business? Why should they be allowed in effect to tax consumers to support their lack of a comparative advantage? As we have discovered, of course, American car manufacturers learned how to make better cars at lower cost under the stimulus of foreign competition. Had they been able to obtain from government as much protection as they had requested, they would not have reformed their ways.

Protection from foreign competitors makes life more comfortable.

The attempt to justify the protection of less efficient producers on the grounds that this will preserve jobs runs quickly into absurdity. Why not push the argument further and produce domestically all the coffee we consume? American soil, climate, and geography are not as well suited for the production of coffee trees as are large areas of Brazil and Colombia. But think of all the jobs we could create by building and operating huge greenhouses in which we try to duplicate the favorable growing conditions in those countries! And why stop with goods currently imported? Think of how many new jobs we could create by outlawing the use of automated equipment in the telephone industry!

In Defense of Comparative Advantage

For more than two centuries, economists have been arguing along these lines against the proponents of restrictions on imports, but not with great success. A French pamphleteer-economist named Frédéric Bastiat (1801–1850) wrote a witty satire in 1845 in the form of a petition by the French candlemakers for protection against the unfair competition of the sun. Their request to the Chamber of Deputies for legislation that would protect the jobs of candlemakers by prohibiting windows brilliantly exposes the absurdity of protectionist logic. Bastiat's satire has been reprinted numerous times, but the arguments he ridiculed don't disappear.

Is free sunlight unfair competition for the lighting industry?

Part of the explanation must be found in the resistance of special-interest groups to mere logic. People are readily persuaded by arguments in which they want to believe and have difficulty understanding arguments that run counter to their interests. More important, however, the political process almost guarantees that those who stand to benefit from restrictions on international trade will have a louder voice in policy formation than will the larger group that stands to lose. Transaction costs prevent automobile purchasers from organizing effectively to oppose domestic automobile producers, and the foreign producers obviously have little influence on domestic policy. The externalities of the political process in a democracy, discussed in Chapter 13, make it almost certain that when government officials come to the point of choosing between the interests of American buyers of automobiles and American producers of automobiles, they will be surrounded by the clamor of producers but will hear almost nothing from consumers. Government officials who wish to survive in their jobs pay attention to that kind of pressure.

A limited but legitimate argument for protection against imports can be constructed from the costs of change. The closing down of an industry unable to meet foreign competition entails losses for its owners and employees. The more narrowly specialized the displaced resources, the greater the losses. There may be a case for protection in such circumstances. Notice, however, that the argument can be applied to the case of an industry hurt by domestic competition as well as foreign. Domestic competitors have political influence, of course, and are therefore harder to exclude by special legislation. Nonetheless, if resources were attracted to an industry because of government restrictions on imports, it may be unfair to yank that protection away suddenly. So there may be a case for the maintenance of prior and long-continued restrictions on imports, or at least for their reduction at a slow rate. Equity considerations along with political realities may also suggest a policy of transitional subsidies, designed to reduce the loss to workers and owners or to help them find new opportunities. But this argument cannot be used to support the introduction of new or additional restrictions against imports. Moreover, given the arguments we presented in Chapter 13 on the bias within democratic policy-making to *concentrate benefits and disperse costs*, we have to be very wary of the strategic use of government by businesses to protect themselves from competition rather than competing in the marketplace.

There is no limit to the number of bad arguments that can be constructed in support of import restrictions, and it would be an exercise in futility to attempt to anticipate and refute each one. The fact that there is a kernel of validity in most such arguments complicates the task of their analysis. The valid reasoning must be winnowed from the chaff that surrounds it before the limitations of its applicability can be shown. Perhaps nothing would contribute more toward raising the quality of public discussion in this area than a firm grasp of the principle of comparative advantage. The principle of comparative advantage shows why and how exchange creates wealth. It keeps insisting that the cost of a transaction is the value of what is given up and the benefit is the value of what is obtained, so that it is nonsense to claim that a country can grow wealthy by exporting more than it imports. The principle of comparative advantage undercuts the claim that one country may be more efficient than another in the production of everything. The logical impossibility of that is apparent from the very definition of efficiency as a ratio between the value of what is produced and what is consequently not produced, between the goods obtained and the goods that had to be sacrificed because production entails genuine opportunity costs. By focusing on the real factors involved in production and trade, the principle of comparative advantage dispels the confusion that so easily arises when trade policy is discussed exclusively in monetary terms.

Variant of Gresham's Law: In politics bad arguments drive out the good arguments!

Unfortunately, there are many parties who hope to gain from fostering this sort of confusion, because they suspect that they have no real chance to obtain the special-interest legislation they're after unless they can obscure what's going on. These are the people who invent deficits in the trade balance, who blame their domestic troubles on the conspiracies of foreign governments, and who regularly discover that their foreign competitors are engaging in unfair trade practices. In the world of political economy, such arguments have weight.

Globalization and Its Discontents[1]

These seemingly mundane issues of international economics have led in recent years to protests in the streets of Seattle, Prague, Genoa, and Washington, DC. Signs were carried, gas masks were worn, and violence broke out all in the name of a rejection of the so-called neoliberal "Washington consensus." Globalization has become the lightning-rod issue in the post–Cold War period. Tina Rosenberg put it this way in an article that was published in *The New York Times Magazine*:

> Globalization is meant to signify integration and unity—yet it has proved, in its way, to be no less polarizing than the cold-war divisions it has supplanted. The lines between globalization's supporters and its critics run not only between countries but also through them, as people struggle to come to terms

[1]Joseph Stiglitz (Nobel Prize winner 2001) published a book under this title in 2002, *Globalization and Its Discontents* (New York: Norton, 2002). Jagdish Bhagwati offers a positive case for globalization in his book *In Defense of Globalization* (New York: Oxford University Press, 2004). Bhagwati's work is particularly important because he writes with sympathy toward those who are critical of globalization, but then divides the antiglobalization camp into two groups. Group A includes those who are willing to listen to argument and evidence and weigh the evidence on economic development and the establishment of effective political freedom and human rights protections; Group B includes those who are unwilling to listen to any argument and/or evidence and instead ignorantly hold to positions about the ill effects of globalization that are not consistent with basic economic reasoning or, in many instances, even casual observation. His book, obviously, is written for those in the first group, but unfortunately many of the protestors on the streets at G-8 summits and similar meetings are from the group that tends to be impervious to argument and evidence. Readers interested in the debate over globalization should also consult Johan Norberg's *In Defense of Global Capitalism* (Stockholm, SW: Timbro, 2001). Norberg surveys in short chapters all the empirical evidence on a variety of measures of human well-being and shows the positive correlation between globalization and improvements in human well-being. The economic way of thinking offers the causal connection that explains the correlation.

> with the defining economic forces shaping the planet today. The two sides in the discussion—a shouting match, really—describe what seem to be two completely different forces. Is the globe being knit together by the Nikes and Microsofts and Citigroups in a dynamic new system that will eventually lift the have-nots of the world up from medieval misery? Or are ordinary people now victims of ruthless corporate domination, as the Nikes and Microsofts and Citigroups roll over the poor in nation after nation in search of new profits?

To the critics, the "Washington consensus" is meant to capture the set of policies of fiscal responsibility and trade liberalization that are "imposed" on less developed countries of the world in exchange for loans and foreign assistance from international institutions. The World Bank, the IMF, and the World Trade Organization are the main targets of criticism by the protestors. One particularly egregious sin committed by the IMF in the minds of the protestors is *conditionality*—which means the IMF will cut off loans to a country unless it meets certain specified policy goals in terms of budget deficits, inflation, and other macroeconomic concerns. But, as Bhagwati points out, once you examine the basic facts as to why poor countries suffer as they do in poverty, you will see that it is no mystery at all that political authorities in these countries commit economically irresponsible public policies, let alone horrendous human rights abuses.[2]

would you lend money to a chronic gambler?

Let's now get down to some particular debating points. Critics of globalization argue that the "Washington consensus" leads to

(a) Growing income inequality in the world as the gap between the rich nations and the poor nations gets wider
(b) A "race to the bottom" in terms of environmental policy as large capitalist firms seek to relocate in areas with lower-cost regulations with regard to the environment and thus bring environmental damage to less developed countries as these less developed countries are compelled to keep their regulatory environment friendly to business in order to attract the investment
(c) A "race to the bottom" in terms of labor policy as large capitalist firms seek to relocate in areas with lower costs associated with wages and workplace regulations

In each instance, however, the evidence suggests that globalization actually achieves the *opposite* of the effects so described and

[2]It is not our purpose in this book to discuss the interdependence between political and economic freedom, but the interested reader can consult two classic texts by economists who explore this question in depth: F. A. Hayek, *The Road to Serfdom* (Chicago: University of Chicago Press, 1944) and Milton Friedman, *Capitalism and Freedom* (Chicago: University of Chicago Press, 1962). There are two empirical tracking sources that touch upon these topics as well—the *Economic Freedom Index* (Fraser Institute) and the *Index of Economic Freedom* (Wall Street Journal/Heritage Foundation).

leads to a lifting of the world's poor up from miserable poverty through integration into the global marketplace; that environmental quality in less developed countries actually *improves* through time with the increase in wealth and the greater availability of technology that globalization provides; that workers in less developed countries are *better off* in terms of income and working conditions than previously.

The Power of Popular Opinion

But if this is so, why does the idea that globalization hurts the poor of the world remain so popular and widespread?

Strong opinions are not the same as valid arguments.

Everybody has a right to their own opinion, of course, and everybody seems to have strong opinions—pro and con—about globalization. We are concerned with the *analysis* that they employ to back their opinions. Many people have strong opinions about economic issues without having *any* training in economics at all. Studying economics—like acquiring any scarce good—comes at a cost, and apparently many people act as if it's not worth the cost. Let's not forget that the economic way of thinking is part of a long chain of reasoning, the kind that many people grow tired of before it reaches its conclusions. Just consider how many chapters you've read and tried to understand *before* you've reached the globalization issue! Imagine, instead, if we *began* the book by discussing the hot issues of this chapter. It simply wouldn't work. We would have to retreat all the way back to Jack and Jim swapping a basketball and a baseball glove and *then* work our way forward through comparative advantage, supply and demand, competition, money and banking, and so forth. We have instead introduced the basic building blocks and, over many chapters and several weeks, further developed and applied them until we've (we hope!) become adept at thinking about the complex global issues that permeate the evening news.

Popular opinion often focuses on the obvious consequences of public policy. But good economics is not only about both the immediate and obvious consequences of any public policy. It also tries to clarify the longer term and the often hidden, *unintended consequences* that result. That's why we defined our subject as the study of choice and its unintended consequences. We emphasize the hidden, the unseen, the unanticipated. Our emphasis on unintended consequences gives the economic way of thinking about everyday, yet complex, issues an "outside the box" characteristic. It takes time and practice to master. It indeed comes at a cost. It also takes a great deal of patience and understanding to engage in economic argument with people who are not economists, or dismiss economics as "mere theory."

The cost of being a good economist

Back to the issue at hand. Nobody, including economists, doubts that globalization is transformative, and therefore certain traditional ways of life are torn asunder in the move toward global integration. But the pattern of exchange and production that emerges in the wake of this "creative destruction" is more often than not a marked improvement over the previous order that existed. We must always remember that increases in the real income of a people is not a function of money. Increases in real income result only from increases in real productivity. Real productivity increases result from one of three sources: (1) improvements in labor skill, (2) increases in technological knowledge, and (3) improvements in the organization of economic affairs. Globalization brings all three from the more developed world to the less developed world and in so doing provides the transformative power to lift millions of people out of poverty and ways of life that are destined to keep people in poverty.

The Power of Special Interests

That this basic message of the economic way of thinking has such a hard time getting through is both an indictment of the communicative skills of economists since Adam Smith and the power of the sophistry of special interests. It is the power of special interests, as we have explained in Chapter 13 and Chapter 18, that leads to a conflict between good economic policy and good political decisions. Politics, as we have argued, tends to exhibit a shortsightedness and concentrated-benefits bias in decision making, and this bias is even more exacerbated in nondemocratic governments that are not secure in their time horizon of rule.[3] If a ruler is relatively secure in his position (e.g., chances of a military coup are low), there will be a strong tendency for that ruler to adopt an "encompassing interest"—which means he will adopt economic policies that generate long-term economic growth, rather than merely follow his "narrow interest" by pursuing short-term policies that increase only his own wealth and power.

The Outsourcing Controversy: Soundbytes vs. Analysis

Economic development and economic growth will be the subject of the next chapter so we don't want to get ahead of ourselves, but the important point for our current discussion is that basic economic reasoning will lead us to doubt any explanation of the discrepancy between rich and poor nations as a consequence of expanding opportunities for *voluntary trade* between people. Voluntary trade is mutually beneficial, regardless of whether it's

[3]Mancur Olson (1932–1998) is the scholar who explored more than any other contemporary economist or political scientist the effect of the time horizon on politicians' economic policy-making (both democratic and nondemocratic) and how it impacted economic development policies. See, for example, *Power and Prosperity* (New York: Basic Books, 2000).

between Harry and Sam involving baseball cards back in the neighborhood, or between Joe and Mr. Smith at the grocery store, or between Mrs. Smith in Virginia who purchases furniture sold by Mr. Jones in North Carolina, or between Mr. Jones who purchases fine suits from producers in Italy and wine from producers in France. And what is true for baseball cards, furniture, suits, and wine, is also true for the purchase of *labor services*—be that on a factory floor in Latin America or from a radiologist in India.

In a testimony before Congress, Feb. 10, 2004, Gregory Mankiw, a professor of economics at Harvard and the chairman of the White House Council of Economic Advisors, made this basic argument during the heated debate over "outsourcing." The pattern of trade that we are witnessing as a result of globalization is just another manifestation of the gains from trade that we have been talking about throughout this book:

> New types of trade deliver new benefits to consumers and firms in open economies. Growing international demand for goods such as movies, pharmaceuticals, and recordings offers new opportunities for U.S. exporters. A burgeoning trade in services provides an important outlet for U.S. expertise in sectors such as banking, engineering, and higher education. The ability to buy less expensive goods and services from new producers has made household budgets go further, while the ability of firms to distribute their production around the world has cut costs and thus prices to consumers. The benefits from new forms of trade, such as in services, are no different from the benefits from traditional trade in goods. Outsourcing of professional services is a prominent example of a new type of trade. The gains from trade that take place over the Internet or telephone lines are no different than the gains from trade in physical goods transported by ship or plane. When a good or service is produced at lower cost in another country, it makes sense to import it rather than to produce it domestically. This allows the United States to devote its resources to more productive purposes.

Mankiw certainly gets an A in economic analysis. However, he was lambasted in the news media and by politicians on both the left and right for his blunt defense of markets. Former Senate Minority Leader Tom Daschle was quoted as saying that "if this is the administration's position, I think they owe an apology to every worker in America."

We do have to be careful about the political hyperbole involved. The number of jobs lost due to outsourcing in the U.S. economy is miniscule compared to the size of the U.S. economy. Even as jobs are moving overseas, including white-collar jobs in such fields as financial services and information technology, it means that scarce resources are being channeled in a more productive direction. The law of comparative advantage works whether we are trading goods and services across borders by land, by sea, by air or by the Internet. The creation of jobs overseas will tend to create different jobs and higher incomes back in the United States. In short, trade between nations is a positive-sum game. Whether we realize the gains from trade that exists between nations or whether we pursue policies of protectionism and thus forgo those gains from trade is a choice determined by the public policies adopted by political leaders.

Unpopularity: Another cost of being a good economist

The economists' role in this political process is to tell the truth as they best see it and not worry about its political palatability or feasibility within a given climate of popular political opinion. Economists from Adam Smith to Gregory Mankiw have done precisely this only to have their advice disregarded in the name of political expediency. Be that as it may, the human propensity to truck, barter, and exchange is so great that even though protectionism is rampant throughout the democratic world, the force of global economic opportunity is so robust that the wealth of those nations (and their people) who pursue relative free trade is evident in the record of economic history. As Milton Friedman has put it: "The research is unambiguous that freeing people economically unleashes individual drive and initiative and puts a nation on the road to economic growth. In turn, economic prosperity and independence from government promotes civil and political liberty."

Obviously, not everybody agrees. Most haven't looked at the research. And, of course, the data don't speak for themselves. It takes the economic way of thinking to explain the cause-and-effect relationships behind the data. In the next chapter, we shall continue to explore the global economy and the causes of economic growth and decay among nations.

Once Over Lightly

The total credits in a nation's balance of international payments must always exactly equal the total of its debits; any discrepancy reflects errors in record keeping.

If foreigners want to invest more in total in the United States than Americans want to invest in foreign countries, the United States must import more merchandise and services than it exports to make this possible. A disequilibrium in the balance of payments implies that intended credits and intended debits (intended by whom?) are not equal. To assert that the balance of payments is in deficit is therefore to imply that some credit items were unintended or cannot be expected to continue or should not have been allowed to occur. The assertion of a balance-of-payments disequilibrium is thus a complex policy judgment disguised as a simple statement of obvious fact.

Foreign-exchange rates are prices that link the sets of relative prices existing in nations with separate currencies. Exchange rates between national currencies reflect the forces of supply and demand, which are, in turn, guided by the relative domestic purchasing power of the currencies, especially with regard to internationally traded goods, modified by expectations with regard to the future value of holding various currencies or assets exchangeable for these currencies.

Exchange rates can be set arbitrarily only by governments able to enforce arbitrary prohibitions on international exchange of merchandise, services, and financial assets.

Fixed exchange rates promote trade and thus create wealth by reducing uncertainty. But fixed exchange rates between currencies presuppose compatible domestic economic policies. A nation that tries to "peg" its exchange rate to another currency while pursuing monetary and fiscal policies that make its currency progressively worth less and less relative to the other currency is courting trouble. Its currency will eventually have to be devalued, because it will exhaust the supply of foreign exchange it is using to maintain the "peg."

The "Asian Crisis" of 1997–1998 was brought on by the determination of governments to support unsustainable exchange rates and was transmitted by the fear that other developing countries would also soon have to let their currencies depreciate.

In a world of uncoordinated domestic economic policies, floating exchange rates probably produce less uncertainty and more trade than do fixed exchange rates, which in practice are frequently revised. Floating exchange rates allow governments greater policy freedom, for good or for ill.

The attempt of European countries to achieve the advantages of fixed exchange rates through adoption of a common currency, the euro, will not succeed unless the governments of those countries are willing to surrender some of the freedom they now enjoy to pursue divergent domestic policies.

Most arguments in favor of restrictions on international trade ignore the fundamental principle of comparative advantage, a principle that has not fared well in the area of international trade against well-organized producer groups exploiting public ignorance and nationalist sentiments. The debate over globalization is simply another round in this age-old debate between the principles of free trade versus the organized interests of protectionism. When we look deeply into the issue, we can see that globalization is just another manifestation of the mutually beneficial gains from trade between people.

QUESTIONS FOR DISCUSSION

1. Suppose you established an accounting system to keep track of your personal "balance of payments" with your trading partners (i.e., everybody else).

(a) If you "import" a new television set, you must "export" something else to pay for it. What would you have "exported" if you paid cash to the store at which you bought the set? If you traded in your old set and paid cash for the balance? If you wrote a check to cover the purchase? If you put the purchase on a bank credit card? If you simply promised the store owner that you would pay when you got some money this summer?

(b) Could you have a balance-of-payments deficit or surplus?

(c) How would you handle the transaction if your Uncle Miltie gave the set to you as a birthday present?

(d) If you put a lot of large purchases on your bank credit card over several months while making only minimum payments on the account, are you running a deficit of any sort? Why isn't it proper to call it a deficit in your balance of payments? What will happen to prevent this deficit from continuing indefinitely?

2. An American sends $100 in the form of five crisp twenties as a gift to a relative in Vienna. This action counts as a debit in the U.S. balance of payments. The balancing credit item is an increase in foreign investment in the United States as the Viennese relative acquires $100 of U.S. currency. Where does the balancing credit item appear as the following events unfold?

(a) The Austrian relative exchanges the dollars for schillings at a Vienna bank. The bank holds the dollars, because it has customers who frequently want to buy dollars with schillings.

(b) The Vienna bank sells the dollars to the Austrian central bank in exchange for schillings.

(c) The Austrian central bank gives the dollars to the German central bank in exchange for schillings that the German central bank had been holding.

(d) The German central bank sells the dollars to the Volkswagen Company in exchange for marks.

(e) The Volkswagen Company gives the dollars as expense money to a company executive who is taking a business trip to Pennsylvania. He spends them at a motel in Scranton.

(f) If the dollars had remained permanently in Europe, would this imply that the United States had a deficit in its balance of international payments?

3. Is a disequilibrium price something we can observe? What would you look for in each of the following cases to decide whether the situation is in fact a disequilibrium situation?

(a) The government is allegedly holding the price of oil down below its equilibrium level.

(b) Someone asserts that the current price of wheat is not an equilibrium price, that it is in fact "too high."

(c) The U.S. balance of trade is said to be in disequilibrium because our imports of merchandise and services are regularly exceeding our exports.

4. Is it better for a country to export more merchandise and services than it imports or to import more than it exports? If you're in doubt, ask the

same question about a single household, such as yourself. Which is better for you: a surplus or a deficit in your personal exporting and importing of goods and services?

5. What are the consequences of heavy net investment in the United States by foreigners?
   (a) Does this mean foreigners are obtaining control of our economy?
   (b) What advantages does the United States receive from net investment by foreigners?
   (c) If foreigners invest in U.S. agricultural land, do they acquire the power to control our food supply?
   (d) If foreigners buy stock in U.S. corporations, do they acquire the power to use these corporations in ways that run counter to the security interests of the United States?
   (e) If foreigners purchase controlling interest in a U.S. corporation, do they acquire the power to use this corporation's assets in ways that run counter to the security interests of the United States?
   (f) Who benefits and who loses if foreign nationals start buying large amounts of prime farming land in the Midwest? Who would want to see the price of such land raised and who would not?
   (g) Why have foreigners been so eager to invest in the United States over the past 30 years or so rather than in their own countries, even when their own countries are hurting for lack of capital?
6. Canadian firms trying to attract tourists from the United States will sometimes claim in their advertising that U.S. tourists can benefit from the low price of the Canadian dollar.
   (a) Does the U.S. dollar buy more goods in Canada when one Canadian dollar exchanges for 75 U.S. cents than when one Canadian dollar exchanges for one U.S. dollar?
   (b) If the exchange rate of one Canadian dollar for 75 U.S. cents reflects purchasing power parity, how much should Americans expect to pay, in Canadian dollars, for a hotel room that would cost $90 in the United States? Why might hotel rooms cost considerably more or less than this even if the exchange rate reflects purchasing power parity?
   (c) Suppose you are a Canadian retailer of some sort and you're interested in making as much money as possible from the tourist trade. Would it pay for you to place this sign in your shop window: "U.S. dollars exchanged for $1.50 Canadian on all purchases"?
7. For many years before the mid-1970s, Mexico maintained the price of its peso at 8 U.S. cents.
   (a) Could Mexico have succeeded in doing this if the Mexican inflation rate had been much faster or slower than the U.S. inflation rate during these years?
   (b) From 1963 to 1972, the rate of inflation in Mexico averaged 5 percent per year; in the United States, over the same period, the inflation rate averaged about 4 percent. From 1972 to 1975, however, the U.S. inflation rate ran at 8 percent, while the rate in Mexico leaped to 17 percent. Was there any way the Mexican government could have maintained the 8 cents per peso exchange rate after 1975?

(c) After a series of devaluations, beginning in 1976, the Mexican government in 1982 abandoned all attempts to fix the rate of exchange between pesos and dollars. Throughout this period, the supply of pesos was growing at annual rates in the vicinity of 30 percent. The peso tumbled steeply when the peg was abandoned. For a few months thereafter, Americans found Mexican goods remarkably cheap. Why did Mexican goods become major bargains for Americans in 1982? Why didn't the bargain prices last very long?

8. The Japanese yen was said by many to be *overvalued* relative to the dollar in 1995 when one dollar was exchanging for fewer than 100 yen.
   (a) What do people usually have in mind when they say that a currency is overvalued?
   (b) If some people think the yen is worth less than the price it's currently commanding in the foreign-exchange markets, how can these people profit from this knowledge? What will happen to them if they turn out to be wrong?
   (c) What is the test of whether they are right or wrong? Where do we look to discover the *true* value of one currency relative to another?
9. Some Japanese people were prominent among those complaining in 1995 that the yen had become overvalued.
   (a) Why would anyone living in Japan express unhappiness with a "strong" yen?
   (b) Which Japanese people would be very happy indeed to find the yen "overvalued"?
10. In 1985, when the dollar was exchanging for more than 235 yen, some Americans complained that the dollar was overvalued. One year later the dollar purchased fewer than 170 yen. Would you agree, on the basis of these data, that the dollar really was overvalued in 1985?
11. How did the change described in the preceding question, from 235 yen per dollar to 170, affect all the following groups?
   (a) Americans interested in buying Japanese automobiles
   (b) Americans interested in buying automobiles made in the United States
   (c) American automobile manufacturers and their employees
   (d) Americans planning travel to Japan
   (e) Americans operating businesses that cater extensively to Japanese tourists
   (f) American firms that export extensively to Japan
   (g) American firms that manufacture items with components made in Japan
   (h) American firms that fit both of the two preceding descriptions
12. Under a system of genuinely fixed exchange rates, every nation must experience approximately the same rate of inflation as every other.
   (a) Why is this so?
   (b) How can a country determined to have both a low inflation rate and a fixed rate of exchange between its own and other nations' currencies go about achieving these two objectives if other countries choose high inflation rates?

13. "Floating exchange rates free a nation to pursue the domestic policies it prefers." Is that true? Is it desirable that governments be able to pursue whatever monetary and fiscal policies they wish, free from any constraints that might be imposed by the system of international exchange? From whose point of view might such "freedom" be highly undesirable?
14. What is the difference between exchange rates that are free to fluctuate in response to conditions of supply and demand and exchange rates that are fixed but are periodically altered in accordance with changed conditions of supply and demand?
15. Bonds issued by the government of Italy and denominated in lire have long offered purchasers a substantially higher interest rate than bonds issued by the government of Germany (or West Germany before unification) and denominated in deutsche marks. In 1993, for example, when German bonds were yielding about 7 percent interest per year, the yield on Italian bonds was about 14 percent.
    (a) What does this suggest about the rates of inflation investors expected in Germany and Italy?
    (b) After January 1, 1999, the date for adoption of the euro, interest payments and redemption payments on the bonds of both countries are to be made in euros. How would you expect this to have affected the Italian and German government bond yields *in 1998*, the year before adoption of the euro? (*Hint:* Most of the outstanding government debt of both countries in 1998 was expected to mature *after* January 1, 1999.)
    (c) What actually happened was that the yields on German and Italian bonds steadily converged from 1995 onward, and in 1998 were about 5 percent for both countries. If the euro were to fail quickly as the common currency among the signatory nations, these government bonds would again be redeemed in lire and marks. What does the common 5 percent rate tell you about the expectations of investors with respect to the success of the euro?
16. Footnote 2 in Chapter 16 pointed out that government deposit insurance eliminates the incentive of depositors to examine the soundness of banks or savings and loan associations to whom the depositors entrust their money. How might the existence of the International Monetary Fund have contributed to the Asian Crisis of 1997 as it is described in this chapter?
17. Why can't one country have a comparative advantage over another country in the production of everything if the first country has excellent natural resources, a huge capital stock, a highly skilled labor force, and ingenious technicians and managers while the second country is poor in all four areas?
18. How does the theory of free riders help explain the generally greater legislative influence of producers than of consumers?
19. Estimates published in 1972 predicted that the Concorde SST, the French and British supersonic commercial plane, would not repay its development costs, would create environmental problems, and would not generate sufficient additional revenue to cover the associated costs for the airlines that purchased them. These were essentially the objections that led to cancellation in the 1970s of government financing for an American supersonic commercial plane. A counterargument in both

cases was that these planes would provide many additional jobs, help the balance of payments, and prevent other countries from gaining an advantage. How would you evaluate these counterarguments?

20. Everyone will agree that *some* policies that would create more jobs for Americans are nonetheless not in the national interest. For example, no one recommends that we build highways without using heavy machinery, even though many more jobs would be created if highways were built entirely with hand tools. When is the job-creation argument actually used? Are there any circumstances in which it's a defensible argument?

Promoting Economic Growth 20

Most people in the world today exist continuously in a poverty much worse than anything experienced even at the bottom of recessions by inhabitants of the so-called "developed" countries. Indeed, the most striking fact about economic systems in the world today is how much better some of them work than do others. Although there is no generally accepted yardstick with which we can clearly and unambiguously compare the performances of different economic systems in order to decide whether Canada works better than the United States, Norway better than Sweden, or Switzerland better than any of them, we don't need any sophisticated measures of performance to know that the economy of each of the countries mentioned works far better than the economic systems of Ethiopia, Albania, Bangladesh, or dozens of other poverty-stricken nations in the world today.

An economic system is a social system through which people cooperate in creating and using resources to satisfy one another's wants. Why do some systems accomplish so much more than others? That's the subject of this chapter. Some nations, of course, start off with fewer natural resources than others. But differences of natural endowment cannot begin to explain the enormous differences in wealth and welfare between rich Singapore and poor India, or between rich Switzerland and poor Nigeria. Nor can the ratios of population to land explain all or even most of the observed differences between the wealth of some nations and the poverty of others. The 37,000 square kilometers of the Netherlands support 16 million people far more munificently than the 45,000 square kilometers of Estonia support one-tenth that number—not to mention the fact that the people of the Netherlands created a substantial amount of the land on which they live.

Who is Rich, Who is Poor?

The International Bank for Reconstruction and Development, better known as the World Bank, regularly publishes a World

Development Report in which it tries to summarize the performance of each country's economic system. It divides the countries into high-income, middle-income, and low-income economies.

The high-income economies are those of the United States and Canada, the nations of Western Europe, Israel, Japan, South Korea, Australia, New Zealand, Singapore, a handful of small nations that have grown wealthy by selling oil, such as Brunei, Kuwait, Qatar, and the United Arab Emirates, and a few more very small nations that are or have until recently been dependencies of larger, wealthy nations: French Guiana, Netherlands Antilles, and Guam, for example.

There are far more countries classified by the World Bank as low income whose economies annually generate less than 1,000 current U.S. dollars of income for each resident. They include China and India, which together contain three-eighths of the world's population, and two-thirds of those in low-income countries, Pakistan, Bangladesh, Myanmar (Burma), Cambodia, Laos, Vietnam, the poorer republics from the former USSR, Albania, and almost all of central Africa.

The middle-income economies are those of Latin America, from Mexico to the tip of South America (except for Nicaragua, Honduras, Haiti, and Guyana, which are low income), South Africa and the countries of northern Africa, for the most part the nations of the Middle East from Greece and Turkey to Iran and Saudi Arabia, the nations of central and eastern Europe that were part of the Soviet empire until 1989, most of the republics in the former USSR, plus Thailand, Malaysia, Indonesia, and the Philippines.

The criterion used by the World Bank to classify each country is *gross national product per capita*, which is *GNP divided by population*. Because those who measure the total income and product of the world's nations emphasize gross *domestic* product, and gross national product is for most purposes practically the same as gross domestic product, we'll focus on gross domestic product in explaining the significance and the limitations of this criterion of wealth or poverty.

The Historical Record

Gross domestic product per capita in the United States in 1999 was $30,845. In India it was $2,248, less than 10 percent of the U.S. level. In 1999, GDP in the United States was more than 500 times what it had been in 1820. In India, GDP in 1999 was less than 20 times what it had been in 1820.[1] The difference is

[1]This chapter relies extensively on the voluminous data assembled and analyzed by Angus Maddison and published in *Monitoring the World Economy, 1820–1922*, a publication of the Development Center of the Organization for Economic Cooperation and Development, 1995. We have tried to update the figures since 1995 when possible. However, we would like to reinforce the cautionary note on aggregation that we first raised in the appendix to Chapter 14. The sources of

economic growth. It occurred in the United States at an average annual rate of better than 3 percent over these 175 years; in India over the same period, economic growth was negligible. Why were the experiences of these two countries so different?

In some circles, the confident answer is *exploitation*. Economic growth depends upon the initial existence of a surplus that can be invested in productive capital. The wealthy countries of the world are supposed to have used their military supremacy to subjugate less powerful nations in Asia, Africa, and Latin America, impoverishing the conquered peoples and using the extracted surplus to jump-start their own economies. It is true that at the time when the nations of Europe came into contact with the rest of the world, "the superiority of force happened to be so great on the side of the Europeans, that they were enabled to commit with impunity every sort of injustice in those remote countries." That's Adam Smith speaking, not Karl Marx. But Smith also notes that their injustices were mixed with a great deal of "folly," and his own opinion was that Great Britain, the most ambitious of the colonizing powers, was expending more resources on the maintenance of her empire than she could ever hope to recover in return. He was probably correct. A major reason for the rapid collapse of the European empires after World War II was that they had not yielded many obvious economic benefits to the colonizing powers.

A fundamental objection to exploitation as a general explanation of the great contrast today between wealthy and poor nations arises from the fact that some of the poorest nations of the world, such as Ethiopia, were never subjected to conquest or colonization, and some of the wealthiest, such as Switzerland, never conquered or colonized. Military power seems to have been much more the effect than the cause of economic growth. There can be no doubt, however, that economic growth was first discovered or invented in Western Europe. When Marx and Engels celebrated in 1848 the productive achievements of "bourgeois society" over the preceding 100 years, they were looking almost exclusively at what had happened in Europe and its extensions: the United States, Canada, and Australia. Outside these countries, increases in per capita GDP had been quite unremarkable.

Since 1848, economic growth has come to other parts of the world, and in the quarter century following World War II, every continent, at least for a time, experienced impressive rates of economic growth. The average annual rate of growth of gross domestic product in the world as a whole between 1950 and 1973 has been calculated at 4.9 percent. When we adjust this to take

economic growth and development lay in the structural composition of the political and economic system under study, and aggregate statistics are at best poor estimators that must be used with caution and skepticism. For the inquiring student, the appendix to this chapter provides a further discussion of the difficulties of measuring, comparing, and interpreting GDP among countries.

account of population growth over the period, the average annual rate of growth in per capita GDP comes to a most impressive 2.9 percent, a rate high enough to almost double the average real income of the world's people in just a quarter century. But 1950 to 1973 were exceptionally good years for growth. After 1973, the economies of Latin America slowed down appreciably, and those of the Soviet empire and Africa grew at rates below the rate of population growth so that average per capita incomes in these countries actually fell. In Europe and its offshoots, economic growth generally continued at rates at least sufficient to double per capita income over half a century, while in Asia—up until the crises of the 1990s—average growth rates were high enough to double real per capita income in less than a quarter century.

Sources of Economic Growth

The unprecedented phenomenon of sustained economic growth emerged in human history because some nations of the world managed to create conditions under which the vast majority of their people could specialize and exchange. The essential precondition was and is a stable social order in which the rule of law is well established so that people can initiate projects with reasonable confidence that they will be able to enjoy the results of their efforts.

One way to think about this is that *economic development is really a function of three things: people, resources, and institutions*. People, however, are really a factor that must be treated as given. We might like it if people were friendlier and nicer, but we cannot really control that. We also do not have direct control over the natural endowment of resources. We might hope for better weather and more productive land, but that is not something our choices directly determine. But we do have some command over the institutions that govern the way we interact with one another and the way we utilize resources. This is why fundamental institutions (such as the rule of law), and not the supply of natural resources or the level of human capital investment, are vital to economic development. These institutions provide the rules of the game under which we interact and realize the gains from exchange.

Prerequisites:

- The rule of law
- Low-cost systems of transportation and communications

Another important prerequisite is the possibility of exchanging both goods and ideas at low cost. Specialization cannot proceed if people cannot trade, and they won't be able to trade if the cost of moving goods is higher than the prospective gains from trade. The exchange of ideas is also important, perhaps much more important than Adam Smith and other early economists realized. The geography of Europe was thus a major factor in the nurture of economic growth. Europe's many good harbors along extensive coastlines and its numerous broad rivers, flowing through level plains and kept navigable throughout the year by melting snow from the mountains, enabled the people of Europe to trade goods and ideas over wide areas at low cost.

Extensive specialization cannot progress very far without the accumulation of additional capital. Those who produce goods for the use of others, generally unknown to them and often far away, must be able to live during the steadily lengthening period of time between the beginning of the production process and the receipt of income from the sale of what they have produced. Economic growth consequently presupposes the accumulation of stocks of consumption goods to tide producers over the period of production, goods that function as capital because they are produced goods whose use increases the future rate of production.

• Stocks of capital

The accumulation of capital also makes an obvious and important contribution to economic growth by multiplying the power of labor. No one needs to be told that bulldozers can move a lot more earth than can men with shovels. What may not be quite so obvious is that the accumulation of capital is a qualitative as well as a quantitative process. One of the most important consequences of specialization is technical innovation, and technical innovation implies that a nation adding to its stock of capital goods is not just acquiring *additional* means of production but also *more powerful* means of production. Additional earthmoving equipment tends, over time, to be more effective earthmoving equipment.

• Technical progress

Technical innovation may in fact be the most powerful of the forces that propel economic growth. Take transportation systems, for example, already mentioned as a major factor in the process of economic growth. How did people in the United States move merchandise, ideas, and themselves in 1800? Very slowly, by today's standards. Almost everything went by water if it was to go any long distance. Roads were costly to construct. They had to cross rivers and mountains and remain passable in snow and mud. And the goods or people that traversed them moved mostly by literal horsepower. The accumulation of transportation capital between 1800 and 1870, however, was not primarily the accumulation of additional sailing ships and canals, but rather the accumulation of additional railroad tracks, locomotives, and rolling stock, which moved merchandise far faster per unit of capital. Thus technological innovation was embodied in the additional capital people were acquiring. By 1940, the internal combustion engine had created another huge increase in the productivity of a new unit of transportation capital intended for the movement of merchandise. As for the capital equipment that moves people and their ideas today, we are all familiar with the jet airplane and the Internet and their vast superiority in every dimension when compared with the capital equipment that moved people and ideas in 1800 or even 1940.

The major role of technical progress in propelling economic growth points to a significant advantage enjoyed by nations that have lagged behind the leaders. Technological innovation does not fall from the heavens; it is created by people interacting in the course of trying to promote the projects that interest them. The nation that leads the world in technical progress has to discover better ways of doing things on its own, and it will inevitably incur the costs of the discovery process, including all the costs of making mistakes. The nations that follow behind, however, especially if they follow at a distance, can avoid these costs. An impoverished country with little capital trying at the end of the twentieth century to increase its output and hence its income does not have to pass through the technological stages traversed in the course of history, but can jump immediately from oxcarts and dirt roads to diesel trucks and concrete highways. That's the great advantage of backwardness. Poor countries may be able to grow at rates very much faster than the rates at which the wealthiest nations grew in the past simply by applying the many lessons that the leaders learned only at high cost.

Foreign Investment

Whether poor countries will actually manage to do this, however, is going to depend on a number of factors. Given the technically primitive condition from which they begin, they will not be able to manufacture for themselves the complex capital goods that can increase their productivity. So they will have to import them. But will they have the means to import the capital goods they want? What can they offer in exchange? Being poor, they have by definition very little surplus that they can export in order to acquire the means to import. Would any surplus they might generate even be in demand in the countries from which they want to import? Would it be sufficiently in demand to create favorable terms of trade? What do poor countries produce that rich countries want? Although "raw materials" is an answer that immediately suggests itself to many people, few poor countries actually possess substantial quantities of minerals or other raw materials that are sufficiently demanded abroad to generate export earnings that will purchase new capital equipment. Or if they do have the resources, they most likely lack the knowledge and equipment to extract them at any cost low enough to permit their profitable sale abroad.

· Foreign investment

Here is a role for foreign investment. Investors in wealthy countries can lend the means with which to purchase the capital equipment that poor countries want to purchase. Will they be willing to do that? They will if the expected rate of return on such investments, adjusted for risk, exceeds the expected rate of return on alternative investments. Because a country playing catch-up has an opportunity to grow very rapidly, the rates of return on investment in poor countries ought to be correspondingly high. Unfortunately, the *risk* on such investments is also quite high in many cases. To the high ordinary risks that typically come with investing in an economically undeveloped country, risks caused by uncertainties regarding the ready availability of complementary resources, we must add in many cases the risks created by political instability.

Some of the political risk will arise from the automatic hostility with which so many people regard foreign investors, especially those who invest in poor countries. Return on investment is widely regarded as a "drain" on the resources of poor countries in which the investment occurs, especially if the investors are from wealthy countries. Such attitudes can easily lead to government policies that confiscate part or all of the foreigners' investments by changing the rules of the game. Individuals and corporations aware of these political risks are that much more reluctant to commit their capital—unless they can arrange a deal on the side that reduces the risk! Governments run by dictators or oligarchs are often willing to suppress popular discontent and even to grant special privileges to foreign investors if these investors are willing to share the returns on their investments with the appropriate government officials. This is one of the major reasons why, when economic growth does occur in poor countries, its benefits so often flow just to a privileged few without substantially benefiting the mass of the people.

• Foreign aid

The inability of poor countries to generate internally the capital required for development, the reluctance of foreign investors to supply that capital without an expectation of high returns, and the corrupt relationships this sometimes generates between foreign investors and government officials in poor countries has prompted many to call for investment by the *governments* of wealthy nations rather than private individuals and corporations. This raises problems of its own, however. What would prompt the government of a wealthy country such as the United States to invest in a poor country? Are charitable impulses acceptable reasons for government policies? Do governments ever have charitable impulses? What actual motivations underlie an asserted intention to behave charitably when the allegedly charitable actor is a government? What will be the actual *quid pro quo*? What will the government officials extending the aid want from the government officials receiving the aid? What will the governments of wealthy and presumably powerful nations do when the implicit or explicit terms of their aid are not satisfied? Is not government-to-government assistance a recipe for eventual interference by governments in the affairs of other nations?

Those who believe that these problems can be handled by channeling foreign aid through international agencies must look carefully at the actual record of such international agencies as the World Bank, which has not managed to escape altogether the difficulties and dilemmas associated with government-to-government aid. All these questions arise before we even get around to the question of whether governments are the best agencies to control the direction of investment. How will the governments of poor countries allocate the resources granted to them or loaned to them at subsidized interest rates? Will they allocate the capital to those parties that can use it most effectively? How will they know which parties these are? How confident can we be that corruption will not enter at this point? Waste and corruption have occurred often enough in such circumstances to make the citizens of wealthy countries highly suspicious of "foreign aid" programs. And in a democracy, such suspicions are themselves often sufficient to curtail the programs.

Foreign trade and investment have made large contributions to world economic growth, and those today who stridently insist that "globalization" only makes the rich richer while further impoverishing the poor ought to explain why this should be the case now when it was not the case in the past, even the very recent past. Nations that have been insulated from the world economy or have chosen to insulate themselves have not experienced notable economic growth. On the other hand, the examples of Hong Kong (before its incorporation into China in 1997) and Singapore should be sufficient to refute those who doubt the power of the international division of labor to generate wealth for those who participate in the global economy. These tiny countries, set in hostile environments and almost totally devoid of what we ordinarily think of as natural resources, achieved astounding records of economic growth by throwing themselves wholeheartedly into the whirl of international trade and investment.

• *Globalization*

We worried a moment ago about the danger that governments granting aid to other governments would interfere in the domestic affairs of the recipient country. We need to balance that against the fear that they will *not* interfere. The fact is that many recipient countries use foreign aid in ways that fail to advance economic growth. The aid may even *reduce* the rate of economic growth. How could a gift of capital reduce a country's growth rate? At worst, you might think, it would only do no good. But the capital received from donor countries is almost inevitably going to be employed in conjunction with domestic resources—land, labor, domestic capital—that would otherwise have been employed somewhere else. Thus foreign aid that is allocated to useless projects—useless in the sense that they make no contribution to economic growth, such as a four-lane highway to the ruler's country palace, or a national airline that mainly transports politicians and bureaucrats to Alpine vacations, or even a dam that looks impressive but does not manage to produce valuable electricity or irrigation water—such aid will make a negative contribution to economic growth in the recipient country. The opportunity cost of putting foreign aid to work in a country is not zero.

• *How foreign aid can do damage*

Foreign aid can also prop up bad governments whose policies are designed to enrich a favored few or keep the ruling parties in power even if that retards economic growth. When you think about it carefully you realize that government-to-government aid is interference by the donor government in the domestic affairs of the recipient country. If you don't see why, ask yourself how people who would like to overthrow a tyrannical government regard grants from other countries that flow through their own rulers. The question thus becomes not *whether* but *how* governments or international agencies extending assistance to the governments of poor countries ought to interfere. If the goal is to lift people out of poverty, then aid should be channeled to countries with good economic policies and lots of poor people.[2] Although there is certainly room for disagreement about exactly what constitutes the best economic policy in particular situations, we know a great deal about what works and what does not. The basic problem is not ignorance so much as political incentives that keep those in charge from doing what even they know ought to be done.

• Private investment

There are several reasons why private investment can usually do more to accelerate economic growth than aid from foreign governments or official international agencies. One is that private investment is often accompanied by people who know how to use it. A more important reason is that private investors, at least in the absence of corrupt relations with local officials, urgently want economic growth, because that is what will make their investments profitable. Private investors are not much inclined toward projects that look impressive but don't create more value than they use up. They are fairly diligent about seeing to it that the capital they lend finds productive uses.

Human capital

• Education and human capital

One sound policy that poor nations ought to pursue more diligently than many now do is basic education, especially for women. A literate population is another important precondition for rapid economic growth. And by neglecting the education of girls, many poor countries are willfully depriving themselves of valuable resources. Chapter 11 argued that income inequalities among persons in the United States are attributable primarily to differences not in the amount of physical capital that they own, but differences in the value of their human capital. It is the possession above all of productive knowledge and skills that makes individuals wealthy. How much does human capital contribute to growth in the wealth of nations?

It is difficult if not impossible to give a quantitative answer to this question, in large part because one way in which wealthy nations spend their income is by providing schooling more generously for their citizens. Schooling is a consumption good as well as a capital good. Because increased wealth leads to additional schooling and also to more knowledge acquired in other ways, we can't estimate with any confidence the precise contribution that human capital makes to the process of economic growth. We can

[2]A 1998 World Bank publication makes an impressive case for channeling aid in this way: David Dollar and Lant Pritchett, *Assessing Aid: What Works, What Doesn't, and Why*.

be sure, however, that it is important. Could technical progress have made such a large contribution to economic growth in the absence of an educated populace? It seems most unlikely. The knowledge and skills of the people who develop new products for Microsoft had to be matched by an increase in the knowledge and skills of those who use Microsoft products if those products were to be more than mere toys. The complex machinery that enables us to do so many things so much more easily has to be repaired as well as designed and manufactured.

Oil Comes from Our Minds

• The importance of knowledge

Most people think in terms of *given endowments of factors and the earth's natural resources*. But if we go beyond that common assumption and think outside the box a little, we find *knowledge* to be the *crucial* factor in the process of economic growth. It is not "things" that are lacking in the poor countries of the world. It's *ideas*. For the greater part of human history oil had no practical value. It was nothing less than an act of human *intelligence* that eventually saw a way of using oil to serve human purposes. Julian Simon, an economist who had quite the ability to think outside the box, put it this way: "Resources come out of people's minds more than out of the ground or the air." Natural resources are, of course, *found* in the physical world around us, but Simon's point is that it takes *human minds to discover and employ those resources*. What we might take today as an obvious way to use a natural resource—say, the use of silicon in computer chips—is, in fact, an inherited deposit of *human knowledge and intelligence*.

If the incentives are right, educated people can take advantage of the world's readily available stock of knowledge and transform what they have into what they want. Even the task of getting the incentives right is itself a problem of knowledge. We are learning more all the time about how to assign property rights more clearly so that organizations work more effectively and prisoners' dilemmas less frequently produce failures of cooperation. Although all this is welcome news to those who, like us, earn their living by promulgating ideas, it is not for that reason false.

Economic Freedom Index

Beginning in the 1980s, a group of economists sought to capture these insights using traditional empirical techniques. In consultation with Milton Friedman and other market-oriented economists, Walter Block, James Gwartney, and Robert Lawson developed an Economic Freedom Index and then correlated their index with measures of economic growth. Their results, originally published in 1996, presented data on world development from 1975 to 1995. Since that time, Gwartney and Lawson have annually updated their study and other organizations have joined the effort to measure the magnitude of the effect of various policies on economic growth.[3] The Economic Freedom Index seeks to measure a country's economic policies in the dimensions of regulation, pricing practices, monetary policy, fiscal policy, and international trade. Countries that follow policies of low levels of regulation, freedom of pricing, stable monetary policy, low levels of taxation, and open international trade are graded as having greater degrees of economic freedom; whereas countries with high levels of regulation, administered pricing, inflationary monetary policy, high levels of taxation, and closed international trade will be scored as having a lower degree of economic freedom. The results of their initial measurements can be seen in Figure 20–1.

As can be seen, the countries that followed policies that ranked the highest on the economic freedom index (the A countries) also had the highest levels of per capita GDP. These aggregate correlations are worth considering when discussing why some nations are rich and others are poor, but an examination of the historical record might get underneath these figures a bit more and reveal to us in more detail the institutional prerequisites for economic development and the causal forces that contribute to economic development.

The Developmental Power of Private Property Rights

The Wealth of Nations in one paragraph

This observed correlation between economic freedom and economic development is surely not a mere statistical association. There is a systematic causal force, identified by Adam Smith back in 1776, in *The Wealth of Nations*. People grow wealthier when they have the freedom to participate in the market process. The causal force is precisely what we have been explaining throughout this textbook, starting in Chapter 2. The economic freedom that allows people to cooperate with one another through the voluntary exchange of private property rights—to buy, sell, and trade as each best sees fit under the rule of law—contributes to the development of personal and national wealth. It unleashes a process that allows people to seek their comparative advantage, to find ways to produce and deliver scarce goods and services at

[3]Gwartney, Lawson, and Block, *Economic Freedom of the World, 1975–1995* (Washington, DC: The Cato Institute,1996). For updates see www.freetheworld.com. The Heritage Foundation has also started to publish an annual *Index of Economic Freedom* in cooperation with the *Wall Street Journal*, and Transparency International publishes data on the extent of corruption in countries, which is used by investors in deciding on the relevant risk factors of investing in different regions of the world. Economists have used these indices in their work to better understand the institutional preconditions of economic growth and in particular the importance of institutions such as private property rights, freedom of contract, and the rule of law.

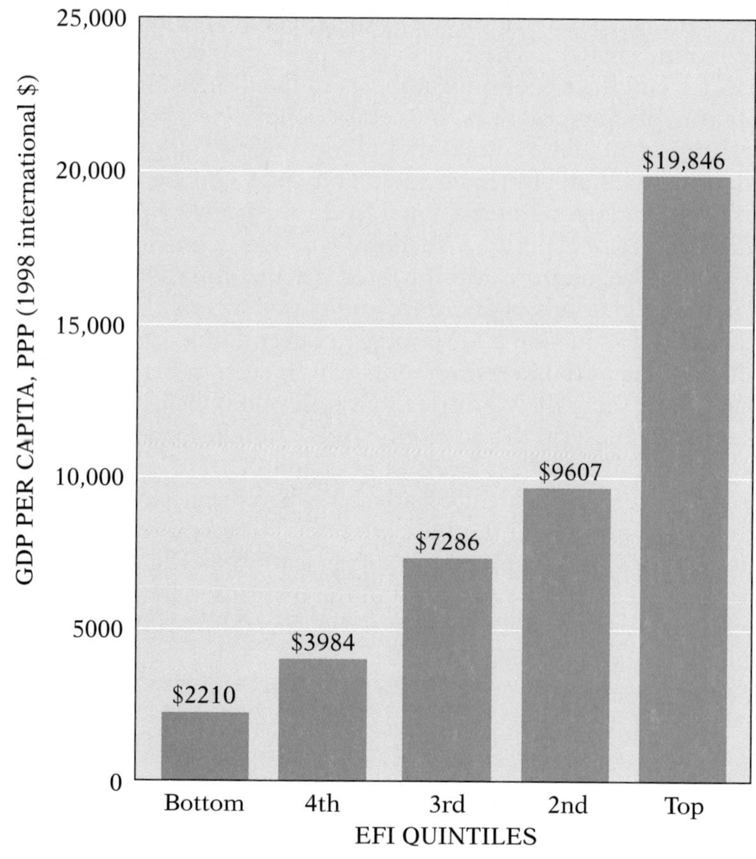

Figure 20–1 **Economic freedom and income**

lower cost, and to tap the entrepreneurial motive that drives the market process.

The Asian Record

There is little anyone can do to alter the handicaps that climate and geography impose on nations. But the rule of law, competent and honest government officials, an educated populace, openness to international trade and investment—these are matters over which governments have a large measure of control. How well have they done? Consider the case of South Korea. From 1960 to 1999, the gross domestic product (in terms of 1995 U.S. dollars) increased more than eighteen-fold, with the average annual rate of increase exceeding 12 percent. Per capita GDP in 1995 dollars (adjusted to express purchasing power parity) rose from $1,256 in 1960 to $12,056 in 1999, or at an average annual rate of nearly 10 percent. What was South Korea doing to raise itself over this period from a poor to a wealthy country?

Causes of growth in Asia

The government and people of South Korea certainly paid adequate attention to education, including the education of women, who currently make up more than a third of the labor force. The country opened itself to the global economy and made effective use of the funds that foreigners were willing to invest in the country. Taking advantage of a boom in international trade during these years, South Korea concentrated on producing exports that could be used to purchase other goods required for development. Who would have predicted in 1960 that 20 years later automobiles manufactured in Korea would be competing for sales with automobiles made in Western Europe and North America?

South Korea was definitely not a country in which the government stepped aside and let the market allocate resources; government officials conspired with industrial leaders to influence at crucial points the investment of resources and the development of particular industries. The forces of supply and demand were nonetheless allowed to generate relative prices to which even government officials regularly paid attention so that economic development generally followed the patterns decreed by comparative advantage. Government spending was kept under reasonable control so that the economy was not subjected to the uncertainties of rapid price inflation. And the people of Korea showed themselves willing to practice a relatively high rate of saving, thus raising the supply of resources available for domestic investment.

The rule of law was generally honored, even if not with religious fervor. Corruption was a problem. Not just low-ranking bureaucrats but also some of the most highly placed government officials were convicted of taking bribes to favor particular economic interests. Political alliances produced policies that arbitrarily favored some regions of the country over others. But these abuses *were* criticized and powerful public officials *were* indicted and convicted, which speaks well for the rule of law. The rules of the game were for the most part known and enforced, so people could make economic decisions with reasonable confidence that they would bear the cost of wrong decisions and reap the benefits of good ones.

The records of Japan and Taiwan over this period were similar to that of South Korea, both in the rates of economic growth achieved and in the policies generally pursued. An educated populace willing to work hard and to save, operating within a framework of stable rules of the game, taking cues from the price system, open to the world economy, and not hampered by excessive government spending or rapid inflation can take advantage of the technology developed by more advanced nations to grow rapidly and to narrow substantially the gap between themselves and the very wealthiest nations of the world. Japan did more than narrow the gap, becoming itself one of the wealthiest countries. In 1960, per capita gross domestic product in Japan was 35 percent of per capita GDP in the United States. In 1999, it was 78 percent.

Some of the other nations in Asia performed far less well. The per capita gross domestic product of India—stated again in 1995 dollars and adjusted for purchasing power parity—was $735 in 1960. It had grown to only $2,248 by 1999, which was approximately twice the per capita GDP that South Korea had enjoyed 40 years earlier. Per capita GDP in India, which had been about 55 percent of South Korea's in 1960, was less than 15 percent of South Korea's in 1999. Some of this is a consequence of population growth; the population of India increased by more than 100 percent from 1960 to 1999. But the population of South Korea increased 47 percent over the period. Most of the explanation for the lagging rate of income increase in India must be attributed to its much slower rate of economic growth. Why was India not able to catch up at anything even remotely resembling the rate of South Korea, Taiwan, and Japan? War and preparation for war are costly drags on economic growth, and India was plagued over this period by internal dissension and conflict with its neighbors, both Pakistan and China. But South Korea and Taiwan also spent considerable sums during this period on military preparations. The answer probably has to be sought in the policies pursued by Indian governments.

Failure to grow

Although there have been signs over the last decade of reform on these counts, India displayed extreme reluctance to let prices allocate resources and a strong preference for lodging authority in government bureaucrats. The government engaged in extensive distortion of prices throughout this period. Some prices were suppressed for the stated purpose of protecting poor people, although they did not always have this effect. As you may remember from earlier chapters, governments that hold down prices do not thereby reduce scarcity. They are much more likely to aggravate scarcity by discouraging suppliers. Moreover, prices held down by law don't assure the poor that they will be able to obtain the goods whose prices are being suppressed ostensibly for their benefit. Competition will move to other margins, and the poor are often no more capable of competing effectively on these margins than they are of competing on the margin of price.

The Indian government also distorted prices, in effect, by refusing to pay attention to the information prices provided. Central planning as practiced in the USSR enjoyed a considerable reputation in the 1960s (largely undeserved, as we subsequently learned), and government leaders in India allowed themselves to be seduced by the Soviet model. The result was a great deal of waste, reckoned again in terms of economic growth forgone, as investment was directed toward projects that ultimately proved incapable of generating revenues in excess of costs. In those sectors of the economy that the government did not attempt to plan, entrepreneurs were systematically discouraged by the regulations of bureaucrats whose authorizations were required to do almost everything. The rule of law does not exist in an economic system where government licenses are required for most economic decisions and those licenses are granted or withheld in an arbitrary manner, according to little more than the will of the relevant bureaucrat. Arbitrary government is the very opposite of the rule of law, and it functions as a crushing damper on enterprise.

Outside of Asia

The countries of Latin America have had a very mixed record on economic growth since World War II. Table 20–1 shows the percentage changes in per capita gross domestic product from 1960 to 1999 for the seven Latin American countries featured in Angus Maddison's *Monitoring the World Economy*. The changes again refer to real GDP adjusted for purchasing power parity.

Mixed records

These figures must be used with great caution. The mixed record of Latin American economies has been mixed over time as well as space. In 1929, per capita GDP in Argentina was 63 percent of the U.S. level and Argentina ranked among the wealthy countries of the world; it was only 38.5 percent of the U.S. level in 1999. Per capita GDP in Venezuela in 1999 was 0.1 percent *below* what it had been in 1960. In Brazil, per capita GDP rose rapidly in the 1970s but fell in the 1980s; in 1990, it was 8 percent *below* what it had been in 1980. In 1999, it was 4 percent higher than where it had been in 1990. Chile went through two economic revolutions during this period, both of which had major effects on its economy. The Chilean economy has seemingly stabilized in recent years, enjoying 19 percent growth from 1990 to 1999. Economic policies in Peru varied during this time between what can only be called absurd to what might be called reasonably sensible.

Variable economic policies have been the rule in Latin America rather than the exception, which makes it difficult to generalize about the causes of economic growth in these countries and the causes of their failure to grow. The safest generalization might be that unstable governments cannot establish the rule of law and that Latin American governments have been notoriously unstable.

Table 20–1 **Changes in Per Capita GDP, 1960–1999**

Country	% Change
Argentina	17.4
Brazil	41.0
Chile	41.5
Colombia	31.1
Mexico	34.3
Peru	1.0
Venezuela	−.1

Source: World Bank, *World Development Indicators;* www.worldbank.org/.

Table 20–2 **Per Capita GDP in 1999 (in 1995 U.S. dollars)**

Country	Per Capita GDP
Ethiopia	$112
Tanzania	188
Nigeria	250
Kenya	337
Ghana	410
Cote d'Ivoire	787
Zaire (Congo)	840

Source: World Bank, *World Development Indicators;* www.worldbank.org.

The record of sub-Saharan Africa, except for Botswana and South Africa, can only be called tragic. Table 20–2 shows per capita gross domestic product in 1999 for seven African countries. Ethiopia is included although it is not actually a sub-Saharan country. These results have not emerged from lack of trying. Tanzania was for many years after World War II the favorite country of development experts and the recipient of much technical assistance and financial aid. All these efforts accomplished little, and per capita GDP in Tanzania has actually been declining for the most part since the mid-1970s.

. . . if anything can go wrong, it will.

Climate and geography have both worked to impede economic growth in this area. Much of the continent lacks fertile soil or adequate rainfall. Heat and humidity discourage exertion, while diseases that thrive only in tropical climates, such as the sleeping sickness transmitted by the tsetse fly, weaken the population and destroy livestock. Water flow in the rivers varies greatly between wet seasons and dry ones because the rivers are fed more by rainfall than by melting snow from mountains; they consequently do not function, as they do in Europe, as corridors for the movement of goods or people. The states of Africa are largely the product of lines drawn arbitrarily by European powers in the nineteenth century, and the diversity of peoples captured by their borders has fostered disunity and civil wars. Occasional periods of respectable economic growth have done little to increase average living levels because that growth has been matched by explosive growth in population. Per capita income in the region as a whole is lower today than it was a quarter century ago. Poor at the outset of the twentieth century, the peoples of sub-Saharan Africa, again excluding the nation of South Africa, remain overwhelmingly poor at its close.

Even an optimist, if inclined at all to realism, must concede that no one currently knows what can be done to put Africa on the road to economic growth. The most discouraging fact has to be the politics of the region, in which stable, honest, and competent regimes are more the exception than the rule. A government preoccupied with the task of remaining in power or suppressing rebellion or resisting aggression from a neighboring power will not be in a position to act on good advice even if good advice is forthcoming.

The experiences of Asia over the past decades assure us that policies do matter. Other Asian countries have not done as well as Japan, Korea, Taiwan, Hong Kong, or Singapore. But Thailand, Malaysia, and China have experienced respectable rates of economic growth, giving us reason to believe that poverty is not the unavoidable fate of any nation in today's world. Policies, however, are set by governments, and we cannot count on those who set policies always to favor economic growth over narrower goals of their own that are not compatible with growth.

An Appendix: *THE DIFFICULTIES OF INTERNATIONAL GDP COMPARISONS*

Recall our earlier concerns in Chapter 14 about aggregate measures: The concept of gross domestic product is based on so many conventions, with so many essentially arbitrary inclusions and omissions, that it should be used only with extreme caution to compare the well-being of different nations—which, of course, is exactly what we have been recklessly doing. The gross domestic product for the most part measures only what passes through the market. Thus the people in the Bureau of Economic Analysis in the U.S. Department of Commerce who calculate the GDP of the United States do not include the services of the spouse who maintains the home. It is too difficult to evaluate such services, despite their enormous importance, so they are completely excluded from the accounts. But the value of hired housekeepers' services can be measured by the payments made to obtain them; hence, they do enter into the accounts. As a result, GDP will tend to *decline* as a direct consequence of marriages and *increase* with a rising divorce rate. Real welfare surely moves in the opposite direction. Also, as more women enter the labor force, the GDP expands by the amount of their contribution to total output, as measured by their earnings. Because there is no deduction, however, for the value of the work they are no longer doing at home, the increase in GDP exaggerates the increase in the value of total output—unless their housework had no value, which seems quite unlikely.

Apply this to the situation of the low-income economies. In these countries a much smaller proportion of the productive work that people do is going to pass through the market. Consequently, the gross domestic product of the low-income countries will be understated. When we look at the numbers that the World Development Indicators provide on per capita GDP in the lowest

$120 per year is $10 per month. Can anyone live on $10 per month?

of the low-income countries, we realize that those numbers have to be vastly understated. The World Development Indicators estimated per capita GDP for Mozambique in 1999 at $198 per year, for Ethiopia at $112, and for Tanzania at $188. Because no one could possibly live for a year on an income that low—and because it's an average, some people would have incomes even lower—we know that the unadjusted figures on gross domestic product seriously exaggerate the poverty of the people in the poorest countries.

They also exaggerate the wealth of those in the wealthier countries by counting income that is used to offset the effects of other income. For example, when a coal-burning plant generates electricity, its output enters GDP. When people are then hired to clean and paint as a consequence of the sooty fallout from the generating plant, GDP rises once more. Similarly, the additional cost of an automobile attributable to its incorporation of a catalytic converter is not so much a "good" as a cost we must accept if we want to drive so many automobiles in densely populated areas and not choke on the exhaust fumes. It would make sense, if we were interested in welfare, to exclude the value of the cleaning and painting and the value of the catalytic converter from the gross domestic product. The problem is that once we started down that path there would be almost no place to stop. We would have to deduct the value of a great deal of our medical care, the costs of commuting to work, and every other good produced and purchased in response to work-related activities.

International comparisons of per capita gross domestic product are seriously distorted also by the common denominator used to make those comparisons. The World Development Indicators reports list the nations of the world from the poorest to the wealthiest in terms of GDP per capita in *U.S. dollars*. But nations outside the United States do not calculate their gross domestic product in U.S. dollars. So each country's GDP, stated in terms of that country's national currency, must be divided by its population and then translated into U.S. dollars, using the current exchange rate.

Foreign-exchange rates, as we discussed in Chapter 19, state the number of units of some other currency that one unit of a particular currency will purchase. Thus the dollar–forint exchange rate, for example, can be stated either as 220 Hungarian forints for one U.S. dollar, or as 0.004545 dollars for one forint. This suggests that an American who is visiting Hungary can expect to pay 220 forints to obtain goods for which he would expect to pay one dollar in the United States. If that were in fact the case, if 220 forints in Budapest purchased what one dollar would purchase in New York, then the dollar–forint exchange rate would express *purchasing power parity*. All through the 1990s, however, for reasons that will be discussed later, Americans in Budapest were pleasantly surprised to discover that their dollars purchased far more by way of restaurant meals and hotel rooms when

Table 20–3 **Annual Income in the Poorest Nations (1999 data in 1995 U.S. dollars)**

	GDP per Capita	Adjusted for PPP
Ethiopia	112	628
Sierra Leone	138	448
Burundi	143	578
Malawi	156	586
Eritrea	173	881
Guinea-Bissau	183	678
Tanzania	188	501
Mozambique	198	861
Niger	209	753
Chad	218	850

Source: World Bank, *World Development Indicators,* 2001.

transformed into forints that were spent in Hungary than when left in dollars and spent in the United States. The dollar–forint exchange rates did not express purchasing power parity at any time in the 1990s. The implications for international comparisons of exchange rates that depart from purchasing power parity can be enormous.

The World Development Indicators reported, for example, that per capita GDP in Hungary in 1999 was $5,151 (compared with $30,845 in the United States). But when Hungarian GDP per capita for 1999 is adjusted to reflect estimated purchasing power parity, it rises to $11,430. That's considerably higher—approximately 120 percent higher, as a matter of fact. These adjustments must be made if international comparisons are to be meaningful. And when they are made, per capita incomes in the poorest countries rise substantially. Table 20–3 shows per capita gross domestic product in the 10 lowest-income countries for 1999 and then the same measure of income when estimates of purchasing power parity (PPP) have been used to adjust the figures. The table supports what we stated earlier: No one can live on an income of $100 per year and no one did.

220 Hungarian forints buy a much better lunch in Budapest than $1 buys in New York.

Once Over Lightly

Economic growth entered the world only within the past few centuries, in company with a rapidly expanding division of labor or specialization, making its first appearance in Europe and its offshoots.

Low-cost means of transporting people, merchandise, and ideas have been an important precondition for increasing specialization and the economic growth that it generates.

Another essential condition for economic growth within a society is the establishment of clear, generally accepted, and well-enforced rules of the game, or the rule of law.

Economic growth has depended upon the accumulation of capital, both because capital increases the productive power of labor and because capital embodies the technical progress that has contributed so greatly to the process of economic growth.

Openness to the global economy facilitates economic growth. In addition to permitting a fuller exploitation of comparative advantages, it enables primitive economies to benefit from the technological achievements of already developed economies. If a nation establishes favorable conditions, foreign investment can also make a large contribution to the accumulation of initial capital in a developing economy.

The willingness of the population to save a large part of its income can make a significant contribution to capital accumulation and economic growth.

Human capital is an important part of a society's capital stock. Economic growth proceeds more rapidly in a society of educated people. A growing amount of evidence suggests that knowledge is the single most important factor in promoting economic growth.

The knowledge essential to economic growth includes knowledge about the effective organization of political life. Whether a nation experiences rapid economic growth or an economic growth rate below its rate of population growth will depend largely on whether it develops appropriate institutions of governance.

The reliability of aggregate GDP analysis is further aggravated when trying to compare per capita GDP across different countries with differing currencies.

QUESTIONS FOR DISCUSSION

1. How important is economic growth? Does it really make people better off in the long run? Or, as the question is sometimes misleadingly put, "Can money buy happiness?"
   (a) Why is that last question misleading?
   (b) The behavior of almost everyone indicates that people believe they will be better off if they earn a larger income, because a larger income means the ability to acquire more of what they want almost, but not quite, without regard to what it is that they want. But to what extent is this desire for more relative to what others have? If everyone else in the society is also acquiring more, how much satisfaction will I obtain from getting more? Will the marginal benefit exceed the marginal cost?

(c) Our desires and satisfactions are often relative not only to what others have but also to what we ourselves have become accustomed to. A small amount of tasteless food can be the source of immense satisfaction to a very hungry person. Is the marginal satisfaction gained by upgrading from codfish to jumbo prawns or from processed cheese to brie as great as the marginal satisfaction in going from one cup of rice per day to two? The marginal cost of the last improvement is surely far less.

(d) Is per capita GDP an appropriate measure of well-being, even after we have made all the adjustments suggested in this chapter's appendix? Do the procedures used to calculate GDP take adequate account of the social and psychological costs associated with turning out a larger gross domestic product?

(e) Per capita GDP can be increased by enlarging GDP or by shrinking the population. If rising GDP per capita indicates that the people of a society are becoming better off, then each additional child born into the society lowers the average level of well-being. Do the parents of the children usually reason this way? They are, after all, the only ones whose per capita income falls significantly with the birth of an additional child.

(f) Advocates of zero economic growth are principally concerned about the deleterious effects of economic growth on the environment. Does economic growth necessarily lower the quality of the environment?

(g) Rising GDP makes a lot of things possible that were previously impossible. What these things will be is going to depend largely on the level of GDP already obtained. In Ethiopia or Bangladesh, rising GDP could make possible for millions of people adequate nutrition as well as dental care that would enable them to avoid considerable pain and to keep their teeth into old age. What would a 2 percent growth rate in per capita GDP make possible for people in the United States over the next 35 years, the time that it will take at that rate for GDP to double? (For those who have serious doubts about the value of economic growth in today's world, we strongly recommend a small book by Peter Berger, a sociologist who has done extensive research on economics and culture: *The Capitalist Revolution: Fifty Propositions about Prosperity, Equality, and Liberty*, Basic Books: NY, 1986. Berger will fortify some doubts, but he will probably overcome a lot more.)

2. Has the economic growth of European countries and their offshoots been achieved at the expense of poor nations in Asia, Africa, and Latin America? Those who believe it has usually point to the fact that European nations used their military power in the past to subjugate weaker nations and in some cases to impose unequal trading relationships by force. Those who disagree point out that many of the poorest countries of the world had almost no contact until very recent times with the outside world and that in other cases Western countries introduced resources that initiated economic growth. What evidence would resolve this contentious issue?

3. How would you account for the fact that the United States and Canada experienced so much faster rates of economic growth in the nineteenth and twentieth centuries than did the countries of Latin America?
4. The textbook has several times emphasized the importance of the rule of law. The antithesis of the rule of law is arbitrary governance, or governance according to the will of whoever is in charge.
   (a) Does democracy promote the rule of law?
   (b) The governments of South Korea, Taiwan, Hong Kong, and Singapore—four countries that experienced very rapid economic growth from 1950 to 1990—were not distinguished during most of this period for the democratic character of their political systems. Is the rule of law more likely to be established in a highly democratic society or in one with a somewhat authoritarian government?
5. Should the wealthy nations of the world make grants to the poorer nations, as many now argue?
   (a) What arguments can you present in favor of such grants?
   (b) What arguments can you present against such grants?
6. Should the foreign aid that is extended to poor countries either by wealthy nations or by international agencies be extended without strings, or should the donors exercise some control over the uses of the foreign aid that they extend?
7. The text offers two reasons why private investment might be better for poor countries than assistance tendered by foreign governments or international agencies. One is that technical assistance often comes along with private investment as part of the package. The other is that private investors may be more determined to see their funds invested profitably and therefore less likely to subsidize projects that do not promote economic growth. Can you think of any reasons for the opposite view: why government assistance or assistance by international agencies would be better for poor countries than private investment?
8. The culture of some poor countries militates against letting women enter the labor force or even, in some cases, of providing for women more than a very limited education.
   (a) Do you think that potential aid donors should insist upon changes in such policies and practices as a condition of aid?
   (b) How would you respond to someone who claimed that this would be unwarranted interference in the affairs of another nation and culture (and maybe even religion)?
9. Here are the 1999 figures for per capita GDP, adjusted for purchasing power parity, for five wealthy countries.

United States	$30,845
Norway	28,433
Switzerland	27,171
Canada	26,251
Japan	24,898

In which of these countries was average wealth the greatest? Why do you say so? If there is anything else you would like to know before deciding, what is it you want to know?

10. Can you think of ways in which economic growth makes at least some of the people in a society worse off? As more people acquire enough income to purchase cars, do those who cannot afford cars or who dislike their operation in cities become worse off? Do people ever become worse off simply because others have become better off?

The Limitations of Economics

21

The possibility of civilization depends largely on how well societies work. What does the economic way of thinking reveal about the working of society? And is there anything of importance that it conceals? If you can bring yourself to return to the first chapter of this book, you will find a brief discussion of the biases of economic theory. You might want to read that section again, now that you've completed the book. Are those really biases? Or are they something more like useful working hypotheses?

What Economists Know

The economic way of thinking employs such concepts as demand, opportunity cost, marginal effects, and comparative advantage to make sense out of the everyday world around us. The economist knows very little about the real world that is not better known by business executives, artisans, engineers, and others who make things happen. What economists do know is *how things fit together*. The concepts of economics enable us to make better sense out of what we observe, to think more consistently and coherently about a wide range of complex social interactions.

This turns out in practice to be a largely negative kind of knowledge about mostly impersonal transactions. The economic way of thinking, as you may have noticed, contributes relatively little to a better understanding of relationships within the family or other small groups where people can know one another well enough to cooperate on a personal basis. Economics mostly explains how cooperation occurs among people who don't know one another at all, but who nonetheless manage to work together with extraordinary effectiveness.[1] Perhaps you also detected, as you read through the chapters of this book, a greater emphasis

[1]Adam Smith argued in *An Inquiry into the Nature and Causes of the Wealth of Nations* (Chicago: University of Chicago Press, 1976 [1776], p. 18) that in a civilized society we are in constant need of the cooperation and assistance of a

on what *should not* be done than on what *should* be done. But negative conclusions are important. The economist Frank Knight used to defend the heavily negative character of economic reasoning with a quotation: "It ain't ignorance that does the most damage; it's knowin' so derned much that ain't so."

Too many people claim to "know" how to solve pressing social problems. Their mental picture of the economic universe is a simple one, in which intentions can easily be realized and the only obstacle to a better society is therefore a lack of good intentions. They therefore often dismiss economists as "mere theorists," who unnecessarily complicate things and call good intentions into question. Indeed, John Stuart Mill tried to defend not only economics but all the social sciences against the layman's charge in an article published in 1831 called "The Spirit of the Age." He observed that

> every dabbler thinks his opinion is as good as another's. Any man who has eyes and ears shall be judge whether, in point of fact, a person who has never studied politics, for instance, or political economy systematically, regards himself as anyway precluded thereby from promulgating with the most unbounded assurance the crudest opinions, and taxing men who have made those sciences the occupation of a laborious life, with the most contemptible ignorance and imbecility. It is rather the person who *has* studied the subject systematically that is regarded as disqualified. He is a *theorist*: and the word which expresses the highest and noblest effort of human intelligence is turned into a bye-word of derision.

Social actions have consequences that run far beyond those that can be easily predicted or foreseen. The economic way of thinking—a theory, no doubt—gets our "sights" in order to help anticipate or explain the unintended consequences. Restricting textile imports into the United States, for example, does, for the present at least, protect the jobs and income of textile producers; that's clear enough. But it takes a tutored eye to notice that this will shift even more income away from *other* Americans, by raising textile prices, reducing American export opportunities, and in general inhibiting the exploitation of comparative advantage. Again, it is easy to see that rent controls hold down the money

great multitude for our well-being and even our very survival, whereas in our lifetime we will only be able to make friends with a few. Explaining how we achieve this cooperation among strangers has been a constant source of intellectual puzzlement since the founding of our discipline. In fact, the Greek word for exchange—*Katallaxy*—has the dual meaning of bringing a stranger into friendship, as has been stressed in the work of F. A. Hayek, James Buchanan, and more recently David Levy. For a fascinating discussion of how, through exchange activity, strangers are brought into cooperative relationships with distant others as if they were close friends, see Paul Seabright, *The Company of Strangers: A Natural History of Economic Life* (Princeton: Princeton University Press, 2004).

payments that tenants must make to landlords. But how many advocates of such controls are aware of the alternative payments that tenants will have to make, of the *new* forms of discrimination that will replace discrimination on the basis of money price, and of the short- and long-run effects on the supply of rental housing? They just don't have the conceptual tools to think outside the box.

Nonetheless, people easily become impatient with those who warn against the inadvisability of actions that will make matters worse without proposing solutions of their own. And in a society such as ours, accustomed to the almost miraculous accomplishments of science and technology, the demand for "doing something" tends to exceed by a wide margin the supply of constructive responses to social problems.[2] We have probably erred in assuming that social problems can be handled in the same way that we manage technological problems. We admit that conflicting interests create hard problems for social policymakers. But we still underestimate the difficulties in the way of bringing about planned social change, largely because we underestimate the complexity of social systems, of the networks of interaction through which behavior is coordinated in a society and people are induced to cooperate in the achievement of their goals. In *The Theory of Moral Sentiments*, Adam Smith's great book on virtue, he warned about "the man of system" who

> seems to imagine that he can arrange the different members of a great society with as much ease as the hand arranges the different pieces upon a chess-board. He does not consider that the pieces upon the chess-board have no other principle of motion besides that which the hand impresses upon them; but that, in the chess-board of human society, every single piece has a principle of motion of its own.

[2]See Robert Nelson, *Economics as Religion: From Samuelson to Chicago and Beyond* (University Park, PA: Penn State University Press, 2001) for a discussion of the presuppositions that underlie much of modern economic analysis. In doing so, Nelson highlights the mode of justification that is relied on for the claims being made on behalf of different economic arguments and the public-policy advice that follows from these arguments. Nelson's book, it might be of interest to the readers to note, is dedicated to the memory of Paul Heyne. One of the most important problems in twentieth-century economics, we contend, is that our arrogance leads us to expect economics to be able to provide information that is beyond its limits as a scientific discipline. Economics is mistakenly seen as a tool of social control, rather than as an intellectual tool of social inquiry. This is obviously true in the instances of socialism, but it is no less true in the Keynesian reconfiguration of economics. As a matter of historical record, however, it should be noted that in societies where economics has been deployed most vigorously as a tool of social control, such as the former Soviet Union, the consequences for the economy, as well as the population as a whole, have been disastrous in terms of both material well-being and the protection of human rights. The economic way of thinking might make a claim to be universal in its application, but the claim when examined closely is actually one of extreme humility.

Perhaps that's why economic theory often treats proposals for reform of the economic system so unkindly: It assumes that each single piece has a principle of motion of its own. It's not that economists are themselves uninterested in reform, much less that they're the paid lackeys of the privileged classes. But economic theory, by revealing the interdependence of decisions, calls attention to the unexamined consequences of proposals for change. "It won't work out that way" is the economist's standard response to many well-intentioned policy proposals. Realism is not necessarily conservatism, but it often looks quite similar. And there is a sense in which knowledge does promote conservatism. Even physicists have been accused of hopeless conservatism by would-be inventors of perpetual-motion machines.

Beyond Mere Economics

John Maynard Keynes once proposed a toast to economists as "the keepers of the possibility of civilization." The *possibility* of civilization—that is all. The efficient allocation of resources and effective social cooperation on complex tasks enlarge the realm of possibility, but they do not by themselves guarantee the progress of civilization. A well-coordinated and smoothly functioning society gives individuals more opportunity to choose; it does not guarantee that they will choose well. The economic way of thinking, especially in a democracy, is an important preliminary. But it is no more than that.

Economists are for the most part prepared to admit that the concepts they employ sometimes distort the reality they study. And they are willing to submit their analysis and conclusions to the test of rational criticism. But *some* point of view is indispensable to any inquiry, in the physical sciences as well as the social sciences. If the economic way of thinking sometimes leads to distortions, to misplaced emphasis, or even to outright error, the appropriate corrective is rational criticism. The application of that corrective has frequently altered the conclusions of economics in the past. It will probably continue to do so in the future.

Let us add one final comment. Being a good economist means more than being skilled in the economic way of thinking. A knowledge of mathematics and statistics is a must, of course, as any decent economist must be able to speak the language of the profession. But a *better* economist ought to realize that there are *gains from trade* with specialists in other disciplines. The specialist in the economic way of thinking might very well be enriched through the *exchange of ideas* with other specialists who study the human condition, from philosophers, political theorists, and sociologists to literary types, art historians, and cultural anthropologists. Should you decide to continue on with your studies in economics, you might want to consider resisting the temptation to ignore or dismiss outright the other human sciences. Should you instead choose to specialize in another discipline outside of economics, we hope you won't forget some of the lessons you've learned in this book. Either way, the choice is up to you.

Glossary

Accounting Profit: Total revenue minus total (explicit) cost. Does not take into account the opportunity costs associated with the profit-seeker's resources. Compare this to economic profit.

Arbitrage: The attempt to obtain economic profit by purchasing a good at a relatively low price, and selling it at a relatively higher price.

Bad: Anything whereby less of it is preferred to more. Compare this to Good.

Balance of Trade: A situation in which the money value of a nation's exports equals the money value of its imports.

Barter: The direct exchange of two goods, without the use of money.

Budget Deficit: A situation whereby the total expenditures made by government officials exceed the total tax revenues. The difference must by financed by the issuance of national debt.

Budget Surplus: A situation whereby the total tax revenues collected by government officials exceed the total government expenditures.

Capital: A good that is used to produce other goods and services. (Also see Human Capital.)

Cartel: An agreement among a group of sellers to regulate prices, output, or a combination of the two.

Checkable Deposits: Deposits in a financial institution that can be transferred to others through the writing of a check.

Coercion: To induce cooperation by threatening to reduce people's options. The opposite of persuasion.

Commercial Society: A society that is founded on an advanced market economy, with a highly specialized division of labor, monetary profit-and-loss calculations, and the exchange of private property rights.

Comparative Advantage: The ability to produce a good or service at a lower opportunity cost, compared to another potential producer. (Also see Law of Comparative Advantage.)

Competition: The process that occurs when people strive to meet the criteria (whether prices, status, or the willingness to stand in long lines) that are being used to ration scarce goods.

Deadweight Cost: The cost that a purchaser must bear to obtain a good, but is not transferred as benefits to the seller.

Deflation: A sustained rise in the purchasing power of money, often experienced as a fall, on average, of the monetary value of goods and services.

Demand: A concept that relates the amounts of a good people plan to obtain to the sacrifices they must make to obtain these amounts. (Also see Law of Demand.)

Demand Curve: An illustration of the inverse relationship between the price of a good and the quantity demanded, holding other variables constant. With a *given* demand curve, a change in the price of good X leads only to a change in the *quantity demanded* of good X. (Also see Law of Demand.)

Depression: An unusually severe and long-lasting recession. (See Recession.)

Discount Rate: The interest rate that the Federal Reserve charges when it extends a loan to a commercial bank. The Federal Reserve can use the discount rate as a tool to manipulate the overall money supply in the economy: the money supply tends to increase if the Fed reduces the discount rate, and it tends to decrease if the Fed raises the discount rate.

Disinflation: A slowing down (lowering) of the inflation rate.

Division of Labor: Another term for specialization, or the following of one's comparative advantage.

Economic Growth: A sustained increase in real GDP over time.

Economic Profit: Total revenue minus total (explicit plus implicit) cost. Takes into account the opportunity costs associated with the profit-seeker's resources. Compare this to Accounting Profit.

Economics: The study of choice, and its consequences. Because unintended consequences are so often overlooked by non-economists, economists often define their discipline as the study of choice and its unintended consequences, for emphasis.

Economizing Behavior: The way individuals choose because they are faced with scarcity. One economizes by selecting those courses of action in which the expected additional benefits exceed the expected additional costs. Economizing behavior is actually another term for efficient behavior. (Also see Efficiency.)

Economy: The set of institutions through which people coordinate their production and consumption plans.

Efficiency: For economists, this term refers to a comparison between expected additional benefits and expected additional costs. An action or a project is deemed efficient if, in the eyes of the chooser, he feels the additional benefits outweigh the additional costs.

Elasticity: The sensitivity of choosers to changes in price. (Also see Price Elasticity of Demand, Price Elasticity of Supply.)

Employment Rate: The number of people employed divided by the number of people in the noninstitutional population.

Entrepreneur: The person who strives to earn an economic profit, but also faces the possibility of bearing the burden of economic loss. Entrepreneurs therefore are also called "residual claimants": they claim the residual (the profit or loss) after all prior agreements have been honored.

Entrepreneurship: The act of engaging in arbitrage and innovation in the search for economic profit.

Externality: The benefit or the cost that is unintentionally enjoyed by, or imposed upon, third-parties who are not directly involved in a market exchange. (Also see Negative Externality, Positive Externality.)

Federal Funds Market: The process of lending short-term loans between commercial banks.

Federal Funds Rate: The interest rate that commercial banks charge one another when they extend short-term bank-to-bank loans.

Federal Reserve: The central bank of the United States, created in 1913 by an act of Congress.

Fiat Money: Something official declared by law to serve as money. In some situations, however, fiat money does not actually serve as money!

Final Good: In the context of national income accounting, a final good is a good that has been acquired by a final demander. That is, a good that is purchased without the intention of resale.

Fiscal Policy: The manipulation of the federal government's budget in order to bring about desired levels of total spending in the overall economy.

Foreign-Exchange Rate: The price of one country's currency expressed in another country's currency.

Free Good: A good that can be obtained without sacrificing something else of value.

Free Rider: An individual who enjoys consuming a good without having to pay their share of the costs of producing that good.

Futures Contracts: Agreements to deliver or to accept, at some specified date in the future, amounts of a commodity at a price determined at the time of the agreement.

Futures Market: The process through which futures contracts are agreed upon and settled. Compare this to Spot Market.

Good: Anything in which more of it is preferred to less. (Also see Final Good, Free Good, Inferior Good, Intermediate Good, Normal Good, Scarce Good.)

Government: A generally conceded monopoly of coercion over a group of people within a specific geographical location.

Gresham's Law: The observation that poor-quality money tends to drive high-quality money out of circulation.

Gross Domestic Product (GDP): The total market value of all final goods and services produced within a country, during a particular period of time. (Also see Nominal GDP, Real GDP.)

Gross National Product (GNP): The total market value of all final goods and services produced by permanent citizens of a country, during a particular period of time.

Hedge: An attempt to reduce one's exposure to risk and uncertainty.

Human Capital: The knowledge and skills that people accumulate through education, training, or experience and that enable them to supply valuable productive services to others.

Inferior Good: Relates to the way demand changes with a change in income. A good is inferior, by definition, if the demand for it increases (decreases) when one's income decreases (increases). Compare this to Normal Good.

Inflation: A fall in the purchasing power of money, often experienced as a rise, on average, of the monetary value of goods and services.

Interest: The price that people pay to obtain resources sooner rather than later. Interest is the premium paid to enjoy current command of resources. (Also see Time Preference, Nominal Interest Rate, Real Interest Rate.)

Intermediate Good: In the context of national income accounting, an intermediate good is a good that is purchased with the intention of further manufacturing and/or resale.

Labor Force: Anybody 16 years or older in the noninstitutional population who is either employed or unemployed.

Law of Comparative Advantage: States that individuals within a society can enjoy greater wealth by specializing in the activities that they do more efficiently than others, and exchanging the goods and services that they produce for the goods and services produced more efficiently by others.

Law of Demand: States that the quantity demanded of a good increases as the relative price of the good falls, and decreases as the relative price of the good rises, *holding other influences on demand (such as tastes, income, expectations, the prices of substitute goods and complementary goods) constant*.

Law of Supply: States that the quantity supplied of a good increases as the relative price of the good rises, and decreases as the relative price of the good falls, *holding other influences on supply (such as prices of factors of production, or expected prices of the output) constant*.

Margin: In economics, margin means "the edge," the particular moment when an action is undertaken. Being "at" or "on" the margin is like standing at a "fork in the road."

Marginal: Means additional.

Marginal Benefit: The additional benefit that will be expected to occur if an action is undertaken.

Marginal Cost: The additional cost that will be expected to be incurred if an action is undertaken. Compare this to Sunk Cost.

Marginal Revenue: The additional expected revenue that will be created by selling more output.

Market: The process through which people coordinate their consumption and production plans through the exchange of private property rights.

Market Clearing: The condition whereby quantity demanded (the plans of consumers) are fully coordinated with quantity supplied (the plans of suppliers). Compare this to Shortage, Surplus.

Middleman: Someone who specializes in lowering the transaction costs among suppliers and demanders.

Minimum Wage: A legally-mandated price floor in the unskilled labor market.

Monetary Calculation: The use of money and market-based prices to calculate the expected (and realized) costs and benefits of one's projects. Business accounting is a clear example of the use of monetary calculation.

Monetary Policy: The attempt by a nation's central bank to manipulate the overall money supply, often with the goal of influencing overall spending in the economy.

Money: Anything that serves as a general or common medium of exchange. (Also see Fiat Money.)

Money Supply: A measure of the total amount of money in the economy. The M1 money supply measure includes all currency in circulation, plus money on deposit in checking accounts, plus any issued traveler's checks.

The M2 measure includes all of the above, plus money on deposit in savings accounts and money market accounts.

Monopoly: Literally means "single seller."

National Debt: The total dollar amount of principle plus interest owed by the federal government.

Negative Externality: The cost imposed upon a third party to an exchange. Also called a "spillover cost."

Nominal GDP: A measure of GDP using current dollars, which does not account for any inflationary or deflationary circumstances. Compare this to Real GDP.

Nominal Interest Rate: The rate of interest quoted in a contract. Compare this to Real Interest Rate.

Normal Good: Relates to the way demand changes with a change in income. A good is normal, by definition, if the demand for it increases (decreases) when one's income increases (decreases). Compare this to Inferior Good.

Not-for-Profit: A firm that has no residual claimant. The firm might actually make an accounting profit (TR > TC) but nobody in particular has rights to that profit.

Open Market Operations: The purchase and sale of U.S. government bonds by the Federal Reserve, in an attempt to manipulate the overall money supply. The Fed's purchase of bonds tends to increase the money supply (and lower interest rates), and the Fed's sale of bonds tends to decrease the money supply (and raise interest rates).

Opportunity Cost: The next-best alternative that is sacrificed when a choice or action is undertaken.

Perfect Competition: The hypothetical state characterized by (1) large numbers of buyers and sellers, (2) perfect information, (3) homogeneous (or identical) products, (4) zero transaction costs, and (5) price taking behavior among all participants. Compare this to Competition.

Positive Externality: The unintended benefit enjoyed by a third party to an exchange.

Predatory Pricing: The attempt to compete with one's rivals by cutting prices, with the hope that it might drive them out of business, providing the opportunity to raise prices in the future.

Present Value: A calculation of the current value of a future income stream.

Price Control: Another term for either a price ceiling or price floor.

Price Elasticity of Demand: The percentage change in quantity demanded divided by the percentage change in price. A measure of consumer sensitivity to changes in price.

Price Elasticity of Supply: The percentage change in quantity supplied divided by the percentage change in price. A measure of seller sensitivity to changes in price.

Price Ceiling: A legally-mandated maximum price set on a good or service.

Price Floor: A legally-mandated minimum price set on a good or service.

Price Searcher: A supplier who enjoys some degree of market power, and has the ability to raise or lower his price. In this context, he has to "search" for the best price to charge for his goods or service. Compare this to Price Taker.

Price Taker: A supplier who is such a small player in an overall market that he has no ability to raise, nor any incentive to lower, the price he charges. He simply "takes" the prevailing market price as a given.

Private Property Rights: Legal rights assigned to a particular person which allow him to use, depreciate, or exchange his title to somebody else. Compare this to Social Property Rights.

Production: In its broadest sense, production is the creation of value, the creation of wealth.

Production Possibilities Frontier: Illustrates the maximum amounts of two goods that can be produced with a given set of resources.

Profit: Total revenue minus total costs. Also referred to as "residual" or "net revenue," or, in Not-for-Profit circles, as an "inurement." (Also see: Accounting Profit, Economic Profit.)

Property Rights: Legal rules that establish who owns what, and how their property can be used. (See also Private Property Rights, Social Property Rights.)

Purchasing Power Parity: A situation in which a unit of a nation's currency can be used to purchase the same quantity of goods in all countries.

Rarity: A measure of the amount of a particular thing in existence. Compare this to Scarcity.

Real GDP: A measure of GDP which uses a price level established in a base year. Real GDP is an adjustment of nominal GDP for any inflationary or deflationary effects, and attempts to provide a clearer picture of the actual performance of the economy. Compare this to Nominal GDP.

Real Interest Rate: The nominal (quoted) interest rate minus the rate of inflation.

Recession: Traditionally defined as a decrease in real GDP over two consecutive quarters (six months). More recently, economies that experience a slowing down of the rate of economic growth are also said to be in a recession. (Also see Depression.)

Rent: The income generated by the leasing of property to others.

Required Reserve Ratio: The percentage of a bank's total deposits that it must hold in the form of vault cash or cash on deposit at a Federal Reserve Bank.

Residual Claimant: One who has ownership rights to the profit of a firm. (Also see Entrepreneur.)

Scarce Good: A good that can be obtained only by sacrificing something else of value.

Scarcity: A condition under which an individual must choose, incur a cost or a trade-off, in order to obtain more of what he or she values.

Seignorage: The net revenue from the minting of coins calculated as the difference between the coin's face value and the value of the metal contained in the coin.

Shortage: The situation of plan discoordination, whereby the quantity demanded of a good exceeds the quantity supplied. Compare this to Surplus.

Social Property Rights: Legal rights that assign ownership to society as a whole, and therefore to nobody in particular.

Socialism: An economic system based upon comprehensive economic planning and social ownership of the means of production.

Specialization: The pursuit of one's comparative advantage. Another term for Division of Labor.

Speculator: In its broadest sense, a speculator is anybody who faces an uncertain future. In that way every human being is a speculator. A professional speculator, on the other hand, is a specialist who tries to profit on the futures market.

Spot Market: The exchange of goods and services with immediate payment and acceptance. Compare this to Futures Market.

Sunk Cost: The non-recoverable cost that was incurred in the past, and reflects no current opportunity for choice. Compare this to Marginal Cost.

Surplus: A situation of plan discoordination whereby the quantity supplied of a good exceeds the quantity demanded. Compare this to Shortage.

Theory: A systematic way of thinking about cause and effect relationships in the world around us.

Time Preference: The term for the tendency for an individual to place a higher value on goods and services when they're obtained sooner in time, rather than later in time.

Transaction Cost: The cost of arranging exchanges between buyers and sellers.

Unemployed: Somebody who is currently not employed and is either looking for a job or waiting to begin or return to a job.

Unemployment Rate: The number of people unemployed divided by the number of people in the civilian labor force.

Wage: Income earned by people who sells their labor to others.

Wealth: In its broadest definition, wealth is anything that a person values.

Index

D

E

G

H

I

J

N

O

P

S

T

U

photo credits

p. 1	Getty Images Inc.—Hulton Archive Photos
p. 20	Getty Images Inc.—Hulton Archive Photos
p. 44	Getty Images Inc.—Hulton Archive Photos
p. 74	Corbis/Bettmann
p. 98	Getty Images Inc.—Stone Allstock
p. 126	Getty Images Inc.—Hulton Archive Photos
p. 162	Stockbyte
p. 204	Spanish National Tourist Office
p. 220	Getty Images Inc.—Hulton Archive Photos
p. 242	Getty Images Inc.—Hulton Archive Photos
p. 264	Corbis/Reuters America LLC
p. 290	Getty Images Inc.—Stone Allstock
p. 316	Getty Images Inc.—Hulton Archive Photos
p. 344	Getty Images, Inc.—Taxi
p. 370	Stockbyte
p. 394	Getty Images Inc.—Hulton Archive Photos
p. 418	Getty Images Inc.—Hulton Archive Photos
p. 448	Aurora & Quanta Productions Inc.
p. 472	Getty Images Inc.—Hulton Archive Photos
p. 504	Corbis/Bettmann
p. 528	Getty Images, Inc.—Taxi